Advance Praise for
Critical Transformative Educational Leadership and Policy Studies

Paraskeva's *Critical Transformative Leadership and Policy Studies* is a masterpiece in education for social justice and creative freedom, a crucial oeuvre for those really committed with the struggle for dignified living conditions for humanity. It is a timely volume which emerges in the midst of a world crisis, caused by covert investigations in laboratories in which genes are mutated, viruses and bacteria are altered, all of which at the (warlike) service of the empire— of all empires—, of an elite that leads international corporations and institutions, and owns all the goods on the planet—to the detriment of life, of all humanity. Paraskeva's volume is an imperative reading in a world of exhausted, stagnant, a world that faces the collapsed capitalism, a world with no other effects, other than human pain and suffering. It is a work that disagrees with and challenges the imperial reason; the dehumanization and denaturalization, which it has brought with it. Paraskeva's *Critical Transformative Leadership and Policy Studies* works away from the abysmal thought, from the violence and cruelty of conservative neoliberal policies, which have given the epistemic basis to the capitalist—and imperial—order of that North, imposed on the Planetary South. Paraskeva's volume provides valuable approaches de-linked from the academy deliberately involved in the constitution of that substratum, epistemicide! Hence its educative tinge (which is no longer scholarly, instructional), its decolonized, libertarian and fraternal touch, which allows to cultivate hope—in a world in which social justice radiates. This magnificent work brings together, the most relevant critical radical voices of libertarian education, which dissect the nonsense of neoliberal political economy, examine the roots of colonial power, and, in the face of it, give an account of the possibilities opened by educational programs of political, critical-radical transformative, leadership, such as the Doctoral program created and led by João M. Paraskeva at UMass, Darmouth—a program which provided a critical space to alternative ways (to the canon) to think about education, towards its full democratization. Furthermore, the volume suggests the urgency of transcending, the challenges of the empire, now tending to colonize every trace of life.

However, education will never kneel, and will never lead such a crime against humanity. The 'education' that is wisdom and creative freedom—as it was advocated, by the Millennial South of Anahuac, Abya Yala—will never bend, because per se it is irredentant, re-evolutionary. It transmutes all power, however deadly it may be, because as wisdom and freedom, it is life, which only corresponds to life. Hence such education turns in a radical different direction from 'epistemic occidentosis' as Paraskeva's argues, from neoliberal globalization which is eugenic and genocidal. It is such critical education that these leading voices point to, which is represented in this work by an unrepentant educator, João. M. Paraskeva, who bravely confronts hostile tendencies—to life, and defends it, with manifestos, and declarations of independence. João M. Paraskeva—and those who with him write this radical work, dispel the imperial fog, the myth of colonial reason and its epistemic power, and illuminate the path of poetic, social justice. Thus, as eminent creators, they show the way of change—towards respect for life. Although the night of the world, spread its darkness, the light of the sun, will continue to shine! Of this, it is a commendable example, and this work is priceless.

—Jacqueline Zapata
Universidade de Querétaro, México

Judging from most of this book's authors, the University of Massachusetts, Dartmouth, has put together an excellent series of talks involving some of the finest committed and progressive public intellectuals around. Thanks to their commitment and the efforts of João M. Paraskeva, himself a very inspiring and insightful public intellectual, based at the same US University, their talks are now made available to a wider global public. As somebody ensconced in a Mediterranean island, Malta, I am grateful to Myers Education for extending the contents beyond North America.

The team of writers/public intellectuals, while mainly composed of scholars ensconced in North America, a presence conditioned by the logistics of travel and the convenience of geographical proximity, besides funding considerations, also includes voices originating in a variety of other contexts. These include Argentina, Brazil, Mozambique, Puerto Rico (though part of the USA, it strikes me as a distinct context) Portugal and Spain. The list of contributors/ speakers is truly impressive which renders the book a who's who of leading public intellectuals. They offer different 'takes' on some of the most burning world issues and the challenges they pose to humanity. These challenges include those posed by pandemics laying bare the Darwinian selection processes exacerbated by neoliberalism, itself a pandemic creating an ever burgeoning sector of disposable beings, some living precariously, others denied life tout court. They also include more evident global imperial politics in which manufactured consent and, increasingly, brutal force are evident; more domination than hegemony, in Gramsci's distinction? While there is constant appeal to the democratic imaginary, true of many of the authors in this volume, there is prima facie little evidence of 'democracy from above' as the voices of international capital, and the military-industrial complex, condition the lives of many. This notwithstanding, as exemplified by some of the authors, there are, thankfully, beacons of hope. There are exemplars of 'democracy from below' which prefigure that which is possible but 'not yet' on a global scale. Hope springs eternal and education, in its wider context, not limited to institutions but extending to an array of sites, including popular (not necessarily left-wing populist) sites, plays its part. It represents a part, albeit a significant part, of the struggle for change. Education, we ought to be reminded, is not an independent variable. Paulo Freire wrote that it cannot be accorded powers it does not have; it cannot bring change on its own. On the other hand, there cannot be change, rooted in popular consciousness, a popular revolution rather than what Gramsci calls a 'passive revolution', without education in its broadest context. Viewed this way, education is crucial to the workings of Hegemony. By drawing on a number of public intellectuals, not all easily identified with Education as an area of specific enquiry, this book helps generate discussions around the connections between educational critiques (not just criticisms) and larger social-economic and political efforts sounding either discordant or complementary notes. This is a great book, quite refreshing and insightful in its scope.

—Peter Mayo
University of Malta

In a world turned upside down by the reciprocally generative antagonisms of capitalism and racism, by the far-reaching kleptocratic machinations of a luxury real estate developer and former reality television star, and by the world-historical ramifications of The Great Lockdown associated with the misery and death surrounding the coronavirus pandemic, this important volume could not have arrived at a more urgent time. Too many struggles against genocide, ecocide, epistemicide and omnicide that have emerged from the wheelhouse of the academy have been tragically undermined not necessarily by the policy wonks themselves but by the toxic fix of neoliberalism that for decades has been rushing through the veins of college planning councils and boards of trustees, turning universities and colleges into little more than ivy covered crack houses where a fatal addiction to profit augmentation result in an ideological pathocracy more suited to hustling on the Vegas Strip than for the nourishment of critically transformative leadership and policy practices. Neo-Marxist sallies into education, while bringing some temporary correctives to the increasingly moribund field of transformative leadership, what Paraskeva calls a "false cult," have thankfully given way to an actual engagement with Marx's own works and the development of revolutionary critical pedagogy. Yet truly transformative critical programs remain too few and far between. Engagements with the pathfinding work of the decolonial school and the politics of indigeneity are more scarce, still. This is not surprising since schools and colleges of education have overwhelmingly adopted a model of consumer citizenship and have shucked off the idea of critical citizenship as a liberal fantasy that needs to be cast into the trash can of history. Ever since governments made the decision not to exert control over their capital markets and fixed currencies, it became obvious that there would only be a very limited range of possible public policy choices both inside and outside of education. In this way neoliberalism has struck a huge blow against democracy. Yet the struggle for democracy has not ceased, thanks to the efforts of João Pareskeva, his colleagues, and his comrades throughout the field of education. Which is why this magisterial collection of essays becomes so urgent. The model of transformative leadership cultivated by Paraskeva and his colleagues that helped to birth this volume should be held up as a path for moving the field of education forward and out of the shark tank. Time has not run out completely, and educators need not succumb to the sirens of despair. The ill-fated response to the recent pandemic by the transnational capitalist state and Black Lives Matter protests have ripped the curtain away from capitalism's swindle of fulfilment, making it clear that we cannot recapitulate to the problems that initiated these current crises. The essays included in this stellar collection can provide the necessary seedbed of ideas and practices for rethinking how to refashion our leadership and policy agendas for the refurbishing of a radical democracy for a post-pandemic era.

—Peter McLaren
Distinguished Professor in Critical Studies,
Chapman University

Critical Transformative Educational Leadership and Policy Studies is a timely and needed volume in an era framed by the pandemonium triggered by COVID-19 crisis, the George Floyd murder among others, which fanned the flames of a paradoxical time opening the ground for more oppression from the totalitarian regimes, yet facing strong and solid resistance from the oppressed majority. This volume is not only a call for international solidarity in critical times but also an example of it. Background to the book, there is a constructed community of 'intellectual relatives' when Paraskeva engaged the faculty and students at UMD in conversations with scholars and practitioners from different fields, thus modeling a critical transformative praxis, a microcosm of the community. This tightly exceptional volume addresses real problems and emerging trends in education, matters on the intersection of politics and education, on critical issues concerning democracy such as the educational and curriculum epistemicide, public schooling, minorities, curriculum, teaching, and learning.

Drawing from critical theories and pedagogies, the contributors of this volume dissected diverse set of contemporary complexities and challenges related with democracy, critical curriculum theory, epistemology, among others. The chapters that make up this volume recognize the deeply neoliberal political nature of education and curriculum, the political economy that captured education, and the struggles to be taken both by the scholars and educators. Thus, the contributors of *Critical Transformative Educational Leadership and Policy Studies* take the reader to an intellectual journey for taking responsibility, for promising humanity for a better society which is currently under the threat of totalitarian regimes emerging around the world.

This exceptionally valuable collection calls us to struggle for critical transformative leadership and democratic education by presenting examples of alternative ways to think alternatively within neoliberal policies. A perfect reading to unpack the challenges facing radical, critical progressive intellectuals to lead a sustainable, critically transformative educational leadership in the current anti-intellectual environment. This book is a production of a collective intellectual commitment to social justice and equity for democratic education in culturally rich environments. It is an intellectual reading with a strong message of solidarity especially in the times of isolation, closed schools, and shut down homes with endless uncertainties. Last but not the least, the message produced by contributors of this volume is one of hope so well highlighted by Noam Chomsky who invites us to a commitment to 'international solidarity which can take new and more constructive forms as the great majority of the people of the world come to understand that their interests are pretty much the same and can be advanced by working together'.

—Fatma Mizikaci
Ankara University, Turkey

Critical
Transformative
Educational Leadership
& Policy Studies:
A READER

Copyright © 2021 | Myers Education Press, LLC

Published by Myers Education Press, LLC
P.O. Box 424
Gorham, ME 04038

Myers Education Press is an academic publisher specializing in books, e-books, and digital content in the field of education. All of our books are subjected to a rigorous peer review process and produced in compliance with the standards of the Council on Library and Information Resources.

LIBRARY OF CONGRESS CATALOGING-IN-PUBLICATION DATA AVAILABLE FROM LIBRARY OF CONGRESS
13-digit ISBN 978-1-9755-0288-1 (paperback)
13-digit ISBN 978-1-9755-0287-4 (hardcover)
13-digit ISBN 978-1-9755-0289-8 (library networkable e-edition)
13-digit ISBN 978-1-9755-0290-4 (consumer e-edition)

Printed in the United States of America.

All first editions printed on acid-free paper that meets the American National Standards Institute Z39-48 standard.

Books published by Myers Education Press may be purchased at special quantity discount rates for groups, workshops, training organizations, and classroom usage. Please call our customer service department at 1-800-232-0223 for details.

Cover design by Teresa Lagrange.

Visit us on the web at **www.myersedpress.com** to browse our complete list of titles.

Critical Transformative Educational Leadership & Policy Studies: A READER

Discussions & Solutions from the Leading Voices in Education

EDITED BY
João M. Paraskeva

Myers
Education
Press

Gorham, Maine

2021

To Jean MacCormack and Tony Garro

To the Students

Contents

PART V
THE STRUGGLE TO DEMOCRATIZE EDUCATION

Introduction

Critical Transformative Educational Leadership and Policy Studies

João M. Paraskeva

THE OUTBREAK OF the current pandemic is just one symptom of the great regression we are living. For some, COVID-19 is not that different from the normal flu; it is *una invenzione* used to pave the way to implement a state of exception and fear as a normal governing paradigm (Agamben, 2020a, 2020b). Others argue that the current pandemic certifies the death of the vanguard intellectuals that "write about the world, but not with the world" (Santos, 2020, p. 9) and the need of *"rearguard* intellectuals attentive to the needs and aspirations of ordinary citizens and how to start theorizing from them." To make matters worse, George Floyd, brutally and ruthlessly murdered by four policemen, has unmasked the violent racism that black and minority communities face in the United States, which is so ingrained in our institutions. Racism, classism, and genderism are not abstract "things."

Humanity is indeed facing a paradoxical time. On one hand, our current time "is marked by huge developments and thespian changes, an era that is referred to as the electronic revolution of communications, information, genetics and the biotechnological" (Santos, 2005, p. vii); on the other, "it is a time of disquieting regressions, a return of the social evils that appeared to have been or about to be overcome" (Santos, 2005, p. vii). Great achievements in areas such as space conquest and technologies have been reduced to a pale inconsequentiality for the massive majority of the world's population, which is facing slavery, genocide, holocaust, poverty, inequality, social and cognitive apartheid, and intergenerational injustice. Painfully, all of these sagas are at the very root of such modern societal tech advancements.

Such paradoxes speak volumes about "modern humanity which is not conceivable without a modern sub-humanity" (Santos, 2007b, p. 52). It looks like modernity, what Quijano (1992) coined *el patron colonial de poder*, has exhausted its limits. The "coloniality matrix of power" (Mignolo, 2018; Dussel, 2013), the Western Cartesian modernity reasoning as a hegemonic matrix, is not just moribund, it is dead. Modernity was/is a "misleading dream"

(Harding, 2008, p. 23). The twentieth century "was the last Eurocentric century" (Thernborn, 2010, p. 59). As Fanon (1963) beautifully stated, "let's go comrades, the European game is definitely finished, it is necessary to find something else" (p. 239).

Education is deeply implicated in this puzzle. It determines and has been determined by the logic of Eurocentric modernity, fundamentally derivative (Santos, 2014), selective (Williams, 1989), positivistic (Giroux, 1981), and patriarchal (hooks, 1994). Why, Santos (1999, p. 197) asks, "in a world where there is so much to criticize, it has become so difficult to produce a critical theory?" (Santos, 1999, p. 197).

Through the educational system, modern Western Eurocentric thinking has been able to impose itself hegemonically as abyssal thinking. It consists

> of a system of visible and invisible distinctions, the invisible ones being the foundation of the visible ones. The division is such that "the other side of the line" vanishes as reality becomes nonexistent, and is indeed produced as non-existent. What most fundamentally characterizes abyssal thinking is thus the impossibility of the co-presence of the two sides of the line. This side of the line only prevails by exhausting the field of relevant reality. Beyond it, there is only nonexistence, invisibility, non-dialectical absence. (Santos, 2007a, p. 45)

Such abyssal lines constitute the very core of "the epistemological foundation of the capitalist and imperial order that the global North has been imposing on the global South" (Santos 2007b, p. ix). There is no "incomplete other" (Todorova, 1997). Invisibility and nonexistence of the "one side" are the roots of visibility and existence of the "another side." Education is the carburetor of the colonial zone, a zone that is *par excellence*, the realm of incomprehensible beliefs and behaviors which in no way can be considered knowledge, whether true or false" (Santos, 2007b, p. ix). Education is thus the stage of an epistemicide (Santos, 2014), a curricular epistemicide and reversive epistemicide (Paraskeva, 2021, 2017, 2016a, 2016b, 2014, 2011).

While one of the great living curriculum scholars, Dwayne Huebner (1967, p. 174), insightfully argues that one of the problems in education "is no longer one of explaining the change, but of explaining non-change," education is still a site of hope and possibility for a world we all wish to see (Amin, 2008).

This book needs to be framed in such context, a context that is related with the critical transformative struggles done by so many educators against the educational structures of inequality for a more just society. Like any other volume, this one has a history and numerous stories associated with it, ones related to the design and development of a PhD program in critical transformative leadership and the founding of an Educational Leadership Department at the University of Massachusetts Dartmouth (UMD), which speaks volumes to some of the challenges facing progressive radical critical intellectuals in academia and translates some of the issues facing the very radical critical progressive onto-epistemological terrain.

A brief bio is crucial here. I was hired in the fall of 2009 by UMD after a fantastic year that I had spent in the College of Education, Health, and Society at Miami University in Oxford, Ohio, with colleagues and close allies, such as Richard Quantz, Michael Dantley, Lisa Weems, Denis Carlson, Denise Taliafero Baszile, and others. As I never stop saying, in Oxford I saw a space that cultivated humanity, as Nussbaum would have certainly put it. At UMD, I was charged with the responsibility of building a doctoral program—PhD/EdD—in educational leadership and policy studies, and a department of educational leadership, as a clear 'response to a growing local, state and national imperative to improve K-12 educational standing and attainment.'

The program and department were part of one of the great achievements and legacies of the MacCormack-Garro administration, which was the creation of the "School of Education, Public Policy and Civic Engagement." For the first time, in 2007, UMD—formerly Southern Massachusetts University—established an autonomous School of Education, Public Policy, and Civic Engagement, a graduate school closely linked to the South Coast communities. The other great legacy was the creation of the UMass School of Law at Dartmouth, the first law school in a public institution in the state. When I arrived, I found in the MacCormack-Garro administration a very clear notion of the public mission of a university, as was also demonstrated, for example, by the creation of the first and only School of Law at a public university in the state of Massachusetts, done during a time of great financial challenges.

The commitment to social justice was clear. The institution was, in a sense, attempting to promote a *Deweyan–Douglass* spirit, to be a microcosm of the community, addressing the needs of the minorities in a region economically devastated yet culturally enormously rich—important commitments for the establishment and success of any critically transformative project. Naturally, the battles were enormous, exhausting but also comforting. As in all of them, they have revealed the good and the very worst of the state of academia in an era hammered by the power of neoliberal policies that tortured public higher education financially.

However, as I have been arguing, the great challenge to public higher education and, above all, to the critical political pedagogical projects in public institutions does not come only from the violence and cruelty of neoliberal, neoconservative policies but also, among other things, is due to many complex issues within our radical critical platform—some of them insightfully dissected by the authors of the chapters of this book. Antonia Darder explains how

> the university today exists as a disturbing battleground, where ideas and practices can easily degenerate into a nightmare of undemocratic repression and bureaucratic madness. This phenomenon is fueled by wholesale abandonment of the public good and a full-fledged institutional divestment from the welfare of the commons. In the process, liberal values of equality and public responsibility have been precariously been undermined by an

> unrelenting neoliberal culture of rampant greed, racism, increasing public surveillance, and the social regulation and containment of subaltern populations. In the wake of this fiasco, critical notions of multiculturalism and diversity within the university, along with scholarship anchored in community concerns, have been rampantly undermined by an economic ethos that has rendered difference a whore to its utilitarian pursuits. (p. 217)

Consistent with the mission and vision of the university at that time, an interdisciplinary and integrated critical transformative program in educational leadership and policy studies was created, 'combining different fields of study and disciplines to break with traditional epistemological boundaries to better address contemporary local and global challenges.' The program 'blended theory and practice, recognized as essential the creation and nurturing of community-school environments, and supported the development of innovative pedagogy and critical transformative leadership.' As the result of a collective process that involved faculty, administrators, community members, community leaders, social activists, principals, and superintendents, a program was 'designed to prepare future practitioners and scholars who will work as professors, researchers, administrators, or executives in leadership roles in a variety of institutional settings.' The utopia was to 'develop a new generation of professional practitioners and scholars, highly trained in educational policy and management who could exercise critical transformative leadership and to prepare intellectuals 'committed to transforming students and institutions alike in pursuit of a more ethical, just and fair society and to improving educational achievement in environments that are dynamic, interactive, culturally diverse, and democratic.'

To accomplish such a task, the program was driven by a set of beliefs, namely, that "human growth and development are transformative lifelong pursuits; that schools are political and cultural artifacts of local and global contexts; that diversity strengthens organizations; that while transformative leadership implies individual and teamwork that stimulates differences, it is also 'driven by moral and ethical imperatives'; and that 'one can only have an impact globally if one is capable of making a difference locally."

The program was approved with flying colors, in record time, and at a moment when the university was facing financial challenges. Yet, in the summer of 2011, I was quite honored to teach the first course of the program—ELP 551: Introduction to Educational Leadership and Public Policy—to the first cohort of students. As part of the course requirements, the program delivered '18 courses and 10 colloquia each academic year in three sessions (summer, fall, and spring).' The colloquia were just one of the secrets of the success of the program. The rationale for such a series of colloquia was clear in the proposal:

> A set of two colloquia is provided to engage the faculty and students in conversations with invited scholars and practitioners from well-known or emerging fields. While colloquia topics will change from semester to semester, responding in real-time to real problems and emerging trends in education, their focus will

be on the intersection of politics and education and on critical issues (what's new, what is controversial) concerning teaching and learning. The colloquia will be open to other faculty and practitioners in the region so that these can serve as professional or academic forums. The colloquia also will engage the faculty and students in the program in an active dialogue and build community. Expert faculty, researchers, and practitioners may be invited to present papers or to be keynote speakers from time to time and encouraged to dissert with the faculty and students afterward. The colloquia are a hallmark of this program.

Students and faculty participated in the construction of a unique intellectual environment within and beyond traditional doctoral courses, with a clear impact on the students' success. In addition to traditional doctoral courses (such as Introduction to Educational Leadership and Public Policy; Organizational Behavior in Educational Settings; Transformative Educational Leadership; Social, Historical and Philosophical Foundations of American Education; Research Methods; Design and Evaluation of Educational Systems; Public Finance in Education; Law, and the Education of Disenfranchised Groups and Subaltern Communities Contemporary Policy and Reform in American Education; Critical Curriculum Theory and Inquiry in Education; Globalization, Cosmopolitanism, Democracy and Social Justice in Education; Education, Work and Emancipation; Indigenous Knowledge and Methodologies; Educational Reform, Accountability and the Achievement Gap; Political Economy and Education), students and faculty participated in colloquia that covered issues such as politics and education, critical issues in teaching and learning, innovations in instructional design and technology, global contexts in education policy, global challenges, local demands and solutions, language planning and education, and promoting parental and civic engagement in schools.

Open to the public, leading intellectuals within and outside of the field were invited to lecture on such crucial issues. During my tenure as chair and graduate program director, the colloquia structure provided an opportunity to bring world-renowned school administrators to our campus, such as Antonio Carvalho of Miami-Dade County Public Schools and National Superintendent of the Year; Matthew Malone, who was the superintendent of Brockton, Massachusetts, Public Schools and, at the time, the Massachusetts secretary of education; and national and state legislators, such as Massachusetts Senator Joe Kennedy and Massachusetts State Representative Tony Cabral. In addition, African poets, such as Vera Duarte and Ondjaki, and educators, such as Noam Chomsky, Henry Giroux, Stanley Aronowitz, Angela Valenzuela, Gary Anderson, Antonia Darder, Sonia Nieto, Lilia Bartolome, Kenneth Zeichner, John Willinsky, David Berliner, Donaldo Macedo, Thomas Popkewitz, Thomas Pedroni, Gloria Ladson Billings, Pauline Lipman, Richard Quantz, Susan Searls Giroux, Lois Weis, Garry Anderson, David Hursh, Bernadette Baker, Mike Peters, Khalil Saucier, Leigh Patel, Jurjo Torres Santome, Ana Bello, Clyde Barrow, Ines Oliveira, Alvaro Hypolito,

Wayne Au, Vanessa Andreotti, Alex Means, and Gustavo Fischman. Victor Borges, former minister of education in Cape Verde, honored us by giving the first lecture in the first colloquia of the program. Students and faculty also organized an annual meeting in which the students formed and created TRED—Transformative Researchers and Educators for Democracy—which became the name for this international conference, constituting another great accomplishment for the program.

The chapters that make up this volume reflect some of the lectures of such colloquia and what used to represent the intellectual atmosphere that the program collectively produced. Lectures that addressed current contentious issues on neoliberal political economy and education, leadership, policy, and reform, examining the colonial power matrix, alternative ways to think alternatively on education, and the struggles to democratize education, compose the five parts of this volume. The approaches that structure this volume help to better understand how education has been determined and how it determines our contemporary social havoc. Leading intellectuals in the field examine the current complex momentum facing public education and explore new possible alternative avenues to address present and future challenges for our field, thus unpacking the real epistemological colors of such great regression. I am confident that from many different perspectives, *Critical Transformative Educational Leadership and Policy Studies: Discussions and Solutions from the Leading Voices in Education* will help better unpack the challenges facing radical, critical progressive intellectuals to edify a sustainable, critically transformative educational leadership in the current anti-intellectual environment (Paraskeva, 2020, 2013) with authoritarian impulses framing public education. Such impulses—quite visible in the daily praxis—are very difficult to challenge though, since they have captured and undermined one of the great advances and achievements of progressive movements—the field of identity politics. Unfortunately, this field is one of the wide-open doors through which the dominant power has managed to disguise and camouflage a false cult of equity and social justice.

In its first five years, the program graduated 40 students, mostly minorities. This book is dedicated to all that made the program possible, especially the students of the program and to both Jean MacCormack and Tony Garro, former UMD chancellor and provost, respectively. Special thanks to Massachusetts legislators such as Michael Rodrigues, Tony Cabral, and Marc Pacheco for their tremendous support and care. A word of gratitude to Chris Myers and Stephanie Gabaree from Myers Educational Press. Chris's commitment to progressive education is crucial as he provides an important space for the struggle for social and cognitive justice. Last but not least, as Santos (2019, p. xi) once beautifully stated, without a doubt I know painfully well that "most of those to whom I owe this book will not be able to read it."

References

Agamben, G. (2020a). The State of Exception Provoked by an Unmotivated Emergency. *Positions Politics*. Retrieved from http://positionswebsite.org

Agamben, G. (2020b) Giorgio Agamben: Normalising the State of Exception Under the Covid-19 Epidemic. *Biopolitics*. Retrieved from https://non.copyriot.com

Amin, S. (2008). *The World We Wish to See: Revolutionary Objectives in the Twenty-First Century*. New York: Monthly Review Press.

Dussel, E. (2013). *Ethics of Liberation: In the Age of Globalization and Exclusion*. Edited by A. Vallega. Translated by E. Mendieta, N. Maldonado-Torres, Y. Angulo, and C. Pérez Bustillo. Durham: Duke University Press.

Fanon, F. (1963). *The Wretched of the Earth*. New York: Grove Press.

Geiselberger, H. (2017). *O Grande Retrocesso. Um Debate International sobre as Grandes Questoes do Nosso Tempo*. Lisboa: Objectiva.

Giroux, H. (1981). *Ideology, Culture & the Process of Schooling*. Philadelphia: Temple University Press.

Harding, S. (2008). *Sciences from Bellow. Feminisms, Postcolonialities and Modernities*. Durham: Duke University Press.

Huebner, D. (1967). Curriculum as Concern of Man's Temporality." *Theory into Practice*, 6 (4), pp. 172–179.

hooks, b. (1994). *Teaching to Transgress. Education as a Practice of Freedom*. New York: Routledge.

Mignolo, W. (2018). The Invention of the Human and the Three Pillars of the Coloniality Matrix of Power. In C. Walsh and W. Mignolo (Eds.), *On Decoloniality: Concepts, Analytics, Praxis*. Durham: Duke University Press, pp. 153–176.

Paraskeva, J. (2011). *Conflicts Curriculum Theory*. Challenging Hegemonic Epistemologies. New York: Palgrave

Paraskeva, J. (2014). *Conflicts Curriculum Theory*. Challenging Hegemonic Epistemologies. New York: Palgrave (upgrade paperback edition).

Paraskeva, J. (2016a). *Curriculum Epistemicides*. New York: Routledge.

Paraskeva, J. (2016b). The Curriculum: Whose Internationalization? In J. Paraskeva (Ed.), *Curriculum: Whose Internationalization*. New York: Peter Lang, pp. 1–10.

Paraskeva, J. (2017). *Towards a Just Curriculum Theory. The Epistemicide*. New York: Routledge.

Paraskeva, J. (2021). *Curriculum: The Generation of Utopia*. New York: Routledge.

Pinar William (2004). *What Is Curriculum Theory?* Mahwah: Lawrence Erlbaum Associates Publishers.

Quijano, A. (1992). Colonialidad y Modernidad-Racionalidad. In En H. Bonilla (Ed.), *Los Conquistadores*. Bogota: Tercer Mundo, pp. 437–447.

Santos, B. (1999). Porque é tão difícil construir uma teoria crítica? *Revista Crítica de Ciencias Sociais*, 54, Junho, pp. 197–215.

Santos, B. (2005). *Another Democracy Is Possible*. London: Verso.

Santos, B. (2007a). *Another Knowledge Is Possible*. London: Verso

Santos, B. (2007b). Beyond Abyssal Thinking. From Global Lines to Ecologies of Knowledges, *Review*, XXX (1), pp. 45–89.

Santos, B. (2014). *Epistemologies of the South: Justice Against Epistemicide*. Boulder: Paradigm.

Santos, B. (2019). *The End of the Cognitive Empire*. Durham: Duke University Press.

Santos, B. (2020). *A Cruel Pedagogia do Virus*. Coimbra: Almedina.

Thernborn, G. (2010). *From Marxism to Post-Marxism?* London: Verso.

Todorova, M. (1997). *Imagining the Balkans*. Oxford: Oxford University Press.
UMD Doctoral Proposal. (2010). Program in Educational Leadership and Policy Studies. North Dartmouth: University of Massachusetts Dartmouth.
Williams, R. (1989). *Resources of Hope*. London: Verso.

PART I
NEOLIBERAL POLITICAL ECONOMY
OF EDUCATION

CHAPTER ONE

Market Democracy in a Neoliberal Order: Doctrines and Reality

Noam Chomsky[1]

I HAVE BEEN asked to speak on some aspect of academic or human freedom, an invitation that offers many choices. I will keep to some simple ones. Freedom without opportunity is a devil's gift, and the refusal to provide such opportunities is criminal. The fate of the more vulnerable offers a sharp measure of the distance from here to something that might be called "civilization." While I am speaking, 1000 children will die from easily preventable disease, and almost twice that many women will die or suffer serious disability in pregnancy or childbirth for lack of simple remedies and care (UNICEF, 1997, 1996). UNICEF estimates that to overcome such tragedies and, to ensure universal access to basic social services, would require a quarter of the annual military expenditures of the "developing countries," about 10% of U.S. military spending. It is against the background of such realities as these that any serious discussion of human freedom should proceed.

It is widely held that the cure for such profound social maladies is within reach. The hopes have foundation. The past few years have seen the fall of brutal tyrannies, the growth of scientific understanding that offers great promise, and many other reasons to look forward to a brighter future. The discourse of the privileged is marked by confidence and triumphalism: the way forward is known, and there is no other. The basic theme, articulated with force and clarity, is that "America's victory in the Cold War was a victory for a set of political and economic principles: democracy and the free market." These principles are "the wave of the future – a future for which America is both the gatekeeper and the model." I am quoting the chief political commentator of the *New York Times*, but the picture is conventional, widely repeated throughout much of the world, and accepted as generally accurate even by critics. It was also enunciated as the "Clinton Doctrine," which declared that our new mission is to "consolidate the victory of democracy and open markets" that had just been won. There remains a range of disagreement: at one extreme "Wilsonian idealists" urge continued dedication to the traditional mission of benevolence; at the other, "realists" counter that we may lack the means to conduct these crusades of "global meliorism," and should not neglect our own interests in the service of others.[2] Within this range lies the path to a better world.

1   Version of the keynote address, Department of Education Leadership, University of Massachusetts Dartmouth, Town Hall, December, 4 2012.
2   Thomas Friedman, *NYT*, June 2, 1992; National Security Adviser Antony Lake, *NYT*, Sept. 26, 1993; historian David Fromkin, *NYT Book Review*, May 4, 1997, summarizing recent work.

Reality seems to me rather different. The current spectrum of public policy debate has as little relevance to actual policy as its numerous antecedents: neither the United States nor any other power has been guided by "global meliorism." Democracy is under attack worldwide, including the leading industrial countries, at least, democracy in a meaningful sense of the term, involving opportunities for people to manage their own collective and individual affairs. Something similar is true of markets. The assaults on democracy and markets are furthermore related. Their roots lie in the power of corporate entities that are totalitarian in internal structure, increasingly interlinked and reliant on powerful states, and largely unaccountable to the public. Their immense power is growing as a result of social policy that is globalizing the structural model of the third world, with sectors of enormous wealth and privilege alongside an increase in "the proportion of those who will labor under all the hardships of life, and secretly sigh for a more equal distribution of its blessings," as the leading framer of American democracy, James Madison, predicted 200 years ago (Clairmont, 1960; Chossudovsky, 1997). These policy choices are most evident in the Anglo-American societies but extend worldwide. They cannot be attributed to what "the free market has decided, in its infinite but mysterious wisdom," "the implacable sweep of 'the market revolution,'" "Reaganesque rugged individualism," or a "new orthodoxy" that "gives the market full sway."[3] The quotes are liberal to left, in some cases quite critical. The analysis is similar across the rest of the spectrum but generally euphoric. The reality, on the contrary, is that state intervention plays a decisive role, as in the past, and the basic outlines of policy are hardly novel. Current versions reflect "capital's clear subjugation of labor" for more than 15 years, in the words of the business press,[4] which often frankly articulates the perceptions of a highly class-conscious business community, dedicated to class war.

If these perceptions are valid, then the path to a world that is more just and more free lies well outside the range set forth by privilege and power. I cannot hope to establish such conclusions here but only to suggest that they are credible enough to consider with care and to suggest further that prevailing doctrines could hardly survive were it not for their contribution to "regimenting the public mind every bit as much as an army regiments the bodies of its soldiers," to borrow the dictum of the respected Roosevelt–Kennedy liberal Edward Bernays in his classic manual for the public relations industry, of which he was one of the founders and leading figures.

Bernays was drawing from his experience in Woodrow Wilson's state propaganda agency, the Committee on Public Information. "It was, of course, the astounding success of propaganda during the war that opened the eyes of the intelligent few in all departments of life to the possibilities of regimenting the public mind," he wrote. His goal was to adapt these experiences to the needs of the "intelligent minorities," primarily business leaders, whose task is "the conscious and intelligent manipulation of the organized habits

---

3   See Buell (1997) *The Progressive*, March; J. Cassidy (1995) *New Yorker*, Oct. 16; H. Cox (1997) *World Policy Review*, Spring; N. Nolan (1997) *BG*, March 5.
4   John Liscio, *Barron's*, April 15, 1996.

and opinions of the masses." Such "engineering of consent" is the very "essence of the democratic process," Bernays wrote shortly before he was honored for his contributions by the American Psychological Association in 1949. The importance of "controlling the public mind" has been recognized with increasing clarity as popular struggles succeeded in extending the modalities of democracy, thus giving rise to what liberal elites call "the crisis of democracy" as when normally passive and apathetic populations become organized and seek to enter the political arena to pursue their interests and demands, threatening stability and order. As Bernays explained the problem, with "universal suffrage and universal schooling, at last even the bourgeoisie stood in fear of the common people. For the masses promised to become king," a tendency fortunately reversed – so it has been hoped – as new methods "to mold the mind of the masses" were devised and implemented (Bernays, 1928; also Crozier, Huntington, and Watanuki, 1975).

Quite strikingly, in both of the world's leading democracies there was a growing awareness of the need to "apply the lessons" of the highly successful propaganda systems of World War I "to the organization of political warfare," as the chairman of the British Conservative Party put the matter 70 years ago. Wilsonian liberals in the U.S. drew the same conclusions in the same years, including public intellectuals and prominent figures in the developing profession of political science. In another corner of Western civilization, Adolf Hitler vowed that next time Germany would not be defeated in the propaganda war, and also devised his own ways to apply the lessons of Anglo-American propaganda for political warfare at home (Cockett, 1994; Lasswel, 1933; Chomsky, 1982; Carey, 1995).

Meanwhile the business world warned of "the hazard facing industrialists" in "the newly realized political power of the masses" and the need to wage and win "the everlasting battle for the minds of men" and "indoctrinate citizens with the capitalist story" until "they are able to play back the story with remarkable fidelity" and so on, in an impressive flow, accompanied by even more impressive efforts, and surely one of the central themes of modern history (Cockett, 1994; Lasswel, 1933; Chomsky, 1982, 1991; 1992; Carey, 1995; Fones-Wolf, 1995; Ewen, 1996).

To discover the true meaning of the "political and economic principles" that are declared to be "the wave of the future," it is of course necessary to go beyond rhetorical flourishes and public pronouncements and to investigate actual practice and the internal documentary record. Close examination of particular cases is the most rewarding path, but these must be chosen carefully to give a fair picture. There are some natural guidelines. One reasonable approach is to take the examples chosen by the proponents of the doctrines themselves, as their "strongest case." Another is to investigate the record where influence is greatest and interference least so that we see the operative principles in their purest form. If we want to determine what the Kremlin meant by "democracy" and "human rights," we will pay little heed to *Pravda*'s solemn denunciations of racism in the United States or state terror in its client regimes, even less to protestation of noble motives. Far more instructive is the state of affairs in the "people's democracies" of Eastern Europe. The point is elementary, and applies to the self-designated "gatekeeper and model" as well. Latin America is the obvious testing ground, particularly the Central America–Caribbean region. Here Washington has faced few external challenges for almost a century, so the guiding principles of policy, and of today's neoliberal "Washington Consensus," are revealed most clearly when we examine the state of the region and how that came about.

It is of some interest that the exercise is rarely undertaken, and if proposed, castigated as extremist or worse. I leave it as an "exercise for the reader," merely noting that the record teaches useful lessons about the political and economic principles that are to be "the wave of the future."

Washington's "crusade for democracy," as it is called, was waged with particular fervor during the Reagan years, with Latin America the chosen terrain. The results are commonly offered as a prime illustration of how the U.S. became "the inspiration for the triumph of democracy in our time," to quote the editors of the leading intellectual journal of American liberalism.[5] The most recent scholarly study of democracy describes "the revival of democracy in Latin America" as "impressive" but not unproblematic; the "barriers to implementation" remain "formidable," but can perhaps be overcome through closer integration with the United States (Lakoff, 1996). The author, Sanford Lakoff (1996), singles out the "historic North American Free Trade Agreement (NAFTA)" as a potential instrument of democratization. In the region of traditional U.S. influence, he writes, the countries are moving towards democracy, having "survived military intervention" and "vicious civil war."

Let us begin by looking more closely at these recent cases, the natural ones given overwhelming U.S. influence and the ones regularly selected to illustrate the achievements and promise of "America's mission."

The primary "barriers to implementation" of democracy, Lakoff (1996) suggests, are the "vested interests" that seek to protect "domestic markets"—that is, to prevent foreign (mainly U.S.) corporations from gaining even greater control over the society. We are to understand, then, that democracy is enhanced as significant decision-making shifts even more into the hands of unaccountable private tyrannies, mostly foreign-based. Meanwhile the public arena is to shrink still further as the state is "minimized" in accordance with the neoliberal "political and economic principles" that have emerged triumphant. A study of the World Bank points out that the new orthodoxy represents "a dramatic shift away from a pluralist, participatory ideal of politics and towards an authoritarian and technocratic ideal . . . ," one that is very much in accord with leading elements of twentieth century liberal and progressive thought, and in another variant, the Leninist model; the two are more similar than often recognized (Toye, Harrigan, and Mosley, 1991; Mihevc, 1995; Chomsky, 1973)

Thinking through the tacit reasoning, we gain some useful insight into the concepts of democracy and markets, in the operative sense. Lakoff (1996) does not look into the "revival of democracy" in Latin America, but he does cite a scholarly source that includes

---

5   Editorial, *New Republic*, March 19, 1990.

a contribution on Washington's crusade in the 1980s. The author is Thomas Carothers, who combines scholarship with an "insider's perspective," having worked on "democracy enhancement" programs in Reagan's State Department (Carothers, 1991a, 1991b). Carothers (1991a, 1991b) regards Washington's "impulse to promote democracy" as "sincere" but largely a failure. Furthermore, the failure was systematic: where Washington's influence was least, in South America, there was real progress towards democracy, which the Reagan administration generally opposed, later taking credit for it when the process proved irresistible. Where Washington's influence was greatest, progress was least, and where it occurred, the U.S. role was marginal or negative. His general conclusion is that the U.S. sought to maintain "the basic order of . . . quite undemocratic societies" and to avoid "populist-based change," "inevitably [seeking] only limited, top-down forms of democratic change that did not risk upsetting the traditional structures of power with which the United States has long been allied."

The last phrase requires a gloss. The term "United States" is conventionally used to refer to structures of power within the United States; the "national interest" is the interest of these groups, which correlates only weakly with interests of the general population. So the conclusion is that Washington sought top-down forms of democracy that did not upset traditional structures of power with which the structures of power in the United States have long been allied. Not a very surprising fact, or much of a historical novelty. To appreciate the significance of the fact, it is necessary to examine more closely the nature of parliamentary democracies. The United States is the most important case, not only because of its power but because of its stable and long-standing democratic institutions. Furthermore, the United States was about as close to a model as one can find. America can be "As happy as she pleases," Thomas Paine (cited in Wood, 1991) remarked in 1776: "she has a blank sheet to write upon." The indigenous societies were largely eliminated. There is little residue of earlier European structures, one reason for the relative weakness of the social contract and of support systems, which often had their roots in pre-capitalist institutions. And to an unusual extent, the sociopolitical order was consciously designed. In studying history, one cannot construct experiments, but the U.S. is as close to the "ideal case" of state capitalist democracy as can be found.

Furthermore, the leading Framer of the constitutional system was an astute and lucid political thinker, James Madison, whose views largely prevailed. In the debates on the Constitution, Madison pointed out that in England, if elections "were open to all classes of people, the property of landed proprietors would be insecure. An agrarian law would soon take place," giving land to the landless. The system that he and his associates were designing must prevent such injustice, he urged, and "secure the permanent interests of the country," which are property rights. It is the responsibility of government, Madison declared, "to protect the minority of the opulent against the majority." To achieve this goal, political power must rest in the hands of "the wealth of the nation," men who would "sympathize sufficiently" with property rights and "be safe depositories of power over them," while the rest are marginalized and fragmented, offered only limited public participation in the political arena. Among Madisonian scholars, there is a consensus that "the Constitution was intrinsically an aristocratic document designed to check the democratic tendencies of the period," delivering power to a "better sort" of people and excluding "those who were not rich, well born, or prominent from exercising political power" (Chomsky, 1996a, 1996b).[6]

These conclusions are often qualified by the observation that Madison, and the constitutional system generally, sought to balance the rights of persons against the rights of property. But the formulation is misleading. Property has no rights. In both principle and practice, the phrase "rights of property" means the right *to* property, typically material property, a personal right which must be privileged above all others, and is crucially different from others in that one person's possession of such rights deprives another of them. When the facts are stated clearly, we can appreciate the force of the doctrine that "the people who own the country ought to govern it," "one of [the] favorite maxims" of Madison's influential colleague John Jay, his biographer observes (Monaghan, 1935).

One may argue, as some historians do, that these principles lost their force as the national territory was conquered and settled, the native population driven out or exterminated. Whatever one's assessment of those years, by the late 19th century the founding doctrines took on a new and much more oppressive form. When Madison spoke of "rights of persons," he meant humans. But the growth of the industrial economy, and the rise of corporate forms of economic enterprise, led to a completely new meaning of the term. In a current official document, "'Person' is broadly defined to include any individual, branch, partnership, associated group, association, estate, trust, corporation or other organization (whether or not organized under the laws of any State), or any government entity,"[7] a concept that doubtless would have shocked Madison and others with intellectual roots in the Enlightenment and classical liberalism—precapitalist, and anti-capitalist in spirit.

These radical changes in the conception of human rights and democracy were not introduced primarily by legislation but by judicial decisions and intellectual commentary. Corporations, which previously had been considered artificial entities with no rights, were accorded all the rights of persons, and far more, since they are "immortal persons" and "persons" of extraordinary wealth and power. Furthermore, they were no longer bound to the specific purposes designated by state charter but could act as they chose, with few constraints. The intellectual backgrounds for granting such extraordinary rights to "collectivist legal entities" lie in neo-Hegelian doctrines that also underlie Bolshevism and fascism: the idea that organic entities have rights over and above those of persons. Conservative legal scholars bitterly opposed these innovations, recognizing that they undermine the traditional idea that rights inhere in individuals, and undermine market principles as well (Horwitz, 1992; Sellers, 1991). But the new

---

6   Lance Banning, the leading scholarly proponent of the libertarian interpretation of Madison's views, citing Gordon Wood.
7   *Survey of Current Business,* (1996) Vol. 76, no. 12, Dec. Washington, D.C.: U.S. Department of Commerce.

forms of authoritarian rule were institutionalized, and along with them, the legitimation of wage labor, which was considered hardly better than slavery in mainstream American thought through much of the 19th century, not only by the rising labor movement but also by such figures as Abraham Lincoln, the Republican Party, and the establishment media (Sandel, 1996; Peck, 1987: Chomsky, 1996a; 1971).[8]

These are topics with enormous implications for understanding the nature of market democracy. Again, I can only mention them here. The material and ideological outcome helps explain the understanding that "democracy" abroad must reflect the model sought at home: "top-down" forms of control, with the public kept to a "spectator" role, not participating in the arena of decision-making, which must exclude these "ignorant and meddlesome outsiders," according to the mainstream of modern democratic theory. I happen to be quoting the essays on democracy by Walter Lippmann, one of the most respected American public intellectuals and journalists of the century (Carey, 1995). But the general ideas are standard and have solid roots in the constitutional tradition, radically modified, however, in the new era of collectivist legal entities.

Returning to the "victory of democracy" under U.S. guidance, neither Lakoff nor Carothers asks how Washington maintained the traditional power structure of highly undemocratic societies. Their topic is not the terrorist wars that left tens of thousands of tortured and mutilated corpses, millions of refugees, and devastation perhaps beyond recovery—in large measure wars against the church, which became an enemy when it adopted "the preferential option for the poor," trying to help suffering people to attain some measure of justice and democratic rights. It is more than symbolic that the terrible decade of the 1980s opened with the murder of an archbishop who had become "a voice for the voiceless" and closed with the assassination of six leading Jesuit intellectuals who had chosen the same path, in each case by terrorist forces armed and trained by the victors of the "crusade for democracy." One should take careful note of the fact that the leading Central American dissident intellectuals were doubly assassinated: both murdered and silenced. Their words, indeed their very existence, are scarcely known in the United States, unlike dissidents in enemy states, who are greatly honored and admired; another cultural universal, I presume.

Such matters do not enter history as recounted by the victors. In Lakoff's study, which is not untypical in this regard, what survives are references to "military intervention" and "civil wars," with no external factor identified. These matters will not so quickly be put aside, however, by those who seek a better grasp of the principles that are to shape the future, if the structures of power have their way.

Particularly revealing is Lakoff's description of Nicaragua, again standard: "a civil war was ended following a democratic election, and a difficult effort is underway to create a more prosperous and self-governing society." In the real world, the superpower attacking Nicaragua escalated its assault *after* the country's first democratic election: the election

---

8   His interpretation in terms of republicanism and civic virtue is too narrow, in my opinion, overlooking deeper roots in the Englightenment and before.

of 1984, closely monitored and recognized as legitimate by the professional association of Latin American scholars (LASA), Irish and British Parliamentary delegations, and others, including a hostile Dutch government delegation that was remarkably supportive of Reaganite atrocities, as well as the leading figure of Central American democracy, Jos Figueres of Costa Rica, also critical observer, though regarding the elections as legitimate in this "invaded country" and calling on Washington to allow the Sandinistas "to finish what they started in peace; they deserve it." The U.S. strongly opposed the holding of the elections and sought to undermine them, concerned that democratic elections might interfere with its terrorist war. But that concern was put to rest by the good behavior of the doctrinal system, which barred the reports with remarkable efficiency, reflexively adopting the state propaganda line that the elections were meaningless fraud. (Chomsky, 1988, 1993a; Herman and Chomsky, 1988; Carothers, 1991).[9]

Overlooked as well is the fact that as the next election approached on schedule[10], Washington left no doubt that unless the results came out the right way, Nicaraguans would continue to endure the illegal economic warfare and "unlawful use of force" that the World Court had condemned and ordered terminated, of course in vain. This time the outcome was acceptable, and hailed in the U.S. with an outburst of exuberance that is highly informative (Chomsky, 1992).[11]

At the outer limits of critical independence, columnist Anthony Lewis of the *New York Times* was overcome with admiration for Washington's "experiment in peace and democracy," which showed that "we live in a romantic age." The experimental methods were no secret. Thus, *Time* magazine, joining in the celebration as "democracy burst forth" in Nicaragua, outlined them frankly: to "wreck the economy and prosecute a long and deadly proxy war until the exhausted natives overthrow the unwanted government themselves," with a cost to us that is "minimal," leaving the victim "with wrecked bridges, sabotaged power stations, and ruined farms" and providing Washington's candidate with "a winning issue," ending the "impoverishment of the people of Nicaragua," not to speak of the continuing terror, better left unmentiond. To be sure, the cost to them was hardly "minimal": Carothers notes that the toll "in per capita terms was significantly higher than the number of U.S. persons killed in the U.S. Civil War and all the wars of the twentieth century *combined.*"[12] The outcome was a "Victory for U.S. Fair Play," a headline in the Times exulted, leaving Americans "United in Joy," in the style of Albania and North Korea.

9   For details, see Chomsky (1988, chapter 11, and sources cited), including long quotes from Figueres, whose exclusion from the media took considerable dedication. See also Chomsky (1993, chapter 6; on the record, including the long obituary in the *NYT* by its Central America specialist and the effusive accompanying editorial, which again succeeded in completely banning his views on Washington's "crusade for democracy." On media coverage of Nicaraguan and Salvadoran elections, see Herman and Chomsky (1988, chapter 3). Even Carothers, who is careful with the facts, writes that the Sandinistas "refused to agree to elections" until 1990.

10   Another standard falsification is that the long-planned elections took place only because of Washington's military and economic pressures, which are therefore retroactively justified.

11   On the elections and the reaction in Latin America and the U.S., including sources for what follows see Chomsky (1992, chapter 10).

12   His emphasis, op. cit.

The methods of this "romantic age," and the reaction to them in enlightened circles, tell us more about the democratic principles that have emerged victorious. They also shed some light on why it is such a "difficult effort" to "create a more prosperous and self-governing society" in Nicaragua. It is true that the effort is now underway, and is meeting with some success for a privileged minority, while most of the population faces social and economic disaster, all in the familiar pattern of Western dependencies (Garfield, 1993; Chomsky, 1994a). Note that it is precisely this example that led the editors to laud themselves as "the inspiration for the triumph of democracy in our time," joining the enthusiastic chorus.

We learn more about the victorious principles by recalling that these same representative figures of liberal intellectual life had urged that Washington's wars must be waged mercilessly, with military support for "Latin-style fascists, regardless of how many are murdered," because "there are higher American priorities than Salvadoran human rights." Elaborating, editor Michael Kinsley, who represented "the left" in mainstream commentary and television debate, cautioned against unthinking criticism of Washington's official policy of attacking undefended civilian targets. Such international terrorist operations cause "vast civilian suffering," he acknowledged, but they may be "perfectly legitimate" if "cost-benefit analysis" shows that "the amount of blood and misery that will be poured in" yields "democracy," as the world rulers define it. Enlightened opinion insists that terror is not a value in itself but must meet the pragmatic criterion. Kinsley later observed that the desired ends had been achieved: "impoverishing the people of Nicaragua was precisely the point of the contra war and the parallel policy of economic embargo and veto of international development loans," which "wreck[ed] the economy" and "creat[ed] the economic disaster [that] was probably the victorious opposition's best election issue." He then joined in welcoming the "triumph of democracy" in the "free election" of 1990[13] (Chomsky, 1992, 1988).

Client states enjoy similar privileges. Thus, commenting on yet another of Israel's attacks on Lebanon, foreign editor H.D.S. Greenway of the *Boston Globe*, who had graphically reported the first major invasion 15 years earlier, commented that "if shelling Lebanese villages, even at the cost of lives, and driving civilian refugees north would secure Israel's border, weaken Hezbollah, and promote peace, I would say go to it, as would many Arabs and Israelis. But history has not been kind to Israeli adventures in Lebanon. They have solved very little and have almost always caused more problems." By the pragmatic criterion, then, the murder of many civilians, the expulsion of hundreds of thousand of refugees, and the devastation of southern Lebanon is a dubious proposition.[14] It would not be too hard, I presume, to find comparable examples here in the recent past. Bear in mind that I am keeping to the dissident sector of tolerable opinion, what is called "the left," a fact that tells us more about the victorious principles and the intellectual culture within which they find their place.

13   Kinsley, *Wall Street Journal*, March 26, 1987; *New Republic*, March 19, 1990.
14   Greenway, *BG*, July 29, 1993.

Also revealing was the reaction to periodic Reagan administration allegations about Nicaraguan plans to obtain jet interceptors from the Soviet Union (the U.S. having coerced its allies into refusing to sell them). Hawks demanded that Nicaragua be bombed at once. Doves countered that the charges must first be verified, but if they were, the U.S. would have to bomb Nicaragua. Sane observers understood why Nicaragua might want jet interceptors: to protect its territory from CIA overflights that were supplying the U.S. proxy forces and providing them with up-to-the-minute information so that they could follow the directive to attack undefended "soft targets." The tacit assumption is that no country has a right to defend civilians from U.S. attack. The doctrine, which reigned challenged, is an interesting one. It might be illuminating to seek counterparts elsewhere.

The pretext for Washington's terrorist wars was self-defense, the standard official justification for just about any monstrous act, even the Nazi Holocaust. Indeed Ronald Reagan, finding "that the policies and actions of the Government of Nicaragua constitute an unusual and extraordinary threat to the national security and foreign policy of the United States," declared "a national emergency to deal with that threat," arousing no ridicule.[15] Others react differently. In response to John F. Kennedy's efforts to organize collective action against Cuba in 1961, a Mexican diplomat explained that Mexico could not go along, because "If we publicly declare that Cuba is a threat to our security, forty million Mexicans will die laughing" (Leacock, 1990). Enlightened opinion in the West takes a more sober view of the extraordinary threat to national security. By similar logic, the USSR had every right to attack Denmark, a far greater threat to its security, and surely Poland and Hungary when they took steps towards independence. The fact that such pleas can regularly be put forth is again an interesting comment on the intellectual culture of the victors, and another indication of what lies ahead.

The substance of the Cold War pretexts is greatly illuminated by the case of Cuba, as are the real operative principles. These have emerged with much clarity once again in the past few weeks, with Washington's refusal to accept World Trade Organization (W.T.O.) adjudication of a European Union challenge to its embargo, which is unique in its severity, and had already been condemned as a violation of international law by the organization of American States and repeatedly by the United Nations, with near unanimity, more recently extended to severe penalties for third parties that disobey Washington's edicts, yet another violation of international law and trade agreements. The official response of the Clinton administration, as reported by the Newspaper of Record, is that "Europe is challenging 'three decades of American Cuba policy that goes back to the Kennedy administration,' and is aimed entirely at forcing a change of government in Havana." (Morley and McGillion, 1997).[16] The Administration also declared that

15   NYT, May 2, 1985.
16   David Sanger, "U.S. Won't Offer Testimony on Cuba Embargo," NYT, Feb. 21, 1997. The actual official wording is that the "bipartisan policy since the early 1960s [is] based on the notion that we have a hostile and unfriendly regime 90 miles from our border, and that anything done to strengthen that regime will only encourage the regime to not only continue its hostility but, through much of its tenure, to try to destabilize large

the W.T.O. "has no competence to proceed" on an issue of American national security and cannot "force the U.S. to change its laws."

At the very same moment, Washington and the media were lauding the W.T.O. Telecommunications agreement as a "new tool of foreign policy" that compels other countries to change their laws and practices in accord with Washington's demands, incidentally handing over their communications systems to mainly U.S. megacorporations in yet another serious blow against democracy.[17] But the W.T.O. has no authority to compel the U.S. to change its laws, just as the World Court has no authority to compel the U.S. to terminate its international terrorism and illegal economic warfare. Free trade and international law are like democracy: fine ideas but to be judged by outcome, not process.

The reasoning with regard to the W.T.O. is reminiscent of the official U.S. grounds for dismissing World Court adjudication of Nicaragua's charges. In both cases, the U.S. rejected jurisdiction on the plausible assumption that rulings would be against the U.S.; by simple logic, then, neither is a proper forum. The State Department legal adviser explained that when the U.S. accepted World Court jurisdiction in the 1940s, most members of the UN "were aligned with the United States and shared its views regarding world order." But now "a great many of these cannot be counted on to share our view of the original constitutional conception of the U.N. Charter," and "this same majority often opposes the United States on important international questions." Lacking a guarantee that it will get its way, the U.S. must now "reserve to ourselves the power to determine whether the Court has jurisdiction over us in a particular case," on the principle that "the United States does not accept compulsory jurisdiction over any dispute involving matters essentially within the domestic jurisdiction of the United States, as determined by the United States." The "domestic matters" in question were the U.S. attack against Nicaragua.[18]

The media, along with intellectual opinion generally, agreed that the court discredited itself by ruling against the United States. The crucial parts of its decision were not reported, including its determination that all U.S. aid to the contras is military and not humanitarian; it remained "humanitarian aid" across the spectrum of respectable opinion until Washington's terror, economic warfare, and subversion of diplomacy brought about the "Victory for U.S. Fair Play" (Chomsky, 1989a, 1989b).

Returning to the W.T.O. case, we need not tarry on the allegation that the existence of the United States is at stake in the strangulation of the Cuban economy. More interesting is the thesis that the U.S. has every right to overthrow another government, in this case, by

---

parts of Latin America," so that Cuba is a national security threat to the U.S. and to Latin America – much as Denmark has been to Russia and Eastern Europe.

17   David Sanger, "Playing the Trade Card: U.S. Is Exporting Its Free-Market Values Through Global Commercial Agreements," *NYT*, Feb. 17, 1997. On the same day, *Times* editors warned the EU not to turn to the W.T.O. on Washington's sanctions against Cuba. The whole affair is "essentially a political dispute," they explain, not touching on Washington's "free-trade obligations."

18   Sofaer (1995) *The United States and the World Court*. U.S. Dept. of State, Bureau of Public Affairs, Current Policy, December, No. 769.

aggression, large-scale terror over many years, and economic strangulation. Accordingly, international law and trade agreements are irrelevant. The fundamental principles of world order that have emerged victorious again resound, loud and clear.

The Clinton administration declarations passed without challenge, though they were criticized on narrower grounds by historian Arthur Schlesinger. Writing "as one involved in the Kennedy administration's Cuban policy," Schlesinger maintained that the Clinton administration had misunderstood Kennedy's policies. The concern had been Cuba's "troublemaking in the hemisphere" and "the Soviet connection," Schlesinger explained.[19] But these are now behind us, so the Clinton policies are an anachronism, though otherwise unobjectionable, so we are to conclude.

Schlesinger did not explain the meaning of the phrases "troublemaking in the hemisphere" and "the Soviet connection," but he has elsewhere, in secret. Reporting to incoming President Kennedy on the conclusions of a Latin American Mission in early 1961, Schlesinger spelled out the problem of Castro's "troublemaking"—what the Clinton administration calls Cuba's effort "to destabilize large parts of Latin America": it is "the spread of the Castro idea of taking matters into one's own hands," a serious problem, Schlesinger added, when "the distribution of land and other forms of national wealth greatly favors the propertied classes . . . [and] the poor and underprivileged, stimulated by the example of the Cuban Revolution, are now demanding opportunities for a decent living." Schlesinger also explained the threat of the "Soviet connection": "Meanwhile, the Soviet Union hovers in the wings, flourishing large development loans and presenting itself as the model for achieving modernization in a single generation."[20] The "Soviet connection" was perceived in a similar light far more broadly in Washington and London, from the origins of the Cold War 80 years ago.

With these (secret) explanations of Castro's "destabilization" and "troublemaking in the hemisphere," and of the "Soviet connection," we come closer to an understanding of the reality of the Cold War, another important topic I will have to put aside. It should come as no surprise that basic policies persist with the Cold War a fading memory, just as they were carried out before the Bolshevik revolution: the brutal and destructive invasion of Haiti and the Dominican Republic, to mention just one illustration of "global meliorism" under the banner of "Wilsonian idealism."

It should be added that the policy of overthrowing the government of Cuba antedates the Kennedy administration. Castro took power in January 1959. By June, the Eisenhower administration had determined that his government must be overthrown. Terrorist attacks from U.S. bases began shortly after. The formal decision to overthrow Castro in favor of a regime "more devoted to the true interests of the Cuban people and more acceptable to the U.S." was taken in secret in March 1960, with the addendum that the operation must be carried out "in such a manner as to avoid any appearance of U.S. intervention," because of the expected reaction in Latin America and the need to ease

19   Letter, *NYT*, Feb. 26, 1997.
20   *Foreign Relations of the United States*, 1961–63, vol. XII, American Republics, 13f., 33.

the burden on doctrinal managers at home. At the time, the "Soviet connection" and "troublemaking in the hemisphere" were nil, apart from the Schlesingerian version. The CIA estimated that the Castro government enjoyed popular support (the Clinton administration has similar evidence today). The Kennedy administration also recognized that its efforts violated international law and the charters of the UN and Organization of American States, but such issues were dismissed without discussion, the declassified record reveals[21] (Gleijeses, 1995; Benjamin, 1990, p. 186ff; Vigil, 1995; Chomsky, 1997).

Let us move on to NAFTA, the "historic" agreement that may help to advance U.S.-style democracy in Mexico, Lakoff suggests. A closer look is again informative. The NAFTA agreement was rammed through Congress over strenuous popular opposition but with overwhelming support from the business world and the media, which were full of joyous promises of benefits for all concerned, also confidently predicted by the U.S. International Trade Commission and leading economists equipped with the most up-to-date models (which had just failed miserably to predict the deleterious consequences of the U.S.–Canada Free Trade Agreement but were somehow going to work in this case). Completely suppressed was the careful analysis by the Office of Technology Assessment (the research bureau of Congress), which concluded that the planned version of NAFTA would harm most of the population of North America, proposing modifications that could render the agreement beneficial beyond small circles of investment and finance. Still more instructive was the suppression of the official position of the U.S. labor movement, presented in a similar analysis. Meanwhile, labor was bitterly condemned for its "backward, unenlightened" perspective and "crude threatening tactics," motivated by "fear of change and fear of foreigners"; I am again sampling only from the far left of the spectrum, in this case, Anthony Lewis. The charges were demonstrably false, but they were the only word that reached the public in this inspiring exercise of democracy. Further details are most illuminating, and reviewed in the dissident literature at the time and since, but kept from the public eye, and unlikely to enter approved history (Chomsky, 1996a, p. 131ff.; Burke, 1995).[22]

By now, the tales about the wonders of NAFTA have quietly been been shelved, as the facts have been coming in. One hears no more about the hundreds of thousands of new jobs and other great benefits in store for the people of the three countries. These good tidings have been replaced by the "distinctly benign economic viewpoint" – the "experts' view" – that NAFTA had no significant effects. The Wall Street Journal reports that "Administration officials feel frustrated by their inability to convince voters that the

---

21   On recent polls by a Gallup affiliate. See *Miami Herald* Spanish edition, Dec. 18, 1994.

22   On the predictions and the outcome, see economist Burke (1995). Also, see *Social Dimensions of North American Economic Integration*, report prepared for the Department of Human Resources Development by the Canadian Labour Congress, 1996. On World Bank predictions for Africa, see Mihevc, op. cit., also reviewing the grim effects of consistent failure – grim for the population, that is, not for the bank's actual constituency. That the record of prediction is poor, and understanding meager, is well known to professional economists. See, for example, "Cycles of Conventional Wisdom on Economic Development," *International Affairs* 71.4, Oct. 1995. He is, however, a bit selective in exempting professional economists from his withering censure.

threat doesn't hurt them" and that job loss is "much less than predicted by Ross Perot," who was allowed into mainstream discussion (unlike the OTA, the Labor movement, economists who didn't echo the party line, and of course dissident analysts) because his claims were sometimes extreme and easily ridiculed. "'It's hard to fight the critics' by telling the truth – that the trade pact 'hasn't really done anything,'" an administration official observes sadly. Forgotten is what "the truth" was going to be when the impressive exercise in democracy was roaring full steam ahead (Cooper, 1997).

While the experts have downgraded NAFTA to "no significant effects," dispatching the earlier "experts' view" to the memory hole, a less than "distinctly benign economic viewpoint" comes into focus if the "national interest" is widened in scope to include the general population. Testifying before the Senate Banking Committee in February 1997, Federal Reserve Board Chair Alan Greenspan was highly optimistic about "sustainable economic expansion" thanks to "atypical restraint on compensation increases [which] appears to be mainly the consequence of greater worker insecurity" – an obvious desideratum for a just society. The February 1997 Economic Report of the President, taking pride in the administration's achievements, refers more obliquely to "changes in labor market institutions and practices" as a factor in the "significant wage restraint" that bolsters the health of the economy.

One reason for these benign changes is spelled out in a study commissioned by the NAFTA Labor Secretariat "on the effects of the sudden closing of the plant on the principle of freedom of association and the right of workers to organize in the three countries." The study was carried out under NAFTA rules in response to a complaint by telecommunications workers on illegal labor practices by Sprint. The complaint was upheld by the U.S. National Labor Relations Board, which ordered trivial penalties after years of delay, the standard procedure. The NAFTA study, by Cornell University Labor economist Kate Bronfenbrenner, has been authorized for release by Canada and Mexico but not by the Clinton administration. It reveals a significant impact of NAFTA on strike-breaking. About half of union organizing efforts are disrupted by employer threats to transfer production abroad, for example, by placing signs reading "Mexico Transfer Job" in front of a plant where there is an organizing drive. The threats are not idle: when such organizing drives nevertheless succeed, employers close the plant in whole or in part at triple the pre-NAFTA rate (about 15% of the time). Plant-closing threats are almost twice as high in more mobile industries (e.g., manufacturing vs. construction).

These and other practices reported in the study are illegal, but that is a technicality, on a par with violations of international law and trade agreements when outcomes are unacceptable. The Reagan administration had made it clear to the business world that their illegal antiunion activities would not be hampered by the criminal state, and successors have kept to this stand. There has been a substantial effect on destruction of unions – or in more polite words, "changes in labor market institutions and practices" that contribute to "significant wage restraint" within an economic model offered with great pride to a backward world that has not yet grasped the victorious principles that are to lead the way to freedom and justice.[23]

What was reported all along outside the mainstream about the goals of NAFTA is also now quietly conceded: the real goal was to "lock Mexico in" to the "reforms" that had made it an "economic miracle," in the technical sense of this term: a "miracle" for U.S. investors and the Mexican rich, while the population sank into misery. The Clinton administration "forgot that the underlying purpose of NAFTA was not to promote trade but to cement Mexico's economic reforms," *Newsweek* correspondent Marc Levinson loftily declares, failing only to add that the contrary was loudly proclaimed to ensure the passage of NAFTA while critics who pointed out this "underlying purpose" were efficiently excluded from the free market of ideas by its owners. Perhaps someday the reasons will be conceded too. "Locking Mexico in" to these reforms, it was hoped, would deflect the danger detected by a Latin America Strategy Development Workshop in Washington in September 1990. It concluded that relations with the brutal Mexican dictatorship were fine, though there was a potential problem: "a 'democracy opening' in Mexico could test the special relationship by bringing into office a government more interested in challenging the US on economic and nationalist grounds"[24] – no longer a serious problem now that Mexico is "locked into the reforms" by treaty. The U.S. has the power to disregard treaty obligations at will, not Mexico.

In brief, the threat is democracy, at home and abroad, as the chosen example again illustrates. Democracy is permissible, even welcome, but again, as judged by outcome, not process. NAFTA was considered to be an effective device to diminish the threat of democracy. It was implemented at home by effective subversion of the democratic process, and in Mexico by force, again over vain public protest. The results are now presented as a hopeful instrument to bring American-style democracy to benighted Mexicans. A cynical observer aware of the facts might agree.

Once again, the chosen illustrations of the triumph of democracy are natural ones, and are interesting and revealing as well, though not quite in the intended manner. Markets are always a social construction, and in the specific form being crafted by current social policy they should serve to restrict functioning democracy, as in the case of NAFTA, the W.T.O. agreements, and other instruments that may lie ahead. One case that merits close attention is the Multilateral Agreement on Investment (MAI) that is now being forged by the Organisation for Economic Co-operation and Development (OECD), the rich men's club, and the W.T.O. (where it is the MAI). The apparent hope is that the agreement will be adopted without public awareness, as was the initial intention for NAFTA, not quite achieved, though the "information system" managed to keep the basic story under wraps. If the plans outlined in draft texts are implemented, the whole

---

23   Editorial, "Class War in the USA," *Multicultural Monitor*, March, 1997; Bronfenbrenner, "We'll Close"
ibid., based on the study she directed: "Final Report: The Effects of Plant Closing or Threat of Plant Closing on the Right of Workers to Organize." The massive impact of Reaganite criminality is detailed in a report in *Business Week*, "The Workplace: Why America Needs Unions, but not the Kind it Has Now," May 23, 1994.
24   Levinson, *Foreign Affairs*, March/April 1996. Workshop, Sept. 26–27, 1990, Minutes, 3.

world may be "locked into" treaty arrangements that provide transnational corporations with still more powerful weapons to restrict the arena of democratic politics, leaving policy largely in the hands of huge private tyrannies that have ample means of market interference as well. The efforts may be blocked at the W.T.O. because of the strong protests of the "developing countries," notably India and Malaysia, which are not eager to become wholly owned subsidiaries of great foreign enterprises. But the OECD version may fare better, to be presented to the rest of the world as a fait accompli, with the obvious consequences. All of this proceeds in impressive secrecy, so far (OECD, 1997).[25]

The announcement of the Clinton Doctrine was accompanied by a prize example to illustrate the victorious principles: What the administration had achieved in Haiti. Since this is again offered as the strongest case, it would only be appropriate to look at it. True, Haiti's elected president was allowed to return but only after the popular organizations had been subjected to three years of terror by forces that retained close connections to Washington throughout; the Clinton administration still refuses to turn over to Haiti 160,000 pages of documents on state terror seized by U.S. military forces – "to avoid embarrassing revelations" about U.S. government involvement with the coup regime, according to Human Rights Watch.[26] It was also necessary to put President Aristide through "a crash course in democracy and capitalism," as his leading supporter in Washington described the process of civilizing the troublesome priest.

The device is not unknown elsewhere, as an unwelcome transition to formal democracy is contemplated. As a condition on his return, Aristide was compelled to accept an economic program that directs the policies of the Haitian government to the needs of "Civil Society, especially the private sector, both national and foreign": U.S. investors are designated to be the core of Haitian civil society, along with wealthy Haitians who backed the military coup but not the Haitian peasants and slum-dwellers who organized a civil society so lively and vibrant that they were even able to elect their own president against overwhelming odds, eliciting instant U.S. hostility and efforts to subvert Haiti's first democratic regime (Farmer, 1994; Chomsky, 1996a, 1994b; McFadyen and LaRamee, 1995).

The unacceptable acts of the "ignorant and meddlesome outsiders" in Haiti were reversed by violence, with direct U.S. complicity, not only through contacts with the state terrorists in charge. The Organization of American States declared an embargo. The Bush and Clinton administrations undermined it from the start by exempting U.S. firms and by secretly authorizing the Texaco Oil Company to supply the coup regime and its wealthy supporters in violation of the official sanctions, a crucial fact that was prominently revealed

---

25   See OECD, Multilateral Agreement Investment: *Consolidated Texts and Commentary* (OLIS 9 Jan., 1997; DAFFE/MAI/97; Confidential). Scott Nova and Michelle Sforza-Roderick of Preamble Center for Public Policy, Washington, "M.I.A. Culpa" *The Nation*, Jan. 13; Martin Khor, "Trade and Investment: Fighting over Investors' rights at W.T.O.," *Third World Economics* (Penang) Feb. 15; Laura Eggerston, "Treaty to Trim Ottawa's Power," *Toronto Globe and Mail*, April 3; Paula Green, "Global Giants: Fears of the Supranational," *J. of Commerce* (Canada), April 23. George Monbiot, "A Charter to Let Loose the Multinationals," *Guardian* (UK), April 15, 1997.

26   Kenneth Roth, Executive Director, HRW, Letter, *NYT*, April, 12, 1997.

the day before U.S. troops landed to "restore democracy,"[27] but has yet to reach the public, and is an unlikely candidate for the historical record.

Now democracy has been restored. The new government has been forced to abandon the democratic and reformist programs that scandalized Washington, and to follow the policies of Washington's candidate in the 1990 election, in which he received 14% of the vote.

The prize example tells us more about the meaning and implications of the victory for "democracy and open markets." Haitians seem to understand the lessons, even if doctrinal managers in the West prefer a different picture. Parliamentary elections in April 1997 brought forth "a dismal 5 percent" of voters, the press reported, thus raising the question, "Did Haiti Fail US Hope?"[28] We have sacrificed so much to bring them democracy, but they are ungrateful and unworthy. One can see why "realists" urge that we stay aloof from crusades of "global meliorism."

Similar attitudes hold throughout the hemisphere. Polls show that in Central America, politics elicits "boredom," "distrust," and "indifference" in proportions far outdistancing "interest" or "enthusiasm" among "an apathetic public . . . which feels itself a spectator in its democratic system" and has "general pessimism about the future." The first Latin America survey, sponsored by the EU, found much the same: "the survey's most alarming message," the Brazilian coordinator commented, was "the popular perception that only the elite had benefited from the transition to democracy."[29] Latin American scholars observe that the recent wave of democratization coincided with neoliberal economic reforms, which have been very harmful for most people, leading to a cynical appraisal of formal democratic procedures. The introduction of similar programs in the richest country in the world has had similar effects. By the early 1990s, after 15 years of a domestic version of structural adjustment, over 80% of the U.S. population had come to regard the democratic system as a sham, with business far too powerful and the economy as "inherently unfair." These are natural consequences of the specific design of "market democracy" under business rule.

Natural, and not unexpected. Neoliberalism is centuries old, and its effects should not be unfamiliar. The well-known economic historian Paul Bairoch points out that "there is no doubt that the Third World's compulsory economic liberalism in the nineteenth century is a major element in explaining the delay in its industrialization," or even "deindustrialization," while Europe and the regions that managed to stay free of its control developed by radical violation of these principles (Bairoch, 1993). Referring to the more recent past, Arthur Schlesinger's secret report on Kennedy's Latin American mission realistically criticized as having "the baleful influence of the International Monetary Fund" than pursuing the 1950s' version of today's "Washington Consensus" ("structural adjustment," "neoliberalism"). Despite much confident rhetoric, not much is

27   See Chomsky (1994b) "Democracy Restored," citing John Solomon, AP, Sept. 18, 1994 (lead story).
28   Nick Madigan, "Democracy in Inaction: Did Haiti Fail US Hope?," *Christian Science Monitor*, April 8, 1997, AP, BG, April 8, 19
29   John McPhaul, *Tico Times* (Costa Rica), April 11 May 2, 1997.

understood about economic development. But some lessons of history seem reasonably clear and not hard to understand.

Let us return to the prevailing doctrine that "America's victory in the Cold War" was a victory for democracy and the free market. With regard to democracy, the doctrine is partially true, though we have to understand what is meant by "democracy": top-down control "to protect the minority of the opulent against the majority." What about the free market? Here, too, we find that doctrine is far removed from reality, as several examples have already illustrated.

Consider again the case of NAFTA, an agreement intended to lock Mexico into an an economic discipline that protects investors from the danger of a "democracy opening." Its provisions tell us more about the economic principles that have emerged victorious. It is not a "free trade agreement." Rather, it is highly protectionist, designed to impede East Asian and European competitors. Furthermore, it shares with the global agreements such anti-market principles as "intellectual property rights" restrictions of an extreme sort that rich societies never accepted during their period of development but that they now intend to use to protect home-based corporations: to destroy the pharmaceutical industry in poorer countries, for example – and, incidentally, to block technological innovations, such as improved production processes for patented products; progress is no more a desideratum than markets, unless it yields benefits for those who count.

There are also questions about the nature of "trade." Over half of U.S. trade with Mexico is reported to consist of intrafirm transactions, up about 15% since NAFTA. For example, already a decade ago, mostly U.S.-owned plants in Northern Mexico employing few workers and with virtually no linkages to the Mexican economy produced more than 1/3 of engine blocks used in U.S. cars and 3/4 of other essential components. The post-NAFTA collapse of the Mexican economy in 1994, exempting only the very rich and U.S. investors (protected by U.S. government bailouts), led to an increase of U.S.-Mexico trade as the new crisis, driving the population to still deeper misery, "transformed Mexico into a cheap [i.e., even cheaper] source of manufactured goods, with industrial wages one-tenth of those in the US," the business press reports. Ten years ago According to some specialists, half of U.S. trade worldwide consists of such centrally managed transactions and much the same is true of other industrial powers (Cable, 1995); Barkin and Rosen, 1997; Greider, 1997),[30] though one must treat with caution conclusions about institutions with limited public accountability. Some economists have plausibly described the world system as one of "corporate mercantilism," remote from the ideal of free trade. The OECD concludes that "oligopolistic competition and strategic interaction among firms and governments rather than the invisible hand of market forces condition today's competitive advantage

30   Cable (1995), citing UN *World Investment Report* 1993, which, however, gives quite different figures, noting also that "relatively little data are available." Crawford, L. (1997) Legacy of Shock Therapy, *Financial Times*, Feb. 12, Crawford reviews the increasing misery of the vast majority of the population, apart from "the very rich." Post-NAFTA intrafirm transactions, Greider (1997, p. 273), citing Mexican economist Carlos Heredia.

and international division of labor in high-technology industries," (Tyson, 1992)[31] implicitly adopting a similar view.

Even the basic structure of the domestic economy violates the neoliberal principles that are hailed. The main theme of the standard work on U.S. business history is that "modern business enterprise took the place of market mechanisms in coordinating the activities of the economy and allocating its resources," handling many transactions internally, another large departure from market principles (Chandler, 1977). There are many others. Consider, for example, the fate of Adam Smith's principle that free movement of people is an essential component of free trade – across borders, for example. When we move on to the world of transnational corporations, with strategic alliances and critical support from powerful states, the gap between doctrine and reality becomes substantial.

Free market theory comes in two varieties: the official doctrine and what we might call "really existing free market doctrine": Market discipline is good for you, but I need the protection of the nanny state. The official doctrine is imposed on the defenseless, but it is "really existing doctrine" that has been adopted by the powerful since the days when Britain emerged as Europe's most advanced fiscal-military and developmental state, with sharp increases in taxation and efficient public administration as the state became "the largest single actor in the economy" and its global expansion (Brewer, 1989), establishing a model that has been followed to the present in the industrial world, surely by the United States, from its origins.

Britain did finally turn to liberal internationalism – in 1846, after 150 years of protectionism, violence, and state power had placed it far ahead of any competitor. But the turn to the market had significant reservations. Forty percent of British textiles continued to go to colonized India, and much the same was true of British exports generally. British steel was kept from U.S. markets by very high tariffs that enabled the United States to develop its own steel industry. But India and other colonies were still available and remained so when British steel was priced out of international markets. India is an instructive case; it produced as much iron as all of Europe in the late 18th century, and British engineers were studying more advanced Indian steel manufacturing techniques in 1820 to try to close "the technological gap." Bombay was producing locomotives at competitive levels when the railway boom began. But "really existing free market doctrine" destroyed these sectors of Indian industry just as it had destroyed textiles, shipbuilding, and other industries that were advanced by the standards of the day. The U.S. and Japan, in contrast, had escaped European control, and could adopt Britain's model of market interference.

When Japanese competition proved to be too much to handle, England simply called off the game: the empire was effectively closed to Japanese exports, part of the background of World War II. Indian manufacturers asked for protection at the same time—but against England, not Japan. No such luck, under really existing free market doctrine (Mukerjee, 1967; Bayly, 1988; Rothermund, 1993; Bairoch, 1993).

---

31   1992 OECD study cited by Clinton's former chief economic adviser Tyson (1992).

With the abandonment of its restricted version of laissez-faire in the 1930s, the British government turned to more direct intervention into the domestic economy as well. Within a few years, machine tool output increased five times, along with a boom in chemicals, steel, aerospace, and a host of new industries, "an unsung new wave of industrial revolution," Will Hutton writes. State-controlled industry enabled Britain to outproduce Germany during the war, even to narrow the gap with the U.S., which was then undergoing its own dramatic economic expansion as corporate managers took over the state-coordinated wartime economy (Hutton, 1995; Hooks, 1991).

A century after England turned to a form of liberal internationalism, the U.S. followed the same course. After 150 years of protectionism and violence, the U.S. had become by far the richest and most powerful country in the world, and like England before it, came to perceive the merits of a "level playing field" on which it could expect to crush any competitor. But like England, with crucial reservations.

One was that Washington used its power to bar independent development elsewhere, as England had done. In Latin America, Egypt, South Asia, and elsewhere, development was to be "complementary," not "competitive." There was also large-scale interference with trade. For example, Marshall Plan aid was tied to purchase of U.S. agricultural products, part of the reason why the U.S. share in world trade in grains increased from less than 10% before the war to more than half by 1950, while Argentine exports reduced by two-thirds. U.S. Food for Peace aid was also used both to subsidize U.S. agribusiness and shipping and to undercut foreign producers, among other measures to prevent independent development. (Haines, 1989; Godfried, 1987; Weis, 1993; Rock, 1987) The virtual destruction of Colombia's wheat growing by such means is one of the factors in the growth of the drug industry, which has been further accelerated throughout the Andean region by the neo-liberal policies of the past few years. Kenya's textile industry collapsed in 1994 when the Clinton administration imposed a quota, barring the path to development that has been followed by every industrial country, while "African reformers" are warned that they "must make more progress" in improving the conditions for business operations and "sealing in free-market reforms" with "trade and investment policies" that meet the requirements of Western investors. In December 1996 Washington barred exports of tomatoes from Mexico in violation of NAFTA and W.T.O. rules (though not technically, because it was a sheer power play and did not require an official tariff), at a cost to Mexican producers of close to $1 billion annually. The official reason for this gift to Florida growers is that prices were "artificially suppressed by Mexican competition" and Mexican tomatoes were preferred by U.S. consumers. In other words, free market principles were working, but with the wrong outcome[32] (LaFeber, 1986[33]; Philips, 1997).

These are only scattered illustrations.

One revealing is example is Haiti, along with Bengal the world's richest colonial prize and the source of a good part of France's wealth, largely under U.S. control since

---

32   David Sanger, "President Wins Tomato Accord for Floridians," *NYT*, Oct. 12, 1996.

33   Phillips, M. (1997) "U.S. is Seeking to Build its Trade with Africa," *Wall Street Journal*, June 2

Wilson's Marines invaded 80 years ago, and by now such a catastrophe that it may scarcely be habitable in the not-too-distant future. In 1981, a USAID–World Bank development strategy was initiated, based on assembly plants and agroexport, shifting land from food for local consumption. USAID forecast "a historic change toward deeper market interdependence with the United States" in what would become "the Taiwan of the Caribbean." The World Bank concurred, offering the usual prescriptions for "expansion of private enterprises" and minimization of "social objectives," thus increasing inequality and poverty and reducing health and educational levels; it may be noted, for what it is worth, that these standard prescriptions are offered side by side with sermons on the need to reduce inequality and poverty and improve health and educational levels, while World Bank technical studies recognize that relative equality and high health and educational standards are crucial factors in economic growth. In the Haitian case, the consequences were the usual ones: profits for U.S. manufacturers and the Haitian superrich, and a decline of 56% in Haitian wages through the 1980s – in short, an "economic miracle." Haiti remained Haiti, not Taiwan, which had followed a radically different course, as advisers must surely know.

It was the effort of Haiti's first democratic government to alleviate the growing disaster that called forth Washington's hostility and the military coup and terror that followed. With "democracy restored," USAID is withholding aid to ensure that cement and flour mills are privatized for the benefit of wealthy Haitians and foreign investors (Haitian "Civil Society," according to the orders that accompanied the restoration of democracy), while barring expenditures for health and education. Agribusiness receives ample funding, but no resources are made available for peasant agriculture and handicrafts, which provide the income of the overwhelming majority of the population. Foreign-owned assembly plants that employ workers (mostly women) at well below subsistence pay under horrendous working conditions benefit from cheap electricity, subsidized by the generous supervisor. But for the Haitian poor – the general population – there can be no subsidies for electricity, fuel, water, or food; these are prohibited by International Monetary Fund rules on the principled grounds that they constitute "price control." Before the "reforms" were instituted, local rice production supplied virtually all domestic needs, with important linkages to the domestic economy. Thanks to one-sided "liberalization," it now provides only 50%, with the predictable effects on the economy. The liberalization is, crucially, one-sided. Haiti must "reform," eliminating tariffs in accord with the stern principles of economic science – which, by some miracle of logic, exempt U.S. agribusiness; it continues to receive huge public subsidies, increased by the Reagan administration to the point where they provided 40% of growers' gross incomes by 1987. The natural consequences are understood, and intended: a 1995 USAID report observes that the "export-driven trade and investment policy" that Washington mandates will "relentlessly squeeze the domestic rice farmer," who will be forced to turn to the more rational pursuit of agroexport for the benefit of U.S. investors, in accord with the principles of rational expectations theory[34] (Chomsky, 1993b; Farmer, 1994; McGowan, 1997)

By such methods, the most impoverished country in the hemisphere has been turned into a leading purchaser of U.S.-produced rice, enriching publicly subsidized U.S. enterprises. Those lucky enough to have received a good Western education can doubtless explain that the benefits will trickle down to Haitian peasants and slumdwellers – ultimately. Africans may choose to follow a similar path, as currently advised by the leaders of "global meliorism" and local elites, and perhaps may see no choice under existing circumstances – a questionable judgment, I suspect. But if they do, it should be with eyes open.

The last example illustrates the most important departures from official free trade doctrine, more significant in the modern era than protectionism, which was far from the most radical interference with the doctrine in earlier periods either though it is the one usually studied under the conventional breakdown of disciplines, which makes its own useful contribution to disguising social and political realities. To mention one obvious example, the industrial revolution depended on cheap cotton, just as the "golden age" of contemporary capitalism has depended on cheap energy, but the methods for keeping the crucial commodities cheap and available, which hardly conform to market principles, do not fall within the professional discipline of economics.

One fundamental component of free trade theory is that public subsidies are not allowed. But after World War II, U.S. business leaders expected that the economy would collapse without the massive state intervention during the war that had finally overcome the great depression. They also insisted that advanced industry "cannot satisfactorily exist in a pure, competitive, unsubsidized, 'free enterprise' economy" and that "the government is their only possible savior" (Fortune, Business Week, expressing a general consensus). They recognized that the Pentagon system would be the best way to transfer costs to the public. Social spending could play the same stimulative role, but it has defects: it is not a direct subsidy to the corporate sector, it has democratizing effects, and it is redistributive. Military spending has none of these unwelcome features. It is also easy to sell, by deceit. President Truman's air force secretary put the matter simply: we should not use the word "subsidy," he said; the word to use is "security." He made sure the military budget would "meet the requirements of the aircraft industry," as he put it. One consequence is that civilian aircraft is now the country's leading export, and the huge travel and tourism industry, aircraft-based, is the source of major profits (Kofsky, 1993; Chomsky, 1994a, chapter 2; 1985, chapters 4 & 5)

It was quite appropriate for Clinton to choose Boeing as "a model for companies across America" as he preached his "new vision" of the free market future, to much acclaim. A fine example of really existing markets, civilian aircraft production is now mostly in the hands of two firms, Boeing-McDonald and Airbus, each of which owes its existence and success

---

34   *Labor Rights in Haiti*, International Labor Rights Education and Research Fund, April 1989; *Haiti after the Coup*, National Labor Committee Education Fund (New York), April 1993.

to large-scale public subsidy. The same pattern prevails in computers and electronics generally, automation, biotechnology, communications, in fact just about every dynamic sector
of the economy (Kofsky, 1993; Chomsky, 1994a, chapter 2; 1985, chapters 4 & 5)

There was no need to explain this central feature of "really existing free market
capitalism" to the Reagan administration. They were masters at the art, extolling the
glories of the market to the poor at home and the service areas abroad while boasting
proudly to the business world that Reagan had "granted more import relief to U.S. industry than any of his predecessors in more than half a century" – in reality, more than all
predecessors combined, as they "presided over the greatest swing toward protectionism
since the 1930s," shifting the U.S. from "being the world's champion of multilateral free
trade to one of its leading challengers," the journal of the Council on Foreign Relations
commented in a review of the decade. The Reaganites led "the sustained assault on [free
trade] principle" by the rich and powerful from the early 1970's that is deplored in a
scholarly review by GATT secretariat economist Patrick Low, who estimates the restrictive effects of Reaganite measures at about three times those of other leading industrial
countries[35] (Low, 1993, p. 271, 70ff).

The great "swing toward protectionism" was only a part of the "sustained assault"
on free trade principles that was accelerated under "Reaganite rugged individualism."
Another chapter of the story includes the huge transfer of public funds to private power,
often under the traditional guise of "security," a "defense buildup [that] actually pushed
military R&D spending (in constant dollars) past the record levels of the mid-1960s,"
Stuart Leslie notes (Leslie, 1993). The public was terrified with foreign threats (Russians,
Libyans, etc.), but the Reaganite message to the business world was again much more
honest. Without such extreme measures of market interference, it is doubtful that the
U.S. automotive, steel, machine tool, semiconductor industries, and others, would have
survived Japanese competition or been able to forge ahead in emerging technologies,
with broad effects through the economy.

There is also no need to explain the operative doctrines to the leader of today's
"conservative revolution," Newt Gingrich, who sternly lectures 7-year-old children on
the evils of welfare dependency while holding a national prize for directing public subsidies to his rich constituents. Or to the Heritage Foundation, which crafts the budget
proposals for the congressional "conservatives," and therefore called for (and obtained)
an increase in Pentagon spending beyond Clinton's increase to ensure that the "defense
industrial base" remains solid, protected by state power and offering dual-use technology to its beneficiaries to enable them to dominate commercial markets and enrich
themselves at public expense. All understand very well that free enterprise means that
the public pays the costs and bears the risks if things go wrong, for example, bank and
corporate bailouts that have cost the public hundreds of billions of dollars in recent
years. Profit is to be privatized, but cost and risk socialized, in really existing market

---

35   Citing Secretary of the Treasury James Baker; Shafiqul Islam, *Foreign Affairs, America and the World*
(Winter 1989–90).

systems. The centuries-old tale proceeds today without notable change, not only in the United States, of course.

Public statements have to be interpreted in the light of these realities, among them, Clinton's current call for trade-not-aid for Africa, with a series of provisions that just happen to benefit U.S. investors and uplifting rhetoric that manages to avoid such matters as the long record of such approaches and the fact that the U.S. already had the most miserly aid program of any developed country even before the grand innovation. Or to take the obvious model, consider Chester Crocker's explanation of Reagan administration plans for Africa in 1981. "We support open market opportunities, access to key resources, and expanding African and American economies," he said, and want to bring African countries "into the mainstream of the free market economy." The statement may seem to surpass cynicism, coming from the leaders of the "sustained assault" against "the free market economy." But Crocker's rendition is fair enough, when it is passed through the prism of really existing market doctrine. The market opportunities and access to resources are for foreign investors and their local associates, and the economies are to expand in a specific way, protecting "the minority of the opulent against the majority." The opulent, meanwhile, merit state protection and public subsidy. How else can they flourish, for the benefit of all?

To illustrate "really existing free market theory" with a different measure, the most extensive study of Transnational Corporations found that "virtually all of the world's largest core firms have experienced a decisive influence from government policies and/or trade barriers on their strategy and competitive position" and "at least twenty companies in the 1993 Fortune 100 would not have survived at all as independent companies, if they had not been saved by their respective governments," by socializing losses or simple state takeover when they were in trouble. One is the leading employer in Gingrich's deeply conservative district, Lockheed, saved from collapse by $2 billion government loan guarantees. The same study points out that government intervention, which has "been the rule rather than the exception over the past two centuries, . . . has played a key role in the development and diffusion of many product and process innovations – particularly in aerospace, electronics, modern agriculture, materials technologies, energy and transportation technology," as well as telecommunications and information technologies generally (the Internet and World Wide Web are striking recent examples), and in earlier days, textiles and steel, and of course energy. Government policies "have been an overwhelming force in shaping the strategies and competitiveness of the world's largest firms"(Ruigrock and van Tulder, 1995). Other technical studies confirm these conclusions.

As these examples indicate, the United States is not alone in its conceptions of "free trade," even if its ideologues often lead the cynical chorus. The gap between rich and poor countries from 1960 is substantially attributable to protectionist measures of the rich, the UN Development Report concluded in 1992. The 1994 report concluded that "the industrial countries, by violating the principles of free trade, are costing the developing countries an estimated $50 billion a year – nearly equal to the total flow of foreign assistance"—much of it publicly subsidized export promotion (Toussaint & Drucker, 1995). The 1996 Global Report of the UN Industrial Development Organization estimates that the disparity between the richest and poorest 20% of the world population increased by over 50% from 1960 to 1989 and predicts "growing world inequality resulting from the globalization process." That growing disparity holds within the rich societies as well, the U.S. leading the way, Britain not far behind. The business press exults in "spectacular" and "stunning" profit growth, applauding the extraordinary concentration of wealth among the top few percent of the population while for the majority, conditions continue to stagnate or decline. The corporate media, the Clinton administration, and the cheerleaders for the American Way generally, proudly offer themselves as a model for the rest of the world; buried in the chorus of self-acclaim are the results of deliberate social policy during the happy period of "capital's clear subjugation of labor," for example, the "basic indicators" just published by UNICEF (1997), revealing that the U.S. has the worst record among the industrial countries, ranking alongside of Cuba – a poor Third World country under unremitting attack by the hemispheric superpower for almost 40 years – by such standards as mortality for children under five, and also holding records for hunger, child poverty, and other basic social indicators. All of this takes place in the richest country in the world, with unparalleled advantages and stable democratic institutions but also under business rule, to an unusual extent. These are further auguries for the future, if the "dramatic shift away from a pluralist, participatory ideal of politics and towards an authoritarian and technocratic ideal" proceeds on course, worldwide.

It is worth noting that in secret, intentions are often spelled out honestly, for example, in the early post war II period, when George Kennan, one of the most influential planners and considered a leading humanist, assigned each sector of the world its "function": Africa's function was to be "exploited" by Europe for its reconstruction, he observed, the U.S. having little interest in it. A year earlier, a high-level planning study had urged "that cooperative development of the cheap foodstuffs and raw materials of northern Africa could help forge European unity and create an economic base for continental recovery," an interesting concept of "cooperation" (UNICEF, 1997).[36] There is no record of a suggestion that Africa might "exploit" the West for its recovery from the "global meliorism" of the past centuries.

If we take the trouble to distinguish doctrine from reality, we find that the political and economic principles that have prevailed are remote from those that are proclaimed. One may also be skeptical about the prediction that they are "the wave of the future," bringing history to a happy end. The same "end of history" has confidently been proclaimed many times in the past, always wrongly. And with all the sordid continuities, an optimistic soul can discern slow progress, realistically I think. In the advanced industrial countries, and often elsewhere, popular struggles today can start from a higher plane and with greater expectations than those of the past. And international solidarity can

---

36   Kennan, PPS 23, Feb. 24, 1948 (FRUS, vol I, 1948), p. 511; Also, Hogan (1987), 41, paraphrasing the May 1947 Bonesteel Memorandum.

take new and more constructive forms as the great majority of the people of the world come to understand that their interests are pretty much the same and can be advanced by working together. There is no more reason now than there has ever been to believe that we are constrained by mysterious and unknown social laws, not simply decisions made within institutions that are subject to human will – human institutions, which have to face the test of legitimacy, and if they do not meet it, can be replaced by others that are more free and more just, as often in the past.

Skeptics who dismiss such thoughts as utopian and naive have only to cast their eyes on what has happened right here in the last few years, an inspiring tribute to what the human spirit can achieve, and its limitless prospects – lessons that the world desperately needs to learn, and that should guide the next steps in the continuing struggle for justice and freedom here too, as the people of South Africa, fresh from one great victory, turn to the still more difficult tasks that lie ahead.

References

Bairoch, P. (1993) *Economics and World History*, Chicago: Univ. of Chicago Press.

Barkin, D. and Rosen, F. (1997) Why the Recovery Is Not a Recovery, *NACLA Report on the Americas*, Jan./Feb.

Bayly, C.A. (1988) *The New Cambridge History of India*. Cambridge: Cambridge Univ. Press.

Benjamin, J. (1990) *The United States and the Origins of the Cuban Revolution*. Princeton Princeton Univ. Press.

Bernays, E. (1928) *Propaganda* New York: Liveright.

Brewer, J. (1989) *Sinews of Power*. New York: Knopf.

Burke, M. (1995) NAFTA Integration: Unproductive Finance and Real Unemployment, *Proceedings from the Eighth Annual Labor Segmentation Conference*, April Notre Dame and Indiana Universities.

Cable, V. (1995) The diminished nation-state: a study in the loss of economic power. *Daedalus*, 124 (2), pp. 23–34.

Carey, A. (1995) *Taking the Risk out of Democracy*. Sidney: Univ of New South Wales Press.

Carothers, Th. (1991a) "The Reagan Years" in A. Lowenthal, ed., *Exporting Democracy*. Baltimore: Johns Hopkins Univ. Press.

Carothers, Th. (1991) *In the Name of Democracy*. Berkeley: Univ. of California Press.

Chandler, A. (1977) *The Visible Hand*. Cambridge: Belknap Press.

Chomsky, N. (1971) *The Problems of Knowledge and Freedom*. New York: Pantheon.

Chomsky, N. (1973) *For Reasons of State*. New York: Pantheon.

Chomsky, N (1982) *Toward a New Cold War*. New York: Pantheon.

Chomsky, N. (1985) *Turning the Tide*. Boston: South End Press.

Chomsky, N. (1988) *Turning the Tide*. Boston: South End Press.

Chomsky, N. (1989a) *Necessary Illusions* Boston: South End Press.

Chomsky, N. (1989b) *Culture of Terrorism*. Boston: South End Press.

Chomsky, N. (1991) Force and Opinion. *Z Magazine*, July August.

Chomsky, N. (1992) *Deterring Democracy*. New York: Will and Wang.

Chomsky, N. (1993a) *Letters from Lexington*. Monroe: Common Courage.

Chomsky, N. (1993b) *Year 501*. Boston: South End Press.

Chomsky, N. (1994a) *World Orders, Old and New.* New York: Columbia University Press.

Chomsky, N. (1994b) Democracy Restored, *Z Magazine,* Nov.

Chomsky, N. (1996a) *Powers and Prospects.* Boston: South End Press.

Chomsky, N. (1996b) Consent without Consent, *Cleveland State Law Review*

Chomsky, N. (1997) Passion for Free Markets," *Z Magazine,* May.

Clairmont, F. (1960) *The Rise and Fall of Economic Liberalism.* Goa: Asia Publishing House.

Chossudovsky, M. (1997) *The Globalization of Poverty.* Penang: Third World Network.

Cockett, R. (1994) The Party, Publicity, and the Media." In Anthony Seldon and Stuart Ball, (Eds.), *Conservative Century: The Conservative Party Since 1900.* Oxford: Oxford University Press.

Cooper, H. (1997) Experts' View of NAFTA's Economic Impact: It's a Wash. *Wall Street Journal,* June 17.

Crozier, M. P., Huntington, S. J., and Watanuki, J. (1975) *The Crisis of Democracy: Report on the Governability of Democracies to the Trilateral Commission.* New York: New York University Press.

Ewen, S. (1996) *PR!: A Social History of Spin.* New York: Basic Books.

Farmer, P. (1994) *The Uses of Haiti.* Monroe: Common Courage Press.

Fones-Wolf, E. (1995) *Selling Free Enterprise: the Business Assault on Labor and Liberalism, 1945-1960.* Urbana: Univ. of Illinois Press.

Garfield, R. (1993) Desocializing Health Care in a Developing Country. *Journal of the American Medical Association,* Aug. 25, 1993, vol. 270, no. 8

Gleijeses, P. (1995) Ships in the Night: The CIA, the White House and the Bay of Pigs. *Journal of Latin American Studies* vol.27, part 1 (Feb), pp. 1-42.

Greider, W. (1997) *One World, Ready or Not.* New York: Simon & Schuster.

Godfried, N. (1987) *Bridging the Gap between Rich and Poor.* Westport: Greenwood.

Haines, G. (1989) *The Americanization of Brazil.* Wilmington: Scholarly Resources.

Herman, E. and Chomsky, N. (1988) *Manufacturing Consent.* New York: Pantheon

Hogan, M. (1987) *The Marshall Plan.* Cambridge: Cambridge Univ. Press

Hooks, G. (1991) *Forging the Military-Industrial Complex.* Urbana: Univ. of Illinois Press,

Horwitz, M. (1992) *The Transformation of American Law, 1870-1960.* Cambridge: Harvard Univ. Press.

Hutton, X. (1995) *The State We're In.* London: Jonathan Cape, London.

Kofsky, F. (1993) *Harry Truman and the War Scare of 1948.* New York: St. Martin's Press.

LaFeber, W. (1986) The Alliances in Retrospect. In Andrew Maguire and Janet Welsh Brown, (Eds). *Bordering on Trouble.* Bethesda: Adler & Adler.

Lakoff, S. (1996) *Democracy: History, Theory, Practice.* Boulder: Westview, Boulder.

Lasswel, H. (1933) Propaganda. In *Encyclopedia of the Social Sciences,* vol. 12. New York: Macmillan.

Leacock, R. (1990) *Requiem for Revolution.* Kent: Kent State Univ. Press.

Leslie, S. (1993) *The Cold War and American Science.* New York: Columbia Univ. Press.

Levinson (1990) *Foreign Affairs,* March/April 1996. Workshop, Sept. 26 & 27

Low, P. (1993) *Trading Free.* New York: Twentieth Century Fund New York.

Madigan, N. (1997) Democracy in Inaction: Did Haiti Fail US Hope? *Christian Science Monitor,* April 8, 1997, AP, *BG,* April 8, 1997.

McFadyen, D. and LaRamee, P. (1995) (Eds) *Haiti, Dangerous Crossroads NACLA.* Boston: South Ends Press.

McGowan, L. (1997) *Democracy Undermined, Economic Justice Denied: Structural Adjustment and the AID Juggernaut in Haiti.* Washington: Development Gap.

Mihevc, J. (1995) *The Market Tells Them So*. London: Zed.

Monaghan, F. (1935) *John Jay*. New York: Bobbs-Merril.

Morley, M. and McGillion, Ch. (1997) *Washington Report on the Hemisphere*. Council on Hemispheric Affairs.

Mukerjee, R. (1967) *The Economic History of India: 1600-1800*. Allahabad: Kitab Mahal,

Peck, J. (1987) *The Chomsky Reader*. New York: Pantheon

Phillips, M. (1997) U.S. is Seeking to Build its Trade with Africa, *Wall Street Journal*, June 2.

Rock, D. (1987) *Argentina*. Berkeley: Univ. of California Press.

Rothermund, D. (1993) *An Economic History of India*. London: Croom Helm

Ruigrock, W. and van Tulder, R. (1995) *The Logic of International Restructuring*. London: Routledge.

Sandel, M. (1996) *Democracy's Discontent*. Cambridge: Harvard Univ. Pres

Sellers, Ch. (1991) *The Market Revolution*. Oxford: Oxford Univ. Press.

Social Dimensions of North American Economic Integration, (1996) Canadian Labour Congress

Survey of Current Business (1996) vol. 76, no. 12, Dec. Washington, D.C: U.S. Department of Commerce.

Toussaint, E. and Drucker, P. (1995) (Eds) *IMF/World Bank/WTO, Notebooks for Study and Research*. (International Institute for Research and Education, Amsterdam, 24/5.

Toye, J., Harrigan, J., and Mosley, P. (1991) *Aid and Power*. London: Routledge

Tyson, L. (1992) *Who's Bashing Whom?* Washington: Institute for International Economics.

UNICEF (1996) *The Progress of Nations*. New York: UNICEF House

UNICEF (1997) *State of World's Children*. New York: UNICEF House.

Vigil, M. L. (1995) *Envío*. June. Managua: Jesuit Univ. of Central America

Weis, M. (1987) *Cold Warriors & Coups d'Etat*. Albquerque: Univ. of New Mexico Press.

Wood, G. (1991) *The Radicalism of the American Revolution*. New York: Vintage.

CHAPTER TWO

Against Schooling:
Education and Social Class[1]

Stanley Aronowitz

> The crisis in American education, on the one hand, announces the bankruptcy of progressive education and, on the other hand, presents a problem of immense difficulty because it has arisen under the conditions and in response to the demands of a mass society.
>
> —*Hannah Arendt (1961)*

AT THE DAWN of the new century no American institution is invested with a greater role to bring the young and their parents into the modernist regime than public schools. The common school is charged with the task of preparing children and youth for their dual responsibilities to the social order: citizenship and, more important, learning to labor. On the one hand, in the older curriculum on the road to citizenship in a democratic, secular society, schools are supposed to transmit the jewels of the Enlightenment, especially literature and science. On the other, students are to be prepared for the work world by means of a loose but definite stress on the redemptive value of work, the importance of family, and, of course, the imperative of love and loyalty to one's country. As to the Enlightenment's concept of citizenship, students are, at least putatively, encouraged to engage in independent, critical thinking.

But the socializing functions of schooling play to the opposite idea: children of the working and professional and middle classes are to be molded to the industrial and technological imperatives of contemporary society. Students learn science and mathematics not as a discourse of liberation from myth and religious superstition but as a series of algorithms, the mastery of which are presumed to improve the student's logical capacities, or with no aim other than fulfilling academic requirements. In most places the social studies do not emphasize the choices between authoritarian and democratic forms of social organization, or democratic values, particularly criticism and renewal, but offer instead bits of information that have little significance for the conduct of life. Perhaps the teaching and learning of world literature where some students are inspired by the power of the story to, in John Dewey's terms, "reconstruct" experience is a partial

---

1   Keynote address, Department of Educational Leadership, University of Massachusetts Dartmouth, October 3, 2014, Grand Reading Room, Claire T. Carney Library.

exception to the rule that for most students, school is endured rather than experienced as a series of exciting explorations of self and society.[2]

In the wake of these awesome tasks, fiscal exigency and a changing mission have combined to leave public education in the United States in a chronic state of crisis. For some the main issue is whether schools are failing to transmit the general intellectual culture, even to the most able students. What is at stake in this critique is the fate of America as a global model of civilization, particularly the condition of its democratic institutions and the citizens who are, in the final analysis, responsible for maintaining them. Of course, we may contend that the "global model" is fulfilled by the relentless anti-intellectual bias of schools and by a ruthless regime of the virtual expulsion of the most rebellious students, especially by secondary schools. Hannah Arendt goes so far as to ask whether we "love the world" and our children enough to devise an educational system capable of transmitting to them the salient cultural traditions. Other critics complain that schools are failing to fulfill the promise of equal opportunity for good jobs for working-class students, whether black, Latino, or white. Schools unwittingly reinforce the class bias of schooling by ignoring its content. The two positions, with respect both to their goals and to their implied educational philosophies, may not necessarily be contradictory, but their simultaneous enunciation produces, with exceptions to be discussed below, considerable tension for the American workplace, which has virtually no room for dissent. Individual or collective initiative is not sanctioned by management. The corporate factory, which includes sites of goods and symbolic production alike, is perhaps the nation's most authoritarian institution. But any reasonable concept of democratic citizenship requires an individual who is able to discern knowledge from propaganda, is competent to choose among conflicting claims and programs, and is capable of actively participating in the affairs of the polity. Yet the political system offers few opportunities, beyond the ritual of voting, for active citizen participation.[3]

Even identifying the problem of why and how schools fail has proven to be controversial. For those who define mass education as a form of training for the contemporary workplace, the problem can be traced to the crisis of authority, particularly school authority. That some of the same educational analysts favor a curriculum that stresses critical thinking for a small number of students in a restricted number of sites is consistent with the dominant trends of schooling since the turn of the twenty-first century. In the quest to restore authority, conservative educational policy has forcefully caused schools to abandon, both rhetorically and practically, the so-called child-centered curriculum and pedagogy in favor of measures that not only hold students accountable for passing standardized tests and for a definite quantity of school knowledge—on penalty of being

---

2   Dewey, J. (1916) *Democracy and Education: An Introduction to the Philosophy of Education.* Glencoe: Free Press.

3   The literature on the limits of democracy in America is vast. For a searing indictment, see the classic critique: McConnell, Grant (1966) *Private Power and American Democracy.* New York: Knopf.

left back from promotion or expelled—but also impose performance-based criteria on administrators and teachers. For example, in New York City the schools chancellor has issued "report cards" to principals and has threatened to fire those whose schools do not meet standards established by high-stakes tests. These tests are the antithesis of critical thought. Their precise object is to evaluate the student's ability to imbibe and regurgitate information and to solve problems according to prescribed algorithms.

On the other side, the progressives—who misread John Dewey's educational philosophy to mean that the past need not be studied too seriously—have offered little resistance to the gradual vocationalizing and dumbing down of the mass education curriculum. In fact, historically they were advocates of making the curriculum less formal, reducing requirements, and, on the basis of a degraded argument that children learn best by "doing," promoting practical, work-oriented programs for high-school students. Curricular deformalization was often justified on interdisciplinary criteria, which resulted in watering down course content and de-emphasizing writing. Most American high-school students, in the affluent as well as the "inner-city" districts, may write short papers that amount to book reviews and autobiographical essays, but most graduate without ever having to perform research and write a paper of considerable length. Moreover, since the late 1960s, in an attempt to make the study of history more "relevant" to students' lives, students have not been required to memorize dates; they may learn the narratives but are often unable to place them in a specific chronological context. Similarly, economics has been eliminated in many schools or is taught as a "unit" of a general social studies course. And if philosophy is taught at all, it is construed in terms of "values clarification," a kind of ethics in which students are assisted to discover and examine their own values.

That after more than a century of universal schooling the relationship between education and class has once more been thrust to the forefront is just one more signal of the crisis in American education. The educational Left, never strong on promoting intellectual knowledge as a substantive demand, clings to one of the crucial precepts of progressive educational philosophy: under the sign of egalitarianism, the idea that class deficits can be overcome by equalizing access to school opportunities without questioning what those opportunities have to do with genuine education. The access question has dominated higher education debates since the early 1970s; even conservatives who favor vouchers and other forms of public funding for private and parochial schools have justified privatizing instruction on access grounds.

The structure of schooling already embodies the class system of society, and, for this reason, the access debate misfires. To gain entrance into schools always entails placement into that system. "Equality of Opportunity" for class mobility is the system's tacit recognition that inequality is normative. In the system of mass education, schools are no longer constituted to transmit the Enlightenment intellectual traditions or the fundamental prerequisites of participatory citizenship, even for a substantial minority. While the acquisition of credentials conferred by schools remains an important prerequisite for many occupations, the conflation of schooling with education is mistaken.

Schooling is surely a source of training both by its disciplinary regime and by its creden-tialing system. But schools do not transmit a "love for the world" or "for our children," as Arendt suggests; contrary to their democratic pretensions, they teach conformity to the social, cultural, and occupational hierarchy. In our contemporary world they are not constituted to foster independent thought, let alone encourage independent action. School knowledge is not the only source of education for students, perhaps not even the most important source. Young people learn, for ill as well as good, from popular culture (especially music), from parents, and, perhaps most important, from their peers. Schools are the stand-in for "society," the aggregation of individuals who, by contract or by coer-cion, are subject to governing authorities in return for which they may be admitted into the world albeit on the basis of different degrees of reward. To the extent that popular culture, parents, and peers signify solidarity and embody common dreams, they are the worlds of quasi communities that exert more influence on their members.

Access to What?

In the main, the critique of education has been directed to the question of access and its entailments, particularly the idea that greater access presumably opens up the gates to higher learning or to better jobs. Generally speaking, critical education analysis focuses on the degree to which schools are willing and able to open their doors to work-ing-class students, coded in many cities as "black, Asian, and Latino" students, because through the mechanisms of differential access, schools are viewed as, perhaps, the prin-cipal reproductive institutions of economically and technologically advanced capitalist societies. With some exceptions, most critics of schooling have paid scant attention to school authority, the conditions for the accumulation of social capital—the intricate network of personal relations that articulate with occupational access—and to cultural capital, the accumulation of the signs, if not the substance, of the kinds of knowledge that are markers of distinction.[4]

The progressives assume that the heart of the class question is whether schooling provides working-class kids equality of opportunity to acquire legitimate knowledge and marketable academic credentials. They have adduced overwhelming evidence that contradicts schooling's reigning doctrine: that despite class, race, or gender hierarchies in the economic and political system, public education provides every individual with the tools to overcome conditions of birth. In reality only about a quarter of people of working-class origin attain professional, technical, and managerial careers through the credentialing system. Many more obtain general diplomas, but as the saying goes, a high-school diploma and $2 gets you a ride on the New York subway. The professional and technical credential implies that students have mastered specialized knowledge and ac-quired a set of skills associated with the speciality. They find occupational niches but not

---

4   Pierre Bourdieu's concepts of cultural and social capital are introduced in Bourdieu, P. and Passeron, J. C. (1977) *Reproduction in Education, Culture, and Society*. London: Sage.

at the top of their respective domains. Typically graduating from third-tier, nonresearch colleges and universities, they have not acquired knowledge connected with substantial intellectual work: theory, extensive writing, and independent research. Students leaving these institutions find jobs as line supervisors, computer technicians, teachers, nurses, social workers, and other niches in the social service professions.

A small number may join their better-educated colleagues in getting no-collar jobs, where "no collar"—Andrew Ross's term—designates occupations that afford considerable work autonomy, such as computer design, which, although salaried, cannot be comfortably folded into the conventional division of manual and intellectual labor. That so-called social mobility was a product of the specific conditions of American economic development at a particular time—the first quarter of the twentieth century—and was due, principally, to the absence of an indigenous peasantry during the country's industrial revolution and the forced confinement of millions of blacks to southern agricultural lands, which is conveniently forgotten or ignored by consensus opinion. Nor were the labor shortages provoked by World War II and the subsequent U.S. dominance of world capitalism until 1973 taken into account by the celebrants of mobility. Economic stagnation has afflicted the U.S. economy for more than three decades, and, despite the high-tech bubble of the 1990s, its position has deteriorated in the world market. Yet the mythology of mobility retains a powerful grip on the popular mind. That schooling makes credentials available to anyone regardless of rank or status forms one of the sturdy pillars of American ideology.[5]

In recent years the constitutional and legal assignment to the states and local communities of responsibility for public education has been undermined by what has been termed the "standards" movement that is today the prevailing national educational policy, enforced not so much by federal law—notwithstanding the Bush administration's No Child Left Behind program—as by political and ideological coercion. At the state and district levels the invocation to "tough love" has attained widespread support. We are witnessing the abrogation, both in practice and in rhetoric, of the tradition of social promotion whereby students moved through the system without acquiring academic skills. Having proven unable to provide to most working-class kids the necessary educational experiences that qualify them for academic promotion, the standards movement, more than a decade after its installation, reveals its underlying content: it is the latest means of exclusion, whose success depends on placing the onus for failure to achieve academic credentials on the individual rather than the system. Although state departments of education frequently mandate the teaching of certain subjects and have established standards based on high-stakes tests applicable to all districts, everyone knows that districts with working-class majorities provide neither a curriculum and pedagogy, nor facilities that meet these standards, because, among other problems, they are chronically underfunded. The state aid formulas that, since the advent of conservative policy hegemony, reward those districts whose students perform well on high-stakes tests tend to be unequal. Performance-based aid policies mean that school districts where

---

5   Ross, A. (2003) *No-Collar: The Humane Workplace and Its Hidden Costs*. New York: Basic Books.

the affluent live get more than their share; they make up for state budget deficits by raising local property taxes and soliciting annual subventions from parents, measures not affordable by even the top layer of wage workers, or low-level salaried employees. The result is overcrowded classrooms, poor facilities, especially libraries, and underpaid, often poorly prepared teachers, an outcome of financially starved education schools in public universities.

Standards presuppose students' prior possession of cultural capital—an acquisition that almost invariably entails having been reared in a professional or otherwise upper-class family. That, in the main, even the most privileged elementary and secondary schools are ill equipped to compensate for home backgrounds in which reading and writing are virtually absent has become a matter of indifference for school authorities. In this era of social Darwinism, poor school performance is likely to be coded as genetic deficit rather than being ascribed to social policy. Of course, the idea that working-class kids, whatever their gender, race, or ethnic backgrounds, were selected by evolution or by God to perform material rather than immaterial labor is not new; this view is as old as class-divided societies. But in an epoch in which the chances of obtaining a good working-class job have sharply declined, most kids face dire consequences if they don't acquire the skills needed in the world of immaterial labor. Not only are 75 percent assigned to working-class jobs, but in the absence of a shrinking pool of unionized industrial jobs, which often pay more than some professions such as teaching and social work, they must accept low-paying service-sector employment, enter the informal economy, or join the ranks of the chronically unemployed.

The rise of higher education since World War II has been seen by many as a repudiation of academic elitism. Do not the booming higher education enrollments validate the propositions of social mobility and democratic education? Not at all. Rather than constituting a sign of rising qualifications and widening opportunity, burgeoning college and university enrollments signify changing economic and political trends. The scientific and technical nature of our production and service sectors increasingly require qualified and credentialed workers (it would be a mistake to regard them as identical). Students who would have sought good factory jobs in the past now believe, with reason, they need credentials to qualify for a well-paying job. On the other hand, even as politicians and educators decry social promotion, and most high schools with working-class constituencies remain aging vats, mass higher education is, to a great extent, a holding pen: effectively masking unemployment and underemployment. This may account for its rapid expansion over the last thirty-five years of chronic economic stagnation, deindustrialization, and the proliferation of part-time and temporary jobs, largely in the low-paid service sectors. Consequently, working-class students are able, even encouraged, to enter universities and colleges at the bottom of the academic hierarchy—community colleges but also public four-year colleges—thus fulfilling the formal pledge of equal opportunity for class mobility even as most of these institutions suppress the intellectual content that would fulfill the mobility promise. But grade-point averages, which in the standards era depend as much as the Scholastic Aptitude Test on high-stakes testing, measure the acquired knowledge of students and restrict their access to elite institutions of higher learning, the obligatory training grounds for professional and managerial occupations. Since all credentials are not equal, graduating from third- and fourth-tier institutions does not confer on the successful candidate the prerequisites for entering a leading graduate school— the preparatory institution for professional and managerial occupations, or the most desirable entry-level service jobs that require only a bachelor's degree.

Pierre Bourdieu argues that schools reproduce class relations by reinforcing rather than reducing class-based differential access to social and cultural capital, key markers of class affiliation and mobility. Children of the wealthy, professionals, and the intelligentsia, he argues, always already possess these forms of capital. Far from making possible a rich intellectual education, or providing the chance to affiliate with networks of students and faculty who have handles on better jobs, schooling habituates working-class students, through mechanisms of discipline and punishment, to the bottom rungs of the work world or the academic world by subordinating or expelling them.[6] Poorly prepared for academic work by their primary and secondary schools, and having few alternatives to acquiring some kind of credential, many who stay the course and graduate high school and third- and fourth-tier college inevitably confront a series of severely limited occupational choices—or none at all. Their life chances are just a cut above those who do not complete high school or college. Their school performances seem to validate what common sense has always suspected: given equal opportunity to attain school knowledge, the cream always rises to the top and those stuck at the bottom must be biologically impaired, victimized by the infamous "culture of poverty" or just plain distracted. That most working-class high-school and college students are obliged to hold full- or part-time jobs in order to stay in school fails to temper this judgment, for as is well known, preconceptions usually trump facts.[7] Nor does the fact that the children of the recent 20 million immigrants from Latin America, Russia, and especially Asia speak their native languages at home, in the neighborhood, and to each other in school evoke more than hand-wringing from educational leaders. In this era of tight school budgets, English as a Second Language funds have been cut or eliminated at every level of schooling.

But Paul Willis insists that working-class kids get working-class jobs by means of their refusal to accept the discipline entailed in curricular mastery and by their rebellion against school authority. Challenging the familiar "socialization" thesis—of which Bourdieu's is perhaps the most sophisticated version, according to which working-class kids "fail" because they are culturally deprived or, in the American critical version, are assaulted by the hidden curriculum and school pedagogy that subsumes kids under

---

6   Bourdieu, P. and Passeron, J. C. (1977).

7   Cicourel, A. V. and Kitsuse, J. I. (1963) *The Educational Decision-Makers*. Indianapolis, Ind.: Bobbs Merrill. This is one of the most persuasive studies demonstrating the salience of phenomenological investigations of social life. It is a tacit repudiation of the reliance of much of social science, especially sociology and political science, on what people say rather than what they do.

the prevailing order—Willis recodes kids' failure as refusal of (school) work, which lands them in the world of factory or low-level service work. Willis offers no alternative educational model to schooling: his discovery functions as critique. Indeed, as Willis himself acknowledges, the school remains, in Louis Althusser's famous phrase, the main "ideological state apparatus," but working-class kids are not victims. Implicitly rejecting Richard Sennett and Jonathan Cobb's notion that school failure is a "hidden injury" of class insofar as working-class kids internalize poor school performance as a sign of personal deficit, he argues that most early school leavers are active agents in the production of their own class position. While students' antipathy to school authority is enacted at the site of the school, its origins are the working-class culture from which they spring. Workers do not like bosses, and kids do not like school bosses, the deans and principals, but often as well the teachers, whose main job in the urban centers is to keep order. The source of working-class kids' education is not the school but the shop floor, the places where their parents work, the home, and the neighborhood.[8]

In the past half-century, the class question has been inflected by race and gender discrimination, and, in the American way, the "race, gender, class" phrase implies that these domains are ontologically distinct, if not entirely separate. Nor have critics theorized the race and gender question as a class issue but as an attribute of bioidentities. In fact, in the era of identity politics, for many writers, class itself stands alongside race and gender as just another identity. Having made the easy, inaccurate judgment that white students—regardless of their class or gender—stand in a qualitatively different relation to school-related opportunities than blacks, class is often suppressed as a sign of exclusion. In privileging issues of access, not only is the curriculum presupposed, in which case Bourdieu's insistence on the concept of cultural capital is ignored, but also the entire question is elided of whether schooling may be conflated with education. Only rarely do writers examine other forms of education. In both the Marxist and liberal traditions, schooling is presumed to remain—over a vast spectrum of spatial and temporal situations—the theater within which life chances are determined.

Education and Immaterial Labor

Education may be defined as the collective and individual reflection on the totality of life experiences: what we learn from peers, parents (and the socially situated cultures of which they are a part), media, and schools. By reflection I mean the transformation of experience into a multitude of concepts that constitute the abstractions we call "knowledge." Which of the forms of learning predominate are always configured historically. The exclusive focus by theorists and researchers on school knowledges—indeed, the implication that school is

---

8   The best analysis of the relation of schools to the lives of working-class kids remains Willis, P. (1981) *Learning to Labor: How Working Class Kids Get Working Class Jobs.* New York: Columbia University Press.

the principal site of what we mean by education—reflects the degree to which they have, themselves, internalized the equation of education with school knowledge and its preconditions. The key learning is they (we) have been habituated to a specific regime of intellectual labor that entails a high level of self-discipline, the acquisition of the skills of reading and writing, and the career expectations associated with professionalization.

To say this constitutes the self-reflection by intellectuals—in the broadest sense of the term—of their own relation to schooling. In the age of the decline of critical intelligence and the proliferation of technical intelligence, "intellectual" in its current connotation designates immaterial labor, not traditional intellectual pursuits such as literature, philosophy, and art. Immaterial labor describes those who work not with objects or the administration of things and people, but with ideas, symbols, and signs. Some of the occupations grouped under immaterial labor have an affective dimension. The work demands the complete subordination of brain, emotion, and body to the task while requiring the worker to exercise considerable judgment and imagination in its performance. For example, at sites such as "new economy" private-sector software workplaces; some law firms that deal with questions of intellectual property, public interest, or constitutional and international law; research universities and independent research institutes; and small, innovative design, architectural, and engineering firms, the informality of the labor process, close collaborative relationships among members of task-oriented teams, and the overflow of the space of the shop floor with the spaces of home and play evoke, at times, a high level of exhilaration, even giddiness, among members, and at other times utter exhaustion and burnout because the work invades the dreamwork and prohibits relaxation and genuine attention to partners and children.

To be an immaterial worker means, in the interest of having self-generated work, surrendering much of one's unfettered time. Such workers are obliged to sunder the conventional separation of work and leisure, to adopt the view that time devoted to creative, albeit commodified labor, is actually "free." Or, to be more exact, even play must be engaged in as serious business. For many the golf course, the bar, the weekend at the beach are workplaces, where dreams are shared, plans formulated, and deals are made. Just as time becomes unified around work, so work loses its geographic specificity. As Andrew Ross shows in his pathbreaking ethnography of a New York new economy workplace during and after the dot-com boom, the headiness for the pioneers of this new work world was, tacitly, a function of the halcyon period of the computer software industry when everyone felt the sky was no longer the limit.[9] When the economic crunch descended on thousands of workplaces, people were laid off, and those who remained, as well as those who became unemployed, experienced a heavy dose of market reality.

It may be argued that among elite students and institutions, schooling not only prepares immaterial labor by transmitting a bundle of legitimate knowledges; the diligent, academically successful student internalizes the blur between the classroom, play, and home by spending a great deal of time in the library or ostensibly playing at the computer.

9   Ross, A. (2003) *No-Collar.*

Thus, the price of the promise of autonomy, a situation intrinsic to professional ideology, if not always its practice in the context of bureaucratic and hierarchical corporate systems, is to accept work as a mode of life; one lives to work, rather than the reverse. The hopes and expectations of these strata are formed in the process of schooling; indeed, they have most completely assimilated the ideologies linked to school knowledge and to the credentials conferred by the system. Thus whether professional school people, educational researchers, or not, they tend to evaluate people by the criteria to which they, themselves, were subjected. If the child has not fully embraced work as life, he is consigned to the educational nether land. Even the egalitarians (better read *populists*) accept this regime: their object is to afford those for whom work is a necessary evil entry into the social world, where work is the mission.

The Labor and Radical Movements as Educational Sites

The working-class intellectual as a social type precedes and parallels the emergence of universal public education. At the dawn of the public-school movement in the 1830s, the antebellum labor movement, which consisted largely of literate skilled workers, favored six years of schooling in order to transmit to their children the basics of reading and writing but opposed compulsory attendance in secondary schools. The reasons were bound up with their congenital suspicion of the state, which they believed never exhibited sympathy for the workers' cause. Although opposed to child labor, the early workers' movements were convinced that the substance of education—literature, history, philosophy—should be supplied by the movement itself. Consequently, in both the oral and the written tradition, workers' organizations often constituted an alternate university to that of public schools. The active program of many workers' and radical movements until World War II consisted largely in education through newspapers, literacy classes for immigrants where the reading materials were drawn from labor and socialist classics and world literature. These were supplemented by lectures offered by independent scholars who toured the country in the employ of lecture organizations commissioned by the unions and radical organizations.[10]

But the shop floor was also a site of education. Skilled workers were usually literate in their own language and in English, and many were voracious readers and writers. Union and radical newspapers often ran poetry and stories written by workers. Socialist-led unions sponsored educational programs; in the era when the union contract was still a rarity, the union was not so much an agency of contract negotiation and enforcement as an educational, political, and social association. In his autobiography, Samuel Gompers, the founding American Federation of Labor president, remembers his fellow cigar makers hiring a "reader" in the 1870s, who sat at the center of the shop floor and read

10   Mishler, P. C.(1999) *Raising Reds: The Young Pioneers, Radical Summer Camps, and Communist Political Culture in the United States.* New York: Columbia University Press.

from literary and historical classics as well as more contemporary works of political and economic analysis such as the writings of Marx and Engels. Reading groups met in the back of a bar, in the union hall, or in the local affiliate of the socialist wing of the nationality federations. Often these groups were ostensibly devoted to preparing immigrants to pass the obligatory language test for citizenship status. But the content of the reading was, in addition to labor and socialist newspapers and magazines, often supplemented by works of fiction by Shakespeare, the great nineteenth-century novelists and poets, and Karl Kautsky. In its anarchist inflection, Peter Kropotkin, Moses Hess, and Michael Bakunin were the required texts.[11]

In New York, Chicago, San Francisco, and other large cities where the Socialist, Anarchist, and Communist movements had considerable membership and a fairly substantial periphery of sympathizers, the parties established adult schools that not only offered courses pertaining to political and ideological knowledge but were vehicles for many working- and middle-class students to gain a general education. Among them, in New York, the socialist-oriented Rand School and the Communist-sponsored Jefferson School (formerly the Workers' School) lasted until the mid-1950s when, because of the decline of a Left intellectual culture among workers as much as the contemporary repressive political environment, they closed. But in their heydays, from the 1920s to the late 1940s, for tens of thousands of working-class people—many of them high-school students and industrial workers—these schools were alternate universities. Many courses concerned history, literature, and philosophy, and, at least at the Jefferson School, students could study art, drama, and music, as could their children. The tradition was revived, briefly, by the 1960s New Left that, in similar sites, sponsored free universities where the term *free* designated not an absence of tuition fees but an ideological and intellectual freedom from either the traditional Left parties or the conventional school system. I participated in organizing New York's Free University and two of its successors. While not affiliated with the labor movement or socialist parties, it successfully attracted more than a thousand mostly young students in each of its semesters and offered a broad range of courses taught by people of divergent intellectual and political orientations, including some free-market libertarians attracted to the school's nonsectarianism.[12]

When I worked in a steel mill in the late 1950s, some of us formed a group that read current literature, labor history, and economics. I discussed books and magazine articles with some of my fellow workers in bars as well as on breaks. Tony Mazzocchi, who was at the same time a worker and union officer of a Long Island local of the Oil, Chemical and Atomic Workers Union, organized a similar group, and I knew of several other cases in which young workers did the same. Some of these groups evolved into rank-and-file

---

11   Gompers, S. (1925) *Seventy Years of Life and Labor: An Autobiography.* New York: E. P. Dutton.
12   Gettleman, M. (2002) "No Varsity Teams: New York's Jefferson School of Social Science, 1943-1956," *Science and Society* Fall, pp. 336–59. My reflections on the Free University and other New Left educational projects may be found in Aronowitz, S. (1984) "When the New Left Was New," in S. Sayres, A. Stephanson, S. Aronowitz, and F. Jameson (Eds.) *The Sixties without Apology.* Minneapolis: University of Minnesota Press.

caucuses that eventually contested the leadership of their local unions; others were mainly for the self-edification of the participants and had no particular political goals. But beyond formal programs, the working-class intellectual, although by no means visible in the United States, has been part of shop-floor culture since the industrializing era. In almost every workplace there is a person or persons to whom other workers turn for information about the law, the union contract, contemporary politics, or, equally important, as a source of general education. These individuals may or may not have been schooled, but, until the late 1950s, they rarely had any college education. For schools were not the primary source of their knowledge. They were, and are, largely self-educated. In my own case, having left Brooklyn College after less than a year, I worked in various industrial production jobs. When I worked the midnight shift, I got off at 8:00 a.m., ate breakfast, and spent four hours in the library before going home. Mostly I read American and European history and political economy, particularly the physiocrats, Adam Smith, David Ricardo, John Maynard Keynes, and Joseph Schumpeter. Marx's *Capital* I read in high school and owned the three volumes.

My friend Russell Rommele, who worked in a nearby mill, was also an autodidact. His father was a first-generation German American brewery worker, with no particular literary interests. But Russell had read a wide range of historical and philosophical works as a high-school student at Saint Benedict's Prep, a Jesuit institution. The priests singled out Russell for the priesthood and mentored him in theology and social theory. The experience radicalized him, and he decided not to answer the call but to enter the industrial working class instead. Like me, he was active in the union and Newark Democratic Party politics. Working as an educator with a local union in the auto industry recently, I have met several active unionists who are intellectuals. The major difference between them and those of my generation is that they are college graduates, although none of them claim to have acquired their love of learning or their analytic perspective from schools. One is a former member of a radical organization; another learned his politics from participation in a shop-based study of a group/union caucus. In both instances, with the demise of their organizational affiliations, they remain habituated to reading, writing, and union activity.

Beneath the radar screen, union–university collaborations sprang up in the 1980s. I was among those who founded the Center for Worker Education at City College. It is a bachelor's degree program, begun for union members and their families, but expanded to other working people as well. Worker education meant, in this case, that the emphasis is not on labor studies in the manner of Cornell, UCLA, University of Minnesota's schools of industrial and labor relations, or the Queens College Labor Resource Center. Instead, City College's center offers a liberal arts and professional curriculum as well as a few courses in labor history. While the educational content is often critical, the intention articulates with the recent focus on credentialism of undergraduate institutions. Similar programs have been in operation for two decades in a collaboration between the large New York municipal employees' District Council 37 and the College of New Rochelle, and the Hospital Workers Union's various arrangements with New York–area colleges that offer upgrading, training, and college courses to thousands of its members.

Parents, Neighborhood, Class, Culture

John Locke observes that, consistent with his rejection of innate ideas, even if conceptions of good and evil are present in divine or civil law, morality is constituted by reference to our parents, relatives, and especially the "club" of peers to which we belong:

> He who imagines commendation and disgrace not to be strong motives to men to accommodate themselves to the opinions and rules of those with whom they converse seems little skilled in the nature or the history of mankind: the greatest part whereof we shall find govern themselves, chiefly, if not solely by this law of *fashion* [emphasis in the original]; and so they do what keeps them in reputation with their company, [with] little regard for the laws of God or the magistrate.[13]

William James puts the matter equally succinctly:

> A man's social self is the recognition which he gets from his mates. We are not only gregarious animals, liking to be in the sight of our fellows, but we have an innate propensity to get ourselves noticed, and noticed favorably, by our kind. No more fiendish punishment could be devised, were such a thing physically possible, that that should be turned loose in society and remain absolutely unnoticed by all the members thereof.[14]

That the social worlds of peers and family are the chief referents for the formation of the social self, neither philosopher doubted. Each in his own fashion situates the individual in social context, which provides a "common measure of virtue and vice" (Locke) even as they acknowledge the ultimate choice resides with the individual self. These, and not the institutions, even those that have the force of law, are the primary sources of authority.

Hannah Arendt argues that education "by its very nature cannot forego either authority or tradition." Nor can it base itself on the presumption that children share an autonomous existence from adults.[15] Schooling ignores the reality of the society of kids at the cost of undermining its own authority. The society of kids is in virtually all classes an

---

13   Locke, J. (1958) *An Essay concerning Human Understanding.* New York: Dover, bk. 1, chap. 28, p. 478.

14   James, W. (1955) *The Principles of Psychology.* New York: Dover, 1, p. 293.

15   Arendt, H. (1961) "Crisis in Education," *Between Past and Future.* New York: Harcourt, Brace and World.

alternative and oppositional site of knowledge and of moral valuation. We have already seen how working-class kids get working-class jobs by means of their rebellion against school authority. Since refusal and resistance is a hallmark of that moral order, the few who will not obey the invocation to fail, or to perform indifferently in school, often find themselves marginalized or expelled from the society of kids. While they adopt a rationality that can be justified on eminently practical grounds, the long tradition of rejection of academic culture has proven hard to break, even in the wake of evidence that those working-class jobs to which they were oriented no longer exist. For what is at stake in the resistance of adolescents is their perception that the blandishments of the adult world are vastly inferior to the pleasures of their own. In the first place, the new service economy offers few inducements: wages are low, the job is boring, and the future bleak. And since the schools now openly present themselves as a link in the general system of control, it may appear to some students that cooperation is a form of self-deception.

If not invariably, then in many households parents provide to the young a wealth of knowledges: the family mythologies that feature an uncle or aunt, a grandparent or an absent parent. These are the stories, loosely based on some actual event(s) in which family members have distinguished themselves in various ways that (usually) illustrate a moral virtue or defect, the telling of which constitutes a kind of didactic message. Even when not attached to an overt narrative, parable, or myth, the actions of our parents offer many lessons: How do they deal with adversity? How do they address ordinary, everyday problems? What do they learn from their own trials and tribulations and what do they say to us? What are our parents' attitudes toward money, joblessness, and everyday life disruptions such as sudden, acute illness or accidents? What do they learn from the endless conflicts with their parent(s) over issues of sex, money, and household responsibilities?

The relative weight of parental to peer authority is an empirical question that cannot be decided in advance; what both have in common is their location in everyday life. Parents are likely to be more susceptible to the authority of law and of its magistrates and, in a world of increasing uncertainty, will worry that if their children choose badly, they may be left behind. But the associations with our peers we make in everyday life provide the recognition that we crave, define what is worthy of praise or blame, and confer approbation or disapproval on our decisions. But having made a choice that runs counter to that of "their company" or club, individuals must form or join a new "company" to confer the judgment of virtue on their actions. This company must, of necessity, consist of "peers," the definition of which has proven fungible.

Religion, the law, and, among kids, school authorities face the obstacles erected by the powerful rewards and punishments meted out by the "clubs" to which people are affiliated. At a historical conjunction when—beneath the relentless pressure imposed by capital to transform all labor into wage labor, thereby forcing every adult into the paid labor force— the society of kids increasingly occupies the space of civil society. The neighborhood, once dominated by women and small shopkeepers, has all but disappeared save for the presence of children and youth. As parents toil for endless hours to pay the ever-mounting debts incurred by home ownership, perpetual car and appliance payments, and the costs of health care, kids are increasingly on their own, and this lack of supervision affects their conceptions of education and life.

Some recent studies and teacher observations have discovered a considerable reluctance among black students in elite universities to perform well in school, even among those with professional or managerial family backgrounds. Many seem indifferent to arguments that show that school performance is a central prerequisite to better jobs and higher status in the larger work world. Among the more acute speculations is the conclusion that black students' resistance reflects an anti-intellectual bias and a hesitation, if not refusal, to enter the mainstream corporate world. There are similar attitudes among some relatively affluent white students as well. Although by no means a majority, some students are less enamored by the work world to which they, presumably, have been habituated by school, and especially by the prospect of perpetual work. In the third-tier universities, state and private alike, many students, apparently forced by their parents to enroll, wonder out loud why they are there. Skepticism about schooling still abounds even as they graduate high school and enroll in postsecondary schools in record numbers. According to one colleague of mine who teaches in a third-tier private university in the New York metropolitan area, many of these mostly suburban students "sleepwalk through their classes, do not participate in class discussions, and are lucky to get a C grade."[16]

In the working-class neighborhoods—white, black, and Latino—the word is out: given the absence of viable alternatives, you must try to obtain that degree, but this defines the limit of loyalty to the enterprise. Based on testimonies of high-school and community-college teachers, for every student who takes school knowledge seriously there are twenty or more who are timeservers. Most are ill prepared for academic work, and, since the community colleges, four-year state colleges, and "teaching" universities simply lack the resources to provide the means by which such students can improve their school performance, beyond the credential there is little motivation among them to try to get an education.

In some instances, those who break from their club and enter the regime of school knowledge risk being drummed out of a lifetime of relationships with their peers. What has euphemistically been described as "peer pressure" bears, among other moral structures, on the degree to which kids are permitted to cross over the line into the precincts of adult authority. While success in school is not equivalent to squealing on a friend to the cops, or transgressing some sacred moral code of the society of kids, it comes close to committing an act of betrayal. This is comprehensible only if the reader is willing to suspend the prejudice that schooling is tantamount to education and is an unqualified "good," as compared to the presumed evil of school failure, or the decision of the slacker to rebel by refusing to succeed.

To invoke the concept of "class" in either educational debates or any other politically charged discourse generally refers to the white working class. Educational theory and

16   McWhorter, J. H. (2000) *Losing the Race: Self-Sabotage in Black America.* New York: Free Press.

practice treats blacks and Latinos, regardless of their economic positions, as unified categories. That black kids from professional, managerial, and business backgrounds share as much or more with their white counterparts than with working-class blacks is generally ignored by most educational writers, just as in race discourse whites are an undifferentiated racial identity, which refers in slightly different registers to people of African origin and those who migrated from Latin countries of South America and the Caribbean, and are treated as a unified category. The narrowing of the concept of class limits our ability to discern class at all. I want to suggest that, although we must stipulate ethnic, gender, race, and occupational distinction among differentiated strata of wage labor—with the exception of children of salaried professional and technical groups, where the culture of schooling plays a decisive role—class education transcends these distinctions. No doubt there are gradations among the strata that comprise this social formation, but the most privileged professional strata (physicians, attorneys, scientists, professors) and the high-level managers are self-reproducing, not principally through schooling but through social networks. These include private schools, some of which are residential; clubs and associations; and, in suburban public schools, the self-selection of students on the basis of distinctions. Show me a school friendship between the son or daughter of a corporate manager and the child of a janitor or factory worker, and I will show you an anomaly.

Schooling selects a fairly small number of children of the class of wage labor for genuine class mobility. In the first half of the twentieth century, having lost its appeal among middle-class youth, the Catholic Church turned to working-class students as a source of cadre recruitment. In my neighborhood of the East Bronx two close childhood friends, both of Italian background, entered the priesthood. For these sons of construction workers, the church provided their best chance to escape the hardships and economic uncertainties of manual labor. Another kid became a pharmacist because the local college, Fordham University, offered scholarships.

A fourth was among the tiny coterie of students who passed the test for one of the city's special schools, Bronx Science, and became a science teacher. Otherwise, almost everybody else remained a worker or, like my best friend, Kenny, went to prison. Despite the well-publicized claim that anyone can escape their condition of social and economic birth—a claim reproduced by schools and by the media with numbing regularity—most working-class students, many of whom have some college credits but often do not graduate—end up in low- and middle-level service jobs that do not pay a decent working-class wage. Owing to the steep decline of unionized industrial production jobs, those who enter factories increasingly draw wages substantially below union standards. Those who do graduate find work in computers, although rarely at the professional levels. The relatively low paid become K–12 school teachers and health care professionals, mostly nurses and technicians, or enter the social services field as caseworkers, medical social workers, or nonsupervisory social welfare workers. The question I want to pose is whether these "professional" occupations represent genuine mobility.

During the postwar economic boom that made possible a significant expansion of spending for schools, the social services, and administration of public goods, the public sector workplace became a favored site of black and Latino recruitment, mainly for clerical, maintenance, and entry-level patient care jobs in hospitals and other health care facilities. Within several decades a good number advanced to practical and registered nursing, but not in all sections of the country. As unionization spread to the nonprofit private sector as well as public employment in the 1960s and 1970s, these jobs paid enough to enable many to enjoy what became known as a middle-class living standard, with a measure of job security offered by union security and civil service status. While it is true that "job security" has often been observed in its breach, the traditional deal made by teachers, nurses, and social workers was that they traded higher incomes for job security. But after about 1960, spurred by the resurgent civil rights movement, these "second-level" professionals—white and black—began to see themselves as workers more than professionals: they formed unions, struck for higher pay and shorter hours, and assumed a very unprofessional adversarial stance toward institutional authority. Contracts stipulated higher salaries, definite hours—a sharp departure from professional ideology—and seniority as a basis for layoffs, like any industrial contract, and demanded substantial vacation and sick leave.

Their assertion of working-class values and social position may have been strategic; indeed, it inspired the largest wave of union organizing since the 1930s. But, together with the entrance of huge numbers of women and blacks into the public and quasi–public sector workforces, it was also a symptom of the proletarianization of the second-tier professions. Several decades later, salaried physicians made a similar discovery; they formed unions and struck against high malpractice insurance costs as much as the onerous conditions imposed on their autonomy by health maintenance organizations and government authorities bent on cost containment, often at the physicians' expense. More to the point, the steep rise of public employees' salaries and benefits posed the question of how to maintain services in times of fiscal austerity, which might be due to economic downturn or to probusiness tax policies. The answer has been that the political and public officials told employees that the temporary respite from the classical trade union trade-off was over. All public employees have suffered a relative deterioration in their salaries and benefits. Since the mid-1970s fiscal crises, begun in New York City, they have experienced layoffs for the first time since the Depression. And their unions have been in a concessionary bargaining mode for decades. In the politically and ideologically repressive environment of the last twenty-five years, the class divide has sharpened. Ironically, in the wake of the attacks by legislatures and business against their hard-won gains in the early 1980s, the teachers unions abandoned their militant class posture and reverted to professionalism and a center-right political strategy.

In truth, schools are learning sites, even if only for a handful of intellectual knowledge. For the most part, they transmit the instrumental logic of credentialism, together with their transformation from institutions of discipline to those of control, especially in working-class districts. Even talented, dedicated teachers have difficulty reaching kids and convincing them that the life of the mind may hold unexpected rewards, though the career implications of critical thought are not apparent. The breakdown of the mission of public schools has produced varied forms of disaffection; if school violence has abated in some places, that does not signify the decline of gangs and other "clubs" that represent the autonomous world of youth. The society of kids is more autonomous because, in contrast to 1960s, official authorities no longer offer hope; instead, in concert with the doctrine of control, they threaten punishment that includes, but is not necessarily associated with, incarceration. The large number of drug busts of young black and Latino men should not be minimized. With over a million blacks, more than 3 percent of the African American population—most of them young (25 percent of young black men)—within the purview of the criminal justice system, the law may be viewed as a more or less concerted effort to counter by force the power of peers. This may be regarded in the context of the failure of schools. Of course, more than three hundred years ago John Locke knew the limits of the magistrates—indeed, of any adult authority—to overcome the power of the society of kids.[17]

Conclusion

What are the requisite changes that would transform schools from credential mills and institutions of control to sites of education that prepare young people to see themselves as active participants in the world? As my analysis implies, the fundamental condition is to abolish high-stakes tests that dominate the curriculum and subordinate teachers to the role of drill- masters and subject students to stringent controls. By this proposal I do not mean to eliminate the need for evaluative tools. The essay is a fine measure of both writing ability and of the student's grasp of literature, social science, and history. While mathematics, science, and language proficiency do require considerable rote learning, the current curriculum and pedagogy in these fields includes neither a historical account of the changes in scientific and mathematical theory nor a metaconceptual explanation of what the disciplines are about. Nor are courses in language at the secondary level ever concerned with etymological issues, comparative cultural study of semantic differences, and other topics that might relieve the boredom of rote learning by providing depth of understanding. The broader understanding of science in the modern world—its relation to technology, war, and medicine, for example—should surely be integrated into the curriculum; some of these issues appear in the textbooks, but teachers rarely discuss them because they are busy preparing students for the high-stakes tests in which knowledge of the social contexts for science, language, and mathematics is not included.

17   Aronowitz, S. (1992) *False Promises: The Shaping of American Working Class Consciousness*, 2d ed. Durham, N.C.: Duke University Press; Giroux, H. A. (2003) *The Abandoned Generation: Democracy beyond the Culture of Fear.* New York: Palgrave; Spina, S. U. (2001) Dd., *Smoke and Mirrors: The Hidden Context of Violence in Schools and Society.* Boulder, Colo.: Rowman and Littlefield.

I agree with Hannah Arendt that education "cannot forgo either authority or tradition." But authority must be earned rather than assumed, and the transmission of tradition needs to be critical rather than worshipful. If teachers were allowed to acknowledge student skepticism to incorporate kids' knowledge into the curriculum by making what they know the object of rigorous study, especially popular music and television, teachers might be treated with greater respect. But there is no point denying the canon; one of the more egregious conditions of subordination is the failure of schools to expose students to the best exemplars, for people who have no cultural capital are thereby condemned to social and political marginality, let alone deprived of some of the genuine pleasures to be derived from encounters with genuine works of art. When the New York City Board of Education (now the Department of Education) mandates that during every semester high-school English classes read a Shakespeare play, and one or two works of nineteenth-century English literature, but afford little or no access to the best Russian novels of the nineteenth century, no opportunities to examine some of the most influential works of Western or Eastern philosophy and provide no social and historical con text for what is learned, tradition is observed in the breach more than in its practice.

Finally, schools should cut their ties to corporate interests and reconstruct the curriculum along the lines of genuine intellectual endeavor. Nor should schools be seen as career conduits, although this function will be difficult to displace: in an era of high economic anxiety, many kids and their parents worry about the future and seek some practical purchase on it. It will take some convincing that their best leg up is to be educated. It is unlikely in the present environment, but possible in some places. One could elaborate these options; this is only an outline. In order to come close to their fulfillment at least three things are needed. First, we require a conversation concerning the nature and scope of education and the limits of schooling as an educational site. Along with this, theorists and researchers need to link their knowledge of popular culture, culture in the anthropological sense—that is, everyday life—with the politics of education. Teachers who, by their own education, are intellectuals who respect and want to help children obtain a genuine education regardless of their social class are in the forefront of enabling social change and are entrusted with widening students' possibilities in life. For this we need a new regime of teacher education founded on the idea that the educator must be educated well. It would surely entail abolishing the current curricula of most education schools, if not the schools themselves. Teacher training should be embedded in general education, not in "methods," many of which are useless; instruction should include knowledge other than credential and bring the union/movement/organic intellectuals into [the] classroom. In other words, the classroom should be a window on the world, not a hermetically sealed regime of the imposition of habitus, that is, making the test of academic success equivalent to measuring the degree to which the student has been inculcated with the habit of subordination to school and pedagogic authority.[18]

---

18   Bourdieu, P. and Passeron, J. C. (1977).

And we need a movement of parents, students, teachers, and labor armed with a political program to force legislatures to adequately fund schooling at the federal, state, and local levels, and boards of education to deauthorize high-stakes tests that currently drive the curriculum and pedagogy.

To outline a program for the reconstruction of schooling does not imply that the chances for its success are good, especially in the current environment. Indeed, almost all current trends oppose the concept of public education as a school of freedom. But if the principle of critique is hope rather than the most rigorous form of nihilism—the suspension of action pending an upsurge from below—we have an obligation to resist but also to suggest alternatives. These will, inevitably, be attacked as utopian, and, of course, they are. But as many have argued, utopian thought is the condition for change. Without the "impossible," there is little chance for reform.

CHAPTER THREE

Rationality Crisis in Higher Education[1]

Clyde Barrow

> *By the second section of the intelligible world you may*
> *understand me to mean all that unaided reasoning*
> *apprehends by the power of dialectic . . . like a flight of steps*
> *up which it may mount all the way to something that is*
> *not hypothetical, the first principle of all . . . never making use*
> *of any sensible object, but only of Forms, moving through*
> *Forms from one to another, and ending with Forms. I*
> *understand, he said, though not perfectly; for the procedure*
> *you describe sounds like an enormous undertaking.*

—Plato, *The Republic*

Capitalism, Crisis Theory, and the University[2]

THE CAPITALIST SYSTEM is frequently conceptualized as a matrix of three interdependent, but relatively autonomous subsystems: the economic system, the political system, and the ideological system.[3] The most important institutions associated with the economic subsystem are the relations of production between classes in the workplace and relations of exchange between buyers and sellers in the marketplace. The ideological subsystem, from which individuals derive normative values, includes the family, educational institutions, religion, and cultural outlets. Finally, in late capitalism, the political subsystem consists primarily of those institutions organized as the state and the policies implemented through the state apparatuses.

Although each subsystem encompasses concretely identifiable institutions, the capitalist system as a whole is often posited as the *network of relationships* among these institutions, which produces consequences *through* institutions, but is therefore never

1   Keynote Address - Department of Educational Leadership, University of Massachusetts Dartmouth, October 14, 2011, The Kaput Center Conference Room, 200 Mill Road, Fairhaven, MA.
2   This section is an abridged and revised version of the argument in Barrow (1993b), Chap. 4.
3   Miliband (1969: 1–15); Poulantzas (1978a: 1–33).

reducible *to* institutions.[4] Claus Offe maintains, for example, that the capitalist system is a "superordinate level of mechanisms that generate 'events.'"[5] However, the superordinate reality of the system is only observable empirically when the institutional mechanisms that fulfill systemic maintenance functions fail to suppress or displace the underlying contradictions of the capitalist mode of production. A contradiction, according to Offe, "is the tendency inherent within a specific mode of production to destroy those very pre-conditions on which its survival depends."[6] Consequently, the historical development of a contradiction must inevitably culminate in some crisis event that makes the contradiction empirically perceptible as a crisis.[7]

Jurgen Habermas provides the most comprehensive and analytically coherent typology of potential crisis conditions within late capitalism.[8] Habermas argues that "crises arise when the structure of a social system allows fewer possibilities for problem solving than are necessary to the continued existence of the system. In this sense, crises are seen as persistent disturbances of system integration."[9] Importantly, the difference between a crisis and a mere problem is that crises ultimately cannot be resolved within the system's boundaries, because they are generated by system imperatives that are mutually incompatible, that is, contradictory.

Habermas suggests that crises of capitalism may be generated from within any of its three subsystems. However, it is generally agreed—at least among radical political economists influenced by Marx—that the underlying economic contradictions of capitalism are often displaced onto the political and ideological subsystems that become responsible for managing, deflecting, or absorbing the economic crisis in various ways.[10]

The Fiscal Crisis of the State

In *The Fiscal Crisis of the State* (1973), James O'Connor argues that beginning in the early twentieth century, contemporary capitalist states have managed the economic contradictions of capitalism by socializing many of the costs of production in capital intensive sectors of the economy.[11] O'Connor observes that the steady increase in state spending throughout the last century provided the basis for continuing economic growth in these sectors,

---

4   Poulantzas (1978a: 115, fn. 24) defines an institution as "a system of norms or rules which is socially sanctioned . . . On the other hand, the concept of structure covers the *organizing matrix* of institutions." Similarly, Gold, Lo, and Wright (1975: 36) observe that the concept of a structure "does *not* refer to the concrete social institutions that make up a society, but rather to the systematic functional interrelationships among these institutions."

5   Offe (1984: 37).

6   Offe (1984: 132).

7   Offe (1984: 116 fn.15).

8   Habermas (1975: Part 2, Chaps. 1–8). See also, O'Connor (1987); Dunleavy and O'Leary (1987: 259–70).

9   Habermas (1975: 2).

10   O'Connor (1973).

11   On the continuing relevance of this analysis, see the latest edition of this book with a new introduction by the author O'Connor (2002).

because their profitability is heavily dependent on state outlays for physical, human, and more recently, intellectual capital. At the same time, and to insure its popular legitimacy, the state must respond to escalating material demands from classes seeking access to the public goods and services required to participate in economic growth or to ameliorate the costs of capitalist economic growth, such as unemployment, injury and disability, environmental damage, and urban deterioration. Thus, there is constant political pressure on state elites to increase state expenditures on education, social insurance, social welfare, housing, health care, and environmental remediation. A structural gap develops between the expenditures necessary to maintain both capital accumulation and popular legitimacy and this structural contradiction becomes a fiscal crisis of the state that is empirically observable as a chronic structural deficit.

The Rationality Crisis of the State

Claus Offe and Jurgen Habermas have each suggested that efforts by state elites and state managers to surmount the political contradiction between accumulation and legitimation are hindered by systemic limitations on state rationality.[12] Offe calls attention to a potential contradiction between the democratic legitimacy and capitalist functions of the state apparatus. In modern states, the legitimacy of state policy inheres in formal rules and procedures whose observation by political authorities obligates citizens to comply with the state's laws and decisions. However, Offe makes the important observation that the legitimating status of formal rules and procedures is linked to an assumption that their application and observation by state officials will systematically result in functional consequences that contribute to the common and individual welfare. Thus, while the formal legitimacy of bureaucratic procedures is based on strict adherence to bureaucratic rules and consistent enforcement of those rules, over the long-term their substantive legitimacy resides in our common expectation that these rules are functionally effective in achieving an identified outcome, whether that outcome is new job creation, environmental protection, a fair trial, or student learning.

However, as Habermas (1975: 47) notes:

> During the course of capitalist development, the political system shifts its boundaries not only into the economic system, but also into the socio-cultural system. While organizational rationality spreads, cultural traditions are undermined and weakened. The residue of tradition must, however, escape the administrative grasp, for traditions important for legitimation cannot be regenerated administratively.

---

12   For purposes of this analysis, federal officials, governors, state legislators, boards of trustees, system offices, and other high-ranking higher education boards are considered state elites, while campus-based administrators are considered state managers. On the distinction, see Barrow (1993b: 28–29).

Thus, according to Habermas (1975: 46) systemic output crises of the state apparatus take:

> the form of a *rationality* crisis in which the administrative system does not suc-
> ceed in reconciling and fulfilling the imperatives received from the economic
> system . . . . The rationality crisis is a displaced systemic crisis which, like
> economic crisis, expresses the contradiction between socialized production
> for non-generalizable interests and steering imperatives. This crisis tendency
> is converted into the withdrawal of legitimation by way of a disorganization
> of the state apparatus.

The dilemma faced by state managers is that they must simultaneously balance two competing forms of rationality: (1) a formal rationality that inheres in the strict observation of formal-bureaucratic procedure and (2) substantive rationality that inheres in functional effectiveness (Marcuse 1965). The ability to balance these two forms of rationality requires that means and ends be aligned with each other, but to the extent that the two forms of ratio-nality diverge, state managers must choose between short-term formal legitimacy based on appeals to position and authority or substantive legitimacy based in the long-term functional effectiveness of their decisions and administrative practices. However, Offe and Habermas suggest that the two forms of rationality are diverging as a systemic effect of capitalist de-velopment and this divergence leads to a dichotomy in state administrative practices and decision-making processes. The result is a type of state administration that constantly oscil-lates between the two horns of this dilemma, but which does not resolve the contradiction itself. Moreover, state managers cannot resolve the contradiction within current systemic constraints, because the wholesale pursuit of either strategy risks a legitimation deficit or substantive failure.[13] Both outcomes have the potential to implode the administrative system and generate popular upheavals demanding a new system of relationships that restore dem-ocratic accountability and functional effectiveness to the failed state administrative system. The other alternative is for state elites to relieve pressure on the state administrative system by shrinking its boundaries and withdrawing from public functions through privatization, marketization, and commodification policies, which ostensibly "de-politicize" these social relations by transferring them back to the private sector.[14]

These contradictory pressures in the administration of higher education are now gen-erating a form of decision-making that I call *fictitious rationality*. Fictitious rationality is a derivative of formal rationality, which as Herbert Marcuse observed almost a half-century ago, focuses exclusively on administrative *means*, such as rules, procedures, and efficiency

---

13   Offe (1985: 303-7); Habermas (1975: 47). Offe's and Habermas's hypothesis on the possibility of rationality crisis is non-empirical in the sense that it does not examine the actual rules that govern action in specific state bureaucracies. Thus, they only postulate a hypothetical divergence between the two criteria of administrative rationality.
14   Offe (1996).

calculations.[15] Substantive rationality focuses on *ends* and it is therefore evaluative, normative, and even political. It asks whether an administrative process achieves its purpose, however narrowly or broadly conceived, and even questions whether that purpose is worthwhile or in the best interests of those who are the objects of formal rationality. Consequently, an administrative process based exclusively in formal rationality does not incorporate the *substantive reasons* for its existence or understand the normative purposes it serves as an instrumentality. Thus, when the failure of formal rationality is challenged by substantive rationality, its adherents solipsistically justify the need for *more* formal rationality with redundant appeals to the need for more rules, more process, greater efficiency, and more productivity without questioning why there is a crisis in the first place. Marcuse (1965: 6) observes that the climax of formal rationality in late capitalism occurs when this rationality appears "in a new light— in the light of its [substantive] irrationality." Formal rationality becomes fictitious rationality when it is divorced from social or organizational ends and no longer subjects itself to the evaluative requirement that it be functionally effective.

In higher education, fictitious rationality is the structural ideological effect of occupying a position within the administrative system where managers exclusively monitor and regulate the academic labor process, rather than produce educational values, such as teaching (learning) or research (information and knowledge).[16] Fictitious rationality is the ideological illusion of individuals who observe the academic labor process, but are *not* directly part of that process. Consequently, as I will subsequently illustrate, higher education administrators who occupy this position in the social relations of production increasingly seek to regulate that labor to achieve greater efficiency, because they view it as a net cost to the organization, rather than the producer of its value. Thus, the illusory solution to the fiscal crisis in higher education is to monitor, regulate, and reduce the costs of intellectual production, but to do so requires an ever larger, and more coercive, administrative apparatus. This rationality crisis leads to an intensification of the fiscal crisis in higher education, which leads to a deepening of the rationality crisis, as higher education administrators seek to suppress this contradiction coercively with authoritative appeals to formal legitimacy, which potentially transforms the rationality crisis in higher education into a political crisis of the university.

The University and the Crises of the State

Over the course of the last century, many of the stresses and contradictions of advanced capitalism have been displaced onto colleges and universities, which are now directly attached to the state—whether legally, politically, or financially—as an important component of the ideological and economic state apparatuses.[17] Consequently, the problems associated

15   Marcuse (1968: 201–26).

16   For background, see Smyth (1995).

17   Althusser (1978: 127–86). On the concept of the state economic apparatus and its increasingly important role, see Poulantzas (1978b: 170). For this reason, college and university faculty occupy a social location

with fiscal crises have often been a catalyst to institutional reform in American higher education and a persistent theme of those reforms has been to promote increased "academic efficiency."[18] Orthodox economists define academic efficiency as a policy that uses "the minimum necessary resources for *intended* (as opposed to actual) results."[19]

It is now clear that the recession of 1990–91 marked the beginning of a prolonged fiscal crisis in American higher education. In fact, during the last fifteen years, state appropriations to U.S. colleges and universities per Full-Time Equivalent (FTE) student have declined substantially after adjusting for inflation, while dependence on tuition and fees as a primary source of revenue has grown during the same time.[20] Moreover, the fiscal crisis in higher education emerged just as corporate and state elites began to pressure colleges and universities to assume a more prominent role in the general maintenance function by increasing their direct support for business through expanded workforce development and technology transfer.[21] Corporate and state elites began demanding that faculties reorient their teaching and research toward the immediate problems of global economic competitiveness, while also becoming more efficient and productive in their use of financial and physical resources.[22] The contradictory imperative that universities respond to the challenges of building a globally competitive post-industrial economy and the demand for increased access to higher education, while simultaneously coping with a fiscal crisis has generated a rationality crisis in college and university administrative systems that is leading to their disorganization and functional collapse.

The Fetishism of Planning[23]

By the spring of 1991, 71% of college and university administrators in the United States had come to view adequate finances as the main challenge facing higher education

at the nexus of the economic, political, and ideological subsystems. They not only fulfill multiple functions within the capitalist system, but are peculiarly subject to its many contradictions and, therefore, they are in a position to experience and observe those contradictions in the *quotidian*, see Lefebvre (2008).

18   For historical studies, see Barrow (1990); Scott (1983); Smith (1974). On the class war character of institutional responses to the current fiscal crisis in higher education, see the excellent argument by Phillips (2009).

19   Halstead (1989: 41). This concept was first introduced by Cooke (1910).

20   For empirical documentation, see Delta Cost Project (2009: 14–15).

21   Commission on the Skills of the American Workforce (1990); Rodriguez (1992).

22   Slaughter (1990) identifies numerous organizations created during this period specifically to promote a new strategic alliance between business, government, and higher education. Slaughter (1990, 2) documents how such organizations have argued convincingly that higher education policy should be linked explicitly to the goal of regaining a competitive advantage for American business mainly by promoting "advanced applied technology, technology transfer, and the training of a competitive scientific and professional labor force." See also, Barrow (1993a), pp. 25–39; Barrow (1996a). More recently, see Slaughter and Rhoades (2004).

23   I have applied the anthropological concept of a fetish to strategic planning in higher education, because a fetish is an object or ritual that is believed to have magical properties. Thus, a shaman believes that if a rain dance is performed properly, it will rain. However, if it does not rain, this does not lead the shaman to conclude that the ritual is a superstition. It leads the shaman to demand more dancing or to accusations that the dancers lack the appropriate faith or that the dance was performed incorrectly in some minor detail. If the shaman is lucky, and

institutions.[24] Similarly, two-thirds of state higher education executive officers, such as governing and coordinating board officials, identified declining state support as the dominant issue in higher education policy.[25] Consequently, administrators responded to the burgeoning fiscal deficits in higher education budgets by rapidly shifting from short-term problem solving to crisis management and then strategic planning for a prolonged fiscal crisis. Strategic planning is a direct descendant of Frederick Taylor's principles of scientific management.[26] Strategic planning quickly became the fetish *de jour* among the state elites and state managers who oversee the higher education apparatus,[27] but unfortunately the proponents of strategic planning rarely stopped to consider that its pitfalls, fallacies, and exaggerated claims had already rendered it a dubious venture by the time it was implemented in colleges and universities.[28] Strategic planning originated in the 1950s primarily as a budget planning exercise among corporate financial officers. It spread quickly through the corporate sector, particularly in the United States, and by the mid-1960s, it was a virtual obsession within American corporations.[29] Yet, even at the pinnacle of its popularity with U.S. corporate elites, management consultants from within the private sector were already observing that "the word 'planning' is currently used in so many and various senses that it is in some danger of degenerating into an emotive noise" (Loasby 1967: 300–08). The identified limitations of strategic planning included (1) the inability of strategic planners to agree on how best to implement a strategic planning process, (2) a lack of real commitment to strategic plans by high level managers, who were disempowered by strategic plans, (3) a tendency toward risk aversion and a reluctance to embrace change among middle managers who therefore obstruct implementation of the strategic plan once it is adopted, and (4) a strategic plan's tendency to generate an obsession with micro-management and financial controls that not only stifles real creativity, independence, and entrepreneurialism in large organizations, but overloads the management system with decision-making bottlenecks and an endless quest for more information through centralized data systems, official forms, and multiple signature authorities.[30]

Indeed, the strategic planning movement failed to prevent the collapse of moribund U.S. corporations in the 1970s, but the recognized limitations and failures of strategic planning did not forestall its export to government by political conservatives, who saw it as a key to running government like a business.[31] The fundamental problem, of course, is not only that government is not a business; that is, it produces public goods and services and not private

---

the dance continues long enough, eventually it will rain, although not because of the dance; or the entire village may die of thirst and starvation, because they keep dancing, but it never rains.

24   *The Almanac of Higher Education, 1992* (1992: 72).

25   Russell (1992: 13–19).

26   Mintzberg (1994: 21–22, 225–26).

27   For a sampling of the early strategic 1990s' planning movement, see, Western Interstate Commission for Higher Education (1992); Western Interstate Commission for Higher Education (1992); Heydinger and Simsek (1992); Johnstone (1993: 3–24); Massy and Meyerson (1992); Finifter, Baldwin, and Thelin (1991).

28   Mintzberg (1994: Chaps. 3–4).

29   Mintzberg (1994: 6).

30   Mintzberg (1994: 159–60).

31   Bluestone and Harrison (1982).

goods and services, but it was now going to be managed using a business planning and de-cision-making system that by the 1980s was already being abandoned by U.S. corporations for leaner, flatter, and more flexible forms of organization and decision-making.[32] Indeed, as early as 1973, the political scientist Aaron Wildavsky was reiterating these warnings for the public sector that

> Planning has become so large that the planner cannot encompass its dimen-sions. Planning has become so complex planners cannnot keep up with it. Planning protrudes in so many directions the planner can no longer discern its shape. (Wildavsky 1973: 127)

Nevertheless, as I have documented elsewhere, by the early 1990s state elites and state managers in higher education ostensibly began linking system- and campus-level resource allocations to a strategy of selective excellence that depended on strategic plan-ning.[33] The strategy of selective excellence is a form of strategic planning designed to rationalize the American higher education system by clearly differentiating the missions of individual institutions, eliminating programs that do not support that mission, and by shifting research activities into applied research that directly supports government and business. The central objective of this strategy was to manage the burgeoning fiscal crisis in higher education by downsizing individual institutions, while enabling the system as a whole to adjust to the needs of the new economy. Thus, higher education elites began adopting a business strategy that had been abandoned by corporate elites at least a de-cade earlier and it was already failing in the wider state sector for reasons that were well understood by corporate elites, business consultants, scholars, and government officials.

University of Massachusetts: A Case Study of the Rationality Crisis

The ongoing attempt to systematically restructure public higher education in the Commonwealth of Massachusetts exemplifies the strategy of selective excellence as a response to the fiscal crisis, and I use it to illustrate the limitations and failures of stra-tegic planning as a form of crisis management.[34] The combination of a fiscal crisis and the collapse of the state's economic base in the late 1980s and early 1990s resulted in the exertion of two simultaneous pressures on the public higher education system. First, the size and persistence of reduced state appropriations created chronic financial pressures that were only partially offset by student fees increases. Second, corporate and state

32   For example, Davidow and Malone (1992); Hammer and Champy (1993).
33   Barrow (1996b: 447–69). See also Barrow (1991).
34   In June of 1992, the Massachusetts Higher Education Coordinating Council (HECC) adopted "The Mission of the Public Higher Education System of the Commonwealth," which states "The public college and university system of Massachusetts exists to make accessible to the people of the Commonwealth programs of excellence in higher education."

elites officials increasingly turned to the state's public colleges and universities as an untapped source of human and intellectual capital that could support the implementation of state and regional economic development strategies.[35] In the context of these dual pressures, governors, state legislators, and boards of trustees initiated a long-term effort to systematically restructure the state's entire public higher education system.

The blueprint for restructuring the university system was prepared in 1989 by the Commission on the Future of the University of Massachusetts. The Commission, chaired by David Saxon, former president of the University of California, was created by the University of Massachusetts Board of Trustees to build support for increased funding for the University. The Commission recommended that Massachusetts "build a world-class public university" beginning with the consolidation of the state's five university-level campuses into a single University of Massachusetts System with campuses at Amherst, Boston, Dartmouth, Lowell, and Worcester.[36] The Commission's political objective in proposing a five-campus system was to stabilize funding for the University of Massachusetts by creating a statewide base of support, because the proposed system would now have a campus in each of the state's five major regions. However, the report failed to capture the state legislature's attention until the depth of the 1990–1991 recession, at which point, university officials adopted the opposite rationale and suggested that consolidation would yield cost efficiencies at the system level. Thus, amid promises of renewed fiscal efficiency, rather than increased funding, a five-campus University of Massachusetts System was created in September 1991.[37]

The new Board of Trustees (consisting mainly of Massachusetts business executives) spent its first year consolidating the new system's central administration, instituting a series of tuition and fee increases, and preparing a "Vision Statement" for the new five-campus system. The Vision Statement identified "centers of excellence" on each campus that were supposed to build on existing campus strengths and deliver greater efficiency within the system by differentiating each campus through its leading programs. The Amherst campus was designated as the system's traditional research university that would continue to offer a broad range of Ph.D.s where quality and student demand continued to justify such effort. The Boston campus was designated as the state's "urban university" with the goal of serving non-traditional students and providing applied research on urban problems. The Dartmouth campus was identified as a small undergraduate teaching university with selected emphasis on graduate education and

---

35   Massachusetts Executive Office of Economic Affairs and The University of Massachusetts (1993); Massachusetts Department of Economic Development and The University of Massachusetts (2002); Massachusetts Department of Housing and Economic Development (2009).

36   Commission on the Future of the University of Massachusetts (1989); Commission on the Future of the State and Community College System (1992).

37   In line with this commitment, state funding for the UMass System is currently below its 1988 funding level in real dollars. The state appropriation for UMass Dartmouth has fallen from 72% of university revenues in 1989 to 25% of revenues in 2009, see Welker (2009c), who reports that "the state's share of the UMass budget has fallen–from $441 million in fiscal 2001 to $310 million in fiscal 2009, when adjusted for inflation." Also, MacCormack (2009) and Welker (2009a).

applied research in marine- and technology-related fields and in applied professional areas, such as technical writing, public policy, and education. The Lowell campus was to build on long-standing strengths in high-technology and engineering, while Worcester is the system's medical school focused on training general practitioners.[38]

At the same time, the Trustees created a Public Policy Working Group (1992), which initiated an extensive planning process that resulted in a document titled *Planning to Plan*.[39] This process resulted in a new vision statement and a comprehensive framework to guide further strategic planning by the individual campuses. The central thesis of the Trustee's vision statement was that the University of Massachusetts should define a distinctive niche by reclaiming its original land-grant mission, which they defined as student access, program excellence, economic development, and public service. The long-range objective was to strive for world-class status by renewing the university–state partnership and by creating university–business partnerships and this vision was reaffirmed in a *Statement of System Priorities* the following year.[40]

In February 1995, former president Michael Hooker released an *Action Plan for the Year 2000* that was supposed to implement the strategic plans adopted by the system and by each of the individual campuses.[41] The Action Plan 2000 was based on the assumption that the University of Massachusetts is in a "permanent state of fiscal stress," but notwithstanding the fiscal crisis it must provide qualified citizens with access to a first-rate education (while raising tuition and fees) "in order to ensure their own success in the workplace and to ensure the State's competitiveness in the global economy." The Action Plan also emphasized the University's special obligation to provide quality research and technology transfer in areas important to the state's economy. As the final step in a four-year strategic planning process, the Action Plan required each campus to evaluate all existing programs on the basis of centrality to campus mission, quality, cost, and student demand. By December 1995, every program, center, and department was to be rated on the basis of these evaluative categories and designated for expansion, stasis, or reduction/elimination. In accordance with these decisions, each campus was required to document that it was reallocating 3% of its base budget each year over the next five years toward designated areas of selective excellence.

Each UMass campus administration responded to the system level imperative by initiating a campus-based (top-down) strategic planning process that was supposed to operate within the limitations laid down in the system level vision statement and the planning framework articulated in *Planning to Plan* (1992). For example, in 1992, the University of Massachusetts Dartmouth released its first campus strategic plan titled *Building on Our Strengths*, which reaffirmed the commitment to "access and excellence" for students while stimulating regional economic development through technology

---

38   University of Massachusetts (1991).
39   Public Policy Working Group (1992).
40   University of Massachusetts (1993).
41   Hooker (1995).

transfer and innovation in selected areas, such as advanced technology, marine science and technology, textiles, education, business management, and public policy.[42]

The main outcome of *Building on Our Strengths* was the creation of a new Academic Planning Task Force that, in response to faculty resistance to the established plan, was supposed to incorporate more faculty input into the strategic planning process. The campus had just completed its first strategic plan, but the Academic Planning Task Force was charged by the Chancellor with "developing a planning process" for the campus. Although the five-campus consolidation had promised "economies of scale" and "systemic efficiencies," while identifying UMass Dartmouth as an undergraduate institution, the campus-based planning process immediately veered off unrestrained in the opposite direction. The new task force was charged by the campus administration with exploring a variety of new initiatives that would increase costs to the campus and fundamentally diverge from the campus mission established at the system level by the president and board of trustees. These initiatives included increasing student enrollment by 50% over ten years, doubling dormitory capacity, increasing the number of graduate programs, including at the doctoral level, and increasing non-academic support staff while contracting out academic decisions to paid education and management consultanting firms in areas such as new program development and academic space utilization.[43] These expanded campus goals were reaffirmed three years later, when a reconstituted Academic Planning Task Force issued *Building on Our Strengths Revisited* (1995), which was followed two years later by the Task Force's *Shared Academic Agenda* (1997).

Each iteration of the campus-based strategic planning process was launched by a new chancellor, an interim chancellor, a new provost, or an interim provost, who wanted to expand the campus mission with new initiatives attributable to them. Thus, following the appointment of yet another new chancellor at UMass Dartmouth, the campus launched another round of strategic planning in 1999. This round of planning, which was the most extensive to date, involved 150 faculty, staff, and administrators in focus groups, sub-committees, and research groups over a one-year period only to conclude that henceforth: "Planning is an on-going activity at the University." Strategic planning has become a fetish that consumes more and more faculty, staff, administrative, and clerical time in deliberating what faculty should do, and how to evaluate it, rather than doing it. The new report titled *Engaged, Embedded, and Evolving* layered new priorities on top of the old ones, including greater community involvement and public service by faculty, and new programs, staff, and buildings to support those goals.[44] A significant outcome of this strategic planning process was the addition of a $12 million Advanced Technology

---

42   University of Massachusetts Dartmouth (1992).

43   In fiscal year 2009, when UMass Dartmouth ostensibly faced a structural deficit of nearly $10 million on a total budget of $184 million, the institution spent $45.3 million on consultants. Approximately one-third of the total consultant budget was for accounting consultants, management consultants, and education consultants, which illustrates the new era of "decision-making by consultant" in higher education as opposed to decision-making by consultatation with faculty.

44   University of Massachusetts Dartmouth (2000).

Manufacturing Center in Fall River, Massachusetts, a downtown arts school in New Bedford, Massachusetts, and a $10 million School of Marine Sciences and Technology. Each of the new facilities was supposed to be a "self-supporting revenue generator," a "profit center," or it was funded by direct state appropriations outside the university budget, which were terminated due to the state's current budget deficit.[45]

After seven years, the campus convened another group that produced *Engaged, Embedded, and Evolving, 2000–2007: The University of Massachusetts Strategic Plan; A Report on Progress*,[46] and the campus recently completed its third iteration of *Engaged, Embedded, and Evolving, 2008–2012*.[47] During this time, each college and school at UMass Dartmouth was also required to develop a strategic plan. These plans built around the core mandates established at the system and campus level, but just as the campus had done, each of them went beyond the boundaries of higher level plans, by capitalizing on vaguely stated or overly broad objectives to justify new departments, programs, research centers, and other initiatives. Consequently, each new iteration of "the" strategic plan became more expansive, more costly, and more self-contradictory so that it came to replicate, institutionalize, and intensify all the original problems of the multiversity model. Thus, as the strategic planning process evolved it became clear that neither the UMass System, nor its individual institutions, were really prepared to break radically with the post–World War II model of the multiversity.[48] Indeed, the chasm between the bold rhetoric of state elites and the self-serving incrementalism of university managers has produced more institutional chaos than institutional change.

First, faculty resistance to strategic planning has moved administrators toward a form of politicized irrationality, where despite elaborate planning models and formal criteria for program development and evaluation, the administrative implementation of strategic planning objectives becomes a highly charged political process. Administrators attempt to soften political resistance to planning objectives with concessions to internal and external constituencies that often have competing visions of higher education, which results in strategic plans that not only accrete over time but also incorporate contradictory or self-defeating objectives. For example, prior to the first strategic plan at UMass Dartmouth, an interim chancellor had identified the departments of textiles chemistry and textiles technology for elimination, because they were legacy programs introduced early in the twentieth century, when the region was a center of global textiles production. However, in response to intense political pressure from local textiles company executives, a new chancellor successfully inserted the textiles industry in the first strategic plans as a key area for academic program development and technology

---

45   In fact, the New Bedford arts building and the ATMC combined now account for $4.3 million (44%) of a $9.7 million structural deficit in the UMass Dartmouth budget, see, Welker (2009b). In the last twenty years, there has not been a single new program, building, or laboratory at UMass Dartmouth has achieved self-sufficiency or evolved into a profit center for the university.
46   University of Massachusetts Dartmouth (2007).
47   University of Massachusetts Dartmouth (2008).
48   Barrow (1995).

transfer. Ironically, textiles was already a declining regional industry, but the campus invested in faculty, students, and capital equipment to support an industry that has virtually disappeared from New England.[19] Similarly, in response to the state's 1990–1991 budget crisis, the same interim chancellor had slated the education department for a phased elimination. This process was well underway when the new chancellor immediately reversed course and began expanding the undergraduate department just as the Massachusetts Education Reform Act of 1993 abolished the undergraduate education degree and rendered the program obsolete. Meanwhile, later strategic plans called for the establishment of a new department of public policy, but other social science departments concerned about a reallocation of resources successfully blocked its creation for seven years even though it was mandated by a faculty approved campus strategic plan.

In this respect, strategic planning becomes a forum for intensified and concentrated political conflicts that inject an additional centrifugal force into an already diffuse multiversity. Departments and colleges compete against each other for funding and personnel. Faculty salaries are juxtaposed against the provision of additional student services. Facilities and capital improvements compete with personnel needs. In the end, the strategic planning process generates more competition within the campus, rather than any agreement on strategic goals with the result that fragmentation and chaos ensue as smaller and smaller units of organization seek to institutionalize some minor advantage in a strategic plan that will not guide administrative decision-making anyway.

Second, most university administrators have proven to be poor strategic planners. They embrace the rhetoric of twenty-first-century business enterprise while clinging to an outdated model of corporate bureaucracy. Administrators promote the concept of faculty entrepreneurialism, but they attempt to manage and control it with an industrial era corporate bureaucracy. In fact, administrators' commitment to the corporate ideal that I examined in *Universities and the Capitalist State* (1990) has actually intensified in response to the contemporary fiscal crisis as exemplified by the fact that universities no longer have chancellors, provosts, and vice-chancellors but chief executive officers, chief academic officers, chief financial officers, and chief information officers. University administrators refer to deans, directors, and chairs as middle managers. This change in nomenclature also signals a shift in the composition of administrative personnel from career academic administrators, who at least started out as faculty and often had a distinguished record of teaching and scholarship, to a new stratum of career education managers, who often come from business or politics with no previous experience in higher education. It is becoming more and more difficult to find a Ph.D. in university management, which is now populated by assistant chancellors, special assistants, assistant vice-chancellors, executive directors, and assistant or associate deans without Ph.D.s or other academic experience but who enter the university with a bachelor's degree in accounting, management information

---

49   Barrow (2000b).

science, an M.B.A., a law degree, or the now ubiquitous doctorate in educational administration.[50] Given this stratum's lack of substantive academic knowledge, and their reluctance to incorporate faculty expertise in a system of codetermination, the new managerial stratum has come to rely more and more on outside consultants, auditors, and lawyers when making academic policy decisions.

Third, despite all the rhetoric, the fact is that most administrators will not survive the implementation of a strategic plan and, consequently, decisions are actually made around short-term considerations of individual advancement intended to launch them into their next position at a new institution, where the entire process begins anew. Administrators are short-term, but strategic plans are long-term, usually with a five- to ten-year horizon. Successful plans require long-term consistency, but turnover among administrators is frequent. Each new administration starts its own planning process and rarely builds on prior efforts. Strategic plans accrete over time or veer off in competing directions that whipsaw the entire institution. The result is a strategic planning and restructuring movement that creates chaos rather than change while plunging higher education institutions into deeper fiscal and rationality crises.

Moreover, as short-timers, top university administrators typically lack the political will to actually implement strategic plans even when directed to do so by state elites. The result is that bureaucratic decision-making devolves to lower and lower levels of the administration, who move to fill this vacuum, where non-academic middle managers compete with each other like warlords in a failed state while admonishing the faculty that they "do not understand" the magnitude of the institution's fiscal crisis. As non-academic middle managers grasp for more and more control of the minutiae of university operations, the institution spirals further out of control as a confused network of administrative diffusion makes it more and more difficult for faculty to fulfill their role in implementing institution's basic educational mission.[51]

The Center for Policy Analysis (CFPA) at UMass Dartmouth illustrates this pattern of administrative diffusion and organizational disintegration. A decade ago, the director of the Center for Policy Analysis reported directly to the provost for administrative purposes, although its day-to-day operations were supervised by the director, while its mission, budget, and project development was governed by a faculty executive board. The director had full scope of authority over day-to-day operations, including hiring, project development, purchasing, accounts payable, and billing, subject to oversight by the faculty executive board.[52] As an organized research unit, most of its financial operations, purchasing, personnel, and research contracts were organized through the UMass Dartmouth Foundation (a 501(c)3 non-profit corporation) under the double signature authority of the CFPA director and the foundation's executive director. Financial

---

50   Rhoades (1998).

51   Barrow (2000a).

52   It is not surprising that strategic planning experiments throughout the world have consistently found that people are more productive and more satisfied with their jobs when they operate under their own unit plans instead of externally imposed plans; see Bass (1972).

operations and expenditures were post-audited annually by an accounting firm retained
by the foundation.

However, in 2008, the CFPA was transferred to a new School for Education, Public
Policy, and Civic Engagement (SEPPCE), which entailed dispersing most of its administrative and financial operations from the CFPA and foundation director to the
university's Division of Administrative and Fiscal Services. This division is an umbrella
that houses independent departments of Administrative Services, Human Resources,
Purchasing, Accounts Payable, and Auditing. The CFPA's facilities management was
transferred to the Division of Facilities and Planning, while its research operations were
placed under the Office of Grants and Research Contracts, although some semblance
of academic authority was retained by the dean of SEPPCE and the provost. In this
manner, a fundamentally academic enterprise was turned into an administrative and
facilities function. Moreover, the effort to establish centralized controls and accountability over an independent research unit actually dispersed its operations among so
many competing non-academic middle managers that it became impossible to execute
contracts, hire personnel, or complete research projects in a timely manner.

As Figure 3.1 documents, an organization that previously operated under the supervision of an academic director and faculty governing board had its operations dispersed
among fifteen different non-academic administrative supervisors, each of which has the
authority to veto the decision of the academic director, faculty executive board, and academic dean without any requirement that they consult with each other or with academic
personnel on such decisions. If one extrapolates this "disorganization chart" across 65

**FIGURE 3.1. DISORGANIZATION CHART:
ADMINISTRATIVE FRAGMENTATION AS VIEWED FROM BELOW**

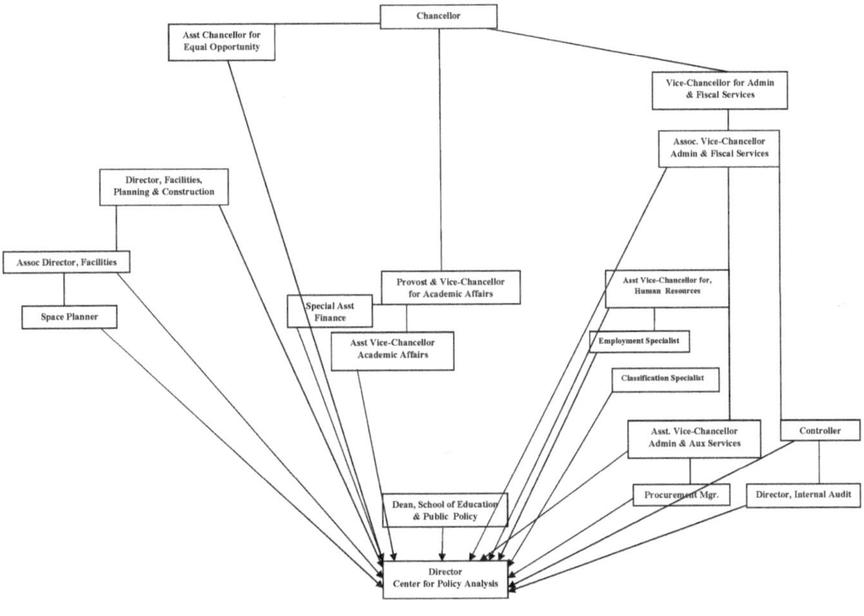

academic departments and programs; 46 research centers, projects, and partnerships; 100 student clubs; and other student services, then one begins to glean the daily chaos generated by this administrative system, not to mention the plethora of decision-making bottlenecks created by non-academic middle managers, who have neither the time nor the expertise to make decisions in a timely or informed manner.[53]

The daily stresses of organizational disintegration and its decision-making bottlenecks are politically charged in a university, because non-academic middle managers lack any of the formal symbols that convey substantive legitimacy within the university, such as an earned doctorate in a substantive field, teaching experience, scholarly publications, or even significant administrative experience within the university's academic division. Consequently, their decision-making authority must rely entirely on strict adherence to the external rules of formal-legal legitimacy, appeals to their "superior" place in the organizational hierarchy, their command of arcane administrative and accounting rules, and their acumen with official forms. However, the middle managers have no real independent authority but must invoke the formal authority of their own superiors or the external authority of laws and regulations. Consequently, middle-management decisions are inherently risk aversive and it is this pattern of decision-making characteristic that was one of the primary failures of corporate strategic planning.

Middle managers constantly work in fear of their organizational superiors, internal and outside auditors, lawyers, press investigations, faculty criticism, and mutual sabotage for purposes of self-advancement. This form of administration not only loses any semblance of substantive legitimacy within the university faculty, administrators' attempts to legitimate their authority in the name of "efficiency" are directly undermined by the daily routines of faculty, who must spend more and more of their time doing clerical and administrative work created by the middle managers. Meanwhile, decisions about teaching, curriculum, and research are made by accountants, auditors, clerks, grants officers, compliance officers, controllers, and other career education managers. The university gradually devolves into a chaos of dispersed administration, where non-academic middle managers make the important academic and personnel decisions, while the bureaucratic processes that implement these decisions are shifted onto faculty, who become an extension of the administrative system. As faculty time is diverted into non-academic activities, the university is less and less able to produce the substantive outputs and values—teaching and research—that generate revenue for the institution. Thus, strategic planning intensifies the fiscal crisis in higher education by institutionalizing a fictitious rationality that generates political dissensus on campus and further deepens the fiscal crisis by implementing structural inefficiencies justified by this fictitious rationality.

---

53   One such example is the UMass Dartmouth "Classification and Compensation Specialist," who blocked the hiring of a research associate due to the claim that such an employee belonged in the clerical union. It was pointed out that the director of the Center for Policy Analysis had authored the language on research associates in the faculty union contract while serving as the union's treasurer, and only then did the Classification "Specialist" reluctantly concede the point, and only after two sponsored research projects had been lost due to the hiring delay.

Despite the strategic planning rhetoric about system integration and administrative streamlining, the University of Massachusetts Dartmouth is actually a welter of overlapping, inconsistent, and self-contradictory administrative practices that generate operational chaos as the primary system output. The strategic planning process, and the numerous policies and administrative practices it generates, now consume so much administration, staff, clerical, and faculty time, that the university's former vice-chancellor for Administrative and Fiscal Services eventually issued a "Policies on Policies" in an effort to slow down the proliferation of new policy and planning initiatives across the campus.[54] However, the *Policy for Creating and Establishing UMass Dartmouth Policies and Procedures* has been completely ignored by the administration as the university's equivalent of a central bank has been unable to steer the institution out of its fiscal crisis or to reestablish control over its own internal administrative procedures.[55] This theoretical conclusion is again illustrated with two case studies that should be read as a phenomenology of the fiscal crisis, because the cases reveal how faculty experience the fiscal crisis as a rationality crisis in their everyday routines on campus.

Forms as the Metaphysics of Strategic Planning

One outcome of the strategic planning process at the University of Massachusetts Dartmouth has been an "administrative streamlining" initiative designed to reduce costs and increase employee productivity. A phenomenological reconstruction of that process from below demonstrates how this initiative systematically generates policy failure within the institution that intensifies administrative chaos throughout the administrative system. When the five-campus University of Massachusetts System was created in 1991, it was soon discovered that the various campuses utilized three different financial software systems that prevented system integration and centralized system management, monitoring, and control from the President's Office in Boston. After a great deal of debate, and in the midst of a financial crisis, the university agreed to purchase PeopleSoft software for $150 million, notwithstanding that it is a system plagued with numerous difficulties, including a level

---

54   The purpose of the Policy on Policies "is to establish a formal mechanism to create, approve, rescind, and periodically revise campus policies and procedures, including a standardized format and reference numbering system"; see University of Massachusetts Dartmouth (2007).

55   This process exactly parallels the restructuring of central state apparatuses worldwide, where an internal realignment of power within the state apparatus privileges the institutions, offices, and agencies in closest contact with the centers of the global economy while subordinating or disempowering those offices and agencies that draw support from domestic constituencies. The offices of presidents and prime ministers, treasuries, and central banks now assume the leading role in state policy, while ministries of commerce, labor, health, welfare, and education, among others, are being subordinated ideologically to the tenets of international competitiveness and further disempowered through budget and staffing reductions, see Panitch (1994: 72). In universities, it is the academic and student divisions that are being subordinated to divisions of administrative and fiscal services.

of user unfriendliness that requires extensive training and retraining at considerable additional expense.[56]

PeopleSoft was corporate America's dominant supplier of software for human resource operations when it decided to first enter the higher education market in 1994. Thus, it had an immediate appeal to state elites and state managers intent on running the university like a business. PeopleSoft first entered the higher education market with its financial-management systems, and then introduced "integrated" applications for managing human resources, student information, fund raising, and grants. One could write an entire paper on the continuing problems with PeopleSoft, particularly how it takes control of routine decision-making processes, rather than implementing or facilitating them. However, this paper will focus on UMass Dartmouth's travel reimbursement process, because it is an administrative practice familiar to all faculty. The travel reimbursement system at UMass Dartmouth was comparatively simple ten years ago before the adoption of PeopleSoft. Faculty submitted a travel reimbursement form with copies of receipts for airfares, meals, lodging, conference fees, and so forth. The form was filled out by a department secretary, signed by the department chair and dean, submitted to a payroll clerk, and then a reimbursement check was mailed within one or two weeks. This system was deemed "inefficient," because it lacked the multiple managerial controls that administrators and trustees considered necessary to reign in non-essential or excessive spending by the academic division.

In contrast, PeopleSoft mandates management "controls" that require multiple additional signature authorities and approvals, including the budget control officer, the human resources director, purchasing director, an associate vice-chancellor for administration and finance, and finally a payroll clerk. Thus, once again, what was previously an administrative practice performed within the academic division for academic purposes was transformed into an administrative and fiscal services function controlled entirely by non-academic middle managers. The new controls were ostensible to insure that sufficient funds existed in the travel account being billed, and to insure compliance with university travel policies, but the additional controls assume therefore that department chairs and deans are either not capable of understanding their own budgets and travel policies, or they are inherently prone to overspend their travel budgets and to authorize reimbursements in violation of university policies. Not only does PeopleSoft infantilize faculty and academic administrators, but the new reimbursement procedures also turned a two-week process into a six-week process, primarily because middle managers were frequently off-campus attending system-level "software integration" meetings, off-site PeopleSoft training sessions, or they simply did not consider faculty reimbursements a daily priority. The significant element of this change, however, is the subtle transformation of an

---

56   Olsen (1990); Leibowitz (1999) reports that "the provosts and vice-presidents of seven of the eight 'Big Ten' universities that use PeopleSoft software on their campuses wrote a joint letter to the company last month, complaining that the 'performance of the systems, in terms of responsiveness, is simply unacceptable.'" See, also, Huston (2009).

academic function previously controlled by academic personnel with Ph.D.s (chairs and deans) and *implemented* by administrative and fiscal clerks into a middle management function supervised by accountants, payroll clerks, and human resource managers with the authority to veto the decisions of academic chairs, deans, and directors.[57] It also institutionalizes the anti-intellectual culture that academic personnel are not capable of managing budgets or complying with reasonable procedures without the constant supervision and monitoring by non-academic personnel. The assumption underlying this managerial anti-intellectualism is that faculty are responsible for the fiscal crisis in higher education, because of their uncontrolled spending or low productivity, although faculty generally have less control over university budgets than administrators and it is actually the growth of middle management and professional staff that accounts for the largest increases in higher education spending over the last two decades.[58]

This logic of academic disempowerment was carried further when it was decided by middle managers that the reporting details on business expense reimbursements were not sufficient to allow for "proper controls" over how faculty spent funds for academic and business purposes, such as faculty recruitment dinners. UMass Dartmouth previously required faculty to submit a "Direct Reimbursement Form" with a credit card receipt, which identified the purpose of the business expense, such as a faculty recruitment dinner. This form too was signed by the department chair and the dean, who then submitted it directly to an accounts payable clerk for payment from a department or college account.

In its effort to clamp down on "unnecessary expenses" by implementing "appropriate financial controls," the UMass Board of Trustees issued a new policy discouraging, but not prohibiting, the expenditure of university funds on alcohol at official dinners or functions. Consequently, to encourage compliance with the policy, middle management decreed that faculty would now have to attach the original itemized restaurant receipt—not the summary credit card receipt—in order to be reimbursed for a faculty recruitment dinner or other academic function, such as a guest lecturer's dinner. When the itemized restaurant receipts failed to have the anticipated stigma necessary to discourage the purchase of alcohol, a new Direct Reimbursement Form was issued that requires one to attach the original itemized receipt, state the purpose of the dinner, and the location, date, names, titles, and affiliations of all persons who attended the dinner. What was previously a two-minute process became a twenty-minute process with the obvious result that more time was being spent filling out and processing forms across the campus than money was being "saved" as a result of the new process.

---

57 Ironically, after the author had completed this paper for presentation at the annual meeting of the American Anthropological Association, he received an email from the Accounts Payable Department informing him that "the system will not allow it [his travel] to be approved." Evidently, the PeopleSoft "system" has now commandeered the authority to veto academic travel arrangements even after they have been approved by the department chair and college dean.

58 Delta Cost Project (2009: 17–20), which documents that most increases in higher education spending are due to increased expenditures on operations, student services, and academic support personnel, while direct research and instructional budgets have languished during the same time.

However, it was eventually determined by the middle managers in administrative and fiscal services that the Direct Reimbursement Form could properly be used only for the reimbursement of out-of-pocket expenses, such as emergency office supplies.[59] Instead, faculty recruitment and guest lecturer expenses had to now be submitted on a new "Business Expense Reimbursement Form," which is submitted by the department chair directly to the Division of Administration and Finance (bypassing the dean), where it must be approved by the human resources director, purchasing manager, an associate vice-chancellor for administrative and fiscal services and, finally, an accounts payable clerk. When this procedure met resistance from deans, who no longer had signature authority over expenditures from their own accounts, middle managers decided that *in addition to* the new Business Expense Reimbursement Form, faculty would now *also* submit the old Direct Reimbursement Form with all required documentation. The problem with this integrated procedure was that Direct Reimbursement Forms went from the dean to payroll, while the Business Expense Reimbursement Forms went from the associate-vice chancellor to an accounts payable clerk and the two forms sat on two desks unpaid until an irate faculty would call to find out why two months had passed without a reimbursement.

Thus, the author and his dean met with the vice-chancellor of Administrative and Fiscal Services, who ostensibly supervises these myriad functions, and explained the "irrationality" of the campus reimbursement system and they were informed that a "streamlined electronic solution" would be implemented as soon as possible. The PeopleSoft solution was supposed to streamline the reimbursement process, but it actually added new layers of forms and costs to an already cumbersome system. The PeopleSoft reimbursement process starts with a "self-service" function that now requires each faculty member, rather than a department secretary, to electronically enter their Business Expense Reimbursement Form. What was previously performed by employees earning $15 to $20 per hour is now performed by employees earning $50 to $75 per hour, and faculty who attempt to circumvent these new responsibilities are continually reminded by the IT middle managers that it is a punishable violation of the university's information technology policy to give another person, such as a departmental secretary, access to their PeopleSoft password or account.

Once the new streamlined electronic reimbursement system was implemented in the fall of 2009, faculty were also informed that after entering the reimbursement information into the electronic Business Expense Reimbursement Form, one then has *to print out a hardcopy*, sign it, secure the department chair's signature, and then have it signed by the purchasing manager. Furthermore, after submitting the new "electronic" hardcopy to purchasing, one must *also* submit the old paper Business Expense Reimbursement Form *and* the old paper Direct Reimbursement Form. Consequently, the

59   It should be noted that any cost–benefits analysis of these policy changes should incorporate the fact that middle managers actually held numerous "strategy meetings," which involved the expenditure of significant amounts of administrative payroll to arrive at these monumental decisions. Those decisions then had to be communicated to faculty, while clerks and faculty had to be retrained on the new forms and procedures.

electronic system not only duplicates the old paper system at a much greater expenditure of labor and capital, it actually adds a third layer of paperwork—three forms instead of two forms—becomes administrative streamlining in the world of doublethink, because it now incorporates the use of a user-unfriendly $150 million software system. The true impact of this streamlining has probably been to triple or quadruple the total cost of implementing reimbursement processes, which has essentially done nothing more than shift a clerical and non-academic administrative function onto the faculty workload. However, layered on top of what even Frederick Taylor would recognize as a basic inefficiency has been the expenditure of millions of dollars on multiple rounds of training and retraining for clerks, faculty, and staff, which has also diverted administrative and fiscal staff time into training as opposed to administration, but it also requires the continuing support of PeopleSoft consultants and trainers (at considerable additional expense).

By "streamlining" the reimbursement system with PeopleSoft, UMass Dartmouth added a third form, another layer of signature authority, and added further delays to the process, because it is still the case that none of these forms ever intersect in a single place, so a department clerk still has to track them down, reassemble them, and finally insure that they all end up on one desk, which is difficult because no one person is actually responsible for concluding the process. The standard time for a reimbursement is now three months and it requires more time and more people than previously and it requires the use of more expensive labor, not less expensive labor.[60]

The LaGrassa Paradox

The LaGrassa Paradox was first identified at the University of Massachusetts Dartmouth in 2009 following a decision by Michael LaGrassa, the assistant vice-chancellor for Administrative Services, to terminate all purchases of Poland Spring water on the campus.[61] The rationale for the decision was that it would save the university approximately $30,000 to $50,000 annually and, thereby, reduce the institution's $9.8 million structural deficit.[62] The small benefit of this "strategic decision" was quickly offset by the costs of its implementation in faculty time, clerical time, and lost productivity, as well as the administrative payroll expended on more "strategy meetings," audits, notices, and other enforcement actions by the middle management authority. These costs, while

---

60   In an electronic mail received December 14, 2009, from Administrative Services, the university explicitly refers to the travel reimbursement system just described as "administrative streamlining," when in fact the new procedure actually costs more money to capitalize, requires more signatures, and takes more time to implement than the previous system while relying on faculty labor, rather than clerical labor; see LaGrassa (2009b).

61   On December 1, 2009, the Center for Policy Analysis received an official "Bottled Water Reminder" from Michael LaGrassa (2009a), assistant vice-chancellor for Administrative Services at UMass Dartmouth, restating "that effective as of July 1, 2009 the University will no longer support with University funds, the purchase of bottled water, associated dispensers or rental of such. This includes small personal sized bottled water as well as jugs of water used in conjunction with dispensers."

62   This alleged savings is equal to 0.51% of the institution's structural deficit.

difficult to quantify, no doubt far exceed the savings attributable to this strategic decision. For example, when the institution's Center for Policy Analysis refused to comply
with the unilateral decree on grounds that it purchased Poland Spring water with privately generated funds, the response on November 30, 2009, was a one-inch-thick audit
report from the university controller. This extensive audit package documented that the
UMass Dartmouth Center for Policy Analysis had spent $163.27 on Poland Spring water
from July 1, 2009, through October 30, 2009. It is estimated that several thousand dollars
were expended in audit, clerical, and other middle management payroll to document
this small figure and to demand that the center's employees "pitch in" to personally
reimburse the university for their drinking water. When this example is extrapolated
to the entire campus, it becomes readily evident that the cost of implementation was
exceeding any savings to the campus.

The audit confrontation reached its crisis when the UMass Dartmouth Director
of Physical Plant forwarded an email from the Town of Dartmouth to all university
employees (informing them four days late and after most units had discontinued the
purchase of Poland Spring water) that the town water available on campus was contaminated with *E. coli* bacteria. According to the official communication,

> these microbes can make you sick, and are a particular concern for people
> with weakened immune systems. Dartmouth Water Division routinely pro-
> vides disinfection adequate to remove fecal bacteria, but it does not reach
> the current standard to confidently remove viruses from drinking water.
> (Ferguson 2009)

Thus, not only did the Poland Spring ban *not* save university funds, but it also incurred additional financial and health care costs that were shifted onto employees at
precisely the same time that contributions to health insurance premiums (+67%), phy-
sician co-pays (+33%), prescription co-pays (+25%), and annual deductibles (+$250-$750)
were being increased for all UMass employees, but under the new campus policy no
other source of public drinking water was available to faculty. The health costs and lost
workdays were not factored into the original decision. The alternative option proposed
by faculty was to eliminate the position of the assistant vice-chancellor for Administrative Services for a real savings of $98,000 annually, which would have yielded cost
savings two to three times greater than the decision to terminate the purchase of Poland
Spring water, even before accounting for the payroll, auditing, and health care costs of
a fundamentally irrational decision which ultimately generated the opposite output of
its stated objective.[63]

63   The author eventually filed a grievance against the assistant vice-chancellor of Administrative Services
on grounds that the Poland Spring decree violated the university's own *Policy for Creating and Establishing
UMass Dartmouth Policies and Procedures*, because it had not gone through the review and approval process
required by this policy. The grievance was withdrawn after it was agreed that the Center for Policy Analysis
would be allowed to provide its employee with Poland Spring water so long as the water was purchased with
non-state revenues.

The LaGrassa Paradox is not an isolated occurrence in American higher education but an example of the fact that higher education managers rarely incorporate the cost of implementation, the cost of their own time, or the cost of lost faculty productivity into their calculations about institutional efficiency. This fictitious rationality generates an economic contradiction of precisely the type hypthosized by Offe. For example, UMass Dartmouth has grown from 4,800 students in 1998 to more than 9,500 (+98%) students in 2009, while the number of full-time tenure line faculty employed by the campus increased by only 7.3% in the same time (from 303 to 313).[64] Concurrently, UMass Dartmouth has faculty increased their sponsored research and public service efforts as sponsored research increased from $5 million to $20 million annually during the same period. These figures would lead a rational manager to the conclude that teaching and research productivity by tenure line faculty was increasing dramatically, even the fiscal crisis was intensifying throughout this period. For that reason alone, a rational administration would calculate that the diversion of this high-value, revenue-generating labor power into lower cost clerical and low-level administrative tasks (that generate no new revenue) is a net loss in real dollars to the university's revenue streams in the form of lost student tuition and research grants. In fact, as middle managers have continued diverting more and more faculty time away from their primary missions of teaching and research, the dollar value of sponsored research has begun to decline in the last two years (−15%), while UMass Dartmouth was the only UMass campus to experience a decline in undergraduate applications for academic year 2009–10.

The institution's managers concluded that these declines were due to a lack of strategic planning support personnel, professional grants administrators, grants compliance officers, and enrollment management personnel, and, thus it has become the rationale for hiring more administrative personnel and adopting even tighter fiscal controls on such minutae as how many pages of paper students and faculty will be allowed to print per semester.[65] In contrast, as faculty productivity increases, publicly available data provided by the UMass Dartmouth administration indicate that the Chancellor's Office was the fastest growing division of the university over the last 3 years (2006–2009), which expanded from 11 to 24 FTE. This 112% growth in personnel compares to average campus FTE growth of 12.4% over the same time. Similarly, FTE employees in the Provost's Office grew by 33%, which is nearly three times the campus average during the same three years. These figures do not include the addition of purchasing and auditing personnel to monitor and enforce compliance with minute financial controls or administrative personnel whose cost to the campus has been disguised by been shifting their lines from the campus payroll to the system payroll, which has grown exponentially over the last 10 years. The growth in administration is also disguised by converting various positions and functions into educational or

---

64   University of Massachusetts Dartmouth (2009).

65   This decision exemplifies the fictitious rationality of non-academic middle managers. What faculty member would ever conclude that students chose to attend a college or university because of its enrollment manager or that faculty chose not to write grants, because the institution lacks a sufficient number of grants compliance officers?

management consultants.[66] Consequently, the campus has been on a middle management hiring spree even as it lays off clerical personnel and part-time faculty, zeroes out faculty pay raises for some years, and defers them for other years. Thus, as faculty productivity increases, these gains are being expropriated through an uninterrupted expansion of managerial personnel, whose ongoing proliferation is now beginning to undermine the institutional foundation of the earlier productivity gains.

On its surface, the LaGrassa Paradox appears to be a radical exception to the rational actor market logic of neoclassical economics. Indeed, how does one explain decisions taken in the midst of a fiscal crisis to adopt and implement policies with costs that far exceed the benefits, when alternative rational decisions are readily available, for example, to eliminate an assistant vice-chancellor whose irrational decisions are systematically imposing new costs on the institution? The solution to this paradox exemplifies the continuing relevance of Marxian value theory; namely, the mere fact that a fictitious commodity commands an exchange value does not mean that it has a use-value.[67] Marx's distinction between the value of a commodity and the price of a commodity is useful in understanding and solving the LaGrassa Paradox.

Marx (1974: 30) observes that

> as the *exchangeable values* of commodities are only *social functions* of those things, and have nothing at all to do with the *natural* qualities, we must first ask: What is the common *social substance* of all commodities? It is *labour* . . . And I say not only *labour*, but *social labour*. A man who produces an article for his own immediate use, to consume it himself, creates a *product*, but not a *commodity*.

While Marxian value theory takes us part of the way toward solving the LaGrassa Paradox, a complete solution of the problem must draw on the related concept of un-productive labor, which according to Marx (1978: 208) "creates *neither a product, nor a commodity*," but is incorporated into systems of higher education accounting as having use value, but no price.[68] The fictitious rationality that underlies the LaGrassa Paradox is that university administrators place a high use value on their own labor but incorrectly price that at $0, because they regard it as a necessary and indispensable fixed cost.

---

66   It is a well accepted principle of state theory that state elites and state managers are self-interested max-imizers whose main interest is to enhance their own institutional power, prestige, and financial resources; see Barrow (1993: 125).

67   On the concept of a fictitious commodity, see Polanyi (1949).

68   The basis of this distinction is Marx (1978: 208), who observes that "the dimensions assumed by the conversion of commodities in the hands of capitalists can naturally not transform this labour, which does not create value, but only mediates a change in the form of value, into value-creating labour . . . These third parties will certainly not put their labour-power at the disposal of the capitalists for the sake of their blue eyes. It is similarly immaterial for the rent collector of a landlord or the porter at a bank that their labour does not add one iota to the magnitude of the value of the rent, nor to the gold pieces carried to another bank by the sackful."

Thus, the cost of administration is effectively excluded from all budget deliberations by administrators so it has a functional price of zero dollars. In contrast, university administrators incorrectly assign a use value of zero to the work of academic employees, whom they regularly denigrate in their private cabinet meetings, because they are unable to conceptualize that faculty labor (and by extension some students) is *the only revenue producing labor in a university*. Thus, if we assume that all unproductive administrative labor has zero cost and a high use value then the expenditure of administrative labor will be factored into a cost–benefits equation as zero cost, while faculty labor is factored into the equation as having zero value, but a high price. In fact, the *price* we pay for administration now far exceeds its benefits, while the *price* we pay for faculty labor generates the only real outputs of a university in the form of teaching and research. The idea that the university should be run "like" a business collapses in contradiction, because if it was run like a business, it would be out of business.[69]

Conclusion

The rationality crisis in American higher education manifests itself politically in the struggle between faculty and students, on one hand, and a strata of state elites and state managers in the higher education system, on the other hand. As the fiscal crisis in higher education continues to intensify, these elites and managers will increasingly choose strict adherence to ever more complex, arcane, and authoritarian administrative rules over fulfilling the substantive functions of the college and university. One choice adheres to the external rules of formal-legal legitimacy and fictitious rationality, backed by the coercive legal authority of the state, while the other relies on the internal substantive legitimacy of faculty expertise within the college and university and a commitment to access and affordability for students. The traditional cultural norms of faculty and students are focused on teaching and research, and the ability to perform these functions effectively is the cornerstone of substantive legitimacy, which is being withdrawn from the university by faculty at every type of institution.

However, within the current boundaries of the corporate university, higher education administrators cannot respond to demands for substantive legitimacy, because it would mean shifting the focus of administration away from the fictitious rationality of formal rules and financial controls onto those areas where faculty rightly claim substantive expertise, that is, educational goals, curriculum, and research techniques.[70] It would also require

---

69   Habermas (1975: 47–48), identifies motivation crisis as a third crisis possibility within the cultural subsystem, but it is beyond the scope of this paper to address that hypothesis. The intensification of the labor process in higher education, as in other sectors of the economy, is stressing the balance between work and family (and leisure). Faculty can devote less time to family and personal matters, which contributes to a motivational crisis or faculty can reconcile the contradiction by attending to family and personal matters, which feeds back into the economic system as suboptimal performance.

70   Steck (2003).

a greater focus on affordability and access for students as opposed to viewing them as a source of revenue and profit.[71] This shift in focus would undermine the very foundations of the new managerial apparatus in higher education and deprive it of its claim to formal legitimacy, which is based in the authoritative enforcement of rules and procedures and its alleged (though failed) efforts to bring greater efficiency and profitability to the higher education institutions.[72]

The rationality crisis in the administrative apparatus has been explored through an analysis of the strategic planning process at the University of Massachusetts, but it is the author's contention that this case is not *sui generis* but one that illustrates a systemic rationality crisis in U.S. higher education and the state apparatuses. In fact, Marcuse suggests that the extension of formal rationality from the economic system to the political and ideological subsystems of capitalism is a structural characteristic of late capitalism that unfolds as it subsumes and commodifies ever wider swaths of the social order. However, he also observes that

> when the bureaucratic administration of the capitalist apparatus in all its rationality remains a means, and thereby dependent, it reaches its own limits as rationality. Bureaucracy subordinates itself to a power above and beyond bureaucracy—a power 'alien to administration'. And when rationality is incorporated into administration and *only* incorporated there, then this law-enforcing power must be *irrational*. (Marcuse 1965: 13)

The rationality crisis has also been illustrated through an examination of two case studies at the University of Massachusetts Dartmouth. If these examples are extrapolated across the entire campus and then multiplied by layering these policies on top of still more policies, then one can start to conceptualize the degree to which fictitious rationality has become so embedded in the organizational structure of the institution that it is incapable of extracting itself from the rationality crisis while working within its existing structures of fictitious rationality.[73] Furthermore, the irrationality of this administrative system layers cost upon cost and, thus, the administrative apparatus that is charged with resolving the fiscal crisis in higher education is incapable of doing so, because its decision-making process *is* the problem. However, the perceived administrative solution to this problem is to do more of the same—the very essence of a fetish—a bureaucratic system that culminates with an administration administering an administration.

The logical outcome of the fiscal and rationality crises would seem to be an implosion of the university. Structural implosions of the state apparatus open political space for the

71   The author recently attended a meeting called by a UMass Dartmouth administrator to discuss the importance of websites as a source of student recruitment, where said administrator referred to students as "human ATMs."

72   Aronowitz (2000); Giroux and Myrsiades (2001).

73   It is assumed that readers will empathetically recognize equivalent, or even identical processes, at their own colleges and universities. It is hoped that similar case studies will be produced by other scholars as a measure of the rationality crisis throughout the U.S. higher education system.

organization of new state forms.[74] In contrast, the general tendency of economic globalization has been to ease the rationality crisis by ceding state sovereignty to global markets and transnational corporations, and this process is evident too in higher education.[75] At the present time, the fastest growing sector in American higher education is the for-profit private sector, while the transnationalization of this sector is being actively facilitated through the General Agreement on Trade in Services and various regional free trade agreements.[76] These trends, and numerous other forms of privatization, may potentially resolve the rationality crisis and its underlying fiscal crisis by marketizing higher education and shifting system boundaries in a way that remove the state from this region of the economic and ideological subsystems. A more progressive resolution of the crisis would be a new social compact between higher education, the state, and the public, which must include a restoration of faculty and students to a central place in higher education decision-making processes. the progressive alternative will not be realized until faculty and students retake physical control of their campuses and join with other social movements to reconstruct power relations within those institutions and redefine their relationship to the state.

References

Academic Planning Task Force. 1995. *Building on Our Strengths Revisited*. North Dartmouth: University of Massachusetts Dartmouth.

Academic Planning Task Force. 1997. *Shared Academic Agenda*. North Dartmouth: University of Massachusetts Dartmouth.

"Administrators' Views of Challenges Facing Institutions in the Next Five Years." *The Almanac of Higher Education, 1992*. Chicago: University Chicago Press.

Althusser, Louis. 1978. *Lenin and Philosophy and Other Essays*. New York: Monthly Review Press.

Aronowitz, Stanley. 2000. *The Knowledge Factory: Dismantling the Corporate University and Creating True Higher Education*. Boston: Beacon Press.

Barrow, Clyde W. 1990. *Universities and the Capitalist State*. Madison: University of Wisconsin Press.

Barrow, Clyde W. 1991. "Social Investment in Massachusetts Public Higher Education: A Comparative Analysis." *New England Journal of Public Policy* 7 (1): 85–110.

Barrow, Clyde W. 1993a. "Will the Fiscal Crisis Force Higher Education to Restructure?" *Thought and Action: The NEA Higher Education Journal* (9): 25–39.

Barrow, Clyde W. 1993b. *Critical Theories of the State: Marxist, Neo-Marxist, Post-Marxist*. Madison: University of Wisconsin Press.

Barrow, Clyde W. 1995. "Beyond the Multiversity: Fiscal Crisis and the Changing Structure of Academic Labour," in John Smyth, ed., *Academic Work: The Changing Labour Process in Higher Education*. Buckingham, England: Open University Press, pp. 159–78.

Barrow, Clyde W. 1996a. "The New Economy and the Restructuring of Higher Education." *Thought and Action: The NEA Higher Education Journal* (12): 37–54.

---

74   See Marx (1940). Specifically, on higher education, see Barrow (2001); Barrow (1990: 175–77); Giroux and Myrsiades (2001).

75   Barrow (2004).

76   Bassett (2006); Barrow, Didou-Aupetit, and Mallea (2003); Barrow (2003).

Barrow, Clyde W. 1996b. "The Strategy of Selective Excellence: Redesigning Higher Education for Global Competition in a Postindustrial Society." *Higher Education* 31 (4): 447–69.

Barrow, Clyde W. 2000a. "Author's Post-Script." *Thought and Action: The NEA Higher Education Journal* (16): 77–88, available at http://www.nea.org/he/hetaoo/footoc.pdf.

Barrow, Clyde W. 2000b. *Economic Impacts of the Textile and Apparel Industries in Massachusetts.* Boston: Donahue Institute of Governmental Affairs.

Barrow, Clyde W. 2001. "What is to Be Undone?: Academic Efficiency and the Corporate Ideal in American Higher Education." *Found Object* (10): 149–80.

Barrow, Clyde W. 2003. "Globalization, Trade Liberalization, and the Higher Education Industry," in Stanley Aronowitz and Heather Gautney, eds., *Implicating Empire: Globalization and Resistance in the 21st Century.* New York: Basic Books, pp. 229–54.

Barrow, Clyde W. 2004. "Trade Liberalization and the Emergence of Multinational For-Profit Colleges and Universities." *Global Education* (8): 88–109.

Barrow, Clyde W., Sylvie Didou-Aupetit, and John Mallea. 2003. *Globalisation, Trade Liberalisation, and Higher Education in North America: The Emergence of a New Market Under NAFTA?* Dordrecht, The Netherlands: Kluwer Academic Publishers.

Bass, B.M. 1972. "When Planning for Others." *Journal of Applied Behavioral Science* 6 (2): 151–71.

Bassett, Roberta M. 2006. *The WTO and the University: Globalization, GATS, and American Higher Education.* New York: Routledge.

Bluestone, Barry and Bennett Harrison. 1982. *The Deindustrialization of America.* New York: Basic Books.

Commission on the Future of the University of Massachusetts. 1989. *Learning to Lead: Building a World-Class Public University in Massachusetts.* Boston: University of Massachusetts.

Commission on the Future of the State and Community College System. 1992. *Responding to Change: New Directions for Public Colleges in Massachusetts.* Boston: Massachusetts Higher Education Coordinating Council.

Commission on the Skills of the American Workforce. 1990. *America's Choice: High Skills or Low Wages!* Rochester, N.Y.: National Center on Education and the Economy.

Cooke, Morriss L. 1910. *Academic and Industrial Efficiency.* New York: Carnegie Foundation for the Advancement of Teaching.

Davidow, William H. and Michael S. Malone. 1992. *The Virtual Corporation: Structuring and Revitalizing the Corporation for the 21st Century.* New York: Harper Collins Publishers.

Delta Cost Project. 2009. *Trends in College Spending.* Washington, D.C.

Dunleavy, Patrick and Brendan O'Leary. 1987. *Theories of the State.* New York: Macmillan.

David Ferguson. 2009. "Memorandum on Town of Dartmouth Drinking Water Notice (December 5)." North Dartmouth: University of Massachusetts Dartmouth.

Finifter, D.F., R.G. Baldwin, and J.R. Thelin. 1991. *The Uneasy Public Policy Triangle in Higher Education: Quality, Diversity, and Budgetary Efficiency.* New York: American Council on Education and MacMillan Publishing Co.

Giroux, Henry A. and Kostas Myrsiades, eds. 2001. *Beyond the Corporate University: Culture and Pedagogy in the New Millennium.* Lanham, MD: Rowman & Littlefield.

Gold, David, Clarence Lo, and Erik Olin Wright. 1975. "Recent Developments in Marxist Theories of the Capitalist State, Part I." *Monthly Review,* 27 (5): 29–43.

Habermas, Jurgen. 1975. *Legitimation Crisis.* Boston: Beacon Press.

Halstead, Kent. 1989. *State Profiles: Financing Public Higher Education, 1978 to 1989.* Washington, D.C.: Research Associates.

Hammer, Michael and James Champy. 1993. *Reengineering the Corporation: A Manifesto for Business Revolution.* New York: Harper Business.

Heydinger, Richard B. and Hasan Simsek. 1992. *An Agenda for Reshaping Faculty Productivity: State Policy and College Learning*. Denver, Co.: State Higher Education Officers.

Hooker, Michael K. 1995. *The President's Action Plan for the Year 2000: Improving Quality and Responsiveness at UMASS Through Restructuring, Reallocation, and Reinvestment*. Boston: University of Massachusetts President's Office.

Huston, John. 2009. "Village Dumps PeopleSoft." *Oak Leaves* (Oak Park, Illinois), January 14.

Johnstone, D. B. 1993. "The Costs of Higher Education: Worldwide Trends for the 1990s," in Philip G. Altbach and D. B. Johnstone, eds., *The Funding of Higher Education: International Perspectives*. New York: Garland Publishing, Inc., pp. 3–24.

LaGrassa, Michael. 2009a. "Bottled Water Reminder (December 1) Memorandum." North Dartmouth: University of Massachusetts Dartmouth.

LaGrassa, Michael. 2009b. "Administrative Streamlining Memorandum (December 14)." North Dartmouth: University of Massachusetts Dartmouth.

Lefebvre, Henri. 2008. *Critique of Everyday Life*. London and New York: Verso.

Leibowitz, Wendy. 1999. "Officials of 7 Large Universities Complain to PeopleSoft About Its Programs." *Chronicle of Higher Education*, December 14.

Loasby, B. J. 1967. "Long-Range Formal Planning in Perspective." *The Journal of Management Studies* 4 (3): 300–08.

MacCormack, Jean F. 2009. *Campus-wide Town Meeting Presentation*. North Dartmouth, Mass. Available at http://www.umassd.edu/chancellor/updates/campus_town_meeting051409.pdf.

Marcuse, Herbert. 1965. "Industrialization and Capitalism." *New Left Review* (30): 3–17.

Marcuse, Herbert. 1968. *Negations: Essays in Critical Theory*. Boston: Beacon Press.

Marx, Karl. 1940. *The Civil War in France*. New York : International Publishers.

Marx, Karl. 1974. *Value, Price, and Profit*. New York: International Publishers.

Marx, Karl. 1978. *Capital: A Critique of Political Economy*, Vol. 2. London: Penguin Books.

Massachusetts Department of Economic Development and the University of Massachusetts. 2002. *Toward a New Prosperity: Building Regional Competitiveness Across the Commonwealth*. Boston: Commonwealth of Massachusetts.

Massachusetts Department of Housing and Economic Development. 2009. *Regional Economic Development Framework*. Boston: Commonwealth of Massachusetts. Available at http://www.mass.gov/?pageID=ehedmodulechunk&L=1&L0=Home&sid=Ehed&b=terminalcontent&f=Framework_For_Action&csid=Ehed.

Massachusetts Executive Office of Economic Affairs and the University of Massachusetts. 1993. *Choosing to Compete: Statewide Strategy for Job Creation and Economic Growth*. Boston: Commonwealth of Massachusetts.

Massachusetts Higher Education Coordinating Council. 1992. *The Mission of the Public Higher Education System of the Commonwealth*. Boston.

Massy, William F. and J. W. Meyerson. 1992. *Strategy and Finance in Higher Education*. Princeton, N.J.: Peterson's Guide.

Miliband, Ralph. 1969. *The State in Capitalist Society*. New York: Basic Books.

Mintzberg, Henry. 1994. *The Rise and Fall of Strategic Planning*. New York: Free Press.

O'Connor, James. 1973. *The Fiscal Crisis of the State*. New York: St. Martin's Press.

O'Connor, James. 1987. *The Meaning of Crisis: A Theoretical Introduction*. New York: Basil Blackwell.

O'Connor, James. 2002. *The Fiscal Crisis of the State*, with a new introduction. New Brunswick, N.J.: Transaction.

Offe, Claus. 1984. *Contradictions of the Welfare State*. Cambridge, Mass.: MIT Press.

Offe, Claus. 1985. *Disorganized Capitalism*. Cambridge, Mass.: MIT Press.

Offe, Claus. 1996. *Modernity and the State*. Cambridge, Mass.: MIT Press.

Olsen, Florence. 1990. "Delays, Bugs, and Cost Overruns Plague PeopleSoft's Services." *Chronicle of Higher Education*, September 22.

Panitch, Leo. 1994. "Globalisation and the State," in Ralph Miliband and Leo Panitch, eds., *Socialist Register, 1994*. London: Merlin Press, pp. 60–93.

Phillips, Peter. 2009. "The Fiscal Crisis in Higher Education Protects the Wealthy." *The Daily Censored*, November 22, see, http://dailycensored.com/2009/11/22/the-higher-education-fiscal-crisis-protects-the-wealthy/.

Polanyi, Karl. 1949. *The Great Transformation*. Boston: Beacon Press.

Poulantzas, Nicos. 1978a. *Political Power and Social Classes*. London: Verso.

Poulantzas, Nicos. 1978b. *State, Power, Socialism*. London: Verso.

Public Policy Working Group. 1992. *Planning to Plan: A Proposal for Trustee Action*. University of Massachusetts Board of Trustees.

Rhoades, Gary. 1998. *Managed Professionals: Unionized Faculty and Restructuring Academic Labor*. Albany: State University of New York Press.

Rodriquez, Esther. 1992. *Building a Quality Workforce: An Agenda for Postsecondary Education*. Denver: State Higher Education Executive Officers.

Russell, Alene Bycer. 1992. *Faculty Workload: State and System Perspectives*. Denver: State Higher Education Executive Officers.

Scott, Barbara Ann Scott. 1983. *Crisis Management in American Higher Education*. Westport, Conn.: Praeger Press.

Slaughter, Sheila. 1990. *The Higher Learning and High Technology: Dynamics of Higher Education Policy Formation*. Albany: State University of New York Press.

Slaughter, Sheila and Gary Rhoades. 2004. *Academic Capitalism and the New Economy: Markets, State, and Higher Education*. Baltimore: Johns Hopkins University Press.

Smith, David N. 1974. *Who Rules the Universities?* New York: Monthly Review Press.

Smyth, John, ed. 1995. *Academic Work: The Changing Labour Process in Higher Education*. Buckingham, England: Open University Press.

Steck, Henry. 2003. "Corporatization of the University: Seeking Conceptual Clarity." *Annals of the American Academy of Political and Social Science* 585 (1): 66–83.

University of Massachusetts. 1991. *Vision Statement*. Boston: University of Massachusetts Board of Trustees, Revised Doc. T91-107, 1991. Available at http://www.umb.edu/about/mission.html.

University of Massachusetts. 1993. *Statement of System Priorities*. T-Doc. 93-122. Boston: University of Massachusetts Board of Trustees. Available at http://media.umassp.edu/massedu/policy/Land%20Use%20Policy.pdf

University of Massachusetts Dartmouth. 2007. *Policy for Creating and Establishing UMass Dartmouth Policies and Procedures*. North Dartmouth, Mass. Available at http://www.umassd.edu/policies/gov/001.cfm.

University of Massachusetts Dartmouth. 2007. *Engaged, Evolving, Embedded: A Progress Report*. North Dartmouth, Mass. Available at http://www.umassd.edu/chancellor/strategicplanupdate.pdf.

University of Massachusetts Dartmouth. 2009. *NEASC Draft Report: Standard Five Faculty*. North Dartmouth, Mass.: Office of the Provost. Available at http://www.umassd.edu/provost/neasc/standard5_11-16-09.doc.

University of Massachusetts Dartmouth. 2008. *Engaged, Embedded, and Evolving, 2008–2012*. North Dartmouth.

Welker, Grant Welker. 2009a. "Another Round of Cuts Coming to UMD." *Fall River Herald News*, May 15.

Welker, Grant. 2009b. "UMD Still Scrambling Due to Cuts in Funding." *Fall River Herald News*, May 21.

Welker, Grant. 2009c. "A 'Tale of Two Stories'." *Fall River Herald News*, August 14.

Western Interstate Commission for Higher Education. 1992a. *Meeting Economic and Social Challenges: A Strategic Agenda for Higher Education*. Boulder, Colo.

Western Interstate Commission for Higher Education. 1992b. *Joined or Unconnected?: A Look at State Economic Development and Higher Education Plans*. Boulder, Colo.

Wildavsky, Aaron. 1973. "If Planning Is Everything Maybe It's Nothing." *Policy Sciences* 4 (2): 127–53.

CHAPTER FOUR

Austerity Politics, Coercive Neoliberal Urbanism and the Challenge of Counter-Hegemonic Education Movements[1]

Pauline Lipman

You never want a serious crisis to go to waste. And what I mean by that is an opportunity to do things you think you could not do before. In the area of education there's got to be fundamental reforms there as it relates to making sure that we are effectively training the workforce.

(Rahm Emanuel, Nov. 7, 2008, to Wall Street Journal)

THE 2008 GLOBAL economic crisis was in many respects an urban crisis. It was triggered by the collapse of the sub-prime mortgage market, which was an outgrowth of neoliberal urban growth strategies rooted in speculative real estate development and deregulation of financial and land markets (Oosterlynck & Gonzalez, 2013). The crisis quickly spiraled from the sub-prime market to global financial markets, sparking the worst recession since the Great Depression. Because the U.S. neoliberal urban growth model relied on debt financing and real estate development, cities were particularly vulnerable to the crisis (Peck & Theodore, 2012). Debt-financing requires consistent access to credit markets controlled by the Wall Street banks, so the recession and shrinking tax revenues made city governments even more subject to their discipline (Harvey, 2012). Instead of making the banks pay for a crisis they had created, a financial crisis on Wall Street was reframed as a debt crisis that required everyone (except the banks) to "tighten their belts." Narrating a discourse of inevitability, city governments insisted the only alternative was "the new normal" of fiscal restraint implemented through public austerity, cutting labor costs, and selling off public assets.[2]

In a version of "disaster capitalism" (Klein, 2008), the crisis was an opportunity to extend the neoliberal agenda to privatize the public sector, weaken public sector unions, and shrink public institutions on the premise that city governments were

---

1   Revised keynote address at the 3rd TREd—Transformative Researchers and Educators for Democracy—Annual Conference, Department of Educational Leadership, University of Massachusetts, Dartmouth, November 15, 2014, Woodland Commons.

2   Commentary of city officials at an urban governance conference, Metropolitan Resilience in a Time of Economic Turmoil, at the University of Illinois at Chicago, December 2012. Author field notes.

broke and simply could not afford it. The Organization for Economic Co-operation and Development (OECD), a powerful organisation for the creation and distribution of global policy discourses on urban development, made "Don't waste the crisis" the first of its 2009 Barcelona Principles (Oosterlynck & Gonzales, 2011). The Principles were adopted to mitigate and even capitalize on the impacts of the economic crisis on cities. But Oosterlynck and Gonzales also point to the dialectics of this moment:

> Crises are moments at which hegemonic understandings of the operation of political economies are called into question. This tends to repoliticize identities, institutions and societal structures, and hence opens up space for a proliferation of discourses attempting to interpret the causes of and solutions to the crisis. (p. 1077)

Focusing on education, I build on the dialectic of crisis and opportunity to examine neoliberal urban responses to the crisis and counterhegemonic movements and possibilities. In *The New Political Economy of Urban Education* (Lipman, 2011), I argue education policy is constitutive of the contested dynamics of power that shape the urban context, especially the role of capital and race in structuring urban space. Building on that framework, I situate public education in the foreground of discourses of urban fiscal crisis and city governments' attempts to impose austerity. Education has also been a stage of fierce resistance against attempts to further commodify public institutions and make working class families and communities and teachers pay for the crisis. My analysis centers mainly on Chicago, a laboratory for neoliberal policy experiments in education and an incubator of grassroots organizing and resistance. I locate the turn to urban austerity as part of a broader shift to racialized coercive neoliberal governance.

This chapter is a revised version of a presentation at the 3rd Annual Transformative Researchers and Educators for Democracy Conference, University of Massachusetts, Dartmouth in 2014. Despite claims that the recession is over, austerity policies continue. The American Federation of Teachers (2018) reports that in 2016, 25 states were still funding K–12 schools less than before the recession. Following in the footsteps of the Chicago teachers strike in 2012, a wave of teacher uprisings in conservative southern and western states, and in Los Angeles, demonstrate how deeply austerity continues to bite into classrooms and the lives of teachers and the resistance to them.

"Fiscal responsibility is the new normal"

Though neoliberal capital accumulation strategies triggered the global financial crisis, federal, state and local governments in the U.S.A. responded by doubling down on neoliberal policies. In addition to a one-trillion-dollar federal bailout of the Wall Street banks, the state at all scales attempted to make workers and sectors of the middle class pay for the ensuing fiscal crisis created by debts they owed to the financial institutions (Harvey, 2012; Peck, 2012). To manage loss of revenue caused by the recession and unsustainable urban debt, city governments defunded and/or sold off public institutions (e.g., schools, hospitals) and infrastructure (e.g., bridges, parking meters, airports, sports stadiums) to private investors. Under the mantra that "there is no alternative," they imposed cut to wages, health care, and pensions of public sector employees and undermined the power of trade unions. This was a form of structural adjustment typically reserved for indebted economically "developing" countries (Harvey, 2012). Opportunistically, the crisis legitimated doubling down on the neoliberal agenda to shrink the social state, weaken unions, expand markets, and redistribute wealth upward. This was reflected at a conference of city officials held in Chicago in 2012 ("Metropolitan Resilience in a Time of Economic Turmoil," University of Illinois at Chicago, December 6, 2012), where austerity was framed as not only necessary but also a "practical" and "realistic" corrective to outdated lavish public spending:

> "Business as usual is over. We couldn't continue if we wanted to. The financial markets won't tolerate it." "We have to have difficult conversations" about "inflated" pensions and wages and "engage" unions to "adjust." "There is no choice." (Author field notes)

Urban austerity is, however, a path dependent neoliberal strategy, applied differently in different contexts but in the U.S. always deeply racialized, ideologically and materially. Cuts to social welfare programs and attacks on public sector workers are legitimated by claims that public sector unions—where workers of color are concentrated, the "undeserving poor" who receive social benefits (constructed as "entitlements"), and the public sector itself (coded Black) is irresponsible, lazy, and underserving. This racially coded discourse of "irresponsibility" and indolence (coded Black) that is a "burden" to the public (coded White) is a central pillar of neoliberal ideology. American studies scholar George Lipsitz (2014) argues:

> By making public spaces and public institutions synonymous with communities of color, neoliberals seek to taint them in the eyes of white working-class and middle-class people, who then become more receptive to privatization schemes that undermine their own stakes in the shared social communities that neoliberalism attempts to eliminate. (p. 11)

Moreover, the impact of the crisis and the government's protection of the Wall Street banks, not home owners, has fallen disproportionately on people of color. Mass home foreclosures following the 2008 crisis produced the greatest loss of Black wealth in U.S. history (Cooper & Bruenig, 2017), increasing the dramatically expanded racial wealth gap created by 30 years of neoliberalism (Collins, Asante-Muhammed, Hoxie, & Nieves, 2016).

Education is a focus of neoliberal crisis management, with the state imposing budget and program cuts and using the structural crisis of capitalism to extend neoliberal restructuring of public education. This strategy was initiated at the national level with President Obama's $4.35 billion Race to the Top competitive education grant to states (and later cities), as part of the 2009 economic stimulus package. Race to the Top incentivized school closings, the expansion of charter schools, and other neoliberal initiatives (Lipman, 2016). While consent for these policies is cultivated through discourses of (racialized) "school failure" and the need for "reform," hegemonic strategies of consent are dialectically related to the deployment of coercive state power to disenfranchise parents and the public in general, expropriate public institutions for private gain, and intensify state abandonment of low-income Black communities. At the same time, the cumulative effects of nearly three decades of neoliberal education policy and the state's crisis driven austerity strategies have opened up fissures in neoliberal hegemony, creating space for counter-hegemonic alternatives. This is a conjectural moment and what teacher unions and social movements do is crucial.

Hegemony and coercion

I want to put this is in a broader perspective. Over the past three decades, neoliberal political and economic forces were able to implement their agenda by strategically building broad support for their values and goals. (See, for example, Harvey, 2005; MacLean, 2017.) Political elites mobilized particular "socioeconomic imaginaries" and institutional arrangements to develop, institutionalize, and politically entrench neoliberal, market-based and finance-driven economic, political, social, and spatial urban restructuring. And as Michael Apple (2006) argued, they assembled various social forces under their hegemonic, albeit unstable, umbrella. In education, neoliberal ideology of personal responsibility, choice, standards, and accountability permeates discourse, policy, and practice in schools, university education departments, and education policy-making bodies and think tanks. The discourse of neoliberal "reform" ushered in high-stakes testing, value added assessment of teaching (based partly on student test scores), teacher and parent bashing, attempts to disable teacher unions, the Common Core State Standards (promoted by the Gates Foundation to support human capital development), charter schools (the principle vehicle for school privatization in the U.S.), and more (Saltman, 2015). While this discourse is deeply racialized, linking failure and irresponsibility with people of color, neoliberal antiracism (Melamed, 2011) positions education markets as the new civil rights agenda of our time.

But the weakness of the hegemonic strategy is that consent of subordinated classes and social groups depends on the state cultivating expectations for social well-being and advancement that it cannot necessarily meet. In Gramsci's (1971) conception of the integral state, hegemony and coercion are dialectically related in the exercise of power. Although ruling classes deploy technologies of consent to persuade various social sectors and classes to support their political, economic, and social agendas, for Gramsci, coercion "remains the indispensable condition of social order" (Gramsci, 1971, p. 57, cited in Davies, 2012, p. 3). The nature of this dialectic—which strategies predominate—is situated in specific time and specific context; it is shaped by specific social conjunctures. At this historical moment, the state cannot meet public expectations without cutting into capital's profits and institutionalized privileges, undermining hegemony. With its room for maneuver constrained, the state resorts to coercive measures to shore up its fiscal obligations to the banks. The crisis has thus opened up cracks in neoliberal hegemony, and for the first time in decades, the legitimacy and inevitability of capitalism itself is being widely questioned.[3]

While critical scholarship has focused productively on the role of media, neoliberal think tanks, and the discursive construction of consent for neoliberal education policies, my focus here is on coercive education policy as crisis management. The social contradictions created by neoliberal racial capitalism have led governments to increasingly deploy racialized coercive processes of incarceration, surveillance, and punishment to maintain order in society and contain and exclude those redundant and dangerous to the exiting order (Davis, 2005; Gill, 2003; Wacquant, 2001). In the U.S., governance through coercion has always been a fact of life for African Americans, Native peoples, and specific immigrant groups and was central to the accumulation of capital and development of racial capitalism (Robinson, 2000). Over the past two decades, surveillance, curtailment of civil liberties, militarization of schools and policing of students, incarceration and the entire carceral apparatus aimed primarily at low-income African American men and recently women have grown explosively—both qualitatively and quantitatively. But the economic crisis and the state's attempt to shift its costs onto the mass of people has intensified the state's coercive strategy *through public policy*, and that is my focus here in education.

From financial crisis to debt crisis

To be clear, there is a structural crisis of capitalism, a long term crisis of stagnation and over accumulation, for which neoliberalism, financialization, and globalization were meant to be "fixes" (Bello, 2002). But the 2008 financial crisis (a manifestation of the structural crisis) was quickly reframed as a "public debt crisis." Naming and constituting the problem this way opened space for certain policies and solutions and foreclosed others (Clarke & Newman, 2010). From Greece to Chicago, political and economic elites used "deficit panic" to further dismantle social programs and the social wage to offload

3   See, for example, explicitly anti-capitalist programs of social movements such as the Movement for Black Lives (https://policy.m4bl.org/platform/); the Bernie Sanders's campaign critique of the "one percent," an August 2018 Gallop Poll that found that Democrats have a more positive image of socialism than they do of capitalism (https://news.gallup.com/poll/240725/democrats-positive-socialism-capitalism.aspx).

bank losses onto working class and low-income people. As economist Paul Krugman argued, "[E]conomic recovery was never the point; the drive for austerity [is] about using the crisis, not solving it" (quoted in Peck, 2012, p. 3).

Cities were particularly vulnerable to the politics of "deficit panic." As city governments turned to downtown development as an economic growth strategy in the 1980s and 1990s, they increasingly relied on debt financing, real estate development, and urban place marketing (Harvey, 2005). It was this reliance on revenue from property taxes and debt financing that left cities exposed to the financial crisis triggered by the collapse of the subprime mortgage sector and loss of housing values. In order to function, debt financed cities need consistent access to credit markets controlled by the Wall Street banks. The 2008 recession and shrinking tax revenues made city governments even more subject to their discipline (Harvey, 2012). In 2012, the U.S. municipal debt market was $3.7 trillion (Larson, 2012). As the crisis rolled downhill from the federal to state and local governments, cities became laboratories for the discursively constructed "necessity" to impose austerity and privatize public goods as the only way to restore fiscal solvency and investor confidence, promote growth, and compete globally (Peck, 2012; Peck, Theodore, & Brenner, 2010).

In the discourse of "the new normal," union wages, retirement security, health benefits, and public provision of social services were framed as excesses of an extravagant, profligate era. Working and middle classes were expected to endure an even deeper decline in income and living standards and extension of the economic polarization and transfer of wealth upward that has characterized the past 30 years, with the worst born by those most economically vulnerable. A 2012 report by the Pew Charitable Trust projected the "local squeeze" as the new normal far into the future. The U.S. government accounting office estimates local expenditures will have to be cut by 12.7% each year until 2062 (Peck, 2012, p. 627)! Emphasizing the racialized nature of austerity discourses as a capital accumulation strategy, Rose Brewer (2012) notes that "austerity is a construction of financial urgency rooted in the relentless press by global capital for more and more profit. In the United states the call for austerity is framed as a debt crisis caused by too much public spending on unneeded social programs" (p. 233).

Education, the politics of austerity, and coercive governance

Education is a primary target of austerity and coercive governance. The "budget crisis" provided a warrant for city governments to cut school budgets and teacher pensions and benefits, close public schools, eliminate elected governing bodies, and dismantle portions of public school systems. Teachers, parents, and students were expected to pay for the crisis but not equally. The concentrated impact was on low-income communities of color. This is a form of coercive neoliberal governance in which the state colludes with capital in a racialized process of state abandonment, accumulation by dispossession, and political exclusion.

School closings as "organized abandonment"

Economically impoverished communities of color, particularly Black communities that have been demonized in the White racial imagination, have been targets of public and private disinvestment for decades, what geographer Ruth Wilson Gilmore (2007) terms "organized abandonment." The most marginalized communities are now subject to a new round of public disinvestment as local school boards and mayors authorize mass school closings, charter school expansion, and handing over public schools to private "turnaround" management organizations. These education policies compound the abandonment of marginalized Black communities, in particular, through dismantling public housing, home foreclosures, closing public health clinics and hospitals, and privatizing public services.

After years of inequitable education (Journey 4 Justice Alliance, 2018), decisions to close schools in Black communities solidify the state's further abandonment of its responsibility to educate Black children. The Journey 4 Justice Alliance (2014), a national alliance of grassroots community, parent, and youth-led organizations in communities of color, reported in 2014 that in recent years, Detroit, New York, and Chicago had all closed more than 100 public schools. Columbus (OH); Pittsburgh; St. Louis; Houston; Philadelphia; Washington, D.C.; Kansas City; Milwaukee; and Baltimore have all closed more than 25. The District of Columbia closed 39 neighborhood public schools since 2008; Newark closed 13 since 2009.

In Philadelphia, after months of protest by a citywide coalition of parents, teachers, and students, in the summer of 2013, the board of education closed 23 schools, one quarter of all schools in the school district. Over 80 percent of affected students were Black in a district that was 58 percent Black. Just 4 percent of affected students were White (Lee, 2013). Washington, D.C.'s, closure of 15 schools in 2013 affected about 2,700 students; just two students (less than 0.01 percent) were White, and 93 percent were African American, although 72 percent of the students in the district are African American (Khalek, 2013). Detroit, a school district that is 80 percent African American, closed 195 schools since 2000 (Loveland Technologies, 2016).

Since 2001, the Chicago Board of Education has closed, phased out, consolidated, or handed over to private managers more than 170 neighborhood public schools, almost all in Black and Latinx communities. Eighty-seven percent of affected students were African American (the district is 40.5% African American; Lipman, Vaughan, & Gutierrez, 2014). Serial school closings since 2004 have left some Chicago Black community areas with few public neighborhood schools. Parents are forced to shop around for charter schools, and children travel to schools outside their community. In 2013, an investigative journalist reported that in five (Black) community areas, more than 60% of children were attending schools outside their neighborhoods (Karp, 2013).

The reality of state abandonment of public schools in Black communities was dramatized by the closing of Dyett High School. The Chicago Board of Education, appointed by the mayor, voted in 2012 to phase out Dyett, despite popular protest and even as parents and community members developed their own plan for school improvement.

Dyett was the last open-enrollment neighborhood high school in the historic, and gentrifying, African American Bronzeville area in Chicago. The campaign to "Save Dyett" was the focus of an intense community struggle that elevated citywide resistance to school closings and exposed the connection between closing schools in working-class Black communities and gentrification. Petitions, community meetings, rallies, civil disobedience actions, and years of community and youth organizing forced the board to agree to reopen the school. Over three years and dozens of community meetings, a coalition of parents, students, educators, education researchers, and community organizations worked together to draft a comprehensive and visionary educational proposal to revitalize the school (Dyett High School RFP, 2015). When it was clear the board, at the direction of the mayor, would disregard the community plan, in August 2015, 12 parents, grandparents, and teachers launched a 34-day hunger strike that ultimately forced the board to reopen Dyett as a neighborhood high school. The hunger strike dramatized the extremes of school closings as state abandonment and the measures Black parents would have to take to contest them.

The grounds for closing schools as a "commonsense" solution to budget crises were laid by historical inequities in African American and Latinx schooling and by two decades of neoliberal education policy and urban development that concentrated resources and investment in affluent white areas, the city center, and gentrifying neighborhoods (Lipman, 2004). Education in many public schools serving low-income students of color in Chicago was degraded by an overemphasis on standardized tests, failed accountability measures, limited curricula and course offerings, and crumbling facilities and lack of resources such as libraries and up-to-date science labs (Chicago Teachers Union, 2012; Journey 4 Justice, 2018; Lipman, 2004). Closing schools was the last step in persistent racist politics of disposability. A Black parent interviewed about the effects of school closings in her community summarized: "You know, I feel they don't care about the African American communities. They don't care if we get an education" (Lipman, Vaughan, & Gutierrez, 2014, p. 22).

Accumulation by dispossession

Marxist geographer David Harvey (2005) argues a key feature of neoliberal capitalism is the proliferation and extension of the primitive accumulation of capital through a violent process of "accumulation by dispossession"—the commodification and privatization of human value and the natural world. This includes sucking into the market: land, indigenous crops, and other elements of the natural world; public institutions and resources; and whatever else remains of the commons.

The economic crisis provided a rich opportunity to expand the appropriation of public institutions for private gain. Education is a primary target. Venture capitalists, hedge fund operators, tech corporations, and for-profit education companies recognize the enormous profits to be made from every component of public education. Dun & Bradstreet (2018), an investment and business consulting firm, estimates the value of the U.S. K–12 education market at $700 billion. Following the economic crisis, Stephanie Simon (2012) reported in Reuters, investors are "pouring private equity and venture capital into scores of companies that aim to profit by taking over broad swaths of public education." Citing school district budget crises, pension fund shortfalls, and a friendly political climate, investors are optimistic. The manifesto of the venture capitalist GSV Capital states, "we believe the opportunity to build numerous multi-billion dollar education enterprises is finally real" (Fang, 2014, p. 4).

Charter schools, publicly funded but privately operated, are an expanding sector of the education industry that directly benefits from the state's organized abandonment of public schools. From 2005–06 to 2012–13, 20 large urban school districts (including Detroit, Los Angeles, Newark, Baltimore, and Houston) had a 35 percent increase in charter school enrollment, and charter enrollment more than doubled in 13 of the districts (Journey 4 Justice Alliance, 2015, p. 3). This is a lucrative opportunity for for-profit charter school companies and charter school management organizations that get a hefty fee to manage schools for nonprofit charter organizations. Money is also to be made by investing in bonds floated by charter school operators. And banks and equity funds reap huge federal tax credits, called New Market Tax Credits, by investing in charter schools in "underserved" communities. According to one estimate (Gonzalez, 2010) investors who put up millions of dollars to build charter schools can double their money in seven years through a 39 percent tax credit from the federal government. Black and Latinx students are both consumers and commodities in the growing charter school industry.

Detroit is a radical case of accumulation by dispossession as the collapse of the economy and accumulated debt provoked state officials to impose structural adjustment on the city. No austerity measure seemed to be too extreme, including gutting pensions, slashing wages, cutting basic services (including water, streetlights, and garbage collection), closing schools, and clearing out neighborhoods where the city's Black working class bought homes, raised families, and created community. The land is to put in reserve for future development. This amounted to a class/race war on the city's mostly Black, mostly poor, working class whose labor made Detroit "Motor City." Some city leaders suggested turning "vacant" land into corporate farms as part of a scheme to rebrand Detroit a "green city." Education scholar Tom Pedroni (2011) writes, school closings are part of an "effort to unlock real estate value currently 'contaminated' by a population in need of containment" (p. 210). While Detroit lost significant population, closing public schools was also linked to expansion of charter schools. By 2013, more students were enrolled in charter schools than Detroit Public Schools (Loveland Technologies, 2016).

This is a form of both material and symbolic violence in which public assets in Black communities and Black children are converted to investment opportunities. Schools in historically segregated Black communities have been central to urban placemaking and resistance in the face of White supremacy and struggle for a right to the city (Haymes, 1995).

Although depicted in the dominant neoliberal narrative as "failing," shuttered schools are far more complex. While city governments pointed to low test scores or under- enrollment, parents and community members also pointed to their educational strengths and the historical significance of these schools as centers of Black intellectual and cultural life. Many were community, housing adult education programs, after-school activities, community exercise and athletic facilities, community clinics, and more. Some had served generations of the same families. As Pedroni (2011) argues in relation to school closings in Detroit, "within this struggle over for whom the city exists, schools in Detroit play a vital role in maintaining or relinquishing one's stake in the city, which is why they are central to both the fostering of and resistance to neoliberal urbanism" (p. 213). Closing schools to force people from the city is a racial strategy of coercive urban governance.

Governance by exclusion

While Chicago's global city discourse foregrounds downtown skyscraper development, corporate headquarters, Magnificent Mile luxury shopping, and a world-class restaurant scene, behind the scenes Chicago's Black communities endure extreme rates of incarceration, economic poverty, public and private disinvestment, and a growing affordable housing crisis. And low-wage immigrant workers form the hidden backbone of the city's booming service economy. The exodus of over 250,000 African Americans since 2000 is in direct relation to the emergence of Chicago as a "world-class city." Peck and Theodore (2012) argue, "These communities have effectively no productive role, in socially selective narratives of globalization, which as a promotional necessity render them discursively and socially invisible" (p. 188). Discourses of social invisibility help to legitimate policies of political and social erasure that explicitly constitute coercive neoliberal urban governance by exclusion.

The crisis has legitimated state takeovers of school districts and appointment of financial managers with nearly unlimited powers to impose structural adjustment. Michigan has been the urban epicenter of Black political exclusion. Under the state's Emergency Financial Manager law, state officials appointed Emergency Financial Managers (EM) with sweeping powers to run seven majority Black cities, including Detroit. The EM's authority includes the power to sell city assets, remove elected leaders, privatize or eliminate public services, and restructure union contracts. These extreme measures are designed to ensure that debts to Wall Street banks are paid, at the expense of Black residents. A representative of the Michigan State Treasury office explained, the takeovers are "to show bond rating agencies that we are working aggressively. We think that they will look favorably on this" (Russ Bellant, redemocratize-detroit blog, Feb. 9, 2011).

In 2011, Michigan's governor abolished the authority of Detroit's elected school board and appointed a former General Motors executive to run the school system. His charge was to close public schools and convert others to charter schools. The state legislature also created a state-run "recovery school district" composed of Detroit's "worst" schools, similar to that in New Orleans after Hurricane Katrina. Downsizing the city and positioning for a new round of capital accumulation depends on pushing out the people who once made the city an industrial powerhouse—Detroit's Black working class. Fast-tracking this project depends on excluding Detroit's Black voters from having any say in their destiny.

This neoliberal strategy of governance by political exclusion is repeated in other major cities where elected school boards have been replaced by mayor-appointed boards (Lipman, Gutstein, Gutierrez, & Blanche, 2015). Chicago's mayor-appointed Board of Education has been predominantly made up of corporate CEOs, investment bankers, and real estate magnates. The Board makes decisions behind closed doors on the fates of nearly 400,000 Black and Latinx school children. It has approved nearly every school closing proposed by the mayor despite mass public opposition.

This is neoliberal urban governance by exclusion, a "form of economic, spatial and symbolic violence against the poor where hegemonic actors do not see the potential, need or possibility of organizing a more inclusionary enrolment strategy" (Davies, 2010, p.25; see also Davies 2012.). Directed primarily at Black communities, it is a fundamentally colonial strategy. But the resort to coercive governance also reveals the fundamental weakness of liberal democracy in the face of the inability of capitalism to deliver on its promises. Default to authoritarianism lays bare the logics of race and capital behind neoliberal urban development, opening up a space of opportunity for progressive, transformative solutions to the crisis.

Emergent education movements

The assault on public education, teachers and teacher unions and the devastating effects of neoliberal policies have opened cracks in the hegemony of the neoliberal logics in education. The congealed consequences of a decade of high-stakes testing, top-down accountability, blaming teachers, school closings, and privatization erupted in the historic 2012 Chicago Teachers Union (CTU) strike—the first truly mass resistance to these policies. Organized opposition to school closings by coalitions of Black and Latinx community organizations, parents, and teachers, and the CTU strike made education the focal point of opposition to neoliberal policies in Chicago. This was demonstrated concretely when Karen Lewis, the president of the CTU, was poised to seriously contest Rahm Emanuel in the 2015 race for mayor of Chicago. Before she became ill and had to withdraw, Lewis was significantly ahead of Emanuel in the polls.

School closings, privatization, and political exclusion have incited coalitions of parents, students, and teachers, led primarily by people of color, in cities across the U.S. National organizing by the Journey 4 Justice Alliance compelled the U.S. Department of Education under Obama to make sustainable community-driven school transformation a fifth option for federal School Improvement Grants. Journey 4 Justice also pressed the Department's Office of Civil Rights to investigate school closings in Black and Latinx communities as civil rights violations. And the rebirth of the CTU as a social movement union spawned radical teacher caucuses nationally. As the protracted effects of austerity continue, in 2018 there was a wave of teacher strikes and mass organizing in some of the seemingly most conservative states—West Virginia, Oklahoma, Arizona, North Carolina, Kentucky. The "Education Spring" was a grassroots uprising led and organized by classroom teachers against four decades of neoliberal "reforms" magnified by austerity policies that have starved classrooms, pushed teachers into poverty, and degraded teaching (Weiner, 2018).

These grassroots education movements are beginning to coalesce around analyses that challenge the intersection of race and capital and advance programmatic alternatives to neoliberal policies (e.g., Caref, Hilgendorf, Jankov, Hainds, & Conwell, 2015; Chicago Teachers Union, 2012; Schools and Communities United, 2014). They are connecting quality neighborhood public schools, living wages, and affordable housing. And they are targeting the financial and corporate interests responsible for impoverishment and profiteering on low-income communities. For example, the Chicago Teachers Union indicted Chicago Public Schools for wasting millions of dollars on charter schools, outsourcing services to private companies, and excessive testing and for risky speculative financial deals that put the school district in debt billions of dollars to Wall Street banks (Jankov, 2015). The CTU's call to put funds back into the classroom and its progressive revenue solutions, including a tax on millionaires (Illinois has a flat income tax), taxing corporations (many pay little or no taxes), and a tax on financial transactions (Chicago is home to the Chicago Board of Trade and Mercantile Exchange) are concrete proposals for economic redistribution.

Conclusion: shifting neoliberal strategies and new social imaginaries

Peck (2012) reminds us that neoliberalism has evolved as a "roiling" process of crisis and experimentation, with neoliberals opportunistically capitalizing on crises, including those of their own making. Neoliberalism has been surprisingly flexible but is also highly unstable. Jody Melamed (2011) demonstrates that racial capitalism and its regimes of accumulation are integrally linked to the state's flexible appropriation and incorporation of various antiracisms. In education, neoliberals have rolled out a seeming endless variety of market-oriented experiments: vouchers, charter schools, turnaround schools, virtual schools, alternative teacher certification programs, value-added evaluation of teachers, high-stakes testing and top-down accountability, state takeovers of schools and school districts, school choice and portfolio districts, outsourcing and privatization of education services, standards geared to workforce preparation, privatized alternative schools for school push-outs, the Common Core Standards industry in testing and textbooks, and more (see Ross & Gibson, 2007; Saltman, 2015; Weiner, 2012). This is the shifting terrain educators and education activists have to negotiate. Understanding neoliberalism as an unruly, opportunistic, and highly unstable and variegated project is crucial to frame strategies to contest and supplant it.

Missing the racialized core of neoliberal capitalism, the integral relationship of austerity and politics of White supremacy and ways in which policies have differential effects by race and class, disarms the emerging education justice movement. School closings predominantly impact low-income students of color, yet they central to the generalized neoliberalization of education, the loss of unionized teachers, and a gateway to privatization. The loss of Black teachers undermines the militancy of teacher unions and undermines the education of all students. Thus, any struggle against education privatization has to be a struggle for racial justice. Moreover, Nancy Fraser (1990) reminds us that the bourgeois public sphere was constituted by raced and gendered exclusions. The public schools neoliberals seek to dismantle are neither equitable nor just. Indeed this is part of the "good sense" of neoliberal solutions, such as charter schools and vouchers (Pedroni, 2007). Thus any defense of public schools or demands for economic redistribution in education have to center racial and gender justice if they are not to reproduce existing inequalities.

Crises open up space for alternative political-economic and social solutions. Yet, as Colin Leys points out, "for an ideology to be hegemonic it is not necessary that it be loved. It is merely necessary that it have no serious rival" (quoted in Peck, et al., 2009). This is the urgency of the present social conjuncture. The persistent, extended crisis of capitalism and failures of neoliberal policy beg for new social imaginaries, concrete reinventions of public education that are far more inclusive, democratic, humane, culturally relevant, invigorating, and critical. In organized opposition to school closings, parents and students and committed teachers claim, "We are the people who can save our schools." The starting point for an alternative agenda is the aspirations and knowledge of parents and expertise of teachers and committed school leaders. Interviews with parents from closed schools in Chicago show they have a holistic, humanistic, and justice-driven vision of education (Lipman, et al., 2014). There are kernels of antiracist, anti-capitalist, antiheteropatriarchal social imaginaries in teachers' practices of critical pedagogy (see, for example, publications of Rethinking Schools, https://www.rethinkingschools.org/), in the platform of the Movement for Black Lives (https://policy.m4bl.org/platform/), and in the growing education justice movements and coalitions, including resistance to racialized policing and the school-to-prison pipeline, for example, Dignity in Schools Campaign (https://dignityinschools.org/about-us/mission/). These protagonistic practices hold the potential to not only disrupt neoliberal education agendas but also develop counter-hegemonic alternatives.

References

American Federation of Teachers. (2018). A decade of neglect: Public education funding in the aftermath of the great recession. Retrieved from https://www.aft.org/decade-neglect

Apple, M. W. (2006). *Educating the "right" way: Markets, standards, God, and inequality, 2nd Ed.* New York: Routledge Falmer.

Bello, W. (2002). *Deglobalization: Ideas for a new world economy.* London: Zed

Brewer, R. M. (2012). 21st Century capitalism, austerity, and Black economic dispossession. *Souls, 14* (3-4), pp. 227–239.

Caref, C. R., Hilgendorf, K., Jankov, P., Hainds, S., & Conwell, J. (2015). *A just Chicago: Fighting for the city our students deserve.* Chicago: Chicago Teachers Union.

Chicago Teachers Union. (2012). The schools Chicago students deserve. Chicago: Author. Retrieved from http://www.ctunet.com/quest-center/research/the-schools-chicagos-students-deserve

Clarke, J., & Newman, J. (2010). Summoning spectres: Crises and their construction. *Journal of Education Policy, 25*(6), 709–715.

Collins, C., Asante-Muhammed, D., Hoxie, J., & Nieves, E. (2016). *The ever-growing gap.* Institute for Policy Studies. Retrieved from http://ips-dc.org/wp-content/uploads/2016/08/The-Ever-Growing-Gap-CFED_IPS-Final-2.pdf

Cooper, R., & Bruenig, M. (2017, December 7). *Destruction of Black wealth during the Obama presidency.* Peoples Policy Project. Retrieved from http://peoplespolicyproject.org/2017/12/07/destruction-of-black-wealth-during-the-obama-presidency/

Davies, J. (2010). Neoliberalism, Governance and the Integral State. Paper presented at Critical Governance Conference, University of Warwick, 13–14 December. Retrieved from: http://www2.warwick.ac.uk/fac/soc/wbs/projects/orthodoxies/papers

Davies, J. (2012). Network governance theory: A Gramscian critique. *Environment and Planning A, 44*(11), 2687–2704.

Davis, A. (2005). *Abolition democracy: Beyond prisons, torture, and empire.* New York: Open Media.

Dun & Bradstreet. (2018). MDR in the news. New report from MDR provides insights into $700 billion K–12 education market. Retrieved from https://mdreducation.com/news/report-insights-k-12-education-market/

Dyett High School RFP. (2015, April 6). The coalition to revitalize Dyett High School. http://cps.edu/SiteCollectionDocuments/DyettRFP_DyettGlobalAndGreenTechnology-HSProposal.pdf

Fang, L. (2014, September 25). Venture capitalists are poised to 'disrupt' everything about the education market. *The Nation.* Retrieved from https://www.thenation.com/article/venture-capitalists-are-poised-disrupt-everything-about-education-market/

Fraser, N. (1990). Rethinking the public sphere: A contribution to the critique of actually existing democracy. *Social Text, 25/26,* 56–80.

Gill, S. (2003). *Power and resistance in the new world order.* New York: Palgrave Macmillan.

Gilmore, R. W. (2007). *Golden Gulag: Prisons, surplus, crisis, and opposition in globalizing California.* Berkeley: University of California Press.

Gonzalez, J. (2010, May 7). Albany charter cash cow: Big banks making a bundle on new construction as schools bear the cost. *New York Daily News.* Retrieved from http://articles.nydailynews.com/2010–05-07/local/29438011_1_charter-law-albany-charter-state-aid

Gramsci, A. (1971) *Antonio Gramsci: Selections from the Prison Notebooks.* Edited by Q. Hoare and G. Smith. New York: International Publishers.

Harvey, D. (2005). *A brief history of neoliberalism*. Oxford: Oxford University Press.

Harvey, D. (2012). The urban roots of financial crises. *Socialist Register*, 48, 1–35.

Haymes, S. N. (1995). Race, culture and the city. Albany: SUNY Press.

Jankov, P. (2015). Broke on purpose: Chicago Public Schools budget brief. Retrieved from https://ajustchicago.org/wp-content/uploads/2015/07/budget-brief-layout-WEB.pdf

Journey 4 Justice Alliance. (2014). Death by a thousand cuts: Racism, school closures, and public school sabotage. Retrieved from http://www.j4jalliance.com/wp-content/uploads/2014/02/J4JReport-final_05_12_14.pdf

Journey 4 Justice Alliance. (2018). Failing Brown v. Board: A continuous struggle against inequity in public education. Retrieved from https://www.dropbox.com/s/f60dvoxk8ottjzz/Final%20Failing%20Brown%20v%20Board%20Abridged.pdf?dl=0

Karp, S. (2013). A sign of stability. *Catalyst Chicago, XXIV* (3), Spring, 2013, pp. 11–15.

Khalek R. (2013, May 31). Racist school closings in Washington, DC. *Truthout*. Retrieved from http://www.truth-out.org/news/item/16672-racist-school-closings-in-washington-dc

Klein, N. (2008). *The shock doctrine: The rise of disaster capitalism*. New York: Holt and Company.

Larson, Ann. (2012, November 16). Cities in the red: Austerity hits America [Blog]. *Dissent*. Retrieved from http://www.dissentmagazine.org/blog

Lee, T. (2013). Mass school closings' severe impact on lives of black, Latino students. MSNBC. Retrieved from: http://nbclatino.com/2013/10/15/mass-school-closings-severe-impact-on-lives-of-black-latino-students/

Lipman, P. (2004). High Stakes Education: Inequality, globalization, and urban school reform. New York: Routledge.

Lipman, P. (2011). *The new political economy of urban education: Neoliberalism, race, and the right to the city*. New York: Routledge.

Lipman, P. (2016). Obama's education policy: More markets, more inequality, new urban contestations. In J. DeFilippis (Ed.), *Urban policy in the time of Obama*. Minneapolis: University of Minnesota Press, pp. 132–148.

Lipman, P., Gutstein, R., Gutierrez, R. R., & Blanche, T. (2015, February). *Should Chicago have an elected representative school board: A new review of the evidence*. Chicago Collaborative for Equity and Justice in Education, UIC College of Education.

Lipman, P., Vaughan, K. & Gutierrez, R. R. (2014). Root shock: Parents' perspectives on school closings in Chicago. Chicago: Collaborative for Equity and Justice in Education, University of Illinois at Chicago. Retrieved from http://www.ceje.edu

Lipsitz, G. (2014). Introduction: A new beginning. *Kalfou: A journal of comparative and relational ethnic studies, 1*(1), 7–14. Retrieved from http://tupjournals.temple.edu/index.php/kalfou/article/view/7

Loveland Technologies. (2016). A school district in crisis: Detroit's Public Schools 1842-2015. Detroit, MI: Author. Retrieved from https://makeloveland.com/reports/schools

MacLean, N. (2017). *Democracy in chains: The deep history of the radical right's steal plan for America*. New York: Viking.

Melamed, J. (2011). *Represent and destroy: Rationalizing violence in the new racial capitalism*. Minneapolis: University of Minnesota Press.

Oosterlynck, S., & Gonzalez, S. (2013). 'Don't waste a crisis': Opening up the city yet again for neoliberal experimentation. *International Journal of Urban and Regional Research, 37*(3), 1075–1082.

Peck, J. (2012). Austerity urbanism: American cities under extreme economy. *City, 16*(6), 626–655.

Peck, J. & Theodore, N. (2012). Chicago beyond Fordism: Between regulatory crisis and sustainable growth. In F. Martinelli, F. Moulaert & A. Novy (Eds.), *Urban and regional development trajectories in contemporary capitalism*. London: Routledge.

Peck, J., Theodore, N., & Brenner, N. (2009). Postneoliberalism and its malcontents. *Antipode, 41*, 94–116.

Pedroni, T. C. (2007). *Market movements: African American involvement in school voucher reform*. New York: Routledge.

Pedroni, T. (2011). Urban shrinkage as a performance of whiteness; Neoliberal urban restructuring, education, and racial containment in the post-industrial, global niche city. *Discourse: Studies in the Cultural Politics of Education, 32*(2), 203–216.

Pew Charitable Trust. (2012). *The local squeeze: Falling revenues and growing demand for services challenge cities, counties, and school districts*. Washington, DC: Author. Retrieved from http://www.pewstates.org/research/reports/the-local-squeeze-85899388655

Robinson, C. (2000). *Black Marxism: The making of the Black radical tradition*. Chapel Hill: University of North Carolina Press.

Ross, E. W., & Gibson, R., Eds. (2007). *Neoliberalism and educational reform: Marxian perspectives on the impact of globalization on teaching and learning*. Cresskill, NJ: Hampton Press.

Saltman, K. J. (2015). *The failure of corporate school reform*. New York: Routledge.

Schools and Communities United. (2014). *Fulfill the promise The schools and communities our children deserve*. Milwaukee: Author.

Wacquant, L. (2001). The penalization of poverty and the rise of neo-liberalism. *European Journal of Criminal Policy and Research, 9*(4), 401–412.

Weiner, L. (2012). *The future of our schools: Teachers Unions and social justice*. Chicago: Haymarket Books.

Weiner, L. (2018). Walkouts teach U.S. labor a new grammar for struggle. *New Politics, 17*(1). Retrieved from http://newpol.org/content/walkouts-teach-us-labor-new-grammar-struggle-0

CHAPTER FIVE

The Failure of Corporate School Reform: Towards a New Common School Movement[1]

Kenneth Saltman

IN THE UNITED States, a corporate model of schooling has overtaken educational policy, practice, curriculum, and nearly all aspects of educational reform. While this movement began on the political right, the corporate school model has been heralded across the political spectrum and is aggressively embraced by both major parties. Corporate school reformers champion private sector approaches to reform including, especially, privatization, deregulation, and the importation of terms and assumptions from business, while they imagine public schools as private businesses, districts as markets, students as consumers, and knowledge as product. Corporate school reform aims to transform public schooling into a private industry nationally by replacing public schools with privately managed charter schools, voucher schemes, and tax credit scholarships for private schooling. The massive expansion of de-unionized, non-profit, privately managed charter schools with short term contracts is an intermediary step towards the declaration of their failure and replacement by the for-profit industry in Educational Management Organizations (EMOs). EMOs extract profit by cutting teacher pay and educational resources while relying on high teacher turnover and labor precarity.[2] Corporate school reform seeks solutions to public problems in private sector ways, from contracting out schools and services, to union-busting, a wholesale embrace of numerical benchmarking and database tracking, and the modeling of schooling and administration on multiple aspects of corporate culture. Policy hawks make demands, for example, for teacher entrepreneurialism, or insist that students dress like retail chain workers and call school heads "CEO," or install corporate models of numerical "accountability" paying students for grades and teachers for test scores, or leaders play intricate Wall Street–style shell games with test performance to show rising "return on investment" or teachers assign

---

1   Keynote address, Department of Educational Leadership, UMass Dartmouth, May, 21, 2012, The Kaput Center Conference Room.

2   The visions of the right-wing think tanks such as AEI, Hoover, and Heritage is made particularly clear by Andy Smarick. (2010). "The Turnaround Fallacy" *Education Next* 10 (1). Smarick suggests that public schools should be thought of as private businesses competing against one another and most importantly suggests that the "advantage" of charter schools is that they can be easily closed and replaced with other privatized solutions. Paul T. Hill of the Center for Reinventing Public Eduction regularly champions this aim in advocating "urban portfolio districts."

students the task of crafting a resume for Benjamin Franklin, BP was involved in creating California's new science curriculum: the examples are endless.

Despite the fact that corporate school reforms have expanded at an exponential speed, the dominant corporate school reforms have failed on their own terms. Such reformers have insisted on "accountability" through test scores and lowering costs, but it is precisely in reference to these accountability measures that corporate school reforms have failed. The failing policies that are being aggressively implemented nonetheless include contracting out management to privately managed charters or for-profit educational management organizations[3] putting in place voucher schemes or neo-voucher scholarship tax credits;[4] expanding commercialism;[5] imposing corporate "turnaround" models on schools and faculty[6] that often involve firing entire faculties and administrations; reducing curriculum and pedagogy to narrow numerically quantifiable and anti-intellectual, anti-critical test-based forms, the creation of "portfolio districts" that imagine districts as a stock portfolio and schools as stock investments;[7] reorganizing teacher education and educational leadership on the model of the MBA degree;[8] and the

---

3   Miron, G. (2011). Review of "Charter Schools: A Report on Rethinking the Federal Role in Education." Boulder, CO: National Education Policy Center. Retrieved [March 13, 2011] from http://nepc.colorado. edu/thinktank/review-charter-federal; Molnar, A., Miron, G., & Urschel, J.L. (2010). *Profiles of for-profit education management organizations: Twelfth annual report - 2009-2010*. Boulder, CO: National Education Policy Center. Retrieved [March 13, 2011] from http://nepc.colorado.edu/publication/EMO-FP-09-10; Miron, G., & Urschel, J. L. (2010). *Profiles of nonprofit education management organizations: 2009- 2010*. Boulder, CO: National Education Policy Center. Retrieved [March 13, 2011] from http://nepc.colorado.edu/publication/ EMO-NP-09-10; Murray, C. (2010, May 4). Op-Ed: Why Charter Schools Fail the Test. *The New York Times*. Retrieved May 4, 2010, from http://www.nytimes.com/2010/05/05/opinion/05murray.html 56 ; Byrnes, V. (2009). Getting a feel for the market: The use of privatized school management in Philadelphia. *American Journal of Education, 115*, 437–455; Peterson, P. E., & Chingos, M. M. (2009). *Impact of for-profit and nonprofit management on student achievement: The Philadelphia intervention 2002–2008* (Working Paper PEPG 09-02). Cambridge, MA: Harvard University, Program on Education Policy and Governance.

4   See Kevin G. Welner, *Neo-Vouchers: The Emergence of Tuition Tax Credits for Private Schooling* Lanham, MD: Rowman & Littlefield 2008.

5   See Patricia Burch, *Hidden Markets: The New Education Privatization* New York: Routledge 2009. For the most thorough tracking of commercialism see Alex Molnar's Schoolhouse Commercialism annual reports available at www.nepc.colorado.edu.

6   Turnaround consulting in schools has been based not on evidence of effectiveness or a cohesive program but rather a metaphor of corporate turnaround consulting and a massive public subsidy for this market experiment. For excellent coverage of the appalling lack of public oversight see Sam Dillon, "Inexperienced Companies Chase U.S. School Funds" *The New York Times* August 9, 2010, available online at www.nytimes. com; see also my discussion of Alvarez and Marsal's "turnaround consulting" that slashed millions in funding for public schools while netting millions in consulting fees in New Orleans before and after Katrina in Kenneth J. Saltman, *Capitalizing on Disaster: Taking and Breaking Public Schools* Boulder: Paradigm Publishers 2007.

7   Kenneth J. Saltman, "Urban School Decentralization and the Growth of "Portfolio Districts" June 2010 *The Great Lakes Center for Education Research and Practice* available online at: www.greatlakescenter.org.

8   I take this up in Kenneth J. Saltman *The Gift of Education: Public Education and Venture Philanthropy* Palgrave Macmillan 2010.

elimination of advanced degrees and certification in favor of pay for test performance schemes such as value added assessment.[9]

These corporate school reforms are deeply interwoven with commercial interests in the multibillion-dollar test and textbook publishing industries, the information technology and database tracking industries, and the contracting industries.[10] The corporate sector has in the last decade positioned education in the United States as a roughly $600 billion per year "industry," ripe for takeover.[11] As directions for future economic growth are uncertain, public tax money in public services appears to corporations and the super-rich who are flush from decades of upward redistributions as tantalizing to pillage.[12] These upward redistributions of public wealth and governance are particularly obvious in Wisconsin and New Jersey as tax cuts on the super-rich and corporations and slush funds for business development are funded by defunding public and higher education; attacking teacher pay, benefits, and unions; expanding privatization schemes including vouchers, charters, and tuition fee hikes; and shifting educational costs onto individual working class and professional class individuals. The same agenda is being enacted in Michigan, Indiana, Florida, Ohio, and Pennsylvania, to name a few. Chicago could be considered the blueprint with its Renaissance 2010 plan designed by the Commercial Club and implemented by Arne Duncan. That plan, which resulted in failure to raise test scores or lower costs, succeeded in privatizing and deunionizing about a hundred of the six hundred schools in the district.

The Original Common School Movement

The U.S. public school system has its origins in the common school movement spearheaded first in Massachusetts by Horace Mann in the early nineteenth century. The movement eventually spread throughout the United States. Mann's emphasized the need for an educated public for a functioning democracy, a system of publicly financed schools, that schools should be composed of children of different backgrounds, that

---

9   Kenneth J. Saltman, "'Value Added' Assessment: Tool for Improvement or Educational 'Nuclear Option'" September 14, 2010 available at: www.truthout.org; Eva L. Baker, Paul E. Barton, Linda Darling-Hammond, Edward Haertel, Helen F. Ladd, Robert L. Linn, Diane Ravitch, Richard Rothstein, Richard J. Shavelson, and Lorrie A. Shepard, "Problems with the Use of Student Test Scores to Evaluate Teachers" EPI Briefing Paper #278 August 29, 2010 available at www.epi.org.

10   Patricia Burch *Hidden Markets: The New Education Privatization* New York: Routledge 2009.

11   "Special Report Education a New Push to Privatize" *Businessweek* January 14, 2002.

12   Usually such pillage is described as introducing "private sector" efficiencies which fits the classic definition of ideology as a camera obscura inverting reality as private sector involvement skims wealth out of the system. McKinsey, whose education sector is headed by globe-trotting neoliberal consultant Michael Barber, makes the agenda quite clear: **"Drive productivity gains in the public and regulated sectors.** Public and regulated sectors such as health care and education represent more than 20 percent of the US economy, but has persistently low productivity growth. McKinsey analysis has demonstrated that, if the US public sector could halve the estimated efficiency gap with similar private sector organizational functions, its productivity would be 5 to 15 percent higher and would generate annual savings of $100 billion to $300 billion." Available at http://www.mckinsey.com/mgi/publications/growth_and_renewal_in_the_us/index.asp.

education should be non-sectarian, that students should be taught by professionally trained teachers and that the educational disciplines and methods should express the values of a free society. The common school movement was promoted as a means of political inclusion, workforce preparation, and individual character building aiming to bring together children of different classes and provide a common learning experience. The common school movement sought to increase provision of educational resources including the quality of schools, increased duration of schooling to the age of sixteen, better pay for the mostly female teacher workforce and a broader curriculum.

While many aspects of public schooling have been struggled over since the common school movement including racial segregation and integration, the question of secular versus religious-based moral instruction, the politics of the curriculum, and the role of public schools in workforce preparation, neoliberal privatization in the last twenty years has in many respects undone many socially valuable aspects of the legacy of the common school movement. The aspirations for a common educational experience, the commitment to non-sectarian schooling, and the value of educated citizenry for public participation are collateral damage in the privatization trend. Voucher schemes, home-schooling, and scholarship tax credits have contributed to an effort by especially the Christian right to capture public resources to pay for religious education. The neoliberal emphasis on schooling for work and consumption has dramatically undermined the central value on promoting democratic citizens imbued with the knowledge and dispositions for self-governance. The relentless push for charter schooling has worsened racial segregation in public schools. Magnets were transformed as well during Reagan from being an effort in racial integration and equity into being seen as a "market" in schools. The values on universal and equal provision and the common benefit to publicly paying for schooling has been damaged severely by the centrality of the metaphors of "competition" and consumer "choice." In addition to transforming schooling into something that is more class stratified, neoliberal privatization redefines schooling into an individualized responsibility undermining the sense of shared value for the benefit of others.

Corporate school reform represents hopelessness for the future and an assumption that unlimited capitalist growth is the only alternative. That is, corporate school reform not only actively contributes to the reproduction of economic exploitation, political marginalization, and the crushing of imagination as all social and individual values are reduced to market concerns. It also contributes to planetary destruction that makes life on the planet a kind of terminal illness while waiting out the imminent cascade of ecological collapse and human disaster in responding to it. As a number of scholars have suggested, capitalism and its imperative for unlimited growth of consumption is a waste production system, despoiling not only the planet but also rendering wasted lives and disposable populations.[13]

13   See Georges Batailles, *The Accursed Share Volume One* New York: Zone Books 1995; Jean Baudrillard *The Consumer Society* Thousand Oaks: Sage 1998 was an important early work that recognized this while more recently Zygmunt Bauman *Wasted Lives* 2005 and Henry Giroux *Youth in a Suspect Society* New York: Palgrave

Corporate School Reform Is an Enclosure of the Commons

Corporate school reform represents not merely better or worse school reform approaches—adjusting pedagogical methods, tweaking the curriculum, on so on. It is crucially about redistributed control over social life and as such is part of a much broader trend. It represents a capitalist enclosure of the commons—that is the violent taking of "the shared substance of our social being."[14] As Zizek points out there are three crucial enclosures of the commons at present:

> *the commons of culture*, the immediately socialized forms of "cognitive capital", primarily language, our means of communication and education, but also the shared infrastructure of public transport, electricity, the postal system, and so on; *the commons of external nature*, threatened by pollution and exploitation (from oil to rain forests and the natural habitat itself); *the commons of internal nature* (the biogenetic inheritance of humanity); with new biogenetic technology, the creation of a New Man [*sic*] in the literal sense of changing human nature becomes a realistic prospect.[15]

A fourth enclosure of the common involves the de facto apartheid situation of new "walls and slums" that physically enclose people separating the Excluded from the Included. These four enclosures of the common are being struggled over and the stakes in the struggle are, for Zizek, the very survival of the species and the planet itself. Capitalist enclosure of the natural commons produces ecological catastrophe. Capitalist enclosure of the knowledge commons makes ideas into private property rather than freely shared and exchanged knowledge of use and potential universal benefit. Capitalist enclosure transforms the biological information that is the stuff of life into property setting the stage for new forms of bio-slavery and profit-based control. Corporate school reform colludes with and deepens these enclosures of the commons. It makes knowledge into a commodity rather than being shared and freely exchanged. It naturalizes a natural world defined by private ownership rather than public care. It privatizes the process of maturation and socialization making human development into business and children into product. Finally, the lower tier of privatized public schooling expands repression in the form of new walls and slums.

The most significant aspect of corporate school reform involves privatizing the public schools. In an economic sense privatization involves enclosing commonly held wealth, assets, and land. Value is produced by collective labor in any enterprise. But capitalism individualizes the profits from collective labor. As David Harvey points out, the common

---

Macmillan 2010 make important interventions. Giroux's book significantly links the death of futurity signified in the ramped up hard and soft war on youth to the dead-end of consumer capitalism and ecological disaster.

14   Slavoj Zizek, *First as Tragedy, Then as Farce* New York: Verso 2009, p. 91.

15   Slavoj Zizek, *First as Tragedy, Then as Farce* New York: Verso 2009, p. 91.

as a form of collective laboring must ground collective rather than individualized property rights and result in collective control over the production process.[16] Public schools are not simply commonly held property, but the collective labor of teachers, administrators, and staff comprises the common of the public schools as well. As Harvey explains,

> the collective laboring that is now productive of value must ground collec-
> tive, not individual, property rights. Value, socially necessary labor time, is
> the capitalist common, and it is represented by money, the universal equiva-
> lency by which common wealth is measured. The common is not, therefore,
> something extant once upon a time that has since been lost, but something
> that, like the urban commons, is continuously being produced. The problem
> is that it is just as continuously being enclosed and appropriated by capital in
> its commodified and monetary form.[17]

Corporate school reform encloses and appropriates for capital the collective *labor* of teachers, administrators, staff, and students. And it does so by using public financing for privatizing public schooling. In fact, as real estate schemes by charters and the vast array of contracting deals exemplify, corporate school reform also encloses the collective *property* of the public school. In some cases the actual public school building is given to a private entity such as a charter school. More frequently, the contracting arrangements that districts do with for profit firms results in the extraction of surplus wealth, most often by decreasing teacher pay and skimming off profit by contractors and inflating administrator salaries. For Harvey, the problem of the commons is that unregulated individualized capital accumulation threatens to destroy the laborer and the land that are the two basic common property resources.

The promise of corporate school reform for its proponents is that it increases the effi-
ciency of the teacher-laborer through the enforcement of discipline (tighter controls over time, subject matter, and pedagogical methods) and that such efficiency increases the de-
livery of knowledge to the student-consumer, increasing, in turn, the potential economic efficiency of the future student-worker. The promise is false at every point. For example, chartering which has become captured by a corporate logic and much of it exists for profit ex-
traction, aims to replicate and scale up the most efficient delivery models, extend the teacher day, pay the teacher less, burn the teacher out, turnover the teacher workforce. All of these are proven effects of chartering and there is no doubt that these are good means of maximizing short term profit for for profit management companies and other contractors. The problem is not only, as a liberal like Darling-Hammond emphasizes, that these destructive reforms are bad for test-based student achievement.[18] More significant, these are means of worsening

16   David Harvey, "The Future of the Commons" *Radical History Review* (Winter 2011), p. 105.
17   David Harvey, "The Future of the Commons" *Radical History Review* (Winter 2011), p. 105.
18   See Linda Darling-Hammond *The Flat World and Education* New York: Teachers College Press 2010
for abundant empirical evidence as to the destructive effects of these anti-teacher policies on the "quality"
of teaching as measured by test outputs.

the creative, intellectual, curiosity-fostering, and critically engaged qualities of teaching and also worsening the future productive force of the students' labor.[19] But controlled, rigid, anti-critical teaching results not in subjects with a greater capacity for economic productivity but the opposite. If the goal is to produce docile, disciplined low-skill workers or marginalized people who are excluded from the economy altogether, then these corporate school reforms are right on target. However, ethics and politics aside, this is shortsighted as an economic strategy if as the corporate school reformers allege, the aim of public schooling is to produce future high-tech workers with knowledge of math and science and the creativity to create new projects and create new value. The dominant justification for corporate school reform is for the U.S. to develop its labor capacity in the high technology arena towards the end of winning global economic competition. Usually, proponents of the dominant justification call for encouraging students to develop their capacities for entrepreneurialism. It is difficult to see how eroding the capacity of teacher labor to inspire vigorous, creative thinking and intellectual curiosity could contribute to such a capitalist goal. The point not to be missed here is that even on its own bad terms of education for capitalist accumulation corporate school reform undermines it own aims. Enclosure of the public school through privatization does create short-term profit, turning kids into commodities and creating a new two-tiered system that is privatized at the bottom. But enclosure destroys the labor and resources of the public school—that is, it destroys the value of it by pillaging it as productive force. Perhaps the ultimate failure of corporate school reform is that it does nothing to challenge the historical reality of a two-tiered public education system that reproduces the labor force: the upper tier produces the professional class managers while the bottow tier reproduces the low-paid, low-skill workforce, hence the respective different emphases on critical thinking as problem solving in professional class schools and the emphasis on discipline and docility in working class and poor schools.

If we consider corporate school reform in terms of the recent literature on the commons, we can ask the question of how it helps us formulate a response to the problems posed by public school privatization in terms of economic control, political control, and cultural control. The issue at stake here is not whether privatization threatens critical, public, and democratic forms of education. We begin with assuming that as a given. Rather the question is, *How do critical forms of education create the conditions for collective labor towards collective benefit and how do private forms of education create the conditions for collective labor towards private benefit?*

Part of what is at stake in the privatization of schools is the diminishment of the public sphere. We should recognize that there are at least four clear ways that those committed to democratic education must understand how public control differs from private control. These differences in control are crucial for expanding the public schools as a common and resisting its enclosure.

---

19   By critically engaged I am referring not to critical thinking as problem-solving skills but rather critical in the tradition of critical pedagogy that takes up questions of knowledge in relation to broader power struggles, interests, and social structures.

1) Public versus private ownership and control: for-profit education companies are able to skim public tax money that would otherwise be reinvested in educational services and shunt it to investor profits. These profits take concrete form as the limousines, jet airplanes, and mansions that public tax money provides to rich investors. These profits also take symbolic form as they are used to hire public relations firms to influence parents, communities, and other investors to have faith in the company. This is a parasitical financial relationship that results in the management of the schools in ways that will maximize the potential profit for investors while cutting costs. This has tended to result in antiunionism, the reduction of education to the most measurable and replicable forms, assaults on teacher autonomy, and so on. There is no evidence that the draining of public wealth and its siphoning to capitalists has improved public education or that it is required for the improvement of public education. If the state is going to use privatization as a tool (as the advocates of the Third Way in the United Kingdom do), then it could exercise authoritative state action directly in ways that do not upwardly redistribute wealth or funnel such wealth into misrepresenting the effects of privatization. Moreover, such a redistribution over economic control shifts the collective control over the processes of teaching and learning to the owner or private manager of the privatized educational approach. It captures such educational labor and channels it towards profit making for owners in the short term and future exploitable capitalist labor relations in the long term.

2) Public versus private cultural politics: privatization affects the politics of the curriculum. A for-profit company and a nonprofit dependent on a private venture philanthropy (Gates, Broad, Walton) cannot have a critical curriculum that makes central, for example, the ways privatization threatens democratic values and ideals. While most public schools do not have wide-ranging critical curricula, the crucial issue is that some do, and most could. This is a matter of public struggle. Privatization forecloses such struggle by shifting control to private hands and framing out possibilities that are contrary to institutional and structural interests of corporations. The possibility of developing and expanding critical pedagogical practices are a major casualty of privatization. Democratic society requires citizens capable of debate, deliberation, dissent and the tools of intellectual engagement. Privatization fosters antidemocratic instrumental and transmission-oriented approaches to pedagogy such as standardized testing and standardization of curriculum. The privatization of mass media represents an important parallel to the privatization of public schooling with regard to cultural politics. For profit media disallows representations and questioning that runs counter to the institutional interests of corporations.[20] The corporate takeover of schooling means the overemphasis on standards and standardization, testing, and "accountability" that replicates a corporate logic in which measurable task performance and submission to authority become central. Intellectual curiosity, investigation, teacher autonomy, and critical pedagogy, not to mention critical theory, have no place in this view. "Critical" in this context means

---

20   See Edward Herman and Noam Chomsky *Manufacturing Consent* and the work of Robert W. McChesney such as *Rich Media, Poor Democracy*.

not merely problem-solving skills but also the skills and dispositions for criticizing how particular claims to truth secure particular forms of authority. Democratic forms of education enable critical forms of agency fostering political interpretation that can form the basis for collective social action. Critical curriculum and school models could provide the means for theorizing and acting to challenge the very labor exploitation to which schools such as these prepare students to submit.

3) Public versus private forms of publicity and privacy including secrecy and transparency. Private companies are able to keep much of what they do secret. EMOs and charters that straddle the line between public and private selectively reveal financial and performance data that would further their capacity to lure investors. Such manipulation is endemic to privatization schemes. Such secrecy represents a tactic on the part of privatizers to disallow collective control over school financing and budgets. The secrecy of privatization prevents collective educational labor for common benefit.

4) Public versus private forms of selfhood. Privatization produces social relations defined through capitalist reproduction that function pedagogically to instantiate habits of docility and submission to authority at odds with collective control, dialogue, debate, dissent and other public democratic practices. Privatization fosters individualization in part by encouraging everyone to understand education as a private service primarily about maximizing one's own capacity for competition. This runs counter to valuing public schooling for the benefit to all. A new common school movement can be involved with producing a new public person imbued with the capacity to recognize and value both the collective labor of social life and imagine ways of common benefit from such labor.

In both the neoliberal and liberal visions of schooling, the collective labor of teaching and learning aims for accommodation to the existing economic structure and political forms that foster it. This is an economic structure that individualizes benefit from such labor. The task ahead for the critical perspective is to imagine pedagogical practices, curriculum, and school organization that enact the global commons. How can critical pedagogy make central common labor for common benefit? What path should teachers and students take with communities in recovering control over the work of teaching and learning? How can the struggle against corporate school reform not simply demand limits on testing and a cessation to privatization in all its guises but also demand that public education be the basis for reimagining the economy in truly democratic forms, reimagining the political system and political action not beholden to purchased and commercialized elections, and reimaging the culture as a public rather than a private one.

Corporate school reform threatens the possibility for public schools to develop as places where knowledge, pedagogical authority, and experiences are taken up in relation to broader political, ethical, cultural, and material struggles informing competing claims to truth. While the battle for critical public schools and against privatization and other manifestations of neoliberalism are valuable struggles in themselves, they should also be viewed as an interim goal to what ought to be the broader goals of developing practices, modes of organizing and habits of social and self questioning that aim towards the redistribution of state and corporate power from elites to the public while expanding critical consciousness and a radically democratic ethos.

A new common school movement has an inevitably hopeful dimension to it. The common can be built and expanded (like it has been through the Occupy movement), and it can never be fully enclosed because there are parts of human experience that can't be turned into property and have to be held in common. Compassion, ideas, and the planet itself must be held in common.

A first step for educators and others committed to equality and justice to enact a new common school movement is to propagate some key "talking points" to transform public discourse about public education:

Talking Points

- Corporate school reform has failed.
- Charters, vouchers, privatization, educational management companies have failed. to come through on what they promised—namely, higher "student achievement" and lower costs.
- Corporate school reform worsens racial segregation.[21]
- Corporate school reform deepens inequality in educational resources.
- Corporate school reform introduces a new "audit culture" and "new market bureaucracy" that is expensive, misdirects educational resources, and promotes misery and inefficiency.
- Corporate school reform has no way of dealing with ecological crisis.
- Corporate school reform is linked to the values of an economic system designed to expand profit and consumerism over human values such as love, care, and common living.
- As the capitalist economy falters, why should control over education be handed over to business people?
- As the corporate sector realizes the limitations of corporate bureaucracy, why should schooling inherit what doesn't work for business?
- We need a new commitment to public education for public rather than corporate values.

Finally, a second step is to plan to occupy the Board of Education, the Commercial Club, Chicago Public Schools, suburban schools, and the schools being targeted for closure and privatization to teach in collective human values and disrupt corporate schooling. The public schools belong to the 99%. It is time to take them back.

21   Miron, G., Urschel, J. L., Mathis, W. J., & Tornquist, E. (2010). Schools without Diversity: Education-Management Organizations, Charter Schools and the Demographic Stratification of the American School-System. Boulder and Tempe: Education and the Public Interest Center & Education Policy Research Unit. Retrieved (2012) from http://epicpolicy.org/publication/schools-without-diversity.

PART II

CRITICAL TRANSFORMATIVE LEADERSHIP,
POLICY, AND REFORM

CHAPTER SIX

Effects on Inequality and Poverty Versus Teachers and Schooling on America's Youth[1]

David Berliner

WHAT DOES IT take to get politicians and the general public to abandon misleading ideas, such as "Anyone who tries can pull themselves up by the bootstraps," or that "Teachers are the most important factor in determining the achievement of our youth"? Many ordinary citizens and politicians believe these statements to be true, even though life and research informs us that such statements are usually not true.

Certainly people do pull themselves up by their bootstraps and teachers really do turn around the lives of some of their students, but these are more often exceptions, and not usually the rule. Similarly, while there are many overweight, hard-drinking, cigarette-smoking senior citizens, no one seriously uses these exceptions to the rule to suggest that it is perfectly all right to eat, drink, and smoke as much as one wants. Public policies about eating, drinking, and smoking are made on the basis of the general case, not the exceptions to those cases. This is not so in education.

For reasons that are hard to fathom, too many people believe that in education the exceptions are the rule. Presidents and politicians of both parties are quick to point out the wonderful but *occasional* story of a child's rise from poverty to success and riches. They also often proudly recite the heroic, remarkable, but *occasional* impact of a teacher or a school on a child. These stories of triumph by individuals who were born poor or of success by educators who changed the lives of their students are widely believed narratives about our land and people, celebrated in the press, on television, and in the movies. But in fact, these are simply myths that help us feel good to be American. These stories of success reflect real events, and thus they are certainly worth studying and celebrating so we might learn more about how they occur (cf. Casanova, 2010). But the *general* case is that poor people stay poor and that teachers and schools serving impoverished youth do not often succeed in changing the life chances for their students.

America's dirty little secret is that a large majority of poor kids attending schools that serve the poor are not going to have successful lives. Reality is not nearly as comforting as myths. Reality does not make us feel good. But the facts are clear. Most children born

1   Keynote address, Department of Educational Leadership, University of Massachusetts Dartmouth, November 15, 2012.

into the lower social classes will not make it out of that class, even when exposed to heroic educators. A simple statistic illustrates this point: In an age where college degrees are important for determining success in life, only 9 percent of low income children will obtain those degrees (Bailey and Dynarski, 2011). And that discouraging figure is based on data from before the recent recession that has hurt family income and resulted in large increases in college tuition. Thus, the current rate of college completion by low-income students is now probably lower than suggested by those data. Powerful social forces exist to constrain the lives led by the poor, and our nation pays an enormous price for not trying harder to ameliorate these conditions.

Because of our tendency to expect individuals to overcome their own handicaps and teachers to save the poor from stressful lives, we design social policies that are sure to fail since they are not based on reality. Our patently false ideas about the origins of success have become drivers of national educational policies. This ensures that our nation spends time and money on improvement programs that do not work consistently enough for most children and their families, while simultaneously wasting the good will of the public (Timar and Maxwell-Jolly, 2012). In the current policy environment we often end up alienating the youth and families we most want to help while simultaneously burdening teachers with demands for success that are beyond their capabilities.

Detailed in what follows is the role that inequality in wealth, and poverty, plays in determining many of the social outcomes that we value for our youth. It is hoped that our nations' social and educational policies can be made to work better if the myths we live by are understood to be just that, simple myths, and we learn instead to understand reality better.

A wrongheaded educational policy. Bipartisan congressional support in the US for the No Child Left Behind Act (NCLB), passed in 2001, demanded that every child in every public and charter school in the country be tested in grades 3 through 8, and grade 10. There were severe consequences for schools that did not improve rapidly. The high-stakes accountability program at the center of the policy was designed to get lazy students, teachers, and administrators to work harder. It targeted, in particular, those who attended and worked in schools with high concentrations of poor children. In this way it was believed that the achievement gap between poor students and those who were middle class and wealthy could be closed, as would the gaps in achievement that exist between black, Hispanic, American Indian, and white students. It has not worked. If there have been gains in achievement they have been slight, mostly in mathematics, but not as easily found in reading (see Amrein and Berliner, 2002; Smith, 2007; Lee, 2008; Chudowsky, Chudowsky, and Kober, 2009; Braun, Chapman, & Vezzu, 2010; Nichols, Glass, and Berliner, 2006, 2012). It may well be that the gains now seen are less than those occurring before the NCLB act was put into place. In fact, the prestigious and non-political National Research Council (2011) says clearly that the NCLB policy is a failure, and all the authors of chapters in a recently edited book offering alternative policies to NCLB reached the same conclusion (Timar and Maxwell-Jolly, 2012). Moreover, a plethora of negative side effects associated with high-stakes testing are now well documented (Nichols and Berliner, 2007; Ravitch, 2010).

By 2008–2009, after at least five years of high-stakes testing in all states, about 1/3 of all US schools failed to meet their targeted goals under NCLB (Dietz, 2010). Estimates in 2011 by the US secretary of education are that more than 80 percent of all US public schools will fail to reach their achievement targets in 2012 (Duncan, 2011), and almost every school in the nation will fail by 2014. And this widespread failure is with each state using their own testing instruments, setting their own passing rates, and demanding that their teachers prepare students assiduously. The federal government at the time this paper is being written is now quickly backing off the requirements of the failed NCLB act and granting waivers from its unreachable goals to those states willing to comply with other "reform" effort that also will not work. These other inadequate reforms required by the federal government include the forced adoption of the Common Core State Standards, using numerous assessments from prekindergarten to high school graduation that are linked to the Common Core and evaluating teachers on the basis of their students' test performance.

In addition, and long overdue, as this paper is being written a backlash against high-stakes testing from teachers, administrators, and parents has begun (see "Growing National Movement Against 'High Stakes' Testing," 2012). Still, most state legislatures, departments of education, and the federal Congress cling to the belief that if only we can get the assessment program right, we will fix what ails America's schools. They will not give up their beliefs in what is now acknowledged by the vast majority of educators and parents to be a failed policy.

Still further discouraging news for those who advocate testing as a way to reform schools comes from the PISA (the Programme for International Student Assessment). Nations with high-stakes testing have generally gone down in scores from 2000 to 2003 and then again to 2006. Finland, on the other hand, which has no high-stakes testing and an accountability system that relies on teacher judgment and school-level professionalism much more than tests, has shown growth over these three PISA administrations (Sahlberg, 2011).

Finland is often considered the highest achieving nation in the world. Their enviable position in world rankings of student achievement at age 15 has occurred with a minimum of testing and homework, a minimum of school hours per year, and a minimum of imposition on local schools by the central government (Sahlberg, 2011). Although we are constantly benchmarking American school performance against the Finns, we might be better served by benchmarking our school policies and social programs against theirs. For example, Finland's social policies result in a rate of children in poverty (living in families whose income is less than 50% of median income in the nation) that is estimated at well under 5 percent. In the US that rate is estimated at well over 20 percent!

The achievement gaps between blacks and whites, Hispanics and Anglos, the poor and the rich are hard to erase because the gap has only a little to do with what goes on in schools, and a lot to do with social and cultural factors that affect student performance (Berliner, 2006, 2009). Policy makers in Washington and state capitals throughout the US keep looking for a magic bullet that can be fired by school "reformers" to effect a cure for low achievement among the poor, English language learners, and among some minorities. It is, of course, mostly wasted effort if the major cause of school problems stems from social conditions beyond the control of the schools. The evidence is that such is the case.

Virtually every scholar of teaching and schooling knows that when the variance in student scores on achievement tests is examined along with the many potential factors that may have contributed to those test scores, school effects account for about 20 percent of the variation in achievement test scores, and teachers are only a part of that constellation of variables associated with "school." Other school variables such as peer group effects, quality of principal leadership, school finance, availability of counseling and special education services, number and variety of AP courses, turnover rates of teachers, and so forth also play an important role in student achievement. Teachers only account for a portion of the "school" effect, and the school effect itself is only modest in its impact on achievement.

On the other hand, out-of-school variables account for about 60 percent of the variance that can be accounted for in student achievement. In aggregate, such factors as family income; the neighborhood's sense of collective efficacy, violence rate, and average income; medical and dental care available and used; level of food insecurity; number of moves a family makes over the course of a child's school years; whether one parent or two parents are raising the child; provision of high-quality early education in the neighborhood; language spoken at home; and so forth, all substantially affect school achievement.

What is it that keeps politicians and others now castigating teachers and public schools from acknowledging this simple social science fact, a fact that is not in dispute: Outside-of-school factors are three times more powerful in affecting student achievement than are the inside-the-school factors (Berliner, 2009)? And why wouldn't that be so? Do the math! On average, by age 18, children and youth have spent about 10 percent of their lives in what we call schools, while spending around 90 percent of their lives in family and neighborhood. Thus, if families and neighborhoods are dysfunctional or toxic, their chance to influence youth is 9 times greater than the schools! So it seems foolish to continue trying to affect student achievement with the most popular contemporary educational policies, mostly oriented toward teachers and schools, while assiduously ignoring the power of the outside-of-school factors. Perhaps it is more than foolish. If one believes that doing the same thing over and over and getting no results is a reasonable definition of madness, then what we are doing is not merely foolish; it is also insane.

How Inequality of Income, and Poverty, Affects the Achievements of Our Youth

Few would expect there to be equality of achievement outcomes when inequality of income exists among families. The important question for each nation is the magnitude of the effect that social class has on test scores within countries. In the recent PISA test of reading achievement, socioeconomic variables (measured quite differently than is customarily done in the USA) explained about 17% of the variation in scores for the USA (OECD, 2010). But socioeconomic status explained less than 10 percent of the variance in outcomes in counties such as Norway, Japan, Finland, and Canada. Although in some nations a family's social class had a greater effect on tested achievement, it is also quite clear that in some nations the effects of familial social class on student school achievement are about half of what they are in the USA. Another way to look at this is to note that if a Finnish student's family moved up 1 standard deviation in social class on the PISA index, that student's score would rise 31 points on the PISA test, which has a mean of 500 and a standard deviation of 100. But if that same happy family circumstance occurred in the USA, the student's score would rise 42 points, indicating that social status has about 30 percent more of an effect on the test scores among American youth than in Finland.

The PISA data were also looked at for the percentage of children in a nation that came from disadvantaged backgrounds and still managed to score quite well on the test. That percent is over 80 percent in Hong Kong, over 50 percent in Korea, over 40 percent in Finland, but not even 30 percent in the US. Somehow other nations have designed policies affecting lower social class children and their families that result in a better chance for those youth to excel in school. The US appears to have social and educational polices and practices that end up limiting the numbers of poor youth who can excel on tests of academic ability.

How does this relation between poverty and achievement play out? If we broke up American public schools into five categories based on the percent of poor children in a school, as in Table 5.1, it is quite clear that America's youth score remarkably high if they are in schools where less than 10 percent of the children were eligible for free and reduced lunch. These data are from the international study of math and science trends completed in 2007. The data presented are fourth grade mathematics data but eighth-grade mathematics and science data at both the fourth and eighth grade, provide the same pattern (Gonzales, Williams, Jocelyn, Roey, Kastberg, and Brenwald, 2008). If this group of a few million students were a nation they would have scored the highest in the world on these tests of mathematics and science. Our youth also score quite high if they are in schools where between 10 and 24.9 percent of the children are poor. These two groups of youth, attending school where under 25 percent of the students come from impoverished families, total about 12 million students and their scores are exceeded by only four nations in the world (Aud, Hussar, Johnson, Kena, Roth, Manning, Wang, and Zhang, 2012).

Our youth perform well even if they attend schools where poverty rates of youth are between 25 and 49.9 percent. And these three groups of students total about 26 million students, over half of the US elementary and secondary public school population. It is quite clear that America's public school students achieve at high levels when they attend schools that are middle or upper middle class in composition. The staff and cultures of those schools, as well as the funding for those schools, appears adequate, overall, to give America all the academic talent it can use.

TABLE 5.1. SCHOOL LEVEL OF FAMILY POVERTY AND TIMSS SCORES,
WHERE THE US AVERAGE WAS 529 AND THE
INTERNATIONAL AVERAGE WAS 500 (GONZALES ET AL., 2008).

Percent of Students at a School whose Families are in Poverty

	Less than 10%	10% to 24.9%	25% to 49.9%	50% to 74.9%	More than 75%
Score on TIMSS	583	553	537	510	479

On the other hand, children and youth attending schools where over 50 percent of the children are in poverty, the two categories of schools with the highest percentage of children and youth in poverty, do not do nearly as well. In the schools with the poorest students in America, those where over 75 percent of the student body is eligible for free and reduced-price lunch, academic performance is not merely low, it is embarrassing. Almost 20 percent of American children and youth, about 9 million students, attend these schools. The lack of academic skills acquired by these students will surely determine their future lack of success, and pose a problem for our nation.

The schools that those students attend are also funded differently than the schools attended by students of wealthier parents. The political power of a neighborhood and local property tax rates have allowed for apartheid-light systems of schooling to develop in our country. For example, 48% of high poverty schools receive less money in their local school districts than do low poverty schools (Heuer and Stullich, 2011). Logic would suggest that the needs in the high poverty schools were greater, but the extant data shows that almost half of the high poverty schools were receiving less money than schools in the same district enrolling families exhibiting less family poverty.

Table 5.2 presents virtually the same pattern using a different international test, the PISA test of 2009 (Fleischman, Hopstock, Pelczar, and Shelly, 2010). When these 15-year-old American youth attend schools enrolling 10 percent or fewer of their classmates from poor families, achievement is well above average in reading, and the same pattern holds for science and mathematics. In fact, if this group of American youth were a nation, their reading scores would be the highest in the world! And if we add in the youth who attend schools where poverty levels range between 10 and 24.9 percent we have a total of about 26 million youth, constituting over half of all American public school children whose average score on the PISA test is exceeded by only two other developed countries. Given all the critiques of public education that exist, this is a remarkable achievement. But the students in schools where poverty rates exceed 75 percent score lower, much lower than their wealthier age-mates. In fact, their average scores are below every participating OECD country except Mexico.

TABLE 5.2. SCHOOL LEVEL OF FAMILY POVERTY AND PISA SCORES IN READING, WHERE THE US AVERAGE WAS 500 AND THE INTERNATIONAL AVERAGE WAS 493 (FLEISCHMAN ET AL., 2010).

	Percent of Students at a School Whose Families are in Poverty				
	Less than 10%	10% to 24.9%	25% to 49.9%	50% to 74.9%	More than 75%
Score on PISA	551	527	502	471	446

The pattern in these data is duplicated in Australia (Perry and McConnery, 2010). And this pattern is replicated in other OECD countries, though not always as dramatically. The pattern seen in our country and many non-OECD nations exists because of a hardening of class lines that, in turn, has been associated with the development of ghettos and hyperghettos to house the poor and minorities (Wacquant, 2002). The hardening of class lines results also in some overwhelmingly wealthy and white and enclaves. The neighborhood schools that serve these ghettos and hyperghettos are often highly homogenous. Currently, white students attend schools that are between 90 and 100 percent minority at a rate that is under 1 percent. But about 40 percent of both Hispanic and black students attend schools that are 90 to 100 percent minority (Orfield, 2009). A form of apartheid-light exists for these students and to a lesser but still too large an extent for Native Americans, as well.

The grouping of poor minorities into schools serving other poor minorities seems frequently to produce social and educational norms that are not conducive for high levels of school achievement. For example, recently radio station WBEZ in Chicago (WBEZ, 2010) reported that of 491 Illinois schools where the students are 90 percent poor and also 90 percent minority, only one school, a magnet school enrolling 200 students, was able to demonstrate that 90 percent of its students met or exceeded basic state standards. In most states "basic" is an acceptable, but not a very demanding standard to meet. Still, this school beat the odds that quite realistically can be computed to be about 491 to 1 in Illinois. Schools with the kinds of demographics these schools have rarely achieve high outcomes. Nevertheless, there is a wide spread and continuing myth in America that schools that are

90 percent minority and 90 percent poor can readily achieve 90 percent passing rates on state tests if only they had competent educators in those schools (cf. Reeves, 2000). This apparently can happen occasionally, as seems to be the case in Chicago, but like other educational myths, this is a rare phenomenon, not one that is commonplace.

The believers in the possibilities of "90/90/90," as it is called, are part of a "No Excuses" group of concerned citizens and educators who want to be sure that poverty is not used as an excuse for allowing schools that serve the poor to perform inadequately. But the "No Excuses" and the "90/90/90" advocates can themselves become excuse makers, allowing vast inequalities in income and high rates of poverty to define our society without questioning the morality and the economic implications of this condition. Ignoring the powerful and causal role of inequality and poverty on so many social outcomes that we value (see the following discussion), not merely school achievement, is easily as shameful as having educators use poverty as an excuse to limit what they do to help the students and families that their schools serve.

Our data on school performance and segregation by housing prices ought to be a source of embarrassment for our government, still among the richest in the world and constantly referring to its national commitment to equality of opportunity. Instead of facing the issues connected with poverty and housing policy, federal and state education policies are attempting to test more frequently; raise the quality of entering teachers; evaluate teachers on their test scores and fire the ones that have students who perform poorly; use incentives for students and teachers; allow untrained adults with college degrees to enter the profession; break teachers unions; and so forth. Some of these policies may help to improve education, but it is clear that the real issues are around neighborhood, family, and school poverty rates, predominantly associated with the lack of jobs that pay enough for people to live with some dignity. Correlated with employment and poverty issues are the problems emanating from a lack of health care, dental care, and care for vision; food insecurity; frequent household moves; high levels of single-parent homes; high levels of student absenteeism; family violence; low birth weight children; and so forth.

Another way to look at this is by interrogating data we already have. For example, if national poverty rates really are a causal factor in how youth perform on tests, then Finland, one of highest achieving nations in the world on PISA tests, with a childhood poverty rate of about 4 percent, might perform differently were it instead to have the US childhood poverty rate of about 22 percent. And what might happen if the US, instead of the appallingly high childhood poverty rate it currently has, instead, had the childhood poverty rate that Finland has? A bit of statistical modeling by Condron (2011) suggests that the Finnish score on mathematics would drop from a world leading 548 to a much more ordinary (and below the international average) score of 487. While the US below average score of 475 would rise to a score above the international average, a score of 509! A major reduction of poverty for America's youth might well improve America's schools more than all other current educational policies now in effect, and all those planned by the president and the Congress.

The Effects of Poverty and Inequality on Social Indicators

Poverty can exist without great inequalities, but in societies where inequalities are as great as in ours, poverty may appear to be worse to those that have little, perhaps because all around them are those that have so much more. So relative poverty, that is, poverty in the midst of great wealth, rather than poverty per se, may make the negative effects of poverty all that more powerful. This is a problem for the US because the US has the greatest level of inequality in income of any wealthy nation in the world (Wilkinson and Pickett, 2010). This hurts our nation in many ways. For example, when you create an index composed of a number of factors reflecting the health of a society, including such things as teenage birth rate, infant mortality rate, ability to achieve in life independent of family circumstances, crime rate, mental illness rate, longevity, PISA performance, and so forth, a powerful finding emerges. The level of inequality within a nation—not its wealth—strongly predicts poor performance on this index made up of a multitude of social outcomes! In the US this finding also holds across our 50 states: inequality within a state predicts a host of negative outcomes for the people of that state.

Indicator 1. Child well-being. As measured by UNESCO, children fare better in Finland, Norway, or Sweden, each of which has a low rate of inequality. But child well-being is in much shorter supply in England and the US, each of which has high rates of inequality (Wilkinson and Pickett, 2010). Schools, of course, suffer when children are not well taken care of. The problems associated with inequality and poverty arrive at school at about 5 years of age, and continue through graduation from high school, except for the approximately 25 percent of students who do not graduate on time, the majority of whom are poor and/or minority (Aud et al., 2012).

Indicator 2. Mental health. The prevalence of all types of mental illness is greater in more unequal countries, so the US with its high rate of inequality has more than double the rate of mental illness to deal with than does Japan, Germany, Spain, and Belgium. The latter countries each have relatively low rates of income inequality (Wilkinson and Pickett, 2010). How does this affect schools? The prevalence rate for severe mental illness is about 4 percent in the general population, but in poor neighborhoods it might be 8 percent or more, while in wealthier neighborhoods that rate might be about 2 percent. Imagine two public schools each with 500 youth enrolled, one in the wealthy suburbs and one in a poor section of an inner city. As in most public schools, administrators and teachers try to deal sympathetically with students' parents and families. The wealthier school has 10 mentally ill families and their children to deal with, while the school that serves the poorer neighborhood has 40 such families and children to deal with. And as noted, almost 50 percent of these schools get less money than do schools in their district that are serving the wealthier families. Thus, inequality and poverty, through problems associated with mental health, can easily overburden the faculty of schools that serve poor youth, making it harder to teach and to learn in such institutions.

Indicator 4. Illegal drug use. Illegal drug use is higher in countries with greater inequalities. And the USA is highest in inequality among wealthy nations. So rates of illegal drug use (opiates, cocaine, cannabis, ecstasy, and amphetamines) are dramatically higher than in the Northern European countries, where greater equality of income and lower rates of poverty exist (Wilkinson and Pickett, 2010). High-quality schooling in communities where illegal drugs are common among youth and their families is hard to accomplish. That is especially true when the commerce in the neighborhood the school serves is heavily dependent on drug sales. This occurs in many urban and rural communities where employment in decent paying jobs is unavailable.

Indicator 5 and Indicator 6. Infant and maternal mortality. The tragedy associated with infant mortality occurs much more frequently in more unequal countries than in more equal countries. Thus, the US has an infant mortality rate that is well over that of other countries that distribute wealth more evenly than we do (Wilkinson and Pickett, 2010). Recent data reveal that 40 countries have infant mortality rates lower than we do (Save the Children, 2011). American children are twice as likely as children in Finland, Greece, Iceland, Japan, Luxembourg, Norway, Slovenia, Singapore, or Sweden to die before reaching age five. A woman in the US is more than seven times as likely as a woman in Italy or Ireland to die from pregnancy-related causes. And an American woman's risk of maternal death is 15-fold that of a woman in Greece (Save the Children, 2011). The average overall American rate is much worse in poor states like Mississippi. And the rate of those tragedies are even higher still for African Americans and other poor people who live in states like Mississippi. Comparisons with other nations make it quite clear that our system of medical care is grossly deficient.

But here is the educational point: Maternal and Infant mortality rates, and low birth weights, are strongly correlated. Every low birth weight child has oxygen and brain bleeding problems that produce minor or major problems when they show up at school 5 years later. So inequality and poverty—particularly for African Americans—is affecting schooling though family tragedy associated with childhood deaths and through low birth weights that predict poor school performance.

Indicator 7. School dropouts. In the US if you scale states from those that are more equal in income distribution (for example, Utah, New Hampshire, Iowa) to those that are much more unequal in the distribution of income (for example, Louisiana, Alabama, Mississippi) a strong trend appears. Dropout rates are much higher in the more unequal states (Wilkinson and Pickett, 2010). Poverty and a lack of hope for a good future take its toll on youth in the more unequal states and they drop out of school at high rates. This costs our society a great deal of money through increased need for public assistance by these youth, the loss of tax revenues from their work, and the higher likelihood of their incarceration. Inequality and the poverty that accompany it take a terrible toll.

Indicator 8. Social mobility. Despite the facts, the US prides itself on being the nation where a person can be anything they want to be. But if that was ever true, and that is debatable, it is now less true than it has been. In reality, social mobility is greater in nations that have greater equality of income than our country does (Wilkinson and Pickett, 2010). We now know that the correlation of income between siblings in the Nordic countries is around .20, indicating that only about 4 percent of the variance in the incomes of siblings could be attributable to joint family influences. But in the US the correlation between the income of siblings is over .40, indicating that about 16 percent of the variance among incomes of siblings in the US is due to family (Jantti, Osterbacka, Raaum, Ericksson, and Bjorklund, 2002). These data support the thesis that the Nordic countries are much more meritocratic than the US.

Family, for good or bad, exerts four times the influence on income earned by siblings in the US than in the Nordic countries. Sibling income also provides evidence that class lines in the US are harder to overcome today than previously. Sibling incomes have grown quite a bit closer in the US over the last few decades, indicating that family resources (having them or not having them) play an increasing role in a child's success in life. Data inform us that only 6 percent of the children born into families in the lowest 20 percent of income (often about $25,000 a year or less) ever get into the top 20 percent in income (about $100,000 or more per year). Now, in the US, our parents are a greater determiner of our income in life than either our weight or our height. That is, your parents' station in life determines your station in life to a much greater degree than we ever thought. Despite our myths, it turns out that among the wealthy nations of the world, except for Great Britain, we have the lowest level of income mobility, that is, the highest rate of generational equality of income. (Noah, 2012). Income heritability is greater and economic mobility therefore lower in the US than in Denmark, Australia, Norway, Finland, Canada, Sweden, Germany, Spain and France. "Almost (arguably every) comparably developed nation for which we have data offers greater income mobility than the United States" (Noah, p. 35). Yet we are the nation with the most deeply ingrained myths about how we are a self made people!

Indicator 9. School achievement. At least one reason for this lack of movement in generational income is the increasingly unequal schooling provided to our nation's middle- and to our nation's lower-class children. Shaun Reardon (2011) has built a common metric for test data from the 1940s through to the mid-2000s. He convincingly shows that the gap in scores between youth whose families are in the 90th percentile in income and youth whose families are in the 10th percentile in income is now dramatically greater than it was. In the 1940s the gap between rich and poor youth (youth from families in the 90th percentile vs. youth from families in the 10th percentile in income) was about .6 of a standard deviation on achievement tests. This is a large difference, but still, the curves of achievement for poorer and richer youth overlap a great deal. Many poor students score higher than many rich students, and many rich students score lower than many poor students. But in recent times—the 2000s—the gap between youth from the 90th percentile and youth from the 10th percentile families has grown wider. Now the difference between children from these two kinds of families is about 1.25 standard deviations, with much less overlap between the two groups of young Americans. Since we live in a world where income and income stability are highly correlated with education, these data mean that more of the better-off children will succeed and more of the less-well-off youth will fail to make a good living. The rich are getting richer (in educational terms, which translates into annual salary), and the poor are getting poorer (in both educational opportunities and in the income that accompanies educational achievement). Our nation cannot stand as we know it for much longer if we allow this inequality in opportunity to continue.

Indicator 10. Teenage birth rate. Despite the fact that the birth rate for teens in the US is going down, we still have the highest teenage birth rate in the industrialized world. That is surely related to the strong relationship between income inequality in a society and teen pregnancy rates (Wilkinson and Pickett, 2010). The US has, by far, the highest level of inequality among wealthy nations. So, not surprisingly, the US also has by far the highest rate of teenage pregnancy. Poverty, the result of great inequality, plays a role in this, as demonstrated with some California data (Males, 2010). In Marin County, one of the wealthiest counties in America, with a poverty rate for whites in 2008 of about 4%, the teenage birth rate per thousand woman aged 15 to 19 was 2.2. In Tulare County, one of the poorest counties in the US, Hispanic teens had a poverty rate of about 41% in 2008, while the teenage birth rate was 77.2 per thousand woman aged 15 to 19. While that difference is astounding, among Tulare County black teens, with a similar poverty rate, the teenage birth rate was about 102 for woman between 15 and 19 years of age. Inequality and poverty are strongly associated with rate of teenage pregnancies.

But poverty has relationships with other characteristics of families, and among them is a higher rate for impoverished youth to experience abuse, domestic violence, and family strife during their childhood (Berliner, 2009). Girls who experience such events in childhood are much more likely to become pregnant as teenagers, and that risk increases with the number of adverse childhood experiences she has. This kind of family dysfunction in childhood has enduring and unfavorable health consequences for women during the adolescent years, childbearing years, and beyond. And this all ends up as social problems, because teenage pregnancy is not only hard on the mother; it is hard on the child, and it is also hard on the school that tries to serve them.

Indicator 11. Rates of imprisonment. Imprisonment rates are higher in countries with more unequal income distribution (Wilkinson and Pickett, 2010). The US, with its high rate of inequality, not only has, by far, the highest rate of imprisonment among the wealthy countries but also appears to have more prisoners per capita than almost every other country in the world. We punish harshly, and the poor and poor minorities are punished a lot more, and for longer times, than are their white and wealthier fellow citizens. Michelle Alexander (2010) vividly describes the new "Jim Crow" laws that incarcerate poor black youth at much higher rates than wealthy white students, even when the laws that were broken were identical. Human Rights Watch (2000, 2002) identifies the US as quite unique in its desire to punish and particularly to punish by social class. Their data show that in many states whites are more likely to violate drug laws than people of color, yet black men have been admitted to prison on drug charges at rates 20 to 50 times greater than those of white men. They found, as well, that Hispanics, Native Americans, and other people of color who are poor are incarcerated at rates far higher than their representation in the population.

For example, a decade ago in Connecticut, for every 11 white males incarcerated, there were 254 black men and 125 Hispanics, suggesting a strong bias in sentencing (Human Rights Watch, 2002). While some of these males were family men, and their imprisonment hurt their family, many of the poor and minority people incarcerated were woman and their imprisonment was much more likely to hurt their children's chances for success. In 15 states, black women were incarcerated at rates between 10 and 35 times greater than those of white women, while in eight states, Latinas were incarcerated at rates between four and seven times greater than those of white women. And if we hope that youthful offenders would be helped by sentencing to prison, we must wonder why six states incarcerated black youth under the age of 18 in adult facilities at rates between 12 and 25 times greater than those of white youth. Similarly, in four states, Hispanic youth under the age of 18 were incarcerated in adult facilities at rates between 7 and 17 times greater than those of white youth. In these states, particularly, rehabilitation and education seem not to be the goal of the state. Rather, the goal seems to be the development of a permanent criminal class for black and Latino youth. It is not far fetched to point out that in a nation with a large and growing private prison system, a permanent prison class ensures permanent profits!

As tragic as the biases seen in the ways US law is administered in many states, the after effects for incarceration may even be worse! That is because once released, former prisoners find it difficult or impossible to secure jobs, education, housing, and public assistance. And in many states, they cannot vote or serve on juries. Alexander (2110) rightly calls this situation as a permanent second-class citizen a new form of segregation. For the men and woman who hope to build better lives after incarceration, and especially for the children and youth in their families, family life after paying back society for their crimes seems much more difficult than it should be.

Policies for Improving Education and Income Equality

It is hard to argue against school reformers who want more rigorous course work, higher standards of student performance, the removal of poor teachers, greater accountability from teachers and schools, higher standards for teacher education, and so forth. I stand with them all! But in various forms and in various places all that has been tried, and the system has improved little—if at all. The current menu of reforms simply may not help education improve as long as we refuse to notice that public education is working fine for many of America's families and youth and that there is a common characteristic among families for whom the public schools are failing. That characteristic is poverty brought about through, and exacerbated by, great inequality in wealth. The good news is that this can be fixed.

First, of course, is through jobs that pay decently so people have the dignity of work and can provide for their children. To do that we need a fair wage, or a living wage, rather than a minimum wage. This would ensure that all workers could support themselves and their families at a reasonable level. The current minimum wage is set at $7.25 an hour and would net a full-time worker under $15,000 per year. That is not much in our present economic system. The U.S. government sets the poverty level at $22,050 for a family of four in most states. But for a family to live decently on $22,050 is almost impossible. At this writing, fair wages/living wages might well require more like $12.00 an hour in many communities. That would certainly raise the price for goods and services, but it would also greatly stimulate local economies and quite likely save in the costs for school and the justice system in the long run.

Our nation also needs higher taxes. You cannot have a commons, that is, you cannot have teachers and counselors, librarians and school nurses, athletics and technologically adequate schools, without resources to pay them. Nor can you have police and fire services, parks and forest service personnel, bridges and roads, transportation systems, medical care, service to the elderly and the disabled, and so forth, without taxes to pay for jobs in these areas. Schools, parks, health care, public support of transportation, police and fire protection, and so forth, are either basic rights that citizens in a democracy enjoy, or not. If the former, then government needs to employ directly or through private enterprise the people to provide those services. Either of those two strategies, government jobs or government support for private jobs that help to preserve the commons, requires revenue.

Despite the distortions in the press and the vociferous complaints by many of its citizens, the facts are clear: The US has an extremely low tax rate compared to any of the OECD countries, the wealthier countries of the world. Only two countries pay a lower rate of taxes relative to its gross domestic product, while 29 countries pay more in taxes, and countries like Denmark, Finland, France, Italy, Norway, and Sweden pay about 75% more in taxes than we do to support civic life (Citizens for Tax Justice, 2011). This provides the citizens of those countries such things as free preschools; medical, dental, and vision care; support for unemployed or single woman; no food insecurity among the poor; free college if you pass the entrance examination; and so forth.

Beyond the low tax rate the US also has many highly profitable corporations that pay *less* than nothing in taxes. That is, they not only pay no taxes; they also get rebates! Table 5.3 shows that much more tax revenue should be obtainable from US corporations if we would elect politicians who understand that the commons will disappear if corporations are not contributing to its maintenance.

Increased tax revenues could provide more public sector jobs to help both our nation and our schools do better. Some of the money raised for the betterment of the commons could be used for high-quality early childhood education for the children of poor families. Replicable research teaches us a near certain method to reduce the population of poor youth that end up in jail. That is reliably accomplished by providing poor children with access to high-quality early childhood education. Nobel laureate economist James

TABLE 5.3. CORPORATE PROFITS, TAXES PAID, AND REBATES OBTAINED
BETWEEN 2008–2010 (MCINTYRE, GARDNER, WILKINS, & PHILLIPS, 2011).

Corporation Name	Profits	Taxes Paid	Rebates Obtained
General Electric	$10,460,000,000	ZERO	$4,737,000,000
Verizon	$32,518,000,000	ZERO	$951,000,000
Boeing	$9,735,000,000	ZERO	$178,000,000
Wells Fargo	$49,370,000,000	ZERO	$681,000,000
Honeywell International	$4,903,000,000	ZERO	$34,000,000

Heckman studied the Perry Preschool program, in which children from poverty homes attended a high quality preschool. The effects of that program in adulthood are remarkable.

A high-quality preschool, of course, requires "up-front" tax dollars to be spent, but ultimately saves society billions of dollars. Heckman and colleagues (Heckman, Seong, Pinto, Savelyev, and Yavitz, 2010) showed a 7 percent to 10 percent per year return on investment based on increased school and career achievement of the youth who were in the program, as well as reduced costs in remedial education, health care, and avoidance of the criminal justice system. Similarly, the Chicago Child Parent Center Study (Reynolds, Temple, Robertson, and Mann, 2001) was estimated to return about $48,000 in benefits to the public, per child, from a half-day public school preschool for at-risk children. In the Chicago study, the participants, at age 20, were more likely to have finished high school—and were less likely to have been held back, to have needed remedial help, or to have been arrested. The estimated return on investment was about $7.00 for every dollar invested. In the current investment environment these are among the highest returns one can get. Sadly, however, America would rather ignore its poor youth and then punish them, rather than invest in them, despite the large cost savings to society in the long run!

Another policy proven to improve the achievement of poor youth is to provide small classes for them in the early grades. There is ample proof that this also saves society thousands of dollars in the long run, though it requires extra funding in the short run. Biddle and Berliner (2003) reviewed the famous randomized study of small class size in Tennessee, the Milwaukee STAR study, some reanalyses by economists of original research on class size, a meta-analysis, and review of classroom processes associated with lower class size and found that class sizes of 15 or 17 in the early grades has long-term effects on the life chances of youth who come from poverty homes and neighborhoods. Instead of firing teachers and raising class size, as we have done over the last few years because of the great recession, we should instead be adding teachers in the early grades to schools that serve the poor. Using those teachers to reduce class size for the poor will result in less special education need, greater high school completion rates, greater college attendance rates, less incarceration, and a more just society, at lower costs, over the long run.

Another policy with almost certain impact is the provision of summer educational opportunities that are both academic and cultural for poor youth (Cooper, Nye, Charlton, Lindsay, and Greathouse, 196). Youth of the middle class often gain in measured achievement over their summer school holiday. This is a function of the cultural and study opportunities that their parents arrange. Youth from the lower classes have fewer such opportunities, and so, as a group, they either do not gain in achievement or lose ground over the summer. Small investments of dollars can fix that, leading to better school achievement. This is why we need more money invested in the commons now, so our nation will be a more equitable one in the future.

Another educational reform policy, like imprisonment, is based on a punishment- oriented way of thinking, not a humane and research-based way of thinking. This is the policy to retain children in grade who are not performing at the level deemed appropriate. As this paper is being written about a dozen states have put new and highly coercive policies into effect, particularly to punish third graders not yet reading at the level desired. Although records are not very accurate, reasonable estimates are that our nation is currently failing to promote almost 500,000 students a year in grades 1 through 8. Thus, from kindergarten through eighth grade it is likely that about 10 percent of all public school students are left back at least once, a total of about 5 million children and youth. Research informs us that this policy is wrong for the overwhelming majority of the youth whom we do leave back. Research is quite clear that on average, students left back do not improve as much as do students who are allowed to advance to a higher grade with their age-mates. Furthermore, retention policies throughout the nation are biased against both boys and poor minority youth. Moreover, the retained students are likely to drop out of school at higher rates than do their academic peers who were advanced to the next grade.

Of course, mere advancement in grade does not solve the problem of poor academic performance by some of our nation's youth. But there is a better solution to that problem *at no more cost than retention*. Children not performing up to the expectations held for their age group can receive tutoring, both after school and in the summer. On average, the cost to a school district is somewhere about $10,000 per child per year to educate in grades K through 8. That $10,000 is the fiscal commitment made by a district or a state when it chooses to leave a child back to receive an additional year of schooling. That same amount of money could be better used for small-group and personal tutoring programs over a few years to help the struggling student to perform better. This is precisely the method used by wealthy parents of slow students to get their children to achieve well in school. As Dewey reminded us many years ago, what the best and wisest parents want for their children should be what we want for all children. Thus, that same kind of opportunity to catch up in school should not be denied youth who come from poorer families. And for the record, Finland, whose school system is so exceptional, shuns retention in grade. It retains only about 2 percent of its students, not 10 percent, using special education teachers to work with students who fall significantly behind their age-mates, ensuring that for most slow students there are chances to catch up with their classmates, without punishing them.

Other policies that would help the poor and reduce the inequities we see in society include reducing teacher "churn" in schools. Lower class children experience more of that, and it substantially harms their academic performance (Ronfeldt, Lankford, Loeb, and Wyckoff, 2011). Policies to help experienced teachers stay in schools with poorer students also need to be developed. New teachers rarely can match a veteran of five or more years in accomplishing all the objectives teachers are required to meet in contemporary schools.

A two-year visiting nurse service to new mothers who are poor costs over $11,000 per family serviced. But results 10 years later show that in comparison to matched families, both the mothers and the children who were visited were significantly better off in many ways, and the cost to the local community was $12,000 less for these children and families over those 10 years. Even greater benefits to the community are expected in the future (Olds et al., (2010). In essence, there is really no cost at all for a humane and effective program like this, but humaneness, *even when cost-effective*, seems noticeably lacking in many of our communities.

Related to the visiting nurse study is the high likelihood of success by providing wraparound services for youth in schools that serve poor families. Medical, dental, vision, nutrition, and psychological counseling, if not accessible by the families in a community, need to be provided so the children of the poor have a better chance of leaving poverty in adulthood. These programs have become increasingly of interest since both the social sciences and the neurosciences have now verified through studies of brain functioning and cognitive processing that the stress associated with extreme poverty reduces a child's ability to think well. Stress and academic problem-solving ability, and stress and working memory, correlate negatively. Thus, the cognitive skills of many poor youth are diminished, making life much harder for them and their teachers. The greater the physical and psychological stress experienced during childhood, the higher the likelihood that a child will not do well in school or in life. Noted earlier, however, is that the American media loves the story of the child from awful surroundings—war, famine, family violence, drug use, crime, and so forth—who grows to become a respected pillar of the community. But that is the exception not the rule! Educational and social policies need to be made on the basis of the general rule, not on the occasional exception, dramatic and nobel as that exception may be.

Adult programs also need to be part of schools so the school is part of its community: health clinics, job training, exercise rooms, community political meetings, technology access and training, libraries, and so forth—often help schools to help poor families. It is not good for children, their adult caretakers, or a school district if the public schools are seen as remote, alien, foreign, hostile, or anything other than a community resource. What seems evident is that America simply cannot test its way out of its educational problems. Our country has tried that and those policies and practices have failed. It is long past the time for other policies and practices to be tried, and as noted, some fine candidates exist.

Conclusion

During the great convergence in income, from World War II until about 1979, American wealth was more evenly spread and the economy hummed. With the great divergence in income, beginning in about 1979, and accelerating after that, American wealth became concentrated and many factors negatively affected the rate of employment. The result has been that despite our nations great wealth, inequality in income in the US is the greatest in the Western world. Sequelae to high levels of inequality are high levels of poverty. Certainly poverty should never be an excuse for schools to do little, *but poverty is a powerful explanation for why they cannot do much!*

Although school policies that help the poor are appropriate to recommend (preschool, summer programs, health care, and so forth), it is likely that those programs would be less needed or would have more powerful results were we to concentrate on getting people decent jobs and reducing inequality in income. Jobs allow families, single parents or otherwise, to take care of themselves and offer their children a more promising future. Too many people without jobs do bad things to themselves and to others. Literally, unemployment kills: the death rates for working men and woman increase significantly as unemployment increases (Garcy and Vagero, 2012). The death of adult caretakers obviously affects families, particularly children, in profound ways. Government promotion of decent paying jobs, and a low unemployment rate, is a goal around which both conservatives and liberals who care about the American education system ought to unite. That is the single best school reform strategy I can find.

But more than that, it is part of my thinking about rights we should expect as citizens of our country, in order that our country thrives. President Franklin Delano Roosevelt articulated these rights as he addressed the nation, shortly before he died (Roosevelt, 1944). His experience with both the great depression, the rise of fascism, and the second world war led him to offer Americans a second bill of rights that would help promote what was originally offered to Americans a century and half before—the right of our citizens to pursue happiness. Roosevelt said:

> We have come to a clear realization of the fact that true individual freedom cannot exist without economic security and independence. "Necessitous men are not free men." People who are hungry and out of a job are the stuff of which dictatorships are made. [It is now self evident that the American people have] The right to a useful and remunerative job . . . . The right to earn enough to provide adequate food and clothing and recreation; The

right of every family to a decent home; The right to adequate medical care and the opportunity to achieve and enjoy good health; The right to adequate protection from the economic fears of old age, sickness, accident, and un-employment; *The right to a good education.*

I think we need to fight as hard for our second bill of rights as we did for our first. Among the many reasons that might be so is that the performance of our students in our schools cannot be thought about without also thinking of the social and economic policies that characterize our nation. Besides the school policies noted earlier, and the need for decent jobs, if we had a housing policy that let poor and middle-income children mix in schools, that might be better than many other school improvement strategies designed specially to help the poor. This is a policy that works for Singapore, a nation with great inequalities in wealth and greater equalization of achievement outcomes between its richer and poorer students. If we had a bussing policy based on income, not race, so that no school had more than about 40 percent low-income children it might well improve the school's performance more other policies we have tried. This is the strategy imple-mented by Wake County, North Carolina, and it has improved the achievement of the poor in Raleigh, North Carolina, the county's major city, without subtracting from the achievements of its wealthier students (Grant, 2009). My point is that citizens calling for school reform without thinking about economic and social reforms are probably being foolish. Poverty is certainly not destiny, but maintaining impoverishment for so many does appear to be the policy of the US. Thus, the likelihood of affecting school achievement positively is more likely to be found in economic and social reforms, in the second bill of rights, than it is in NCLB, the Common Core standards, early childhood assessments, and the many assessments after that, value-added assessment of teachers, and the like. *More than educational policies are needed to improve education.*

I think everyone in the US, of any political party, understands that poverty hurts families and affects student performance at the schools their children attend. But the bigger problem for our political leaders and citizens to recognize is that inequality hurts everyone in society, the wealthy and the poor alike. History teaches us that when income inequalities are large, they are tolerated by the poor for only so long. Then there is an eruption, and it is often bloody! Both logic and research suggest that economic policies that reduce income inequality throughout the United States are quite likely to improve education a lot, but they have greater consequences than that. Such policies might once again establish this nation as a beacon on a hill and not merely a light that shines for some, but not for all, of our citizens.

References

Alexander, M. (2010). *The New Jim Crow: Mass incarceration in the age of colorblindness.* New York: The New Press.

Amrein, A. L. & Berliner, D. C. (2002, March 28). High-stakes testing, uncertainty, and student learning. *Education Policy Analysis Archives, 10*(18). Retrieved June 15, 2012, from http://epaa.asu.edu/epaa/v10n18/

Aud, S., Hussar, W., Johnson, F., Kena, G., Roth, E., Manning, E., Wang, X., & Zhang, J. (2012). *The condition of education 2012* (NCES 2012-045). Washington, DC: U.S. Department of Education, National Center for Education Statistics. Retrieved June 30, 2012, from http://nces.ed.gov/pubsearch

Bailey, M. J., & Dynarski, S. M. (2011, December). *Gains and gaps: Changing inequality in U.S. college entry and completion.* (Working Paper No. 17633). Cambridge, MA: National Bureau of Economic Research.

Berliner, D. C. (2006). Our impoverished view of educational reform. *Teachers College Record, 108*(6), 949–995. Retrieved June 24, 2012, from http://www.tcrecord.org/content.asp?-contentid=12106

Berliner, D. C. (2009). *Poverty and potential. Out-of-school factors and school success.* Boulder, CO, and Tempe, AZ: Education and the Public Interest Center, University of Colorado/ Education Policy Research Unit, Arizona State University. Retrieved June 10, 2012, from http://epicpolicy.org/publication/poverty-and-potential

Biddle, B. J., & Berliner, D. C. (2003). *What research says about unequal funding for schools in America.* San Francisco, CA: WestEd. Retrieved July 1, 2012 from http://www.wested.org/cs/we/view/rs/694

Braun, H., Chapman, L., & Vezzu, S. (2010). The Black–White achievement gap revisited. *Education Policy Analysis Archive, 18*(21). Retrieved June 14, 2012, from http://epaa.asu.edu/ojs/article/view/772

Casanova, U. (2010). *Si Se Puede!: Learning from a school that beats the odds.* New York: Teachers College Press.

Chudowsky, N., Chudowsky, V., & Kober, N. (2009). *State test score trends through 2007–2008: Are achievement gaps closing and is achievement rising for all?* Washington, DC: Center on Education Policy. Retrieved June 30, 2011, from http://www.cep-dc.org/index

Citizens for Tax Justice. (2011). U. S. is one of the least taxed developed countries. Retrieved July 2, 2012, from http://ctj.org/ctjreports/2011/06/us_one_of_the_least_taxed_developed_countries.php

Condron, D. J. (2011). Egalitarianism and educational outcomes: Compatible goals for affluent societies. *Educational Researcher, 40*(2), 47–55.

Cooper, H., Nye, B., Charlton, K., Lindsay, J., & Greathouse, S. (1996). The effects of summer vacation on achievement test scores: a narrative and meta-analytic review. *Review of Educational Research, 66* (3), 227- 268.

Dietz, S. (2010). *How many schools have not made adequate yearly progress under the No Child Left Behind Act?* Washington, DC: Center for Educational Policy. Retrieved June 24, 2010, from http://www.cep- dc.org/index.cfm?fuseaction=document_ext.showDocument-ByID&node ID=1&DocumentID=303

Duncan, A. (2011). *Winning the future with education: Responsibility, reform and results.* Oral testimony of US Secretary of Education Arne Duncan given to the US Congress, March 9, 2011. Retrieved June 20, 2011, from http://www.ed.gov/news/speeches/winning-future-education-responsibility- reform-and-results

Fleischman, H. L., Hopstock, P. J., Pelczar, M. P., & Shelley, B. E. (2010). *Highlights from PISA 2009: Performance of U.S. 15-year-old students in reading, mathematics, and science literacy in an international context* (NCES 2011-004). Washington, DC: U.S. Government Printing Office.

Garcy, A. M., & Vagero, D. (2012). The length of unemployment predicts mortality, differently in men and women, and by cause of death: A six year mortality follow-up of the Swedish 1992-1996 recession. *Social Science and Medicine, 74*(12), 1911–1920.

Gonzales, P., Williams, T., Jocelyn, L., Roey, S., Kastberg, D., & Brenwald, S. (2008). *Highlights From TIMSS 2007: Mathematics and science achievement of U.S. fourth- and eighth-grade students in an international context* (NCES 2009–001). Washington, DC: National Center for Education Statistics, Institute of Education Sciences, U.S. Department of Education.

Grant, G. (2009). *Hope and despair in the American city: Why there are no bad schools in Raleigh.* Cambridge, MA: Harvard University Press.

Growing national movement against "high stakes" testing. (2012). Retrieved, June 30, 2012, from https://www.youtube.com/watch?feature=player_embedded&v=gbdTheK9uqY

Heckman, J. J., Seong, H. M., Pinto, R., Savelyev, P. A., & Yavitz, A. (2010). The rate of return to the High/Scope Perry Preschool Program. *Journal of Public Economics, 94*(1–2), 114–128.

Huer, R., & Stullich, S. (2011). *Comparability of state and local expenditures among schools within districts: A report from the study of school-level expenditures.* Washington, DC: U.S. Department of Education, Office of Planning, Evaluation and Policy Development, Policy and Program Studies Service.

Human Rights Watch Reports. (2000). *United States punishment and prejudice: Racial disparities in the war on drugs* (Vol. 12, No. 2). Retrieved July 1, 2012, from http://www.unhcr.org/refworld/pdfid/3ae6a86f4.pdf

Human Rights Watch Reports. (2002). *Collateral casualties: Children of incarcerated drug offenders in New York* (Vol. 14, No. 3). Retrieved July 1, 2012, from http://www.hrw.org/sites/default/files/reports/USA0602.pdf

Jantti, M., Osterbacka, E., Raaum, O., Ericksson, Y., & Bjorklund, A. (2002). Brother correlations in earnings in Denmark, Finland, Norway and Sweden compared to the United States. *Journal of Population Economics, 15*(2), 757–772.

Lee, J. (2008). Is test driven accountability effective? Synthesizing the evidence from cross state causal-comparative and correlational studies. *Review of Educational Research, 78* (30), 608–644.

Males, M. (2010). *Teenage sex and pregnancy: Modern myths, unsexy realities.* Santa Barbara, CA: Praeger/ABC-CLIO

McIntyre, R. S., Gardner, M., Wilkins, R., & Phillips, R. (2011, November). *Corporate tax dodgers.* Washington, DC: A Joint Project of Citizens for Tax Justice & the Institute on Taxation and Economic Policy.

National Research Council. (2011). *Incentives and test-based accountability in education.* Washington, DC: The National Academies Press.

Nichols, S. L., & Berliner, D. C. (2007). *Collateral damage: How high-stakes testing corrupts America's schools.* Cambridge, MA: Harvard Education Press.

Nichols, S. L., Glass, G. V., & Berliner, D. C. (2006). High-stakes testing and student achievement: Does accountability pressure increase student learning? *Education Policy Analysis Archives, 14*(1). Retrieved June 25, 2012 from http://epaa.asu.edu/epaa/v14n1/

Nichols, S. L., Glass, G. V., & Berliner, D. C. (2012). High-stakes testing and student achievement: Updated analyses with NAEP data. *Education Policy Analysis Archives, 20* (20). Retrieved July 22, 2012, from http://epaa.asu.edu/epaa/v20n20/

Noah, T. (2012). *The great divergence.* New York: Bloomsbury press.

OECD (2010). *PISA 2009 results: Overcoming social background – Equity in learning opportunities and outcomes (Volume II).* Retrieved June 30, 2012, from http://dx.doi.org/10.1787/9789264091504-en

Olds, D. L., Kitzman, H. J., Cole, R. E., Hanks, C. A., Arcoleo, K. J., Anson, E. A., Luckey, D. W., Knudtson, M. D., Henderson, C. R., Bondey, J., & Stevenson, A. J. (2010). Enduring effects of prenatal and infancy home visiting by nurses on maternal life course and government spending: Follow-up of a randomized trial among children at age 12 years. *Archives of Pediatric Adolescent Medicine, 164*(5), 419–424.

Orfield, G. (2009). *Reviving the goal of an integrated society: A 21st century challenge.* Los Angeles: The Civil Rights Project/ Projecto Derechos Civiles, University of California at Los Angeles.

Perry, L. B., & McConney, A. (2010). Does the SES of the school matter? An examination of socioeconomic status and student achievement using PISA 2003. *Teachers College Record, 112*(4), 1137–1162.

Ravitch, D. (2010). *The death and life of the great American school system: how testing and choice are undermining education.* New York: Basic Books

Reardon, S. F. (2011). The widening academic achievement gap between the rich and the poor: New evidence and possible explanations In R. Murnane & G. Duncan (Eds.), *Whither opportunity? Rising inequality, schools and chidren's life chances.* New York: Russell Sage Foundation.

Reeves, D. B. (2000). *Accountability in action.*Lanham, MD: Advanced Learning Press.

Reynolds, A. J., Temple, J. A., Robertson, D. L., & Mann, E. A. (2001). *Age 21 cost-benefit analysis of the Title I Chicago Child-Parent Center Program, executive summary.* Retrieved June 30, 2012, from http://www.waisman.wisc.edu/cls/cbaexecsum4.html

Ronfeldt, M., Lankford, H., Loeb, S., & Wyckoff, J. (2011). *How teacher turnover harms student achievement* (Working paper 17176). Cambridge, MA: National Bureau of Economic Research. Retrieved, July 20, 2012, from http://www.nber.org/papers/w17176

Roosevelt, F. D. (1944). State of the nation address, January 11,1944. Retrieved July 30, 2012 from http://www.youtube.com/watch?v=3EZ5bx9AyI4

Sahlberg, P. (2011). *Finnish lessons: What can the world learn from educational change in Finland.* New York: Teachers College Press.

Save the Children. (2011). *State of the world's mothers 2011.* Westport, CT: Save the Children.

Smith, M. S. (2007, October 10). *NAEP 2007-What about NCLB?* Powerpoint presentation made by Marshall S. Smith at Berkeley, CA, cited with permission of the author.

Timar, T. B., & Maxwell-Jolly, J. (Eds.) (2012). *Narrowing the achievement gap: Perspectives and strategies for challenging times.* Cambridge, MA: Harvard Education Press.

Wacquant, L. (2002, April/May). Deadly symbiosis. *Boston Review, 27*(2). Retrieved July 30, 2012, from http://bostonreview.net/BR27.2/wacquant.html

WBEZ. (2010). Retrieved July 1 2012 from http://www.wbez.org/story/2010-report-card/high-poverty-high-scores

Wilkinson, R., & Pickett, K. (2010). *The spirit level: Why greater equality makes societies stronger.* London: Penguin.

CHAPTER SEVEN

Dominant Issues, Themes, and Prospects in the Education of Mexican Americans in the United States: An Overview[1]

Cori Salmerón & Ángela Valenzuela

Introduction

THIS LITERATURE REVIEW will focus on the experiences of K–12 public school students in the United States who identify as being of Latina/o origin. In particular, we will focus on the experience of Mexican origin students, beginning with a general portrait of Mexican Americans in the U.S. Then we move on to historical issues facing Mexican Americans, including the practice of subtractive schooling, the impact of the No Child Left Behind Act (NCLB), high-stakes testing, the history of bilingual education, misidentification in special education, the role of Latina/o teachers, and demographic realities that help illustrate how the education system generally fails to support Mexican and Mexican American students adequately. Second, we review opportunities that reflect Mexican Americans' growing political power. Such opportunities include the DREAM Act, pedagogical shifts that call upon teachers to draw on the resources that students bring to school, increased family engagement and advocacy, and a rethinking of bilingual education. We conclude with promising future prospects embodied in today's Mexican American movement for Ethnic Studies and a Grow Your Own educator movement both of which share an agenda for community empowerment.

Dominant Issues and Themes

Demographic Makeup: Mexican Americans and Latina/os in the United States

As of 2010, Latinas/os are the largest minority group in the United States (U.S. Census, 2011). In 2016, around 63% of people who identify as Latina/o were of Mexican origin and Puerto Ricans, the next largest group, comprised 9% of the population (Flores, 2017, p. 7). In addition to being the largest subgroup, Mexican Americans have deep historical roots

---

[1] Revised keynote address, Department of Educational Leadership, University of Massachusetts Dartmouth, November 22, 2013, at the Grand Reading Room, UMass Dartmouth.

in the United States, dating back to the period before 1848 when the American Southwest was a part of Mexico (San Miguel & Valencia, 1998). From mariachis to tacos, many of the cultural components that Americans associate with Latinas/os are actually Mexican. In addition, even Latino communities that do not identify as Mexican have adopted typical aspects of Mexican culture and have become "Mexicanized" (Gándara & Contreras, 2009). Going along with this idea, researchers often group Latinas/os together and do not identify the subgroups they are researching when they describe their participants as Latina/o. As a result, while Latinos exhibit a great deal of diversity, we can use the Mexican American experience as a way to examine the experiences of Latinos as a whole in the United States (Gándara & Contreras, 2009).

It is important to note that like the Latino experience, the Mexican American experience is not homogenous. The interchangeably used terms herein, namely, "Mexican American," "Mexican origin," and "U.S.-born Mexicans," refer to a diverse group that also includes recent immigrants. Many recent immigrants and some Mexican-origin youth get further referred to in policy as "English Language Learners" (ELLs). We prefer the term "bilingual learner" because it does not pit languages against each other. In the context of immigrant children, it is important to know that, according to the U.S. Supreme court decision in *Plyler v. Doe* (1982), all children in the United States are guaranteed a free public elementary and secondary education.

This review of the literature encompasses the experiences of Mexican-origin students living in the United States writ large that otherwise reflect an array of different generational statuses. That is, some are born in Mexico (first generation); others have one or more parents born in Mexico (second generation); and then there are those who were born along with their parents in the U.S. (third generation). Third- and later-generation youth emanate from families that have lived continuously in the United States for many generations and are predominantly English dominant (Krogstad & Gonzalez-Barrera, 2015). A final group, mostly first generation, is transnational, living alternately in two countries, the United States and Mexico (Salas, Jones, Perez, Fitchette, & Kissau, 2013).

Subtractive Schooling

Valenzuela (1999) contends that schools subtract value from the cultural capital that Mexican American students bring to school in two significant ways. First, schools are actively involved in the practice of "de-Mexicanization" which de-emphasizes and marginalizes students' languages, cultures, and community-based identities. This is significant because this systematic exclusion of students' cultures, languages, and identities impacts both their engagement in school and their academic achievement. A social effect of "de-Mexicanization," is that by assimilating or "whitewashing" U.S.-born, Mexican American youths' identities (Urrieta, 2016), schools undermine the possibility of connections forming between immigrant and U.S.-born Mexican youth. In this way, the youth are unable to access the social capital important to academic success that can potentially be found in these relationships (Coleman, 1988).

In addition to "de-Mexicanization," there is a misalignment between how Mexican American students view education and the prevailing view on education in that "teachers expect students to *care about* school in technical fashion before they *care for* them, while students expect teachers to *care for* them before they *care about* school" (Valenzuela, 2005, p. 83). These factors combine to create school environments that are unsupportive of the cultural and linguistic resources that Mexican American students bring to school, fostering a sense of estrangement from the dominant culture embodied in a school curriculum that is itself chauvinistic, privileging the histories, stories, and experiences of the dominant Anglo group in U.S. society. This situation is exacerbated by curricular impacts from the No Child Left Behind Act (NCLB), issues facing bilingual learners, and a dearth of Latina/o K–12 teachers.

NCLB and Every Student Succeeds Act (ESSA): Accountability, High-Stakes Testing, and the Narrowing of Curricula

The NCLB of 2001 ushered in a period of reform that is based on four main principals, accountability, state and district autonomy in their expenditure of federal education grants, school choice, and a focus on instructional practices and programs that the NCLB narrowly defines as effective by the standards of "scientifically-based research" (U.S. Department of Education [DOE], 2004). Although this may seem like a helpful framework for school reform, unfortunately mandated high-stakes tests, standardized testing, and school metrics to which they attach foster a rigid school environment that has particularly negative consequences on Latina/o youth (McNeil, 2000; McNeil & Valenzuela, 2001; Valenzuela, 2004). For example, the use of standardized test scores as the sole or primary indicator of a school's quality results in a harmful labeling of schools as "underperforming" when average scores fall below the cut scores. Such consequences range from narrowing the curriculum to aligning with high-stakes tests to intense district oversight of mandated changes to school closure (DOE, 2004).

Unfortunately, a disproportionate number of Latina/o students attend high-poverty schools that are often also labeled as "underperforming" (National Center for Education Statistics, 2017a). One reason that Latino/a students are more likely than Anglo majority students to attend high poverty schools is that according to a 2015 U.S. Census Bureau survey, the Latino/a poverty rate was 24%, in comparison to the 9% Anglo majority poverty rate (U.S. Census Bureau, 2016a). As a result, Latino/a students often attend schools where the pressure to raise test scores is acutely felt (McNeil, 2000; McNeil & Valenzuela, 2001; Valenzuela, 1999).

In many classrooms, the pressure to raise test scores is palpable in a shift to curriculum focused on teaching how to take a standardized test rather than teaching content (McNeil, 2000; McNeil & Valenzuela, 2001; Valenzuela, 2005). In part due to this excessive focus on test scores, little extra room exists for curriculum that builds on students' cultures, native languages, and community-based identities. A compounding factor is a dearth of books written about and by Latinas/os. For example, in 2016, out of a total 3,400 children's books published, 103 were written by Latinas/os and 169 were about Latinas/os (Cooperative Children's Book Center, 2016). Moreover, many schools across the nation have discontinued the teaching of multicultural education (also referred to as Ethnic Studies) courses (Fine et. al., 2007; Romero, 2010). In 2015, NCLB was replaced by the ESSA (DOE, 2017). Under ESSA many of the NCLB reforms were kept, albeit under the guise of putting the control of the reforms in the hands of the states with the high stakes accountability system under NCLB remaining largely in place (Texas Association of School Boards, 2017).

Bilingual Education

In 1968, the U.S. federal government passed the Bilingual Education Act (BEA). In its original form, it signaled a shift from assimilationist or "Americanization" goals of U.S. education and recognized the harm that children suffered under "English-only" policies in school (Ovando, 2003). Valenzuela (1999) distinguishes between additive and subtractive cultural assimilation to underscore the lack of a neutral ground in the schooling of U.S. Mexican youth. Schools are either adding or subtracting resources from youth through the very process of schooling, with the latter being the predominant mode.

Unfortunately, this period of support for bilingual education did not last long and starting in the 1980s, there was a growing public sentiment among non-Latinas/os against bilingual education (Santa Ana, 2002). For example, in 1981, President Reagan said, "It is absolutely wrong and against American concepts to have a bilingual education program that is now openly, admittedly dedicated to preserving their native language" (Crawford, 1999, p. 53). Another important event was the passage of Proposition 227 in California that stated that English should be the main language of instruction for language minority students (Santa Ana, 2002; Ovando, 2003). The backlash against bilingual education continued in 2002, with the passage of NCLB and the subsequent increased emphasis on high-stakes testing. The BEA was renamed, the English Language Acquisition, Language Enhancement, and Academic Achievement Act (Gándara, 2015). This name change reflects a change in the pedagogical approach towards bilingual education. The elimination of "bilingual" and the addition of terms like "English language" and "academic achievement" shows how the purpose of the bill is to increase English proficiency, and not develop bilingual or biliterate students, much less multilingual students. Another negative impact of NCLB was the symbolic conflation of the labels "English Language Learner" and "remedial student" (Collins, 2015).

Assimilation rather than bilingualism and biculturalism have been the goals of bilingual education programs historically. The goal of using the native language in order to transition students to English only rather than maintaining Spanish, and thusly developing competency in two languages, has been a pervasive practice and policy goal (Hernandez, 2017). Within this context, Latina/o, primarily Mexican immigrant bilingual learners face difficulties in school that are an artifact of poor teacher preparation in multiculturalism and bilingual learner instructional methods, and a dearth of support for frequently highly mobile families adjusting to a new community and schooling contexts (Good, Maseqicz, & Vogel, 2010).

Another problem facing bilingual learners is misidentification for special education (Scull & Winkler, 2011). Bilingual learners face both overrepresentation and underrepresentation in special education. In certain contexts, there is an overrepresentation of bilingual learners in special education that stems from biased assessments that rely on IQ deficit models and assessments that are not attuned to the needs of bilingual learners (García & Ortiz, 2006; Baca & Cervantes, 2004; Valdés & Figueroa, 1994). In other contexts, there is an underrepresentation of bilingual learners in special education that results largely from schools not distinguishing well between the needs of bilingual learners and students that have learning disabilities (Ovando, Combs, & Collier, 2006; Ramírez, 2005). Another layer of complexity regards students with specific learning disabilities who vary with respect to specific skills deficits (Pieters, Roeyers, Yves, Rosseel, Van Waelvelde, & Desoete, 2015). The pedagogical best practice is for each student to have an Individual Education Plan, which is also required by law (Individuals with Disabilities Education Act, 2004).

Increasing the pool of general education and special education Latina/o teachers who can help bridge the linguistic and cultural differences between students' home and school lives is coming into greater focus, particularly in light of research that observes the predictive power of racial and ethnic congruence between classroom teachers and students (e.g., Meier, Wrinkle, & Polinard, 1999).

Lack of Latina/o Teachers and Why This Matters

Latina/o students face a range of institutional obstacles and a final one we want to explore is the lack of Latina/o teachers. Research from the Schools and Staffing Survey 2011–12 data conducted by National Center for Education Statistics (NCES; 2012), shows wide racial and ethnic disparities in the teacher workforce. Anglo teachers represent 82.9% of all teachers in comparison to 7.1% of Latinas/os, 7.0% of African Americans, 1.9% of Asians, and .4% of American Indians. Making matters worse is a notable decline in the number of students pursuing teaching careers (Sutcher, Darling-Hammond, & Carver-Thomas, 2016).

A large and growing body of data point to the academic benefits of having a teacher from the students' racial and ethnic background (Dee, 2004; Egalite et al., 2015; Clewell, Puma, & McKay, 2001; Villegas & Lucas, 2004; Villegas & Irvine, 2009). For example, teachers who are Latina/o and have the experience of being classified as an ELL can draw on their cultural capital and possible shared experiences of oppression to connect with Latina/o students designated as ELLs in ways that Anglo, monolingual teachers are typically less able to (Lucero, 2010; Monzó & Rueda, 2001). For Mexican-origin students, generally, having teachers of their same ethnic background means a presence of role models in their lives, resulting in strong, positive correlations to higher academic achievement (Meier et al., 2001).

How Do These Practices Impact Students' Educations?

Subtractive schooling often produces students who are neither connected to Mexico and things Mexican nor prepared to be successful in majoritarian U.S. society. This is associated with their increased disengagement in school and lower graduation rates in comparison to their Anglo peers (Cabrera, Milem, Jaquette, & Marx, 2014; Valenzuela, 1999). In addition, the aforementioned narrow, high-stakes testing focused academic environment fostered by the NCLB Act (2001), coupled with struggles facing bilingual learners, and a dearth of Latina/o teachers have contributed to a situation where Latina/o students are not achieving at the same rate as the dominant Anglo group. In 2017, the NCES (2017b) reported that 9% of Latina/os aged 16 to 24 years old are not enrolled in school and have not earned a high school degree, in comparison to 5% of Anglos. While this prevailing gap is not encouraging, it is critical to put these numbers in context. The same study found that the number of Latina/os dropping out of high school went from 28% in 1996 to 9% in 2015. In comparison, the number of Anglo students dropping out stayed relatively the same, 7% to 5% over this same time period. The statistics for Mexican Americans mirror the numbers for Latina/os in general. In terms of preparation for college, a recent study published by the ACT and Excelencia in Education, found that almost half of the Latina/o high school graduates that took the ACT did not meet any of the ACT College Readiness Benchmarks (ACT & Excelencia in Education, 2015). Despite this disheartening statistic, it is important to note that the percentage of Latina/o students enrolling in college has increased from 35% in 1996 to 47% in 2016 (Gramlich, 2017). Unfortunately, Latina/os still obtain a four-year college degree at lower rates than other groups in the United States (Krogstad, 2016). One reason could for this could be because Latina/os are less likely to attend an academically selective university or to attend school full-time (Fry & Taylor, 2013). Looking at these statistics from a broad view shows us that while the education of Latina/os has been improving, there are still many changes to policy and practice that need to be made for them to reach parity with Anglos.

Prospects

Mexican Americans Growing Political Power

Mexicans in the United States are growing in their percentage of the population and, with this, political power (Wright, 2017). Higher college enrollment and college graduation rates not only reflect, but also suggest as much. In 2016, the total percentage of Latinos hit a record number at 18% of the national population and were the largest racial/ethnic group behind Anglos (U.S. Census, 2016b). This increase in shear number of Latina/os has also translated to increased political power. For example, in terms of educational leadership, for the first time in Texas, Latino superintendents lead four of the six largest school districts (Smith, 2016).

Another example of the growing political power of Latinos is the United We Dream immigrant, youth-led organization and the Dream Act movement. This organization is comprised of over 100,000 immigrant youth, allies, and 55 affiliate organizations in 26 states. It began to mobilize in the mid-2000s. Their original goal was to pass at act that would open up higher education access and a pathway for legal status for undocumented immigrant youth. While the Dream Act did not pass in 2012, they achieved a major success when President Obama declared that the Department of Homeland Security would allow temporary relief from deportation for eligible undocumented youth through the Deferred Action for Childhood Arrivals program (United We Dream, n.d.). In addition, eligible undocumented youth have access to higher education. Since this success, United We Dream has expanded its goal to include a pathway for citizenship for the 11 million families and communities of undocumented youth.

Family Engagement and Advocacy

Latina/o engagement has also increased in spaces that have traditionally been disparaging of many Latina/o students and families. Bourdieu argues that schools have historically served as institutions that privilege the cultural resources that upper class students and families bring to school (Bourdieu, 1977). "Upper class" is often a code word for Anglos. The act of privileging the cultural resources of "higher class" students maintains their higher class status by transforming their cultural resources to cultural capital. Lareau (1987) connects the ways that schools privilege certain cultural capital to how they privilege specific types of family engagement. Desired family engagement is based upon the norms of social elites and families who do not fit this category face being perceived as not being invested in their child's education (Lareau, 1987). In the context of this bleak portrayal of family engagement, it would seem that Latina/o families are doomed to not be accepted as legitimate actors in school communities because they often do not participate in ways that are deemed socially acceptable.

Fortunately, there is a growing body of scholarship to counter this traditional view of family involvement in schools. In this vein, there is a greater number of schools that recognize and build upon families' *funds of knowledge* (Moll, Amanti, Neff, & Gonzalez, 1992). Such schools understand that there are specific categories of knowledge that families share and that valuing this knowledge supports children's development. To learn about a family's *funds of knowledge*, schools must organize opportunities for families to share their cultural knowledge (Riojas-Cortez & Flores 2009). For example, Huerta and Riojas-Cortes (2011) studied a program intended to develop a deeper understanding of how multiple forms of literacy at home and school support the literacy development of young Mexican and Mexican American children. The program at the elementary school focused on literacy within the context of *cuentos tipicos* that are shared among families to teach children about the medicinal properties of specific herbs. In one part of the weeklong, parent–child program, parents, and their children came together to write about their knowledge of *remedios caseros*. In this experience, parental involvement was predicated on valuing the cultural knowledge that the parents brought to school. Huerta and Riojas (2011) found that as a result of this type of family engagement, parents, children, and leaders of the program developed a deeper appreciation for the families' home literacy practices. This is an important example of how family engagement is not solely a way to assimilate families into the school community but rather a way to enrich the school community.

In addition to family engagement being a way to integrate families' *funds of knowledge* into school, it is also a mechanism for families to advocate for what is best for their children and community. In this way it can turn the idea of school accountability upside down and approach it from a bottom-up, rather than a top-down, perspective (Johnson, 2011). One such example of this type of parental engagement is the Parent U-Turn Program (Johnson, 2011). This program was founded by three parents that participated in the University of California, Los Angeles Parent Curriculum Project.

The Parent U-Turn program is "an autonomous, multicultural, and nonprofit parent organization consisting of approximately 200 parents from South Los Angeles County cities" (Johnson, 2011, p. 148). They are focused on taking on roles as advocates for their children and breaking the stereotype of allegedly uninvolved, working class, families of color. The parents are involved in the schools in myriad ways. For example, parents are a part of the interview process for new teachers, members of the textbook selection committee, and elected to be a part of decision-making panels. In this way, parent engagement is not about getting parents to fit a mold of desired behavior or solely about gaining a deeper understanding of families' *funds of knowledge*. Rather, parents are seen as respected and active participants in their children's education.

Culturally Relevant Curriculum Reform

Schools and universities across the United States are taking up the idea that we need to adjust our curriculum to meet the needs of all students. This movement has many names; from multicultural education to critical pedagogy to culturally responsive pedagogy, to culturally relevant teaching. This movement is rooted in Freire's vision of critical pedagogy and Ladson-Billings's work on cultural relevant pedagogy (Freire, 1985; Ladson-Billings, 1995). A fresh articulation of this vision is conveyed by a national group of Latina/o educational scholars and community advocates, namely, the National Latino/a Education Research and Policy Project (or "NLERAP"; see Valenzuela, 2016, for a detailed explanation of this national-level effort). In particular, they call for reforms to higher education, teacher preparation programs to incorporate critical frameworks, topics, and themes germane to the Latino experience, and students of color, generally.

The NLERAP concurs with Ladson-Billings's definition of culturally relevant teaching as follows: "an ability to develop students academically, a willingness to nurture and support cultural competence, and the development of a sociopolitical or critical consciousness," (Ladson-Billings, 1995, p. 483). One example of a district enacting this type of teaching is Shannon's (2008) study of a progressive school district in the Northwest that primarily serves Mexican-origin students. It implemented a culturally relevant curriculum and transformed its late exit bilingual education program that was focused on transitioning students to English to a dual language program focused on developing bilingual and biliterate students. In this dual language program, English-dominant students and Spanish-dominant students learn both languages together. Shannon's (2008) larger point is that culturally relevant teaching and dual language programs should optimally go hand in hand.

On the other coast of the United States, the Education Department at the University of North Carolina at Charlotte is implementing a culturally relevant professional development program for public middle school teachers that primarily serve Mexican-origin students. Their professional development perspective incorporates the lived experiences of transnational students with a specific focus on the home–school relationships in order to promote constructive teacher-parent relationships. They focus on the importance of talking to students directly about their experience as Mexican-origin youth rather than talking about Latina/os, in general. The researchers found that this approach helps Mexican-origin students overcome stereotypes that hamper their progress in school (Salas et al., 2013).

In the Southwest of the United States, a local public library, university teacher preparation program, and a school district came together to start the Stories to Our Children Program (Rosado, Amaro-Jiménez, & Kieffer, 2015). The goal of this program is to support predominantly Mexican American parents to write culturally relevant literature about diverse groups of Mexican Americans living in the Southwest. This program serves the multiple purposes of drawing on parents' *funds of knowledge* and giving them an active role in school while also creating culturally relevant literature.

Finally, in addition to school districts implementing more culturally responsive teaching (CRT), research is also filling in the gap on how CRT relates to academic achievement outcomes. López (2016) looked at three schools in the Southwest with predominately Latina/o, Mexican American populations and examined the link between CRT as evidenced by teacher's beliefs and actions and students' identities and reading achievement. López (2016) found that the students had higher reading achievement when they had teachers who both valued students' *funds of knowledge* and possessed a critical awareness of how societal structures function to maintain social inequalities. Valenzuela (2016) similarly advocates not solely for more Mexican American teachers but for critically conscious ones, as well.

Bilingual Education Movement

While bilingual education has a tumultuous history in the United States, the problem is not with bilingual education, per se, but rather with the nation's complicated and racist history with language. There is a historically strong English-only movement that sees non-English languages as the root of educational and economic problems (Ruiz, 1984). Despite the prevalence of this view, the opposite is actually true. In terms of the pedagogical value of bilingual education, research shows that culturally responsive, additive bilingual instruction is helpful by simultaneously developing the student's native language and English language proficiency (Escamilla, 2006; Rao & Morales, 2015; Hornberger & Link, 2012). Research has also found that bilingualism has cognitive (Bialystok, 2009; Bialystok & Majumder 1998; Peal & Lambert, 1962), social (Cho, 2000), psychosocial (Colzato et al., 2008; Portes & Hao, 2002), and sociocultural benefits (Zhou & Bankston, 1998). In addition to these advantages, more recent research has shown that there are economic benefits to being bilingual (Callahan & Gándara, 2011). For example, research has shown that bilingual applicants have an advantage in the hiring process (Porras et al., 2014). Aside from the instrumental value of bilingualism, Mexican Americans and Latinos, generally, construe bilingual education as a civil and human right (Valenzuela, 2016).

Prospects

Most promising in the current policy and practice environment, particularly in Texas, California, New Mexico, Arizona, and Colorado—albeit to varying degrees across states and localities—is the presence of strong bilingual programs and a vision of coupling Ethnic Studies, bilingual or dual language education, and grow your own (GYO) educator programs. GYO programs establish pathways for the recruitment of future educators from the local community into higher education, teacher preparation settings. Upon graduation and armed with teaching degrees and credentials and a deep connection to their communities, they can return as teachers in the very schools and communities from which they emanate. Organizations like the NLERAP envision populating our nation's classrooms with community-based, culturally anchored GYO teachers that can establish a platform for growing the critically conscious administrators, school board members, and city and national leadership that the Mexican American community so desperately needs.

References

ACT. (2017). Hispanic students lag behind peers in college readiness. Retrieved from http://www.act.org/content/act/en/newsroom/hispanic-students-lag-behind-peers-in-college-readiness.html

ACT & Excelencia in Education. (2015). The condition of College & Career Readiness 2014 – Hispanic students. Retrieved from: http://www.edexcelencia.org/research/college-career-readiness-201

Bialystok, E. (2009). Bilingualism: The good, the bad, and the indifferent. *Bilingualism: Language and Cognition, 12*(1), 3–11.

Bialystok, E., & Majumder, S. (1998). The relationship between bilingualism and the development of cognitive processes in problem solving. *Applied Psycholinguistics, 19*(1), 69–85.

Bourdieu, P. (1977). Cultural reproduction and social reproduction. In J. Karabel & A. H. Halsey (Eds.), *Power and ideology in education* (pp. 487–511). Oxford: Oxford University Press.

Cabrera, N. L., Milem, J. F., Jaquette, O., & Marx, R. W. (2014). Missing the (student achievement) forest for all the (political) trees empiricism and the Mexican American Studies controversy in Tucson. *American Educational Research Journal, 51*(6), 1084–1118.

Cho, G. (2000). The role of heritage language in social interactions and relationships: Reflections from a language minority group. *Bilingual Research Journal, 24*(4), 369–384.

Clewell, B. C., Puma, M., & McKay, S. A. (2001). *Does it matter if my teacher looks like me? The impact of teacher race and ethnicity on student academic achievement.* New York: Ford Foundation.

Coleman, J. S. (1988). Social capital in the creation of human capital. *The American Journal of Sociology, 94*, 95–120.

Collins, J. (2015). Migration, language diversity and education policy: A contextualized analysis of inequality, risk and state effects. *Policy Futures in Education, 13*(5), 577–595.

Colzato, L. S., Bajo, M. T., van den Wildenberg, W., Paolieri, D., Nieuwenhuis, S., La Heij, W., & Hommel, B. (2008). How does bilingualism improve executive control? A comparison of active and reactive inhibition mechanisms. *Journal of Experimental Psychology. Learning, Memory, and Cognition, 34*(2), 302–312.

Cooperative Children's Book Center. (2016). Publishing statistics on children's books about people of color and First/Native Nations. Retrieved from https://ccbc.education.wisc.edu/books/pcstats.as

Crawford, J. (1989). *Bilingual education: history, politics, theory, and practice.* Trenton, NJ: Crane Publishing

Dee, T. S. (2004). Teachers, race, and student achievement in a randomized experiment. *Review of Economics and Statistics, 86*(1), 195–210.

Egalite, A. J., Kisida, B., & Winters, M. A. (2015). Representation in the classroom: The effect of own-race teachers on student achievement. *Economics of Education Review, 45*, 44–52.

Escamilla, K. (2006). Semilingualism applied to the literacy behaviors of Spanish-speaking emerging bilinguals: Bi-illiteracy or emerging biliteracy? *Teachers College Record, 108*(111), 2329–2353.

Fine, M., Jaffe-Walter, R., Pedraza, P., Futch, V., & Stoudt, B. (2007). Swimming: On oxygen, resistance, and possibility for immigrant youth under siege. *Anthropology and Education Quarterly, 38*(1), 76–96.

Flores, A. (2017). Facts on U.S. Latinos, 2015: Statistical portrait of Hispanics in the United States. Retrieved from: http://www.pewhispanic.org/2017/09/18/facts-on-u-s-latinos

Freire, P. (1985). *Pedagogy of the oppressed.* New York, NY: Continuum.

Fry, R., & Taylor, P. (2013). Immediate entry into college. Retrieved from http://www.pewhispanic.org/2013/05/09/ii-immediate-entry-into-college/

Gándara, P. C., & Contreras, F. (2009). *The Latino Education Crisis: The Consequences of Failed Social Policies.* Cambridge, MA: Harvard University Press.

Gándara, P. (2015). Charting the Relationship of English Learners and the ESEA: One Step Forward, Two Steps Back. *The Russell Sage Foundation Journal of the Social Sciences, 1*(3), 112–128.

García, S. B., & Ortiz, A. A. (2006). Preventing disproportionate representation: culturally and linguistically responsive prereferral interventions. *TEACHING Exceptional Children, 38*(4), 64–68.

Good, M. E., Masewicz, S., & Vogel, L. (2010). Latino English language learners: bridging achievement and cultural gaps between schools and families. *Journal of Latinos and Education, 9*(4), 321–339

Gramlich, J., (2017). Hispanic dropout rate hits new low, college enrollment at new high. Retrieved from http://www.pewresearch.org/fact-tank/2017/09/29/hispanic-dropout-rate-hits-new-low-college-enrollment-at-new-high/

Hernandez, S. J. (2017). Are they all language learners?: Educational labeling and raciolinguistic identifying in a California middle School dual language program. *CATESOL Journal, 29*(1), 133–154.

Hornberger, N. H., & Link, H. (2012). Translanguaging in today's classrooms: A biliteracy lens. *Theory into practice, 51*(4), 239–247.

Huerta, M. E. S., & Riojas-Cortez, M. (2011). Santo remedio: Latino parents & students foster literacy through a culturally relevant folk medicine event. *Linguistically Diverse Students and Their Families, 18*(2), 39–43.

Individuals with Disabilities Education Act, 20 U.S.C. § 1400 (2004).

Johnson, M. (2011). A parent advocate's vision of a 21st century model for bicultural parent engagement. In E.M. Olivos, O. Jiménez-Castellanos, & A.M. Ochoa (Eds.), *Bicultural parent engagement, advocacy, advocacy, and empowerment* (145–158). New York, NY: Teachers College Press.

Krogstad, J. M. (2016). 5 facts about Latinos and education. Retrieved from http://www.pewresearch.org/fact-tank/2016/07/28/5-facts-about-latinos-and-education/

Krogstad, J. M., & Gonzalez-Barrera, A. (2015, October 24). A majority of English-speaking Hispanics in the U.S. are bilingual. Retrieved from http://www.pewresearch.org/facttank/2015/03/24/a-majority-of-english-speaking-hispanics-in-the-u-s-are-bilingual/

Ladson-Billings, G. (1995). Toward a Theory of Culturally Relevant Pedagogy. *American Educational Research Journal, 32*(3), 465–491.

Lareau, A. (1987). Social class differences in family-school relationships: The importance of cultural capital. *Sociology of Education, 60*(2), 73–85.

López, F. A. (2016). Culturally responsive pedagogies in Arizona and Latino students' achievement. *Teachers College Record, 118*(5), 1–42.

Lucas, T., & Villegas, A. M. (2011). A Framework for preparing linguistically responsive teachers. In T. Lucas (Ed.), *Teacher preparation for linguistically diverse classrooms: A Resource for teacher educators* (pp. 55–72). New York, NY: Routledge.

Lucero, A. (2010). Dora's program: A constructively marginalized paraeducator and her developmental biliteracy program. *Anthropology & Education Quarterly, 41*(2), 126–143.

McNeil, L. (2000). Contradictions of school reform: Educational costs of standardized testing. New York, NY: Routledge.

McNeil, L., & Valenzuela, A. (2001). The harmful impact of the TAAS system of testing in Texas: Beneath the accountability rhetoric. In G. Orfield & M. Kornhaber (Eds.), *Raising standards or raising barriers? Inequality and high-stakes testing in public education* (pp. 127–150). New York, NY: Century Foundation Press.

Meier, K. J., Wrinkle, R. D., & Polinard, J. L. (1999). Representative bureaucracy and distributional equity: Addressing the hard question. *Journal of Politics, 61*(November), 1025–1039.

Monzó, L. D., & Rueda, R. S. (2001). Professional roles, caring, and ccaffolds: Latino teachers' and paraeducators' interactions with Latino students. *American Journal of Education, 109*(4), 438–471.

Morales, A. R., & Shroyer, M. G. (2016). Personal agency inspired by hardship: Bilingual Latinas as liberatory educators. *International Journal of Multicultural Education, 18*(3), 1–21

Moll, L. C., Amanti, C., Neff, D., & Gonzalez, N. (1992). Funds of knowledge for teaching: Using a qualitative approach to connect homes and classrooms. *Theory into Practice, 31*(2), 132–141.

National Center for Education Statistics. (2012). Schools and Staffing Survey (SASS). Retrieved from https://nces.ed.gov/surveys/sass/index.asp

National Center for Education Statistics. (2017a). The condition of education: Status dropout rates. Retrieved from https://nces.ed.gov/programs/coe/indicator_coj.asp

National Center for Education Statistics. (2017b). Concentration of public schools eligible for free or reduced-price lunch. Retrieved from https://nces.ed.gov/programs/coe/indicator_clb.asp

Ovando, C. J. (2003). Bilingual education in the United States: Historical development and current issues. *Bilingual Research Journal, 27*(1), 1–24.

Ovando, C. J., Combs, M. C., & Collier, V. P. (2006). *Bilingual and ESL classrooms: Teaching in multicultural contexts* (4th ed.). Boston: McGraw-Hill.

Peal, E., & Lambert, W. E. (1962). The relation of bilingualism to intelligence. *Psychological Monographs: General and Applied, 76*(27), 1.

Pieters, S., Roeyers, H., Yves Rosseel, Y., Van Waelvelde, H., & Desoete, A. (2015). Identifying subtypes among children with developmental coordination disorder and mathematical learning disabilities, using model-based clustering, *Journal of Learning Disabilities, 48*(1), 83–95.

Porras. D.A., Ee, J. & Gándara, P. (2014). Employer preferences: Do bilingual applicants and employees experience an advantage? In R.M. Callahan & P.C. Gándara (Eds.), *The bilingual advantage: Language, literacy, and the US labor market.* Tonawanda, NY: Multilingual Matters.

Portes, A., & Hao, L. (2002). The price of uniformity: language, family and personality adjustment in the immigrant second generation. *Ethnic and Racial Studies, 25*(6), 889–912.

Powers, J. M. (2014). From segregation to school finance: The legal context for language rights in the United States. *Review of Research in Education, 38*(1), 81–105.

Pyler v. Doe, (1982). 457 US 202.

Rao, A. B., & Morales, P. Z. (2015). Creating a climate for linguistically responsive instruction: The case for additive models. *Mid-Western Educational Researcher, 27*(4), 296–316.

Reardon, S.F., & Robinson, J.P. (2008). Patterns and trends in racial/ethnic and socioeconomic achievement gaps. In H.F. Ladd & E.B. Fiske (Eds.), *Handbook of research in education finance and policy* pp. 497–515. (New York, NY: Routledge.

Riojas-Cortez, M., & Flores, B. B. (2009). Sin olvidar a los padres: Families collaborating within school and university partnerships. *Journal of Latinos and Education, 8*(3), 231–239.

Romero, A. F. (2010). At war with the state in order to save the lives of our children: The battle to save ethnic studies in Arizona. *The Black Scholar, 40*(4), 7–15.

Rosado, L., Amaro-Jiménez, C., & Kieffer, I. (2015). Stories to our children: A program aimed at developing authentic and culturally relevant literature for Latina/o children. *School Community Journal, 25*(1), 73–93.

Ruiz, R. (1984). Orientations in language planning. NABE: *The Journal for the National Association of Bilingual Education, 8*(2), 1–23.

Salas, S., Jones, J. P., Perez, T., Fitchett, P. G., & Kissau, S. (2013). Habla con ellos—Talk to them: Latinas/os, achievement, and the middle grades. *Middle School Journal, 45*(1), 18–23.

San Miguel, Jr., G., & Valencia, R. (1998). From the Treaty of Guadalupe Hidalgo to Hopwood: The educational plight and struggle of Mexican Americans in the Southwest. *Harvard Educational Review, 68*(3), 353–413.

Santa Ana, O. (2002). *Brown tide rising: Metaphors of Latinos in contemporary American public discourse.* Austin: University of Texas Press.

Scull, J., & Winkler, A. M. (2011). *Shifting trends in special education*. Washington, DC: The Thomas B. Fordham Institute.

Shannon, S. M. (2008). Mexicans in the Pacific Northwest: Lessons from progressive school leaders for progressive educational policy. *Journal of Educational Research & Policy Studies, 8*(2), 16–40.

Smith, C. (2016, October 24). Latino superintendents lead the way in Texas' largest school districts. *Dallas News*. Retrieved from https://www.dallasnews.com/news/education/2016/10/24/latino-superintendents-lead-the-way

Sutcher, L., Darling-Hammond, L., & Carver-Thomas, D. (2016). *A coming crisis in teaching? Teacher supply, demand, and shortages in the US*. Washington, DC: Learning Policy Institute. Texas State Association of School Boards. (2017). Update on the Every Student Succeeds Act. Retrieved from https://www.tasb.org/Services/Legal-Services/TASB-School-Law-eSource/Governance/documents/update_on_essa.pdf

United We Dream. (n.d.). History. Retrieved from https://unitedwedream.org/about/history/

Urrieta, L. (2016). Colonial structures, identities, and schooling: My take on multicultural education and White supremacy. In F. E. Objakor & J. Martinez (Eds.), *Latin@ voices in multicultural education: From invisibility to visibility in higher education*. Hauppauge, NY: Nova Science Publishers.

U.S. Census (2011). 2010 Demographic Profile Data. Retrieved from: https://factfinder.census.gov/faces/tableservices/jsf/pages/productview.xhtml?pid=DEC_10_DP_DPDP1&src=ptU.S.

U.S. Census Bureau. (2016a). Income poverty and in the United States: 2015. Retrieved from https://www.census.gov/content/dam/Census/library/publications/2016/demo/p60-256.pdf

U.S. Census Bureau. (2016b). 2016 population estimates. Retrieved from https://www.census.gov/quickfacts/fact/table/US/PST045216

U.S. Department of Education. (2004). Four pillars of NCLB. Retrieved from https://ed.gov/nclb/overview/intro/4pillars.html

U.S. Department of Education. (2017). Every Student Succeeds Act (ESSA). Retrieved from https://www.ed.gov/esea

Valdés, G., & Figueroa, R. A. (1994). *Bilingualism and testing: A special case of bias*. Westport, CT: Ablex Publishing.

Valenzuela, A. (1999). Subtractive Schooling: U.S.–Mexican Youth and the Politics of Caring. Albany, NY: SUNY Press.

Valenzuela, A. (2004). *Leaving children behind: How "Texas-style" accountability fails Latino youth*. Albany: State University of New York Press.

Valenzuela, A. (2010). *Subtractive schooling: U.S.-Mexican youth and the politics of caring*. Albany: State University of New York Press.

Valenzuela, A. (2016). *Growing critically conscious teachers for Latina/o youth: A social justice curriculum for educators of Latina/o youth*. New York, NY: Teachers College Press.

Valenzuela, A. (2017). *Grow your own educator programs: A review of the literature with an emphasis on equity-based approaches*. San Antonio, TX: Intercultural Development Research Association.

Villegas, A. M., & Irvine, J. J. (2010). Diversifying the teaching force: An examination of major arguments. *The Urban Review, 42*(3), 175–192.

Wright, L. (2017, July 17). America's future is Texas. *The New Yorker*. Retrieved from https://www.newyorker.com/magazine/2017/07/10/americas-future-is-texas

Zhou, M., & Bankston, C. (1998). *Growing up American: How Vietnamese children adapt to life in the United States*. New York: Russell Sage Foundation.

CHAPTER EIGHT

Turn Around Schools:
Towards Authentic School Reform:
Eroding Authenticity and the Need for
Advocacy Leadership[1]

Gary Anderson

WE LIVE IN an increasingly inauthentic world. In 2005, the Department of Education got its hand slapped by the General Accounting Office (GAO) because it paid $186,000 to a public relations firm to produce favorable news coverage of President Bush's education policies. The GAO described the activities engaged in by the Bush administration as "covert propaganda." What did the Education Department get for the money it paid the public relations firm Ketchum, Inc.? According to a front-page *New York Times* story (Pear, 2005),

> The auditors denounced a prepackaged television story disseminated by the education department. The segment, a "video news release" narrated by a woman named Karen Ryan, said that President Bush's program for providing remedial instruction and tutoring to children 'gets an A-plus.' (p. A13)

The narrator ended the news video by saying, "In Washington, I'm Karen Ryan reporting," giving the unsuspecting public the impression that this was a network news report, not government-sponsored propaganda, paid for by taxpayer dollars.

In a blow to campaign finance reform and media authenticity, in June 25, 2007, the Supreme Court encouraged this kind of deception by upholding the right of corporations and unions to run phony "issue ads" that promoted a particular candidate's views or attacked another's. A previous decision in 2003, with a differently constituted court, had found that these issue ads were an attempt to circumvent the provisions of the McCain-Feingold Act that limits spending in federal campaigns. The day after the 2007 decision, the *New York Times* (2007, June 26) editorialized against the decision:

---

1   Keynote address, October 14, 2011, Department of Educational Leadership, University of Massachusetts Dartmouth.

> The 2003 ruling correctly found that the bogus issue ads were the functional equivalent of campaign ads and upheld the Congressional restrictions on corporate and union money. Yet the Roberts court shifted course in response to sham issue ads run on radio and TV by a group called Wisconsin Right to Life with major funding from corporations opposed to Senator Russell Feingold, the democrat who co-authored the act. (p. A24)

Rather than increase transparency, these politically motivated ads "purport to just educate voters about a policy issue, but are really aimed at a particular candidate" (*New York Times*, 2007, June 26, p. A24). Given the importance of media in our political lives, such decisions help to erode the authenticity of our political system. It is increasingly difficult for the average viewer to tell what looks like a public service ad or a news report from political indoctrination or propaganda.

The Iraq war provides a tragic list of inauthentic government sponsored hype: The famous aluminum tubes discovered in Iraq that were purportedly part of a program to build nuclear weapons, the media attention to Jessica Lynch's staged rescue, and all-American athlete Pat Tillman's heroic death, which we later learned was from friendly fire. As an examples of political spectacle produced by a co-dependent relationship between a government committed to deception and a compliant media, these may appear to be extreme examples of inauthentic behavior. However, they set the tone for the American public's increasing levels of cynicism toward American institutions.

There are many other signs of an erosion of authenticity in American society. In baseball, Barry Bonds, Sammy Sosa, and Mark McGuire blasted more home runs than legendary hitters like Babe Ruth, Roger Maris, and Hank Aaron, not merely through hard work or talent, but—as it turns out—through the aid of muscles bulked up by illegal steroids.

Disney movie sets used to imitate towns; now towns, like the town of Celebration in Florida, imitate Disney movie sets. Movies like the *Truman Show* spoof a social world increasingly saturated by phoniness and round-the-clock media, in which television "reality" shows appeal to a craving for some semblance of authentic life even if it isn't one's own. Meanwhile, private shopping malls have replaced the public square where shopping wasn't the only thing that brought citizens together.

In American schools, teachers feel pressured to teach to standardized tests and use scripted curricula mandated by non-educators and marketed by multinational corporations. Increasingly administrators are pressured to engage in impression management by playing fast and loose with data, and students join service clubs, less to serve than to build their resumes for college (Pope, 2001).

While it is easy to point to ways we live in an inauthentic world, it's also easy to assume that there was some golden age of authenticity in which things were as they seemed, in which word and deed were always in sync, in which impersonal and inane bureaucracies did not exist and in which democracy was not distorted by media spin doctors and monied interests. Examples of inauthenticity can be drawn from all historical periods. For instance, anyone who has followed Major League Baseball over the years knows that scandals are not new, nor is the Iraq war the first war that garnered support through deception and untruths.

And yet, we live in an age in which new technologies make it easier to distort, manipulate, and spin information (while at the same time providing possibilities for grassroots resistance). These same technologies and the corporate money and culture that has grown up around them, have also created a society in which flexibility, transiency and mobility are prized over stability and community (Sennett, 2006). The line from the old Carole King song, "Doesn't anybody stay in one place anymore," seems quaint in an age in which chat rooms, text messaging and email threaten to replace face-to-face communication—an age in which "brick and morter" institutions are moving into cyberspace. Ironically, most of us will not have to stay in one place anymore, because job, friends, and even family are now scattered across the country and can be accessed in cyberspace. While technology has saved millions of lives and made our daily lives more comfortable, it can also divorce people from reality. While a real war rages, many upper and middle-class young people spend hours a day fighting cyber wars on computers, only vaguely aware that their mostly poor and working-class peers are real soldiers, fighting a real war in Iraq and Afghanistan.

While the scope of inauthenticity in our society and institutions seems greater than ever, it is difficult to provide empirical evidence of such an elusive phenomenon. The search for an authentic self or human nature has long been a project of philosophers as distinct as Rousseau, Freud, Marx, and Kierkegaard. But we can, at least, say with some authority that authenticity has been a social theme for many during the second half of the 20th century, though sometimes for different reasons. David Riesman's *The Lonely Crowd* and William Whyte's *The Organization Man,* both books published in the mid 1950s, documented a new outer-directed, organizational way of life in post-war America that was replacing tradition and personal autonomy. Existential and Marxist accounts of alienation, particularly the work of Jean Paul Sartre was immensely popular during the 1960s as was J. D. Salinger's *The Catcher in the Rye* and Marcuse's *One Dimensional Man.* All expressed a concern with how to live an authentic life in a society becoming increasingly inauthentic.

Authenticity became a central theme of the 1960s' youth movement, in which many young people criticized what they perceived to be an inauthentic and even hypocritical society that failed to live up to its espoused values. Many youth, mostly middle class and suburban, pursued "authentic lifestyles" through an emphasis on being natural: less makeup for women, more informal dress, beards and long hair for men. Angela Davis's large "Afro," besides being a political symbol of Black power, became part of a quest for an authentic self. Authenticity also meant organic farming, a reconnection to the land, and a return to breastfeeding and herbal remedies, and in many cases breaking out of perceived repression and social constraints through free love and the use of drugs.

While the sons and daughters of ethnic, hyphenated Europeans were becoming "white," many African-Americans, Latinos, American Indians, and Asian-Americans were attempting to seek authenticity by recapturing a largely lost ethnic and cultural past. While postmodernists have critiqued the notion of authentic identities of any kind, there was a strong impulse in the counterculture movement to expose the incongruence between cherished ideals and modern realities, including historical racial, gender, and class oppressions.

The result of these political and cultural movements was that many individuals could lead more authentic lives. Spanish speakers were no longer punished for speaking the language of their parents. Gays and lesbians could more easily be themselves in public. The physically disabled were able to move about more easily. Many groups have achieved greater authenticity though social struggle. But as we have seen with movements like labor, the gains can be rolled back if citizens become complacent, and fail to protest those public and democratic spaces in which political redress can be obtained.

Today we continue to yearn for greater authenticity in our government, our organizations, our communities, and our relationships. Erosions to authentic democracy and community life are well documented by communitarians (Barber, 1984; Bellah, Madson, Sullivan, Swidler, and Tipton, 1985; Putnam, 2000) and philosophers (West, 2004). Movements for greater authenticity in education have occurred thoughout the 20th century. Perhaps the most important was led by John Dewey's call for experience-based, child-centered education that taught children to live in an *authentic* democracy, which he contrasted with *formal* democracy with its emphasis on voting. He wanted schools to create citizens that infused the notion of democratic participation into our everyday activities. While Dewey's progressive education became popular during the counter-culture movement of the 1960s, it was never as prevalent in public school classrooms as some believed (Goodlad, 1970).

But Dewey's (1929) call for authenticity transcended the classroom and the school. Writing in the late 1920s, a period much like our own, with giant disparities of wealth and the hegemony of a business culture, he warned that

> If we Americans manifest, as compared with those of other countries who have had the benefits of higher schooling, a kind of infantilism, it is because our own schooling so largely evades serious consideration of the deeper issues of social life: for it is only through induction into realities that mind can be matured. Consequently the effective education, that which really leaves a stamp on character and thought, is obtained when graduates come to take their part in the activities of an adult society which puts exaggerated emphasis on business and the result of business success. Such an education is at best extremely one-sided; it operates to create the specialized "business mind" and this, in turn, is manifested in leisure as well as in business itself. The one-sidedness is accentuated because of the tragic irrelevancy of prior schooling to the controlling realities of social life. There is little preparation to induce hearty resistance, discriminating criticism, or the vision or desire to direct economic forces in new channels.

Ultimately, it was not schooling, but a major economic depression and an organized labor movement that directed economic forces in new channels. Although schooling in America was widely expanded and facilities modernized throughout the 20th century, the essence of education and its lack of engagement with social reality has continued to the present. I quote Dewey at length, because he articulates many of the elements of authenticity I discuss later. As Dewey suggests, authenticity is multileveled. It can't exist unless it exists at all levels, the individual, the relational, and the societal. In many ways, Dewey anticipated Vygotsky's notion that the individual cannot exist outside of the social. If our social environment is impoverished then we are diminished as individuals and our social relationships are impoverished as well. Thus, education has to be linked to the realities of social life and the political controversies of the day. Lacking these connections, education becomes one-sided, in the sense that students are being prepared merely to be depoliticized, docile, and replaceable fodder for either the corporate workplace; the low-wage, service sector; or the military, which looms ever larger in American life.

Scholars on the political right and left, armed with empirical research, battle each other over how to close the achievement gap, without ever stopping to ask what it is rich and poor black and white students are actually learning. While closing the achievement gap is important as an equity issue, the test scores that are fought over represent a largely inauthentic education devoid of controversy, as testing and scripted curricula banish the last remnants of experiential learning and critical thought from the classroom. One thing that administrators and teachers know and that students quickly learn is what Dewey (1929) knew decades ago; that schooling in a business culture "evades serious consideration of the deeper issues of social life (p. 128) As a result, "there is little preparation to induce either hearty resistance, discriminating criticism, or the vision or desire to direct economic forces in new channels" (Dewey, 1929, p. 129).

Multiple Levels: Authentic Democracy, Authentic Relationships, and an Authentic Self

A library search for "authenticity" will net several specialized uses of the term ranging from linguistic authenticity to philosophical ruminations on the authentic life. For the purposes of this book, authenticity, at an *individual* level, is living a life—personal or professional—that is congruent with one's espoused values. It also assumes that constructing a self is a social process, best done through collective and interactive endeavors. Our identities are constructed in social institutions like families and organizations like schools. Schools, whether we were students in them or whether we work in them, rank only behind family and community in determining the kind of person we become.

In the realm of social *relationships*, authenticity has to do with viewing human beings as ends in themselves, rather than as means to other ends. Corporate CEO George Soros (1998) has observed that *transactions* have replaced *relationships* in human affairs. In schools, it means that the pedagogical relation, the interaction between teacher and student, is essentially a social relation that requires emotional commitment, caring, and a view that one's students deserve as high a quality education as one's own children receive. The current reality of middle-class teachers in low-income schools populated by children of color is a result of historical and continuing social segregation by class and race. Within these unacceptable social arrangements, authentic teaching is not likely unless a symbiotic relationship exists with local communities. Authenticity also means that democratic decision-making is not engaged in merely as a human relations strategy to raise productivity, however that is defined, but also because it respects others views and right to participate in making decisions that affect their lives.

At a *societal* level, it is a state of affairs that is congruent with the shared political and cultural values of a society. In a country with ideals of equal opportunity, we become less authentic to the extent that we become less equal. We become less authentic to the extent that we do not share in society's risks and responsibilities. Authenticity also requires engagement with society as educated and empowered citizens, not merely as consumers with choices. Adam Smith, who is often evoked as the father of market capitalism, was also a moral philosopher who argued that enlightened self-interest was acceptable and desirable in society, but mere greed was not. Collective survival, whether at the national or global level, requires a highly developed sense of the common good.

Given the tendency of individuals to pursue their self-interest, advocacy at all three levels is needed to ensure that the powerful do not oppress the powerless. This notion was written into our constitution by men who had fought the British monarchy and were obsessed with creating a nation in which formal power was dispersed through democratic principles. While their notion of democracy was limited to propertied white males at the time, the constitution and the amendments they wrote were subsequently used to gain rights for other groups. An authentic democracy requires leaders to uphold laws and policies against discrimination and to challenge those that discriminate—defending the powerless from the powerful is the essence of advocacy leadership.

Shifts at any one of these three levels of authenticity—individual, relational, societal—will tend to provoke shifts at other levels. This interconnectedness of authenticity and advocacy at different levels will form a framework I will use throughout the rest of the chapter. Attempts to understand authenticity in social institutions and human relationships cannot be successful unless all levels of society are taken into account. For educators, it means that high academic achievement is tied to what goes on in schools as well as outside of schools. It means that children who lack resources outside of school have as much right to those resources as children who lack resources inside schools. Few teachers or principals would knowingly withhold needed resources from a child in school. The same indignation should be felt for those same children when they are not provided adequate access to health care, food, or shelter outside of school. Authentic education cannot exist unless all children have access to basic social welfare. This will require more than indignation. It will require advocacy.

I'm not suggesting that principals need to lead broad social movements in their spare time. But, sometimes we underestimate the extent to which, in the aggregate, local actions evolve into social movements. The civil rights movement didn't begin in the 1950s. The ground work was laid decades before. Siddle Walker (2005) has documented how black teachers in Georgia in the early 20th century, who could not engage openly in activism under Jim Crow, nevertheless, prepared the ground for social change through their professional associations.

Ways of being an advocate are more obvious at the relational and organizational levels where unjust social arrangements can be challenged, but teachers and leaders have to be able to *see* injustice when it occurs. The elementary school tracking system I described elsewhere (Anderson, 2009) was hidden in plain sight. Nevertheless, the principal and teachers not only failed to address it, but in many instances collaborated with it. These are the times when an advocate leader can truly make a difference, as I was able to examine in another context (Anderson, 2009), but one thing is clear: To the extent that school leaders are not at least asking broader social questions and are buying into their role as scapegoat for society's ills, the status quo will march on with slight fluctuations in test scores. These slight fluctuations will be seized upon by reform advocates to make exaggerated claims of advocacy for low-income children.

The Demise of the Welfare State and the Emergence of the Competition State

The reason I have linked authenticity and advocacy is that historically advocates for social justice have too often engaged in forms of social engineering that have ended up creating inauthentic and even oppressive systems. Soviet-style state socialism was a noble social experiment but ended up creating inauthentic societies in which secrecy, political freedoms, and social trust were major casualties. In the U.S., we bulldozed neighborhoods and put up sterile housing projects in a misguided attempt to improve people's lives.

James C. Scott (1999), in *Seeing Like a State*, asks, "Why have large scale schemes to improve the human condition in the twentieth century so often gone awry?" Using examples like collectivist farming in the Soviet Union and the construction of Brasilia, the Brazilian capital, he argues that any large-scale social planning must take into consideration local practices, customs, and forms of knowledge. He points to what he calls the hubris of *authoritarian high modernism* in which planners think they are smarter than they actually are and that the public is stupider than they actually are. While he focuses on the role of states, he also points out that such planning hubris can also be executed by large corporations. As I have examined elsewhere (Anderson, 2009) throughout the twentieth century, the State has allied itself with corporations to such an extent that it becomes increasingly confusing to tell which is in control at any given point. In fact some have argued that global corporations have made the nation-state largely irrelevant.

Postmodern scholars take this further to argue that new forms of governance or *govern-mentalities* that focus on less visible forms of control through discourse, information, cognition, and spectacle have either replaced or supplanted traditional forms of governance (Lukes, 2005). I have also examined this issue in great detail elsewhere (Anderson, 2009) since today ideology is seldom spread through overt forms of propaganda, but rather through multiple ways of manufacturing consent.

One of the key reasons that NCLB and other business-led reforms are inadequate approaches to advocacy is that they exhibit this same hubris and were formulated and politically negotiated with little input form educators, students, and communities. In other words, they lack an understanding of local practices, customs, and forms of knowledge. So rather than build on forms of authentic practice, they destroy them. They fail to understand the larger social causes of inauthenticity in schools and the ways the policies themselves eviscerate social trust and contribute to inauthentic relations among principals, teachers, students, and communities.

Though we have embraced the notion that schools influence society, the fact is that schools are far more likely to reflect society. In order to engage in authentic advocacy, we first have to understand how our society and social institutions have become less authentic and why authenticity is harder to achieve in classrooms, schools, teachers' professional lives, and in our social lives generally.

Life at the End of the Welfare State

Americans have always believed in progress and the notion that one's children would live in a more humane, democratic, equitable and prosperous society than their parents. These beliefs were at the heart of the liberalism espoused by the first leaders of our republic. Americans have experienced cycles of economic recession and depression over the years, but social struggles leading to the New Deal policies of the Roosevelt administration in the 1940s led to a social safety net for citizens and a fairer distribution of risks and responsibilities among the population. Few Americans alive today remember a world without Social Security, low-interest mortgages, the G.I. bill, unemployment insurance, and employee contributions to pensions and health insurance. Many of these policies have been successful because they responded to demands of authentic grassroots movements.

Perhaps most important, after many years of a bloody labor movement, capital and labor came to a historic agreement. In exchange for management's acceptance of unions and higher wages, labor agreed to be more docile. Business and labor negotiated these agreements largely because of a more even balance of power between them but also because industry recognized that unless it paid workers better wages, there would be few people to purchase their products. This agreement, however, has slowly unraveled over the years as unions became more conservative and receded in size and influence and capital, responding to shareholder pressures went in search of lower wages. These trends became most notable during the 1970s, the decade most historians see as pivotal in our shift to globalization and neoliberal free market policies.

Nevertheless, those of us who lived during the post–World War II years, remember how New Deal policies led to upward social mobility for a large segment of the American working class. Now we are told that in a world of global competition, these hard-won social gains are too costly and must be given up. However, some of us remember that even before globalization became a buzzword, capital was doing what it always does when there is no countervailing force—seeking greater profit through paying lower wages.

I was born in LaPorte, Indiana, a small factory town between Gary and South Bend. For the working-class descendents of Polish, German, and Scandinavian immigrants there, the large Alice Chalmers plant and two other smaller factories made for a decent livelihood in the years after the Second World War. These were primarily union jobs that paid decent wages and included good benefits and pensions. I recall a solid working-class childhood in which most of my relatives worked in one or another of these factories, sent their children to public schools, were pro-union, and saw their lives and their children's lives improve.

Returning from World War II as a young man, my father bought a modest home with government low-interest loans made available to returning servicemen. Later, in his old age, his Social Security and pension made his life relatively comfortable. He was proud of his economic independence and spoke often of a time when old people who could no longer work either lived in poverty or at the mercy of family members. He ultimately became a staunch Democrat, but when I was a child, he was a supporter of Dwight Eisenhower. Eisenhower was a war hero and received the votes of most returning servicemen. Although he was a Republican, his politics were more liberal than most of today's Democrats, warning Americans of an incipient military-industrial complex that could amass inordinate power and usurp the power of a sovereign people.

In a period of a few years in the late 1950s all of the factories in LaPorte closed their doors. In those days, they did not move overseas; they merely moved to nonunion states. The factory where my father worked moved to a small town in Iowa. He was one of the lucky ones, as they were willing to transfer him there to help with the new factory. So he packed his family up and, like so many Americans in those years, we were uprooted from the supports of our communities and extended families. It was in that small Iowa town that I ultimately grew into adolescence.

When we arrived, Iowa was beginning the transition from the family farm to corporate agribusiness. Farmers could no longer survive on 150 acres, and their wives were forced into wage labor to pay the bills. The factory that employed my father moved there explicitly because they could pay women half of what they were paying men in LaPorte, and they knew the farmers' wives needed to work to save the family farm. Women, as is the case today with immigrants, were what Marx called the reserve army of labor that could be tapped to drive down wages. Today businesses use immigrant labor or seek cheaper labor overseas; in the 1950s they found cheaper labor among women and in nonunion states in the South and West.

In my Iowa high school, there were two groups: the townies and the farm kids. Among the townies, there were two sides of the track, those who were sons and daughters of local merchants and professionals and those who were sons and daughters of factory workers or those with more menial jobs. Among the farm kids, there were those few from relatively successful, large farms, and the rest from small, increasingly less viable farms. In school, I often found myself in classes with the sons and daughter of factory workers and small farmers. The higher track classes consisted largely of the more affluent town kids and kids from the more successful farms. Such was the social class tracking in rural schools.

I remember conversations with farm kids who talked endlessly of the advantages of one brand of tractor over another or the best time to plant corn. These were young men with a love of farming who opted for the agriculture curriculum instead of industrial arts or courses for the college-bound. (Their female equivalents were tracked into the secretarial curriculum.) When I returned to my hometown years later and ran into my old classmates who grew up on farms, I discovered that virtually none of them had gone into farming. Without the requisite courses to enter college, most were driving trucks or working at the local factory.

The demise of the family farm was not a natural phenomenon but was rather in part the result of social policies that subsidized agribusiness. Over the years, farm bills in the legislature have provided what Timothy Egan (2007) calls red state welfare:

> The Red State welfare program, also known as the farm subsidy system, showers most of its tax dollars on the richest farmers, often people with no dirt under their fingernails, at the expense of everybody else trying to work the land. (p. A23)

These agribusiness subsidies also affect the U.S. diet as they support large commodity crops like corn, soybeans, and wheat, the foundation for junk foods and obesity, instead of fruits and vegetables.

Meanwhile, back in LaPorte, where the large Allis Chalmers plant was now a vacant and rusting shell, my uncles and cousins were suffering massive unemployment. In and out of work over the years, many began to drink too much. Wives entered the workforce, not as liberated professionals but as pink-collar minimum-wage earners. The economic stress affected marriages; their kids got pregnant and began to drift off to Florida, California, or Texas; some dropped out of school to work to help support their families. Few went to any kind of postsecondary institution. My misfortune of not growing up with extended family was also my salvation, as my father had stable employment and my sister and I ended up going to college. For many working-class youth, academic and economic success is bought at the cost of alienation from one's family and community.

But in spite of the devastation of many local economies, America, in the decades after the war, was an upwardly mobile society, as more Americans attended college, started businesses, and enjoyed union protections. This began to change in the late 1970s, and by the decades of the 1980s and 1990s, two incomes per family replaced the family wage of the post war years. Union membership plummeted to its current private sector low of 7%. It should be mentioned, and will be discussed in more detail below, that this post-war period was not as kind to African-Americans (and, as we saw earlier, working-class women). In order to receive the benefits of the welfare state that whites took for granted, a civil rights struggle was necessary, resulting in legal barriers being removed for African-Americans. Once again social gains were the result of a social movement, not social engineering schemes like NCLB. In a tragic irony, at the point in which African-Americans were beginning to enjoy the fruits of the welfare state, it was beginning to be dismantled. The brunt of the shift from welfare state to neoliberal, competition state has been disproportionately born by African-Americans who had used welfare state institutions as their route to upward social mobility. Over the same period, massive immigration has helped drive down wages in the private service sector, where many African-Americans also had found work.

What the welfare state did, in all of its bureaucratic imperfection, was to try to bring some stability to peoples lives, lives that were exposed to the vagaries of cycles of boom and bust or the whim of factories that closed down and moved to where profits could be increased for the short-term profits of shareholders. In European social democracies, when industries such as textiles became unviable due to foreign competition, corporate CEOs, government representatives, and union leaders would sit down together to make a plan that would avoid the massive dislocations and misery that can accompany the closing a large factory. In such a situation, the Allis Chalmers plant in LaPorte might have been retooled into a more viable industry. In such a process, the CEO would negotiate for government subsidies to aid in the transition. The union would be at the table to look out for the workers' interests, and the government would represent the interests of the commonwealth. The savings to society of such collaboration would be significant in terms of mental health, alcoholism, divorce, unemployment insurance, and the tangible and intangible benefits of saving an intact community. It is social policies like these, not mere academic achievement, that provides the conditions for social advancement. Academic achievement improves as the lives of children, families, and communities improve, not the other way around, as human capital theory and NCLB implicitly argue.

Social Sources of Inauthenticity in U.S. Schooling

In the context of the U.S. (and many other countries that had developed welfare states), the economic and political break is most vividly seem as a move away form viewing the state as a direct provider of services to a regulator of nongovernmental organizations, increasingly profit-driven, that provide services. It has increasingly taken on the role that Milton Freidman and other so-called neoliberals proposed. The state has not so much retreated from the scene as changed its role to one of a security state and promoter of the private sector. The marketplace is the new mechanism though which values and resources are allocated, increasingly in both the private and public sectors. This monumental shift has enormous implications for how we think about our individual selves and our collective endeavor as a society. What does it mean to be an authentic person, professional, and advocate in this new context.

In the sections that follow, I discuss the following six areas in which these shifts have impacted authenticity at the individual, relational, and societal levels:

1) A shift in the primary goals of our educational system toward individual competition and away from individual enhancement or the common good

2) An increasingly segregated and unequal society in which levels of racial segregation and social class disparities are at historic highs, leading to greater inauthenticity as our espoused values fail to match our reality on the ground

3) A new neoliberal workplace culture that replaces stability with flexibility, long-term planning with short-term profit, and that makes living an authentic life more challenging

4) A shift to hyper-accountability systems that create an inauthentic, performance culture that results in greater levels of alienation and fabrication in the workplace

5) The use of political spectacle and misinformation to promote social policies, particularly as this relates to who controls the media

6) A tendency to replace democratic practices with market-driven choices and more generally an inappropriate translation of market and business principals to education in which the core work of educating diverse students is fundamentally different than the production of products or the delivery of other services

1) The Neoliberal Economy and the New Goals of Schooling

Educational historians have documented the multiple goals of public schooling over the years. The functions of our educational system have ranged from providing literacy to read the Bible and thus, save our souls, to the formation of human capital to enhance our competitiveness in a global economy. Along the way, it has served, among other goals, to "Americanize" millions of immigrants, transmit a common set of values, provide homemaking and vocational skills, and socialize the young into our political system.

Labaree (1997) has documented a contemporary shift in how Americans view the goals of schooling. Figure 8.1, adapted from Labaree's work, shows four goals for American schools from an economic and humanistic perspective and with a focus on the individual or the social. As a neoliberal economic model has become more dominant, humanistic goals for schools have receded in importance. Notions of education for *personal fulfillment and enhancement* is currently viewed as elitist by many and appropriate only for affluent children whose vocational concerns are viewed as less salient. Education for *democratic citizenship*, or what we once called "civics," has largely been displaced or replaced by the teaching of authoritarian forms of patriotism in history or JROTC classes. In many cases, especially when the country is at war, teaching the skills of public debate is viewed as risky and controversial in many schools (Westheimer, 2007). While one could argue that the humanistic goals of education were never dominant, the economic goals have undeniably become front and center in the wake of the ascendancy of Neoliberalism with its emphasis on the individual as human capital and its promotion of a competition state that has intensified competition among individuals.

FIGURE 8.1.

	Humanistic	Economic
Individual	Personal Fulfillment and Enhancement	Individual Self-Interest
Social	Democratic Citizenship	Social Efficiency

On the economic side, the goal of *social efficiency* and its link to education has become a rallying cry for school reform since the Soviet Union put Sputnik, the first satellite, into space. The link between schooling and the economy, again, came to the fore when the U.S. economy was perceived as falling behind that of Japan and Germany in the late 1970s (National Commission on Excellence in Education, 1983). More recently, a report of the new Commission on the Skills of the American Workforce, *Tough Choices or Tough Times,* makes a similar argument, replacing competition from Japan and Germany with competition from India and China. It is hard to find any commissioned report that doesn't include international comparisons of America's test scores, linking them to international competitiveness. America's public schools have been blamed during economic bust times, but seldom praised when the economy performs well. The school–economy link is tenuous at best (Levin, 1998), but it does provide a useful argument for the continued funding of public schools. Whether true or not, the rationale that we should provide resources to low-income schools to improve the economy appears to be a more powerful argument to the American public than one merely based on equity arguments.

Social efficiency as a goal of schooling is grounded in human capital theory, which argued that education was more than an expenditure; it was an investment in human capital with a return in increased productivity. The notion that what's good for business is good for America has always informed the social efficiency notion, and for a period of time from the 1930s though the 1960s, the national economic welfare was shared to a great extent among business, unions, and government agencies, ensuring that all would share in the benefits of a strong economy. Since the 1970s, unions have receded in power while business has increasingly gained what many consider inappropriate levels of influence in Washington. This has caused increases in productivity and profitability to be less evenly distributed among the general population.

Human capital theory and school-to-work programs continue to link schooling and economic growth, as well as argue that the "new" economy will produce a need for more highly skilled workers. What is becoming increasingly clearer is that the promise of an increase in demand for highly skilled workers in an information age society has not materialized largely because of automation and outsourcing. According to economist James K. Galbraith (1998),

> what the existing economy needs is a fairly small number of first-rate technical talents combined with a small superclass of managers and financiers, on top of a vast substructure of nominally literate and politically apathetic working people. (pp. 34–35)

So while social efficiency goals may not increase national productivity, or lead to better jobs, it has served as a way to make schools a scapegoat for national ills as well as a way for educators to argue for greater investment in education. In other words, regardless of who appropriates the human capital discourse, it has largely been used as a legitimating ritual for either supporting education funding or scapegoating schools when the economy performs poorly.

This leaves Labaree's fourth goal of schooling: *individual self-interest,* which he argues has become the central motivating force of Americans. But individual self-interest cannot serve as a national ideal to inspire young people and, while it was always a force in American society, it was tempered by larger ideals of democracy and equity. In a world in which students in elementary school are already building resumes for college, education has become "doing school, where they learn a hidden curriculum that includes manipulating the system, lying, sucking up, and doing whatever else it takes to keep a high grade point average" (Pope, 2001, p. 4). As these students take their places as leaders in the neoliberal, competition state, they will find little incentive to change their behaviors.

A similar phenomenon is modeled by middle- and upper class parents. The loss of a sense of the common good has resulted in a growing dissociation between the well-being of one's own and other people's children. It may well be natural that parents should make the welfare of their own children their primary concern. Every parent wants the best for their child. What we are witnessing however is a shift in which parents aren't simply demanding schools provide a quality education for their children. Instead, they are demanding that schools provide their children with more than other children are getting (Kohn, 2000). While upper class parents have always been able to buy a superior education for their children, an economically squeezed middle class are left to fight each other and the working class for privileges for their children.

While academic tracking may well be in part due to a belief that students at the same level are best taught together, McGrath and Kurillof (1999) found that many middle-class parents are adamant that their children not be mixed in with other people's children, unless those children are at similar academic levels. Because academic level tends to correlate so closely with socioeconomic level and race, it is often hard to sort out the real concerns. Regardless of whether middle-class parents are classist, racist, or simply want their child to be competitive in the job market, the result is a society segregated by class and race, even when kids spend the day in the same school.

A society in which individual self-interest becomes a dominant goal, cannot also claim to truly support goals of social equality. The two have to be in balance. Because race is so often absent from discussions of neoliberalism and education, I want to make the link between the two as clearly as possible. We now know that racism is not merely an attitude; it is structured into the very fabric of American society. To take New York City as an example, the creation of white suburbs during the 1950s and 1960s had dire consequences for people of color in the city. Because African-Americans were excluded from many welfare state benefits, including affordable, low-interest suburban housing, they remained in the city as white New Yorkers moved to the suburbs. Not only did this increase racial segregation, but it also meant that homeownership and its economic benefits were out of reach for African-Americans who remained as renters in the city. After the civil rights movement helped to remove these formal obstacles, African-Americans began to move to the suburbs only to find more white flight from their neighborhoods and a consequent lack of appreciation in the price of their homes. Meanwhile manufacturing also left the city for the suburbs and the flight of higher income residents from New York City sapped the tax base, leading to fiscal austerity, the deterioration of the city's public schools and the depletion of public health programs during the 1970s.

"The new white suburban communities could now use their political influence and tax base to develop good jobs, good schools, and public services, high-end stores, and rising property values without the use of legal racial barriers. The result was the creation of a new and powerful cycle of privilege" (Barlow, 2003, p. 41).

In the wake of this structured racism, it no longer was necessary for whites to appeal to a Jim Crow–like legal and state apparatus. Given the inherently unfair competition, it was possible to defend racial privilege merely by appealing to local control of schools, and "neutral," meritocratic practices like high stakes standardized test scores.

Parents know that education is an important economic investment for their children, since attendance at prestigious colleges and universities is the price of admission to high status and high-paying jobs. This has always been understood by the wealthy, but the American middle class has increasingly entered the competition. Barlow (2003) provides an explanation for why individual self-interest has become such a central goal of the middle class and its implications for race. He argues that the growing inequality that neoliberalism has created has produced an American middle class who are seeing their standard of living decline. This decline is not so much because of falling incomes—though they are working more hours to maintain them—but rather the rising cost of housing, college tuition, and health care. As they experience downward pressures, job insecurity, and high levels of debt, they mobilize

whatever social and cultural resources they have. This has created greater opposition to policies like affirmative action, along with a growing anti-immigrant sentiment. During times
when the middle class feel relatively secure, they will support social welfare policies and racial
equality, but in times of insecurity and fear, they embrace more narrow policies that reflect
their individual self-interest.

The goals of schooling, then, seem to be shifting under the competition state to a
greater emphasis on the maximization of individual advantage for one's own children.
The ripple effect of this shift is a pulling back from policies that benefit the common
good and toward policies that allow the middle-upper classes to cash in their relative
advantage in economic, social, and cultural capital.

2) Racial Segregation and Class Disparities at Historic Highs

In the movie *Grand Canyon*, Mack, a white middle-class protagonist takes a wrong
turn and gets lost at night in South Central Los Angeles. He is rescued from a mugging
by Simon, an African-American auto mechanic who lives in the neighborhood. Mack,
days later, is drawn back to Simon, with whom he shared a fleeting but profound experience of solidarity. These two protagonists would otherwise never have occasion to
meet in segregated Los Angeles. The movie is an exploration of the grand canyon of
social distances we have created across racial and social class lines, and it is this divide
that is played out daily in schools, either through the creation of within school barriers
or the absence of human diversity of any kind in many schools. The U.S. is certainly not
the only country in the world experiencing such problems. In fact, some countries have
dissolved into class warfare and ethnic cleansing. My point is not to single the U.S. out
as much as it is to call attention to how far our social reality has strayed from out social
ideals, and how our social policies have contributed to this distance.

The late Christopher Lasch, in *The Revolt of the Elites,* describes an America in which
professional and corporate elites seldom have any reason to have a conversation with
auto mechanics unless they are working on their car. He saw this increasing social segregation by class and race as a betrayal of American democracy. Like Mack, from *Grand
Canyon,* most Americans have a deep-seated desire to live in an equitable and racially integrated society. The reality, however is quite different and getting worse. There are many
books and articles that document in copious detail the growing economic inequalities
and racial resegregation of American society, so I will spare the reader pages of charts
and graphs. Suffice it to say that whether one measures income or wealth (income plus
assets), differences between the haves and have-nots are greater than at any time since
the 1920s, the decade before the Great Depression. The central fallacy of the No Child
Left Behind Act is the notion that we can improve the lives of children in schools without
recourse to social policies that address the massive reallocation of wealth away from poor
children and their families.

Robert Reich, in his influential 1991 book, *The Work of Nations: Preparing Ourselves
for 21st Century Capitalism*, argued that a new class of Americans was emerging that

he called "symbolic analysts." These highly paid professionals and executives and their families are a product of our new high-tech information society and represent roughly one fifth of the working population. Often working as consultants, engineers, lawyers, bankers, real estate developers, systems analysts, entertainment professionals, and advertising executives, they increasingly intermarry and see themselves as a group apart. They share social networks, friendships, and neighborhoods, and their incomes allow them to purchase other people's labor. Their children are likely to attend private schools or public schools in affluent suburbs and are unlikely to serve in the military. Whereas a previous generation of wealthy Americans were heavily taxed to help provide for the national infrastructure and the needs of the bottom one fifth, the tax structure currently insulates this new elite from contributing to the common good.

Furthermore, as economies are globalized, the well-being of a country no longer depends on the performance of national industries, and national elites' loyalties are no longer national but international. Over 15 years ago, Reich projected a 2020 scenario that is fast becoming reality.

Distinguished from the rest of the population by their global linkages, good schools, comfortable lifestyles, excellent health care, and abundance of security guards, symbolic analysts will complete their secession from the union. The townships and urban enclaves where they reside and the symbolic analytic zones where they work will bear no resemblance to the rest of America, nor will there be any direct connections between the two. America's poorest citizens, meanwhile, will be isolated within their own enclaves of urban and rural desperation; an ever larger portion of their young men will fill the nation's prisons. The remainder of the American population, growing gradually poorer, will feel powerless to alter any of these trends (Reich, 1991, pp. 302–303).

This scenario supports the notion of the economically squeeezed middle class described by Ehrenreich (1990) and Barlow (2003). Some members of the middle class have moved into this affluent one fifth, but many more are at risk of slipping back into the working class, out of which many of them emerged a generation or two ago. A large segment of this tenuous middle class struggles with its generally politically liberal values and the anxiety parents feel to provide advantages for their own children. Brantlinger (2003) has documented how liberal middle-class parents manage to maintain espoused theories of equity and social justice while deftly using the system to pass their privileges on to their children. This often creates a gap between our espoused theories of opportunity and public schooling with our need to work the system for our own children. Such gaps are related to the ways inauthenticity plays out in our daily lives. Many resolve this tension by moving into the conservative neoliberal camp. While such a move resolves the tension, it results in more neoliberal social policies and greater social inequality.

Inauthenticity, then, whether at the individual, organizational, or societal level is linked to this growing gap between our cherished ideals and the realities of our lives. In many cases ideals like liberty and equality have come into conflict with each other as well, with equality often losing out to an invigorated belief in individual liberty. When

Christopher Lasch referred to the revolt of the elites, he wasn't just referring to Reich's (1991) top one fifth of Americans. He also took on left-leaning liberals, who have also isolated themselves from working-class Americans, and use their educations and cultural capital to work the system. Thomas Frank (2000) has more recently made a similar point, arguing that political liberals have abandoned the American working class to the political right. Ironically, this conflict of values between liberty and equality were in tension during the social movements of the 1960s as individual-oriented, countercultural movements lived in uneasy tension with democratic socialist movements that stressed social inequalities and collectivist struggles around class, race, and gender. As Duggan (2003), Lakoff (2004) and others have documented, many of these tensions continue to keep political progressives from developing a unified critique of neoliberal and neoconservative movements. The libertarian, autonomous individual of the 1960s and the neoliberal focus on the individual, property rights, and free markets merged in the election of Ronald Reagan and a significant shift in society from the 1970s to the present. Later, it was a "new" Democrat, not a Republican who gave us free trade agreements like the North American Free Trade Agreement (NAFTA) and rolled-back welfare benefits for single mothers. In the contemporary "risk" society, the individual bears greater responsibility for personal and social choices. The idea that an authentic self and authentic society is achieved through democratic social interaction among diverse equals is at risk of becoming viewed as hopelessly utopian.

3) The Neoliberal Economy and the New Workplace: How the New Economy Creates a New Culture

Much new policy language contrasts old bureaucracy with new entrepreneurial approaches that claim to have flattened hierarchies and de-bureaucratized organizations. We still tend to blame bureaucracy for inauthenicity, and the critque of bureaucracy is embedded today in coded language like "the education establishment." As I have discussed elsewhere (Anderson, 2009), one of the sources of this critique was Max Webber's distinction between instrumental and substantive rationality. Max Webber focused heavily on the threat that the instrumental rationality of bureaucracies represented for an authentic society. In such organizations, people tend to be means to ends, rather than ends in themselves. Human relations theories tend to call for treating people well and including them in decisions, not so much because this is the way people should be treated but, rather, because "empowered" employees tend to be more productive. Organizational theorists also warn of goal displacement, in which the real goals of an organization—in schools, educating children—often get displaced by more self-serving goals of organizational members or clients. This is why schools must repeat the mantra that "at our school, kids come first," since in many schools they clearly don't.

Webber sought more substantive forms of rationality in which people were ends in themselves and in which social ends took precedent over individual goals. Newer "network" organizations have changed in form, but as we will see, they continue to operate on the basis of instrumental rationality, a tendency exacerbated in public organizations as they increasingly operate in a marketized environment.

While new business models attempt to manage through network organization, rather than through bureaucratic hierarchies, there is some evidence that this has intensified instrumental rationality, not reduced it. These new flexible organizations are part of a growing neoliberal business model to which some social theorists attribute a growing inauthenticity in organizations (Sennett, 2003). They have developed to respond to markets, not to meet the human needs of those who work in them.

A central thesis of this book is that neoliberal economic shifts at the global and national levels of the last 40 years are creating significant social and cultural shifts at all levels of society, leading to greater levels of inauthenticity. Because of the ways we have thought about authenticity in the past—either limited to more authentic forms of instruction and assessment or more authentic relationships within organizations—new forms of inauthenticity can easily escape our attention. If the cost of getting rid of the ills of bureaucracy is the loss of a democratic public sphere, then the cost may be too high. Only by deepening our critique to include these new forms of inauthenticity can educators effectively contest the current dominance of neoliberal market ideology in education.

Keynesian economics with an emphasis on government provision of social welfare and regulation of markets was gradually replaced in the 1970s by a neoliberal or neoclassical model inspired by Milton Freidman's call for the marketization and privatization of most sectors of society.[2] As market relations become dominant in all aspects of our lives, it becomes increasingly difficult to think beyond individual competition toward any sense of a common good. While most people think of neoliberalism as a purely economic model, it has important social and cultural consequences that we are only beginning to understand. Richard Sennett (2006) provides perhaps the most eloquent account of the ways that shifts in political economy have resulted in cultural shifts in the ways we live our lives. In his qualitative study of several corporations, Sennett has identified characteristics of work in what he calls the new capitalism. I provide a condensed version of his argument here.

Sennett (2006) traces the recent phenomenon of globalization back to the breakdown in 1973 of the Bretton Woods controls on the global movement of money. After Bretton Woods, there were large amounts of new capital seeking short-term investments. Later, stock prices began to replace profit as a goal for many businesses as money was made by trading and later speculation—not owning and producing. This

---

2   The term *neoliberalism* is emerging as the term of choice for the economic shifts that began in the U.S. during the economic crisis of the 1970s. Therefore, I will use the term throughout this chapter, although I have defined it in greater detail in my book "Advocacy Leadership" (Routledge, 2009). In brief, Keynesian economic theories gave way to Freidman's prescriptions that favored free markets and monetarist policies. This view of unregulated markets and the extension of market logic to all social sectors are aspects of neoliberalism. The term is also used to describe a group of "new" Democrats who around the same period began to move to the right on economic issues, while retaining liberal/left views on cultural issues, such as affirmative action and certain welfare provisions. For instance, Bill Clinton's economic policies, such as the NAFTA, are often referred to as neoliberal policies. Scholars outside the U.S. often see neoliberalism as the spread of free markets and privatization through international agencies such as the World Bank, the International Monetary Fund (IMF), and the World Trade Organization (WTO).

new speculative and flexible approach to capital has changed work life and institutional structures, particularly in sectors of capitalism such as finance, insurance, real estate, media, communications and high technology, where short-term exchange replaces long-term relationships. In order to fit into this new fast capitalism, workers have to give up notions of stability of employment and become flexible, mobile, workers in a constantly changing global economy.

Furthermore, workers become disposable as capital continuously seeks to cut labor costs though automation and outsourcing. Neoliberal management books like the best-seller *Who Moved the Cheese?* use a childlike allegory about mice who embrace change to prepare the ideological terrain for the new entrepreneurial worker. The lesson is that it is better to see losing one's job as an opportunity for some better entrepreneurial opportunity that surely lies around the corner. The new entrepreneurial culture that is promoted in all sectors of society prepares employees for this new world of unstable employment in the new "risk" society. Along with this new instability of work comes intensification of work leading to longer work hours and greater levels of stress and anxiety.

However, Sennett (2003) argues that such notions are actually counterproductive for business, since the cost to business of the resulting short-term employment is that it reduces employee loyalty. Moreover, with shorter contracts, work in teams, and a highly competitive internal work environment, authentic relationships are less likely to form because of short timelines. This continuous employee turnover and the tendency to use temporary workers and outside consultants weaken institutional knowledge. He argues that these new tendencies are good for the bottom line and stock prices but are not good for the long-term health of businesses, national productivity, or the building of relationships and personal character. In fact, he titled his book *The Corrosion of Character: The Personal Consequences of Work in the New Capitalism.* The creation of authentic human ties cannot easily occur in transient workplaces and communities. As principals in schools are moved from school to school and teacher turnover, especially in urban districts grows, a similar phenomenon occurs in education. Flexible organizations in a choice environment means teachers and administrators will be more mobile, leading to less stability and a weakening of organizational learning. Increased intensification and standardization of work will be tolerated by newer teachers, but many veteran teachers with families and a strong professional culture are tending to change careers or retire early. The very notion of teaching or administration as a lifelong career is becoming a thing of the past.

Sennett (2003) also identifies other personal deficits associated with this new neoliberal culture. The first is the demise of the work ethic. Only a fool would delay gratification in the new workplace. Employees report feeling a sense of personal betrayal as companies trade loyalty to workers for short-term profits. Second, this loss of long-term employment with its associated benefits and pensions makes it more difficult for newer generations of employees to create life narratives. While much welfare state employment was not exciting, it provided people with a life narrative in which they could pay a mortgage over 30 years, look forward to a pension and social security, and plan for vacations. In the absence of any way to think strategically about one's life, one's sense of purpose, future goals, and sustaining purpose in life is affected.

In flattened hierarchies or network organizations, pyramidal hierarchy is replaced by a horizontal elite core and a mass periphery with minimal mediation and communication between the two. It represents a new concentration of power without centralization of authority. According to Sennett (1998), "this absence of authority frees those in control to shift, adapt, reorganize without having to justify themselves or their acts. In other words, it permits the freedom of the moment, a focus just on the present. Change is the responsible agent; change is not a person" (p. 115). Internal units are created to compete with each other for contracts. Outside consultants are brought in to do the dirty work that management used to do. Senior management can claim they are taking their cue from the expert consultants who come in and leave quickly. In this impersonal environment, no relationships are built, as no one has to take responsibility for decisions. Upper management with its stronger networks move more often as new opportunities arise. Personnel records take the place of humans who are being standardized so "performance" can be compared (just as high-stakes testing in education allows students, teachers, and schools to be compared as a prerequisite for a marketized system). Flexiblity to adjust to changes in the market is gained. This is perhaps good news for stockholders seeking short-term profits, upper level executives and consultancy firms, but it isn't clear who else benefits or what it contributes to the common good. It also, according to Sennett, makes long-term, authentic relationships less likely.

This new model is being intentionally implemented in school districts across the country. Today in New York City, a corporate model is taking shape. Upper level public administrators are contracting out to private companies or taking private sector positions in the burgeoning education services industry. Public–private partnerships are the vehicle for this shift in work culture. This restructuring of the institutional environment will dramatically change the work culture of schools. Whether this will make schools more authentic places for children and teachers remains to be seen. If Sennett's analysis of the new corporate culture is any indication, we can expect to see less employee loyalty, more work stress, and a new performance culture.

4) Alienation and the New Performance Culture

School practitioners have devised forms of "creative compliance" with an accountability system that distorts authentic teaching and learning. Their creative compliance —now well know to most educators and researchers—involves what Elliott (2002) calls "the cynical production of auditable performances" (p. 202) such as teaching to the test, manipulating student dropout rates, recruiting "low-maintenance" students, focusing attention on the "bubble" students who are near the cutoff level, and many more. While such behaviors are clearly inauthentic and, in most cases, unethical, they are predictable based on historical evidence.

Welch (1998) documents parallels between today's reforms and business-led reforms of the 19th and early 20th centuries when forms of efficiency were imposed on schooling through the imposition of a business ethos. In his analysis of the British Revised Code of 1860 whose centerpiece was "payment by results," he documents the audit culture of the time, which, like today, resulted in creative compliance. According to Welsh,

> teachers 'stuffed and almost roasted' their pupils on test items once the teachers knew that the visit of the inspector was imminent. Other teachers secretly trained their pupils so that when they were asked questions they raised their right hands if they knew the correct answer but their left if they did not, thus creating a more favorable impression upon the visiting inspector. (p. 161)

Nearly 150 years later, such pressures are having a similar effect. The following is from the *Columbus Dispatch* in Columbus, Ohio, but newspapers across the country are full of similar stories.

Answer sheets and test booklets arrive at districts in securely taped boxes, shipped by FedEx or UPS. Packets are shrink-wrapped and are supposed to be stored in a locked room until test time. But in some districts, teachers got access last school year. Some made copies. Others shared the questions with students ahead of time, or gave answers during the test. And a few devised nonverbal signals to cue children that their answers were incomplete. For all the lock-and-key procedures and explicit rules, more teachers cheated on Ohio standardized tests than ever before.

Audit cultures not only result in inauthentic practices, they are incapable of achieving real instructional improvement, much less stem the tide of growing class and racial inequalities. What makes NCLB more insidious than the British Revised Code is that in 1860, teachers only had to perform for the intermittent arrival of state inspectors. In the past teachers could close the classroom door and ignore or modify reforms that failed to understand their local context and administrators had considerable autonomy. The lifeworld of schools was often buffered from the constant demands of reforms that came and went. In the new context of high-stakes testing, instructional coaches, administrative "walk-throughs," and school report cards published in local papers, surveillance of teachers is constant, and decisions about instruction and testing are made over the heads of principals and superintendents. In an age of zero tolerance, laying out unrealistic goals for students' annual yearly progress makes many politicians, goaded on by their businessmen partners, score points by appearing to get tough with "failing" public schools, and presenting themselves as advocates for the poor. But this constant demand for forms of accountability that are unrealistic and fail to reflect the nature of authentic teaching and learning have left many educators demoralized and cynical.

Outcomes-based education has created a culture of accountability based on performance indicators. As Ball (2001) points out, a culture of accountability becomes a performance culture. The need to be constantly accountable increases our visibility and requires that we align our performances with external accountability criteria. Ball calls this ongoing requirement to perform for others, *fabrication*, and argues that a culture of performativity creates a need for fabricating performances.

Ironically, a performance culture often lessens efficiency rather than increases it. As anyone who has been involved in an elaborate external evaluation can attest, the generation of performance information, rituals like interviews and exhibit-room documents, and the coding of lesson plans divert energy from the core pursuits of the organization, like teaching and spending time with students. Likewise, a testing culture in schools often decreases rather than increases the amount of authentic (i.e., non-scripted) learning that takes place in classrooms. Of equal importance for Ball (2001), is the impact that a performance culture has on the possibility of authentic institutions and an authentic self. The reduction of persons to "databases" and the constant effort devoted to fabrication empty institutions of authentic practices and relationships. Management becomes

> ubiquitous, invisible, inescapable – part of, embedded in everything we do. We choose and judge our actions and they are judged by others on the basis of their contribution to organizational performance. And in all this the demands of performativity dramatically close down the possibilities for metaphysical discourses, for relating practice to philosophical principles like social justice and equity. (Ball, 2001, p. 216)

By setting up a relationship in which teachers and administrators are viewed as the sources of poor student achievment, their position as subordinates in an overtly punitive system is intensified. Scott's (1990) descriptions of the public and hidden transcripts that are generated whenever unequal relations of power exist is helpful in illustrating how mandated performativity impacts teachers and administrators. The public transcript refers to the tendency of both groups to act out behaviors and attitudes expected of them and which often purposely misrepresent their true feelings or intentions. According to Scott,

> the public performance of the subordinate will, out of prudence, fear, and the desire to curry favor, be shaped to appeal to the expectation of the powerful. I shall use the term public transcript as a shorthand way of describing the open interaction between subordinates and those who dominate. (1990, p. 2)

In other words, social interactions become public performances, and the public transcript fixes the parameters of exchanges between the powerful and the powerless, making authentic communication less likely.

Such performances, according to Scott, also took a psychic toll and many members of subordinate groups, such as peasants or slaves paid with their lives when they could no longer sustain the performance. While recognizing that teachers are hardly in a situation comparable to slaves, something similar happens to teachers when fabrication invades their professional culture. We are seeing an increase in early retirements and workplace stress among teachers and a comparable sense of emotional stress among students who are also subjected to a testing regimen that requires more performativity in the classroom than authentic teaching and learning.

At a policy level, performance and fabrication are used to promote or legitimate particular policy options. An example involves the creation of the appearance of the success of the Texas Accountability system, which later morphed into the national NCLB legislation. Rod Paige, the secretary of education brought to Washington by George W. Bush, was the former superintendent of the Houston Independent School district from 1994 to 2001. The district had been touted as a jewel in the crown of the "Texas miracle" (the assumption that test scores in Texas improved due to a high-stakes standardized testing program) and in 2002 won a $1 million prize as best urban school district in the country from the Los Angeles–based Broad Foundation. During the 2000–2001 school year, Houston schools reported that only 1.5% of its students dropped out. These data, combined with the conservative Broad Foundation's award, attracted much media attention. The success of Page's former district was touted as proof that the Texas Accountability system was an excellent model for the nation.

Then on July 11, 2003, a front-page *New York Times* article reported that "the results of a state audit found that more than half of the 5,500 students who left their schools in the 2000-2001 school year should have been declared dropouts but were not" (Schemo, 2003, p. 1). The audit recommended lowering the ranking of 14 of the 16 audited schools from the best to the worst. Any principal or superintendent knows that there are at least a dozen ways to deflate dropout statistics when under pressure to do so. For example, students can be listed as transfers rather than dropouts, so it looks as though they are moving to another district or program rather than dropping out of school. In some districts students who sign up for GED programs—whether they actually attend or not—are not counted as dropouts. In some states, like New Mexico, dropout rates only include those who drop out during their senior year. The Houston case is a great example of how fabrication promoted a district as a national success story, while in reality its high schools were failing large numbers of students. The "success" of Houston's high schools was particularly important for the Bush administration, since the claims of a "Texas Miracle" had been largely limited to elementary schools. The media had been drawn into covering the Houston district as a success story on an ongoing basis, thus garnering the Houston district, and consequently Paige, a national reputation for making impressive gains.

Perhaps the most devastating effect of an alienated workplace is on the students themselves. (Wexler, Chrichlow, Kern, and Martuswicz, 1992) views the new neoliberal emphasis on the individual and a flight from public solidarity, coupled with a lack of authentic student–adult relationships as creating a sense in schools that "nobody cares." In the absence of authentic relations with adults, students are left to forge identities that are institutionally structured, rather than relationally constructed. As teaching and learning are increasingly defined as measurable cognitive learning, there is an emptying out of socioemotional connection and a neglect of noncognitive aspects of education such as the construction of social identities and social solidarities. Students come to school hoping to "become somebody" in the eyes of their peers and the adults who they look to, albeit, often reluctantly, for guidance in this endeavor. As Wexler puts it, "for many students, school is a disappointment of socio-emotional hope" (p. 136).

In the absence of such authentic relations, students are left to form the institutionally structured identities offered by school subcultures of jocks, rads, gothics, skaters, sluts—all of which boil down in social class terms in one way or another to "loser" or "winner." These are supplemented by the substitute, compensatory identities supplied by the mass cultural images of the entertainment industry or branding options like Abercrombie and Fitch or American Apparel. On the surface, youth are busy, with places to go and people to see. They multitask with cell phones, laptops, and text messaging, and yet underneath all the busy relating, there is too often a lack of authentic, stable relationships or any sense of a stable occupational future.

5) The Creation of a Political Spectacle to Promote Social and Educational Policies

While Karl Rove is credited with masterminding the election of George Bush and the promotion of myriad conservative social policies through the creation of political spectacle, political manipulation, and the dissemination of misinformation have a long and documented history in the U.S. and elsewhere. In *Constructing the Political Spectacle,* Edelman (1988) discusses the elements that make up the spectacle. As citizens gain greater sophistication in decoding it, they may initially become more cynical. Cynicism is fast becoming the emblem of our political culture. Nevertheless, the skill of demystifying these modern elements of political deception are a necessary precondition, along with reforming how political campaigns are funded, for bringing greater rationality to our political system. While the media is a central tool in the creation of spectacle, it is also created in state and local political arenas, as Miller-Kahn and Smith (2001) and Smith, Heinecke and Noble (1999) have demonstrated. Edelman argues that an understanding of the following elements are crucial for an analysis of current social policy formation:

1. *The importance of language and discourse.* Perhaps more than any other political scientist, Edelman (1978) focused on the relationship between language and politics and what he called "the linguistic structuring of social problems" (p. 26). He provides a methodology for studying policy based on the notion that "how the problem is named involves alternative scenarios, each with its own facts, value judgments, and emotions" (p. 29). In my volume, *Advocacy Leadership* (2009), I provide an example of how critical discourse analysis can be used to demonstrate how ideological agendas are embedded in seemingly neutral language.

2. *The definition of events as crises.* "A crisis, like all news developments, is a creation of the language used to depict it; the appearance of a crisis is a political act, not a recognition of a fact or a rare situation" (Edelman, 1988, p. 31). Crises, according to Edelman, "typically rationalize policies that are especially harmful to those who are already disadvantaged."[3] Berliner and Biddle (1995) describe in great detail how a "manufactured crisis" was needed to jump our current school reform policies that date back at least to *The Nation at Risk* report in 1983.

3. *A tendency to cover political interests with a discourse of rational policy analysis.* A crisis is often created through an appeal to scientific, rational, neutral discourses. For example, political advantage on the political right has been gained not through political rhetoric, but rather through privately funded, ideologically driven "think tanks" that sponsor and disseminate so-called objective research.

The linguistic evocation of enemies and the displacement of targets. Those with the power to manage meaning can cast tenured radicals, the welfare state, social promotion, progressive teaching methods, teachers unions, and so on as the villains of educational reform. All displace attention from other possible actors and events. Perhaps the most notable displacement of a target is laying the blame on the education sector for poor economic performance instead of on the State and the corporate sector. NCLB, itself displaces these targets by calling for closing the education gap, while failing to call for closing the growing social and economic gaps. According to Apple (2001), this is not surprising since the state is shifting

> the blame for the very evident inequalities in access and income it has prom-
> ised to reduce, from itself on to individual schools, parents, and children.
> This is, of course, also part of a larger process in which dominant economic
> groups shift the blame for the massive and unequal effects of their own mis-
> guided decisions from themselves on to the state. The state is then faced
> with a very real crisis in legitimacy. Given this, we should not be at all sur-
> prised that the state will then seek to export this crisis outside itself. (p. 416)

1. *The public as political spectators.* Democratic participation is limited to such reactive rituals as voting or being polled: "An individual vote is more nearly a form of self-expression and of legitimation than of influence" (Apple, 2001, p. 97). For instance, recently, in Argentina, where

---

3   Edelman goes on to say that "the class-based result of crisis labeling is unintended" (p. 32), having to do with an already skewed structure of opportunities. Although not wishing to engage in overdeterminism, I tend to see greater intentionality behind the political spectacle than Edelman does. (Flight from Mills notion of elites).

voting is compulsory, a large percentage of voters turned in blank votes as a way to demonstrate their disgust with both candidates and their refusal to participate in the political spectacle.

2. *The media as mediator of the political spectacle*. Edelman (1988) gave news reporting and other forms of media a central place in the construction of the political spectacle. Debord's (1990) "society of the spectacle" explored the influence of the media on social life more generally. The media was used to promote the "Texas Miracle" through the low dropout rates of the Houston school district. When the fabrication was brought to light, it was reported in the media, but by then the original story had already had its political effect.

All of the elements of Edelman's description of the construction of a political spectacle are present in current school reform efforts. Although I have examined these elements elsewhere (Anderson, 2009), a few examples should suffice here to illustrate some of the ways the current school reform spectacle is being constructed through 1) the construction of a crisis by defining the nation as economically "at risk" and displacing blame from the corporate sector onto schools; think tanks release so-called commissioned reports with titles like *Tough Choices or Tough Times* or *Rising above the gathering storm* that use crises language to scapegoat our educational system; 2) the use of language to create heroes and villains, for instance, elevating "education entrepreneurs" and "parental choice" over the "educational establishment" and "educrats"; metaphors often stand in for public debate, such as when we use terms like "customer" or "consumer" of education as a way to make education into a commodity; this sleight of hand creates the internal logic for the marketization, corporatization, and commercialization of schools; in this way the social goals of schooling are shifted without public debate; 3) the promotion of neoliberal ideology as "objective research" produced by right-wing think tanks; 4) the tendency of the media to uncritically use this "research" in their reporting on education; and, 5) finally, the move to replace genuine political participation with choice in an educational marketplace, reducing the public to spectators of politics instead of participants and passive consumers instead of active citizens.

6) The Inappropriate Transfer of Markets, Business Models, and Privatization to Education

Viewing privatization, markets and business models as sources of inauthenticity in education is less a critique of markets and business than an objection to their nonreflective transference to education. While no field should shut itself off from outside influences, public services like education, health, or criminal justice have unique core technologies and purposes that are fundamentally different than business. And while markets may be an efficient way to distribute consumer items and to accumulate capital, they are less effective at allocating services like education (Cuban, 2004). Inappropriate transfers of ideas from one sector to another is like putting a square peg in a round whole; it is inherently inauthentic.

Besides privatization and marketization, two trends I have discussed in more detail in another space (Anderson, 2009), the Business model and what Callahan (1962) called the *cult of efficiency*, has had its most damaging effect through high-stakes testing. While testing didn't suddenly appear during NCLB, this recent obsession with data-based decision-making and statistical control have forced educators to misuse testing in ways unthinkable two decades ago. Not only is a single test score relatively meaningless in the absence of other student and school data, but the current high-stakes use of tests also undermines its reliability. Virtually all testing and measurement experts in the American Educational Research Association have contributed to a statement in protest of this misuse of assessment instruments, and yet the expertise of educators is so marginalized that these misguided and unethical practices continue unabated. It doesn't take a testing expert to know that as teachers teach to a test, it distorts the meticulous norming process of test makers, creating the famous Minnesota phenomenon in which all the children are above average. A test is meant to represent what a student learns in the course of instruction, not how well they are taught to take tests. The problem is not the existence of tests or accountability. Even before tests existed, teachers found ways to assess student learning. The problem is the current near obsession with testing and accountability that has resulted in their misuse, leading to not just unanticipated and perverse incentives but, a more inauthentic relationship between espoused goals of assessment and the reality on the ground.

Increasingly test scores are not merely used to assess students, but also school effectiveness. Popham (2005) and others have argued that tests not designed to assess school effectiveness—such as reading and math scores on standardized tests—should not be used for that purpose. Nevertheless, aggregate test scores are now commonly misused to assess school, and even teacher, quality. McGill-Franzen and Allington (2006) further argue that the results of assessments of school effectiveness are inauthentic because of four key contaminating factors:

1) Low-income students fall further behind their middle class peers over the summer because of a lack of access to text-rich environments. Low-income students can lose two or more years of reading growth across their elementary school careers. So schools that serve low-income children can be very successful during the months they have students but be punished as failing because test scores fail to take disproportionate summer reading loss into account.

2) High-stakes testing has increased the number of students retained-in-grade, or what we used to call "flunking." This is because low-achieving students are often retained the year before high-stakes tests (e.g., for fourth-grade testing, low-achieving students are retained in third grade) in order to increase aggregate test scores. This increase in flunking is particularly ironic in en era of evidence-based practice since decades of research shows that flunking students is not helpful

unless a rigorous remediation program is designed specifically for the student. Well-researched models like Reading Recovery, in which students are remediated immediately and returned to class once they have caught up, have been shown to be more effective. While programs like Reading Recovery are often seen as expensive because they rely on one-on-one tutoring, retaining a student in grade is also expensive as the school system has to pay for an extra year of education with little evidence that it will improve a student's achievement any more than similar students who were not retained. Thus, schools retain more students to create the inauthentic appearance of rising scores rather than engage in more evidence-based practices.

3) High-stakes accountability has diverted massive amounts of teacher time and financial resources away from instruction toward test preparation. While there is some evidence that test prep marginally increases test scores, it represents an attempt to improve scores without improving reading achievement, and is thus considered inauthentic and even unethical by many. It also suggests that in schools where test prep predominates, teachers have no idea how to improve reading proficiencies. In such cases, funds for test prep should be diverted to professional development.

4) The current practice of accommodating students with disabilities by reading passages aloud to them appears to be a cynical attempt to raise test scores. Reading passages aloud to students converts a reading test into a listening test and is inauthentic, depriving disabled students of being taught to read.

Implicit in all these tendencies is a set of assumptions that are based on little empirical evidence: that business-inspired efficiency models are more effective at managing schools, that markets will hold schools accountable, and that privatizing schools will bring the advantages of efficiency and markets to bear on schooling. Clearly, there is some role for nonprofit partnerships in the public sector, but the balance has to be carefully calibrated if we are to retain the essence of a public system.

As conditions for the poor under neoliberal policies continue to deteriorate, some groups, like the Black Alliance for Education Options, have turned to market solutions like vouchers. This is an authentic response to the abandonment of many American low-income schools and neighborhoods and needs to be addressed.

The aftermath of Hurricane Katrina is only the most dramatic case of the abandonment of millions of African-Americans in our urban centers and inner-ring suburbs. Being based on the lived experience of millions of people abandoned by our economic and educational system, I can hardly challenge the sense of desperation and hopelessness that leads to the belief that nothing could be worse than economically and racially segregated public schools in which few students succeed academically. As a parent under such circumstances, I can imagine opting out of my local public school if given a voucher for a Catholic school. After all, as Howard Fuller (1997) and others have pointed out, white and black middle-class parents already have these options, and many, including many political progressives don't hesitate to exercise them. Abandoning the foundering ship of public schooling seems like a survival impulse, one that has been fine-tuned through the vicissitudes of the history of African-Americans in the U.S.

Given a reality of white supremacy, immigrant groups in the U.S. of all shades have strategically defined themselves as not-black in an attempt to avoid the stigma of race. As the competition state further discourages solidarity and promotes the maximization of one's individual advantage, the idea of human solidarity or even the notion of a common good or a public sphere becomes a more distant utopia. While it is understandable that some will give up political struggle for individual solutions along the way, the elimination of a public space in which political activity can take place may foreclose the very notion of collective struggle in the future.

Once we have destroyed those public spaces where citizenship instead of consumerism dwells, what will we replace them with? What is, after all, a theory of democracy that would replace a public sphere? The private sector is just that: private. On private property, we lose many of our rights of citizenship. Private institutions are under no obligation to open their books to the public, no matter how much the private sector preaches transparency. It is ironic that a private sector that wants schools to be more tightly regulated, is itself becoming more deregulated. As markets become the new discipline for the public sector, not only do they distort the essence of what schooling is about, but they also become a poor substitute for the kinds of transparency that a sovereign people should demand from institutions that belong to them.

While public schools in low-income communities desperately need reform, they also represent a public space that belongs to the community. Many children's parents and grandparents went to local public schools, and there is often a strong sense of belonging, in spite of overcrowded classrooms and teachers and administrators who too often are out of touch with local communities. Schools in low-income communities will not learn to be more responsive through high-stakes testing or by being run by a private corporation with headquarters in another state. In fact, they could become worse. As I will argue in more detail later, schools in low-income communities improve as local communities gain resources through more equitable social policies and through the development of local community leaders who can hold their schools accountable. Trading in a public space for a privatized one or one that imposes a system of testing that classifies most low-income schools and children as failures, is a trade-off that many educators and community leaders are not willing to accept.

Scott and Fruchter (in press) have documented another response of low-income communities of color to privatization. In 2001, then mayor Rudolph Giuliani and Chancellor Harold Levy invited Edison, the for-profit EMO, to take over five low-performing middle schools in New York City. In response, the community group Association of Community

Organizations for Reform Now (ACORN) and a coalition calling itself People's Coalition to Take Back Our Schools began organizing to oppose the plan, charging that parents were shut out of the process. These groups were led by and largely made of of African-Americans and Latinos. In spite of mayoral support and a promotional campaign by Edison, the parents of the five schools all voted against letting Edison take over their schools.

Although politics is alive and well in New York City, some social commentators argue that we are experiencing a period of "antipolitics" in which our society is fast becoming depoliticized. As many communitarians and researchers of civic engagement have pointed out, when people lack opportunities to participate in civic life, the result is political atrophy. According to Boggs (2000), a depoliticized public has five broad features in common:

> An unmistakable retreat from the political realm; a decline in the trappings of citizenship and with it the values of democratic participation; a narrowing of public discourse and the erosion of independent centers of thinking; a lessened capacity to achieve social change by means of statecraft or social governance; and the eventual absence of a societal understanding of what is uniquely common and public, what constitutes a possible general interest amidst the fierce interplay of competing private and local claims. (p. 22)

Defending public schools and insisting on retaining distinctions between the public and private have much higher stakes than many realize. The marketization and privatization of the public sphere is not a harmless reform that toys with incentive structures and retools notions of accountability; it represents a new and dangerous concentration of power and is a radical departure from the founding ideals of our nation.

Conclusion

I have made the case in this chapter that a central problem of contemporary American society, including our public schools, is a growing lack of authenticity in our economic, political, and cultural life. This trend has important implications for our ability to enjoy authentic relationships in our homes and workplaces. It also affects how we go about constructing an authentic self out of this new social and cultural environment. I have also argued that a major cause of this growing inauthenticity is a fundamental shift that has occurred in our economic life, led by a series of neoliberal, market-driven reforms that have drastically redistributed wealth upward, created more transiency and less stability in the workplace, rolled back many welfare state programs and policies, shrunk our public spaces, and created a new category of working poor. Because I am holding this "new" economy largely responsible for these changes, in my volume, *Advocacy Leadership* (2009), I explore in greater depth how neoliberalism in its various manifestations has impacted society and, in particular, our schools.

References

Anderson, G. (2009). *Advocacy Leadership.* New York: Routledge

Ball, S. (2001). Performativites and fabrications in the education economy: Towards the performative society. In D. Gleason and C. Husbands (Eds.) *The performing school: Managing, teaching and learning in a performance culture* (pp., 210–226). London: Routledge/Falmer.

Barber, B. (1984) *Strong Democracy: Participatory politics for a new age.* Berkeley: University of California Press.

Barlow, A. (2003). *Between fear and hope: Globalization and race in the United States.* New York: Rowan and Littlefield.

Bellah, R., Madsen, R., Sullivan, W., Swidler, A., & Tipton, S. (1985). *Habits of the heart: Individualism and commitment in American life.* Berkeley: University of California Press.

Berliner, D. and Biddle, B. (1995). *The manufactured crisis: Myths, fraud, and the attack on America's public schools.* Reading, MA: Addison-Wesley.

Boggs, C. (2000). *The end of politics: Corporate power and the decline of the public sphere.* New York: The Guilford Press.

Brantlinger, E. (2003). *Dividing classes: How the middle class negotiates and rationalizes school advantage.* New York: Routledge.

Callahan, R. (1962). *Education and the cult of efficiency.* Chicago: The University of Chicago Press.

Cuban, L. (2004). *The blackboard and the bottom line: Why schools can't be businesses.* Cambridge: Harvard University Press.

Debord, G. (1995). *The society of the spectacle* (D. Nichelson-Smith, Trans.). New York: Zone Books.

Dewey, J. (1929). *Individualism: Old and new.* New York: Putnam.

Duggan, L. (2003). *The twilight of equality: Neoliberalism, cultural politics, and the attack on democracy.* Boston: Beacon Press.

Edelman, M. (1988). *Constructing the political spectacle.* Chicago: the University of Chicago Press.

Egan, T. (June 28, 2007). Red state welfare. *New York Times,* A23.

Ehrenreich, B. (1990). *Fear of falling: The inner life of the middle class.* New York: Perennial Books.

Elliott, J (2002). In D. Gleason and C. Husbands (Eds.) Characteristics of performative cultures. *The performing school: Managing, teaching and learning in a performance culture* (pp. 192–209) London: Routledge/Falmer.

Frank, T. (2000). *One market under God: Extreme capitalism, market populism, and the end of economic democracy.* New York: Doubleday.

Fuller, H. (1997). *The crisis in urban education.* Paper presented at the Annual Meeting of the American Educational Research Association, Chicago, April.

Galbraith, J. (1998) *Created unequal: The crisis in American pay.* New York: Simon and Shuster.

Goodlad, J. (1970). *Behind the classroom door.* New York: C.A. Jones Pub.

Kohn, A. (2000) Opposing View: Focus on Tests Hurt Students, *USA Today,* Retrived (2011) https://www.alfiekohn.org/article/opposing-view

Labaree, D. (1997). *How to succeed in school without really learning: The credentials race in American education.* London & New Haven, CT: Yale University Press.

Lakoff, G. (2004). *Don't think of an elephant: Know your values and frame the debate.* New York: Chelsea Green Publications.

Lash, Ch. (1995). *The Revolt of the Elites.* New York: Norton

Lukes, S. (2005). *Power: A radical view* (revised edition). London: Macmillan.

McGill-Franzen, A. & Allington, R. (2006). Contamination of current accountability systems. *Phi Delta Kappan*, 762-766.

McGrath, D., & Kurillof, P. (1999) "They're going to tear the doors off this place": Upper-middle-class parent school involvement and the educational opportunities of other people's children. *Educational Policy, 13*(5), 603–629.

Miller-Kahn, L. & Smith, M. L. (2001, November 30). School choice policies in the political spectacle. *Education Policy Analysis Archives, 9* (50). Retrieved [2011] from http://epaa.asu.edu/epaa/v9n50.html.

National Commission on Excellence in Education. (1983) *A nation at risk: the imperative for educational reform*. Washington, DC: Government Publishing Office.

Pear, R. (2005). Buying of News by Bush's Aides Is Ruled Illegal. *New York Times*, October 1., pp. A1, A13.

Pope, D. C. (2001). *Doing school: How we are creating a generation of stressed out, materialistic, an miseducated students*. New Haven, CT: Yale University Press.

Popham, J. (2005) *America's "failing" schools: How parents and teachers can cope with No Child Left Behind*. New York: Routledge.

Putnam, R. (2000). *Bowling alone: the collapse and revival of American community*. New York: Simon and Schuster.

Reich, R. (1991). *The work of nations*. New York: A.A. Knopf.

Schemo, D. (2003). Questions on data cloud luster of Houston schools. *The New York Times*, July, 11, p. .1.

Scott, J., & Fruchter, N. (In Press). Community resistance to school privatization: The case of New York City. In R. Fischer (Ed.). *'The people shall rule': ACORN, community organizing, and the struggle for economic justice*. Philadelphia: Temple University Press.

Scott, J.C. (1999). *Seeing like a state: How certain schemes to improve the human condition have failed*. New Haven, CT: Yale University Press.

Sennett, R. (1998). *The corrosion of character: The personal consequences of work in the new capitalism*. New York: Norton.

Sennett, R. (2003). *The culture of the new capitalism*. New Haven, CT: Yale University Press.

Siddle Walker, V. (2005). Organized resistance and black educators' quest for school equality, 1878-1938. *Teachers College Record, 107*(3), 355–388.

Smith, M.L., Heinecke, W, .F. & Noble, A.J. (1999). *Assessment policy and political spectacle. Center for Research on Educational Standards and Student Testing*. Berkeley: UCLA

Soros, G. (1998). *The crisis of global capitalism: Open Society endangered*. London: Little, Brown.

Welch, A.R. (1998). The cult of efficiency in education: Comparative reflections on the reality and the rhetoric. *Comparative Education, 34*(2), 157–175.

Westheimer, J. (Ed.) (2007). *Pledging allegiance: The politics of patriotism in America's schools*. New York: Teachers College Press.

Wexler, P., Crichlow, W., Kern, J., & Martusewicz, R. (1992). *Becoming somebody: Toward a social psychology of school*. London: Falmer.

CHAPTER NINE

Resisting and Rolling Back Neoliberalism: The Opt-Out Movement and Teachers' Unions[1]

David Hursh, Zhe Chen, and Sarah McGinnis

OVER THE LAST several years, teachers, parents, and students are increasingly resisting and pushing back against neoliberal economic, political, and educational policies. As Fraser, Bhattacharyam, and Arruzza write in *Feminism for the 99%: A Manifesto*, a portion of which appears in a recent issue of *The New Left Review* (Fraser, Bhattachary, and Arruzza, 2018), this resistance is exemplified by increasing protests against funding cuts in education, health, housing, and transport and the elimination of environmental protections. As Fraser et al. write, "opposing governmental assaults on 'public goods' imposed at financial capital's behest, women's strikes are becoming the catalyst and model for broad-based effort to defend our communities—demanding bread, but roses too" (p. 117). Ove the last two years, these protests include the women's march in the US, and, at the international level, in other countries, including Spain, where in 2018 a "country wide feminist strike" and "five million marchers" "brought Spain to a halt" (Fraser et al., 2018, p. 116).

In education, we have seen an historically unprecedented outbreak of teacher strikes, some encompassing whole states (Arizona, West Virginia, Oklahoma) and instigated by teachers where there is no union, and others that are union-led district-wide strikes, as in Los Angeles (Weiner, 2019) and Oakland (French, 2019). The teachers are fed up with local, state, and federal governments increasing military and other security spending (such as Immigration and Customs Enforcement) while implementing austerity budgets for education that result in miserly salaries and inadequate funding for school supplies and other materials (Karp & Sanchez, 2018). Moreover, in some strikes, as in Los Angeles, the teachers included in their demands an end to the increasing privatization of public schools through charter schools (Blanc, 2019a). Charter schools, the teachers point out, by taking funds from public schools and handing it over to publicly funded but privately administered charter schools, reduces funding for traditional public schools.

At the same time as the teacher strikes, many parents, students, and teachers are resisting the imposition of corporate produced curriculum and assessments in their

---

1   Revised Keynote address, Department of Educational Leadership, University of Massachusetts Dartmouth, November 14, 2011.

schools. In particular, in 13 of the 19 states (Howell, 2015) that applied for and "won" funding under Obama's Race to the Top (RttT), parents are opting their children out of the required standardized testing in grades three through eight. The state that has the highest opt out rate is New York, where 20% of the students statewide and 50% of the students on the two counties east of New York City have opted out of what were called the Common Core Standards, curriculum and exams, but by 2020 will be little changed except for a new name: The Next Generation Learning Standards. In this chapter, my evidence regarding the opt out movement comes from our research and that of our colleagues (Hursh, Chen, McGinnis, & Lingard, 2019; Hursh, Deutermann, Rudley, Chen, & McGinnis, 2019).

In New York, the Common Core standards, curriculum, and exams for grades three through eight were initially produced by Pearson and Questar with minimal input for teachers. However, parents, teachers, and others have asserted that the standards are poorly written, do not reflect what we know about how children learn, and provide little useful information. Only a few of the questions have been made public and students only receive a score of one, two, three, or four. Moreover, 50% of a teacher's evaluation is based on students' test scores (New York State Allies for Public Education [NYSAPE], 2019), and because tests are given only in grades three through eight in math and language arts, while nonsensical, many teachers who do not teach in grades three through eight or math or language arts are evaluated based on test scores of students in grades or subjects that they do not teach.

As we have described elsewhere (Hursh, Chen, et al., 2019; Hursh, Deutermann, et al., 2019), parents, educators, students and community members have lobbied against the Common Core standards, curriculum, and tests at legislative hearings, state education department–sponsored forums, and more, with no discernable effect on state education policy. Consequently, in order to get the attention of policymakers, many parents have turned to opting their children out of the tests, with the aim, as one parent, Lisa Rudley, who is head of NYSAPE (www.nysape.org) stated, " throwing a wrench in the system" (Hursh, Deutermann, et al., 2019). Members of NYSAPE and another parent-led organization, Long Island Opt Out (LIOO), asserted that even as few as 10% of the students opting out would render the tests more invalid than they already are.

That achieving a 10% opt-out rate might be difficult quickly became apparent as some school districts, including New York City, use the Common Core tests to place students in specific programs and that students opting out of the test often removes them from consideration for specific programs. Furthermore, some school districts, such as the Rochester City School District, have refused to inform parents of their right to opt out. In addition, the state and federal governments try to intimidate parents and teachers into sitting for the test by assigning low scores of zero or one out of four to students who opt out, which are included in the school's assessment, potentially resulting in negative consequences (NYSAPE, 2019). Therefore, it is astonishing that over the last five years 20% of the students statewide in grades three through eight have opted out and, even more astonishing, 50% of the students in the two politically conservative suburban Long Island counties have opted out.

Such successful parent resistance may explain why on April 30th 2019, the New York State Senate has introduced the "right to opt out of the high-stakes testing act" that would prohibit school district from undertaking all the preceding actions described. School districts would have to notify parents of their right to refuse to participate in any high-stakes testing and students could not be punished for not taking the test nor rewarded for doing so. Nor can student participation rates affect state aid or determine whether a school is "low-performing, underperforming, or . . . failing." (New York State Senate 2019, 2).

Whether the "right to opt out of high-stakes testing act" will become a law is unknown at this time, as is the future of the teacher strikes, but there is much we can learn from them.

In this paper we describe some of the similarities and differences between the opt-out movement and the teacher strikes. Both the opt-out movement and teacher strikes are increasingly engaged in resisting and rolling back (Leitner, Peck, & Sheppard, 2007) neoliberal economic, social, and educational policies that promote market-based rather than value-based decision making and privileges private individual rights over the common good. Neoliberal policies conceptualize parents and children as commodities and consumers who choose their child's education from an array of possibilities.

Both overcame skepticism regarding whether they could succeed. The first wave of successful strikes occurred in Republican-dominated states with little support until parents joined on. Likewise, the opt-out movement required parents to organize outside of schools. Both also share similarities in the demographics of their organizations, and their organizing strategy and tactics. To be specific, both organizations are more likely to be headed by women who are White, to be loosely organized, and to lack formal funding streams. Both, we argue, have been successful because they have been organizing and developing at the grassroots level and use their horizontal organizational strength to vertically impact policy making at the statewide and federal levels. And both have worked not to only just resist neoliberal austerity budgets cutting funding for education and other social services and the end of high-stakes testing but also aim to reconceptualize society and education around the concept of the socially just society and school (Smyth, 2019).

Both are pushing back against neoliberal capitalism's objectifying people as numbers. This is especially obvious in the opt-out movement's resistance to reducing teaching and learning to test scores and that the only information they receive about students from the Common Core exams is that they are categorized as a one, two, three or four, with three and four as proficient.

Therefore, we suggest that the opt-out movement and teacher strikes reflect an increasing recognition that an adequate response to the multiple crises we face requires more than minor reforms in capitalism, such as more efficient markets, or encouraging women to "lean in" at work so that more women become corporate leaders (Fraser, Bhattachary, and Arruzza, 2018), or that "personal learning" on computers will better educate students than actual teachers (Boninger, Molnar, & Saldana, 2019).

Instead of working to make schools and society more efficient and tinkering around the edges of capitalism, we argue, along with parents opting out and teachers going on strike, that our economic, environmental, and educational crises are interconnected and have the same root cause: *global capitalism* (Fraser et al., 2018). We cannot respond adequately to any of the crises unless we respond to all of them, and we do so by replacing the currently dominant neoliberal policies with social democratic ones that include examining not only class but also gender and race inequalities.

As we see it, capitalism is at a breaking point. Economic inequality within and between countries continues to increase (Chappell, 2019). In the US, the median income has not increased over the last five decades. Instead, the beneficiaries of economic growth are the top 1% and even more so the top .1%. The six heirs to the Walton fortune (the family that owns Walmart) have as much wealth as about 30% of the US. Globally, about 80 families control the vast majority of the world's wealth" (Oxfam, 2016).

Global survival requires replacing neoliberal policies with social democratic ones that recognize that our economic, environmental, and education policies are interconnected. Neoliberal economic policies emphasizing profit making in unregulated markets are the main cause of the environmental disasters that we face. Because of feedback loops connecting rising temperatures, thawing permafrost, and melting glaciers to rising sea levels and desertification, further temperature increases are baked into the system. Moreover, neoliberal environmental policies assume that markets need no regulations but are most efficient and effective when left to themselves (Hollling, 2001). However, we see no evidence that we can depend on markets to counteract climate change and environmental disaster. Every indicator suggests a worsening world, from rising oceans to increasing toxins in our environment, such as pesticides, herbicides, and plastic.

Scientists are observing that plastic is everywhere in our environment, including plastic microbeads in all living things. Such widespread contamination leads biologist Sandra Steingarber to observe that we all are "born pre-polluted" (Environmental Working Group, 2019) and "contaminated without our consent" (Steingraber, 2004). We agree with Naomi Klein (2014) that climate change and increasing pollution will drastically worsen without significant changes in economic policies. Mitigating the impending disaster of climate change requires replacing neoliberal political, social, and educational policies and practices with social democratic ones (Fraser et al., 2019).

Transforming out political, economic, and education policies will require a massive effort to resist, roll back, and replace neoliberal policies with feminist social democratic ones. However, we have observed in these authoritarian times increasing resistance to neoliberal policies as expressed by the teacher unions and opt-out movement.

Why Feminism?

Women, rather than men, are more likely to be affected by climate change and neoliberal education and economic policies. Climate change will disproportionately affect women and those in the global South who depend on farming for income and food for themselves and their families. It is women who are responsible for fetching firewood and water, two resources that will be further depleted with climate change.

Similarly, it is women who are harmed the most by neoliberal economic policies that cut social spending in education, health, transportation, and social security as the burden of caring for families—including children and the elderly—is increasingly moved from the state to the family. Therefore, Fraser et al. (2019) argue that we must eliminate the tensions between gender, race, and class policies. Further, as Marx recognized over 150 years ago, it is the family that ultimately is responsible for raising children and providing the nourishment workers need to be productive each day. The current crisis is neither about only gender nor class. Instead, we should reject that "stale opposition" and "zero-sum framework" and, instead, "feminists for the 99 percent should aim to unite existing and future movements into a broad-based global insurgency" (Fraser, 2019, 134).

Our unscientific count indicates that most of the leaders of the opt-out movement and teacher strikes are women, which should not be surprising in that in the US and globally the teaching profession is dominated by women: in the US 75% of teachers are women and globally 70%.

It is, of course, women who objected to the first administration of the Common Core exam in New York describing 70% of students in the state as "not proficient" in math or language arts and whom Secretary of Education Arne Duncan disparaged as "White suburban moms who—all of a sudden—their child isn't as brilliant as they thought they were" (Strauss, 2013). And it is suburban moms who lead the opt-out movement in New York *not* because their children weren't as brilliant as they thought but because they rightly understood that the test scores were manipulated by the commissioner to undermine support for public schools (Hess, 2012).

It is primarily women who have been so disgusted with the leaders of public education that, as Lisa Rudley, director of the New York State Allies, states, want to "throw a wrench in the system."

Rolling back neoliberal education policies: What we need is more John Dewey and less Arne Duncan.

In the United States, it is in the last two decades of education policies that neoliberalism has been most visible (see Hursh, 2008). Neoliberalism is guided by the tenets of competitive markets, privatization, and accountability through numbers. No Child Left Behind (NCLB) and RttT both require annual evaluation of students on standardized tests, with significant consequences for teachers and schools if students do poorly on the tests.

Educators, parents, and students have criticized NCLB and RttT for how Annual Yearly Progress (AYP) is designed to portray the more diverse schools as failing and that the remedy for so-called failing schools includes replacing all the school's teachers and administrators and, possibly privatizing the schools as charter schools (publicly funded privately administered schools). Over more than the last two decades, many educators, parents, and students have criticized the NCLB, RttT, and the Every Student Succeeds Act (ESSA) for their emphasis on test scores rather than student learning.

Responding to the multiple crises we face requires more than choosing the best answer to a multiple-choice question. Instead, we need to develop socially just schools. John Smyth has written hundreds of pages describing a socially just school but offers no concise description. The best we can do here is to quote: "The socially just school pursues a curriculum, forms of organization and a pedagogy that put students before the economy. The emphasis is upon the relationships rather than de-humanized, detached and institutional forms of treatment" (2019, 483). In fact, our current dominate approach to education is the main cause of our economic and environmental problems because our education system not only fails to take on interdisciplinary questions but also undermines our ability to do so.

Public schools in the US have been increasingly impacted by neoliberal policies emphasizing holding students and teachers accountable through standardized tests, cutting funding, and privatizing schools as charter schools. The teacher strikes and the opt-out movement are both efforts to roll back high-stakes testing and the scripted curriculum and test prep that goes with it. Both want to reassert teachers into the educational process.

The resistance to the Common Core and the increasingly effective teacher strikes indicate that teachers, parents, students, and the public have not meekly acquiesced to neoliberal policies but have organized to resist and repel the policies. Teachers have led strikes in West Virginia, Arizona, and Oklahoma demanding increased school funding (Bidgood, 2018; Goldstein & Dias, 2018). Similarly, parents and teachers in 13 states have successfully created organizations informing parents of their right to opt their children out of the Common Core exams (Strauss, 2016). In New York, the LIOO and the NYSAPE have been the most effective leaders in working with parents to achieve this goal.

The opt-out movement and the teacher strikes have implemented similar strategies. First, they have both worked hard to develop a grassroots movement with widespread support from parents, teachers, and the public. Both LIOO and the Arizona Teachers' Union have developed liaisons with local schools so they can use their extensive membership to pressure school boards, the legislature, governors, and other officials to support their goals. Both realize that there is strength in numbers, and both organizations have used the strategy of wearing red shirts emblazoned with "red for ed." To that end, Noah Karvelis of the Arizona Teachers' Union describes how seeing the sea of red bolstered their confidence and communicated their strength not just to their adversaries but also to themselves.

Second, they have broadened their campaigns to rollback neoliberal economic policies that have reduced funding not only for school but for social services in general. In this way they are arguing for more funding for most everyone. They have also challenged charter schools for how they negatively impact funding public schools. In this way, the fight is not solely about teachers about school and society in general.

Over the last few years the Los Angeles school public school board has become increasingly pro–charter schools, with little oversight. The Unified Teachers of Los Angeles (UTLA) argue that charter schools drain "millions away from our neighborhood school" and demand that the Los Angeles United School District must regulate the charter industry growth and charter school co-location on neighborhood school campuses" (UTLA, 2019a). The UTLA went on strike on July 24th 2019. One of their major goals was "stopping privatization" through charter schools, which they saw as "an ongoing war for resources and students that we must win." The corporate charter industry is bankrolling their strategy to move 1 million students from public schools into charter schools by 2022" (UTLA, 2019b). The deal contained no binding agreements on charter schools, but it did include a non-binding resolution calling on the state to establish a cap on charter schools.

Likewise, Oakland, another California school district, has been pushing back against charter schools. In a recent report, Adamson (2019b), a senior policy and research analyst at Stanford Center for Opportunity Policy in Education, authored a recent report on how charter harm the Oakland Public School system, wrote that "charter school growth has steadily drained money away from traditional public schools and districts." (1) Further, in 2016–17, " the net cost to Oakland Unified School District the was $5,705 for each student who attended a charter school, because of lost revenue per student, separate from what the charter school spent" (3). In addition, not only do charter schools drain funds from the district, but they also serve fewer special education students. "Charter schools receive 28% of the district's special education funding . . . but only enroll 19% of the special education students, and an even lower percentage of the highest needs students" (Adamson, 2019, 3). The Oakland teachers went on strike on February 25 and settled the strike a week later.

The teacher strikes and the opt-out movement are questioning the basic assumptions under neoliberalism: drastic funding cuts for education and other social services, and tax cuts for corporations and the wealthy. Political science professor Corey Robin observes that the teacher strikes are mounting real resistance to "incoherent Republicans" and "gutted Dems" (Robin, 2018).

Teachers, parents, students, and community members are succeeding in resisting, rolling back, and replacing the neoliberal social order of privatization, austerity, individualism, and accountability through high-stakes testing. They are demonstrating the ability to develop a grassroots movement that can reveal the ways in which our current system favors the rich over the poor, and that can replace neoliberalism with schools and a society that aims for social justice.

Both the opt-out movement and teacher strikes have had success pushing back against the neoliberal agenda. In New York, the NYSAPE and the LIOO have successfully help elect progressive legislators, who, in turn, chose more progressive members of the Board of Regents, who selected a chancellor who more critical of testing and privatization. They also thwarted the state education department's adoption of In-Bloom, a project to collect massive amounts of data on students and their families, and reduced the role of standardized testing in evaluating teachers and schools (New York State Senate 2019; Tyrrell, 2015).

Similarly, the teacher strikes in West Virginia and Oklahoma have achieved remarkable successes. To end the nine-school-day statewide teacher strikes in West Virginia, Governor Justice signed into law a 5% pay raise for public school teachers and staff (Bidgood, 2018). Similarly, in Oklahoma, a Republican-dominated state, in which school funding has been drastically reduced over the last decade and teachers are among the lowest paid in the nation, teachers have won an average raise of $6,000 per year, or roughly a 16% raise (Goldstein & Dias, 2018).

The success of the opt-out movement and the teacher strikes indicates that the message of parents and teachers connecting our economic and educational issues to broader issues of education for the common good and social justice and education as more than test prep are having traction with the public.

Moreover, it is clear that education is central to solving our various economic and environmental crises. Passing standardized tests is insufficient preparation for examining the many issues we face. While Arne Duncan ridicules parents for complaining that the Common Core exams portrayed their children as not leaning as much as they thought, the parents were right in that an educational system that focuses on test prep rather than interdisciplinary complex learning that introduces students to solving real issues means that their children are not learning as much as they desire. Dewey reminds us that "what the best and wisest parent wants for his own child, that must the community want for all its children." Dewey (1916) would want us, like the opt-out parents, to have schools that focus not on test prep but on creating democratic citizens.

We may also need to be reminded that Dewy was an active union organizer. He also had his own column ("John Dewey's Page") in the socialist education journal *The Social Frontier,* which was published between 1934 and 1939. He, like the teachers and parents in the opt-out movement and the teacher strikes, combined analysis and activism. Teachers and parents in both movements have much they can learn from each other.

References

Adamson, F. (2018). Challenges and community responses in Oakland's public school system. Charter Schools increases OIUSD's challenges. Retrieved from https://www.facebook.com/OpenOakPublicEdNetwork/posts/2057588157666273

Bidgood, J. (2018, May 6). West Virginia raises teachers' pay to end statewide strike. *New York Times.* Retrived from https://www.nytimes.com/2018/03/06/us/west-virginia-teachers-strike-deal.html

Blanc, E. (2019a). 'Billionaires can't teach our kids: Why the Los Angeles teachers' strike was historic. *Rethinking Schools* 3:33. https://www.rethinkingschools.org/articles/billion-aires-can-t-teach-our-kids

Blanc, E. (2019b). *Red state revolt: The teachers' strikes and working-class politics.* New York: Verso.

Boninger, F., Molnar, A., & Saldaña, C.M. (2019). *Personalized learning and the digital pri-vatization of curriculum and teaching.* Boulder, CO: National Education Policy Center. Retrieved from http://nepc.colorado.edu/publication/personalized-learning.

Chappell, B. (2019, September 26). *U.S. income inequality worsens, widening to a new gap.* National Public Radio. https://www.npr.org/2019/09/26/764654623/u-s-income-inequality-worsens-widening-to-a-new-gap

Dewey, J. (1916). *The School and Society.* Chicago: University of Chicago Press.

Environmental Working Group (2019, April 8). *Toxic babies.* Retrieved from https://www.ewg.org/enviroblog/2009/04/toxic-babies

Fraser, N., Bhattachary, T., & Arruzza. C. (2018, November/December). Notes for a feminist manifesto. *New Left Review 114*: 13–134.

French, N. (2019, March). A different kind of teachers' strike wave. *Jacobin.* Retrieved from https://jacobinmag.com/2019/03/a-different-kind-of-teachers-strike-wave

Goldstein, D., & Dias, E. (2018, April 12). Oklahoma teachers end walkout after winning raises and additional funding. *The New York Times.* Retrieved from https://www.nytimes.com/2018/04/12/us/oklahoma-teachers-strike.html

Harrington, T. (2019, March 3). After seven day strike, Oakland teachers approve new contract. EdSource. https://edsource.org/2019/tentative-agreement-reached-in-oakland-unified-teachers-strike/609342

Hess, R. (2012, November 30). The Common Core Kool-Aid. *Education Week.* Retrieved from http://blogs.edweek.org/edweek/rick_hess_straight_up/2012/11/the_common_core_kool-aid.html

Holling, C. S. (2001). Understanding the complexity of economic, ecological and social systems. *Ecosystems* 4: 390–405.

Howell, W. G. (2015). Results of President Obama's Race to the Top. Education Next. Retrieved from https://www.educationnext.org/results-president-obama-race-to-the-top-reform/

Hursh, D. (2008). *The end of public schools: The corporate reform agenda to privatize education.* New York: Routledge.

Hursh, D., Chen, Z. McGinnis, S., & Lingard, B. (2019), Resisting the neo-liberal: Parent activism in New York state against the corporate reform agenda in schooling. In M. Hamilton & L. Tett (Eds.), *Resisting the neo-liberal discourse in education: Local, national and transnational perspectives.* London: Policy Press.

Hursh, D., Deutermann, J. Rudley, L., Chen, Z., & McGinnis, S. (2019). *Opting out: The story of the parents' grassroots movement to achieve whole-child public schools* Gorham, ME: Myers Education Press.

Karp, S., & Sanchez, A. (2018, Summer). The 2018 wave of teacher strikes. *Rethinking Schools. 32*(4); 6, 8–11.

Klein, N. (2014). *This changes everything: Capitalism vs. the climate.* New York: Simon & Schuster.

Leitner, H., Peck, J., & Sheppard, E. (Eds.). (2007). *Contesting neoliberalism: Urban frontiers.* New York, NY: Guilford Press.

New York State Allies for Public Education. (2019). *Know the facts … Ignore the noise.*

New York State Senate. (2019, April 29). Senate bill 5394.

Oxfam (2016, January 18). *62 people own the same wealth as half the world.* https://www.oxfamamerica.org/press/62-people-own-same-wealth-as-half-the-world. Retrieved June 2018

Robin, C. (2018, April 12). Striking teachers are "real resistance" to "incoherent" Republicans and "gutted" Dems. Democracy Now. Retrieved from https://www.democracynow.org/2018/4/12/corey_robin_striking_teachers_are_real

Smyth, J. (2019). The socially just school: Transforming young lives. In Saltman, K. J. & Means, A. J. (Eds.) *The Wiley handbook of global education reform*. Medford, MA.

Stenbgarber, S. (2004). Contaminated without consent: Why our exposure to chemicals in air, food and water violates human rights. *Beyond Pesticides* (24-1). Washington, D.C. Retrieved from https://www.beyondpesticides.org/assets/media/documents/infoservices/pesticidesandyou/Spring%2004/Contaminated%20Without%20Consent.pdf

Strauss, V. (2013, November 16). Arne Duncan: 'White suburban moms' upset that Common Core shows their kids aren't 'brilliant.' *The Washington Post*. Retrieved from www.washingtonpost.com/news/answer-sheet/wp/2013/11/16/arne-duncan-white-surburban-moms-upset-that-common-core-shows-their-kids-arent-brilliant/?utm_term=.0945ab8da214

Tyrrell, J. (2015, May 20). Many candidates endorsed by LI Opt-Out group win seats. *Newsday*. Retrieved from https://www.newsday.com/long-island/many-candidates-endorsed-by-li-opt-out-group-win-seats-1.10452800

Unified Teachers of Los Angeles. (2019a). *Give kids a chance: Stop starving our public schools*. One-page flyer.

Unified Teachers of Los Angeles. (2019b). *When we fight, we win!* One-page flyer.

Weiner, L. (2019. January 6). Why the LA teachers strike matters. *Jacobin*. Retrieved from https://jacobinmag.com/2019/01/utla-los-angeles-teachers-strike-privatization/

CHAPTER TEN

Nonrationality, Education, and the Ritual Performance of Sara Palin[1]

Richard Quantz

A RARE ALIGNMENT of perspectives brought a unique convergence among the mainstream press, social media, and the blogosphere when together they belittled Sara Palin's endorsement of Donald Trump in the 2016 Iowa Republican Presidential Caucuses campaign (Rappeport & Haberman, January 19, 2016, http://www.nytimes.com/2016/01/20/us/politics/donald-trump-sarah-palin.html?_r=0). With unabashed glee, professional writers as well as ordinary bloggers and commentors expressed dismay at the incoherent, nonsensical, nonsequitor, inaccurate speech (see, for example, Barbaro, January 20, 2016, http://www.nytimes.com/2016/01/21/us/politics/sarah-palin-endorsement-speech-donald-trump.html). Examined for many of the bizarre claims and impenetrable phrasing, Palin's endorsement was instantly determined to be hurtful to Trump's campaign. I suspect I am one of the very few who considered Palin's speech masterful and most likely very effective in doing what it was supposed to do, which was to legitimize Trump's candidacy for those who admire and support Palin. Perhaps the cause of my divergence from the dominant opinion results from several decades of attention to the nonrational aspects of social behavior. During that time I have come to believe that nonrationality explains more about social behavior than rationality. Those who criticized Palin's talk did so because it was not rationally defensible, in fact, perhaps, not even rationally meaningful. My own judgment of its success is based on the evidence that rationality rarely influenced anyone other than the trained scholar (and even much less of their thinking than they are likely to admit). Instead, I argue that the nonrational aspects of Palin's endorsement likely made it quite effective.

One of the primary instigators for the rise of sociology as a field was the dominance of the rising field of economics with its assumption that human economic activity is fundamentally rational. Beginning with Karl Marx's recognition that the so-called rational economy was based upon a nonrational commitment to capitalist principles such as the right to private property and the moral acceptability of making profit from others' labor, those who have developed social theory have done so against the economists' assumption that humans act rationally. The world's first official sociologist, Emile Durkheim argued

1   Keynote address, Department of Educational Leadershp, University of Massachusetts Dartmouth, April 25, 2014, Grand Reading Room.

that society itself was constructed upon the nonrational sharing of a collective consciousness that emanated from a collective effervescence. And Max Weber, the third of the initial social theory triumvirate, argued that human action arises from a consciousness formed in historically constructed power struggles among associational groups. In fact, since the time of these early thinkers, all but a handful of social theorists have assumed that there are preconscious, nonrational mechanisms at play in the construction of society. While there may be dramatic differences in how they identify, name, and theorize these mechanisms, there is little difference in their dismissal of human rationality as a primary explanatory for social behavior. Let me be clear, "nonrationality" should not be confused with "irrationality." Irrational action is action that goes against rationality whereas nonrational action is simply action taken by people without regard to reason. People act not only from unconscious psychological motivations but also unreflected and not understood social mechanisms. Given the near unanimous assumption by social theorists outside of the field of economics of this reality, I think it strange that so little writing has focused specifically on the mechanisms that form nonrationality. Perhaps one of the reasons for this has been the difficulty in observing or measuring such nonrationality and given the long empirical commitment of the field of sociology, perhaps this difficulty has relegated nonrationality to a theoretical assumption. My own work has suggested that one way we may be able to see the nonrational at work is through the investigation of ritual (Quantz, 2011).

To understand why ritual may be a useful way into this problem, I need to take some space and explain what I mean ritual as one of the most important ways of understanding the influence of nonrationality. Let me start with an anecdote presented by Lauren Isaac, a former high school teacher, about what happened when the call for students to participate in the Pledge of Allegiance came over the loud speakers while her English as a Second Language (ESL) high school class was working in the library.

> I looked around the library and, out of the corner of my eye, caught the librarian staring at our corner. One hand on her hip, she gazed at me with a look that cried, "Why can't you control your disrespectful students?"
> I walked over to my group and, half-heartedly said, "Okay, y'all need to stand up," strategically making sure the librarian saw and heard my authoritarian and normalizing request. Of course, my performance was not convincing to about 80% of the ESL students. Not only did they not stand, they displayed a dramatic performance of "remaining seated." Marco leaned his chair back and propped his feet up on the table, revealing his red, green, and white shoelaces. Dario draped his torso over the table, and a colorful Virgen de Guadalupe shimmered off the back of his t-shirt. Samuel transformed his hands into a pillow and Mexican flag bandanas wristbands peaked out from under his head. Nicolas indifferently turned away from the U.S. flag and exchanged a few words in Spanish Pig Latin to his neighbor, who chuckled at his coded joke.

While the students' performances were taking place, I had a mini-performance of my own. If the librarian began to click-clack her way over to us, I would circulate through the tables, whispering "y'all need to stand up" or "you know, we're gonna lose our library privileges." If I were not under the gaze of the librarian's glasses, I would shuffle through attendance papers and hope this drama ends before any more trouble ensues. By the time all the performances were organized and enacted, the Pledge of Allegiance was over, and we all returned to other activities.[2]

Introduction to Ritual

We humans are not just social animals; we are also pack animals. We are like wolves and dogs. Watch a pack of dogs and note the many gestures given and understood by other members of the pack. For example, note how dogs greet a returning dog to the pack. In fact, if you own a dog, you are probably quite familiar with the greeting you receive every time you come home "to the pack": the wagging of their tails, their noses pushed out to sniff your scent with the expectation that you will reach out and pat them. There is a whole television show (*The Dog Whisperer*) built around the idea that understanding how dogs communicate in their packs is the key to having a well-behaved pet. And much the same can be said about humans. Understanding how humans communicate as part of "packs" will lead teachers to a better understanding of what is happening in their classrooms. Of course unlike dogs, we humans are not limited to communicating through signals; we also use signs. But just because much of our communication is through language does not mean that all communication uses language nor does it mean that when we do use language that we do so rationally. We can gain a much better understanding of what goes on in our classrooms and cafeterias and playgrounds if we also focus on the nonrational aspects of human action.

Even though ritual has been an important concept in social theory from its beginning, education scholars have been slow to recognize its power. I believe that the lack of enthusiasm for ritual results from several factors. One is that most people equate ritual with large ceremonies such as commencement exercises, assemblies, and pep rallies and while there has been some interesting work on such ceremonies (for example, see Lesko, 1988), few could argue that such ceremonies have much impact on the experience of schooling given that, in the full scope of things, so little time is actually spent on such formal exercises. Second, many people equate ritual with empty repetition of actions such as a softball player who repeats the same acts in the same order each time she comes to bat such as tugging on the brim of her cap followed by turning the bat in her hands followed by tapping the home plate followed by three (and only three) half swings at

---

2   Lauren B. Isaac, "Pledges of Allegiance, Bandana Wristbands, and Spanish Pig Latin: A Teacher's Reflections on Rituals, Resistance, and Working toward Multicultural Classrooms." *Multicultural Perspectives* 15, no. 2 (2013): 98.

the plate. While such behavior is often referred to as ritual, it does not fit the meaning of ritual used in this essay.

By ritual I refer to that aspect of action that is a formalized, symbolic performance. This definition uses four important concepts. Performance refers to acting for an audience (always keeping in mind that sometimes we are the audience for our own performances). Ritual is consciously or unconsciously intended to be observed. It is a show. Consider the actions of the Latino students in Lauren Isaac's ESL class described in the earlier anecdote. Surely Marco, Dario, Samuel, and Nicholas intended others to observe their actions—at least by each other, if not by the other students and the teachers in the library—and Isaac performed for the librarian. As she acknowledged, when in their own classroom where they were unobserved by others, Isaac simply allowed these Mexican students to ignore the requirement to participate in this Pledge of Allegiance to the flag of the United States.

Second, not all performances should be considered ritual, only those that use or are themselves symbolic count as ritual. For example, in Isaac's anecdote, we find the students presenting symbols as part of their performances including Dario's Virgen de Guadalupe T-shirt, Samuel's Mexican flag bandana wristbands, and Nicolas's use of Spanish Pig Latin. But these are not merely symbols of Mexican identity because, when combined with their actions, we find body performances that are symbolic of the students' refusal to exchange their Mexican identity for an American one.

To participate appropriately in ritual action requires that we recognize and respect the form expected by the ritual. One thing is clear in Isaac's example, these Mexican boys fail to respect the form of the Pledge of Allegiance to the American flag, and it is that failure to follow form that had the librarian so upset.

Finally, ritual is not a type of action but an aspect of nearly all action. We can think of all social action as consisting of at least two aspects: ritual action and instrumental action. Ritual action is that part of the act that is a formalized, symbolic performance. Isaac's walking around and pointedly telling students to stand up was a performance whose form and substance symbolized to the librarian that Isaac was acting as a teacher should act. Instrumental action is that part of the act that is intended to achieve a particular end. Though perhaps "half-hearted," Isaac also hoped that her request to stand might actually result in students standing. One part of her action was ritual, but another part of it was actually instrumental. Any particular act may be mostly instrumental or mostly ritual, but almost all human action includes some aspects of both. The benefit of ritual analysis is that it helps us to see those aspects of the nonrational influence even in the most rational of human action.

Let us entertain a different example; consider the college lecture. Many professors (perhaps most professors) believe that when they lecture, they teach, and they only teach, when they lecture. The former director of a university's center for teaching and learning once confided to me that whenever a department chair referred professors with low student evaluations to his office for help, the first thing he did was to sit with the professors and help them understand that there were other people in the room with them while they were teaching. The ineffective professors would often come in confused about why they were not successful with students. They would show the center's director their lectures, talk about how hard they work on them, point out how organized and clear the material was, but no matter how good their lectures might be, students continued to score them low in student evaluations. As far as the instructors were concerned, they were excellent teachers; the problems, they thought, were with the students. The center director would point out that teaching required learning and where little learning occurred little teaching transpired either. While there has been a gratifying reduction in the reliance on the lecture in recent years, students' classroom experience still primarily takes the form of listening to lectures. Given that most students find lectures of little help and given that much research suggests lectures as one of the least effective forms of teaching, why might so many college instructors continue to rely primarily on the lecture?

First, let me be clear that while most research suggests lecture as a weak form of pedagogy, there are clear instrumental reasons for lecture. The lecture is an effective way to deliver up-to-date knowledge to a mass of students. Considering that most textbooks are at least two years out of date on the day that they are published and that they are updated only every five to ten years, clearly, if we want our students to have the benefits of the latest research and scholarship, faculty must find a way to supplement the textbooks, and lectures are a good way to do this. But in this new media age, they are not the only way to supplement textbooks. For example, many years ago (before the internet was as well developed as it is now) I would type out lectures and take them to the copy shop each week for students to purchase and read before coming to class. This way they received the most up-to-date information and we could spend the time in class responding to their questions and clarifying their confusions. Of course with the internet, this is even more easily accomplished and something that I continue to do with certain classes that I teach. With the growing reluctance of students to read along with many students' preference for video, some faculty are recording lectures ahead of time and placing the videos online for students to watch before coming to class. This approach has been dubbed the "inverted classroom." There are instrumental reasons for instructors to lecture, but perhaps more convincing reasons for them to move to an alternative such as the inverted classroom; so, why do so many still rely primarily and even exclusively on the traditional live lecture?

If we shift from thinking about lecture as instrumental action designed to achieve specific ends and start to consider it as ritual action, we begin to see some other possibilities as to why faculty continue to lecture. Focus on the body; what happens in a lecture? The professor is in the front of the room and the students sit in seats all facing the instructor. The instructor stands; students sit, which often (though not in amphitheater lecture rooms) places that instructor's head above the students' heads. The professor talks, students listen and write down the words as if they were magic incantations. The student does not talk without the instructor's permission. We can all recognize these elements of a lecture. They are its form and everyone knows their role within this form. While some lecturers try to stop talking and get students talking, the students' frequent reluctance to engage the lecturer may result partly because to do so is to violate the expected form of lectures where the lecturer talks and the student listens. It is just plain hard for a lecturer to step away from the head of the room and, therefore, the head of the discussion. And consider what this form and these roles symbolize. When I ask students what they think it symbolizes, they are very quick to point out authority and hierarchy accrues to the professor. I might also add that it celebrates education as the transference of knowledge from one who knows to those who do not. In other words, it depicts education as the mastery of knowledge given, rather than as the "drawing out" that the Latin root of the word "education" implies. Might this be why professors continue to lecture even when there are more rational approaches to their instrumental ends? Might lecturing be more important for its ritual effects than its instrumental goals? Might reinforcing the idea that professors are the reservoir of all knowledge and that education is merely the acquisition of knowledge from experts be why lecturing remains the primary method of pedagogy in college?

Solidarity

One of the primary benefits of the focus on nonrationality is its explanation for social solidarity. If we return to those early social theorists—Marx, Durkheim, and Weber, we find each explored group solidarity as an aspect of their larger theory. Marx posited class consciousness, Durkheim suggested collective consciousness, and Weber explored the creation and influence of a communal ethic. Social solidarity is not something to be assumed but to be explained. This is true even for conflict theories such as Marx's and Weber's since the conflict is not one among individuals but among groups. In the incredibly diverse societies that exist today, the requirement to understand and explain social solidarity has become even greater if we are not to fall victim to the reductionism of the individual in the way in which neoliberalism has done.

Typically analysts of culture in schools focus on the ways in which conflict arises without paying much attention to the ways in which solidarity and community are created and maintained. In fact, the mechanisms used to create solidarity and community may be the very same mechanisms that divide groups against each other. While it is true that all groups are multivoiced that does not mean that they are merely a cacophonous collection of individuals. Oddly, how these quite varied persons come to experience a sense of connection with others in a group helps contribute to our understanding of conflict.

Because ritual is a performance, it works primarily by what people do together rather than what they think together. When our joint action makes us feel good, we feel connected to the others who participate with us. Church provides an excellent example. Regular churchgoers can attest that at times they arrive at church stressed or out of sorts, but at the end of the service they often leave feeling refreshed, connected, whole. Even though the individuals in the church likely entertain very different thoughts throughout the service, by sharing the hour with others who stand together, sit together, fold their hands together, pray together, and sing together, they start to feel connected within themselves and to those around them. This feeling of connectedness is what we generally mean by community and what I specifically refer to as solidarity. It can be very powerful stuff.

High school principals love championship football teams because when their teams are winning grades go up and fights go down. This is so even when the student body is divided into competing culture groups. Winning teams bring more students out to the game where they cheer together, yell at the enemy together, shout allegiance to our mascot, and, therefore, ourselves, as we cheer our champion warriors in the ritual war we call sport.

Multivoicedness

Rituals are multivoiced. They speak with many different voices to many different participants. This is an advantage of ritual as much as a weakness. Because ritual relies primarily on symbols for its meaning and because rituals are oblique references, they can be interpreted in multiple ways.

Again consider the high school football game that is so central to many American towns. Imagine a soldier just returned from Afghanistan for a scheduled R and R who attends her high school football game to connect with her friends and neighbors. Before the game begins they mill around talking, bringing the still-uniformed soldier up-to-date on all the latest gossip and trying to get her to talk about her experiences of war. Then the band starts to play the National Anthem. What happens? The soldier immediately turns to the American flag, removes her cap, and salutes. What is going through her mind? Of course, it could be anything, but it would not be too hard to imagine her sense of unreality. Forty-eight hours earlier she was driving a Humvee through dangerous territory and now she is standing in this peaceful and comforting space. Perhaps this place, once so ordinary, has become both familiar and strange. I have heard that many soldiers on R and R feel guilty about leaving their fellow soldiers behind in danger and not being there to protect them. Certainly the National Anthem and the flag mean something very important to her.

But then in the stands, a few rows in front of her the social studies teacher rises. You know the one I mean. The one who teaches American history and American government and believes all of the stories he has told high school students for his 22 years of teaching. He believes in the American story and all that the anthem and the flag represent. Like the soldier, he stands at attention oriented toward the flag, his hand is over his heart and he sings the anthem loudly. What is he thinking about? All that the flag represents: how great America is, the hope of the world, the home of the free and the brave.

Down a little and to the side huddles a group of high school juniors. What do they do when they hear the anthem? Settle down—a little. Maybe even orient themselves toward the flag. Maybe a few even stop talking altogether. What is going on in their mind? Yea!!! The game is about to begin!!

We easily understand such a scenario—each participant acting more or less the same while thinking some very different things. The opening ceremony of the high school football game has form and it is symbolic, but its meaning is multivoiced. Still, it brings the people together. Regardless of what they may be thinking as individuals, just participating in the ritual together even while thinking different things, helps build a sense of solidarity, togetherness, and connection. Ritual works because we act together, more than because we think together and that is why the multivoicedness of ritual can be a positive part of the ritual experience. Just by participating in rituals together, it can work on us—but not always. Because ritual allows people to feel in solidarity with others even when they are thinking different things, multivoicedness can be a strength, but that same multivoicedness can also create important divisions between groups of people.

Return to the Friday night high school football game for halftime. The home team's band has just finished its performance and now the visitor's band comes marching quickly on to the field playing its school's fight song, "Dixie." Listen to that tune and sing the song, "Ohhhh, I wish I were in the land of cotton, Old times there are not forgotten . . ." What happens now? A roar of approval from the visitors in the stands across the field! They sing along and wave their Confederate flags and cheer for their "Rebels"! A ritual of solidarity brings them together. What is going through their minds? "Yea us!" But what about those in the home crowd? What do they think? Well, of course they think many things but surely some of them are disturbed by the performance of what is to them an obviously racist anthem and flag. To the home crowd, the fight song and the flag may represent not only their high school's opponent but also a shameful past. Clearly, this song divides the people at the stadium between them and us. We can see that the multi-voicedness of ritual can lead to solidarity among those who are thinking different things, but it can also lead to the division of the population into opposing groups.

And while a championship football team can bring some sense of solidarity to oth-erwise competing culture groups within a high school as they cheer their team under the shared identity marker that is their mascot, what happens when that mascot singles out a minority group within the school, separating them from the other students, making them feel outside the group. For many indigenous Americans, the use of mascots such as Indians, Redskins, and Braves and fight cheers including tomahawk chops and other symbols of indigenous Americans is highly offensive. While such identity markers of a high school athletic team may bring solidarity to a disparate group, it is also likely to di-vide the group against itself. Given this inevitability, why do we wish to create solidarity while also creating division?

To help understand the problem let us return to Isaac's example of the ESL class in the library. The school clearly intended pledging allegiance to the U.S. flag as a ritual to help bind the students and faculty together in the spirit that is America, land of opportunity for all. But to require Mexican students to stand and salute the American flag is to require that they pledge allegiance to a nation in which they are not members and to negate their own nation. Clearly such a ritual does not work to create solidarity between the Mexican and American students but instead helps solidify a border between them.

But even within the population of American students a problem arises with the Pledge of Allegiance around the phrase "under God," words added to the Pledge in the 1950s as part of the Cold War struggle against a alleged "godless communism." Today nearly thirty percent of Americans claim to be nonbelievers. The revised Pledge with the "under God" phrase requires nonbelievers either to lie when they say the pledge or to present the appearance that they are not loyal citizens of the republic. We must begin to ask ourselves why we would want to require a ritual of solidarity in which nearly a third of the students feel dishonest or excluded because they do not believe in a omnipotent God? Why do we wish to make them feel that they are not legitimate citizens of the country in which they are schooled? And also we should ask why we would want to use a symbol of identity such as the Confederate flag or a term offensive to many indigenous Americans that may bring feelings of solidarity to the majority but at the cost of excluding a minority? Ritual can work to create solidarity because our different thinking is not as important as our joint acting, unless, that is, the symbols of our ritual divide us among ourselves.

Potential Effects

Some scholars speak of ritual as having certain effects such as creating solidarity and so advocate that schools promote their symbols of identity though such actions as school T-shirts, uniforms, and pep rallies. But simply assuming that ritual creates these effects is a mistake because there are plenty of examples of rituals failing to achieve any effect at all. These failed ceremonies I call empty rituals because they fail to be filled with the kind of connections necessary for an effective ritual. For that reason, I prefer to think of ritual as having potential effects, which I identify as either individual or social.

Individual Effects

Individual effects occur when what we are thinking about in our mind during the ritual becomes important to us because of our participation in the ritual. When ritual works, we gain good feelings as we participate with others and often what we are cognitively thinking in our minds becomes associated with those good feelings. In other words, through effective ritual the body connects to the mind and we begin to hold strong feelings about the objects of our thinking. We begin to believe strongly in the truth and the goodness of the symbols of our ritual. For example, when rituals work, we begin to believe in the flag itself as well as in the republic for which it stands. We begin to believe in the goodness of our football players and the rightness of our school. Through effective ritual we come to "know," not just "believe," that what our lecturers teach is true, that they represent what is right and that they embody the good. Note, however, that this "knowing" is believed not through some rational reasoning process but through the nonrational mechanism of participating in rituals.

One way we know that knowledge gained, truth proclaimed, goodness embraced through ritual is not arrived at rationally is that these knowledges, truths, and goods become sacred entities to the believers. Durkheim argued that sacred aspects of societies are created through ritual. In Durkheim's last major work, *The Elementary Forms of Religious Life* (1965/1912), he claimed that one characteristic of all religions is their propensity to divide the world into the sacred and the profane. For Durkheim, this division was one of attitude. Those objects toward which we maintain an attitude of "respect" belong to the sacred realm. Those objects toward which we feel no such sentiments belong to the profane realm.

> We get the impression that we are in relations with two distinct sorts of reality and that a sharply drawn line of demarcation separates them from each other: on the one hand is the world of profane things, on the other, that of sacred things. (Durkheim, 1965/1912, p. 243)

Durkheim's division between the sacred and the profane should not be confused with the difference between the religious and the secular because the point is not whether there is some metaphysical spirit or not but whether there is an attitude of reverence or not. In an extended example, Durkheim compares the respect that a king gets to the respect that an ordinary person gets. He points to the way in which people keep an appropriate distance from high personages, the way in which people only approach them with precautions, and the way in which the gestures and language used when interacting is different with kings than with ordinary mortals. "The sentiment felt on these occasions is so closely related to the religious sentiment that many peoples have confounded the two. In order to explain the consideration accorded to princes, nobles, and political chiefs, a sacred character has been attributed to them" (Durkheim, 1965/1912, p. 244).[3] In this example we not only see that sacred attitudes can be taken with secular personages but also that the taking of the sacred attitude is revealed in ritual performance: by the distance one keeps, the manner in which one approaches, and the special gestures reserved for the recipient of the respect. In the same way, any object of our thoughts that develop strong emotional commitments through ritual begins to treat that object as sacred. We must treat the knowledge, truths, and goods symbolized in our rituals with sacred respect. We must not treat them as profane. For this reason, these objects

---

3   For more development of Durkheim's concept of the sacred and profane in ritual, see Quantz (2011, pp. 21–44).

of thought must not be open to the profane treatment of doubt, reason, and analysis. In our contemporary world of education, no amount of reason or evidence is able to sway some policy makers from a belief in mass testing as a positive mechanism for school reform or from the belief that education is a commodity to be treated like any other commodity in a free marketplace. The "Truth" of testing and market-based strategies presents themselves as rational and reasoned, while surely much of the support for these strategies relies primarily on the nonrational results of the individual effects that these people have felt while participating in rituals that treat these "Truths" as sacred.

Social Effects

While one of the important potential effects of ritual is the way in which it connects individuals' bodies to their minds, another important potential effect is the way ritual connects an individual's body with the bodies of others participating in or observing the ritual. While the individual effect is located in the individual mind and body, the social effect is located in the relationships of bodies to bodies.

Rituals enforce a socially accepted set of behaviors. Individuals are assigned roles in rituals and they know what they are to do and they do it—at least when the ritual is effective. Ritual imposes order on bodies by requiring participants to use their bodies in certain ways. When everyone acts as they are required to act, ritual can be quite imposing. To the outsider (even to the observant insider) watching the ordered actions of participants often leads to the conclusion that there is uniformity, conformity, and agreement about the sacred order.

Consider once again the Pledge of Allegiance to the U.S. flag. While I argue that the daily pledge is probably one of the least effective rituals in American schools, there are times in which a local culture, or unique historical moment, or a rigorous enforcement of the practice results in near full participation by students. Consider the students in the photograph in Figure 10.1 that shows students in Public School #8, a school that served a primarily Italian American part of New York City and that was taken about six months before the Allied invasion of Italy in 1943. Clearly this particular ritual performance has achieved its potential social effect. Notice the attitude and orientation of their bodies, every student is performing his or her role as required. We have no doubt that this ritual moment has imposed a clear order in the classroom.

FIGURE 10.1.
LIBRARY OF CONGRESS: HTTP://WWW.LOC.GOV/PICTURES/RESOURCE/FSA.8D25792/

Looking at this picture, you might draw the conclusion that the students are actually committing themselves to their nation and that they actually understand America to be indivisible with liberty and justice for all. But there is no real reason to think that these students actually believe in the sacred objects of this ritual. Ritual has the potential to impose social order and the potential to create sacred commitments by individuals in that society, but it does not have to do either. The ritual may achieve a social effect without an individual effect as well as the other way around. Return to the photo in Figure 10.1, given the students' mien and perhaps the historical moment, we might easily be persuaded that not only the social effect has been achieved but that its potential individual effect has as well. But such an assumption should not be merely presumed because we cannot know through observation alone what is going on in the minds of those students. Perhaps they are only performing for their teacher because they know they are being photographed and to fail to act as required could bring down the wrath of Miss Huff. A ritual can be considered an utterance in a dialogue and like any utterance, one's gesturing may be a lie. Can you be sure that this picture is not a lie?

Too frequently we assume that a ritual whose social effect is obvious indicates that the ritual has gained meaning to the participants. The librarian in Isaac's anecdote makes this mistake. She seems to believe that if Isaac can force the Mexican students to perform their social role in the ritual that they will come to actually develop deeper appreciation for the United States, or, at least she believes that by failing to participate in the pledge, these students are disrespectful, which itself causes cultural conflict (Wegwert, 2008). It probably does not occur to her that it is not the students' disrespect that causes conflict but the institution's disrespect of them when requiring them to pledge a flag that is not their own. When we finally get Isaac's Mexican students to perform their part, we may fail to realize that the individual effect being created is the opposite of its desired one; that is, it creates oppositional attitudes toward the school and the United States. In this case, a ritual that is intended to create solidarity can be seen to actually spawn division.

Understanding Palin's Endorsement

The primary mistake of those who underestimate the power of Sara Palin's endorsement is their focus on the rationality expressed in her talk rather than to see it as simply a ritual performance designed to evoke feelings of solidarity among the audience, herself, and Trump. So, let us return to Palin's endorsement of Donald Trump and examine it in light of the nonrational instead of the rational.

If we examine the visual aspects of the performance we begin with an image of Palin being embraced by Trump and then the two of them standing in front of two American and two Iowa state flags. Add that Palin stands behind a podium with TRUMP written in large letters and we are able to visually see a nascent solidarity between Palin and Trump. Just as the students saluting the American flag in the example achieve a social effect, so too does the ritual performance presented her move toward achieving a social effect that puts Palin and Trump in solidarity with each other and, therefore, with Palin supporters. For some, this physical presence may be enough to make admirers of Palin to consider the possibilities of a Trump presidency, but there is so much more for us to consider.

From her outfits to her voice, Palin performs an identity that some people connect with. Now I confess, and those who know me even slightly can attest, I know little about fashion. But I find it hard to believe that I could find anything like Palin's cloak with its dangling silver and gold metallic strips in Hillary Clinton's closet. Flashy, gaudy, and expensive-looking, such an outfit does not represent the quiet and subtle well-dressed business and social elite but echoes the fashion of country music culture. Her performance is upbeat and enthusiastic and "fun" as she denigrates and demeans those who disagree with her who happen to be the kind of people who might dress likely Hillary Clinton.

Keep in mind that Palin is a trained media presenter. Listen carefully to her enunciation and you will find that most of her words are carefully spoken so that the final consonants are clearly expressed—except when she waves an ideographic phrase or takes an oppositional posture. Then we hear things such as "You betcha." "I'm still standin','" "pussy footin','" "slurpin' off the gravy train," "Things are gonna change under President Trump." The dropping of consonants is clearly intentional and is part of a ritual performance indicating her solidarity with rural, white working-class Americans allowing them to accept that Palin is "is just like us."

Similarly her use of taboo words and expressions such as "kick ISIS ass" and when she equates President Obama's resolution of the American navy incursion into Iraqi waters as "we bend over" (i.e., kowtowing but really a clear reference to a sexual position) are other little ritual acts to indicate solidarity with her audience.

But mostly, Palin strings together, with only slightly clever rhymes, comments that her audience members are telling each other in the kitchen, on the job, in the bar, and on the street—such as phrases to diminish the president of the United States to a weak, effeminate, and naïve do-gooder:

> "a weak-kneed, capitulator-in-chief has decided America will lead from behind. And he, who would negotiate deals, kind of with the skills of a community organizer maybe organizing a neighborhood tea."

> "No more pussy footin' around!"

> "Now, eight years ago, I warned that Obama's promised fundamental transformation of America. That is was going to take more from you, and leave America weaker on the world stage."

> "Exactly one year from tomorrow, former President Barack Obama. He packs up the teleprompters and the selfie-sticks, and the Greek columns, and all that hopey, changey stuff and he heads on back to Chicago, where I'm sure he can find some community there to organize again."

And, of course, Palin's talk evokes Christian symbols such as "You rock an' rollers. And holy rollers!"

> "... can I get a 'Hallelujah!'"

> "Right wingin', bitter clingin', proud clingers of our guns, our god, and our religions, and our Constitution."

And perhaps most disturbing to those of us on the political Left are her appeals to her white, mostly rural, working-class supporters with phrases that, with a little change in their language, come from the Left's playbook, such as this extended ideograph:

> He's [Trump's] been able to tear the veil off this idea of the system. The way that the system really works, and please hear me on this, I want you guys to understand more and more how the system, the establishment, works, and has gotten us into the troubles that we are in in America. The permanent political class has been doing the bidding of their campaign donor class, and

that's why you see that the borders are kept open. For them, for their cheap labor that they want to come in. That's why they've been bloating budgets. It's for crony capitalists to be able suck off of them. It's why we see these lousy trade deals that gut our industry for special interests elsewhere. We need someone new, who has the power, and is in the position to bust up that establishment to make things great again. It's part of the problem.

Palin's speech ritually takes a sacred attitude toward those sacred truths accepted by so many of her rural, white followers: guns and the Second Amendment, God and Christianity, the need to make America militarily stronger, the blaming of immigrants for America's problems including unemployment and low wages, the undignified belittling of a black president, and the admiration of a self-made men and ties them to Trump. It makes no difference that Trump himself is one of those "crony capitalists" who relies on cheap immigrant labor or that Trump is not actually a self-made man. Such facts may count as counter-evidence to her argument, but Palin's performance appealing to these sacred truths places them beyond the profane and, therefore, disallows the appeal to reason. Those whose identities are built through such ritual and sacred truths may not require or even desire rational arguments. They only need a ritual performance that reinforces those sacred truths and ties them to Trump through his presence at the event. Of course, we cannot know how many of the individuals who attended this rally or watched it on television or streamed it online actually felt the individual effect that ritual potentially constructs, but we shouldn't be surprised that at least some were moved in the direction of attaching their belief in Sara Palin as representing their own identity to that of Donald Trump. After all if Palin is one of us, then so too must Trump.

If you are one who found her speech as attractive as fingernails on a chalkboard, you probably identify with a different group than those whom Palin is rallying. Remember, ritual is multivoiced and, while working to create solidarity among some, may also create division against others. Just as a high school's ritual may help bring solidarity to its student body while dividing it against its football rivals, Palin's endorsement may be quite successful in building solidarity among themselves while creating divisions with the rest of us. In fact, our negative reaction so publicly presented in the press and on social media is itself a ritual that works to create solidarity within our anti-Palin, anti-Trump groups while working to convince Palin supporters that we fail to respect them. Our own self-congratulatory ritual to rationality expressed in our delighted denigrations of her performance may be more self-deluding than enlightening. Until we recognize that people primarily act nonrationally, we will never understand why the forces of bigotry, ignorance, fear, and hatred have such a stranglehold on the throat of American democracy.

References

Durkheim, E. (1965). *Elementary forms of religious life*. New York: The Free Press.

Lesko, N. (1988). *Symbolizing society: Stories, rites and structures in a Catholic High School*. New York: Falmer.

Wegwert, J. (2008) Democracy without dialogue. Unpublished doctoral dissertation. Oxford: Miami University.

Quantz, R. (2011). *Rituals and student identity in education: Ritual critique for a new pedagogy*. New York: Palgrave MacMillan.

PART III

OPEN UP *EL PADRON COLONIAL DE PODER*

CHAPTER ELEVEN

Decolonizing University Leadership: Transforming What It Means to Lead[1]

Antonia Darder

> *The more radical the person is, the more fully he or she enters into reality so that, knowing it better, he or she can transform it. This individual is not afraid to confront, to listen, to see the world unveiled. This person is not afraid to meet the people or to enter into dialogue with them. This person does not consider himself or herself the proprietor of history or of all people, or the liberator of the oppressed; but he or she does commit himself or herself, within history, to fight at their side. (Freire, 1971)*

THE UNIVERSITY TODAY exists as a disturbing battleground, where ideas and practices can easily degenerate into a nightmare of undemocratic repression and bureaucratic madness. This phenomenon is fueled by wholesale abandonment of the public good and a full-fledged institutional divestment from the welfare of the commons. In the process, liberal values of equality and public responsibility have been precariously been undermined by an unrelenting neoliberal culture of rampant greed, racism, increasing public surveillance, and the social regulation and containment of subaltern populations. In the wake of this fiasco, critical notions of multiculturalism and diversity within the university, along with scholarship anchored in community concerns, have been rampantly undermined by an economic ethos that has rendered difference a whore to its own utilitarian pursuits.

It is thus impossible to speak about critical leadership for social justice without attempting to systematically unveil the manner in which neoliberalism has eroded culturally democratic possibilities within the U.S. academy. The all-too-common institutional bypassing of complex moral and ethical questions tied to diversity and emancipatory struggles for social justice have resulted in economic policies and practices in higher education that, wittingly or unwittingly, reproduce racialized structures and relationships, despite rhetorical claims to the contrary. This constitutes a one of the most pervasive and destructive exercises of power and privilege in the academy.

In today's corporatized university, college students have become consumers who can now choose across a variety of educational products, rather than cultural citizens preparing to better understand themselves and how to grapple with their world, as both individuals

---

1   Revised version of a keynote address, Department of Educational Leadership, University of Massachusetts Dartmouth, April 12, 2013, New Bedford Whaling Museum, New Bedford, MA.

and participants in insuring the welfare of the commons. Knowledge in the neoliberal context has been reduced to a market commodity, to be bought and sold to the highest bidder. Teaching in many classrooms now resembles a market "quality-controlled" operation, driven by programmatic and curricular standardization anchored in a banking pedagogy (Freire, 1971), overwhelmingly obsessed with the use of expensive and ever-changing technology. Assessment of students has also become more and more tied to the evaluation of faculty, through the use of commonsensical matrices of product satisfaction.

Incessant data gathering and the expansion of accountability regimes substitute for critical engagement with real concerns that shape students' classroom experience, particularly for racialized working-class students. And all this is accompanied by an epistemicidal curriculum that, for the most part, has become deeply instrumentalized and narrowly defined by a colonizing logic that too quickly circumvents questions of criticality (Paraskeva, 2011). Within such a context, the troubled conditions of our world are easily skirted or obscured, despite growing repression of democratic rights, increasing poverty in the midst of obscene wealth accumulation, a nation perpetually at war, the proliferation of police shootings of youth of color, the unprecedented incarceration of subaltern populations, and state-sanctioned attacks against public education by unaccountable billionaires, corporate foundations, and the media (Burns, 2015).

Consequently, few instances of courageous university leadership in opposition to the culture of corporatization have transpired. In this midst of growing authoritarianism justified by way of financial exigencies, often the only form of dissent remaining is public resistance or mass protest, as we witnessed in 2015 at the University of Missouri. In response to racializing practices, workplace benefit concerns, and dissatisfaction with the lack of response by the leadership to these issues, a series of "Racism Lives Here" protests ensued, a hunger strike was held, and the football team staged a boycott. This led to the resignation of the president of the university, Tim Wolfe. However, it should be noted that this decision was an economic decision rather than a moral or ethical one, for had Wolfe stayed and football players continued to strike, the university would have lost millions of dollars (Green, 2015).

There is no question, then, that higher education today is deeply mired in a culture of economic rule, often shrouded by conservative rhetoric that seeks to delimit genuine struggles for social justice in academia and the larger society. Glimpses of this rhetoric are also apparent in conservative responses to university protests across the country. Harvard professor of law Alan Dershowitz, in a recent interview, sternly asserted: "The last thing these students want is diversity. They want superficial diversity of gender; superficial diversity of color; but the last thing they want is diversity of ideas. We're seeing a curtain of McCarthyism descend over many college campuses."[2] He went on to compare the "tyrannical students" involved in campus protests to Nazi book burners of the 1930s.[3] By utilizing inflammatory rhetoric, Dershowitz's comments were meant to foment fear of dissent and undercut protests

---

2   See http://video.foxnews.com/v/4610150912001/alan-dershowitz-students-dont-want-diversity-of-ideas/?#sp=show-clips.
3   Ibid.

on the university campus. Moreover, it is precisely this rhetorical call for the "diversity of ideas" that has been used ad nauseam in diversity debates to subterfuge pressing concerns over social and material inequalities and institutional disregard for establishing a cultural democratic environment—concerns that time and again have been belittled or vilified or simply ignored by an economic rationality that undermines their legitimacy.

Wendy Brown (2006) rightly notes that the American nightmare today constitutes an indefensible alliance of neoliberalism, conservatism, and the undoing of democratic life. Brown rightly argues that neoliberalism and neoconservatism are two distinct and contradictory political rationalities that converge in their devaluation of political liberty, equality, substantive citizenship, and the rule of law, in favor of market-driven governance and institutional policies, on one hand, and valorization of state power for moralistic ends, on the other. This convergence results in undemocratic institutional forms that, despite social justice or diversity claims, are indifferent to veracity and accountability and to political freedom and equality, defying even liberal ideals of the academy—so much so that Brown (2015) warns, "neoliberal reason . . . is converting the distinctly political character, meaning, and operation of democracy's constituent elements into *economic ones*. Liberal democratic institutions, practices and habits may not survive this conversion. Radical democratic dreams may not either" (p. 17).

It should not be surprising then to learn that transformative notions of multiculturalism and diversity tied to community concerns have been effectively derailed by an aggressive and virulent economic ethos of the university. Accordingly, scholarship, leadership, and activism for structural change, political inclusion, economic access, and human rights have given way to multicultural market niches, the management of an international workforce, a colonizing paradigm of international education, and the portrayal of happy colored faces on public relations pamphlets and websites. Yet in this efficient and cost-effective neoliberal world, where difference is well rhetorized and "celebrated," those considered to be "deficient" subjects, unable to march to the homogenizing and bootstrap neoliberal refrain, are cast aside to the margins of society, left abandoned, impoverished, criminalized, and jailed behind iron bars, with little concern for their numbers or well-being. Blatant disregard for those unable to keep step with the dehumanizing accountability culture that neoliberalism promotes is, sadly, as much at work today within the culture of the university as within the corporate world. Accordingly, universities have become overwhelmingly driven by an economic rationalism, where the financial bottom line capsizes expressed commitments to social justice, democratic participation, or community life.

The term "neoliberalism," coined in the late 1930s, did not actually come to serve "as shorthand for the valorization of the minimal state and deregulated market" (Bell, 2014, p. 502) until the 1970s. Michael Peters (2001) argues that "neoliberalism has attempted to provide a Universalist foundation for an extreme form of economic rationalism . . . and a philosophy that is ultimately destructive of any full-fledged notions of community—national or international, imagined or otherwise" (p. 117). Collective social action is thus considered a gross obstacle to the freedom of individuals, unless collective action serves the interests of the military or corporate elite. This point is best illustrated by the politics of the Trans-Pacific Partnership (or TPP)—a wide-reaching trade and investment agreement involving 12 countries. The collective global corporatization of TPP not only portends a further erosion of nation-state regulation but also privileges the rights of corporations over the rights of workers (Gearhart, 2015). As such, neoliberal policies, grounded in this limiting economic ideology, provide the legitimizing lynchpin from which mega-rich conservatives and liberals alike co-conspire for control of not only the labor force and marketplace but also all public and private institutions, including the university.

Economic Darwinism and the University

> As a theater of cruelty and mode of public pedagogy, economic Darwinism extends its reach throughout the globe, undermining all forms of democratic solidarity and social structures that depend on long term investments and are committed to promoting the public and common good.
>
> (Giroux, 2010a)

Henry Giroux's use of *economic Darwinism*—drawing on the notion of Social Darwinism—serves as an accurate term to describe the manner in which neoliberal policies within higher education function, overtly and covertly, to support *the survival of the fittest*. In such a world, the wealthy, white, male, and able still overwhelmingly prevail over the university's resources and decision-making arenas. Giroux further points to policies of deregulation, privatization, and a lack of concern for the public good, rendering both democratic education and the social welfare of the nation endangered species. In this analysis, he implicates the values of "unchecked competition, unbridled individualism, and a demoralizing notion of individual responsibility" (Giroux, 2012, p. 16) as culprits in the legitimation crisis and ethical impoverishment of neoliberal academic leaders who ascribe to a profit logic that undermines possibilities for culturally democratic life.

This disabling logic of neoliberalism entrenched across the university is most evident within graduate school education, where future academics and public intellectuals are initiated into careerist orientations that disconnect them not only from one another and the world, but also from the critical agency and engagement necessary for the construction of decolonizing and transformative knowledge—knowledge with the potential to challenge advancing inequalities orchestrated by the wealthy elite. From the moment that graduate students and young professors are initiated as tenuous agents of the neoliberal academy, they are disciplined and conditioned into a culture of anti-democratic values and expectations of teaching, research, and tenure that erodes their intellectual freedom. Similarly, an infantilizing culture of institutional surveillance is carried out by complicit and loyal gatekeepers of all colors, genders, and sexualities.

The latter point helps to illustrate the limitations of a politics of identity that often "ignores issues of unequal distribution between identities and ultimately issues of the underlying economic structure, which betray democratic ideals" (Fisk, 2005; Fraser, 1997). Hence, a politics of identity alone cannot forge democratic leadership, particularly within the context of the neoliberal university. Rather, what is indispensable is a coherent and lived emancipatory politics, enacted through a critical and decolonizing praxis of leadership (to be discussed later) that extends courageously "beyond the common sense of official power and its legitimating ideologies" (Giroux, 2010b).

This is also important given the disabling structures of accountability, bolstered by bureaucratic regimes of power and hegemonic ideologies solidified in the last decade. Accordingly, colleges and universities have instituted greater expectations that, for example, professors from all disciplines become effective grant writers and fundraisers in their quest for the security of tenured employment. Hence, a great deal of the energy of graduate students and young professors in major public research universities today is directed away from emancipatory efforts and community commitments and toward becoming published in "respected" refereed journals, getting publicly noticed as "rising stars" on the conference circuit, and developing effective grant-writing skills while competitively shaping their research agendas to garner private and public funds. This narrow culture of professorial formation, as one might expect, has also been accompanied by tenure-track faculty who are left to navigate clumsily through the constantly shifting minefield of the tenure process or forced to contend with the mind-bending authoritarian dynamics of faculty mentorship, often fraught with deep anxieties and traditional expectations that young faculty either accommodate or suffer rejection at the time of tenure.

Although this dynamic has long existed within academia, the last two decades have resulted in a decreasing number of new tenure-track positions and an increase in casual employment, along with increasing competition among new doctoral graduates (Darder & Griffiths, 2016). This has proven especially treacherous for those now saddled with unprecedented debt upon completion of their degrees (Meyer, 2015). Moreover, with an exaggerated emphasis placed on STEM (science, technology, engineering, and mathematics), this has made graduates in the humanities and social sciences particularly vulnerable to current neoliberal priorities within higher education. Yet it is worth noting not only that STEM tenured faculty posts are not plentiful, but also that half of the jobs in the field do not even require a bachelor's degree (Rothwell, 2013).

Conditions of Power and Privilege

> *I decided to try to work on myself at least by identifying some of the daily effects of white privilege in my life. I have chosen those conditions that I think in my case attach somewhat more to skin-color privilege than to class, religion, ethnic status, or geographic location, though of course all these other factors are intricately intertwined.*
>
> *(McIntosh, 1988)*

In the face of dwindling academic posts, young graduate students who seek to become tenured faculty or university administrators are counseled to abandon their "idealistic" intentions and to position themselves competitively for a job in ways that will, on one hand, gain them recognition as "innovative" thinkers while, on the other, make them a "good institutional fit." This generally points to possessing an academic pedigree; an entrepreneurial predisposition; core values of individualism and competition; a naïve, centrist, or conservative political orientation; a subdued social justice outlook; and malleability to hierarchical leadership structures. Unfortunately, a "good institutional fit" is too often linked to the subtle (or not-so-subtle) manner in which classism, racism, patriarchy, disabilism, homophobia, and religious chauvinism coalesce to preserve institutional conditions of privilege.

Drawing on Peggy McIntosh's (1988) work on white privilege—where she openly acknowledges that she was not taught to see the "invisible systems conferring dominance on [her] group"—one can point to numerous university conditions of privilege sanctioned by the official power of the university and its Western ideology of domination. A few of these can be briefly expressed in the following ways:

1. I can critique my institution and talk about how much I dislike its policies and behavior without being seen as a cultural outsider.

2. I can feel like I am an authority on social justice even if I have never lived in poverty, experienced racism, or studied the scholarly literature in the field.

3. I look for grants and research that provide me the most acclaim or funding, rather than those tied to emancipatory objectives.

4. My expertise in my field of study is rarely questioned or criticized—in fact, it is valued and often gains me entrance into committees, task forces, etc.

5. I don't worry about being a token scholar, trotted out primarily for diversity initiatives.

6. I can be sure that because of my race, my research will not be questioned as to its legitimacy, limited scope, or if it is a "good fit."

7. I do not have to contend with people constantly mispronouncing my name.

8. I don't worry about being constantly challenged or racialized by affluent students.

9. I don't worry about being perceived as suspect or "second class" in the institutional setting.

10. I don't worry about being labeled as angry when I speak my mind at department meetings or in other university settings.

11. I can be sure that I will not be seen as a numeric minority or ever have to contend with the expectations or distortions this elicits.

12. I can be pretty sure that most of my colleagues will be neutral or pleasant to me.

13. I can conduct my research without undue surveillance or the need to provide an overabundance of proof of its legitimacy.

14. I can, if I wish, arrange to be in the company of students or colleagues of my race most of the time, without due concern from others.

15. My perspective is widely represented in journal articles across all fields of study.

16. When I read books on national heritage or civilization, I am most often shown that people of my skin color are the heroes.

17. I can be sure that my name or skin color won't count against me when applying for jobs.

18. I can swear, get angry, or not respond to emails without having people attribute these to my lack of civility, bad morals, or anger because of my race.

19. I can speak in public to a powerful dominant white audience without putting my race on trial or receiving hostile critiques if there is disagreement with my perspective.

20. I am never asked to speak for all the people of my racial group.

21. I can remain oblivious of the language and customs of others in my society, without experiencing any real penalty for such oblivion.

22. I can be sure that if I ask to talk to the dean, program director, or chair of the department, I will most often be facing a person of my color.

23. If I am called into the office for one of my actions, I can be sure I haven't been singled out because of my race or my politics.

24. The pictures placed on the walls of my institution do reflect stereotypical representations of people of my color.

25. I can go home from most university meetings feeling connected, rather than isolated, out of place, outnumbered, unheard, held at a distance, or feared.

26. I can take a job at any institution without having coworkers on the job suspect that I got it to fill a quota, rather than because of my qualifications.

27. I can be absent from department meetings without fearing that people of my color will be mistreated or issues will be discussed that negatively impact people of my community.

28. When things go badly, I don't need to reflect on each negative episode or situation to decipher whether I am being racialized.

These conditions of privilege are, more often than not, carried out unintentionally by well-meaning subjects, but are nevertheless enacted daily as microaggressions (which must also be linked to macroaggressions) in university relationships with students, faculty, and administrators who persist on the borders. Institutional conditions of privilege are enacted through attitudes and practices of individuals shaped by embedded asymmetrical relations of power—persistent attitudes and practices of privilege that betray the promises of diversity of another time. The outcome of conditions of privilege—reflective of structural inequalities and enacted through institutional relationships by individuals—is that there has been little to no challenge to the oppressive structures of power within the university. As such, we are left to contend with a neoliberal multiculturalism that systematically negates the power of our political agency of difference to challenge racialized inequalities and other social exclusions, whether within the classroom or beyond.

Neoliberal Multiculturalism

> *Neoliberal policy engenders new racial subjects, as it creates and distinguishes between newly privileged and stigmatized collectivities; yet multiculturalism codes the wealth, mobility, and political power of neoliberalism's beneficiaries to be the just desserts of "multicultural world citizens," while representing those neoliberalism dispossesses handicapped by their own "monoculturalism" or other historico-cultural deficiencies.*
>
> *(Melamed, 2006)*

In the midst of the anti-war movement and civil rights struggles of the 1960s and 1970s, the American university was challenged to break with its lily-white, male, and class-privileged tradition. The seeds of the current neoliberal assault on the academic borderland, as Giroux (2007) suggests in *The University in Chains,* can be found in the long-term authoritarian strategies put in place by conservatives who sought "to win an ideological war against liberal intellectuals, who argued for holding government and corporate power accountable as a precondition for extending and expanding the promise of an inclusive democracy" (p. 142). Those working to democratize the university called for inclusion of more students and faculty of color. Alongside this call for inclusive admissions and hiring practices, pressure was placed on colleges and universities to transform the curriculum in ways that would not only be culturally relevant but also would engage the longstanding historical inequalities and social exclusions that persisted.

Multicultural gains made within the larger society and the university at the time were more consistent with the liberal Keynesian-inspired economics, which recognized the importance of using systematic government intervention (Bell, 2014) to alleviate the downside of corporate capital investments. However, conservative *laissez-faire* views of classical macroeconomics, which began to regain currency with the deregulatory policies of Reaganomics, became the powerful precursor to the era of the "New Economy" and its ruthless consequences of inequality. The era was punctuated by a national report issued by Ronald Reagan's National Commission on Excellence in Education in 1983. This federal report was an aggressive political move by neoliberal conservatives to redefine the purpose and practice of public education. *A Nation at Risk*'s proposed antidote for both the doom and gloom of public education and our diminishing global superiority was the assertion that the American public school system should function as an economic engine. The sprouting neoliberal educational vision of the ruling elite who manned the Reagan Commission also began to forcefully tug at diversity debates underway within higher education.

As a greater number of intellectuals from the cultural, economic, gendered, and sexual margins began to enter graduate education, the presence of their politically distinct voices and transgressive views began to rouse backlash in the academy. It's not surprising, then, that by the early 1990s, the politics of difference had become mired in the hyperbole of political correctness, as mean-spirited attacks began to gnaw away at multicultural visions of equality and inclusion within the university—visions inspired by struggles for self-determination. Conservative backlash within the university also extended beyond ethnic studies faculty, targeting women and gender studies, sexuality studies, Marxists, and poststructuralist scholars who, according to Roger Kimball in *Tenured Radicals: How Politics Has Corrupted Our Higher Education* (1990), had became the new "establishment." Similar public assaults on higher education were at work in Allan Bloom's *The Closing of the American Mind* (1987) and Dinesh D'Souza's *Illiberal Education: The Politics of Race and Sex on Campus* (1991), which alleged liberal bias at the university and pointed to the destructive impact of multiculturalism on the integrity of the Western canon and American society.

In place of more culturally democratic values, the proponents of economic Darwinism proposed a focus on entrepreneurship, derailing attention from social and material inequalities. As Brown (2006) has noted, "class and other impediments to servicing the entrepreneurial self are radically depoliticized, what the neoliberals call 'the equal right to inequality' is newly legitimated, thereby tabling democracy's formal commitment to egalitarianism. A permanent underclass, and even a permanent criminal class, along with a class of... non-citizens are produced and accepted as an inevitable cost of such a society" (p. 695). It is, moreover, this cockeyed and insipid conservative platitude of "the equal right to inequality" that has been utilized to justify and rationalize a political economy that requires an immoral concentration of global wealth among a few. Subsequently, over 50% of the global wealth today is held in the hands of 1% of the population, while over 70% of the world's population scrap over a mere 3% of the global wealth (Treanor, 2015).[4]

It is precisely this political culture of greed that has given rise to a toothless "neoliberal multiculturalism" (Darder, 2011; Fisk, 2005; Melamed, 2006)—a conservative ideology of difference that deploys meritocratic justification to explain and legitimate

---

4   See Jill Treanor's article for a stark rendition of *The Global Wealth Pyramid*, a graph derived from research conducted by Credit Suisse and data collected by the Swiss Global Wealth Databook.

inequalities. Adherents to this ideology enact a structure of public recognition, acknowl-edgment, and acceptance of multicultural subjects based on an ethos of self-reliance, individualism, and competition, while simultaneously (and conveniently) rendering suspect or irrelevant decolonizing discourses and socially just practices aimed at the redistribution of power and wealth.

In a culture where a victim-blaming and stigmatizing ideology drives the institu-tional solutions of university leaders, culturally democratic efforts to contend with the oppressor/oppressed contradiction (Darder, 2015; Freire 1971), and the complexities inherent in a politics of difference are often judged as disruptive, divisive, or offensive. This is so even today, when border academics, such as Steven Salaita, considered too closely aligned with anti-imperialist struggles, are chastised, while repressive conditions within the university remain intact. Similarly, more progressive thinkers and leaders who entered the academy during the "diversity era" find themselves today more mar-ginalized at the very moment when their scholarly and political maturity might serve to more effectively challenge current inequalities, as well as forge a decolonizing vision for higher education. This phenomenon may also be associated with an appetite for so-called originality and innovativeness of scholarship—a neoliberal academic expec-tation that inadvertently stifles the evolution of substantive diversity critiques within the university and the larger society.

Not surprisingly, the educational advances of the "diversity era" proved to be a short-lived moment in the history of American higher education, for as more subaltern students and faculty began to find their way into university classrooms, faculty meetings, and governance tables, the more aggressive both conservative and neoliberal forces be-came in an effort to swing the pendulum back to a more homogenous cultural moment when an economically driven meaning of freedom and justice prevailed and the market-place was heralded as the true purveyor of equality. One of the most incisive critiques of the university's hegemonic appropriation, for example, of decolonizing language is posited by the Sisters of Resistance, a revolutionary, anti-racist, anti-imperialist feminist collective in the UK. Their website post, *Is Decolonizing the New Black?*,[5] forthrightly calls out universities who say they aim to "decolonize" the institution or curriculum, while "articulating, promoting and sustaining practices that privilege neoliberal dynamics of exclusion and inclusion." While aggressively fostering neoliberal financial policies, the commodification of learning, repressive ranking systems, and the overwhelming casualization of labor, class, gendered, and racialized inequalities are reproduced, they sing self-congratulatory decolonizing praises—praises that ring hollow, when "accounts and histories of Blackness and its systematic structural oppression are denied presence and scrutiny in institutional narratives, as well as in everyday engagements" between predominantly White management and faculty and students of color.

---

5   See Sisters of Resistance website: https://sistersofresistance.wordpress.com/?s=Decolonizing.

Assault on the Borderlands

To survive the Borderlands, you must live sin fronteras[6] be a crossroads.

(Anzaldúa, 1987)

It should not be surprising to learn that the incessant neoliberal drive to quantify worth, value, or fit by perceived capital return has never proven friendly to university diversity or the *academic borderlands*—a term that draws on Anzaldúa's (1987) revolutionary concept of the Borderlands to refer to a decolonizing intellectual terrain of struggle where the mixing of cultures, philosophies, theories, spiritualities, and everyday practices of life defy "the transcendent character of the traditional canon, because its exclusion—notably of women and people of color—marked it as the product of the white male imagination" (Aronowitz, 1991, p. 205). Significant features of the academic borderlands during the era of diversity included the increasing number of women and students of color entering colleges and universities, the vast flourishing of nontraditional scholarship, and the overwhelming presence of dissident voices calling for cultural, political, and economic change, while pushing forcefully against centuries of colonizing, racializing, and heteronormative patriarchal values (Darder, 2011).

As border intellectuals were transgressing the traditional boundaries of a variety of disciplines, rising neoliberal imperatives were making their way into the university just in time to conveniently push back fiercely against critical interventions designed to challenge the one-dimensionality of inequality in order to invigorate the decolonizing potential of higher education with a quest for borderless possibilities. At many colleges and universities, traditional administrators worked strategically to defuse what they referred to as the "cultural wars" by imposing austerity measures and fiscal pressures to cut programs, institute hiring freezes, harass noncompliant faculty, reject tenure cases, and even move to merge or eliminate entire departments.

As liberal ideals of higher education receded more and more, universities across the country became more deeply aligned with the narrow rationality of neoliberal objectives. Border intellectuals were pushed further into marginal spaces that served to limit their participation in the life of departments and the governance of the university. High-level administrators, now functioning like corporate CEOs, were less and less concerned with past promises of diversity, as they spent more time hobnobbing with corporate executives, foundation officials, and other big business advocates who could potentially help them recover the loss of public monies. In the process, the values, priorities, and private interests of those who held the reins to research dollars more tightly redefined the purpose of higher education, heavily tilting the enterprise with incentives to support economic self-sufficiency, unfettered deregulation, unrelenting privatization, marketized competition, accountability schemes, technological supremacy, and the instrumentalization of the curriculum. Economic incentives became tied to an overdependence on quantitative

6   *Sin fronteras* translation: without borders.

scientific interpretations fueled by a colonizing paradigm privileging a longstanding "evidence-based" discourse of Westernized universities (Grosfoguel, 2013).

Despite protests against priorities that equated profit, progress, and prestige with policies of deregulation, privatization, free-market competition, and bootstrap economics, university administrators have been too easily herded into the fold with promises of dollars to build new buildings, expand technology, instrumentalize curricula, and hire faculty ready to carry out the political agendas of public and private funders. Hence, through both covert and overt means, the political values and financial priorities of corporate rule have sought greater colonizing control of student intellectual formation, the labor of academics, and research agendas in order to legitimate transnational enterprises. With a keen eye on profit, control over resources, and the use of working-class communities for warfare, the neoliberal rhetoric of difference has functioned strategically to increase production, maximize commerce, and support the growing needs of U.S. militarization, while perpetuating the economic impact of global violence.

In fact, a recent report titled "The Most Militarized Universities in America" noted that "seventeen powerhouse research universities traditionally supporting the military-industrial complex rank in the top 100" (Arkin & O'Brian, 2015). Among those included in this elite group are Johns Hopkins (#7), Penn State (#15), Georgia Tech (#26), Harvard, Stanford, the Massachusetts Institute of Technology (#47), and the University of Southern California (#21). The federal government awarded over $3 billion last year to these schools alone. And rather than study traditional weapons systems, these universities primarily carry out classified research on intelligence technologies, cyber security, and big-data analytics. Also, noteworthy here is the fact that most common academic concentrations for military workers are found in the STEM field. The unbridled advance of STEM education must be understood in concert with expanding militarization rather than superficial interpretations of science as "the new frontier," which fail to question the heavy promotion of STEM as an area of study and "career" choice.

As funding sources have diminished for faculty positions and research in the humanities and social sciences that could serve as a countervailing force, fewer resources are available for research that critically examine issues tied to social and material inequalities. A larger consequence here is that the university, now fully in bed with corporate interests, has systematically eroded the potential "to cultivate the next generation of critical scholars and leaders who can offer a counter-narrative to the national security state" (Arkin & O'Brian, 2015). Instead, critical scholars and leaders in the borderland today are expected to align themselves more narrowly within particular disciplines of study, whether history, anthropology, sociology, or economics, in contrast to transdisciplinary decolonizing or *sin fronteras* approaches that have been at the heart of decolonizing efforts within university teaching and research.

In a world where economic Darwinism prevails, traditional disciplinary approaches provide neater and tidier intellectual alliances than does counterhegemonic or decolonizing scholarship produced by scholars in ethnic, feminist, postcolonial, and queer studies. This tyranny of strict disciplinary boundaries has also worked well to police and monitor the scholarship of more mature border intellectuals, as well as discipline the current efforts of graduate students and young faculty from subaltern communities. Similarly, faculty and university leaders of color who persist in their advocacy for decolonizing or community-based research approaches are often marginalized and derisively dubbed "activists," their scholarly work and emancipatory efforts challenged as mere "opinion" and subjected to excessive requests for proof, despite overwhelming historical evidence and plentiful research to substantiate their conclusions.

Unfortunately, at the moment when they are most needed, decolonizing scholars and potential leaders for social change are often exiled from meaningful participation by an anti-democratic conservative wave that banishes formidable findings tied to social justice, human rights, and economic democracy to the wasteland of irrelevancy. In a climate where the international control of knowledge and the maximizing of profits are the greatest concerns, university administrators have often served—wittingly or unwittingly—as colonizing gatekeepers, through a banking form of leadership that thwarts decolonizing praxis needed for social change.

Critical Praxis for Decolonizing Leadership

> *For apart from inquiry, apart from the praxis, individuals cannot be truly human. Knowledge emerges only through invention and re-invention, through the restless, impatient, continuing, hopeful inquiry human beings pursue in the world, with the world, and with each other.*
>
> *(Freire, 1971)*

The dehumanizing impact of colonizing social and material conditions, perpetrated by hierarchical and undemocratic forms of university leadership, impels us to unveil the hidden curriculum with its anti-dialogical values and practices, in an effort to move toward a decolonizing vision of leadership and a more just social order. In so doing, our task is to counter colonizing social arrangements of accountability and institutional priorities that thwart decolonizing aims as we work to create a critical praxis of leadership to support self-determination and culturally democratic life. This begins with the willingness to disrupt epistemicides that exclusively privilege Western assumptions—assumptions attached to classed, racialized, patriarchal, and heterosexist codes of conduct, resulting in what Boaventura de Sousa Santos (2007) calls an *abyssal divide*—where the other is rendered irrelevant, invisible, or nonexistent.

Of this Santos writes: "What most fundamentally characterizes abyssal thinking is thus the impossibility of the co-presence of the two sides of the line. To the extent that it prevails, this side of the line only prevails by exhausting the field of relevant reality. Beyond it, there is only nonexistence, invisibility, non-dialectical absence" (2007, p. 1).

The challenges that Santos poses—moving beyond the abyssal divide—constitutes one of the most difficult epistemological challenges faced by critical decolonizing approaches to university leadership; particularly with respect to establishing alliances across dominant/subordinate cultural divides.

In facing the challenges of laboring within a context where epistemicides prevail, Freire (1998a) calls upon us to engage more profoundly with the question of a universal human ethic. Of this, he writes:

> I am speaking of a universal human ethic, an ethic that is not afraid to condemn the kind of ideological discourse I have just cited. Not afraid to condemn the exploitation of labor and the manipulation that makes a rumor into truth and truth into a mere rumor. To condemn the fabrication of illusions, in which the unprepared become hopelessly trapped and the weak and the defenseless are destroyed. To condemn making promises when one has no intention of keeping one's word, which causes lying to become an almost necessary way of life. To condemn the calumny of character assassination simply for the joy of it and the fragmentation of the utopia of human solidarity. The ethic of which I speak is that which feels itself betrayed and neglected by the hypocritical perversion of an elitist purity, an ethic affronted by racial, sexual, and class discrimination. (p. 23)

What is most evident for those who have felt betrayed by the very issues Freire raises, yet have remained in this intractable emancipatory struggle, is this: if there is to be a genuinely emancipatory and decolonizing approach to university educational leadership, it demands a decolonizing approach that fully supports both individual and community empowerment. This signals a decolonizing vision that embraces the indigenous call of "idle no more" and extends beyond the academy, where the insights and participation of administrators, faculty, students, and community members from historically oppressed communities are central to decolonizing forms of educational leadership—a leadership fundamentally committed to cultural democracy and economic justice. Inherent in such an emancipatory vision are principles and ethical commitments that can inform a critical praxis of leadership for social justice. The following offers a very brief summary and preliminary discussion of some of the vitally important critical principles and ethical commitments that must be in place.

Decolonizing Leadership is Pedagogical: This notion that decolonizing leadership is pedagogical practice moves us beyond the traditionally hierarchical and individualistic banking model of leadership. Instead we are drawn toward to an understanding of leadership as a social phenomenon that must exist communally and evolves pedagogically, through open, democratic structures of participation. The vision here is *to learn together* as a way of life in which we transform the world as community through a humanizing praxis of inquiry and decision making, where the common good stretches across our differences and our institutional priorities.

Decolonizing Leadership is Moral Commitment: In *Pedagogy of Freedom,* Freire (1998a) wrote: "Human existence is, in fact, a radical and profound tension between good and evil, between dignity and indignity, between decency and indecency, between the beauty and the ugliness of the world" (p. 53) Yet it has been the stubborn unwillingness to contend with institutional colonizing structures and difficult moral questions within the university and the larger society that has resulted in an oppressive bureaucratic system of leadership—ruled by absolute, top-down profit centers and expedient policies—which ignores conditions of human suffering and material oppression. In the wake of such neglect, the colonizing dynamics and their consequences are seldom addressed. Instead, a conserving bureaucratic culture of control, contradictions, distortions, denial, manipulation, and hostility permeates the university environment, often tangibly experienced in ways that further alienate and isolate students, faculty, and administrators from their labor and consigns them to institutional lives of banality and routinized existence.

Decolonizing Leadership is a Political Act: Inherent in a decolonizing form of leadership is an understanding that if, as Freire proposed, education is political, then leadership, too, is a political act. As such, it is informed by a question-posing pedagogy of leadership that recognizes that culture and power are inextricably linked to any system of organization. That said, there must be consistent and humanizing protocols for examining, in an ongoing and organic manner, the consequences of decisions that are made and their impact upon the most disenfranchised, as the consequences of those decisions unfold. Through such a process, a decolonizing approach to leadership creates conditions to question "Why?" That is, to question the colonizing conditions that persist, how they came to be this way, and, more important, how we can work together in the interest of democratic life.

Decolonizing Leadership is Not a Neutral Affair: Decolonizing leadership is never a neutral affair. During the struggle against apartheid in South Africa, Desmond Tutu asserted: "If you are neutral in situations of injustice, you have chosen the side of the oppressor."[7] As such, a decolonizing vision of leadership exposes the illusion of neutrality by critically examining the asymmetry of power relations in the face of colonizing policies and practices. Instead of neutrality, a dialogical process of leadership opens the way for honest questioning, open exercise of voice, multiple cultural forms of participation, and genuine structures of democratic decision making, guided by a moral imperative inextricably tied to the consequences of policy decisions and practices, particularly upon the most vulnerable populations.

Decolonizing Leadership is Purposeful: The purposefulness of decolonizing leadership echoes a humanizing intent that informs our critical pedagogical practices. First and foremost, this approach to leadership encompasses an uncompromising commitment to conditions of our labor and of life that create opportunities for collective empowerment and self-determination—with a particular focus on those who most experience conditions of disempowerment, alienation, or isolation. This purpose

7   See http://organizingchange.org/here-is-how-moral-leaders-approach-neutrality/.

signals the transformation of undemocratic relationships, institutional structures, and material conditions that perpetuate colonizing structures of domination and reproduce material inequalities and social exclusions. Moreover, the underlying purpose of such a decolonizing approach encompasses an ethos of leadership that openly nurtures and cultivates loving, hopeful, ethical, and committed relationships of solidarity with others and the world.

Critical Leadership as a Dialectical Process: To understand decolonizing leadership as a dialectical or analectic process is to recognize that the tensions between the needs of individuals and communities are always competing dimensions of our humanity. Hence, the tension is embraced as an important human creative force that permits for individual participation in the evolution of a collective process of self-determination, without degenerating into moral relativism, even in the midst of resistance. Instead, our comfort with a decolonizing dynamic allows us to more fully embrace our social agency, the unfolding of social consciousness, and expressions of resistance as a meaningful and potentially humanizing moral compass. This decolonizing dynamic can also help us to better unveil, challenge, and reinvent together those colonizing institutional forms driven by apolitical and ahistorical readings of the world.

Humanizing Dialogue: In a decolonizing vision of leadership, humanizing dialogue is not only essential but also serves as a political decolonizing means by which we forge relationships of empowerment and establish participatory communities for transformation. The process of dialogue within this context entails purposeful communication that leads to self-determination and political action, a collective process of conscientization, communal labor that supports the development of solidarity, and an open and humanizing process of inquiry. For Freire, humanizing dialogue constitutes a decolonizing way of knowing and being rather than a tactic or skill to be used to persuade others (Darder, 2018). Our dialogical engagements, then, must be understood not merely as individual exchanges but collective processes from whence we are able to both know and act upon our world in order to change it (Darder, 2015). As such, humanizing dialogue constitutes an indispensable component of a decolonizing praxis of leadership.

Conscientization: As would be expected, the Freirean principle of conscientization, or *conscientização*, again defines here the ongoing aim and practice of decolonizing leadership. This requires us to remain ever vigilant in our continuing evolution as cultural workers, as we seek to practice and develop together ways to decolonize our minds and bodies, as we work to support collective forms of social consciousness that integrate the needs of individuals and communal concerns. This points to an awareness of ourselves as individuals, as well as consciousness of our conditions and the social location we hold, that is, consciousness about the social structures that limit us and potentiate our labor and relationships; an understanding of how these two intersect; an awareness of the power relations that inform cultural, political, social, and economic conditions; and acceptance of our individual and social responsibility as cultural citizens and subjects of history to live our pedagogy.

Decolonizing Democratic Negotiation: However, none of the preceding is possible without an ongoing decolonizing process of critical democratic negotiation. This speaks to the process of engaging organically with the dialectical tension between authority and freedom, within the actual contexts and relationships in which colonizing tensions and struggles arise. The dialectical tension between authority and freedom is understood as a significant and necessary aspect of our human condition that cannot be avoided without sacrificing democracy. Regarding this, Freire (1998a) posited: "It is not possible to have authority without freedom or vice versa" (p. 21). Hence, we must be willing to practice a form of leadership that demands our presence in the interest of democratic life, beyond vulgar competition, infantilizing micromanagement, egotistical ambitions, or careerist pursuits of recognition.

Ideological Intersections: A decolonizing leadership calls for personal vigilance and political groundedness in context to our labor and within organizations and communities. These critical qualities assist us in reading the world in way that support our decolonization, particularly with respect to the ideological intersections at work in the organizational structures of universities. We can think of this as an axis relationship in which there is an intersection between a continuum of tyranny and powerlessness, on one hand, and a continuum of absolute authority and absolute freedom, on the other. Contending dialectically with the meaning of these ideological intersections is paramount to our decolonizing struggle, precisely because people in any and all organizations will exhibit different response patterns across these continuums, depending on their histories, political coherence, grounded knowledge, cultural worldviews, and the depth of their personal and communal commitment to a decolonizing political project.

The Cultural Context as Essential: In concert with Freire's philosophy, the cultural context constitutes an essential dimension of decolonizing practice. This is particularly significant given that the hegemony of a Eurocentric worldview often functions systematically to invisibilize other ways of being and knowing. A deep recognition of the fundamental role that the cultural context plays in this work and the lives of the oppressed prompted Freire (2005) to argue, "One cannot expect positive results from an educational or political action program which fails to respect the particular view of the world held by the people. Such a program constitutes cultural invasion, good intentions notwithstanding" (p. 95).

Integration of Our Human Faculties: Another significant aspect of a decolonizing approach to leadership is a commitment to relationships of solidarity, which—through the integration of our human faculties—nurtures the evolution of social agency and collective agency or political grace. Collective agency or political grace refers to that collective power generated by those who seek to consistently connect, labor, and struggle together within communal relationships. Moreover, given its emancipatory purpose, a decolonizing praxis of leadership requires the exercise of this integral process—where mind, heart, body, and spirit are fully welcomed in the service of liberation. This integral dynamic generates the conditions for individual and collective empowerment and generates the creative force, through our communal exchanges, that mobilizes us toward decolonizing possibilities and social transformation. As such, decolonizing leadership encompasses a political intent that counters the fragmenting and fracturing of our humanity and, instead, aims to prepare and support us all to live with a greater sense of love as a political force—a decolonizing force that connects us to the truth of our material conditions that surround us, alerts us to the possibilities, and propels us more openly toward anti-colonial relationships as individuals and social beings.

A Question of Ethics: For Freire, a question of ethics was always at the forefront of his thinking on education, politics, and social transformation. This point is crystallized in *Pedagogy of Freedom: Ethics, Democracy, and Civic Courage* (1998a), where he forthrightly takes up ethical dilemmas and concerns at the heart of a pedagogy for liberation. Four significant needs that can further inform a decolonizing praxis of leadership include (1) the need to counter determinism, (2) the need to assume responsibility for our lives as individuals and communal beings, (3) the need to carry out our practices through fellowship and solidarity, and (4) the need to understand and embrace our unfinishedness.

Our Unfinishedness: Paulo Freire (1998a) wrote: "If this world were a created finished world, it would no longer be susceptible to transformation . . . This unfinishedness is essential to our human condition. Wherever there is life, there is unfinishedness" (p. 32). At the heart of this notion of our unfinishedness is the recognition that colonization is never a permanent condition, and it is precisely because no human condition is ever absolute or finished that the struggle remains viable and hope fertile, even within political moments that may appear desolate and barren. An understanding of our unfinishedness also nurtures and sustains a critical utopian vision that defies both a politics of prescription and determinism and allows us to remain in a permanent state of discovery, creativity, and epistemological curiosity (Freire, 1998a).

Indispensable Qualities of Decolonizing Leadership

There is no question that a decolonizing approach to leadership requires a fundamental shift in how we define our labor and how we understand our purpose as cultural citizens. This calls on us to shed our internalized oppression, eject colonizing ideologies of domination, establish solidarity with others, recognize ourselves as subjects of history, garner the courage to speak out when necessary, and cultivate a strong sense of social agency in order that we can name, critique, decolonize, and reinvent our world anew, in the interest of a just and democratic future. Drawing inspiration from Freire's (1998b) indispensable qualities for those who *dare to teach*, I briefly summarize many of the points included earlier by offering two sets of indispensable qualities for those who *dare to lead*.

The first group of ethical qualities points to those associated with political struggle and the second to those associated with personal struggle. However, given the nature of the work and the decolonizing values and principles that inform these qualities, there is much overlapping of points, thanks to the ongoing interrelationship and interactions between the public and personal conditions of our everyday lives. This phenomenon is readily apparent as one engages these two sets of indispensable qualities, which are not meant to serve as a taxonomy or prescription, but rather as a politically inspired suggestion or reminder of the complexity and multidimensionality we must assume in our emancipatory quest to redefine the ways we think and practice a decolonizing praxis of leadership in the world.

Ethical Qualities of Political Struggle for Social Justice

- Understand the link between culture and power
- Engage consistently with political questions of the economy
- Be rooted in a historical understanding of our collective existence
- Knowledge of micro and macro systems and their connection
- Knowledge of overarching social and political contradictions at work
- Comprehend the underlying dynamics of material inequalities and social exclusions
- Recognize the inextricable connections between all forms of oppression
- Read both formal and impersonal power relations
- Be conscientious of language use and its relationship to power
- Emphasize voice, democratic participation, and collaborative decision making
- Consistently move toward dialogue as a means for transformative action
- Accept the meaningfulness and necessity of resistance
- Enact a decolonizing sense of authority in the interest of freedom
- Be politically strategic; choose battles tied to the greatest common benefit
- Commit to solidarity and community self-determination
- Understand political change as part of the ongoing process of life
- Acknowledge the power and ongoing nature of unfinishedness
- Embody radical hope and possibility
- Embrace a historical or long view of revolutionary struggle

Ethical Qualities of Personal Struggle for Social Justice

- Knowledge of one's personal demons, struggles, and limitations
- Self-vigilant of one's attitudes and behaviors toward self, others, and the world
- Commitment to our kinship and common good—*Tu eres mi otro yo*
- Practice with confidence and humility (be comfortable with knowing and not knowing)
- Express faith and respect for others, in words and deeds
- Embody presence and a humanizing style of communication and participation
- Enact courage and thoughtfulness when challenging others

- Exercise a collective sensibility in decision making
- Be impatiently patient—respect and honor the process
- Commitment to living, working, and loving with integrity
- Focus on nurturing relationships, rather than simply being right
- Embody a revolutionary love, anchored in decolonizing sensibilities
- Forgiveness for human limitations and shortcomings
- Compassion for struggles faced in our effort to become more socially conscious
- Embrace humor, joy, and the sensual dimensions of our humanity
- Respect for the preciousness of all life

The Struggle for Democratic Public Life

> At the very least, academics should be more responsible to and for a politics that raises serious questions about how students and educators negotiate the institutional, pedagogical, and social relations shaped by diverse ideologies and dynamics of power, especially as these relations mediate and inform competing visions regarding whose interests the university might serve, what role knowledge plays in furthering both excellence and equity, and how higher education defines and defends its own role in relation to its often stated, though hardly operational, allegiance to egalitarian and democratic impulses.
>
> (Giroux, 2010a)

For those who embrace a decolonizing praxis of leadership, the university continues to represent an important terrain of struggle and key public pedagogical space from whence we can strive to forge democratic public life. This notion is often directly tied to critical educational efforts by professors and leaders from the borderlands, who seek through their decolonizing praxis to establish political links between the classroom, college campus, the community, and the larger society, in ways that can foster and support the university as an anticolonial site of culturally democratic possibility.

A decolonizing praxis of leadership also seeks to create emancipatory conditions within the university that support meaningful dialogue for seriously questioning the status quo and the ideologies, policies, and practices that betray earlier liberal democratic ideals of intellectual freedom. This, however, requires a sound pedagogical engagement that can move us beyond the conservative rhetorical refrains of a "diversity of ideas." Rather, what is needed are critically communal relationships of leadership that can infuse our labor with the courage and epistemological flexibly to embrace—or at least be open to—our human differences, even when these may seem incomprehensible and we are readily tempted to eliminate them, particularly when these make us anxious, uncertain, or insecure. In the process, we must become more conscious of those historical moments when more progressive ideals of the university prevailed so that we might explore together those decolonizing possibilities that can propel us beyond the current neoliberal nightmare. In fact, if it were not for the work of critical scholars in the academic borderlands, many of us would never have found an opportunity to flourish in the academy, despite the underlying colonizing nature of higher education, both in this country and in other parts of the world. Since democracy is never a given, the political project for democratic public life must be understood as an ongoing decolonial one, rather than a determined destination. As such, the struggle to decolonize our minds, hearts, and bodies necessities courageous forms of leadership that can remain ever vigilant to inequalities and exclusions, constantly pushing against reified boundaries of legitimacy that prevent our movement toward a genuinely humanizing culture of the university and society.

A decolonizing leadership that critically supports public democratic life and political dissent creates the conditions for university administrators, faculty, and students not only to grapple rigorously with theories and practices of democratic life as cognitive phenomena but also asks them to tackle rigorously and in the flesh the meaning and consequences of material inequalities and ideologies of racism, orientalism, Islamophobia, sexism, homophobia, heterosexism, disablism, and other colonizing forms of social exclusion.

In the last three decades, we have seen neoliberalism steadily negate the hard-earned opportunities gained by earlier civil rights struggles. Yet what is made only too clear by this history is that democracy is never guaranteed, which is truer today than ever. And as such, we must keep in mind that democracy necessitates an ongoing emancipatory international struggle for political voice and participation. Higher education, then, persists as a contested terrain of struggle, given the potential of education to function as either a colonizing or a democratizing force. However, we cannot overcome the perils and pitfalls of persistent conditions colonization that exist all around us if our work is not firmly grounded in an imaginative and creative political vision that requires us to consistently reach beyond the comprehensibility of this unjust and racialized economic order.

There is no question that an imaginative, fluid, and grounded political vision of struggle is especially necessary within the context of leadership today, in that our labor for social change is, indeed, made more difficult in this historical moment when neoliberalism has made a farce of the democratic ideal of "civic engagement," undermining the public good and the power of our differences. To counter this travesty, we must move, in *theory and practice,* beyond the usual colonizing reformism and embrace in our daily praxis wider political possibilities that might allow us to "bring something incomprehensible into the world" (Deleuze & Guattari, 1987, p. 78). For this is the creative substance from whence genuine social and political transformation is born.

This demands from us a more profound sense of our human affiliation, the evolution of consciousness, and a reinvestment in the collective power of social movement and political encounters across our differences. Toward this decolonizing end we can strive to become more politically vigilant in our responses to the world so that we do not fall prey to the commonplace contradictions of either neoliberalism or academic elitism, which easily betray our liberatory dreams. This requires that we understand that *no one exists outside the system* (Darder, 2015) and that none of us is free of the colonial contradictions; further, a purity of politics or sectarianism is not the answer to the suffering and alienation we are facing today.

This speaks to a political vision where uncertainty, ambiguity, discomfort, and incomprehensibility exist in dialectical alliance with their negation. Through the latitude that such political awareness affords us, we can more easily redefine what it means it means to lead, entering into critical engagement with the complexities and nuanced ways in which the coloniality of power still impacts our lives as educators and world citizens. At the heart of such awareness lies the recognition that an anticolonial vision, whether in the university, communities, or the larger society, can only be enacted through a radically imaginative, hopeful, and loving political vision, where neither diversity nor unity are sacrificed.

References

Anzaldúa, G. (1987). *Borderlands/La frontera: The new mestiza.* San Francisco, CA: Aunt Lute.

Arkin, W. M., & A. O'Brien (2015). The most militarized universities in America: A VICE news investigation. *Vice News.* Retrieved from https://news.vice.com/article/the-most-militarized-universities-in-america-a-vice-news-investigation

Aronowitz, A. (1991). [Review of the book *Tenured radicals: How politics has corrupted our higher education,* by R. Kimball.] *Teachers College Record, 93*(1), 204–207.

Bell, E. (2014). There is an alternative: Challenging the logic of neoliberal penalty. *Theoretical Criminology, 18*(4), 489–505.

Bloom, A. (1987). *The closing of the American mind.* New York: Simon & Schuster.

Brown, W. (2006). American nightmare: Neoliberalism, neoconservatism, and de-democratization. *Political Theory, 34*(6), 690–714.

Brown, W. (2015). *Undoing the demos: Neoliberalism's stealth revolution.* New York: Zone Books.

Burns, J. (2015, September 1). The moral bankruptcy of corporate education. *Teachers College Record.* http://www.tcrecord.org

Darder, A. (2011). *A dissident voice: Essays on culture, pedagogy, and power.* New York: Peter Lang.

Darder, A. (2015). *Freire and education.* New York: Routledge.

Darder, A, (2018). *The student guide to Freire's* Pedagogy of the Oppressed. London, UK: Bloomsbury.

Darder, A. & T. Griffiths (2016). Labor in the Academic Borderlands: Unveiling the Tyranny of Neoliberal Policies. *Workplace: A Journal for Academic Labor (Special Issue: Marx, Engels and the Critique of Academic Labor).*

Deleuze, G., & Guattari, F. (1987). *A thousand plateaus: Capitalism and schizophrenia.* Minneapolis: University of Minnesota Press.

D'Souza, D. (1991). *Illiberal education: The politics of race and sex on campus.* New York: Simon & Schuster.

Fisk, M. (2005). Multiculturalism and neoliberalism. *Praxis Filosofica, 21,* 21–28. Retrieved from http://www.miltonfisk.org/writings/multiculturalism-and-neoliberalism/

Fraser, N. (1997). Multiculturalism, antiessentialism, and radical democracy. In N. Fraser (Ed.), *Justice interruptus: Critical reflections on the "postsocialist" condition.* New York: Routledge.

Freire, P. (1971). *Pedagogy of the oppressed.* New York: Seabury Press.

Freire, P. (1998a). *Pedagogy of freedom: Ethics, democracy, and civic courage.* Lanham, MD: Rowman & Littlefield.

Freire, P. (1998b). *Teachers as cultural workers: Letters to those who dare teach.* Boulder, CO: Westview Press.

Freire, P. (2005). *Pedagogy of the oppressed* (30th anniversary ed.). New York and London: Continuum.

Gearhart, J. (2015). TPP ignores worker's weeds and fails to address weaknesses from past trade agreements. *The World Post.* Retrieved from http://www.huffingtonpost.com/judy-gearhart/tpp-ignores-worker-needs_b_8537878.html

Giroux, H. (2007). *The university in chains.* Boulder, CO: Paradigm.

Giroux, H. (2010a). The disappearing intellectual in the age of economic Darwinism. *Global Research.* Retrieved from http://www.globalresearch.ca/index.php?context=va&aid=20112

Giroux, H. (2010b, January 1). Rethinking education as the practice of freedom: Paulo Freire and the promise of critical pedagogy. *Truthout.* Retrieved from http://www.truth-out.org/archive/item/87456:rethinking-education-as-the-practice-of-freedom-paulo-freire-and-the-promise-of-critical-pedagogy

Giroux, H. (2012). Higher education, critical pedagogy, and the challenge of neoliberalism: Rethinking the role of academics as public intellectuals. *Revista Aula de Encuentro,* Número especial. Andalucía, España: Servicio de Publicaciones e Intercambo Científico Universidad de Jaén.

Green, A. (2015). The financial calculations: Why Tim Wolfe had to resign. *The Atlantic* (November 9). Retrieved from http://www.theatlantic.com/business/archive/2015/11/mizzou-tim-wolfe-resignation/414987/

Grosfoguel, R. (2013). The structure of knowledge in Westernized universities: Epistemic racism/sexism and the four genocides/epistemicides of the long 18th century. *Human Architecture, 11*(1), Article 8. Retrieved from https://scholarworks.umb.edu/humanarchitecture/vol11/iss1/8/

Kimball, R. (1990). *Tenured radicals: How politics has corrupted our higher education.* Chicago: Ivan R. Dee.

McIntosh, P. (1988). White privilege: Unpacking the invisible knapsack. Excerpted from *White privilege and male privilege: A personal account of coming to see correspondences through work in women's studies.* Working paper 189. Wellesley MA: Wellesley College Center for Research on Women.

Melamed, J. (2006). From racial liberalism to neoliberal multiculturalism. *Social Text, 89*(4), 1–24.

Meyer, J. (2015). *The unprecedented debt burdens facing millennials.* New York: The Manhattan Institute. Retrieved from http://www.economics21.org/files/pdf/HBC%20Testimony%20Meyer.pdf

Paraskeva, J. (2011). *Conflicts in curriculum theory.* New York: Palgrave.

Peters, M. (2001). *Poststructuralism, Marxism, and neo-liberalism: Between theory and politics.* Lanham, MD: Rowman & Littlefield.

Rothwell, J. (2013). *The hidden STEM economy.* Washington, DC: The Brookings Institution.

Santos, B. de Sousa. (2007). Beyond abyssal thinking. *Eurozine.* Retrieved from http://www.eurozine.com/pdf/2007-06-29-santos-en.pdf

Treanor, J. (2015, October 13). Half of world's wealth now in hands of 1% of population. *The Guardian.* Retrieved from http://www.theguardian.com/money/2015/oct/13/half-world-wealth-in-hands-population-inequality-report

CHAPTER TWELVE

Itinerant Curriculum Theory.
An Epistemological Declaration of Independence[1]

João M. Paraskeva

To Dwayne Huebner

For centuries the poet has sung of his near infinitudes; the theologian has preached of his depravity and hinted of his participation in the divine; the philosopher has struggled to encompass him in his systems, only to have him repeatedly escape; the novelist and dramatist have captured his fleeting moments of pain and purity in never-to-be-forgotten aesthetic forms; and the [man] engaged in the curriculum has the temerity to reduce this being to a single term—learner. (Huebner, 1966, p. 10)

THE STRUGGLE FOR the curriculum, since its emergence as a field of studies at the end of the XIX century, was always quite belligerant (Klibard, 1995; Tyack, 1974; Krug, 1969), with dominant and counter dominant groups and movements fighting over the whose knowledge should be (re)produced (Apple, 1979; Paraskeva, 2011). Within the course of the XX century, and within the context of broader complex social—local and global—issues, curriculum became a open political and ideological battlefield, in which dominant and counter-dominant groups re-escalate the animosity with sides basically assuming a "taking no prisoners commitment" (Paraskeva, 2011). However, at the sunset of the XX century, it was already visibile that the clashes between hegemonic and counterhegeminic movements with radical critical impulses and commitments had triggered an involution (Gil, 2009), that is, the struggle between dominant and counter-dominant educational and curriculum movements created what I call "curriculum involution" (Paraskeva, 2018), a state of massive regression; that is, neither of the dominant models were able to pose as unique and completely destroy the counter-dominants, nor were the counter-dominant ones able to impose themselves as dominants and dismantle the dominant ones. There was neither the emergence of a new human being nor the end of the old human being. There was no evolution in either direction. Somehow, we have the dangerous privilege to live a *theoricide* which is not necessarily an absence of theory.

I argue that the best way to unblock such involution, is to deterritorialized curriculum theory that implies a commitment to fight for a different research platform, one that pushes research to a "level of instability, not stability, generating concepts also, in itself,

1   Keynote address Department of Education Leadership, University of Massachusetts Dartmouth, UMass Maw School, March 12, 2019.

unstable" (O'Brien & Penna, 1999, p. 106). In doing so, a deterritorialized curriculum theory increasingly becomes an itinerant theory, a theory of nonspaces (Auge, 2003). In essence, one needs to assume a rhizomatous approach that sees reality beyond dichotomies, beyond beginnings and endings (Gough, 2000), an approach that breeds from the multiplicity of immanent platforms and, from its centerless and peripheryless position, defies the myth of clean knowledge territories (Deleuze & Guattari, 1987; Eco, 1984). Such itinerant position should be seen as subversively transgressive. The "purpose of curriculum theory[ists], is to travel, to go beyond the limits, to move, and stay in a kind of permanent exile" (Said, 2005, p. 41), a theory of non-places and non-times is, in essence, a theory of all places and all times. The curriculum theorist is a constant migrant (Jin, 2008), a "permanent nomad of his own all multifaceted consciousness" (Pessoa, 2014, p. 113) who experiences a series of (epistemological) events (Khalfa, 1999). The itinerant theorist is a "real dinamogenus" (Gil, 2010, p. 13). Such migrant being and thinking situate the itinerant theorist; "it beckons us to recognize that how we perceive and experience the world (individually or communally), how we identify problems and name solutions, and how we locate ourselves in the world are all inseparable to the struggle for cognitive justice" (Darder, 2018, p. xi), thus helping to short-circuit the functionalist trap that is sinking Western Eurocentric dominant and the counter-dominant platforms (Süssekind, 2017; Oliveira, 2017; Moreira, 2017).

In arguing for an itinerant curriculum theory (hereafter ICT), I am claiming an atypical epistemological approach that will be able to deconstruct the images of thought, thus rethinking the utopia through re-utopianizing thinking fueling the emergence of radical collective and individual subjectivtities; ICT is such metamorphoses exhibiting "a double purpose[,] though[,] (a) to reinvent maps of social emancipation and (b) subjectivities with the capacity and desire for using them; that is no paradigmatic transformation would be possible without the paradigmatic transformation of subjectivity" (Santos, 1995, p. 482). In doing so, ICT brings back to the fore social imagination (Berardi, 2012) but within a pluriversal matrix.

Such an approach will unfold naturally into voluntary and involuntary creations (Merelau-Ponty, 1973). Furthermore, the curriculum worker and creator need to be seen as "an *auctor*, which is *qui auget*, or the person who augments, increases, or perfects the act (in fact), since every creation is always a co-creation, just as every author is a co-author" (Agamben, 2005, p. 76). To create, the theorist "needs a foothold" (Pessoa, 2014, 214), and the strength of such foothold comes from his or her "extraordinary exteriority" (Gil, 2010, p. 14); that is, the "interior and exterior constitute a space of implosion" (Gil, 2010, p. 15). The core of ICT is the fact that it ferociously challenges any attempt of a bunker theory-practice, or a bunker praxis. In examining the complex conundrum of the Portuguese identity, the great Mozambique-born philosopher José Gil argues that identity matters are not detached from the cruelty of a "one and only one-dimensional way" (2009, p. 38). That is, the cult of 'the one best theory-practice' "is intimately connected with all the commonsensical commonsense lack of evidence of so-called credible alternatives, that 'cocoonizes' the subject in invisible and visible bunkers" (2009, p. 38). In a way, to upgrade Gil's (2009) arguments, a palpable 'selficide' is systematically produced by blocking 'truth' from itself and from the very own self, a self that can only exist 'in inner violence.' In fact, I argue that our field doesn't have a lack of identity; quite the opposite it has a healthy excess of identity (Gil, 2009). Thus, ICT is not a bunker theory (Gil, 2009); it works under a pluralistic conceptual grammar (Jupp, 2017, p. 4) "emphasizing (a) the coloniality of power, knowledge, and being; (b) epistemicides, linguicides, abyssality, and the ecology of knowledges; and, (c) poststructuralist hermeneutic itinerancy"; such pluriversal grammar allows to think "a prudent knowledge for a decent life" (Santos, 2007a) defending the epistemological as a political. In this context, ICT promises a sense of respect for epistemological diversity. While being an "occupying epistemology" (Santos, 2018, p. 2) its aim is not "to overcome the hierarchical dichotomy between North and South, but rathter to overcome such normative dualism" (Santos, 2018, p. 7). Thus, it is the claim of a just theory that sees the collective struggle for knowledge as a struggle that must go far beyond the Western epistemological platform. ICT is a clear appeal against the precariousness of any ossified and fixed theoretical position (Paraskeva, 2018). ICT walks towards knowledge emancipation thus open up the canon of knowledge regulation; it is not a great narrative of a great theory as "knowledge-emancipation does not aspire to a great theory, it aspires to a theory of translation that serves as an epistemological support for emancipatory practices" (Santos, 1999, p. 206).

It is not a great theory, it is only a theory—perpetually itinerant—of greater knowledge, fully aware that such greater knowledge, as Tse (2017, p. 66) argues, is reachable only through a "full consciousness that everything is continually transformed inside and outside our mind." Itinerancy thus is not real, it's the real(ity). ICT is thus "an epistemic minga, a collective farming for the collective good" (Santos, 2018, p. 146). In this sense, ICT doesn't just face the outside (Gil, 2010, p. 16) as it is indeed the outside—but not an outsider—, yet drives discrete sensacionism—the opposite of sensationalism—"the only reality is the sensation of consciousness" (Gil, 2010, p. 65). ICT is a wordily theoretical approach; it is the theory of *palavrar*. It is an attempt to build a theory *"que palavre e não que diga"* (Pessoa, 2014, p. 226). In this sense, the itinerant theorist is always mining the meaning (Williams, 2013), knowing fully well that what is around is rather more crucial than the dust, noise, and the grain provoked by the minining. Thus, an itinerant curriculum theory is inherently "an exfoliation" (Gil, 1998, p. 127) metamorphosis, a sill of infinite mournings" (Couto, 2008, p. 105), an anti- and post- "mechanotic" (Ahmad, 1984, p. 31) momentum that will seek to create "a powder, gentle, maneuverable, and capable of blowing up men without killing them, a powder that, in vicious service, will generate a life, and from the exploded men will be born the infinite men that are inside him" (Couto, 2008, p. 68). In such context, ICT is a "pluriversal polyphony, a polylectal rather than ideolectal conception of cultural and political imagination" (Santos, 2018, p. 12) so crucial in an era paced by the death of imagination. I argue for a "new form of political affirmation grounded a global pluriversal *epistemological* visions and interests to be favored and courses of action to be followed that are sustained in people's history" (Popkewitz, 1978, p. 28).

The educational and curriculum theorist needs to be understood as an epistemological pariah who is challenging and challenged by a theoretical path that is inexact yet rigorous (Deleuze, 1990). It is, as we will see later on, a theory of frontier and baroque, in perpetual transitionality state (Santos, 1995). In this sense, an itinerant theorist is immersed in a metamorphosis "so perpetually incomplete that even dreams dislike because they have defects" (Pessoa, 2014, p. 126), so perpetually deep that it hurts the imagination (Gil, 2010, 86); it hurts the "physical brain" (Pessoa, 2014, p. 234). ICT is the perfect utopia because its is conscious of the imperfection of what is perfect, conscious of the perfection of the imperfection. Hence, being perfect contradicts being complete, and yet the theorist is thirsty for being complete, leaving him or her in a perennial state of useless pain. ICT reflects a subject that when "he/she thinks sees him/herself in the process" (Pessoa, 2014, p. 73) and fully "understands that if one knew the truth one would see it" (Pessoa, 2014, p. 96). ICT "captures, vampirizes and calls on the subject to complete it" (Gil, 2010, p. 29). Such an itinerant theory(ist) provokes (and exists amid) a set of crises and produces laudable silences. The theory(ist) is a volcanic chain, showing a constant lack of equilibrium, and thus is always a stranger in his or her own language. He or she is an itinerant theory(ist) profoundly sentient of the multiplicities of lines, spaces, and dynamic becomings (Deleuze, 1990). ICT thus echoes Huebner's (1966, 1959) challenges of a radically different semantology, thirstly seeking for a new language. With the term *epistemicide*, Schubert (2017, p. 12) Paraskeva's ICT "enacts the call for new languages for curriculum studies."

ICT does try to say something to the field. It presents new terrains and theoretical situations. ICT participates in the complicated conversation (Pinar, 2000; Trueit, 2000)—that cannot bend under the yoke of Western academicism—challenging Western curriculum epistemicides and alerting us to the need to respect and incorporate non-Western epistemes. Pinar (2012, 2013) acknowledged the influential synopticality of ICT:

> There are other discourses influential now, sustainability perhaps primary among them. Arts-based research is hardly peripheral. . . . One sign is the synoptic text composed by João M. Paraskeva. Hybridity is the order of the day. Pertinent to the discussion is that even Paraskeva's determination to contain in one "critical river" multiple currents of understand- ing curriculum politically floods its banks; he endorses an "itinerant curriculum theory" that asserts a "deliberate disrespect of the canon" (2011, 184). In Paraskeva's proclamation, this "river" has gone "south" (2011, 186). That South is Latin America, where we can avoid "any kind of Eurocentrism" (2011, 186) while not "romanticizing indigenous knowledge" (2011, 187). Addressing issues [such as hegemony, ideology, power, social emancipation, class, race, and gender] implies a new thinking, a new theory . . . an itinerant curriculum theory. (Pinar, 2013, p. 64)

ICT, as new influencial discourse, as Pinar (2012, 2013) put it, is highly relevant, Zhao (2019, p. 27) argues, as it opens up the eugenic colonial sociabilities (Santos, 2018) built on "language, knowledge, culture and educational" cleansing of the South. In this sense doing ICT is "*corazonar,* that is to warm up reason, a reason that has been *corazonada* and thus it "cannot be planned as it occours out of joined struggles building bridges between emotions'affections on one hand, and knowledges/reasons, on the other" (Santos, 2018, p. 101). It goes without saying how "spirituality is toweing in corazonar converting it into a non-Western-centric form of insurgent energy against oppression and unjust suffering" (Santos, 2018, p. 100).

Such a theoretical course is defined by a cutting edge, a *Malangatanian* and *Pollock-ian* set of processes not because it is abstract but because it is oppressive in its freedom. ICT is thus a theory of disquiet (Pessoa, 2014), challenging the "disquiet paralisis" (Gil, 2009, p. 20) yet knowing fully well that it is through disquiet that subjectivities emerge (Gil, 2009). It is not a sole act, however; it is a populated solitude. This itinerant theoretical path claims a multifaceted curriculum compromise and "runs away" from any unfortunate 'canonology.' ICT, as Darder (2018, p. x) unpacks, claims for a political praxis that "must be both epistemologically fierce and deeply anchored in the sensi-bilities of our subalternity—the only place from which we can truly rid ourselves of the heavy yoke of Western sanctioned tyranny, which has wrought bitter histories of impoverishment, colonization, enslavement, and genocide."

Such an itinerant curriculum theory is an anthem against the indignity of speaking for the other (Walsh, 2012; Deleuze, 1990). ICT challenges the sociology of absences, as the only way to grasp "silences, needs and unpronounceable aspirations questions" (Santos, 1999, p. 206); it challenges "how can silence be spoken without it necessarily speaking the hegemonic language that intends to make it speak?" (Santos, 1999, p. 206); it is the curric-ulum praxis of the sociology emergences, as Santos (2018, p. 276) would put it, an itinerant theory "of the sociology of absences and emergences; the former "would be geared to show the measure of the epistemicide caused by northern epistemologies, while the latter would be oriented to amplify the meaning of the latent and potentially liberating sociabilities" (Santos, 2018, p. 276), paving the way for a just pedagogy, one that foster southern episte-mologies. In such a sense, ICT is not an ortonimus theory, quite the opposite (Gil, 2010), it is a heterotheory. The theorist multiplies him- or herself to feel his or her own individual and collective subject (Gil, 2010); to be sincere, the intinerant theorist contradicts himself every minute (Gil, 2010) as reality is massively contradictory. ICT is not a "diminished theory" (Pessoa, 2010, p. 230), nor does it diminish any other epistemological formation.

The itinerary theory(ist) is much more than an eclectic approach; it is actually a profoundly (in)discipline yet doesn't correlate with any disciplinary grid that ossifies modern Western Eurocentric epistemological platforms. It "reacts againt the vegetal academy of silence" (Pessoa, 2014, p. 270). ICT confronts and throws the subject to a permanent, unstable question, 'What is to think?' ICT is a metemorphoses of the endless multifarious epistemological different "alphabet of thought" (Gil, 2009, p. 25).

It is actually a loaf theory. In this sense, ICT "reads differently because it is written and spoken in a different way" (Gil, 2010, p. 20); ICT pushes one "to think differently, but also to learn differently and to better understand what it means to learn, and what does it mean to think" (Gil, 2009, p. 35) epistemologically radically different; it is a new epistemological logic, one of excess so crucial to deterritoralize and delink but above all to reignite—in a radically way—the utopia for a just world.

Moreover, ICT pushes one to think in the light of the future as well as to question how can 'we' actually claim to really know the things that 'we' claim to know if 'we' are not ready specifically to think the unthinkable but to go beyond the unthinkable and mastering its infinitude. In this contex, ICT challenges not just momentism (Paraskeva, 2011) or presentism (Pinar, 2004) but contemporarysm (Paraskeva, 2011). In Gil's (2018, p. 404) terms, "never has a time been so contemporary as to appear to embody much more than the contemporary time. One is no longer 'contemporary of', one is simply 'contemporary', in essence. Everything becomes contemporary." The yoke of the present-now – in which our field is sinking—is viral, a new barbarism that wipes out ethics of memory regarding a past—that was always a future for a given generation at a specific point. Each 'now' is a 'now' of an absent past or future. Each 'present-now' is a 'present-now' of a 'particular now.' Devoided from a future reality—diluted witin the present—societal transformational impulses have been triggered by having the past as reference and naturally commonsensically one thinks about change in terms of "re-covering, re-building, re-habilitate" (Williams, 2013, p. 281). The human being produced by the democratic Cartesian matrix "leaves and exists for the pure present" (Badiou, 2011, p. 13), a present that is the only one, "the present of Europe" (Mignolo, 2018, p. 110). Modernity's present time, Mignolo (2018, p. 110) advances, "was understood to be the only present, the present of Europe." As we are contemporaries of everything—past and future—, Gil (2018, p. 405) adds, and "everything is present, we are only 'contemporaries' because everything is contemporary and present." This dangerous cult of 'the contemporary' completely dilutes any utopian hypothesis—however remote it may be—within common sense. One ceases to be 'contemporaries of'—which puts one in an existence and experience without historical parallel. The context of contemporaneity is contemporaneity itself.

ICT is to be (or not to be) radically unthinkable. Yet it is a theory of another humanity. It is about this world. It is people's theory. ICT is a metamorphosis between what is thought and nonthought and unthought but is fundamentally about the temerity of the colonization of the non-/un-/thought within the thought. ICT attempts to understand to domesticate how big infinite, the infinite of thought and action, is. If one challenges infinity, 'then it is chaos because one is in chaos'; that means that the question or questions (whatever they are) are inaccurately deterritorialized and fundamentally sedentary. ICT "thinks the movement of infinity" (Gil, 2009, p. 97), or the (im)possibility of finitudness of the infinity. ICT implies an understanding of chaos as domestic, as public, as a *punctum* within the pure luxury of immanence. In such a multitude of turfs, ICT needs to be understood as *poesies*. It plays in the plane of immanence. With immanence being 'a life', ICT is 'a life'; ICT "uses what it is not, like it is," as Tse (2017, p. 67) would put it. A life paced by a *poesis* or a revolution? 'Yes please,' in a full Žižekian way. ICT is, above all, the language for/of doing (Deleuze, 1995). ICT is a *poesies* that itinerantly throws the subject against the infinite of representation to grasp the omnitude of the real(ity) and the rational(ity), thus mastering the transcendent. Being more *poesies* than just theory (and not because it is less theory), its itinerant position *epitomizes* a transcendent nomadography, which is not transcendental. To be more precise, ICT, as Tse (2017, p. 104) would put it, "awakens what will never end and is housed in it." To rely on Deleuze and Guattari (1987, p. 143), "it is not death that breaks [the itinerant theorist] but seeing, experiencing, thinking too much life. There's a profound link between signs, events, life and vitalism. Its organisms that die, not life." Such inquiry implies, as Deleuze and Guattari (1987) felicitously unveil, an itinerant theorist that is not just as a war machine that judiciously collides with ossified truths and fossilized realities, but its itinerant existence is actually only possible in a permanent theater of war. Needless to say that ICT is not a cavalier way to grasp history. In this sense, it refuses to "walk backwards towards the future" (Williams, 2013, p. 281). Nor it is just a pale reaction against the way such history has been *quasi* suffocated by hegemonic and particular counterhegemonic traditions. Although also a concept—arguably a geophilosophical one—it goes well beyond an aesthetic wrangle between sedentary theoretical hegemonic and particular counterhegemonic platforms, and nomad(ic) approaches free from walls, dams, and institutionally regressive. ICT implies the beyond nomadic inquiry, one that the foci occupies the truly total itinerant capacity of space(less)ness, a permanent smooth itinerant position, a perpetual search that wholeheartedly aims at saturation yet the saturation of non-saturation. The nomadography of such theory is framed in the nonstop itinerant posture in which creators of *poesies* seemed to be part of the history of thought but escape from it either in a specific aspect or altogether. ICT challenges the irrelevance of modern Western Eurocentric disciplinary knowledge as is. ICT attempts to turn curriculum theory against itself as well. It is a philosophy of liberation, which is sentient of the pitfalls of the internationalization dynamics within the curriculum field. The itinerant posture provides a powerful space in which to engage in a global conversation that is attentive of the globalisms (Santos, 2008), profoundly aware of the multiplicities of public spheres and subaltern counterpublics (Fraser, 1997); truly attentive to the production of localities (Hardt & Negri, 2000) and militant particularism (Harvey, 1998) and to the (de)construction of new, insurgent cosmopolitanism (Santos, 2008; Popkewitz, 2007); conscious of the wrangle between the globalized few and the localized rest (Bauman, 1998); and yet profoundly alert to the dangerous hegemony of the English language. Such conversation needs to occur in languages other than English (Darder, 1991).

ICT challenges modern Western Euroentric abyssal thinking. It challenges one of the fundamental characteristics of abyssal thinking: the impossibility of co-presence of the 'two sides of the abyssal line.' Such theoretical approach is an itinerantology that addresses *las heridas abiertas* (Anzaldua, 2007) of the colonality of power. Such itinerantology is fully aware *que las heridas abiertas* cannot be addressed by ignoring how "how compressed specific dialectical positions of Marxism are—or specific dialectical positions of specific Marxisms—thus obliterating fair and inclusive analysis" (Paraskeva and Sussekind, 2018). That is, ICT is a form of decolonial thinking that recognizes an ecological coexistence of varying epistemological forms of knowledge around the world paying attention to knowledges and epistmologies largely marginalized and descredit in the current world order" (Zhao, 2019, p. 27).

ICT is not merely an invocation or evocation (Schubert, 2017, p. 10). ICT touches the 'real' nerve (Dabashi, 2015) by challenging both dominant and specific counter domi- nant traditions within the modern Western Eurocentric epistemological matrix as part of the epistemicide. However, as a future for the field, ICT alerts for the need to walk away from all forms of romanticism regarding the non-modern non-Western non-Eu- rocentric epistemes. ICT is not a nationalistic theoretical platform. ICT fights any form of indigenoustude (Paraskeva, 2011); it is about decolonizing native narratives by "con- siderin the relationship of language to power and also to empowerment" (Mallon, 2012, p. 3). In so doing it reacts against epistemological blindness, as it opens the veins of a complex beast, dissects its strokes and counterstrokes (Janson & Paraskeva, 2016), denounces and announces the involution phase of the field as well as its occidentotic fungus, and offers just ways out of it, through a just pluriversal epistemological reading and doing of the wor(l)d. ICT reacts against the "the violent power of the identical that becomes invisible," as Byung-Chul (2018, p. 10) would put it; it reacts against the fading of otherness in an era in which "the negativity of the other gives place to the positivity of the identical" (Byung-Chul, 2018, p. 10). In ICT terms, the identical is pornographic, that is "pornography all bodies resemble each other, they break down into identical body parts. Stripped of all language the body is reduced to the sexual that knows no other dif- ference than sexual" (Byung-Chul, 2018, p. 15). ICT is a call agains an "ontic deficit" that permeates society (Byung-Chul, 2018, p. 13). Its pluriverse nature smahes the obscene link "between the identical and the identical" (Byung-Chul, 2018, p. 16).

ICT move towards a just blend beween experiencies and expectations, an alterna- tive logic of utopianism that redirects towards a "possiblity to wait with hope" (Santos, 1999, p. 213), thus making the new utopia—a decolonial one, utopian otherwise—"the desperate realism of a waiting that allows itself to fight for the content of waiting, not in general but in the exact place and time in which it is" (Santos, 1999, p. 213). Thus, hope, in ICT terms, "does not lie in a general principle which provides for a general future. It resides instead in the possibility of creating fields of social experimentation where it is possible to resist locally the evidences of inevitability, successfully promot- ing alternatives that seem utopian at all times and places except those in which they actually occurred" (Santos, 1999, p. 213). Hence, ICT reignites the utopia, since "the existence does not exhaust the possibilities of existence and therefore there are alter- natives susceptible of surpassing what is critical in what exists" (Santos, 1999, p. 198) yet a different utopian logic, though not because the utopian pragmatism disappeared but because "it was not what it used to be" (Gil, 2009, p. 18), nor can it be; an alternative frame towards alternative utopias cannot be framed—and subjugated—within a matrix that actually will never allow the materialization of such utopia. ICT is not a reinvention or a rehabilitation of past utopianist(s) logic(s), although such constitutes some of its pillars. In Darder's (2018, p. xiii) terms, ICT "is meant to guide us in transforming our labor into a living praxis of global cognitive justice."

ICT implies one to "detheorize reality as the only way to reinvent it" (Santos, 1995, p. 513). It is an epistemological declaration of independence (Paraskeva, 2019). It is thus the pluriversal rubber stamp of the death of the logic through which modern Western Eurocentric platforms imposed a mono-episteme. ICT is not a drone theory though; it doesn't speak for the other. ICT is chaos and its rhythms, a chaos that "inaugurates the appearance of things not because it engenders them, but because it withdraws" (Gil, 2018, p. 376). ICT thus offers a way out of the involution volt, out of occidentosis. In Jupp's (2017, p. 5) terms, ICT is call to "preserve and advance the historically specific and localized knowledges and languages that underlie cognition—and through cognition cultural practices and social relations—represent the fundamental struggle for social justice." ICT dissects chaos as normalcy that "presides over the order of the world; as what it establishes because it withdraws—and in withdrawing, allows the emergence of thinkable things because they are discernible, differentiated" (Gil, 2018, p. 376). Chaos, and ICT in this sense, "ends with the unthinkable" (Gil, 2018, p. 376). ICT is thus emancipatory inaugurating a paradigmatic transition from a reactionary (n)eugenic cosmic capacity towards a chaosmic capacity, one that imposed "alterative forms of sociability rather than one form of sociability" (Santos, 1995, p. x). Chaos is bipolar, a consequence and a beginning, so is curriculum. In this context, ICT challenges the cultural politics of denial, that produces a radical absence, the absence of humanity, the modern sub-humanity (Santos, 2015, p. 30). Such new theoretical task understands that modern humanity is not conceivable without a modern sub-humanity (Santos, 2014), and that the denial of a part of humanity is sacrificial, in that it is the condition for the other part of humanity, which considers itself as universal. ICT thus aims precisely 'a general epistemology of the impossibility of a general epistemology.' Such radical co-presence, Santos (2007b) argues—the begin-anew (Darder, 2018)—pushes one towards a postabyssal momentum, a postabyssal epistemology, which spans an ecology of knowledges (Santos, 2007b, p. 40), "a call for the democratization of knowledges that is a commitment to an emancipatory, non-relativistic, cosmopolitan ecology of knowledges, bringing together and staging dialogues and alliances between diverse forms of knowledge, cultures, and cosmopologies in response to different forms of oppression that enact the coloniality of knowledge and power" (Santos, 2007a, p. xiv). ICT respects three fundamental pillars: (1) learning that the South exists, (2) learning to go to the South, and (3) learning from and with the South (Santos, 2015).

That is, in order to learn from the South "we must first of all let the South speak up, for what best identifies the South is the fact that has been silenced" (Santos, 1995, p. 510).

Postabyssal thinking implies a radical break with modern Western ways of thinking and acting. Postabyssality "is always coknowledge emerging from process of knowing--with rather than knowing-about" (Santos, 2018, 147). While an overt challenge against the colonialism of the English language (Darder, 1991), as well as a call to arms against all other forms of linguistic colonialism perpetrated by other modern Western languages (Paraskeva, 2011), is also an alert against what Ahmad (2008) coined as third-world nationalisms and modern Western internationalization and internationalisms, such radical break doesn't mean slurring specific modern Western impulses. The ecology of knowledges needs to be seen as a "destabilizing collective or individual subjectivity endowed with a special capacity, energy, and will to act with *clinamen* experimenting with eccentric or marginal forms of sociability or subjectivity inside and outside Western modernity, those forms that have refused to be defined according to abyssal criteria" (Santos, 2007b, p. 41). ICT is a destabilizing epistemology that aims to defamiliarize the canonic tradition of monocultures of knowledge (Santos, 2014). What is crucial within the ecology of knowledges is what Santos (2007b, p. 40) calls "action-with-*clinamen*," that is "does not refuse the past; on the contrary, it assumes and redeems the past by the way it swerves from it" (p. 41). In claiming a commitment of the radical copresence, ICT is fully engaged in such ecology of knowledges, and the challenge of an itinerant curriculum theorist is to "unpuzzle" the nexus of physical–metaphysical. That is, we are bodies; we are not institutions, although a schizophrenic system institutionalizes us. Our task is to unmask why we do not teach this and how can we teach this. This 'this' is not just physical; it is also metaphysical. In that sense, ICT is an ethical take. I argue though that ICT pushes above and beynd postabyssality towards a nonabyssal *punctum* since not only challenges the modern Western cult of abyssal thinking but also attempts to dilute such fictional vacuum between lines. ICT is not just an act of resistance, but of reexistance (Walsh, 2018) at the metaphysical level. ICT undeniably an epistemological declaration of idependence. It is a "liberated zone" (Santos, 2018, p. 31). In this sense, ICT is a dis/positional thinking concerned "for viewing educational phenomena from alternative perspectives that are nor method driven, but instead derived from insights of a disposition that seeks to disentangle schlarship from its traditional dependence on formalities" (Reyonolds and Webber 2016, pp. 5–6).

The struggle against modern Western abyssal thinking is not a policy matter. It is also above and beyond that. It is an existential and spiritual question so eloquently advocated by Huebner (1966, 1959) and Macdonald (1966a, 1966b) last century. As I keep reminding, Huebner was indeed the *avant la lettre* intellectual, advocating among other crucial issues for the urgent need for a new language to dissect the educational phenomena. In Huebner's (1966, 1959) terms, such abyssality is traped within a dangerous eugenic despotic anthrocentric semiology. In one of his more brilliant works (1966), he insisted that curriculum language is immersed in two tyrannical myths: "one is that of learning—the other that of purpose, almost magical elements the curriculum worker is afraid to ignore, let alone question" (p. 10). He argues that "learning is merely a postulated concept, not a reality and objectives are not always needed for educational planning" (p. 10). For Huebner, the major problem in the world of education, "which has been short-circuited by behavioral objectives, sciences, and learning theory, was the fact that we were not dealing with the autobiography, we were not dealing with life and inspiration" (Huebner, 2002, Tape 1). The language of education is full of "dangerous and non-recognized [and unchallenged] myths" (Huebner, 1966, p. 9), which makes it impossible to question whether the "technologists maybe were going in the wrong direction" (Huebner, 2002, Tape 1). This becomes much more complex and alarming in a society that is facing the fact that "the problem is no longer one of explaining change, but of explaining nonchange" (Huebner, 1967, p. 174), and that a human being, by his transcendent condition, "has the capacity to transcend what he is to become, something that he is not" (p. 174):

> For centuries the poet has sung of his near infinitudes; the theologian has preached of his depravity and hinted of his participation in the divine; the philosopher has struggled to encompass him in his systems, only to have him repeatedly escape; the novelist and dramatist have captured his fleeting moments of pain and purity in never-to-be-for- gotten aesthetic forms; and the [man] engaged in the curriculum has the temerity to reduce this being to a single term—learner. (Huebner, 1966, p. 10)

However, the struggle against the Western Cartesian model cannot signify the substitution of Cartesian model for another one. Also, the task is not to dominate such model or to rap with a more Eurocentric humanistic impulse. The task is to pronounce its last words, to prepare its remains for a respectful funeral. The task is not to change the language and concepts, although that is crucial. The task is to terminate a particular hegemonic geography of knowledge, which promotes an epistemological euthanasia.

ICT's nonabyssality is "informed by its epistemological rupture from the coloniality of power and disaffiliation with hegemonic dogma, a process that liberates our field of consciousness, opening the way for resurgences of subaltern perspectives, new expressions of solidarity, and the powerful regeneration of that political force necessary for transforming the social and material conditions of our present existence—not only in the mind but also in the flesh" (Darder, 2018, p. xiv). ICT is a "deliberate disrespect of the canon, a struggle against epistemological orthodoxy" (Santos, 2005, p. xxv), and it attempts "to bring scientific knowledge face-to-face with nonscientific, explicitly local knowledges, knowledges grounded in the experience of the leaders and activists of the social movements studied by social scientists" (Santos, 2005, p. xxv). This is the very core of its nutritive faculty, to use Agamben's (1999) Aristotelic approach. An itinerant curriculum theory is an exercise of "citizenship and solidarity" (Santos, 2005, p. xxv) and, above all, an act of social and cognitive justice. It is, as Žižek (2006) would put it, the very best way to understand how reality can explode in and change the real.

I am not claiming a way out that will please everybody. In fact, "a coherent theory is an imposed theory which falsely mythologizes a pseudo-scientific process that has no more to do with real science than astrology does" (Quantz, 2011). ICT it is however a consequence of the perpetual lack of a dominant praxis of a "perfect just teaching and learning," as Tse (2017, p. 284). An itinerant theoretical approach dares to violate the methodological canon and attempts to go beyond some interesting (counter-)dominant clashes to overcome some dead-ends and screaming silences, yet it is an epistemological struggle within the insurgent cosmopolitanism platforms (Santos, 2008) both inside and beyond the Western dominant cartography (Paraskeva, 2011a). ICT is to delink towards a polycentric world, as Amin (1990) would put it. There is no question, Darder (2018, p. xv) sternly claims, that the postabysmal terrain of itinerant curriculum constiutes a complex and challenging political project yet one that offers us political solace, philosophical inspiration, and pedagogical nourishment on a long and arduous journey. ICT

> entails navigating dialectically the often-murky realm of dominant/subordinate relations of power. Yet, it is precisely by consistently traversing the turbulence of this dialectical tension that we become politically primed to ruthlessly critique oppression in ways that prevent us from inadvertently collapsing back into oppressive binary contradictions, from which we ourselves must constantly struggle to emerge *anew*. And further, it is only through such sustained labor and unwavering commitment to denounce the epistemological totalitarianism of our times that we can garner together the moral indignation and political will to announce new ways of knowing, loving and being—beyond the abyssal divide of recalcitrant racisms and neoliberal devastation. (Darder, 2018, pp. xiv–xv)

In this regard, an itinerant theoretical path without floodgates because the best sentinel is always to have no floodgates (Couto, 2008). In so doing the itinerant curriculum theory honors a legacy of accomplishments and frustrations, understanding that delinking will always be to make theory, a just theory. To delink and decolonize, while honoring the legacy of the radical critical path taking it into a different level, it is also a decolonial attempt "to do critical theory" (Kellner, 1989, p. 2). Respecting the legacy of such generation of the utopia, such a decolonial attempt needs cannot ignore the rich legacy of such group of phenomenal utopists and needs to keep swiming through a radical critical river yet reaching out and recognizing endless tributaries and other rivers and tributaries beyond the riverbed of such modern Western Eurocentric river and in doing so produce a new logic towards a new needed utopia. ICT it is a just way to "to ruthlessly problematize and rethink consciousness or to *begin anew*, by way of our subaltern engagements of Marx's unfinished political economic project, in an effort to deepen and expand its emancipatory vision, namely, the liberation of our humanity—but only now through the complexity of multi-centered epistemological lenses able to withstand the ever-changing character our cultural formations and political manifestations" (Darder, 2018, p. xiii). ICT is an heretopian theory. It is people's theory.

References

Agamben, G. (1999) "Absolute Immanence," in J. Khalfa (Ed.), *An Introduction to the Philosophy of Gillen Deleuze*. London: Continuum, pp. 151–169.

Agamben, G. (2005) *The State of Exception*. Chicago: Chicago University Press.

Ahmad, A. (2008) *In Theory. Classes, Nations, Literatures*. London: Verso.

Ahmad, J. (1984) *Occidentosis. A Plague from the West*. Iran: Mizten Press.

Amin, S. (1990) *Delinking: Towards a Polycentric World*. London: Zed Books.

Anzaldua, G. (2007) *Borderlands. La Frontera. The New Mestiza*. San Francisco: Aunt Lute Books.

Apple, M. (1979) *Ideology and Curriculum*. New York: Routledge.

Auge, M. (1994) (2003). *Não-Lugares: introdução a uma antropologia da supermodernidade*. Campinas: Papirus Editora.

Badiou, A. (2011) The Democratic Emblem. In A. Ellen (Ed.), *Democracy in What State?* New York: Columbia University Press, pp. 6–15.

Bauman, Z. (1998) *Globalization. The Human Consequences*. London: Blackwell Publishers.

Berardi, F. (2012) *The Uprising. On Poetry and Finance*. Los Angeles: Semiotext(e).

Byung-Chul, H. (2018) *A Expulsao do Outro*. Lisboa: Relogio D'Agua.

Couto, M. (2008) *Terra Sonambula*. Lisboa: Leya.

Dabashi, H. (2015). *Can Non-Europeans Think?* London: Zed Books.

Darder, A. (1991) *Culture and the power in the classroom*. Boulder, CO: Paradigm.

Darder, A. (2018) Ruthlessness and the Forging of Liberatory Epistemologies: An Arduous Journey. In J. Paraskeva (ed). *Curriculum Epistemicides*. New York: Routledge, pp. ix–xvi.

Deleuze, G. (1990) *Pourparlers*. Paris: Les Editions de Minuit

Deleuze, G. (1995) *The Logic of Sense*. New York: Columbia University Press.

Deleuze, G., & Guattari, F. (1987) *A Thousand Plateaus. Capitalism and Schizophrenia*. Minneapolis: University of Minnesota Press.

Deleuze, G., & Guattari, F. (1995) (1987) *A Thousand Plateaus. Capitalism and Schizophrenia*. Minneapolis: University of Minnesota Press.

Eco, U. (1984) *Proscript to the Name of the Rose*. New York: Harcourt, Brace and Jovanovich.

Fraser, N. (1997) *Justice Interrupts. Critical Reflections on the 'Postcolonialist' Condition*. New York: Routledge.

Gil, J. (1998) *Metamorphoses of the Body*. Minnesota: University of Minnesota Press.

Gil, J. (2009) *Em Busca da Idenitidade. O Desnorte*. Lisboa: Relógio D'Água.

Gil, J. (2010) *O Devir-Eu de Fernando Pessoa*. Lisboa: Relógio D'Água.

Gil, J. (2018) *Caos e Ritmo*. Lisboa: Relógio D'Água.

Gough, N. (2000) Locating Curriculum Studies in the Global Village. *Journal of Curriculum Studies*, 32 (2), pp. 329–342.

Hardt, M., & Negri, T. (2000). *Empire*. Cambridge: Harvard University Press.

Harvey, D. (1998) "What's Green and Makes the Environment Go Round?" in F. Jameson & M. Miyoshi (eds) *The Cultures of Globalization. Post-Contemporary Interventions*. Durham, NC: Duke University Press, pp. 327–355.

Huebner, D. (1959) *From Classroom Action to Educational Outcomes. An Exploration in Educational Theory*. Madison: University of Wisconsin-Madison.

Huebner, D. (1966) "Curricular Language and Classroom Meanings," in J. Macdonald & R. Leeper (eds) *Language and Meaning*. Washington: ASCD.

Huebner, D. (2002) Tape # 1, recorded at 3718 Seminary Rd, Alexandria, VA 22304. Washington. USA.

Jin, H. (2008) *The Writer as Migrant*. Chicago: The University of Chicago Press

Jupp, J. (2017) Decolonizing and De-Canonizing Curriculum Studies. *Journal for the American Association for the Advancement of Curriculum Studies*, 12 (1), pp. 1–25.

Kellner, D. (1989) *Critical Theory, Marxism and Modernity*. Baltimore: The John Hopkins University Press.

Khalfa, J. (1999) "Introduction," in J. Khalfa (ed) *An Introduction to the Philosophy of Gillen Deleuze*. London: Continuum, pp. 1–6.

Kliebard, H. (1968) "The Curriculum Field in Retrospect," in P. Witt (ed) *Technology and Curriculum*. New York: Teachers College Press, pp. 69–84.

Krug, E. (1969) *The Shaping of the American High School, 1880–1920*. Madison: The University of Wisconsin Press.

Mallon, F. (1994) The Promise and Dilemma of Subaltern Studies: Perspectives from Latin American History. *American Historical Review*, 99, pp. 1491–1515.

Mallon, F. (2012). *Decolonizing Native Histories*. Durham: Duke University Press.

Macdonald, J. (1966a) "Language, Meaning and Motivation: An Introduction," in J. Macdonald & R. Leeper (eds) *Language and Meaning*. Washington: ASCD, pp. 1–7.

Macdonald, J. (1966b) "The Person in the Curriculum," in H. Robinson (ed) *Precedents and Promise in the Curriculum Field*. New York: Teachers College, Columbia University, pp. 38–52.

Merlau-Ponty, M. (1973) *The Prose of the World*. Evanston: Northwestern University Press.

Mignolo, W. (2018) "The Invention of the Human and the Three Pillars of the Coloniality Matrix of Power," in Catherine Walsh & Walter Mignolo *On Decoloniality. Concepts, Analytics, Praxis*. Durham: Duke University Press, pp. 153–176.

Moreira, M. A. (2017) And the Linguistic Minorities Suffer What They Must?': A Review of Conflicts In Curriculum Theory Through the Lenses of Language Teacher Education? *Journal for the American Association for the Advancement of Curriculum Studies*, 12 (1), pp. 1–17.

O'Brien, M. & Penna, S. (1999) *Theorizing Welfare*. London: Sage.

Oliveira, I. B. (2017). Itinerant Curriculum Theory Against the Epistemcide. A Dialogue Between the Thinking of Santos and Paraskeva. *Journal for the American Association for the Advancement of Curriculum Studies*, 12 (1), pp. 1–22.

Paraskeva, J. (2011) *Conflicts in Curriculum Theory. Challenging Hegemonic Epistemologies*. New York: Palgrave.

Paraskeva, J. (2017) The Epistemicide. New York: Routledge.

Paraskeva, J. (2018) *Towards a Just Curriculum Theory. The Epistemicide*. New York: Routledge.

Paraskeva, J. (2019) "¿Qué sucede con la teoría crítica (currículum)? La necesidad de sobrellevar la rabia neoliberal sin evitarla," in Rosa V. Recio (comp) *Reconocimiento y Bien Comun en Educacion*. Madrid: Morata, pp. 191–230.

Paraskeva, J., & Sussekind, M. L. (2018) Contra a Cegueira Epistemológica nos Rumos da Teoria Curricular Itinerante. *Educação e Cultura Contemporânea*, 15, pp. 54–85.

Pessoa, F. (2010) *Textos Filosóficos*, Volume II. Lisboa: Nova Ática.

Pessoa, F. (2014) *Livro do Desassossego*. Lisboa: Assirio & Alvim.

Pinar, W. (2000) Introduction: Toward the internationalization of curriculum studies. In D. Trueit, W. Doll Jr., H. Wang, & W. Pinar (eds) *The Internationalization of Curriculum Studies*. New York: Peter Lang, pp. 1–13.

Pinar, W. (2004) *What is Curriculum Theory?* Mawah: Lawrence Erlbaum Associates Publishers.

Pinar, W. (2013) *Curriculum Studies in the United States: Present Circumstances, Intellectual Histories*. New York: Palgrave Macmillan.

Pokwewitz, T. (1978) Educational Research: Values and Visions of a Social Order. *Theory and Research in Social Education*, 4 (4) p. 28.

Popkewitz, T. (2007) *Cosmopolitanism and the Age of School Reform. Science, Education, and Making Society, by Making the Child.* New York: Taylor and Francis.

Quantz, R. (2011) *Rituals and Students Identity in Education: Ritual Critique for a New Pedagogy.* New York: Palgrave.

Said, E. (2005) "Reconsiderando a Teoria Itinerante," in Manuela Sanches (org) *Deslocalizar a Europa. Antroplogia, Arte, Literatura e História na Pós-Colonialidade.* Lisboa: Cotovia, pp. 25–42.

Santos, B. (1995) *Towards a New Common Sense. Law, Science and Politics in the Paradigmatic Transition.* New York: Routledge.

Santos, B. (1999) *Porque é tão difícil construir* uma teoria crítica? *Revista Crítica de Ciencias Sociais,* N. 54, Junho, pp. 197–215.

Santos, B. (2005) *Democratizing Democracy. Beyond the Liberal Democratic.* Cannon. London: Verso.

Santos, B. (2007a) *Another Knowledge Is Possible.* London: Verso.

Santos, B. (2007b) Beyond Abyssal Thinking. From Global Lines to Ecologies of Knowledges. *Review,* XXX (1), pp. 45–89.

Santos, B. (2008). A universidade no seculo XXI. Para uma reforma democratica e emancipatoria da universidade. In B. Sousa Santos & N. de Almeida Filho (Eds.), *A universidade no seculo XXI. Para uma universidade nova* (pp. 13–106). Coimbra: Centro de Estudos Sociais.

Santos, B. (2014) *Epistemologies of the South: Justice against Epistemicide.* Boulder: Paradigm.

Santos, B. (2015) *If God Were a Human Rights Activist: Human Rights and the Challenge of Political Theologies. Is Humanity Enough?* Stanford: Stanford University Press.

Santos, B. (2018) *The End of the Cognitive Empire.* Durham: Duke University Press.

Schubert, W. (1986) *Curriculum. Perspective, Paradigm and Possibility.* New York: MacMillan Publishing Company.

Schubert, W. (2017) Growing Curriculum Studies: Contributions of João M. Paraskeva. *Journal for the American Association for the Advancement of Curriculum Studies,* 12 (1), pp. 1–22.

Süssekind, M. L. (2017) Against Epistemological Fascism. A Reading of Paraskeva's Itinerant Curriulum Theory. *Journal for the American Association for the Advancement of Curriculum Studies,* 12 (1), pp. 1–18.

Trueit, D. (2000). Democracy and Conversation. In D. Trueit, W. Doll Jr, H. Wang and W. Pinar (Eds.). *The Internationalization of Curriculum Studies.* New York: Peter Lang, pp., ix–xvii.

Tse, C. (2017) *Chuang Tse.* Lisboa: Relogio D'Agua.

Tyack, D. (1974) *The One Best System. A History of American Urban Education.* Cambridge: Harvard University Press.

Walsh, C. (2012) 'Other' Knowledges, 'Other' Critiques Reflections on the Politics and Practices of Philosophy and Decoloniality in the Other America. *Transmodernity. Journal of Peripheral Cultural Production of the Luso-Hispanic World,* 1 (3), pp. 11–27.

Walsh, C. (2018) Insurgency and Decolonial Prospect, Praxis and Project. In C. Walsh and W. Mignolo (Eds.), *On Decoloniality: Concepts, Analytics, Praxis.* Durham: Duke University Press, pp. 33–56.

Williams, R. (2013) *Long Revolution.* London: Verso.

Zhao, W. (2019) *China's Education, Curriculum Knowledge and Cultural Inscriptions. Dancing with the Wind.* New York: Routledge.

Žižek, S. (2006) *Bem-Vindo ao Deserto do Real.* Lisboa: Relogio D'Agua.

CHAPTER THIRTEEN

Facing the Limits of Modern-Colonial Imaginaries[1]

Vanessa de Oliveira Andreotti

THIS TEXT IS about the possibility of a form of education that can mobilize a non-coercive re-arrangement of desires towards ethical responsibility "before will" (Spivak, 2004). However, academic alphabetic writing itself, being grounded on and reflective of a modern-colonial onto-metaphysics, is inherently very precarious for this task. Therefore, in order to gesture towards other possibilities of education, the text will be interwoven with images, metaphors and two sets of questions. The first set involves practical questions that ground and situate this work in relation to educational concerns. The second set is "po-ethic" (Silva, 2014) and involves questions that attempt to interrupt the linearity of modern logic. These questions are related to "existence and coexistence" within and beyond (with/out) modernity . Here is the first example:

HOW CAN WE EXPERIENCE:
ETHICS WITH/OUT THE MODERN SUBJECT?
POLITICS WITH/OUT NATION STATES?
EDUCATION WITH/OUT THE ENLIGHTENMENT?
BEING WITH/OUT SEPARABILITY?
THE END OF THE WORLD AS WE KNOW IT WITHOUT DESPAIR?

One of the narratives I use to explain this kind of work is that it is concerned with humanity's capacity (and lack of capacity) to figure out how to get out of a mess it has created, a mess that jeopardizes its own survival. The groups I work with (including Indigenous communities and collectives of artists, educators and activists) do not see this as fundamentally a problem of KNOWING (that can be fixed with more information), but a problem of a habit of BEING (restrictive cognitive, affective and relational *contextual* configurations affecting our reasoning, investments, neurobiology and functionality). One of the analogies we use to explain the magnitude of the challenge of interrupting habits of being is that of a tree. In our metaphorical tree, ways of doing are represented by the leaves, ways of thinking are represented by the branches, ways of seeing are represented by the visible part of the trunk, ways of wanting or desiring

---

1   Keynote address, Department of Educational Leadership, University of Massachusetts Dartmouth
May 10, 2013.

represented are by the roots and ways of sensing, yearning and relating are represented by the point of contact between the roots and the earth. While academic knowledge production has often focused on ways of doing and thinking (i.e. changing convictions in order to change behavior), my research is more focused on the limits of our ways of seeing (i.e. questions of intelligibility) and our ways of wanting and feeling (i.e. how we are wired to hope and want in certain ways). For example I am interested in how, within modernity, we seek the security of being in the certainty of knowing and how this is not something we can think our way out of but something that requires the interruption of feedback loops related to enjoyments, pleasures and satisfactions, as well as traumas and fears. Without an interruption of ways of seeing, wanting and sensing, we will tend to reproduce the same kinds of relationships and forms of coexistence.

The research and artistic projects I am involved with highlight the importance of paying attention to the dynamics of resistance as an act of hospicing worlds that are dying (within and outside of ourselves) and assisting with the births of new worlds that are potentially (but not necessarily) wiser—and that are inherently paradoxical. As an illustration of this paradoxical quality, I would like to draw attention to a picture (Figure 13.1) of a bedroom in the *assentamento* Maceio of the Brazilian landless movement that I visited last year, where, on one wall, there is a large graffiti of Che Guevara's face, the opposite wall features a large graffiti of the face of Jesus and the back wall has the logo of Botafogo football club, with Jesus and Che linked together by the hammock where I slept. The second picture (Figure 13.2) is of a bedroom where I slept while visiting a project at the Pincheq community in Peru where the walls displayed similar ideological complexities (both pictures were taken and are shown with permission).

FIGURE 13.1. A BEDROOM IN ASSENTAMENTO MACEIÓ IN BRAZIL

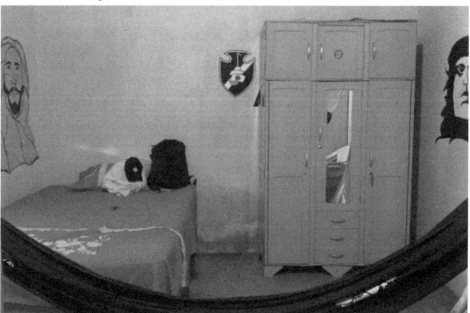

FIGURE 13.2. A BEDROOM IN COMUNIDAD PINCHEQ IN PERU

These images gesture towards the enduring challenges of being present to the pluriverses that exist within complex communities of struggle and the heterogeneities, contradictions, and social tensions that operate within and outside of ourselves (see also Andreotti, Ahenakew and Cooper, 2015).

> HOW CAN WE ENGAGE AND BE TAUGHT BY
> DIFFERENT SYSTEMS OF KNOWLEDGE AND BEING,
> STRUGGLES AND ATTEMPTS TO CREATE ALTERNATIVES,
> (A)CUTELY AWARE OF THEIR GIFTS,
> LIMITATIONS, COMPLEXITIES AND CONTRADICTIONS,
> AS WELL AS OUR OWN (MIS)INTERPRETATIONS,
> PROJECTIONS AND APPROPRIATIONS?

Our socialization into a modern-colonial way of knowing and being through modern institutions focused on coherence, certainty and control does not prepare us for this task. Through a modern/colonial grammar, we are socialized to invest (both intellectually and affectively) in the coherence of a single story of progress, development and human evolution. This story creates patterns of knowledge production that divide humanity between those heading progress (perceived as more intelligent, clean, civilized, educated, authoritative and deserving) and those lagging behind. Research in education has shown that this pattern of knowledge production generates problematic forms of relationships and engagement between those two groups that are very difficult to interrupt. In my research team, we use the acronym HEADS UP to trace these patterns.

H stands for "hegemony" which we translate as an affective (often unconscious) investment in totalizing forms of knowing (i.e. the onto-epistemology that reduces being to knowing);

E stands for "ethnocentrism" translated as the projection of a situated view as universal and the framing of difference/diversity as an "add-on" to a more colourful universal frame (foreclosing incommensurabilities);

A stands for "ahistoricism" translated as the invizibilization of how the past is ever present in the present, specially in terms of colonialism, coloniality and slavery;

D stands for "depoliticized" translated as hiding or minimizing the workings and effects of uneven power relations;

S stands for "salvationist" translated as affective investments feeling and looking good that in turn creates self-congratulatory and often self-serving tendencies that are ultimately ineffective in mobilizing different forms of relationship;

U stands for "uncomplicated solutions" translated as formulaic solutions often geared towards keeping hope, harmony and security, but that invisibilize our complicity in harm and fail to interrupt our satisfactions and feedback loops that keep systemic harmful patterns alive

P stands for "paternalistic" translated as an affective investment in a "thank you" from (often infantilized) "beneficiaries" as an outcome of an intervention. (See Andreotti et al. 2018.)

Even when we realize the single story of progress, development and human evolution is flawed and violent, we tend to resist it from within its own grammar and want to change the content of the single story rather than the process of story-*ing*: to replace it with another story that gives us a similar sense of security, purpose, authority and legitimacy. We tend to look for a theory, a theorist, a leader, a movement or a specific community who can offer a promise and a package of codes, morals, labels, values and virtues that will appease our fears, restore our hope and make things feel right again. In the next part of this text I will use a set of two images to illustrate the (epistemological) grammar and its grip on our sense of (ontological) security: the images of the "house modernity built" (Stein, Hunt, Susa and Andreotti 2017) and "boxhead" (see Andreotti, 2011; 2012; 2016; 2018). I conclude with some reflections on the implications of these questions and analyses.

HOW HAS MODERNITY/COLONIALITY TRAPPED US
IN EXPERIENCES OF LANGUAGE, KNOWLEDGE, AGENCY,
AUTONOMY, IDENTITY, CRITICALITY, ART,
SEXUALITY, EARTH, TIME, SPACE AND SELF . . .
THAT RESTRICT OUR HORIZONS AND WHAT
WE CONSIDER TO BE POSSIBLE/DESIRABLE/INTELLIGIBLE?

"The house modernity built" (Figure 13.3) has its foundations laid on an ontic concrete that separates humans from the land/earth and the rest of nature, constructing land as resource/property and creating hierarchies of value that rank entities of nature against each other according to their perceived utility. The carrying walls of this house are represented, on one side, by bricks of utility-maximizing individual rationalism cemented onto the pillars of Western humanism. On the other side, there is the wet wall of nation states offering (false) securities through borders, rights, illusions of sovereignty, (national) homogeneity and promises of social mobility, cohesion and inclusion. The roof of this house is currently made of roof tiles of investment markets that make up the volatile context of financialized shareholder global capitalism, layered over the beams of continuous growth and consumption as a measure of progress and civilization. The image on the side presents the house mouldy and cracking as it has already exceeded the carrying limits of the planet that it stands on. People inside the house are discussing what to do, as they watch a crowd form at the door. Outside, many of those who have provided the materials, the labour and bore the costs of construction, maintenance and sewage management of the house knock on the door expecting to be allowed in.

FIGURE 13.3. THE HOUSE MODERNITY BUILT

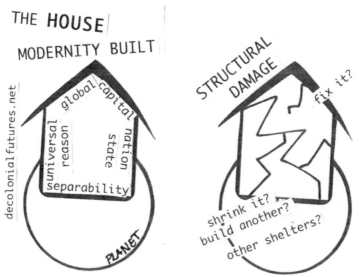

For the people within the house who are noticing the cracks, the first moment of realization of brokenness is one where distractions and denials kick in: people try to fix what is beyond repair by reinforcing the house's structure, specially its roof. The second moment is one where alternatives with guarantees are sought: people try to look for the same securities of the house in another (idealized and romanticized) architectural plan that can replace the one collapsing. Discussions in education have established a circularity between these two moments. However, a possibility exists for a third moment of becoming disillusioned with this circularity and re-orienting our desires towards possibilities of existence outside the promises and parameters of intelligibility that the house has created. This is the moment when we may start to disinvest in the structures of being (not just of 'knowing') that are sustained by the promises and economies of the house. This disinvestment is not about a search for articulated solutions for the crises we face, or an exit from the house coming from aversion, but the insight that for us to exist otherwise, we have to pay attention to the lessons being taught by the limits, failures and eventual collapse of the house itself (i.e. hospicing). This we can only do through facing its death both internal and external to ourselves, and opening up the possibility that the identification or dis-identification with the house will no longer define our existence or allocate our desires and investments.

WHAT HAVE BEEN THE COSTS OF (MODERN/COLONIAL) SEPARABILITY, DESACRALIZATION, DE-COMM(O/U)NIZATION AND UNIVERSALIZATION? HOW CAN DISILLUSIONMENT BE PRODUCTIVE? HOW CAN WE DE-ARROGANTIZE?

"Boxhead" (Figure 13.4) shows how difficult it is to engage in this intellectual and affective process. The image of a large square-headed being with a tiny (unfinished) outlined body represents the modern grammar of intelligibility imprinted on its frame through different and enduring referents that circumscribe his relationship with reality. Although not all referents may surface at the same time, they ascribe coherence to the project of modernity as we know it and create subjects who are versed in a modern-colonial habitus and amenable to the modern dream of seamless progress, development and evolution carried out by human agency through the use of objective knowledge to control the environment and engineer a perfect society. Boxhead 'thinks, therefore he is': his relationship with the world is mediated by his cognitive repertoire of meanings, rather than by his senses.

FIGURE 13.4. BOXHEAD

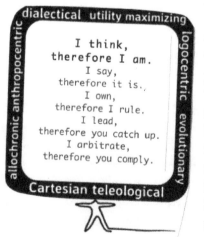

Each referent brackets a way of creating meaning that buffers his sense of reality. Logocentrism compels him to believe that reality can be described in language in its totality. Universalism leads him to understand his interpretation of reality as objective and to project it as the only legitimate and valuable world view. Anthropocentric reasoning makes him see himself as separate from nature and having a mandate to manage, exploit and control it. Teleological thinking makes him want to plan for the engineering of a future that he can already imagine. Dialectical thinking makes him fall in love with a linear logic that is obsessed with consensus, coherence, solutions and averse to paradoxes, complexities and contradictions. Allochronic and evolutionary thinking make him judge others according to criteria where he is represented as being in the present of (linear) time while others are in the past, and where he leads humanity in a single path of evolution.

However, the first reading of this picture is deceiving because it gives us a false idea that there is an outside and an inside of the box. But if we look at the image differently, seeing ourselves not as the box but as the line that draws the picture, we may have two important insights. First, that the very desire for an outside of the box comes from within the box (dialectical aversion to Boxhead generally comes from and reinforces its traits). Second, that we are already free to draw different things, but perhaps not without learning the lessons that being locked in these choices for 500 years has made us repeat (or we will end up making the same mistakes thinking and declaring that we are doing something new). In this sense, we need to hold the Cartesian possibility and modernity itself not as pathologies to be demonized but as interesting and extremely important experiments whose lessons will teach us to make different mistakes in the future. This shift of perception can calibrate our search for what will create the possibility of onto-genesis, understanding that the ways of knowing and being that have created the problems we face are unlikely to provide the solutions.

WHO ARE WE BEYOND OUR PERCEIVED IDENTITIES, SELF-IMAGES AND EGO-LOGICAL DESIRES?

Jacqui Alexander (2005) gestures in this direction in her analysis of a yearning for wholeness that gets codified within modernity/coloniality as a yearning for belonging through categories of representation. She states that the material and psychic dismemberment and fragmentation created by modernity/coloniality produce "a yearning for wholeness, often expressed as a yearning to belong, a yearning that is both material and existential, both psychic and physical, and which, when satisfied, can subvert, and ultimately displace the pain of dismemberment" (p. 281). She suggests that strategies of membership in coalitions, like those of citizenship, community, family, political movement, nationalism and solidarity in identity or ideology, although important, have not addressed the source of this yearning. For Alexander, these coalitions have reproduced the very fragmentation and separation that she identifies as the root of the problem. She states that the source of this yearning is a "deep knowing that we are in fact interdependent—neither separate, nor autonomous" (p. 282). She explains:

> As human beings we have a sacred connection to each other, and this is why enforced separations wreak havoc in our Souls. There is a great danger then, in living lives of segregation. Racial segregation. Segregation in politics. Segregated frameworks. Segregated and compartmentalised selves. What we have devised as an oppositional politics has been necessary, but it will never sustain us, for a while it may give us some temporary gains (which

become more ephemeral the greater the threat, which is not a reason not to fight), it can never ultimately feed that deep place within us: that space of the erotic, that space of the Soul, that space of the Divine. (p. 282)

However, practices that are grounded on forces of interruption (i.e. the erotic, the aesthetic, the divine, the hilarious and the more than human) are essential, but insufficient to the task of honouring the lessons of Boxhead and the House. Without a (self-)ethnography of (egological) boxheads within us these forces are usually instrumentalized and allocated towards the same problematic and often harmful compensatory desires for consumption (based on insecurities designed for the maintenance of modernity-coloniality).

> WHAT IF MODERNITY/COLONIALITY HAS HELD US
> EXISTENTIALLY HOSTAGE BY FEEDING OUR FEARS,
> COMPENSATORY DESIRES AND PERCEIVED ENTITLEMENTS?
> HOW HAVE OUR DREAMS BEEN TAMED?
> HOW CAN THEY BE DECOLONIZED?
> HOW DO WE KNOW WHEN THEY HAVE BEEN?

Boxhead experiences time as (only) linear and the self as uni-dimensional. His life purpose is indexing and codifying reality into units of meaning with a view to engineering something that will control reality itself (and protect us from its inherent plurality and indeterminacy, and, ultimately, from pain and from death). This modern-colonial obsession with the indexing or codification of reality in boxed categories of representation/meaning works like a spell (see Abram, 2012) where making sense codifies all other senses until we can only sense what "makes sense", and we numb to sensorial experiences that cannot be codified. In this context, it is not surprising that the search for meaning (codifying experience) becomes the purpose of existence. In an economy of codifications, meaning is a currency that equates with "value": producing meaning in ways that "stick" confers people authority, credibility, status and legitimacy. When this happens, epistemic certainty becomes the ground for ontological security and being is easily reduced to knowing (see also Andreotti, 2018). Within this neurobiological configuration, fears of worthlessness, indeterminacy, rejection, pointlessness and scarcity generate desires for mastery, coherence, consensus, superiority, accumulation and control. These desires are translated into perceived entitlements of representation (identity), universality and stability. These perceived entitlements are embodied as cumulative "property" in intellectual, affective, relational and material economies, particularly (but not exclusively) within modernity/coloniality (and dialectical attempts to overcome it).

Two implications

In facing the limits of modern-colonial imaginaries, I have attempted to highlight two pedagogical implications: (1) the need to take a step back to examine the discursive and affective regimes of visibility, intelligibility and affectability that police the boundaries of (our) imagination (what we call the 'analectic' dimension), and (2) the need to explore the terms that enable/disable the folding/unfolding of existing and new possibilities (the dimension of ontogenesis). In this sense, the call is for activating our capacity to experience that which exceeds what is intelligible, to imagine beyond categories of thought and affective entrapments, to acknowledge the inevitability of pain, death and (re)birth and to 'sit with' the indeterminacy and plurality of the world without the need for identification and/or dis-identification. This involves looking in the mirror and not turning away when facing both the beauty and ugliness of humanity in each of us, through a deep recognition of our entangled vulnerabilities: our strengths and precariousness, medicines and poisons, light and shadow, capacity for love and violence and, crucially, our own arrogance, unspoken sense of superiority, insecurities, traumas and contradictions (see Andreotti, Pereira, and Edmundo 2017; Andreotti, et al., 2018) This moves the questions we ask from a focus on representation, canonical narratives and normativity towards questions about what lies beyond representability:

> WHAT CONNECTS US BEYOND KNOWLEDGE,
> IDENTITY AND UNDERSTANDING?
> WHAT, BEYOND CONVICTIONS,
> CAN OFFER AN ANTIDOTE TO INDIFFERENCE?
> WHAT WOULD BE POSSIBLE IF
> WE COULD ACT BEYOND
> THE COMPENSATORY DEMANDS
> OF OUR DEEPEST INSECURITIES?

References

Alexander, M. J. (2005). Pedagogies of crossing: Meditations on feminism, sexual politics, memory, and the sacred. Durham: Duke University Press.

Andreotti, V. (2011). Engaging the (geo)political economy of knowledge construction: Towards decoloniality and diversality in global citizenship education. Globalization, Society and Education Journal, 9(3–4), 381, 397.

Andreotti, V. (2012). Education, knowledge and the righting of wrongs. Other Education: The Journal of Educational Alternatives, 1(1), 19–31.

Andreotti, V. (2016). Re-imagining education as an un-coersive re-arrangement of desires. Other Education: The Journal of Educational Alternatives, 5(1), 79-88.

Andreotti, V. (2018). Educação para a expansão de horizontes, saberes, vivências, afetos, sensibilidades e possibilidades de (co)existência. Sinergias: Diálogos educativos para a transformação social, 6, 61–72.

Andreotti, V. (2018). Renegotiating epistemic privilege and enchantments with modernity: The gain in the loss of the entitlement to control and define everything. In J. Paraskeva and S. Steinberg (Eds.), *The Curriculum: Decanonizing the Field.* Frankfurt: Peter Lang, pp. 311–328.

Andreotti, V., Ahenakew, C., Cooper, G. (2011). Towards global citizenship education 'otherwise'. In V. de Oliveira Andreotti, L. de Souza (Eds.), Postcolonial perspectives on global citizenship education (pp. 221–238). New York: Routledge.

Andreotti, V., Pereira, R., Edmundo, E. (2017). O imaginário global dominante e algumas reflexões sobre os pré-requisitos para uma educação pós-abissal. Sinergias: Diálogos educativos para a transformação social, 5, 41–54.

Andreotti, V., Stein, S., Sutherland, A., Pashby, K., Susa, R., Amsler, S. (2018). Mobilising different conversations about global justice in education: Toward alternative futures in uncertain times. Policy & Practice: A Development Edcation Review, 26(Spring), 9–41.

Silva, D. F. (2014). Toward a black feminist poethics: The quest(ion) of blackness toward the end of the world. The Black Scholar, 44(2), 81–97.

Silva, D. F. (2014). Toward a Black Feminist Poethics: The quest (ion) of Blackness toward the End of the World. *The Black Scholar,* 44(2), 81-97.

Spivak, G. C. (2004). Righting wrongs. *The South Atlantic Quarterly, 103*(2), pp. 523-581.

Stein, S., Hunt, D., Suša, R., de Oliveira Andreotti, V. (2017). The educational challenge of unraveling the fantasies of ontological security. Diaspora, Indigenous, and Minority Education, 11(2), 69–79.

CHAPTER FOURTEEN

Beyond US-Centered Multicultural Foundations[1]

James C. Jupp and Miryam Espinosa-Dulanto

THE STATESIAN[2] RACIAL tragedy currently shows no sign of abatement, and within the academy, ways to honestly discuss race in the US continue to present striking silences, awkward exchanges, and hostilities. On the national level, the recent fatal shootings of Michael Brown in Ferguson, Missouri; twelve-year-old Tamir Rice in Cleveland, Ohio; and Tony Robinson in Madison, Wisconsin, as well as the strangulation of Eric Garner in New York, the killing of Freddie Gray in Baltimore, and the Chicago cover-up of the shooting of Laquan McDonald, added to the list of events in the ongoing racialized tragedy in US history. Additionally, we denounce the racial terrorist acts of Dylann Roof in the Mother Emanuel A.M.E. Church in Charleston that left nine murdered and continued attacks on African American churches across the South. We believe that discussing race in the academy is an important component to the national discussion on race, and this essay seeks to create the conditions for continued authentic dialogue within the academy.

We mention these events to somberly recognize the ongoing violent tragedy without using these events as "stand ins" for the larger violence carried out through racialized structurings and segregation since the inception of the United States. Certainly, the historic sweep of racial representation in the US (Omi & Winant, 1986/1994; 2005) demonstrates that discursively structured racialized violence is a constant feature of US society, and recent deaths are but a few more examples of direct violence against people of color in a society historically structured by White supremacy and presently organized through White privilege. Moreover, the punditry of capitalist "news" coverage in its sound bites and polemics seems only to attempt to ignore a history of White supremacy and protect White privilege in the present moment. Truly, a sign of the times is Donald Trump's Republican candidacy. Trump's candidacy is advanced by anti-immigrant media and

---

1   Revised version keynote address, Department of Educational Leadership, University of Massachusetts Dartmouth, UMass Law School, November 14, 2016.

2   Statesian, emerging from *estadounidense* in Latin American traditions, recognizes "American" as pertaining to all territories from the Bering Strait to Patagonia as in *las Américas*. Diminishing colonizing understandings that equate "America" to the US, this essay deploys *Statesian* instead of American, nonetheless, leaving "American" – though we disagree with its usage – in quoted material and titles in references. Our intent is not accidental in using and developing the term *Statesian*, as it suggests a re-provincialization of the US and its influences, especially as it relates to Statesian and Anglophone multicultural foundations of education.

built on the backs of forced emigration from Mexico, and Central and South America and anti-Muslim fearmongering that apparently thinks that building a bigger wall around US White privilege is the final solution for "threats" from both within and without. Surprisingly—much but not at all, efforts to work through or discuss race in the academy continue to elicit striking silences, *un*-dialogic exchanges, and new hostilities (e.g., Bergamo Conference on Curriculum Theory and Classroom Practice, 2015; Curriculum & Pedagogy Group, 2009, 2011; Dixon et al., 2012; Malewski, 2010).

Our essay, perhaps erring in its hope for cosmopolitan interlocution (e.g., Baldwin, 1962, 1998; Dussel, 2005; Freire, 1970; King, 1958/2010, 1968/2010; Oliveira Andreotti, 2011, 2015; West, 2004; X & Haley, 1964/1995), modestly approaches the question, In embattled racial discussions in the academy, can we learn to talk and listen to each other? Attempting to affirmatively answer this question, our conceptual essay[3] develops the following contours. In the sections that come, our essay

a. situates ourselves as implicated in the research question and provides our autobiographical orientations with regard to the question. Situating ourselves in the research, we think, is necessary as part of identity work in which the researchers' identities are always already embedded.

b. briefly characterizes and critiques multicultural foundations so influential in the US academy and, more broadly, Statesian critical-progressive understandings of race. This characterization, understanding the need for broad self-correction, critiques essentializing tendencies *not* with the intention of oppositional dismissal but *rather* with the desire to work through and further advance multicultural foundations in the hegemonic globalizing conditions of the present.

c. provides an analytical synopsis of five books on race and power by Cornel West (1993a, 1993b, 2001, 2004, 2014) that seek to add to and deepen multicultural foundations by developing the following key themes: *race as key criterion, the pitfalls of racial reasoning, the importance of self-identity work*, and *thinking historically*. West, as explained in this essay, effectively moves discussions on race and power toward cross-cultural, cosmopolitan, global-yet-local engagements that we consider important in the present.

---

3   Using the conceptual essay as research methodology (Baldwin, 1962/1998; Careaga Medina, 1972), we emphasize the centrality of the conceptual essay in educational traditions (e.g., Baldwin, 1963/1998; Dewey 1904; Freire, 1970, 1992; Vasconcelos, 1925/1997). As research methodology, the conceptual essay allows for process-oriented research and argumentation organized around a topic of inquiry. The conceptual essay, as taken up here, considers the following texts as "data": personal teaching experience, experience working with preservice teachers, experience working with professional teachers and graduate students, and relevant philosophical and multicultural writing. Let this note stand in the place in what is vulgarly understood "research methodology," a token for those who insist on methods-centered human science understandings.

d.   develops, through West's writings, concepts that challenge, reach back historically, yet renew educational foundation's humanistic commitment to social justice in transforming West's ideas into critical progressive understandings of *identifications* and *relationalities*.

Our essay, in developing identifications and relationalities, moves discussions on race and power into broader contexts and articulates critical cross-cultural, cosmopolitan, global-yet-local exchanges in order to counter hegemonic globalizing conditions in the present moment.

Autobiographical Orientations

As co-authors of the piece, we situate this essay within our autobiographies. Author 1, a White middle-class male from Texas and father of an interracial Latin@ family, spent eighteen years as a classroom teacher working with predominantly Mexican immigrant, Latino, and African American students in inner-city public schools. In his public school teaching, Author 1 strove to develop critical and historically based teaching and learning with special focus on Freirean and culturally relevant approaches to teaching and learning with his students. Author 2, a Peruvian-born educational anthropologist, has spent her life committed to social justice of Latin@ and indigenous populations in Latin American and within the US. Author 2, as activist anthropologist, currently works closely with and researches marginalized mestiza-indigenous populations within the South Georgia Latin@ diaspora. Both researchers, with experience in the southern US and South Texas, seek to take on the critical-progressive task for authentic dialogue and racial understanding. With these experiences and intentions in common, this article emerges from our lifelong commitment to discussions of race and racism in society, schools, and in educational research, and especially, this article springs from our conversation on the topic of stalled and failed discussions on race in the academy. Having attended numerous academic conferences in which discussions on race stall, fail, and create new hostilities (e.g., Bergamo Conference on Curriculum Theory and Classroom Practice, 2015; Curriculum & Pedagogy Group, 2009, 2011; Dixon et al., 2012; Malewski, 2010), we advance this essay that retheorizes multicultural foundations through the work on race and power by Cornel West with the intention of creating new generative discussions on race.

Two Essentializing Tendencies in Multicultural Foundations of Education

Though impossible to detail the vast cultural production of articles, books, and especially, textbooks on race in education,[4] we strategically focus on mainstream confluences in recent formulations of multicultural foundations (Banks, 2001; Bennett, 2007; Gay,

---

4   For a partial list of more than forty textbooks on multicultural education between 1980 and 2003, see Chang (2012) in our references.

2001; Grant, 2006; Grant & Sleeter, 2007; Tozer, Senese, & Violas, 2009). We focus on multicultural foundations because of their established position and influence in understandings of race in educational discourse, educational research, and teacher education that broadly inform the academy in the present moment. In this section, we briefly characterize multicultural foundations with the dual purposes of articulating multicultural foundations' historical location and critiquing two essentializing tendencies inherent in this work.

Multicultural Foundations' Historical Location

As Geneva Gay (2001) correctly commented, "future analysis undoubtedly will reveal that multicultural education is very Western and American in spirit and intent" (p. 41). Our essay, supporting Appelbaum's (2002) historicized understanding of multicultural education as tied the 1960s' Statesian understandings, begins the future analysis to which Gay (2001) insightfully referred.

Influenced by intercultural and intergroup education (Banks, 2001, 2013; Grant, 2006), multicultural foundations of education "is directly linked to the early ethnic studies movement" in the US (Banks, 2001, p. 45). From this link, multicultural foundations of education emerged in the early 1970s in the wake of US civil rights movements (Banks, 2001, 2013; Grant, 2006; Howard, 2006). Privileging Statesian understandings regarding US civil rights movements, multicultural foundations emphasized "a coming together of different groups" (Grant, 2006, p. 10) very much following the unfolding of civil rights movements in the US focusing on race, class, gender, sexuality, and later intersectionalities with differences. In an historical essay, Grant (2006) explains multicultural foundations' intent writ large:

> Multicultural education advocates a long comprehensive, non-patriarchal view of the history and contributions of marginalized groups to the traditional curriculum. . . . Proponents of multicultural education continually challenge the racism and sexism in arguments that contend that achievements have come about because of, for example, Manifest Destiny. (p. 10)

Multicultural foundations of education, emphasizing Statesian historical position and understandings, *universalizes* these understanding to other engagements on difference in education (Banks, 2001; Bennett, 2007; Gay, 2001; Grant, 2006; Grant & Sleeter, 2007; Tozer, et al., 2009) positing 1950s', 1960s', and 1970s' Statesian civil rights struggles as template for understanding differences in all contexts. Particularly apparent in Banks (2013) recent textbook, which awkwardly *adds on* chapters on "global citizenship" (p. 22) to prior editions of multicultural foundations, it becomes increasingly important to critique these Statesian understandings *not* to dismiss them but *rather* to advance relevant multicultural, cross-cultural, and cosmopolitan understandings in the historical present.

West's writings on race and power help us to do that because, as laid out in the following, West (2001, 2004, 2014) attends to Statesian understandings of race yet situates those within historicized, cross cultural, and cosmopolitan contexts. Important in our analysis, as one main argument here, is re-historicizing and provincializing Statesian- and Anglophone-centered understandings of race as a starting point in our discussion. In short, we believe that discussions on race should situate Statesian and Anglophone understandings among other intellectual and historical resources on teaching, learning, and discussing race in academia. This re-historicizing and provincializing of Statesian- and Anglophone-centered understandings are especially important in our discussion and conclusion section at the end of our essay.

Erroneous Tendencies

Besides identifying multicultural foundations as a Statesian and Anglophone project that is often universalized in unspoken ways, this essay asserts that multicultural education's legacy has left us with two erroneous essentializing tendencies in the present moment. In discussing what we consider erroneous tendencies of multicultural foundations, it becomes important to state what we agree with: multicultural education's *commitment to social justice* and its *emphasis on White supremacy* as an overriding historical frame. Though we agree with these two starting points emphasized in US multicultural foundations, we understand our commitments to be worked out within specific social and historical contexts. Important here for us is that social justice be under-determined, relational, dialogic, and subjunctive (Ellsworth, 1989, Freire, 1970; Pinar, 2011; West, 2014) rather than determined, monological, and declarative. Agreeing with multicultural foundations' commitment to social justice, nonetheless, this essay identifies and explains two erroneous essentializing tendencies predominant in multicultural foundations.

Here are the two erroneous essentializing tendencies in multicultural foundations: *First*, we argue that assigning fixed before/after identities in multicultural foundations is an erroneous tendency. This assigning of fixed before/after identities (very often) delineates oppressed person of color and White privilege identities prior the multicultural intervention later to be followed by emancipated person of color and White-ally/race-evasive identities. We argue against multicultural foundations' fixed before/after "conversion" interventions *not* because we oppose racial conscientization and critical political action. To the contrary, we argue against conversion interventions because fixed before/after interventions lack sufficient subtlety, nuance, or attention to process for *actually* capacitating individuals' for critical political action in the present. Following recent breakthroughs on the complexity and historical-constructedness of racial identity within hegemonic globalizing conditions (e.g., Asher, 2007; Hall, 2003, 2004; Lensmire, 2011, 2014; Lowenstein, 2009; McCarthy, 2003; Morales, 2011), we believe that discussions on racial identity must include greater attention to multiple positionalities and identity knowledge about race in discussions while, most important, not diluting critical structural or epistemological content on racialized oppression. Specifically, following recent work representing identity within hegemonic globalizing conditions, we understand that identity work undertaken in academic discussions as complex, narrativized, and process-oriented identities. These complex, narrativized, and process-oriented identities must allow for differing positionalities that move beyond multicultural foundations' conversations. Moving beyond before/after conversions, we argue that new positionalities need to be teased out, elaborated on, and recognized as part of teaching, learning, and discussion on race in the academy. In this way, we believe that richer and more complex discussions on race will better inform contextualized social action.

Second, we argue that multicultural foundations' Statesian and Anglophone (additionally, Puritanical and Manichean) swap of Eurocentric "traditional curriculum" (Grant, 2006, p. 20) for 1960s' US revisionist history is also an erroneous essentializing tendency. We think the swap of Eurocentric traditional curriculum for 1960s' revisionist histories conceals the complexity of historical *relationalities* required to think carefully, clearly, and historically in the present moment (e.g., Appiah, 2006; Baker, 2009; Coronil, 1998; de Sousa Santos, 2009; Dussel, 2005; Hendry, 2012; Paraskeva, 2011; Pinar, 2013; West, 2004, 2014). Drawing particularly on Latino and Hispanophone-influenced scholars such as Fernando Coronil (1998), Boaventura de Sousa Santos (2009), Enrique Dussell (2005), and Joao Paraskeva (2011), this critique of multicultural foundations, rather than dismissing Statesian-based revisionist history, drives at greater understandings within and among collectivities, finer recognitions of identity group differences, and, ultimately, greater ability and understanding to conjugate collective alliances in leveraging projects for social justice in the globalizing present. Of particular importance in this discussion is the notion of ecologies of knowledge elaborated by de Sousa Santos (2009) and Paraskeva (2011) in which differing knowledge landscapes, epistemologies, traditions, and wisdom dialectically interact *not* as a quaint study of the humanities or conversely as an "*indigenoustude*" (Paraskeva, 2011, p. 187) but *rather* as resources for committed political work, strategies, and tactics inside and outside institutions like schools and universities under neoliberal global hegemony.

Having identified the Statesian and Anglophone historical blind spot and its erroneous essentializing tendencies of multicultural foundations, we think West's work on race and power, unheeded for the greater part in educational foundations, helps move us toward contemporary multicultural, cross-cultural, and cosmopolitan understandings needed in the present moment.

Drawing on Cornel West's Work

Moving toward West's (1993a, 1993b, 2001, 2004, 2014) work on race and power, we drive at the purpose of articulating strategies and tactics for alliances to counter hegemony in globalizing conditions. As developed here, this essay develops and articulates four patterns consistent in West's work as a means of advancing critical-progressive understandings of race and power for deployment in the present. The four patterns from West's text are (1) race as key criterion, (2) the pitfalls of racial reasoning, (3) the centrality identity of self-identity work, and (4) thinking historically.

Taking on topics of race and power, West argues that race represents a key criterion for evaluating hypocrisy and progress of democratic projects in the US and elsewhere. West's definition of race as a key criterion refers to *situating race as one key indicator among others of hegemonic oppression*, especially in relation to US national hegemony. In relation to cultural workers and educators laboring in the US, West (2001) recalls that race provides "the fundamental litmus test for American democracy" (p. xix). West (2001) continues:

> Yet the fundamental litmus test for American democracy—its economy, government, criminal justice system, education, mass media, and culture—remains: how broad and intense are the arbitrary powers used and deployed against black people. (p. xix)

Within his focus on race, West recognizes, nonetheless, that race *not* serve as exclusive focus to exclude other questions of progressive-critical alliances. For West (1993b), race represents a key criterion yet certainly not *the* exclusive criterion in a broader critical-progressive project that, ultimately, combats postmodern nihilisms, fights economic imperialism, recognizes the increasing wealth gap, yet promotes "the flowering and flourishing of individuality under the conditions of democracy" (p. 32). In West's vision, race is central but must attend to a broader critical-progressive project that necessarily includes, as examples, Marxian and feminist attentions to indigenous understandings and cosmologies, gay and lesbian rights, and religious equalities. For West, privileging exclusively racial reasoning over other social justice concerns damages and, ultimately, imperils a broad, inclusive, democratic, critical-progressive project, and it dangerously re-centers racialized patriarchal and homophobic understandings. We think that, behind racialized silences and inability to engage in discussions on race, often there lies a hyper-masculinized patriarchy and call for order around single-criterion understandings.

The Pitfalls of Racial Reasoning

Racial reasoning, according to West (1993b, 2001), demonstrates patriarchal and homophobic masculine nationalisms logic that silences women, gays, and other social solidarity projects through its exclusive and masculine call-to-order around race. Racial reasoning, as understood by West (2001), refers to privileging race over other social justice concerns.

As case study in racial reasoning, West (2001) narrates the case of Supreme Court Judge Clarence Thomas's nomination. In the scandal with Anita Hill surrounding Thomas's appointment to the Supreme Court, West (2001) noted a stunning silence on the part of African American leadership due to racial reasoning. West (2001) recounts, first and foremost, that Thomas provided limited credentials for the job, yet racial reasoning functioned to foreclose complex "political discussion in black America about these hearings" (p. 35). Rather than critiquing Thomas for his misogynist and sexist record, African American leadership remained silent and instead supported him through a consensus of silence. Elaborating more completely on racial reasoning, West (2001) explains that racial reasoning undermines complex political representation and instead inserts an exclusive masculinist and patriarchal logic that serves to silence, especially, women's issues along with gay and lesbian rights. In critical-progressive discussions, West (1993a) argues for the need to dismantle exclusively racial reasoning and replace it with moral reasoning in which the racial struggle serves as a particular case of moral-ethical reasoning and "doing the right thing" (p. 67). West (2001) summarizes:

> The fundamental aim of this undermining and dismantling is to replace racial reasoning with moral reasoning, to understand the black freedom struggle not as an affair of skin pigmentation and racial phenotype but rather as a matter of ethical principles and politics, and to combat the black nationalist attempt to subordinate the issues and interests of black women by linking mature black self-love and self-respect to egalitarian relations within and outside black communities. (p. 38)

Seeking an egalitarian moral-ethical position, West affirms the direction of an increasing number of scholars of color (e.g., Appiah, 2006; Hall, 2003; Sen, 2006) who refer to multicultural foundations' essentializing tendencies that seem to reproduce the static identities they purport to change. Exclusive appeals to nationalist logic that West (1993a, 1993b, 2001) calls racial reasoning frequently promotes, not discussions on moral reasoning, but shallow controversies and inter group infighting focusing on *who* – as masculinized leader – *can properly talk for whom*. In short, West holds (2001) that racial reasoning, evinced in catch phrases among Whites who emphasize "playing the race card," damages moral reasoning, narrows the ability to discuss complex moral-ethical questions, and deteriorates the context for authentic democratic exchanges on race. In sum, exclusively racialized reasoning debilitates authentic teaching, learning, and discussion on race in the academy.

Centrality of Self-Identity Work

Building on understandings outlined earlier, West's (1993b, 2004, 2014) writings on race and power emphasize the centrality of self-creation. Drawing on Thomas Stearns Elliot's (1919/1975) essay "Tradition and the Individual Talent," West (1993b) argues that tradition, especially critical-progressive educative traditions, "cannot be inherited . . . and must be earned by great labor" (p. 129). Like Elliot (1919/1975), West (1993b, 2014) argues that individual honor, courage, integrity, and – even – *greatness* emerge through self-identity work in critical-progressive traditions of study. Self-identity work, as West (1993b, 2004) discusses it, refers *to institutionally and self-directed study in multiple traditions that enhances agency and freedom in the face of historical boundedness, obstacles, and structural oppression.* For West (1993b, 2004, 2014), self-creation, which begins institutionally in family and schools and culminates in self-study, is central to historical change, especially in democracies in which "ordinary citizens desire to take their country back from the hands of a corrupt Plutocratic imperial elite" (2004, p. 23).

Resonating with curriculum scholars' recent focus on study (Block, 2001; Pinar, 2006, 2013), West (1993a, 1993b, 2004, 2014) highlights particular educative traditions, especially an international and cosmopolitan Emersonian tradition developing "cross-cultural perspectives on understanding and respecting other traditions from around the world" (2004, p. 77). Among these self-identity work resources, West (2004) indicates Socratic self-examination, prophetic Christianity, and a cross-cultural Statesian tradition emphasizing Emerson, Whitman, Melville, Du Bois, Coltrane, MLK, C. Wright Mills, Jose Carlos Mariatequi, Toni Morrison, and others. In culminating his discussion on self-identity work, West (2004) quotes Toni Morrison at length, emphasizing her message of love for self, other, and community:

> Love. We have to embrace ourselves . . . That's why we're here, We have to do something nurturing in that respect, before we go. We *must*. It is more interesting, more complicated, more intellectually demanding to love somebody. To take care of somebody. (p. 97)

West's thinking on race and power – which identifies *race as key criterion* yet eschews *the pitfalls of racial reasoning* – focuses on *self-identity work* within traditions that, ultimately, strives toward a moral discourse in which, in good faith, everyone comes together to morally do "the right thing" (1993b, p. 67).

Thinking Historically

In addition to forging a good faith moral discourse highlighting historically bounded self-identity work, West (1993b, 2001, 2004, 2014) asks cultural workers and educators to think historically and work carefully with received ideational content. Related to self-creation in resistant traditions, thinking historically refers to *careful self-identity work through study in our own and others' resistant intellectual traditions* not for simplistic revisionisms but rather *for profound understanding of identities' social structurations and malleabilities.*

In this thinking historically, West critiques multiculturalisms found in multicultural foundations for providing but a Manichean shadow of its opposite, Eurocentrism. West, in his critique of multiculturalisms, affirms multicultural recognitions of historical injustices like racism, sexism, and heteronormativity, yet he questions oversimplified reversals seemingly required by multiculturalisms as they simplistically "contest" binary Eurocentrisms (e.g., Bloom, 1987; Hirsch, 1988). Playing multiculturalisms against Eurocentrisms in a binary way, argues West (1993b), allows for theorizing ahistorically "in a rather promiscuous manner" (p. 7). In particular, West (1993b) calls on cultural workers and educators to recognize historical complexities and eschew essentializing and static ideas like Eurocentrism versus multiculturalism and instead bring forth "the best of the past" (p. 126). Transcending essentializing revisionisms, West urges cultural workers and educators to undertake the challenging pathway of historical specificity requiring us to work and think carefully in multiple historical traditions including European and Statesian ones (Du Bois, 1903/2005; West, 1989). Most important, West (2004) teaches that, moving beyond essentialized revisionisms, cultural workers and educators refuse the ahistorical narratives that "simply flip the script and tell new lies about ourselves" (p. 15). Multiculturalisms, like the ones found in multicultural foundations of education, shadowing and mirroring Eurocentrisms, release us from careful thinking about historical relationships both inside and beyond Europe that suggest we might need both European traditions and multicultural, cross-cultural, and cosmopolitan understandings of other cosmologies and traditions.

Thinking historically, says West (1993b), recognizes that Europe and its successor, the US present a complex hybridity of cultural confluences rather than simplistic oppositions (Appiah, 2006; Dussel, 2005; Sen, 2006). Cultural workers and educators need to recognize that Europe and its successor the US do not represent the beginning of oppression nor singular monolithic oppressors as multiculturalisms sometimes suggest. Instead, as West (1993a, 1993b) argues, cultural workers and educators should understand that European-Statesian oppressions provide historically bounded and changeable conditions of oppression as do other historically bounded examples such as the Roman or Ethiopian Amharic traditions previously holding hegemonic positions in the world. Moving beyond understandings of Europe and its successor as monolithic oppressors requires careful discernment in reading historical traditions for crimes and hypocrisies along with radical reappraisals of gifts and progressive resources provided by multiple and paradoxical historical traditions (e.g., Appiah, 2006, Baker, 2009; Connell, 2007; Coronil, 1998; de Sousa Santos, 2009; Dussel, 2005; Paraskeva, 2011; Pinar, 2013; West, 2004).

For example, critical intelligence, as West (1993a, 1993b) highlights, represents one resource and gift clearly exemplified in European-Statesian traditions allowing for continuous critique of illegitimate forms of authority especially as taken up by civil rights movements in the US during the 1950s, 1960s, and 1970s. Only through thinking historically, says West (1993a, 1993b), can cultural workers and educators approach multiple and paradoxical traditions, not in terms of simplistic Manichean reversals that see only binary positionalities but rather in careful, discerning, and hopeful ways that historically reappraise traditions as potential resources to be worked on and worked through.

Discussion

West's thinking, as it identifies *race as a key criterion*, eschews the exclusivity of *racial reasoning*, emphasizes *self-identity work*, and asks cultural workers and educators to *think historically*, begins to remediate multicultural foundations of education's erroneous tendencies. Instead of US multicultural foundations, this essay works through West's ideas (1993a, 1993b, 2001, 2004, 2014) breaking new ground reconceptualizing identities with identifications and relationalities that move toward "a new politics of cultural difference" (1993b, p. 4) in educational foundations that simultaneously renews old progressive commitments yet moves toward local, national, and global progressive alliances.

Identifications

Identifications, by way of definition, refer to *narrative processes through which historically and socially mediated "selves" emerge over time within structuring contexts that recognize race, class, gender, sexual orientation, religion, ability, and other differences.* Identifications, in relation to West's work on race and power, identify race as key a criterion for social justice work yet eschew the pitfalls of exclusively racial reasoning.

Identifications, working through erroneous essentializing tendencies, assume identity as social and historical activities. Understood as social and historical activities, identifications assert West's critical intelligence taking anti-universalist and subversive directions. As anti-universalist, identifications critique both right-appropriated ahistorical and essentialized "individuals" as well as left appropriated masculinist and patriarchal identities that unproblematically equate "spokesmen" to their social history. Rather than "individuals" or "spokesmen" leaders, identifications work through notions of process, coming-to-know, intra- and intergroup dialogue, and vulnerability that listen as well as proclaim injustices and structural inequalities. Requiring critical intelligence in critiquing facile right and left identity appropriations, identifications attend to recognitions of lived experiences within structuring contexts and protect them from the erroneous essentialisms promulgated in facile ways on left–right political continuums. As subversive, identifications seek to destabilize fixed, static, and essentialized identity pre-packagings such as facile "liberated subjects" or simplistic "white allies/race-evasive" identities and instead provide for increased race-cognizance and cross-cultural engagement in historically mediated differences and *not-ever-quite-resolved* questioning and examination (Butler, 1990/1999; Hall, 2003, 2004; Wang, 2004). Conceptually, identifications might include but ultimately supersede multicultural foundations' erroneous tendencies outlined and critiqued earlier in that they seek to articulate narrative processes of becoming within social and historical structurings.

Identifications, superseding erroneous tendencies, focus on how identities emerge narratively within historically and socially structuring contexts (Hall, 2003, 2004; West, 2001, 2004). Identifications, articulating narratively developing identities, recognize that structuring contexts call identities into being. Nonetheless, identifications, in recognizing structured contexts, emphasize that identities emerge through narrative processes of self-identity work within these contexts. Self-identity work, in relation to identifications and structuring contexts, illuminates subjects' narrative processes of interaction, elaboration, and engagement with educative and cultural resources. Important among these structuring contexts are race, class, gender, sexual orientation, religion, ability, and other structuring contexts that mark identifications' power asymmetries; nonetheless, structurings are not considered as an essentializing fixity. Identifications understand boundedness and its importance in day-to-day practices, constructed spaces, social interactions, and social justice projects especially as projects relate to assigned boundedness like race. Yet, contrasting with multicultural foundations' erroneous tendencies, identifications seek cultural workers and educators' working within and development over time. Important in the notion of identification is subjectivities' identity creativity that works within boundedness to differently position self and others in ways that work against the grain of established structuring boundedness.

Relationalities

Relationalities, by way of definition, refer to *identifications' relations with otherness, historical structures and intersections, and historical traditions.* Relationalities, in relation to West's work on race and power, emphasize the centrality of self-identity work through study in historical traditions and his notion of thinking historically.

First, relationalities emphasize *otherness* required in race. Race, as deeply embedded in historical relations of otherness, requires understandings of race as representational and co-performed in an historical present. Race, if understood as representational and co-performed, requires that we understand race as relational set of phenomena embedded in power asymmetries and attendant violence, especially in relation to people of color. Race, if understood as relational otherness, cannot exist in isolation from its historically located relational structurings of oppression, power, and privilege. Existing within a relational structurings, Whiteness and racial otherness are inextricably bound such that Whiteness as hegemonic center, for example, cannot be understood in isolation, and White identifications represent, paradoxically, a shared project with racial others' identifications that requires mutual "undoing." Cameron McCarthy (2003), in relation to Whiteness and racial identity, describes this historically contingent and unstable relationality: "This essay cannot properly understand white identity or whiteness by focusing singularly on white people, assuming a necessary or self-evident unity of whiteness that defines Euro-Americans as a singular group" (p. 133). As other recent work on Whiteness indicates (Lensmire, 2011, 2014; Miele, 2011a, 2011b), White identifications represent, constitute, and perform a complex, unstable, and at times ambivalent relationality with racial otherness that includes be cannot be singularly reduced to White privilege in every analysis. Paradoxically, working against the grain of hegemonic White supremacy, this essay understands race's relationality with otherness as radically contingent and under-determined, and this essay identifies the critical-progressive task, along the lines of West (1993a), as redefining relations that might, developmentally, include or require discussions of ethnic nationalist logic yet should avoid exclusive overdetermined racial reasoning (West, 1993b, 2001). The deployment of ethnic nationalist logic, in avoiding overdetermined racial reasoning, needs to exercise the continual use and development of critical intelligence in working through racial discussions in the academy.

Second, relationalities, rather than focusing on group identities and spokesmen, emphasize identifications' relations with *structures and intersections*. Following West's (1993b, 2001) caveat on "the pitfalls of racial reasoning" (2001, p. 21), relational structures and intersections allow for greater complexity of identifications yet seek, through uses of critical intelligence and self-identity work, identifications that signify "against the grain" (1993b, p. 67). Such an exercise of critical intelligence and self-identity work takes as criterion for evaluation, not who can authentically be a spokesman for whom but rather risks taken and generosity extended in creating conditions for truth telling in authentic and critical exchanges. While recognizing power asymmetries and violences committed by Whites against people of color and critiquing White privilege, nonetheless, relational, dialogical, and pedagogical spaces need to be made that take risks so that people can say what is on their minds in teaching, learning, and discussion on race in the academy. Following West's (1993a, 1993b, 2001, 2004, 2014) work on race and power, the notion of relationalities recognizes and emphasizes identifications' relations with asymmetric power *structures and intersections* in greater complexity and, thereby, works against the grain to "recast, redefine, and revise the very notions of 'modernity,' 'mainstream,' 'margins,' 'difference,' and 'otherness'" (p. 1993a, p. 31).

Third, relationalities value, as educative ideal, profound study (Block, 2001; Pinar, 2013; West, 2004, 2014) in multiple and interrelated historical traditions *not* Procrustean "frameworks" too often related with US graduate school dissertation production. This study in multiple historical traditions include European and Statesian ones as identification resources yet dramatically push beyond those in identifying and reworking alter-traditions currently eclipsed in epistemicides (de Sousa Santos, 2009; Paraskeva, 2011). Relationalities with multiple historical traditions value always problematic cross-cultural and cosmopolitan identifications within complex historical horizons that understand racialized injustices and inequalities but are not reduced to essentialized understandings of race.

Examples of working in multiple historical traditions, reaching back genealogically yet driving forward toward critical-progressive and not-necessarily-"Western" humanistic ideals, include Rubén Darío's (1888/1992) literary creativity, engaging Greek Idealism, Shakespeare's muses, Latin American indigenous history, and Marxian class critique, provides a trajectory for Latin American aesthetic modernist traditions (e.g., García Márquez, 1967/1992; Mistral, 1924/1971; Neruda, 1950/1997; Paz, 1948/1987) that dialectically engage aesthetics for specific historical, social, and political interventions and renewed understandings. Mahatma Gandhi's (1927/1987) intellectual production, taking up Hindu religious resources and practices alongside Christian and English common law traditions, provides a trajectory for traditions of ecumenical solidarity and historically contextualized activisms (e.g., Hahn, 1995; King, 1958/2010; Malewski, 2011a, 2011b) in the face of oppression. D. T. Suzuki's (1958/1998) cross-cultural writings, generating texts in which Buddhism, Christianity, and European traditions communicate, provide for a tradition of dialogue between East and West (e.g., Ikeda, 2006; Wang, 2004; Watts, 1966/1989). W. E. B. Du Bois (1903/1995), drawing on African-American spirituals, European phenomenology, and US pragmatism that he helped articulate, provides a trajectory for a tradition of activists, authors, and writers forming the Harlem Renaissance and beyond (e.g., Hughes, 1959/1990; Hurston, 1937/2006; Wright, 1937/2008; X & Haley, 1964/1999). Sojourner Truth's (1851) provocations and John Stuart Mill and Harriet Taylor Mill's (1970) treatise on sexual equality reflected, constituted, and helped drive enormous production of intellectual critique on gender and gender equality (e.g., Beauvoir, 1949/2009; Friedan, 1963; Stanton, 1848/2015) that intersects both in the Statesian and international contexts with race and indigeneity (e.g., Barrios de Chungara & Viezzer, 1978; Menchú & Burgos, 1985; Wells, 1892/2015) in addition to sexuality (e.g. Butler, 1990/1999; Genet, 1949/2004; Ginsberg, 1956/1973).

Relationalities with multiple historical traditions seems sorely needed for providing resources for creative identifications and greater cross-cultural comprehension that avoids multicultural education's monolithic often unspoken Statesian and Anglophone historical location and erroneous essentializing tendencies. From the examples earlier, an outline of not-necessarily-"Western" yet humanistic cultural resources for self-identity work and associated moral-ethical becoming emerge that value careful study, genealogical historical thinking, cross-cultural exchange, and tensions between historical-social and transcendent truth telling. Such an approach, grounded in thinking historically within multiple traditions contrasts with reductionist-yet-battling categorical "frameworks" typical of university work in the present. Our work here, which drives at historicized, cross-cultural, and cosmopolitan understandings avoid intellectual work that simply wheels in a "framework" to sector off reductionist and idealized "epistemologies" for safe yet divisive academic silos.

Conclusion

In closing, we return to our question: Can we learn to talk and listen to each other about race? In this essay, we have developed the position that erroneous essentializing tendencies, exemplified and lingering in predominant multicultural foundations, have provided a specific Statesian and Anglophone stasis or fixity in embattled discussions on race that, might – rather than improving the discussion – create truncated, awkward, shallow, Manichean, and Puritanical exchanges. In order to unfix and unsettle erroneous tendencies, we have advanced West's multicultural, cross-cultural, and cosmopolitan understandings *not* to dismiss multicultural education's focus on race and social justice *but rather* to better situate and advance a complex study and discussion on race under conditions of globalizing hegemony in the present moment. Conversations on race, too often exemplifying erroneous essentializing tendencies, privilege narrow Statesian and Anglophone understandings and at times advance a simplistic swap of Statesian positions for essentializing revisions and reductions that ignore traditions of cross-cultural and cosmopolitan exchanges. In advancing our reading of West's work on race and power, we drive at un-fixing and unsettling conclusions from a previous (necessary at that time) era of multicultural foundations without dismissing those conclusions. Rather, we have worked through a critique with the intentions of advancing multicultural, cross-cultural, and cosmopolitan understandings that refocus on non-essentializing identifications and relationalities in order to combat hegemonic globalization in the present moment.

In advancing these multicultural, cross-cultural, and cosmopolitan concepts, we critique multicultural education's essentializing erroneous tendencies. Our critique, especially important in academy, seeks to revise and advance multicultural education's insistence on masculinized spokesmen toward more nuanced and subtle critical-progressive exchanges in which feminist, cross-cultural authenticity, vulnerability, alliances, and organizing might find a home (West, 2014). We understand, nonetheless, that the uncritical advance of multicultural foundations, with its residue of masculinized spokesmen, is attractive to many professors (and their students) who wish to *un*critically relive civil rights movements in the academy. Nonetheless, we insist that the task at hand, far from reliving the civil rights movements through the incantation of a newer and more "radical" research epistemology typical of academic work in the present, lies in creating the conditions for broad participation in race-cognizant yet non-essentializing understandings and new related social movements. In drawing on West in articulating identifications and relationalities, we have tried to create the conditions that might ignite broader multicultural, cross-cultural, and cosmopolitan engagement that, instead of *un*critically reliving the civil rights movements of the past, takes on the more onerous task of recreating broad-based social movements within hegemonic globalizing conditions of the present moment. In our vision, discussions of race in the academy play a key role in advancing these new social movements.

Within the contemporary globalizing conditions, we argue that the context has moved, is different, and demands careful cross-cultural, cosmopolitan, global-yet-local understandings of race and identity for supple and movable alliance politics and solidarity in the face of racialized oppressions around the world. We argue that identifications and relationalities, linked to and determined to advance multicultural education in the present, drive more clearly at alliances along a number of identities, contexts, and issues in which cultural workers and educators might work, for example, on the environmental or experiential arts-based teaching or even curriculum history yet still – historically and socially – represent allies in critical-progressive understanding of race and power in the academy.

What do we need, then, in order to engage in race discussions? This essay drives at greater alliances, work on race, culture, and grassroots democracy that emphasize identifications and relationalities outlined earlier. Identifications and relationalities allow for more ample discussions of racialized and other identities, avoid assigning essentialized identities and conversions from the outset, direct us morally and ethically inward toward careful self-identity work through study, and alert us, at times, to the frailty of an ahistorical educational research tied to reductionist university "frameworks" or "paradigms" which, unequivocally now, conceal as much as they reveal. As West (2001) reminds us in our conversations, identifications and relationalities require focusing on race as a key criterion for social justice, as a specific case of doing the right thing. West (2001) comments:

> Based on this uncontroversial criterion [race], the history of American democracy in regard to black people from 1776 to 1965 was a colossal failure. This also holds for red, brown, and yellow peoples. For one generation— thirty five years [forty-five now]—we have embarked on a multiracial democracy with significant breakthroughs and glaring silences. (p. xiv)

This essay offers these concepts, identifications, and relationalities along the line of *otherness, structures, and intersections* and multiple *historical traditions* as a means of keeping the faith and continuing the critical-progressive work moving and vibrant in its resistance to globalizing hegemonic conditions in the present moment.

References

Appelbaum, P. (2002). *Multicultural and diversity education: A reference handbook*. Santa Barbara, CA: ABC-CLIO.

Appiah, K.A. (2006). *Cosmopolitanism: Ethics in a world of strangers*. New York, NY: Norton.

Asher, N. (2007). Made in the (multicultural) U.S.A: Unpacking tensions of race, culture, gender, and sexuality in education. *Educational Researcher, 36,* 65–73.

Baker, B. (2009). Borders, belonging, beyond: New curriculum history. In B. Baker (Ed.) *New curriculum history* (pp. ix–xxxv). Rotterdam: Sense.

Baldwin, J. (1998). The creative process. In T. Morrison's (Ed.) *Collected essays* (pp. 669–672). New York, NY: The Library of America. (Original work published 1962)

Baldwin, J. (1998). A talk to teachers. In T. Morrison's (Ed.) *Collected essays* (pp. 678–686). New York, NY: The Library of America. (Original work published 1963)

Banks, J.A. (2001). Multicultural education: Historical development, dimensions, and practice. In J.A. Banks & C.A. McGee Banks (Eds.) *Handbook of research on multicultural education* (pp. 3–24). San Francisco, CA: Jossey Bass.

Banks, J.A. (2013). *An introduction to multicultural education* (5th ed.). San Francisco, CA: Jossey Bass.

Barrios de Chungara, D., & Viezzer, M. (1978). *Let me speak!* (Trans. V. Ortiz). New York, NY: Monthly Review Press.

Beauvoir, S. (2009). *The second sex* (Trans. C. Borde & S. Malovany-Chavallier). New York, NY: Vintage. (Work originally published in 1949)

Bennett, C. (2007). *Comprehensive multicultural education: Theory and practice* (6th ed.). Boston, MA: Allyn and Bacon.

Bergamo Conference on Curriculum Theory and Classroom Practice. (2015, October). *Why is Bergamo so White*. Program document of the annual meeting of the Bergamo Conference on Curriculum Theory and Classroom Practice. Dayton, OH. (Author 1's personal files)

Block, A. (2001). Essay on ethics and curriculum. Unpublished essay shared in personal communication.

Bloom, A. (1987). *The closing of the American mind*. New York, NY: Touchstone; Simon & Schuster.

Butler, J. (1999). *Gender trouble: Feminism and the subversion of identity*. New York, NY: Routledge. (Work originally published 1990)

Careaga Medina, G. (1972). *Intelectuales, poder, y revolución*. México, DF: Ediciones Oceano, SA.

Chang, H. (2003). A list of analyzed textbooks of multicultural education. http://www.eastern.edu/publications/emme/2003fall/Chang%27s%20list%20of%20analyzed%20textbooks.htm. (Retrieved January 7, 2012)

Connell, R. (2007). The northern theory of globalization. *Sociological Theory, 25*(4), 368–385.

Coronil, F. (1998). Más allá del occidentalismo: Hacia categorías geohistóricas no-imperialistas. In E. Mendieta (Ed.) *Teorías sin disciplina: Latinoamericanismo, poscolonialidad, y globalización en debate* (pp. 121–196). Mexico, DF: Editorial Porrúa.

Curriculum & Pedagogy Group. (2009, October). Town hall meeting. Program document of the annual meeting of the Curriculum & Pedagogy Group in Atlanta, GA. (Author 1's personal files)

Curriculum & Pedagogy Group. (2011, October). Town hall meeting. Program document of the annual meeting of the Curriculum & Pedagogy Group in Akron, OH. (Author 1's personal files)

Darío, R. (1996). *Azul*. Mexico, DF: Editores Mexicanos. (Work originally published 1888)

de Sousa Santos, B. (2009). A non-occidental West? Learned ignorance and ecology of knowledge. *Theory, Culture, & Society 26*(7–8), 103–125.

Dewey, J. (1904). *The educational situation*. Chicago, IL: University of Chicago Press.

Dixon, A.D., Donner, J.K., Gilborn, D., Ladson-Billings, G.J., Solórzano, D.G., & Tate, W.F. (2012, April). *What Derrick Bell knew: The legacy of critical race theory on educational scholarship*. Symposium conducted at the Annual Meeting of the American Association of Educational Research, Vancouver, BC.

Du Bois, W.E.B. (2005). *Souls of black folks*. New York, NY: Signet Classics. (Originally published 1903)

Dussel, E. (2005). 13 Transmodernidad e interculturalidad (Interpretación desde la filosofía de la liberación). http://www.afyl.org/transmodernidadeinterculturalidad.pdf. (Retrieved January 2013)

Elliot, T.S. (1975). Tradition and the individual talent. In F. Kermode (Ed.) *Selected prose of T.S. Elliot* (pp. 37–44). New York, NY: Farrar, Straus & Giroux. (Original work published 1919).

Ellsworth, E. (1989). Why doesn't this feel empowering? Working through the repressive myths of critical pedagogy. *Harvard Educational Review, 59*(3), 297–324.

Friere, P. (1970). *The pedagogy of the oppressed*. New York, NY: Continuum.

Freire, P. (1992). *The pedagogy of hope*. New York, NY: Continuum.

Friedan, B. (1963). *The feminine mystique*. New York, NY: W.W. Norton & Company.

Gandhi, M. (1987). *Lo que yo creo*. Mérida, Yucatán: Editorial Dante. (Originally published 1927)

García Márquez, G. (1992). *Cien años de soledad*. México, DF: Editorial Diana.

Gay, G. (2001). Curriculum theory and multicultural education. In J.A. Banks & C.A. McGee Banks (Eds.) *Handbook of research on multicultural education* (pp. 25–43). San Francisco, CA: Jossey Bass.

Genet, J. (2004). *The thief's journal*. Paris, France: The Olympia Press. (Work originally published 1949)

Ginsberg, A. (1973). America. In *The Norton anthology of American poetry* (pp. 1126–1128). New York, NY: W.W. Norton & Company. (Original work published 1956)

Grant, C. (2006). *The evolution of multicultural education in the United States: A journey for human rights and social justice*. Paper presented at the annual meeting of the International Association of Intercultural Education in Verona, Italy. http://www.iaie.org/download/turin_paper_grant.pdf. (Retrieved January 7, 2012)

Grant, C., & Sleeter, C.E. (2007). *Turning on learning: Five approaches for multicultural teaching plans for race, class, gender, and disability* (4th ed.). San Francisco, CA: Jossey-Bass.

Hahn, N.T. (1995). *Living Buddha, living Christ*. New York, NY: Riverhead Books.

Hall, S. (2003). Introduction: Who needs identity? In S. Hall & P. du Gay (Eds.) *Questions of cultural identity* (pp. 1–17). London: Sage.

Hall, S. (2004). New ethnicities. In D.Morley & K.H. Chen (Eds.) *Stuart Hall: Critical dialogues cultural studies* (pp. 441–449). New York, NY: Routledge.

Hendry, P. (2012, October). *Creating a New Eden: The Ursuline Mission of spiritual universalism in French colonial Louisiana*. Paper presentation at the annual meeting of the Curriculum & Pedagogy Group in New Orleans, LA.

Hirsch, E.D. (1988). *Cultural literacy: What every American needs to know*. New York, NY: Vintage.

Howard, G. (2006). *We can't teach what we don't know: White teachers multiracial schools* (2nd ed.). New York, NY: Teachers College Press.

Hughes, L. (1990). *Selected poems of Langston Hughes*. New York, NY: Vintage Books. (Original work published 1959)

Hurston, Z.N. (2006). *Their eyes were watching God*. New York, NY: Harper Perennial Classics. (Original work published 1937)

Ikeda, D. (2006). *A new era of the people: Forging global networks of robust individuals*. Tokyo, Japan: The Soka Gakkai.

King, M.L. (2010). *Stride towards freedom: The Montgomery story*. Boston, MA: Beacon. (Original work published 1958.)

King, M.L. (2010). *Where do we go from here: Chaos or community?* Boston, MA: Beacon. (Original work published 1968)

Lensmire, T. (2011). Laughing White men. *Journal of Curriculum Theorizing 27*(3), 102–116.

Lensmire, T. (2014). White men's racial others. *Teachers College Record, 116*(3), 1–32.

Lowenstein, K.L. (2009). The work of multicultural teacher education: Reconceptualizing White teacher candidates as learners. *Review of Educational Research, 79*, 163–196.

Malewski, E. (2010). Introduction: Proliferating curriculum. In E. Malewski (Ed) *Curriculum studies handbook: The next moment* (pp. 1–40). New York, NY: Routledge.

Malewski, E. (2011a, October). Part I: *Why Gandhi now? A raced and sexed autoethnographic reading of the Mahatma's life*. Paper presentation at the annual meeting of the Curriculum & Pedagogy Group in Akron, OH.

Malewski, E. (2011b, October). *Part II: Why Gandhi now? Complicity and the implications of Gandhi's life for curriculum studies.* Paper presentation at the annual meeting of the Curriculum & Pedagogy Group in Akron, OH.

McCarthy, C. (2003). Contradictions of power and identity: Whiteness studies and the call of teacher education. *The International Journal of Qualitative Studies in Education 16*(1), 127–133.

Menchú, R., & Burgos, E. (1985). *Me llamo Rigoberta Menchú y así me nació la conciencia.* México, DF: Siglo XXI Editores.

Miele, A. (2011a). *Complicating Whiteness: Identifications of veteran White teachers in multicultural settings* (Unpublished doctoral dissertation). San Francisco State University, San Francisco, CA.

Miele, A. (2011b). *Whiteness as relational phenomena: Literature review.* Unpublished manuscript.

Mill, J.S., & Mill, H.T. (1970). *Essays on sex equality* (A.S. Rossi , Ed.). Chicago, IL: The University of Chicago Press.

Mistral, G. (1971). *Lecturas para mujeres.* México, DF: Porrúa. (Original work published 1924)

Morales, A. (2011). *Factors that foster Latina, English Language Learner, non-traditional student resilience in higher education and their persistence in teacher education* (Unpublished doctoral dissertation). Kansas State University, Manhattan, KS.

Neruda, P. (1997). Canto general. In R. Alberti (Ed.) *Antología poética* (pp. 113-195). México, DF: Planeta Mexicana. (Original work published 1950)

Oliveira Andreotti, V. (2011). (Towards) decoloniality and diversity in global citizenship education. *Globalisation, Societies, and Education, 9*, pp. 381-387.

Oliveira Andreotti, V. (2015, August). Ethics, interdependence, and global change: Imagining global citizenship education otherwise. Paper presented at ICP 2015: 12th Convention of the International Confederation of Principals. Helsinki, Finland.

Omi, M. & Winant, H. (1994). *Racial formation in the United States: From the 1960s to the 1990s* (2nd ed). New York, NY: Routledge. (Original work published 1986)

Omi, M. & Winant, H. (2005). The theoretical status of the concept of race. In C. McCarthy, W. Crichlow, G. Dimitriadis, & N. Dolby (Eds.), *Race, identity and representation in education* (2nd ed.; pp. 3–11). New York, NY: Routledge.

Paraskeva, J. (2011). *Conflicts in curriculum theory: Challenging hegemonic epistemologies.* New York, NY: Palgrave Macmillan.

Paz, O. (1987). *El laberinto de la soledad.* México, DF: El Fondo de Cultura Económica. (Originally published 1948)

Pinar, W. (2013). *Curriculum studies in the United States: Present circumstances, intellectual histories.* New York, NY: Palgrave Macmillan.

Pinar, W.F. (2006). The problem of curriculum and pedagogy. In *The synoptic text today and other essays: Curriculum development after the reconceptualization* (pp. 109–120). New York, NY: Peter Lang.

Pinar, W.F. (2011). Multiculturalism, nationalism, cosmopolitanism. In *The character of curriculum studies: Bildung, currere, and recurring question of the subject* (pp. 49–62). New York, NY: Palgrave-MacMillan.

Sen, A. (2006). *Identity and violence.* New York, NY: Norton.

Stanton, E.C. (2015). Seneca Falls keynote address. http://www.greatamericandocuments.com/speeches/stanton-seneca-falls.html. (Retrieved August 2015) (Work originally performed 1848)

Suzuki, D.T. (1998). *Buddha of infinite light*. Boston, MA: The American Buddhist Academy. (Originally published 1958)

Tozer, S., Senese, G., & Violas, P. (2009). *School and society: Historical and contemporary perspectives* (6th ed.). Boston, MA: McGraw-Hill.

Truth, S. (1851). Ain't I a woman? http://schools.nyc.gov/NR/rdonlyres/E151FA9D-6017-4556-981F-CD076D731A72/0/SecondaryTextGuideAnswerKeyAintWoman.pdf. (Retrieved August 2015)

Vasconcelos, J. (1997). *La raza cósmica/The cosmic race*. Baltimore, MA: Johns Hopkins University Press. (Work originally published 1925)

Wang, H. (2004). *The call from a stranger on a journey home: Curriculum in a third space*. New York, NY: Peter Lang.

Watts, A. (1989). *The book: On the taboo against knowing who you are*. New York, NY: Vintage Books. (Work originally published 1966)

Wells, I.B. (2015). *Southern horrors: Lynch law in all its phases*. http://www.gutenberg.org/files/14975/14975-h/14975-h.htm. (Retrieved August 2015) (Work originally published 1892)

West, C. (1989). *The American evasion of philosophy: A genealogy of pragmatism*. Madison, WI: University of Wisconsin Press.

West, C. (1993a). *Keeping the faith: Philosophy and race in America*. New York: Routledge.

West, C. (1993b). *Prophetic thought in postmodern times*. Monroe, MA: Common Courage Press.

West, C. (2001). *Race matters*. Vintage: New York, NY.

West, C. (2004). *Democracy matters: Winning the fight against imperialism*. New York, NY: Penguin Books.

West, C. (2014). *Black prophetic fire: In dialogue with and edited by Christa Buschendorf*. Boston, MA: Beacon Press.

Wright, R. (2008). *Black boy*. New York, NY: Harper Perennial Classics. (Work originally published 1937)

X. M. & Haley, A. (1999). *The Autobiography of Malcolm X*. New York, NY: Random House. (Work originally published 1964)

CHAPTER FIFTEEN

From Paulo Freire to Boaventura de Sousa Santos: Democracy, Education and Emancipation[1]

Ines Barbosa Oliveira

TWENTY-TWO YEARS AGO, the world of ideas, and especially the field of education, lost one of its greatest icons: Paulo Freire. It was at around the same time that, beginning my career as a researcher in Brazilian universities, I began to become familiar with the work of Boaventura de Sousa Santos. Since then, many occurrences, studies, works and reflections have paved my way. Over the last few years, encouraged by colleagues, activities, events and reflections, I have increasingly returned to Freire's work, as I did in 2013, when I was at the University of Massachusetts, Dartmouth to meet with my esteemed colleague João Paraskeva and some of his students in a fruitful conversation about Freire's work and his contributions, which are still relevant. In fact, more than twenty years after his death, the presence and relevance of his work in educational, political and social debates is becoming increasingly inescapable. Thus, through different contexts and perspectives, researchers in Brazil and worldwide continue to seek bases for their reflections on and approaches to their fields in the key ideas of this author. Personally, pondering Santos's work over the same 20 years, I have recently been searching for a way to delineate some of the similarities that I have noted in both authors and which I believe to be useful not only to address "old" problems but also some of the new issues that have arisen due to the alarming advance of ultraconservatism in politics and morals in today's society.

That is why I have been seeking, when comparing the work of Paulo Freire and Boaventura de Sousa Santos, to discover, through the latter, the unexpected reach of the work of the former, and the possibilities that this dialogue creates to "read today's world" and act in a way that potentializes that which represents more social emancipation, understanding and fighting against that which oppresses, subordinates, dominates and/or denies the imposed invisibility of social groups, actors, cultures and knowledge. I understand that the relevance of reflection on this possible dialogue, not actually carried out by them, resides in the opening that permits greater understanding of some of Freire's most relevant contributions, to think about the relationships between education

---

1 Keynote address, Department of Educational Leadership, University of Massachusetts Dartmouth, March 10, 2013.

and emancipation, dislocating a work produced in the context of the primacy of modern thinking to current affairs and the possibility of inscribing the thoughts weaved into the reading of daily situations observed in research activities.

This is because, after identifying commonalities in the reflection of both authors, we can weave understandings that transcend both, specifically including the educational debate in Santos's work, updating and broadening the political-sociological dimension of Freire's work and potentializing our greater struggle for a liberating education and a more democratic society, given the daily life and privileged space-time in which it unfolds.

This text and the reflections included in it are therefore intended to give readers some of our thoughts on these approaches and their possible contributions to the field of study of School Routines and to the development and consolidation of the notion of curriculum as a daily creation (Oliveira, 2012), in different dimensions, aiming to broaden and deepen these relationships, always seeking to insert elements of social life and concrete educational practices into the reflection, seeking to make our reflections and their potential for confronting hegemonic thinking and the educational practices it leads to more explicit. With this, we understand that it is possible to simultaneously contribute to the perception regarding the sociological and educational reach recognizable in the two works, when compared, and to the social power they possess, when used to understand and intervene in everyday social life, *insideoutside*[2] formal educational spaces.

This text presents theoretical-political-epistemological reflections on the relationships between the thoughts of the two authors. The understanding of both regarding the epistemological diversity of the world helps us understand the formal hierarchies and real challenges that these create, paths to overcome them and perspectives from which to study reality through each's lens. The question of the epistemological diversity of the world and the non-inequality between different types of knowledge allows us, by contemplating the possibilities of relating the thoughts of the two authors, to deepen and consolidate the reading we have been doing of daily life as a space for production and circulation of knowledge and the curricula developed there as creation by *practitionerthinkers* (Oliveira, 2012) involved in educational practices.

From the political point of view, always associated with the epistemological view, we will understand and defend that the relationships between cognitive justice, social justice, solidarity and emancipation, present in the Southern Epistemologies of Boaventura de Sousa Santos, can be associated with the notion of "Orienting towards the South" (*sulear*[3] in Portuguese) developed beginning in the 1930s with the Southern School of Joaquin Torres Garcia, formulated by Marcio Campos (1991) and used

---

2   On many occasions we have invented words formed from pairs of opposites, seeking to express, textually, the need we felt to overcome certain dualisms and binary oppositions and our defense of the complexity of life regarding its characteristic that always integrates them, rather than separating them as modernity intended.

3   In Portuguese, the verb meaning "to orient, to guide" is *nortear*, and its stem is from the word for north, giving the impression that one should orient themselves by looking north. A new word was coined, *sulear*, based on the stem *sul*, meaning south, with the meaning "to orient towards the south."

by Paulo Freire. With this, I believe it is possible to read real and imagined educational situations based on their emancipatory potential, that is, the potential they have for the fabric of cognitive and social justice, through practices aimed at horizontal citizenship and the ecology of knowledge, as Santos teaches us, an activity left for the reader for now.

The plurality of knowledge in the world and the relationships between knowledge in Paulo Freire and Santos[4]

Paulo Freire affirmed, at various times in his life and work,[5] that "no one knows nothing, no one knows everything. That's why we are always learning." With this, he defended the idea that "there is no such thing as knowing more or knowing less: There are different types of knowledge." Although he was an advocate of the idea that access to formal knowledge was a form of emancipation, according to many at the time he wrote his first works, Freire understood the importance of valuing popular knowledge and dialoguing with it. Access to formal knowledge would be, for him, a way of providing the poorer classes with hegemonic knowledge, which could become a weapon against domination. In a more conventional reading of his work, he found problematic the idea that social actors would arrive at school with the "knowledge of experience," with the knowledge of everyday life, and that schooling would allow access to formal scholarly knowledge. This is because from my perspective, based on the thoughts of Santos, there is no a priori hierarchy among these types of knowledge; they are multiple and formal/ scientific knowledge is not superior. This was recognized in a secondary way by Paulo Freire. However, when we study the reflections of each more carefully, using the ideas of Santos and employing them to "read" Freire's thoughts, we notice the similarity between them more than any contradiction.

Concretely, it seems to me today that we can assume that, for Freire, these differences would not necessarily constitute an inequality, in the sense of allowing the suggestion of a hierarchy among types of knowledge; rather, it would mean only that access to the knowledge classified as superior is a necessity and a right of poorer actors, whose cultures lack formal knowledge. To learn this formal knowledge would be a political rather than an epistemic necessity, precisely because the possibility of producing and comprehending formally expressed argumentative discourses, necessary for the political struggle against oppression, would depend on this access. At the same time, if there are multiple types of knowledge in the world, the right to learn is necessarily directed towards learning that which one does not yet know, although it is important to stress that this does not correspond to an assumed superiority of that which is learned

---

4   Editing standards recommend the use of authors.

5   For this reason, in this text we do not identify specific works and pages on which the maxims we are basing our arguments were published. Most of the speeches were retrieved via an internet search and are available at https://www.pensador.com/paulo_freire_frases_educacao/. Retrieved on 10/28/2017.

"in school" compared to what is learned outside of it. Boaventura de Sousa Santos, in producing the critique of modernity and of the processes of knowledge exclusion that modernity produces, which he classifies as epistemicide, states that

> there is, therefore, neither ignorance in general nor knowledge in general. Each form of knowledge arises from a certain type of learning with respect to which a certain type of ignorance is defined. The latter, in turn, is recognized as such when compared to this type of knowledge. All knowledge is knowledge about a certain ignorance, and vice versa, all ignorance is ignorance of a certain knowledge. (Santos, 2000, p. 78)

The validity of knowledge, for Santos, comes from the ability of each piece of knowledge to act, to solve concrete problems. That is, there is no a priori hierarchy, the validity of knowledge is always circumstantial, determined by its utility in solving specific problems, in circumstances that are also specific. Seeking to overcome what he calls the monoculture of knowledge—which presupposes modern science and high culture to embody unique criteria of truth, and are therefore presided over by the logic of formal knowledge, which produces ignorance as a form of nonexistence—Santos understands that his overcoming would be through the development of an *ecology of knowledge* and the transformation of ignorance into applied knowledge. The work, therefore, would be to identify contexts and practices in which the different types of knowledge become operative, surpassing, when being used/applied to effectively solve problems, the ignorance with which they were previously identified.

When we compare the two formulations, it seems evident that the authors are speaking of the same thing: the recognition of the epistemological diversity of the world and the need to think about the relationships between the different types of knowledge beyond modern hierarchies, taking into consideration the interconnections between them and their operability in real situations. The development of this recognition is manifold, and although he has not specifically focused on discussing them beyond the defense of using students' knowledge as a pedagogical starting point for teaching, Paulo Freire would certainly recognize himself in the criticism produced by Santos, as we defend in the following. In developing his reflection, Santos states that

> there is no single, valid form of knowledge. There are many forms of knowledge, as many as the social practices that generate and sustain them [. . .]. Alternative social practices will generate alternative forms of knowledge. Not recognizing these forms of knowledge delegitimizes the social practices that sustain them and, in this sense, promotes the social exclusion of those who foster them. (Santos, 1995, p. 328)

Thus, Santos argues that this process of excluding nonscientific forms of knowledge was present in the European expansion process that included many "epistemicides," that is, annihilation or subalternization, subordination, marginalization and illegalization of practices and social groups with "strange" forms of knowledge because they were sustained by threatening social practices. The principal question of this second way of talking about the hierarchization of knowledge and the trivialization of its plurality lies in the idea that knowledge consists of social practices of knowledge and that each actor and/or social group relates to the world based on what he/it knows. This notion is very useful for comparison with Paulo Freire, because it will show that the Freirean idea of the right of access to formal knowledge does not necessarily mean an a priori hierarchization of them, but rather the right to learn that which you do not yet know, so that your way of relating to the world, developing your social practices of knowledge, is modified and potentialized as more operational elements are available. So, this hierarchical idea of the different types of knowledge, which was more than hegemonic at the time Paulo Freire began writing and reflecting, and still is today, is evidence of his precariousness when we compare it to the thought of Santos, which shows the *needlessness* and the mistake of considering some types of knowledge superior to others, a priori. The ten questions and answers with which Paulo Freire challenges his interlocutor in the classic passage in which he assumes the difference—without inequality—between his knowledge and that of the rural worker with whom he converses is evidence of the same belief, stated at the beginning of this section.

Given this, we can reread Freire's statement regarding the need for access to formal knowledge, understanding it as a necessity of appropriation and acquisition of the dominant knowledge and its language in order to understand the way the ruling classes relate to the world, in order to better engage them in debate. It is also a way of saying that the right to learn what one does not yet know about the world is the essence of the right to education, and this applies to everyone. In the extreme, the bourgeoisie exercises less of its right to education than the poorer classes because it has never been granted the right to know what the poorer classes know, because that is considered ignorance. This is the solution given to this abrogation of rights in order to legitimize the idea that this knowledge denied to members of the favored social classes is, therefore, ignorance and thus dispensable.[6]

That is, the question of the knowledge that Paulo Freire initially expresses as being a pair of opposites between the knowledge of experience and formal knowledge, and intimates that the latter is superior to the former, could lead one to believe that a hierarchy is being described, but when we turn to Santos and some contemporary curricular reflections, we perceive other possibilities of interpretation. After a long period during which this idea bothered me, precisely because it established a hierarchy along the lines of scientific thinking, I could see, especially with the help of Santos but not only through that lens, that this difference did not necessarily constitute inequality for Freire, but rather plurality,

6   In this respect it is worth reading Chapter 6 of the book *Curriculum: Theory and History* (Goodson, 1996) in which the author presents and discusses an episode in England in the nineteenth century in which a study on physics curriculum shows the discomfort of the aristocracy when faced with the knowledge of the students of the populace, which became applied knowledge when they were subjected to a practical curricular proposal, while the "theory" offered to the aristocracy produced learning failure.

inscribed in relationships involving unequal exchanges between them, hence the idea of ascension. Complementarily, the need for dialogue in the educational act comes from the conviction that there will only be learning when what is already known is related to the new information, a premise of Freire's educational work, visible in his experiments with teaching rural people in Brazil's Northeast to read in the late 1950s and early 1960s. The presumption of dialogue is to leave one's experiences and become open to the other. In dialogue, according to Freire (1987, p.81 and 84), "there are no absolutely ignorant people or absolute sages: there are men who, when interacting, seek to know more [...] Authentic education does not result from interactions of the type A to B or A over B, but rather A with B." With this formulation, nothing hierarchizing, Freire approaches what we argue here, with Santos. Moreover, both contribute to a reading of daily educational practices as spaces for collective creation and circulation of plural knowledge.

With this, we can note that, although there is a formulation that gives the impression of a hierarchy, concretely what Freire argues and describes does not conflict with what Santos expresses, which is the need and the right of all individuals to operate with different types of knowledge, weaving networks that amplify and potentiate ways of understanding and interacting with the world—through social practices of knowledge— that respect the epistemological plurality that characterizes it. This recalls Santos's other assertion about the importance of learning not resulting in the "unlearning" of what you already know, from the point of view of your cultural knowledge, and so on.

Santos is concerned with the possibility that learning processes operate to subjugate and discard previous knowledge, understanding that these processes should increase the complexity of the possibilities of understanding the world and of intervening in it. Thus the Freirean idea of ascension that could enhance emancipation would be more an ascension in terms of an understanding of the world that he calls naive—because it is based on more immediate knowledge from the reading of social reality—to a reading based on denser, more detailed knowledge—through the interweaving of the new and what is already known and the consequent increased complexity of the knowledge networks that the process provides—that would allow more conscious, complex readings of the world. That is, the ascension would be made possible by the interweaving of new knowledge with existing knowledge, without loss of epistemological and/or cultural identity. It would be ascension to a better-informed and more conscious "reading of the world."

With this, we come to an understanding of the political and epistemological need to see learning processes as interactive mutual learning systems that value dialogue between the different types of knowledge, and not only as a way to learn. It would be, above all, a process that allows for the enhancement of plural, circumstantially defined interventions on the world based on the dialogue between the types of knowledge. The denser the knowledge networks of those who think and act, the more effective they would be. This association of Freire's thinking with that of Santos makes it possible to understand, from the point of view of educational practices, the risks and tendencies towards reductionism that epistemicide brings to humanity and to society, a debate that leads to an understanding of the epistemicides present in the curricula (Paraskeva, 2018, 2016, 2014, 2011), which also have emancipatory elements (Oliveira, 2012).

Santos considers epistemicide one of the great crimes committed against humanity through colonization and capitalism,[7] since he believes that it resulted in an irreversible impoverishment of the horizon and possibilities of knowledge. In the continuity of his reasoning, he argues that "the new (scientific) paradigm proposes revaluing the non-hegemonic knowledge and practices that are, after all, the overwhelming majority of life and knowledge practices within the global system" (idem, p. 329). And it is in this sense that he proposes honest epistemological competition between the types of knowledge as necessary for the reinvention of the social practice alternatives capable of delimiting the construction of democracy and emancipatory struggles, since this would allow us to overcome the verticality and the hierarchy now predominant in relationships between different types of knowledge. Returning to Freire, we can understand his "ascension" proposal from the perspective of the ascension of the consciousness from naiveté to criticism rather than a trajectory from knowledge-from-experience to formal knowledge. From this perspective, the educational process develops through dialogue in which respect for the prior knowledge of learners, listening to what they bring to the conversation, and the interactions between the different types of knowledge are key. It is a perspective that reassesses nonschool—therefore nonhegemonic—knowledge, recognizing its validity while promoting fair competition among the different types of knowledge while also recognizing the potential uses for solving concrete problems, assuming this criterion of validation to be operational.

Thus, on the basis of Santos's analyses, we have broadened the reach of the Freirean proposal and managed to relate them to Freire's own thinking about the relationships between liberating education and emancipation, insofar as the proposed approach allows us to perceive the reach of Freire's argument in his dialogical pedagogical work in which different types of knowledge are respected as such, raising this argument to the position of a rupture-enhancing element with respect to the epistemicides and their political and social consequences. Both authors work with the conviction that formal scientific knowledge—European, white, bourgeois, capitalist, modern science—is partial, dated knowledge that has been culturally and socially constructed like any other type of knowledge. Because it is hegemonic, this knowledge proclaimed itself as superior, not hesitating to commit all sorts of epistemicides in order to maintain its position. This self-empowered authority of modern scientific thinking that announces and enunciates its own superiority over all others and, further, its universal validity, negating the possibility of validating any other knowledge, has reinforced social hierarchies. In Paulo Freire's text we note that his experience with teaching disadvantaged children and adults how to read is an experience based on knowledge of the working class. What that worker knows is the first big question. Because that which has no meaning cannot be learned. He perceived, through his experiences, from his

---

7   Currently, the author also refers to patriarchalism as the third element of the processes of denial, subalternization and annihilation of the other produced by modern societies (Santos, 2016).

sensitivity as an educator, that if the student does not establish a relationship between what he knows and what he must learn, he does not learn. So, in order to promote learning, one must start from the idea that the learner possesses knowledge,[8] one must recognize him as an actor of knowledge, and dialogue with him, not in a me–you relationship, but to understand "the dialogue (as) this meeting of men, mediated by the world, to pronounce it, therefore not exhausting the me-you relationship" (Freire, 2017, p. 109). Dialogue is therefore only established through the mutual recognition of the words of the other as an expression of his knowledge of the world. In this sense, the illiterate worker possesses knowledge, and the child in front of us in schools does as well. Recognizing that this knowledge, from the epistemological "South" of the hegemonic school model, which presides over the traditional, banking model of educational practices, exists, learning from them (with the South) and seeking to think as they do (in the South) would then be necessary for emancipatory education from the perspective of Freirean dialogue. And, not by chance, these are the premises of the Southern Epistemologies of Boaventura de Sousa Santos, which can also be associated with the idea of orienting towards the South, so dear to Paulo Freire, as we shall see next.

The epistemologies of the South: cognitive justice, social justice, solidarity and emancipation

Boaventura de Sousa Santos (2010) defines his Southern Epistemology as follows: "an epistemology of the South rests on three guidelines: learn that the South exists; learn to go to the South; learn from the South and with the South." This metaphorical South is the South of subalternation, negation, disqualification and invisibility. I think it is correct to affirm that the metaphorical global South to which Santos refers encompasses all epistemologies and their knowledge, existences and ways of being in the world and to understand it that have been inferiorized or made invisible, disqualified and made nonexistent by modernity. Associated with this idea, we have the perspective of orienting towards the South in all its scope, a notion developed based on the work and reflections of Joaquin Torres-Garcia (1992) and that appears to be defined as follows:

> Orienting towards the South is a proposal to think about and represent the world in a different way, an alternative to the global hegemony of the racial, ethnic, geographic-political and economic Norths that have built border walls that separate people, instead of bridges that allow them to travel, communicate and live together. In order to Orient towards the South, that is, to trace intercultural and interethnic trajectories looking for non-hegemonic,

---

8   In a way, the concept of Rancière (2002) in his "Ignorant Teacher" dialogues with this understanding, even when rejecting the explanationism typical of the modern school, opting for more interactive methods based on the recognition of the students' intelligence.

emancipatory references that foster recognition, respect and coexistence between ALL possible worlds, new ways of thinking are needed that "turn the world upside-down" and recognize all of the possible SOUTHS. (Baez, Mariano apud Campos, Marcio, 2016, p. 223)

The metaphorical character of this South encompasses political and epistemological issues, once again in an inseparable way, since the hegemony of the "global North" is inscribed both in the political dimension of life in contemporary societies and in the epistemological perspective of scientific modernity. Once again, the inseparability of these dimensions is evident, and helps us continue the dialogue between Santos and Paulo Freire that we intend to mediate with our studies. Let us then advance towards comprehension of the gestation process of the subversion of hegemony from the North to the South in order to better learn from the potential offered to us by the concept of Orienting towards the South and its dialogues with Southern Epistemology.

The School of the South -
A Escola do Sul - La Escuela del Sur

Joaquin Torres Garcia (1935)

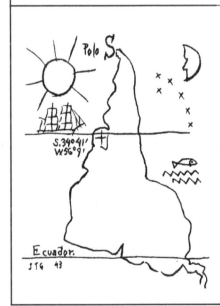

"An important art school had to be created here in our country. I say without hesitation: here in our country. And I have a thousand reasons to affirm it. He called it the School of the South because, in reality, our reference is the South. There should be no North, for us, except in opposition to our South. So now we turn the map upside-down, and then we have a fair idea of our position, and not the way the rest of the world wants it. The tip of South America, from now on, prolongs itself, insistently pointing to the South, our reference. Likewise, our compass is always unforgivably pointing towards the South, to our pole.
The ships, when they depart from here, descend, rather than going up as before, in order to depart towards the North. Because the North is now below. The sunrise, when facing towards our South, is on our left.[9]
This rectification was necessary; so now we know where we are [...]."

Joaquín Torres García. Universalismo Constructivo, Bs. As. : Poseidón, 1941. Available from
http://www.artemercosur.org.uy/artistas/torres/joa.html#anchor255232

---

9   The metaphorical use of this statement leads me to think that for us, Latin Americans who have suffered the process of colonization and the perennial presence of coloniality in our daily lives, the sun of freedom can only rise on the left, through the political choice of the dispossessed, through the subversion of the order instituted by the white, European, scientistic, macho bourgeoisie, by the other hegemonic *knowledgepowers* of the "imperial" North.

This map is fundamental to the debate we propose in this text, because it is the map drawn by Joaquin Torres-Garcia in 1935, and he draws it to say that our guide is the South, which is where the idea of Orienting towards the South will come from. Its purpose is to show that everything always depends on the point of view, which makes it impossible to legitimize any manner of establishing what is true globally for everyone, as points of view vary. This is an important thing, both for Paulo Freire and for Santos, or for those who want to understand why social actors say what they say, believe what they believe, and know what they know, even if it is considered ignorance.

Specifically, we know that the Earth is lost in outer space, revolving around the sun, and that the North is not above, nor is the South below. This is just one way to draw it. Then you can draw it in whichever way you prefer, the traditional way or inverted, and shift the view of the observer. In Brazil, our "south" is the Northeast. The epistemological "south" is the Northeast, which is subalternized culturally, politically and epistemologically. With the Brazilian North it is even worse, for its very existence as specificity is made invisible. That is, the North of Brazil does not exist and the Northeast of Brazil is the epistemological and political "south" of Brazil.

Thus, the idea of recovering the validity of nonscientific knowledge used in solving problems becomes a relevant movement in the struggle against these invisible scientificist hierarchies of the "others" of modernity. This question of the circumstantiality of the validity of knowledge is by no means a "utilitarian" perspective of understanding knowledge, which Santos affirms explicitly. It is the defense of the idea that the validity of knowledge will depend on its capacity for social intervention and not on its degree of scientificity, it will depend on the contribution it can make to solving the problems faced. This idea and the author's defense of it come from the realization that the scientific level, the level of scientificity—which is often difficult to measure—of knowledge does not serve as a criterion for its usability in solving societal problems, according to what we are taught by social experience and its many variables that do not fit scientific readings.

To reach this conviction, Santos will question the pillars of modernity, stating that it is an extremely ambitious project but with fundamental contradictions in its process. We understand that the final conclusion is that capitalism is incompatible with democracy, and this is why modernity could never work as a project. According to the author, modernity has led us to believe that the progress of science corresponds to the progress of society according to the formula: more science means greater social welfare. Since this has clearly not happened, we must accept the impossibility of associating the advancement of science with the advancement of social welfare. This, in the end, will lead to questioning of the validity of scientific knowledge as knowledge capable of explaining the world and therefore able to enable our mediation in it. In this process, scientific knowledge also loses its superiority as knowledge that brings us to a higher level of rationality and, therefore, makes us rationally capable of doing the right thing, since it is not capable of producing the result that modern scientism thought it would produce.

Noting this, and formulating criticisms with epistemological and political solidity, Santos is able to develop the idea that the social validity of knowledge is not measured by its scientificity, from which the need to practice the ecology of knowledge and Southern Epistemologies emerges. That is, far from being faced with any pragmatic utilitarianism, we are facing a high-magnitude political-epistemological exercise. And that is why Santos formulates the idea that we must learn to leave behind the monoculture of formal knowledge to embrace what he calls the ecology of types of knowledge, that is, to recognize the interdependence relationships between different types of knowledge to explain and solve the problems facing society. The solutions will require a conjunction, a constellation of different types of knowledge when addressing the problem, and this changes with each new situation or problem faced that is, the validity of the knowledge will always be given by its capacity to contribute to the solution of the concrete problems of each circumstance.

Santos is also careful to avoid the charge of relativism, as he rejects this idea. That is to say, for him, shifting the ability to solve social problems from modern science to a set of types of knowledge that, seen as equally valid, depending on the relationship of interdependence between them, constitute possible contributions to the production of solutions, does not mean, under any hypothesis, the "everything goes" approach of which the relativists are accused. The a priori lack of hierarchy between scientific and non-scientific knowledge is not an acceptance of permanent equivalence between them. It is the search for greater care and propriety when analyzing problems without pre-defined starting points based on essentialist hierarchies. It is understanding that one can only know what is valuable or not in relation to a problem to be solved at the time in which it is encountered, that is when we can recognize and evaluate the variables and issues involved in order to, only then, determine with which "tools" it should be approached. Both the epistemological and the concrete problems that we are given or face require us to mobilize specific knowledge and actions, which may be scientific and/or non-scientific. So, before formulating and considering a problem, we cannot determine the validity of any type of knowledge to approach it. But this is a priori and does not mean we can approach it with any knowledge/weapon/tool. It does not work for everything. On the contrary, this means that there is no panacea that always works, universally, for everything. Moreover, although there is no neutrality, because there is always an intentionality related to the problem to be addressed, there is also no relativism. There is objectivity—and the more, the better—which is the quest to use the highest degree of conscience possible in relation to the problem in order to employ the knowledge that is needed and most appropriate for the situation.

In the scientific practices we know and coexist with, even in the so-called hard sciences, which as its practitioners know and affirm, are not exact, nor have they ever been, the choices and points of view are the foundation for the production of scientific knowledge. In the field of physics, for example, the debate continues between the more deterministic Newtonian/Einsteinian tradition and the tradition founded by Heisenberg that is based on the uncertainty principle and is one of the pillars of quantum physics but ignored by schools. In mathematics, ethnomathematics and non-Euclidean geometry confirm the in-exactness of these sciences and the knowledge they draw on and develop and, therefore, the impossibility of considering any knowledge as definitive or useful for every circumstance, hence the need to redesign the relationships between different types of knowledge, no longer seeing them as pertaining to a universally valid hierarchical relationship, but rather as existing in a relationship of complementarity and interdependence, which the author proposes that we do through the search for an ecology of knowledge, capable of bringing to the world greater cognitive justice—a more just relationship between different types of knowledge—understood by Santos as a *sine qua non* condition for social justice. In his view, one cannot have social justice if some actors and social groups are considered inferior due to the inferiority of their cultures and knowledge, a conviction that also reaffirms the inseparability of politics and epistemology.

In Freire, the recognition of workers' knowledge, its "use" as a starting point for teaching and the learning that arises from the dialogue between them for teachers and students—premises that fit the principles of the epistemologies of the South, as already mentioned—allow us to perceive these same convictions with respect to the need to not hierarchize the different types of knowledge a priori, recognizing their circumstantial validity according to the problem to be solved. This perspective is, for Freire, necessary for a liberating education, capable of leading the oppressed to an awareness not only of oppression itself, but of its illegitimacy, built precisely on the basis of a priori hierarchies between knowledge, between actors with different types of knowledge and between their ways of being in the world and of intervening in it.

> Hence the need to Orient towards the South, to perceive the ideological character of the word "nortear" and all that is associated with it: "science", scriptural culture (Certeau, 1994), whiteness, "high culture," intellectual work, and life in the city. The sources of the legitimacy of the "superiority" of the North, which lets the knowledge that we "swallow without comparing with the local context" "trickle down." (Campos, 1991, apud, Freire, N. In: Freire, P., 1992, p. 218)

Hence, the need to Orient towards the South, (once again the Epistemologies of the South appear in the work of Freire, in his dialogue with Campos!). With a view to overcoming the desire and the idea that it would be possible to orient interlocutors towards the South through discourses *on* topics considered relevant and that would be dear to them, Paulo Freire takes upon himself the debate and the discussion *with* them as a way of working,[10] assuming, consequently, the need for recognition of knowledge

---

10   Here a tempting comparison with the studies in/of/with daily routines emerges, exactly in this change from work on to work with, a central element of our path towards the formulation of this research methodology with schools, that has been teaching us so much about the epistemological plurality of the world and on daily curricular creation.

and experience, and the dialogue between them as a democratic method and principle of coexistence and of emancipatory education in a perspective that we can recognize as that of autonomy—which does not presuppose disconnection but rather weaving into the collective and through conversations with others—of the actors and social groups to Orient towards the South.

A narrative by Freire (1992, pp. 20–26), about his work with SESC (a social and cultural organization) in the city of Recife in the 1950s, reinforces different aspects of our argument. In this, he first describes his concern and that of his group regarding the spreading of the authoritarian practices present in the undemocratic society in which we live by families and schools. He explains the work he sought to carry out, based on formal knowledge, in opposition to these practices. He therefore perceived, well before writing his first works, the democraticity underlying the scientific work of some authors while trying to understand (rather than explain) the practices and motivations of their interlocutors. He also states that his concern was to increase the involvement of families in school, in order to "widen the political connotation of that involvement in order to open channels for democratic participation to parents in the educational policy of schools" (Freire, 1992, p. 20), demonstrating a democratic, civic conviction far beyond what bourgeois representative democracy and its vertical citizenship—expressed only by citizen–state relationships—can contemplate. Freire also identifies the experience in question as of "real importance" for his

> theoretical understanding of political-educational practice, which, if pro-
> gressive, cannot ignore, as I have always said, the reading of the world that
> the populace has been creating, expressed in their speech, their syntax, their
> semantics, their dreams and their wishes. (idem)

The other appears, therefore, as a partner, as subject of dreams, desires, knowledge and unique ways of expressing them, neither better nor worse, just different. He claims to have learned from a man of the people, the guardian of a student at the school where he worked, the lesson he would remember forever, on the need to recognize the other in his specificity, and to listen to his knowledge as a necessary *modus operandi* for democratic, political-educational practice and even the production of scientific-theoretical knowledge. That is, it is a defense of the ecology of knowledge as a means of producing new knowledge, ecology can only exist when practicing cognitive justice. We cannot therefore accept that our society "turns its back" on the South—as it assumes the Northern point of view as our reference, denounced by Marcio Campos (1991) and discussed further by Nita Freire (In: Freire, 1992, pp. 218–220):

> would "turning our backs" or turning "around" (towards the South) not be
> an attitude of indifference, of contempt, of disdain for our own local possi-
> bilities for construction of a knowledge that is ours, arising from local things
> and concretely ours? [. . .] Would not this "practical pseudo-rule" be a form

of alienation that affects our signs and symbols, passing through detailed knowledge to the production of knowledge that 'turns its back' on itself and turns around, open-breasted, with a greedy mouth and hollow head like an empty container to be filled with signs and symbols from another place, and ultimately to be a continent of knowledge produced by men and women of the "North," from the "top," from "superiors," from the highest point"? (p. 220)

Looking Southward—thus having the sunrise on our left—we can become capable of learning that it exists, and that in it there is knowledge that we can recognize, from which we can learn what the North does not know and cannot teach, which is the presence of the other; the co-presence of the world of these types of knowledge, multiple and independent; and the horizontal dialogue between them, without hierarchies, as means and bases for a democratizing social emancipation based on mutual recognition and the ecology of knowledge at the same time in which it recognizes the concrete social life and the needs that it brings for different types of knowledge to face different circumstances, social relationships that also need to be made horizontal. This is what Santos affirms with his Southern Epistemologies, while at the same time he accepts the need for horizontal social relationships between different social actors, with distinct knowledge and ways of being in the world, as part of the civic dimension of life as part of the need for mutual recognition, for the existence of democracy.

This horizontal citizenship would imply the responsibility of all to build a more just society. This requires recognition of the other and a commitment to collective well-being, ideas that are also present in Freire's work and in the different authors who propose the need to Orient to the South that, among other affirmations, stress that it is not a "celebration of the oppressed, nor a victimization of the dispossessed, it is an invitation to celebrate horizontal globalization" (Campos, 2016). And the comparison with Santos appears once again, from the perspective of necessarily counterhegemonic horizontal globalization, whose path is cosmopolitanism.

Freitas (2013) also contributes by clarifying the notion of Orienting to the South in Freire in his review of the Paulo Freire Dictionary (Streck, Redin, & Zitkoski, 2008). The author says:

> By using the idea of Orienting towards the South (sulear), Paulo Freire draws attention to the ideological character of the term "nortear." Orienting towards the South expresses the intention of providing visibility for the Southern viewpoint as a way of countering the dominant Eurocentric logic in which the North is presented as a universal reference. Orienting towards the South means constructing alternative paradigms in which the South places itself at the center of the "reinvention of social emancipation" (Adams, 2008, p. 397). Orienting thoughts and practices towards the South is a perspective that is announced in

Freirean thought to strengthen the construction of emancipatory educational practices. (Freitas, 2016, pp. 205, 206)[11]

Thus, we discern the similarities between the Southern Epistemologies of Santos, who formulates them after a long international research project that, not coincidentally, sought elements for a "reinvention of social emancipation," and the proposal to Orient towards the South, embraced by Freire, both inscribed in counterhegemonic thinking in the fight against coloniality, capitalism and patriarchalism (Santos, 2016), inseparable dimensions of the construction and legitimation of the processes of domination in modernity. We thus recognize plural knowledge in society and in schools. Because there is no type of knowledge better or worse than any other, or ignorance in general, or knowledge in general, but rather multiple types of knowledge whose validity is circumstantial, given the capacity they have to operate in each situation, reorganizing and equating problems that emerge from everyday life, from our curiosity, from our will to better understand the world. Knowledge that will be usable depending on the circumstances, thereby modifying the impression of truth that they create according to the point of view from which they operate.

With these comments, we conclude this text, understanding that the result of our reflections and associations is, in a way, only the product of a personal intellectual exercise, which seems to allow us to postulate the discovery of characteristics not immediately evident in Paulo Freire's work, in its innovative, creative and relevant aspects, as the production of a new political epistemology which he employed to think about education. A political epistemology that contributes to contemplation of emancipatory education, centered on the possibility for democratization of educational activities and of society, in the search for a way to overcome the processes of social domination. At the same time, based on themes that draw out the similarities in the two authors, I understand this text as a proposal that provides evidence of how the concept of "Epistemologies of the South," developed by Santos, based on his many political-epistemological studies and reflections, not only fits but also already existed as a concern and principle, in an underlying way, in Freirean pedagogy. For these reasons, I believe it is possible to affirm that Freirean pedagogy encompasses the idea of the inseparability between the political and epistemological dimensions and contained and contains possibilities for effective contributions towards democratic social emancipation.

References

Baez, M. (2016). Buscando Un SUR Epistémico. Propuestas para GT-CLACSO.

Campos, M. D. (2016). Por que SULear? Astronomias do Sul e culturas locais. In: Perspectivas Etnográficas e Históricas sobre as Astronomias, Priscila Faulhaber, Luiz C. Borges (orgs.), *Anais do IV Encontro Anual da SIAC*. Rio de Janeiro: Museu de Astronomia e Ciências Afins (MAST), 2016, p. 215-240. http://www.mast.br/publicacoes_do_mast. html#letra_p. Acesso em 10/02/2019.

---

11   Freitas, Ana Lúcia. Rescensão. Revista lusófona de Educação. Available at http://www.scielo.mec.pt/ pdf/rle/n24/n24a16.pdf. Accessed on 10/29/2017.

Certeau, Michel de. (1994). *A Invenção do cotidiano 1*. Artes de fazer. Petrópolis: Vozes.

Freire, P. (1987). *Pedagogia do Oprimido*. São Paulo: Paz e Terra

Freire, Paulo. (1992). *Pedagogia da Esperança*. São Paulo: Paz e Terra, 1992.

Freitas, Ana Lúcia. (2013). Rescensão: Streck, D., Redin, E., & Zitkoski, J. J. (Orgs.). Dicionário Paulo Freire. Belo Horizonte: Editora Autêntica, 2008. *Revista Lusófona de Educação*. n. 24, 2013.

Goodson, I. (1996). Currículo: teoria e história. Petrópolis: Vozes.

Oliveira, Inês B. (2012). *Currículo como criação cotidiana*. Petrópolis/RJ: DP et Alii, 2012.

Paraskeva, João. (2011). *Conflicts in Curriculum Theory*. Challenging Hegemonic Epistemologies. New York: Palgrave.

_____. (2014). *Conflicts in Curriculum Theory*. Challenging Hegemonic Epistemologies. New York: Palgrave, 2. Ed. (revista e ampliada).

_____. (2016). *Curriculum Epistemicides*. Toward an Itinerant Curriculum Theory New York: Routledge.

_____. (2018). *Towards a Just Curriculum Theory*. The Epistemicide. New York: Routledge.

Rancière, Jacques. (2002). *O Mestre Ignorante*. Belo Horizonte: Autêntica.

Santos, B. S. (1995). *Pela mão de Alice*: o social e o político na pós-modernidade. São Paulo: Cortez.

_____. (2000). *A crítica da razão indolente*: contra o desperdício da experiência. São Paulo: Cortez.

_____. (2016). *A Difícil democracia*: reinventar as esquerdas. São Paulo: Boitempo,

_____; Menezes, M. P. (2010). *Epistemologias do Sul*. São Paulo: Cortez.

Streck, D., Redin, E., & Zitkoski, J. J. (orgs.). (2008). *Dicionário Paulo Freire*. Belo Horizonte: Editora Autêntica.

Torres-Garcia, Joaquín (1992). The School of the South (Uruguay, February 1935). In: Ramírez, Mari Carmen, (ed.), *El Taller Torres-García*: the School of the South and its legacy. Austin: University of Texas Press, p. 53–57.

PART IV
ALTERNATIVE WAYS
TO THINK ALTERNATIVELY

CHAPTER SIXTEEN

What Is Really Taught as the Content of School Subjects? Teaching School Subjects as al Alchemy[1]

Thomas Popkewitz

THERE IS GENERAL belief in current reforms that a teacher cannot teach a school subject unless she has adequate knowledge of the disciplinary field of that teaching. Coinciding with this belief is the emphasis in teacher education reforms and research on pedagogical knowledge teachers need for children to learn the content knowledge. The identification of "the best practices" and "the core" teaching knowledge to enact the curriculum exemplifies this belief. "Benchmarks" or standards are indicators of whether the teacher has mastered the core or best practices. The professional, highly skilled teacher is one who exhibits the benchmarks and classified as "effective" and "authentic" in classroom teaching.

The pedagogical knowledge to implement teaching of school subjects is the focus of teacher and teacher education reform. This assumption underwrites the McKinsey reports on educational assessments of national school systems. An international consulting agency that writes public service reports on education, McKinsey uses international assessments of student performances (PISA, the Programme for International Student Assessment) in science and mathematics, for example, to outline models of school change that focus on teacher education and school system recruitment and professional training (Popkewitz, 2017). The models of change focus on the management of pedagogical practices to provide the "pathways" or "highways" for improving science, mathematics, and literary education. The highway metaphor directs attention to change as simply instrumental: "to *get rid of potholes [and] make educators and employers part of the solution by providing 'signs' and concentrate on patch of pavement ahead"* (Barton, Farrell, & Mourshed, 2013, p. 54). Teacher education reform programs follow the same kind of assumptions but at the micro level of classroom interaction. The problem of good teaching is better implementation strategies for students to learn the curriculum. Teacher training is to enable teachers to "approximate" the professional practices of "what teachers *really need to know and be able to do"* (Grossman, McDonald, Hammerness, & Ronfeldt, 2008, p. 247, italics added).

This essay gives attention to the principles of change that organize contemporary teacher and teacher education reforms. It suggests that the models of change are built on

1   Keynote address, Department of Educational Leadership, University of Massachusetts Dartmouth, April 9, 2015.

a chimera or illusion. That illusion is that teaching is about learning science, mathematics, art, or music, and professional competence is finding the "core" pedagogical knowledge. The discussion argues historically that the school curricula for teaching school subjects have little to do with learning disciplinary practices, but rather are models of practices for making kinds of people. They embody cultural principles about who the child is and should be, and who is outside and does not "fit" into the spaces of normalivity.

To explore the principles of the models of curriculum, the analogy is made with the sixteenth- and seventeenth-century alchemists who sought to turn base metals into pure gold. As the medieval alchemy, the school subjects involve magical processes that transform physics and mathematics, for example, into the school curriculum. The alchemy of the school subjects is explored historically to ask how is it possible to think about curriculum reforms as we do and the limits of these models for school change. While it is often pleasing to think of schools as places for children "learning" and teaching as a "help profession," to think of the curriculum as an alchemy directions attention to a different historical quality of schools. Historically they are concerned with the making of kinds of people. Some of these kinds of people are today called the lifelong learner, the adolescent, and the disadvantaged child. Pedagogy (and pedagogical knowledge), the argument continues, links norms and values of collective belonging with the interior of the child in governing "the soul." The second section discusses how theories about the nature of society and collective belonging (the citizen) are brought in to order the curriculum to talk about science, arts, music and mathematics education. The theories in the curriculum and psychologies of the child generate principle about what is thought, talked about and "seen" as the practices of teaching. And embedded in the alchemy of teaching school subjects is the paradox of contemporary reforms. The designing of the curriculum to recognize differences and inclusion so "all children learn" produces, at the same time, divisions that exclude and abject. The final section explores the paradox of the alchemy of making kinds of people and differences in mathematics, science, music, and art education.

The alchemy or translations of disciplinary knowledge into the school curriculum are necessary—translations are needed, as children are not physicists, mathematicians, or professional artists. Current reforms and research, however, obscure the translation practices of the curriculum by privileging pedagogical knowledge and psychological distinctions as the arbiter of what is selected, ordered, and evaluated as learning science and mathematics.

Schools as Making Kinds of People/ The Pedagogical Object as the Soul

The analogy of the alchemy directs attention to the particular translation tools used in the school curriculum. That is, the disciplines of physics and history are produced in social and cultural spaces that entail particular machinery, routines, and cultural practices concerned with the production of specific kinds of knowledge systems—physics, biology, or sociology, for example. Curriculum is a practice that selects some of the knowledge produced in disciplinary practices for children. This practice of curriculum is to treat disciplinary knowledge as discrete "entities" for children to learn. Curriculum is the translation of geometry as a field of inquiry in mathematics, for example, into content for children to learn. The categories and classifications about children's learning and teacher pedagogical knowledge perform as the translation technologies for organizing teaching subjects. To talk about children's learning and development, for example, entails a range of theories, stories, narratives, and social organization of time and space that are not present in the disciplinary fields. No good-standing scientist is going to break the tasks of the laboratory into cognitive knowledge, skills, and affect. What is important for the deliberation of this article is to consider historically the social and cultural principles generated in curriculum models and not to assume that they follow their namesake—the study of physics or music.

Thinking of alchemy of the curriculum, then, is to step back a bit to think historically about how what happens in school become possible and given the labels of science, music, art, or mathematics education. The school curriculum in school subjects, the theories of learning and teaching, and the ordering of lessons and assessments were not invented for children to learn science or mathematics. This inquiry about what is taught starts with recognizing that schools are places of making kinds of people. To learn how to do a science experiment or to do the problem solving through mathematics entails practices that are not only what you should know but also the dispositions, sensitivities, habits, and manners about how you are to know, recognize, and act on what you know. The translation of sports into Brazilian physical education, for example, was about making a moral order. Physical education, as a school subject, was tied to particular narratives about how to form an efficient, healthy, and productive society through the regulation of its citizens (Ilha, 2017). Physical education was to discipline children and their bodies (Ilha, 2017). Sport activity and movement of bodies were tools to inscribe cultural norms that simultaneously created social stability and progress, particularly through the work of its teachers.

I start with thinking about school as making kinds of people to consider how the practices of learning and ideas about childhood are not just there to figure out the best ways of teaching. The distinctions and differentiations about kinds of people in pedagogy emerge as ways of dealing with things happening in the world. If the idea of the child as an adolescent is considered, it appeared in the Child Studies of G. Stanley Hall (1893/1924) as a scientific psychological category to think about childhood as a transition to adulthood. This "problem" of transition of youth was directed to urban populations coming into the US schools at the time. Eastern and Southern European immigrations and African American migrations from the south at the turn of the century brought into the school a different kind of child that was considered deviant. Adolescence was a way for the teacher to think about these different populations through psychological theories. Today, the idea of the child as an adolescent is no longer a way of thinking about how psychology can help in planning who children are. It has become what children are, given as a "reality" for instructional programs to help the child navigate the transition to adulthood.

If this psychology of the child is taken as an example, pedagogy embodies cultural theses about kinds of people; today there are different narratives about the adolescent who spends too much time with computer games or who is in need of remediation because of the achievement gap, the mathematically abled child, the creative child, the at-risk child, the lifelong learner, and the child who has or lacks motivation. The curriculum and its theories of the child and theories of learning are, in fact, about designing the child as practices of governing conduct, something explored later.

When the psychologies in teaching are looked at as making kinds of people, the question of children's learning morphs into a different object. Pedagogy is concerned with "the soul." In previous times, learning about how to think about the objects of the world was directed through theology. The focus of pedagogy is, as Foucault (1988) suggests in his arguments about the changing operation of power, (re)visions of the early church's interest in rescuing the soul. Previous church conceptions of revelation were transferred to strategies of ordering personal self- reflection, self-criticism, and the inner self that guided moral development of the individual.[2] Today, modern psychology no longer talks about the soul but about the mind, learning, problem-solving, and motivation as the object of schooling. Yet this change of language still maintains the interest in governing the soul. The "soul" enters, through reform of teacher education and the curriculum of school subjects, including its notions of "critical literacy education," through focusing on change as "the habits of mind." This objects of changing the interior qualities of the teacher in teacher research and reform are spoken about as making teaching a profession, "nurturing" teacher activists, and the "weeding out" the bad teachers. Stripped of the language of science and moral certitude, the changing the teacher's "habits of the mind" and "nurturing" do not erase the soul as the object governed—in practice if not in name—and the making of kinds of people. To talk of producing "habits of the mind" is to focus on the interiority of the teacher, that is, the inner dispositions and attitudes of the teacher's "soul."

The formal education of the teacher was to make a particular kind of person who could administer changes that were to change the interior of the child. The teacher was to learn how to reason about the child through organizing classroom lessons and observing the child through the new psychologies of child development. The object of observation was to change was the modes of living and the internal qualities of the child, later spoken about as the appropriate attitudes, motivation, and "civic" virtues to participate in society, a language of science but about "the soul." Contemporary discourses about children's learning and teacher effectiveness are talked about as "[t]eachers also need to understand the person, the spirit, of every child and find a way to nurture that spirit" (Darling-Hammond, 2006, p. 310).

---

2   See, for example, discussions about transmogrification of religious cosmologies into theories of social change in Popkewitz (1991, 2008), Tröhler (2011), and Tröhler, Popkewitz and Labaree (2011).

Historically, schools were places to make children into kinds of adults they would not be if they had not attended schools. The early founders of the nation understood this well. The citizen is not born but made. The new republican forms of government needed the kind of person who participated in the processes of government. Education was central in the cultural production of the individual necessary for governing and government. In the US, the self-monitoring ethical techniques of the Puritans tied to themes of religious salvation were (re)visioned as the application of self-watchfulness through notions of the common good (McKnight, 2003; Popkewitz, 2008).

I realize at the outset that speaking of schooling as the struggle for the soul might seem odd, yet this focus is historically obvious. The concern with the soul as the object of schooling was embodied in the formation of the modern school in the late nineteenth century. Paz (2017) argues that the idea of genius in the middle of the nineteenth century was about the student's soul and body. The child who was a genius had a special soul, the result of a gift—from either heaven or earth. Portuguese music education focused on the students' relationship with time and space to convey social values. These values were the dispositions of studying, acquiring knowledge that linked individuality with norms for participating in the new republican form of governing and as a selective process in a secular society. Psychology transferred religious confessional practices to the realm of personal self-reflection and self-criticism.

The earlier discussion of the alchemy and teacher education brings into relation the dual objects of change that simultaneously exist in school reforms. The soul to be changed is plural. It involves the continual relation between the habits of the mind of child and the teacher. The latter is spoken about in teacher education research as the background, invisible knowledge, and unseen qualities and characteristics of the teacher that enables effective teaching.

To consider the object of curriculum as the calculation of the "soul" is to rethink the standards and benchmarks in contemporary reforms. Standards are typically treated as formal goals and outcomes, such as in the Common Core curriculum standards in the US. The standards of benchmarks given attention here are kinds of people. The models of curriculum are cultural theses about the characteristics, qualities, and capabilities embodied in children's modes of reflection and action.

Fabricating People

I focused on schooling *as* the making kinds of people. To further explore this, the distinctions that order and classify children in schools can be explored as a fabrication. Fabrication directs attention to two different qualities that are part of the same phenomenon. One, the classifications kinds of people are fictions. They are ways to think about the social world and often responses to social issues. One such example is the category of "at risk" as a classification to think about equitable and just education.

Second, fabrication directs attention to how these fictions about populations loop into the world and are given a reality; programs, theories stories are produced to treat children as adolescent and for children to think of themselves in that manner. To think about schools as fabricating kinds of people is to bring into focus the productive and material qualities of schooling—how discourses are social practices that order thought and action (Popkewitz, 2013a, p. 1).

First, the fiction. If I use the idea of "healthy person," it is a fabrication of kinds of people. It forms through a mixture of principles that entail, for example, political, commercial, scientific, and gender discourses. This is apparent if I look at a simple box of food that says it is designed for making people healthy. The box of food carries a table of ingredients, percentages of different nutrients, and number of calories to exemplify its qualities. This table of ingredients is formed through political laws, negotiations with commercial groups and science, including and omitting "facts" such as whether it was produced with insecticides. These qualities of the food are also related to qualities of the person whose way of life and consumption is "rational," who organizes meals in particular ways to have the right mixtures of proteins, minerals, "right" fats, sodium, and so on. At the same time, this person is mindful of the dangers to life of unhealthy consumption, such as too many bad fats, sodium, and calories.

The images and narratives of the nutrition table connect science with social and political practices to make up or fabricate the healthy person. This grid connects political rationalities about a healthy society and citizenry (the grid of facts about food content), medical discourses about growth and disease, commercial interests in food production, scientific discourses about diet, and gendered discourses that embody images of sexuality. The gender comes in often in the images represented on the packaging, typically a woman and family. The listing of calories high on the charts of food "facts" connect with cultural images of the "trim" and "fit" body.

The simple classification systems on boxes of food, then, embody cultural theses about kinds of people. The principles are formed through a grid of practices, such as scientific observations; theories of sociology, psychology, genetics, and biology; and technologies of governance. The intersections of theories, practices, and technologies—as tools for knowing and governing people—provide ways to experience oneself as a kind of person. The principles generated about the healthy person or the adolescent are formed as a system of reason to think about kinds of people (the healthy) that "act" as the "self"-governing through the discursive practices about what is desirable, healthy, and personally satisfying.

The making of people entails notions of normalcy that simultaneously produce differences and abjections; that is, those kinds of people placed as outside the livable spaces through evaluating their habits as "unhealthy" and "poor" decisions. This double gesture of normalcy and pathology will be returned to when looking at the school subjects more closely.

The double nuance of fabrication brings into view a particular way of thinking about power and the political. Traditionally, studies of power seek to locate the subjects as who rules and who are ruled. The distinctions are about what actors dominate and are repressed through institutional and structural forces that govern society. This focus on making of people reverses traditional question of who occupies positions of authority, or of what constitutes the economic arrangements of wealth and privilege.

While these analyses are important, my focus is historically on the cultural rules produced to shape and fashion what is talked about, seen, and done. This governing at a distance is what Michel Foucault (1979) called *governmentality, governing through the distinctions, differentiations, and divisions that order and classify who we are and should be.* Lesko and Niccolini (2017), for example, discuss the fabrication of the teacher as a kind of person who learns to think and feel in the "right" ways in order to know youth as haunted by aesthetic conventions and political theories that exceed the boundaries granted by psychological discourses of teachers' personalities and attitudes. They explore how questions of teacher satisfaction and cognition are linked and generated through images and narratives about, for example, the good child and the ineffective teacher who "threatens" student learning.

The political of schooling addresses, then, in the principles generated about kinds of people and the difference and divisions produced. The approach to the power directs attention to the system of reason that orders and classifies what is said, thought, and done. The argument continually focuses on the principles generated in pedagogy, models of curriculum, and psychologies of learning as embodying rules and standards that act on particular populations and produce difference.

Psychology, the Alchemy and Making Kinds of People

If the previous argument is pursued, teaching school subjects is about making kinds of people and differences. What is selected and organized as teaching science or mathematics is, I will argue, designed historically to change children's dispositions, sensitivities and modes of living, that is, to make kinds of people. This making of kinds of people as the school curriculum entails, first, *translations.* What people do and produce in biology, history, and art, for example, require translations into ways of thinking and acting appropriate for children. Since the formation of the nineteen-century modern school, the translation tools have originated primarily through psychological theories.

Traveling with the emergence of the modern school and its curriculum were the social sciences. One of the hallmarks often given to the formation of mass schooling and Progressive education in the US is its reliance on science, particularly the new sciences of sociology and the psychologies of the child. These sciences were designed to think about and order daily life. If the psychologies of the family, community, and the child are given focus, they are not only about understanding and describing what is happening in the world. They are to perform as principles to organize how to see and effectuate change—personal as well as social life. Further, the sciences that enter the school were considered with deviancies, the moral disorder of urban life at the turn of the twentieth century.

Science as a mode of thinking about people has particular historical qualities. During the nineteenth century, it was called "the moral science." In the US, science became part of the national imaginary. For many Americans, the crises of unbridled capitalism, the perceived breakdown of moral order in the city, and the brutality of modern warfare coupled with the struggle over slavery of the American Civil War, among others, cast doubt on the prior American narrative of the idyllic reincarnation of a biblical Garden of Eden and its religiously bound notion of the New World (see, e.g., Menand, 2001). The moral grace of the New World was (re)visioned as the millennial potential of the future. The new epic tale of the nation was told through the technological sublime: narratives of the natural power of Niagara Falls, the Grand Canyon, and the technologies represented in the railroad, bridge, and city skyscrapers as triumphs of art and science in the liberation of the human spirit realized by the young republic. Science and technological changes were made into the apotheosis of cosmopolitan reason and science in the making of the nation. The exceptionalism was of the technological promise of the future in which individuals would overcome the evils of modernization that inhibited progress.

This notion of science was radically different from what preceded it. The practices of science for the Swedish botanist Linnaeus in the seventeenth century, for example, was to create taxonomies of plants as a method to find the rules and order given by God. Reason in the Enlightenment was separate from science (Erickson et al., 2013, pp. 33–34). The former was concerned with wisdom, moral questions, and the highest of mental faculties, including understanding, memory, judgment, and imagination. Science was about rationality, methods, and rules. Quantitative and calculative capacities, for example, from the eighteenth century and throughout the nineteenth century were considered debased mechanical functions unrelated to invention, genius, or consciousness (Halprin, 2014, p. 150). Enlightenment probabilists like Condorcet conceived their mathematics of games as a reasonable calculus but not as one that could have been mechanically implemented by following rules without judgment or interpretation. The idea of the relation of mind and machine that is embedded in today's cybernetics and its offshoots in the learning sciences, for example, were not possible.

Science as the study of the child and in the modern school was different. Science was a social practice of making kinds of people. Its practices were given as "reason" and wisdom in and of itself. The sciences of schooling were designed as technologies to act on the spirit and the body of children and the young (Ó, 2003). Psychology was its technology.

The new psychological sciences were central to the translation of disciplinary knowledge into the school curriculum. The emergence of scientific psychologies of the curriculum in the nineteenth century—the same moment when mass schooling was institutionalized in the republics that dotted Europe and the Americas—embodied the new beliefs in science in social reform. The practices of education were thus tied to questions about moral development and the making of good and productive citizens to function in liberal democracies. It gave attention to social principles of moral order that were conceptualized as the "mind," a word that seemed to emphasize secular and scientific interests but reenvisioned previous theological concerns with governing the soul.

The concept of the "mind" was to satisfy the new scripture of science by replacing metaphysical notions. The psychological distinctions of the mind were to instantiate the spiritual/moral life associated with attitudes and dispositions of a rational and active child. Child psychology entailed new sets of distinctions to direct attention to moral conduct and the self in connection to earlier interests in saving the soul but under the names of intelligent actions, problem-solving, attitudes, and motivation (see Danziger, 1990).

Psychological theories were to respond to problems that schools encountered and provide its solutions. This is evident at the early decades of the twentieth century. The opening up of American schooling for children of immigrants and racial groups produced distinctions of the "backward" child who did not succeed in schools. This distinction, however, was soon expanded on as the phenomena of different populations attending the American common school. It became possible to talk about the differences in the interior of the child through new objects of administration, such as distinctions about motivation, IQ, achievement, and environment that directed attention to low-income families (Franklin, 1994).

Reflection replaced revelation in finding human progress in order to "bring home its truth to the consciousness of the individual" (Dewey, 1967/1990, p. 5). Personal salvation and redemption were tied to personal development and "fulfillment," words that signaled religious motifs placed in secular discourses of science and rational progress. The concept of adolescence was cast as a particular kind of person who represented moral panic about degeneration that threatens the future (Lesko & Talburt, 2011).[3] The moral panic was grounded in racialized, gendered, and class distinctions.

Expressed in and developed through the languages of psychology, the curriculum was a translation process to fashion the "soul." One common assumption of teaching that children develop in particular stages emerged in the nineteenth century as a strategy to govern the child. Martins (2017) argues, for example, that the art education was made possible through ideas intersected with the Child Study Movement. The idea that a child grows and develops made possible the study of children's drawings. Drawings offered a lens into a presumably deeper knowledge about each child, framed by notions of normal and abnormal development. This image of the developing child organized the categories by which to filter a child's progress toward the norm. The analysis of children's art and drawings were not about art *per se* but about a way of reasoning about who the child was and how they might develop in the school. The drawings were about the process by which art is made and how to find the child within through the art.

The distinctions and classification to "see" the child were not only about child development and growth. It embodied a comparativeness, producing a continuum of value about not only who the child is and who the child should be but also who is not that child.

---

3   The title of G. Stanley Hall's book on the psychology of adolescence exemplifies the intersection: *Adolescence: Its psychology and its relation to physiology, anthropology, sociology, sex, crime, religion, and education.*

The psychological sciences were to make self-managed and responsible families and children from those who were cast as outside of livable spaces (Popkewitz, 2008). Turn of the twentieth-century Child Studies, for example, talked about the psychic development of the urban child's "soul." G. Stanley Hall (1893/1924) argued that psychology was to replace moral philosophy and the Bible in seeking human perfection (Bloch, 1987). Hall was concerned with "the urban hothouse" and argued that scientific psychology was the pinnacle of school pedagogy. It was to change "the unwashed and sinful soul" in order to bring purity of the spirit into being. The trope embodied a Calvinist language of fulfilling human destiny by achieving in what G. Stanley Hall called "the beautiful, and the true social, moral and religious good." Portuguese art education in the late nineteenth century differentiated the artist through eugenic theory about different human types: the genius, idiot, insane, and normal (Martins, 2013).

Alchemy of School Subject and "The Social Question"

The school "subject" has two overlapping meanings when talking about the curriculum. One meaning had to do with the translation of external knowledge systems into school subjects—giving consideration to the content selected and organized about what children are supposed know. The other meaning of subject is how the curriculum creates the reason and "reasonable people" by governing the "soul." The soul here, as discussed earlier, refers to an interior of the child that is observed and administered by pedagogical practices and its sciences that mark the "good," "productive," and "right" kind of child.

If the previous analysis is joined with the formations of school subjects at the turn of the century, the human sciences drawn into pedagogical theories were concerned with social deviancy and moral disorder in the new urban contexts of immigration, industrialization, and urbanization. This concern with deviancy and moral disorder were expressed as *The Social Question*. Political and social reforms brought together theories and methods of the social sciences with Protestant themes about intervention in moral and social life. The reforms were to mitigate the economic dislocations and moral disorder associated with urbanization and industrialization (Rodgers, 1998). The social sciences were to liberate urban populations from existing social conditions and produce self-managed and responsible urban children and families (Popkewitz, 2008).

The school subjects were the mapping of knowledge around psychologies of the urban child linked to the Social Question. The teaching of modern English literature in British mass schooling of the nineteenth century, for example, emerged through two different historical movements that did not evolve from the prior "cultivating" aspects of writing or reading (Hunter, 1988). First was the public administration of social problems. Mass schooling was opened to the "inarticulate and illiterate" of the working classes. The child was to learn English literature to develop a cosmopolitan outlook but within the hierarchy of the existing social structure. Second, the subject of English related to the governmental provisions for social welfare. The narrative structures and ethical messages of literary texts were to help the reader become the moral agent who embodied cosmopolitan values and its notions of "civility." The rules of moral conduct were accomplished by making the stories of literature relevant to the everyday experiences of working-class children. Relevancy was to show how the rules and standards for moral conduct could be practiced in daily life.

The Social Question intersected with the sciences of the child and the pedagogical practices of the modern school. The school mathematics curriculum prior to progressive education, for example, was to provide for the mental discipline of the child. Character training was to occur by mentally exercising and training the mind. Faculty psychology ordered pedagogical practices to produce "higher emotions and [the] giving [of] mental pleasure" (Stanic, 1987, p. 155). In this context, school subjects were represented as stable "entities" for children to reflect on and to order the possibilities of their worlds.

Later in the century, the principles of school subjects shifted to giving relevancy to planning of everyday life. Mathematics education, for example, was seen as a practical subject that students needed for understanding everyday activities as well as necessary in "the practical needs in building homes, roads, and commerce" (Reese, 1995, p. 111). The new curriculum produced new ways of thinking about the relationship between the child's development in mathematics and the hope of progress for the nation. Mathematics education articulated cultural theses about modes of living. The translation tools to make mathematics into the objects of teaching were psychology (Diaz, 2017). The translations inscribe moral principles and difference in making kinds of people.

The "new mathematics curriculum" of the post–World War II United States generated normative principles that differentiated the qualities associated with the creative, innovative, and independent child from other children, who were not this kind of child (Diaz, 2017). The language of today's reform was articulated as a salvation theme about mathematics as a "tool for modern life" and economic and social progress (Valero, 2017). The words *creative*, *innovative*, and *independent* are not about some general and universal properties of the mind. They are bound to the particular logic and theories of learning and communication that order the pedagogical practices of teaching. The mathematics curriculum "for all" was entangled with the imperative of social equality. The new curriculum established the identities and differences that distinguished the psychological traits of the child as a mathematically able citizen from the child who was not. What constituted the space of "all children" was also an inscription of difference. The differences embodied qualities and characteristics of children that stand outside the unity inscribed in the signification of "all children" populations recognized for the need to include but inscribed as different and dangerous to the unspoken inscriptions of the normalcy of the "all"—the "disadvantaged" child and the child left behind.

Music education, seemingly with different priorities about learning and knowledge than the orderly worlds of mathematics, has a similar social trajectory in making kinds of people and inscribing differences. Introduced in the 1830s, American music curriculum marked fears of moral decay and degeneration, with mass education civilizing the child (Gustafson, 2009). Horace Mann's 1844 "Report to the Boston School Committee" supported vocal instruction classes as a practice in which the harmony of song was the model for the child's own self-regulation in society. Vocal instruction was to provide regimens to stimulate circulation that would serve to prevent poor health among the urban populations. Teaching the proper songs would remove the emotionalism of tavern and revival meetings and provide a way to regulate the moral conditions of urban life with a "higher" calling related to the nation.

Music appreciation joined vocal instruction in the curriculum by the beginning of the twentieth century. Physiological psychology about the proper amount of stimulation for the brain and body was coupled with notions of musical aesthetics, religious beliefs, and civic virtue. Singing, for example, was to give expression to the home life of industriousness and patriotism that was set against racial stereotypes of Blacks and immigrants. Minstrelsy, a satiric version of Black music and spirituals, were contrasted with the complexity of music of European "civilization." A medical expert in the 1920s, employed by the Philadelphia High School for Girls, described jazz as causing disease in young girls and society as a whole. Choral music in Portuguese education, as well, was considered as medically important as "hygienically, intellectually, morally and disciplinarily" beneficial to the child's health (Paz, 2017, p. 6).

Psychology ordered the selection and organization of music education. The scaling of musical response in the classroom classified listening habits with age-appropriate behavior. A scale of compared immature or primitive human development with those of a fully endowed capacity that corresponded to race and nationality. The progression of musical knowledge outlined in teacher manuals calculated music as a form of psychometrics associated with psychoacoustics. The "attentive listener" was one who embodied cosmopolitan values of the civilized life. That child was contrasted with the distracted listener. Carl Seashore, a psychology researcher, claimed that a full 10% of the children tested for musical talent were unfit for musical appreciation. In teaching manuals, the child who did not learn to listen to the music in a particular way was "distracted," a determinate category bound to moral and social distinctions about the child as a drifter, a name caller, a gang joiner, a juvenile offender, a joke maker, or a potential religious fanatic, having acute emotional stress and an intense interest in sex.

Psychometric tests were used to scale differences in ability. The formation of the US science curriculum in the 1920s measured "scientific ability" that has little to do with science but rather with a cultural view of science as a mode of thinking and acting as a "reasonable" person (Kirchgasler, 2017). The turn-of-the-twentieth-century general science drew on social science techniques to translate disciplinary knowledge into curricula through techniques like the developmental scale, standardized test, and the home survey. The techniques in school science became constituted as a set of norms differentiating the good, rational American citizen from children seen as belonging to populations with "unscientific minds." In stabilizing the science to be learned, difference was defined as deviation from cultural norms. The translations of science into psychological processes positioned children in developmental scales that ordered racial distinctions alongside stages of mental maturity.

The historical transformations have links to present-day science education reforms that seek to adapt science instruction for diverse subgroups, producing new distinctions and exclusions. Further, when contemporary science education is examined internationally, science is taught is not taught as a mode of inquiry or generating knowledge about the world. Textbooks project science as the mode of authority in the management of the natural world. Problem solving is learning the majesty of the procedures, styles of argument, and science as social expertise to apply to daily life (McEneaney, 2003a). When textbooks are examined in relation to scientific literacy, there is no commonalty to what constitutes its "literacy" (McEneaney, 2003b). The construction of scientific literacy embodies cultural theses about the citizen of the nation.

The Alchemy and Making Kinds of People

The alchemy of school subjects was used to consider the ways in which curriculum is developed and reformed as inscriptions of kinds of people. Through examination of its translations it becomes possible to see the cultural norms that operate to define and divide the subjects of the school—as "living up" to social commitments or in need of reform in teaching and teacher education.

The strategy of this article is to treat what is taught as the sensible, the practical, or the necessary in schooling as strange—its practices of ordering and classifying children and school subjects as fragile— and to explore the historical contingency of what otherwise is taken as naturals to the objects of schooling. The rules of school were treated as cultural practices that embody principles and norms that differentiate what is sensible, what counts as practical, and who are seen as "reasonable people." Central was how schooling and research operate to fabricate kinds of people and how these fabrications embody hopes and fears of who does and does not fit into this project. To make visible the fabrications of kinds of people is a strategy for change. It is to make fragile what is given as natural to how schools govern children and children are to govern themselves. Challenging what is taken for granted in the everyday life of teaching and the curriculum is to create potential spaces for opening up other possibilities than those that are given within contemporary frameworks.

References

Barton, D., Farrell, D., & Mourshed, M. (2013). *Education to employment: Designing a system that works.* http://www.mckinsey.com/industries/social-sector/our-insights/education-to-employment-designing-a-system-that-works

Bloch, M. (1987). Becoming scientific and professional: an historical perspective on the aims and effects of early education. In T. Popkewitz (Ed.), *The formation of school subjects: the struggle for creating an American institution* (pp. 21–62). New York: The Falmer Press.

Danziger, K. (1990). *Constructing the subject: Historical origins of psychological research.* New York: Cambridge University Press.

Darling-Hammond, L. (2006). Constructing 21st century teacher education. *Journal of Teacher Education, 57*(3), 300–314.

Dewey, J. (1990). Christianity and democracy. In J. A. Boydston (Ed.), *The collected works of John Dewey, 1882–1953. The early works of John Dewey, 1882–1898 (Electronic edition).* Carbondale, IL: Southern Illinois University. (Original work published 1967)

Diaz, J. (2017). *The paradox of making in/equality: A cultural history of reforming math for all.* New York: Routledge.

Erickson, P., Klein, J., Daston, L., Lemov, R., Sturm, T., & Gordin, M. (2013). *How reason almost lost its mind. The strange career of Cold War rationality.* Chicago: The University of Chicago Press.

Foucault, M. (1988). The political technology of individuals. In L. Martin, H. Gutman, & P. Huttan (Eds.), *Technologies of the self* (pp. 145–162). Amherst: University of Massachusetts Press.

Foucault, M. (1979). Governmentality. *Ideology and Consciousness, 6,* 5–22.

Franklin, B. (1994). *From "backwardness" to "at-risk": Childhood learning difficulties and the contradictions of school reform.* Albany: The State University of New York.

Grossman, P., McDonald, M., Hammerness, K., & Ronfeldt, M. (2008). Dismantling dichotomies in teacher education. In M. Cochran-Smith, S. Feinman-Nemser, & D. J. McIntyre (Eds.), *Handbook of research on teacher education: Enduring questions in changing contexts* (3rd ed., pp. 243–248). New York: Routledge.

Gustafson, R. (2009). *Race and curriculum: Music in childhood education.* New York: Palgrave-MacMillan.

Hall, G. S. (1924). Aspects of child life and education: The contents of children's mind on entering school. *The Princeton Review, II,* 249-272. (Original work published 1893)

Halprin, O. (2014) *Beautiful data. A history of vision and reason since 1945.* Durham: Duke University Press.

Hunter, I. (1988). *Culture and government: The emergence of literary education.* Hampshire, England: Macmillan.

Ilha, F. R. d. S. (2017). The alchemy of Brazilian physical education, the regulating of the body, and the making of kinds of people. In T. S. Popkewitz, J. Diaz, & C. Kirchgasler (Eds.), *A political sociology of educational knowledge: Studies of exclusions and difference* (pp. 135–146). New York: Routledge.

Kirchgasler, K. L. (2017). Scientific Americans: Historicizing the making of differences in early 20th-century US science education. In T. S. Popkewitz, J. Diaz, & C. Kirchgasler (Eds.), *A political sociology of educational knowledge: Studies of exclusions and difference* (pp. 89–104). New York: Routledge.

Lesko, N., & Niccolini, A. D. (2017). Progressive: Historicizing affect in education. In T. S. Popkewitz, J. Diaz, & C. Kirchgasler (Eds.), *A political sociology of educational knowledge: Studies of exclusions and difference* (pp. 70–86). New York: Routledge.

Lesko, N., & Talburt, S. (Eds.). (2011). *Youth studies: Keywords and movement.* New York: Routledge.

Martins, C. S. (2013). Genius as a historical event: Its making as a statistical object and instrument for governing schooling. In T. S. Popkewitz (Ed.), *The "reason" of schooling: Historicizing curriculum studies, pedagogy, and teacher education* (pp. 99–114). New York: Routledge.

Martins, C. S. (2017). From scribbles to details: The invention of stages of development in drawing and the government of the child. In T. S. Popkewitz, J. Diaz, & C. Kirchgasler (Eds.), *A political sociology of educational knowledge: Studies of exclusions and difference* (pp. 105–118). New York: Routledge.

McEneaney, E. (2003a). Elements of a contemporary primary school science. In G. S. Drori, J. W. Meyer, F. O. Ramirez, & E. Schofer (Eds.), *Science in the modern world polity: Institutionalization and globalization* (pp. 136–154). Stanford, CA: Stanford University Press.

McEneaney, E. (2003b). The worldwide cachet of scientific literacy. *Comparative Education Review, 47*(2), 217–237.

McKnight, D. (2003). *Schooling: The Puritan imperative and the molding of an American national identity. Education's "errand into the wilderness."* Mahwah, NJ: Lawrence Erlbaum.

Menand, L. (2001). *The metaphysical club.* New York: Farrar, Straus, and Giroux.

Ó, J. R. do. (2003). The disciplinary terrains of soul and self-government in the first map of the Educational Sciences (1879–1911). In P. Smeyers & M. Depaepe (Eds.), *Beyond empiricism: On criteria for educational research, Studia Paedoagogica 34* (pp. 105–116). Leuven, Belgium: University Press.

Paz, A. (2017). Can genius be taught? Debates in Portuguese music education (1868–1930). *European Educational Research Journal.* pp. 1–13

Popkewitz, T. (1991). *A political sociology of educational reform: Power/knowledge in teaching, teacher education and research.* New York: Teachers College Press.

Popkewitz, T. S. (2008). *Cosmopolitanism and the age of school reform: Science, education, and making society by making the child.* New York: Routledge.

Popkewitz, T. S. (2013a). The empirical and political "fact" of theory in the social and education sciences. In G. Biesta, J. Allan, & R. G. Edwards (Eds.), *Making a difference in theory: The theory question in education and the education question in theory* (pp. 13–29). London & New York: Routledge.

Popkewitz, T. S. (2013b). The impracticality of *practical knowledge* and *lived experience* in educational research. *Nordic Studies in Education, 33,* 24–39.

Popkewitz, T. S. (2017). Anticipating the future society: The cultural inscription of numbers and international large scale assessment. In S. Lindblad, D. Pettersson, & T. Popkewitz (Eds.), *Numbers, education, and making society: International assessments and its expertise* (pp. 168-194). New York: Routledge.

Reese, W. (1995). *The origins of the American high school.* New Haven, CT: Yale University Press.

Rodgers, D. T. (1998). *Atlantic crossings: Social politics in a progressive age.* Cambridge, MA: Belknap Press of Harvard University Press.

Stanic, G. (1987). Mathematics education in the United States at the beginning of the twentieth century. In T. Popkewitz (Ed.), *The formation of the school subjects: The struggle for creating an American institution* (pp. 145–175). New York: Falmer Press.

Tröhler, D. (2011). *Languages of education: Protestant legacies in educationalization of the world, national identities, and global aspirations (T. Popkewitz, Foreword).* New York: Routledge.

Tröhler, D., Popkewitz, T. S., & Labaree, D. F. (Eds.). (2011). *Schooling and the making of citizens in the long nineteenth century: Comparative visions.* New York: Routledge.

Valero, P. (2017). Mathematics for all, economic growth, and the making of the body and the making of kinds of people. In T. S. Popkewitz, J. Diaz, & C. Kirchgasler (Eds.), *A political sociology of educational knowledge: Studies of exclusions and difference* (pp. 119–134). New York: Routledge.

CHAPTER SEVENTEEN

Image Management?
Sites of the Real, Visual Culture, and
Digital Present-Futures in Education[1]

Bernadette Baker

Introduction

IN THE SECOND decade of the 2000s the Australian government reported that the country had reached a digital tipping point where the majority of citizens had access to digital media in the home and engaged in multiscreening (Australian Communications and Media Authority, 2016-17). Such tipping points are generally seen as positive achievements and tied to a plethora of perceptions of advantage and access, from greater facility with digital literacies, to information retrieval on an unprecedented scale, to new employment opportunities, global connectivity, and hope for innovation. From education to economics, such events take for granted the truth, morality and fecundity of visual culture meeting digital media, positioning such thresholds as indicators of resources to be tapped and mined. In the field of education, for instance, while concern has been raised by teachers over perceived shortened attention spans of students in one direction, in another direction visual culture meeting digital media has been positioned as providing additional tools in a toolbox of instruction that enhances and includes different learning styles and addresses participation issues for previously disengaged students.[2]

---

1   Revised keynote address, Department of Educational Leadership, University of Massachusetts Dartmouth, November 10, 2014.

2   This chapter is not focused on social media use in classrooms, where teachers in some countries have raised what are believed to be negative impacts. *The Washington Post* in the US, for instance, reported the following results:

> A Pew Research Center survey found that nearly 90 percent of teachers believe that digital technologies were creating an easily distracted generation with short attention spans. About 60 percent said it hindered students' ability to write and communicate face to face, and almost half said it hurt critical thinking and their ability to do homework. Also, 76 percent of teachers believed students are being conditioned by the internet to find quick answers, leading to a loss of concentration (Porter, 2013, https://www.washingtonpost.com/blogs/therootdc/post/the-problem-with-technology-in-schools/2013/01/28/cf13d-c6c-6963- 11e2-ada3-d86a4806d5ee_blog.html?noredirect=on&utm_term=.90bfa5d5964c

Such issues will be underscored in the section on typical challenges.

If there is a wider or bigger-picture critical aspect to reports of events such as digital tipping points it is usually about unwarranted unevenness in access (OECD, 2017) and in the non-objective nature of internet/film/television content (Anderson, Rainie & Luchsinger, 2018), both of which are legitimate concerns.

Rather than glorify or vilify events such as tipping points, however, this chapter examines some legacies and implications from a curriculum studies perspective, drawing more heavily on history, philosophy and the politics of knowledge in tracing conditions of possibility for phenomena at hand. In particular, the chapter reapproaches the intersection of visual culture and digital media through a "quantum genealogy" which draws together several nonlinear layers that enable questions about how sites of the real became tied to conceptions of self and knowledge, and the role that the changing destiny of "the image" has and may continue to play within such triangulations. A quantum genealogy takes up a Foucauldian-inspired analytics without presuming a neat or consecutive ordering of timespace (Foucault, 1977). Timespace in this sense may be integral but not indexical, a series of references to "location" that does not, as Itty Abraham (2006) underscores within postcolonial technoscience, automatically reduce "knowledge" to "place" and that does not at the same time presume a decontextualized universal horizon or avoid marking chronological time, "ages," "epistemes" and so on as facilitators. Disparate events may be drawn into the same neighborhood, linked not by presumptions about spatiotemporal proximity but by quantum leaps, by compelling formalist discursive features that enable insights through the non-linearity of coincidence. As such, the chapter focuses selectively here on the vicissitudes of the image across various incarnations of so-called Western thought not because to do so solves multiple urgent problems in the field but because not to may inadvertently cause many more in the age of the *technium*. Given the "Westernness" of the invention of technologies such as television, film, the arparnet, the internet, social media and so on, it remains important to put issues on the table that help us think about what might be elaborations of prior tendencies, including forms of domination, and what may be altering the landscape of education so profoundly that we need to engage with it rather than be passively positioned by it.

I. Visual Culture, Digital Media

What gets to count as an image has been contested moreso than many other concepts or things, in part because more recently whether "something" called an image is a concept or thing or inbetween circularly plays into the concern for quiddity. In everyday usage, we might concede that today an image is a representation of something else, that it stands in for either object or for reputation, that you can hang a picture but not an image and that reference to an image entails ambiguity.

If we were to examine the intersection of visual culture and digital media in contemporary circumstances, drawing upon commonsensical notions of the visual and the digital and of what an image might refer to, ignoring the historico-philosophical vagaries, we might document the coming of *moving pictures* in a variety of formats as of importance, historicize this is in terms of nationalized units (recording digital tipping points "in Australia," for example), attribute it a linguistic code such as Anglophone and map the uptake of new technologies accordingly.

Such a standard analytical move with its mainstream historiography could then proceed rather smoothly as a History of Firsts in Australia. Important moments to mention would subsequently arise such as the first government made film worldwide in 1899 (produced by the state of Queensland's department of agriculture), the first full-length narrative feature film ever, *The Story of the Kelly Gang*, shown in 1906, the first experimental broadcast of television in Melbourne in 1929, the coming of moving pictures into the living room via black-and-white television amid the official launch of television in 1956, and the controversy over color television in which government agencies debated whether the Australian population was potentially too vulnerable to withstand the seduction of color in the living room (http://aso.gov.au/chronology/1970s/). The list might also include the invention of arparnet in the US (1969), internet in the US (1983) and the World Wide Web in the US (first commercial providers 1989–1993, with Australia's adoption rates in the 2000s being one of the fastest in the world), and it could additionally note forthcoming satellite-free and infrastructure-free inventions (http://www.rogerclarke.com/II/OzIo4.html#Beg).

Such a chronology could then be layered with statistics pointing to the digital tipping point or positing that 49% of employed Australians could be classified as digital workers. Further notable records could then be narrated: between 2013 and 2015 Australia did not just reach but exceeded the digital tipping point, meaning that over 50% of the country owned three electronic devices—a smartphone, a tablet and a laptop—while 15.8 million Australians had internet access at home by June 2015. Moreover, youth usage indicated that 70% of 14- to 30-year-olds chose the internet instead of traditional offline sources such as television, listening to music, reading books or going to the movies. Of this, long-form content dominated, meaning that 72% binged on such content by watching several episodes at once, whether via download, television or streamed.

Moreover, international comparisons could then be mined. Australia had more "digital omnivores," for example, at 53%, than the US (37%) and Japan (17%), but fewer than Norway and China (57% and 63% respectively) in the same year. The international focus could be modified, however, by noting the problems within: while the internet is now a part of most Australians' daily lives, there's an estimated 1.1 million who have never accessed the internet (as of June 2014). Age and income, rather than race or gender alone, remained the key factors associated with being offline, with 7% of people aged 65 and over, and 83% earning an annual income of less than $30,000, indicating the continued existence of the "digital divide."

Typical Challenges

These kinds of statistics-as-facts reported within official government agencies such as ACMA are the common genre of federal reports in many locations, not just Australia, presuming the subject is a sighted observer, that the numbers are about a collective self and how a "we" consumes things. In addition to all the "good things" and possibilities that the intersection of visual culture and digital media has opened, critical educational commentary has raised some by-now familiar and common challenges. The educational technology, digital media and programming literature is replete with questions around issues such as those already raised like the digital divide and inequality of access, as well as biases in screen-based subject matter and the conservative value sets of computer programmers and coders (Caliskan, Bryson & Narayan, 2017; O'Neil, 2016; Van Deursen & Van Dijk, 2015).

Such general criticisms are rarely delivered from the perspective of frameworks like post-, anti-, and decolonial studies or postcolonial technoscience, however. In those fields, more provocative questions are able to emerge, such as which worldviews made digital media and visibilizing technologies matter and why? (Prasad, 2008). What do the "trading zones" around the "network society" mean for the future of distributive logics? (Castells, 2010). What relationships does visual culture and digital media have to communities, indigenous and beyond, that survived for centuries with rich cosmologies and different kinds of travel, transportation, and transmogrification strategies that do not always entail a screen? (DuBois, 2009). And have such screen-based inventions simply been highways for American military enhancement? (Naughton, 2016).

In teacher education, the typical challenges revolve less around geopolitics and more around instrumentality, such as questions of edutainment, of raced and gendered biases in educational software, of dis/ability in/exclusion, in the repositioning of teachers-as-facilitator and their elision as knowledge-holders, in the production of children-as-citizen-consumers, and in perceptions of anti-social or anti-engagement behavior even in the midst of peer-group-based collaborative projects (Lewin, 2015; Olsson & Edman-Stålbrant, 2008).

In broader techno-literature, however, the classroom is not the focus. Rather, the structures of coding in its binary format, the ontological flattening this entails, the limits on creativity and memory this imposes, the reduction of depth of understanding to breaking a whole down into component parts, the transformation of the "social" and "individuation" and the minimization of the "transcendent" or "ineffable" can and have been raised (Hansen, 2012; Hayles, 2012; Stiegler, 2009, 2014).

Last, the meeting point between visual culture and digital media has not been challenged simply around sales and products but potentially critiqued for "the brave new world" kinds of scenarios feared which sometimes shade into the apocalyptic. Rather than just positioning new technologies as salvific and as rescuer from the most deleterious aspects of human behavior like environmental destruction, they can also be seen as vestiges of other logics—from neugenics (selective human eradication) to human genocide (total eradication of all humans). This scenario is painted especially via engagement with transhumanist movements that are seeking to store human consciousness in a machinic, non-human unit and the research into artificial intelligence (AI) inventions that exceed and make obsolete the question of what is the human good at and what is the machine good at (Bostrom, 2014; Tegmark, 2017).

II. Quantum Counter-Histories, the Image, and the Real

A quantum genealogical approach suggests different pathways for rethinking such nationalized and quantified narratives and the typical critical challenges that are raised in their wake. In particular, it makes available counter-histories that do not "embody" the theme as if it is understood a priori. That is, the points below will not be made by using a slew of "visual images" as if both terms are somehow settled and operational. Rather, I want to take a step back from such obviousness and ask how explanations for current depictions of "the state of affairs" came to be commonsensically staged in the above ways, what the heritages entailed in contemporary narratives imply in terms of challenges for digital present-futures and how image management has come to matter as a result and might now be reconsidered.

Ambiguity over the whatness of an image has many and long heritages that pertain at a minimum to a metaphysics of presence, where at issue is whether there is a transcendental organizing principle behind and beyond that which we think we encounter as real. Crucial in this is a different understanding of labeling heritages, such as "Western," which operate not as unperturbed or predetermined (Said, 1979) but as deployed, as being made and made to matter (Baker, 2013). For instance, for Itty Abraham (2006) Western becomes western through nation, science and colonialism yet not without having to continuously invent and reinvent such belief:

> Modernity, nation, and later, state all pass through and are interpellated in the institutions and cultures of modern western science. However, colonial and later postcolonial science was always a contradictory formation. Though science presents itself as universal knowledge, it is never able to do so unambiguously in a location distant from its putative origins in Western Europe. Science's conjoint history with colonial and imperial power implies a constant representation of its condition in order to pass as universal knowledge in the colony. (Abraham, 2006, p. 211)

For His Holiness the Dalai Lama, however, it is the tendency to explain everything in rational terms, through the un/conscious mind, and without the tools of previous lives that point to the West as western and as limited in what can be challenged:

Underlying all Western modes of analysis is a strong rationalistic tendency—an assumption that all things can be accounted for. And on top of that, there are constraints created by certain premises that are taken for granted. For example, recently I met with some doctors at a university medical school. They were talking about the brain and stated that thoughts and feelings were the result of different chemical reactions and changes in the brain. So I raised the question: Is it possible to conceive the reverse sequence, where the thought gives rise to the sequence of chemical events in the brain? However, the part I found most interesting was the answer the scientist gave. He said, "We start from the premise that all thoughts are products or functions of chemical reactions in the brain." So it is simply a kind of rigidity, a decision to not challenge their own way of thinking. (His Holiness the Dalai Lama, & Cutler, 1998, pp. 5-6)

Whereas for Michael Sells, the points of reference in the construction of Western-ess involve forms of interpenetration and hybridity preceding, including and beyond modernist science/religion or body/mind divides. Rather, the West is

the legacy of the encounter of Semitic prophetic traditions with the Graeco-Roman cultural world. These traditions shared both a highly de-veloped Ptolemaic symbolic cosmology and a central assertion of one, transcendent principle of reality. Rather than focusing upon the textual borrowings of one tradition from another, it seems more profitable to see these traditions as competing within a partially shared intellectual and symbolic world, defining themselves in conversation with one another and against one another. (Sells, 1994, pp. 4–5)

As this cursory trace of conflicting approaches indicates, mapping trajectories in "Western" thought is a controversial affair that often but not always begins with what postcolonial studies calls "the tyranny of Greece" (Bernal, 1987) or a "first in Europe, then elsewhere" mentality (Chakrabarty, 2000). In regard to the destiny and vagaries of the image, ancient Athens is, however, a significant meeting point, trading zone and timespace, not for what it offers but for what it cannot. The orientation to the image in Socratic times poses a counter-narrative to contemporary trust in digital media and filmic representation in ways that have largely been forgotten or buried. For instance, a core feature of philosoph-ical life in ancient Athens was an obsession with that which appears to moves on its own or has a "self-moving soul" relative to that which appeared to require something else to make it move (Baker, 2001). In a world without electricity, while it seemed clear that a hand imparts speed and direction to a javelin, one could not see a hand moving the sun or moon. The fascination for the difference between stillness and movement and which kind of soul inheres in which object arguably today inhabits a Western curiosity around kinetics and locomotion and belief in movement as equaling some kind of change (Baker, 2001). While very differently rendered in a "religious" Plato relative to a "scientistic" Aristotle and their interlocutors centuries later, invoking prime movers, God, Creator or gods; first principles; power; causality; or their analogues is part of this legacy of the obsession with dynamics, movement, change of place, shift in appearance and apparent independence in locomotion.

This obsession with movement, change, forms of locomotion, and so on, does not attribute high status to that which is fleeting in scholars such as Plato and, in fact, the reverse. The image, like all objects and unalike objects, is not to be fully trusted. It is not the site of the real or the site of the experience of the real, nor of Truth. In Platonic revelationalist epistemology, especially in *The Sophist*, *image*, *imitation* and *likeness* arise in the context of "self" as a problem that needs education to be "fixed." Soul-self sits behind and above behavior, speech, art production and writing, which are inferior pursuits. Because soul-self is both human and beyond human, it is not the case that there is a solid, fleshy objective perceiver sitting behind the eyes. Perception of daily things through the flesh, like phenomenological accounts, participates in deception and is subject to changeability:

> STRANGER: We know, of course, that he who professes by one art to make all things is really a painter, and by the painter's art makes resemblances of real things which have the same name with them; and he can deceive the less intelligent sort of young children, to whom he shows his pictures at a distance, into the belief that he has the absolute power of making whatever he likes.

> THEAETETUS: Certainly.

> STRANGER: And may there not be supposed to be an imitative art of reasoning? Is it not possible to enchant the hearts of young men by words poured through their ears, when they are still at a distance from the truth of facts, by exhibiting to them fictitious arguments, and making them think that they are true, and that the speaker is the wisest of men in all things?

> THEAETETUS: Yes; why should there not be another such art?

> STRANGER: But as time goes on, and their hearers advance in years, and come into closer contact with realities, and have learnt by sad experience to see and feel the truth of things, are not the greater part of them compelled to change many opinions which they formerly entertained, so that the great appears small to them, and the easy difficult, and all their dreamy speculations are overturned by the facts of life?

> THEAETETUS: That is my view, as far as I can judge, although, at my age, I may be one of those who see things at a distance only.

> STRANGER: And the wish of all of us, who are your friends, is and always will be to bring you as near to the truth as we can without the sad reality. And now I should like you to tell me, whether the Sophist is not visibly a magician and

imitator of true being; or are we still disposed to think that he may have a true knowledge of the various matters about which he disputes?

THEAETETUS: But how can he, Stranger? Is there any doubt, after what has been said, that he is to be located in one of the divisions of children's play?

STRANGER: Then we must place him in the class of magicians and mimics. (Plato, 360 BCE/2013, *The Sophist*, pp. 155–156)

Discussions of knowing, Being, image and "seeing" across Platonic texts further indicate that while seeing through the eyes may be considered the highest of the senses it is still not to be trusted (Baker, in press). Accordingly, image, simulacra, shadow, project, art are negative, low-status terms that are referred to as illusions—as non-objects because they do not have real presence. Since perception has no access to Being, it has no access to Truth. The site of capital "T" Truth is the Forms and of the experience of the real, the soul-self. Forms can be apprehended as Absolute only through putting "oneself" in the right condition—shutting sensory portals down which in turn purifies, brings "light," brings one "home" and delivers discernment of utter Truth.

Technologies of Self

Platonic considerations unravel presumptions about a sighted observer sitting behind the eyes, looking out, making use of digital media and multiscreening in Australia or elsewhere. While it raises to the threshold of noticeability how belief in "self"—individual, collective, soulful, conscious, unconscious and so on—has become a repetitive pattern in many forms of literature it leaves open the question of how a sense of self emerges out of a unit often characterized as social, such as a nationalized self, literate self, and so on. How is "self" thought to contain "matter" especially, a matter that ought to be inspected, dissected and assigned different roles and meaning? While space does not permit forays into such transitions and translations which have been taken up elsewhere, especially in histories of human dissection (see Baker & Saari, 2018; Carlino, 1999; Sawday, 1995), the disconnect between Platonic revelationism and the so-called Scientific Revolution of empiricism and materialism is a massive one.

For Foucault, different technologies of self that produced perception of and belief in self and others emanated side by side with some becoming more dominant and others more or less lost. The different technologies emerged across Greco-Roman, Christian and post-Christian tracts (with the Gnostic exception) and heralded unique relations between "truth" and "the Subject," embodied in different practical and everyday "arts of existence." Post-Descartes, for Foucault, recognition of self has to go through "mind." Consciousness is defined as access to Being and the idea of "care of the self" atrophies. Such technologies refer to practices "which permit individuals to effect by their own means or with the help of others a certain number of operations on their bodies and souls, thoughts, conduct, and way of being, so as to transform themselves in order to attain a certain state of happiness, purity, wisdom, perfection or immortality" (Foucault 1985, p. 18). Such technologies or operations were considered integral to subjectivation—believing in "self" as an entity that can be worked upon practically and producing a self–knowledge–reality triad. Crucially, the post-Cartesian version of technologies of self operate almost as capstone, as the apex of believing that self-experience-the real were one and the same or more accurately "the movement by which, in ancient thought, from the Hellenistic and imperial period, the real was thought as the place of the experience of the self" (Foucault, 1985, p. 465).

From Oral to Written: Visual Culture as Reading/Writing

While all the effects of print do not reduce to its effects on the use of visual space, many of the other effects do relate to this use in various ways. (Ong, 2002, p. 115)

With the focus on the relationship between truth and subject-formation, Foucault's analysis of technologies of self posited that spirituality, philosophy, and science were roughly distinguishable in a post-Cartesian timespace. Science in the main became focused on methods of producing truth, whereas philosophy considered whether true and false could be separated, with spirituality differently concerned with the condition of the subject: "I think we could call 'spirituality' the search, practice, and experience through which the subject carries out the necessary transformations on himself in order to have access to the truth. We will call 'spirituality' then the set of these researches, practices, and experiences, which may be purifications, ascetic exercises, renunciations, conversions of looking, modifications of existence, etc., which are, not for knowledge but for the subject, for the subject's very being, the price to be paid for access to the truth" (Foucault, 2005, p. 15).

Accompanying such separations, operations and practices was the invention and spread of what is now called literacy. For Ong, more widespread reading/writing technologies and experiences produced not just new possibilities and new daily practices, but new *minds*: "Without writing, the literate mind would not and could not think as it does, not only when engaged in writing but normally even when it is composing its thoughts in oral form. More than any other single invention, writing has transformed human consciousness" (Ong, 2002, p. 77). For Ong, the visual-as-optical, as seeing code through the ocular portal and on a slate that could be returned to, was a pivotal rearrangement of human relationships, subjectivity-formation and sense of interiority:

> The critical and unique breakthrough into new worlds of knowledge was achieved within human consciousness not when simple semiotic marking was devised but when a coded system of visible marks was invented whereby a writer could determine the exact words that the reader would generate from the text. This is what we usually mean today by writing in its sharply focused

sense . . . Writing, in this ordinary sense, was and is the most momentous of all human technological inventions. It is not a mere appendage to speech. Because it moves speech from the oralaural to a new sensory world, that of vision, it transforms speech and thought as well. (Ong, 2002, p. 83)

It is beyond the scope of this chapter to reiterate the multifarious analyses of discourses of vision—from *revelation* to *ocularcentrism* to *postoptical ecologies*—and their implications for education and perception (see Baker, 2017; Crary, 2001; Tomas, 1988). Shifting sensorial hierarchies have been analyzed especially throughout the 1990s and early 2000s with typical divides between Hellenic (seeing) and Hebraic traditions (hearing) and between medieval (ocularphobic) and modern (ocularcentric) modalities postulated (Clark, 2007; Jay, 1993). What are of significance here are the inherently double-edged references unevenly involved in vision-truth couplets across Hellenic, Hebraic, medieval and modern epistemes in which there were multiple appeals to an "inward turn" similar to a "mind's eye" for viewing an interior and to an "outward turn" to "physiological eyes" as organs of sight (Jay, 1993). Such double-edgedness operated not just in "modernist" texts but in the Platonic revelationism considered earlier. For Plato, "knowledge" of the Forms—as both a teleological ascent/goal and as unobjectifiable—is considered the highest point in the epistemological pyramid. His analyses rely simultaneously upon eyesight being distrusted when cast upon paintings, images, shadows on walls, and so on (*The Republic*); on eyesight being elevated above smell, hearing, touch and taste as portals (such as in the *Timaeus*); and on the Forms being knowable only through a kind of introspection that exceeds the interior/exterior problematic and "empirical" senses of knowing (such as in the *Phaedrus*, *Sophist* and *Republic*) (Baker, in press).

Such recognition of double-edges raises the question of visual essentialism—the presumption that the visual is the optical and the optical is the sighted. Even if terminology associated with "the visual" is understood as beyond the eyes, eyewitnessing, and the ocular, how is the beyond decided? Does appealing to a beyond imply the continued operational presence of that which it supposedly exceeds in order to notice that something else is beyond? And in that case, isn't noticing more of a "'visual" act than any other? Visual essentialism seems difficult to avoid as the circle starts to close, that is, when "language" and "the visible" or "noticeable" are assumed interrelated.

Thing, Sensorium, Representation, Rationality

Significantly, however, not all "languages" link terms for vision, the visual, the optical or the eyes to terms for truth, knowledge and Being. While even approaching such questions via the presumption that "language" is an isolated unit of signifier–signified relationships is problematic and while separating words from things or verbal from visual is a recent Western epistemic assumption that is difficult to suspend, the very terms used, including the sensorium, remain part of a problem that can be explicated. Tyler (1984) argues, for instance that *thing, sensorium representation,* and *rationality* are mutually implicated in SAE (Standard Average European, i.e., Indo-European root languages), for it is the role of the senses in such languages to represent the things thinking thinks: "The sensorium 'makes sense,' and the only quarrel in the philosophical traditions of SAE is over the functions and priorities of the different sensory modes; for questions about the sensorium are meaningful only in the context of representation" (Tyler, 1984, p. 23). For Tyler, such self-implicating terminology restricts what it is possible to challenge:

> True challenges to all of these key limiters are practically nonexistent in the philosophical tradition of SAE, for such a challenge would only be classified as nonthought, irrational, beyond the limit of language. Our thinking about thinking presupposes the commonsense meaningfulness of these tropes and rejects whatever falls outside them. That is the reason 'reason' is not universal; it is relative not to an a priori form of thought, but to a discourse that forms a cultural a priori sedimented from common sense. (Tyler, 1984, p. 36)

This is not the case in the Dravidian group of languages in South Asia that includes Koya, that is, where thought and thinking do not involve the idea of ideas as representation. Tyler notes how the structure of SAE sensory concepts implicates representation as a central issue in a way that Koya does not. The absence of a metaphysical category corresponding to "thing," which is the enabling concept for representation means that South Indian and SAE ideas of "substance" do not correspond. In Koya, substance is not a permanent unchanging essence, it is the stuff of *maya,* the illusory, endlessly changing flux. It is further linked to concepts of transmigration, and beyond "Western" concern for or conceptions of representing. Dravidian terms for "knowing/thinking," for instance, do not separate knowing and feeling in the way SAE terms do. "Rationality" is not just knowing/thinking but a way of *feeling/knowing.* The material world and the meaning of knowing is derived from intentionality and desire:

> These "feelings" are not irrational sources of subjective error that rationalism must contest and defeat in the quest for objective truth, but are instead the very source and enabling condition of any rationality whatever. What for SAE is only a disturbing philosophical afterthought in the form of phenomenology is, in Indian tradition, the starting point and foundation of philosophy. (Tyler, 1984, p. 36)

In sum, the idea of "visual culture" and "the image," their relationship to knowledge-claims, in mainstream Western philosophies and in non-SAE languages such as the Dravidian group are not tied to the same value systems, conceptual clusters or analytical strategies for truth-production, nor are they framed by the same cosmological investments or onto-epistemological spatializations. "Western" obsessions with movement, change of place, locomotion and shift in appearance, as well as metaphors of light/dark, metaphors of seeing-knowing, metaphors of perspective, angles, horizons, and so on have not only become linked but have also garnered cultural authority. Significantly, however, that cultural authority is not simply able to be equated with "high"- and "low"-status explanations or practices, as the following section indicates.

III. Destiny of the Image?

The destiny of the image, if there is one, is one that has been continuously haunted by whether an image "exists" and can be described as a "real" object (thing), as standing in for a real object (representation of "thingness") or as in-between subject/object and object/non-object. Such a trajectory does not match up neatly to isolated theories of sight and the ocular. It parallels instead those moments when becoming/being, truth, knowledge and appeals to the real move into different alliances and hierarchies in onto-epistemological scales, and especially those pertaining to belief in a self. Plato's versions of the image accords it a lesser place, for the image is outside truth, associated with becoming, as simulacrum. Medieval religious debates in Europe posited different roles for that which were declared as images. Debates over iconology, over metaphysics of presence and whether representing God in pictorial form was circumscribing a deity and therefore sacrilegious abounded. The advent of the seeming Scientific Revolution deployed witnessing, observation and images differently, positing images as representation of representations supported by verbal or written struts, placing increasing emphasis on pictures in textbooks with the aid of words.

This raises the issue of when veracity is attributed to "the image" and when it is or has been withheld. Since the Scientific Revolution, for example, mistrust in the consistency and objectivity of what comes through a visual portal—visual-as-optics—has been a significant driver of new theories of perception, the unconscious, and observer bias. This was especially salient in the late nineteenth-century questioning of the effects of drugs, alcohol, magic shows, head injuries and hypnosis in clinical trials, medical practice and public demonstrations (Baker, 2013). Alongside the "denigration of vision" since then, however, has come a renewed contemporary trust in practices such as medical imaging, like the colorful pictures generated from brains scans, MRI and the like today (de Rijcke & Beaulieu, 2014; Prasad, 2008). To that end, the role of the image seems to have moved from *illusion* to the *unrepresentable* to *representation* to *emanation of the real* to contemporary *aesthetics as like/dislike*, attraction/repulsion, delight/aversion.

Such vicissitudes point to the complexity of what is *claimed* as "the human" amid such shifts. For, if there is such a claim related to the destiny of the image it pertains to the image's transportive effects on particular kinds of beings with particular kinds of subjectivities: "if there is beauty in the image this is because of what it takes us to—as in an evocation" (Lechte, 2012, p. 136). Lechte's recognition that the image has been recuperated in much contemporary life as a positive and sometimes as seemingly incontestable in terms of both truth-production and the aesthetics of attraction points to "the fusion of audience and art work" (Lechte, 2012, p. 141) that now requires new analytical strategies. In particular, it underscores the need for new *aesthetic theories of epistemology* to reapproach twenty-first-century challenges of and in visual culture, digital media and teaching-learning.

More Than Digital Media and Generation Multiscreen: Digital Present-Futures

New aesthetic theories of epistemology focus moreso today on reception than perception. Aesthetic theories are now considering the dynamism produced through the death of the artist-scientist, where the "reality" manifested is modified by the immediacy and immanence of reception (not perception)—extending notions of "agency" (Lechte, 2012). Several examples suggest some new directions for aesthetic theories of epistemology and significantly such outlines are not meeting at a common point or drawing the same analytical arcs but rather underscoring the use-by date of standard critical theories that offer prepackaged and essentialized human qualities. Lechte, for instance, points to the problem that ensues in the wake of the death of the artist-scientist—the operationality of an older transcendence/immanence binary: "an investigation is required in order to find out whether there is a place for quality and transcendence in digital art in relation to experience, as opposed to what I call the *subjection of aesthetics to experimentation* and thus to a description of *how* art things work or are constructed" (Lechte, 2012, p. 141, original emphasis). Here, Lechte's question and intervention underscores how the reconfiguration of the verbal–visual couplet entails reversible relations between the oral and the pictorial, a reversal that seems to urge a decontextualization focused on a "how to" and that is increasingly understood as neuralized rather than historicized.

Lechte's concern regarding the collapse of everything into an instrumental, descriptive and potentially neural "how to" is echoed in what Stiegler (2014) identifies as the intensification of decontextualization. The decline of print after alphabetization arguably enables a first wave of decontextualization. With digitization, comes another, where event–input–reception collapse and become co-incident. One upshot of this is that "local" is always the same. It becomes the version of "reception" while standardization/decontextualization operate as a structural feature in background.

This points to a third, major related concern articulated in a somewhat different realm for a discussion of aesthetics—contemplative turn research. For Ergas, there is a hierarchy of disciplines with experimental science at the top of the food chain operating as the structural feature in the background. Ergas (2017) addresses this hierarchy differently, however, and aesthetically, from a different direction of what might be opened and not simply foreclosed. The emergence of phenomena such as the contemplative turn and contemplative inquiry coupled with experimental science and random control approaches around practices like meditation or mindfulness can not only reaffirm "science's" primal position but potentially undermine it, pointing to beyond-Kantian notions of reason and enlarging what can count as reception, perception, method and art:

> The suggestion of "contemplative inquiry" as part of science means not merely exploring what could be conceived as a "spiritual practice" through conventional second and third person inquiry . . . It rather pushes the boundaries of scientific methodology for its current methodology delimits our understanding of phenomena. . . . This is a science that does not settle for Kantian reason that is confined to perceive phenomena within time and space. It rather considers a perceptional apparatus that takes us perhaps as fartherest from a cold-objectivist reason as one can get, and conceives of it as a legitimate and complementary source for knowing; a science that in fact leads to an *epistemology of love*. (Ergas, 2014, pp. 14–15, original emphasis)

Ergas can be understood to suggest how the intersection of visual culture and digital media is not simply being left to binge television watching, social media or educational gaming in classrooms, but is simultaneously impacting scientific methods in ways they might not be able to account for in the present. The meeting of the neuro turn and the contemplative turn *through visual imaging* portends the blurring of fact/fiction in new ways, highlighting one of "the image's" old roles. Here, the reliance upon imaging re-marks our inability to tell what is being "seen" as the object and whether it is "real" or not in "empirical" terms. This time, however, there is a rerouting of sensation that places the uncertainty within the domain of *cognification* rather than "spirituality," which then structures the hope and the holding out for a recuperation—what Ergas describes as an epistemology of love—but which now must pass through neuroscience and "learnification" for affirmation.

Conclusion: Beyond Images— Techno-literacies, Networks and the New?

> While visibility can signal recognition and empowerment of formerly "invisible others," it can also imply an erasure of difference or a hypervisibilization of certain bodies within the normalizing gaze of racial discourse, medicine, or regimes of gender. Invisibility, however, is also a double-edged sword. Even as the workings of police corruption and the unresponsiveness of the law depended upon techniques of obfuscation in Trinidad, the justice-seeking tactics of my interlocutors also utilized rumored presences and invisible forces to expand the limits of political struggle. These considerations ask us to think about how "invisibility" and forms of hypervisibility might work in concert, questioning the tacit assumption that visibility is necessarily equated with power and recognition while invisibility signifies the obverse. (Crosson, 2013)

The earlier quantum genealogy gestures toward three related sets of implications or imagined present-futures, not as resolutions for the nationalized narratives of digital tipping points, uneven access and consumption patterns, but as incitements to wider and deeper discourse in a field bound up by and in the collapse between visual culture, digital media, truth claims and the generational transmission of values. The implications reach into (1) reworked conceptions of selfhood and techno-literacies, (2) knowledge-production and networks and (3) reality-claims and the new. Together, these couplings and tropes point to both a more traditionally humanist concern over "agency" and the very redefinition or refiguration of such possibilities in light of new aesthetic epistemologies that may no longer lie strictly in "human" hands.

First in regard to the more traditionally humanist orientations, the implications for the rewriting of selfhood at the intersection of visual culture, digital media and the image are profound yet predictable at a certain level. One of the key eventuations to consider, matched by current curriculum trends in the secondary school, may be the deployment of such a nexus for the fabrication of entrepreneurial selves. Entrepreneurial selves with techno-literacies embody expectations to live in a constant state of dynamism and change, where lifelong learning produces both innovation and stress and where the profit motive is normalized as the only purpose of schooling. In this scenario, Becoming over Being is the reversal achieved relative to Platonic cosmology, a reversal where competition and pressure are thought to unleash new potentials as well as reinforce the infantilization of teachers, instructors, students and more. In this projection, teachers, instructors, professors, parents and students are "themselves" simply objects of software's enactment, moving and being moved from instruct or perish, publish or perish, parent or perish and pass or perish mentalities to an innovate/entertain or perish approach. This begs the question of why digital tipping points or multiscreening would subsequently matter; what diffusion, uptake and a mainstream History of Firsts were/are actually thought to achieve beyond records of consumption; and, whether the "inclusion" and spread of such technologies has or can facilitate responses to older forms of domination or just spreads them in new guise? More widespread adoptions of AI and VR (virtual reality) technologies challenge such for/against narratives, however. Via AI and VR, rewriting the self or challenging self/other dynamics is less the question than who or what is "the subject" that "acts"? Here, "the human" in any recognizable or familiar form is at stake. Redefining an interior/exterior problematic, under the auspices of neuralization, cognification and automation, raises questions over where causality lies within behavioral analysis, "self"-shaping, and innovation. It leaves open to consideration what explanations—if even tolerated or desired—would be suited to whatever the markers of "change" or "movement" might become, especially in scenarios where the machine "thought" of the "innovation" first.

This intersects directly with how and whether knowledge-production is "seen" and the fundamental arrangements that are currently shifting to reposition "Man" as not the main knowledge-carrier, repository, or inventor. The emergence of the *technium* signals that programmable units are becoming more lifelike in the everyday sense, blurring the line between human and non, potentially spawning a super-organism that has its own urges and tendencies. Such an eventuation would require what Cooper Ramo (2016) calls a *seventh sense*—an appreciation and understanding of how connection changes the nature of an object, anticipating how something from anywhere could impact everywhere and rethinking power as networked rather than sovereign, not simply human, and beyond the formation of "networked learning communities." The kind of analytics suited to such redefined circumstances where "Man's" knowledge within the container of "the body" no longer necessarily equals power Khanna (2016) calls *connectography*—a process that could potentially generate new "maps" that exceed the geopolitics of the nation-state and that examine networks, infrastructure, data ownership and beyond-satellite positionings of new federations and alliances and not just from or via the human observer's resources.

Reality-claims often presume the conscious human observer who is making them, however. In a scenario where taking AI and combining it with something else will be a major trope of innovation, cognifying becomes the main mode of Becoming and Life becomes Information. Here, potentially, augmented "humans" plus AI can redefine the nature of thought, of will and of learning, bringing into relief the relative youth of the internet, with the most massive transformations yet to come. In particular, virtual, augmented and mixed reality where "knowledge" is coded differently as "bits" can raise not just accessibility questions, from democratized to exclusivity of access, but also ontological questions regarding the nature of what endures and what not. If analysis, data mining and programming are bequeathed increasingly to AI and bots, then what forms would processing information, efficiency and productivity take, what purposes would such analytics fulfill, and what would be the point or the "Aha!" in visual culture meeting digital media?

I want to end here, however, on a less predictable note that again refuses the good/bad, salvific/apocalyptic tendencies of the educational and techno fields and places a different kind of plate at the buffet of food for thought, projections, or imagined present-futures. Specifically, I want to raise the provocations posed by non-philosophy and by so-called non-Western cosmologies such as that being approached in the opening quote to this final section. For non-philosophy, such concerns, envisionings or questions as outlined earlier around shifting dynamics of human–self-knowledge–reality are philosophical, stuck within the circle that composes them, pointing to the perpetual mixture of transcendence/immanence that constitute debates over Being and the Other. In "non-Western" cosmologies such as those being invoked in reapproaching the role of spirits of the dead, rumored presences and "invisible forces" against the policing strategies used in Trinidad, invisibilization and hypervisibility can work in curious ways, both in concert and beyond the perceptual-experiential structures of Western anthropology. The challenges posed by non-philosophy and more-than-philosophy, such as Laruelle (2013) and Crosson (2013), from very different starting points and concerns, are not about sustaining a contemporary status quo or order of things. It is not to keep the visible/invisible binary, the image/real binary, non-philosophy or "non-Western cosmologies" within a margin that helps to constitute what philosophy is by periodically "pricking" its consciousness and giving it its title. Rather, in unplugging the tacit assumption that "visibility is necessarily equated with power and recognition, while invisibility signifies the obverse" (Crosson) and in pushing beyond societies headed toward "a perpetual state of producing novelty" (Laruelle) a different ethical burden, responsibility and location for "action" is called up, simultaneously questioning the very need for the education-of-the-human while underscoring its necessity: "It is toward a global change of terrain that we must proceed, abandoning that of Being then that of the Other for a terrain of the One or of radical immanence that has shown us the Real itself. On this new basis, it is the whole continent of thought, particularly but not only the relationships of science and philosophy, that is re-organized" (Laruelle, 2013, p. 3).

References

Abraham, I. (2006). The contradictory spaces of postcolonial techno-science. *Economic and Political Weekly, XLI*(3), 210, 217.

Anderson, J., Rainie, L., & Luchsinger, A. (2018). *Artificial intelligence and the future of humans.* Washington, DC: Pew Research Center. http://www.pewinternet.org/2018/12/10/artificial-intelligence-and-the-future-of-humans/

Australian Communications and Media Authority. (2016-17). *Annual report 2016-17.* Source: https://www.acma.gov.au/-/media/mediacomms/Report/pdf/ACMA_OeSC-annual-reports-2016-17-pdf.pdf?la=en.

Baker, B. (in press). Activate or evacuate to educate? Roles of a sensorium in onto-epistemologies. In W. Gershon (Ed.), *The sensuous curriculum* (pp. 1–37). Charlotte: Information Age Publishing.

Baker, B. (2017). To show is to know? Conceptions of evidence and discourses of vision in social science and education research. *Curriculum Inquiry, 47*(2), 151–174. DOI: 10.1080/03626784.2017.1283593.

Baker, B. (2013). *William James, sciences of mind, and anti-imperial discourse.* New York: Cambridge University Press.

Baker, B. (2001). *In perpetual motion: Theories of power, educational history, and the child* (Vol. 14). New York: Peter Lang.

Baker, B., & Saari, A. (2018). "The anatomy of our discontent": From braining the mind to mindfulness for teachers. *Discourse: Studies in the cultural politics of education, 39*(2), 169–183. DOI: http://dx.doi.org/10.1080/01596306.2018.1394425

Bernal, M. (1987). *Black Athena: The Afroasiatic roots of classical civilization.* New Brunswick: Rutgers University Press.

Bostrom, N. (2014). *Superintelligence: Paths, dangers, strategies.* Oxford: Oxford University Press.

Caliskan, A., Bryson, J., & Narayanan, A. (2017). Semantics derived automatically from language corpora contain human-like biases. *Science, 356*(6334), 183–186. DOI: 10.1126/science.aal4230.

Carlino, A. (1999). *Books of the body: Anatomical ritual and renaissance learning* (J. Tedeshi & A. C. Tedeschi, Trans.). Chicago: University of Chicago Press.

Castells, M. (2010). *The rise of the network society* (2nd ed.). West Sussex: Wiley and Sons Ltd.

Chakrabarty, D. (2000). *Provincializing Europe: Postcolonial through and historical difference.* Princeton: Princeton University Press.

Cooper Ramo, J. (2016). *The seventh sense.* New York: Hachette.

Crary, J. (2001). *Suspension of perception: Attention, spectacle, and modern culture.* Cambridge: MIT Press.

Crosson, J. B. (2013). Invisibilities: Translation. Spirits of the dead, and the politics of invisibility. *Cultural anthropology.* DOI: https://culanth.org/fieldsights/346-invisibilities-translation-spirits-of-the-dead-and-the-politics-of-invisibility

de Rijcke, S., & Beaulieu, A. (2014). Networked neuroscience: Brain scans and visual knowing at the intersection of atlases and databases. In M. L. C. Coopmans, J. Vertesi, & S. Woolgar (Eds.), *Representations in scientific practice revisited* (pp. 131–152). Cambridge: MIT Press.

DuBois, T. (2009). *Introduction to shamanism.* New York: Cambridge University Press.

Ergas, O. (2017). *Reconstructing "education" through mindful attention: Positioning the mind at the center of curriculum and pedagogy.* London: Palgrave Macmillan.

Foucault, M. (1977). Intellectuals and power: Language, counter-memory, practice (D. F. Bouchard & S. Simon, Trans.). In D. F. B. (Introduction) (Ed.), *Selected essays and interviews* (pp. 205-217). Ithaca, NY: Cornell University Press.

Foucault, M. (2005). *The hermeneutics of the subject: Lectures at the Collége de France, 1981-1982* (G. Burchell, Trans.; F. Gros, Ed.). New York: Palgrave Macmillan.

Foucault, M. (1985). *The history of sexuality, Vol. 2: The use of pleasure.* New York: Pantheon Books.

Hansen, M. (2012) *Bodies in code: Interfaces with digital media.* New York: Routledge.

Hayles, N. K. (2012). *How we think: Digital media and contemporary technogenesis.* Chicago: University of Chicago Press.

His Holiness the Dalai Lama, & Cutler, H. C. (1998). *The art of happiness: A handbook for living.* London: Hodder & Stoughton.

Jay, M. (1993). *Downcast eyes: The denigration of vision in twentieth-century French thought.* Berkeley: University of California Press.

Khanna, P. (2016). *Connectography: Mapping the future of global civilization.* New York: Random House.

Laruelle, F. (2013). *Principles of non-philosophy.* London: Bloomsbury.

Lechte, J. (2012). *Genealogy and ontology of the Western image and its digital future.* New York: Routledge.

Lewin, D. (2015). Technology, attention, and education. In E. Duarte (Ed.), *Philosophy of education* (pp. 312–320). Urbana: University of Illinois.

Naughton, J. (2016). The evolution of the internet: From military experiment to general purpose technology. *Journal of Cyber Policy, 1*(1), 5–28.

OECD. (2017). *OECD digital economy outlook 2017* Paris: OECD Publishing. DOI: https://doi.org/10.1787/9789264276284-en.

O'Neil, C. (2016). *Weapons of math destruction: How big data increases inequality and threatens democracy.* New York: The Crown Publishing Group.

Olsson, L., & Edman-Stålbrant, E. (2008). Digital literacy as a challenge for teacher education: Implications for educational frameworks and learning environments in IFIP International Federation for Information Processing. In M. Kendall & B. Samways (Eds.), *Learning to live in the knowledge society* (Vol. 281; pp. 11–18). Boston: Springer.

Ong, W. (2002). *Orality and literacy: The technologizing of the world.* London: Routledge.

Plato. (2013). *Sophist.* CreateSpace Independent Publishing. https://www.createspace.com

Prasad, A. (2008). Science in motion: What postcolonial studies can offer. *RECIIS electronic Journal of Communication Information and Innovation in Health, 2*(2), 35–47.

Said, E. W. (1979). *Orientalism.* New York: Random House Trade Paperbacks.

Sawday, J. (1995). *The body emblazoned: Dissection and the human body in Renaissance culture.* London: Routledge.

Sells, M. (1994). *Mystical languages of unsaying.* Chicago: University of Chicago Press.

Steigler, B. (2009). *Technics and time 2: Disorientation.* Palo Alto: Stanford University Press.

Stiegler, B. (2014). *The re-enchantment of the world: The value of spirit against industrial populism* (T. Arthur, Trans.). London: Bloomsbury.

Tegmark, M. (2017). *Life 3.0: Being human in the age of artificial intelligence.* New York: Random House.

Tomas, D. (1988). From the photograph to postphotographic practice: Toward a postoptical ecology of the eye. *Substance, 17*(1), 59–68.

Tyler, S. (1984). The vision quest in the West, or what the mind's eye sees. *Journal of Anthropological Research (40th anniversary issue, 1944–1984), 40*(1), 23–40.

Van Deursen, A., & Van Dijk, J. (2015). New media and the digital divide. In J. Wright (Ed.), *International encyclopedia of the social & behavioral sciences* (2nd Ed.; pp. 787–792). Philadelphia: Elsevier. DOI: 10.1016/B978-0-08-097086-8.95086-4

CHAPTER EIGHTEEN

Critical Transformative Leadership: Seeming to Change Only One Thing[1]

John Willinsky

THIS CHAPTER ADHERES to the title that João M. Paraskeva originally proposed for this book—*Critical Transformative Leadership and Policy Studies: Lessons from Dartmouth*—like a rainy-day rivulet following a roadside curb down an incline. Edited-collection chapters tend to pay their book's title a slight nod as they slip between the covers, but in this case João's title is my touchstone. Its theme is the focus of the lessons that I try to extract from the last two decades or so of my work. As teachers, we often labor within the given structures and policies while still finding ways of introducing what we judge to be critical and transformative, especially on reflection. This is, for me and others in this volume, a second go at addressing the challenge that João sets out with this title. Some years before composing this chapter, we all had the chance to join him, his students and colleagues in the New England seaside town of Dartmouth to consider our work in light of the leadership that he and others have shown, and this opportunity to reconsider how our work stands up to the gauntlet laid down by this title is one that I, for one, welcome.

Still, I tell my story fully aware that you may well regard me as an unreliable and self-serving witness in such matters. I do so, as well, in the face of João Paraskeva's own example of having set out his own gracious demonstration of how to assess critical transformative leadership in others. I am referring to his examination of the deft manner in which the distinguished critical scholar Michael Apple has repeatedly dismantled the magisterial educational policies of the state, with João aptly comparing Michael's work at one point to a Jackson Pollack canvas, in which "tentative and aggressive lines of colors render a profound renting of the social fabric" (Paraskeva, 2002, p. 118). Yes, Michael wields a fierce, dare I say critical transformative, brush. As a result many of us have comes to see the schools in new ways. Prepare yourself, readers, for a more pedestrian depiction of a less accomplished career through which I invite you to reflect on your own critical transformations around this book's theme. (This is about you, after all, not me.)

During the first half of the 1990s, I scribbled away on a project inspired by the Christopher Columbus quincentenary and the wave of counter-commemorations in

1   Keynote address, Department of Educational Leadership, University of Massachusetts Dartmouth, October 4, 2015.

response to that celebration in 1992. In looking back, three aspects proved critical to undertaking such work, each of which can help us reflect how on the term *critical* operates. It struck me as critical to bring the Colombian counter-narrative to the schools. Education was far too central to perpetuating the myths and misapprehensions of imperialism's malfeasance to have its part overlooked to protect the children. I was aided in this by the critical role played by mentors and colleagues in bringing the work into focus by their own example and their willingness to hear one out.[2] And finally, I needed a critical school of thought to give some coherence, edge, and intellectual interest to such a project, which in this case was to be postcolonial theory. Even before the 1990s, postcolonialism had become very much the thrust of theory and critique amid a handful of Euro-American humanities departments.[3] Yet it had emerged out of anti-colonial activism from the likes of Gandhi, Fanon, and Freire in Asia, Africa, and Latin America. The task, as I envisioned it, was to apply the weight of this thinking to what went on in the schools, without losing sight of its origins in the action of opposing colonialism.[4]

I was particularly motivated by what Edward Said had achieved in his celebrated *Orientalism*. The book serves as a reminder not to underestimate the critical transformative leadership provided by such a work. It can serve as a model and inspire a project and a plan. Said sets out his project this way: "What I am interested in doing now is suggesting how the general liberal consensus that 'true' knowledge is fundamentally non-political (and converservely that overtly political knowledge fundamentally is not 'true' knowledge) obscures the highly if obscurely organized political circumstances obtaining when knowledge is produced" (1978, p. 10). I decided to be no less keen in setting out how the political circumstances of imperialism's educational legacy continued to infuse the school curriculum under the guise of being true, non-political knowledge. Education's role in imperialism's great historical pageant needed to be identified and made plain. Where else but the schools did the young learn to honor and celebrate the Christian West's inheritance of the Spirit of Freedom, much as the story had been told in Georg Wilhelm Friedrich Hegel's philosophy of history lectures published in 1837: "The

2   My work in this area, for example, had been greatly advanced by the serendipity of an extended walk through San Francisco in April 1992 with Roger I. Simon (who'd been my teacher nearly twenty years earlier when he had flown into a northern Ontario town to give a graduate class where I was teaching school); he was working at the time on a pedagogy of counter-commemoration with regard to Columbus, which was showing up around the Bay Area that year, and in which he considered "the complementarity and contradictions among all the ways in which a sense of the past is constructed" (1994, p. 128).

3   Let me note some of the significant scholars of postcolonialism and their continuing contributions, such as Gayatri Spivak (2016), Homi K. Bhabha (2015), and Ania Loomba (2016), continued to pursue vital theoretical work. As well, the concept proved effective in "displacing systemic discrimination against Indigenous peoples," as Marie Batiste, Lynne Bell and L. M. Finlay put it, which is "created and legitimized by the cognitive frameworks of imperialism and colonialism," and "remains the single most crucial cultural challenge facing humanity" (Battiste, Bell, and Finlay, 2002, p. 82; see also Coombes, 2006; Snelgrove, Dhamoon, and Corntassel, 2014).

4   Among those who continue to apply postcolonial perspectives to education are Fazal Rizvi (2014), Anne Hickling-Hudson (2014), and Peter Mayo (2016), with Hickling-Hudson and Mayo creating opportunities for others by founding journals such as *Postcolonial Directions in Education* in 2012 (with more on such journals later).

History of the world is none other than the progress of the consciousness of Freedom"—which he explains is derived from "the Christian principle of self-consciousness—"a progress whose development according to the necessity of its nature, it is our business to investigate" (1956, p. 19).

The colonial empires may have been swept away by the mid-twentieth-century wave of independence movements (if only to be replaced some decades later by corporate globalization), but traces of their influence and sensibility were easy to find among in the curriculum of American, British, and Canadian schools. Beyond the Hegelian approach to global history, geography classes were devoted to dividing the world by who belongs where; science classes obfuscated the discipline's role in creating the concept of race; and English classes were sanctuaries of monolingualism. There were signs aplenty that we were still teaching what had been made of the world by centuries of conquest and colonization. Yet when *Learning to Divide the World: Education at Empire's End* (1998) was finally published, some six years late to the quincentenary it was meant to counter, I was then confronted with what an educator is to do with this knowledge.

In universities, postcolonial studies fit neatly enough into the humanities' shift to theory. With the schools, the postcolonial critique seemed thoroughly and bluntly opposed to education's very mission. It seemed to take exception to the school's core assumption. Think of it as neatly summed up by Matthew Arnold, in his school inspector guise, as he promoted a school-age "pursuit of our total perfection by means of getting to know, on all the matters which most concern us, the best which has been thought and said" (1869, p. viii). For Arnold, this "getting to know" was an act of *"Political and Social Criticism"* (as his book's subtitle puts it) in what he saw as the great battle between *Culture and Anarchy* (the title proper). The better half of that pair was best served, he believed, by an English education whether at home or abroad. But a century and a bit later, the political and social criticism of postcolonialism strongly suggested that what Arnold called for was simply not the best. It was too often a thinly veiled racism in the guise of a sound curriculum.

The question of what is to be done after such critical work was more immediately brought home to me by Larry Wolfson, a teacher and a friend who invited, well, more like, challenged me to come into his grade-twelve English class and teach some aspect of what I had learned in writing that book. The case may be compelling, he allowed, but how will it work in the schools? What postcolonial lesson could I bring to his classroom? It gave me pause, but seemed exactly the right sort of question that the aspiring critical transformative leader needed to confront.

Over a number of weeks that spring, I worked with the students on preparing an alternative poetry anthology for the English classroom. This anthology was intended to present poems in languages other than English, which set it apart from the other anthologies in the school, which was our starting point. The poems were to be selected and translated by the students, their families, and other sources from the languages of the community. At least one of the students' responses ran ahead of my own so-called postcolonial thinking, as I did not at first get why his suggestion of Saul Williams's hip-hop, complete with the student's translation, fit the assignment (Willinsky, 2006). The students then photocopied a class set of their postcolonial anthology and set out to market it among the school's English teachers. They did seem to enjoy wandering the halls and knocking on teachers' doors to recommend it to the teachers as just the sort of text to use with their classes next year, pointing out that it also included student questions for each of the poems, just like the other anthologies used in their teaching. On looking back at this episode, the critical transformative leadership lessons might seem threefold: Accept the challenge of trying to apply to the world you have analyzed what you have learned of that world, attempt to change that world by transforming a single aspect of it, and be ready to have shaken what you thought you had learned in the first place about that world.

Sharp-eyed readers may notice that on concluding this incident, I, first of all, make no mention here of what happened to the postcolonial anthology—Larry let me down easy by saying something like, "not much"—and that, second, there is a slight issue of scale between my postcolonial analysis of the schools and my role as visiting teacher. Further on the point of scale, my strategy of constraining the change (by using the standard anthology format) runs contrary to the broader critical pedagogy movement, which excels at identifying how, as one of its leading figures Joe Kincheloe put it, "every dimension of schooling and every form of educational practice are politically contested spaces" (2008, p. 2).

Learning to Divide the World had gone after every educational dimension and form, while my brief classroom stint altered the language of the anthology. I also came to see a further intellectual liability to the totality of contested spaces. It tends to encompass internecine struggles within the critical theories themselves. Consider how the historian Anne McClintock takes issue with the postcolonial label itself: "If 'post-colonial' theory has sought to challenge the grand march of western historicism with its entourage of binaries (self-other, metropolis-colony, center-periphery, etc.), the term 'post-colonialism' nonetheless re-orients the globe once more around a single, binary opposition: colonial/post-colonial" (1992, p. 85). For me, the McClintock binary in which I found myself caught was that of center–periphery. To briefly explain this geometry, the European centers of the empire treated their colonies as peripheral field stations from which botanists, anthropologists, connoisseurs, and opportunists gathered boatloads of specimens and artifacts, while filling notebooks with local lore and data. These goods were funnelled through the hands of Europe's great collectors as well as into the universities, libraries, and museums. This led to exhibitions and books, knowledge and theories, some of which gradually made their way back to the colonial schools, where the very best of these peripheral students dreamed of making their way, in turn, to the center.

Following McClintock's point, my postcolonial work did not exactly break with this binary of center and periphery. My book issued from one of the centers in the scholarly world system (Schott, 1998). Its critique may have been necessary but I was again struck by how it was not sufficient. What dent did it make in the sheer enormity of Said's "highly if obscurely organized political circumstances obtaining when knowledge is produced" (1978, p. 10)? I had to regroup, rather than reengage another layer of postcolonial critique. I ended up moving away from the study of education, uncertain about how and whether I would be able to redress some small part of what I had learned about this imperial legacy. I have now to show how, if after a good number of years, I was able to return to that center–periphery binary through a very different path of activism, but before doing that I should point out another point for readers to reflect on, in light of their own tendencies compared to mine. Among academics, I have seemed to favor the fox's flitting pursuit of many things, compared to the more generally encouraged hedgehog's research trajectory of going after one big idea without fail, achieving a depth of analysis and level of expertise denied foxes.[5]

My pulling back from postcolonialism made me susceptible to the distractions posed by the next shiny thing. I was increasingly drawn to what seemed, brightly enough, the more-than-critical possibilities of the internet welling up around us. It seemed capable of bringing the world into the classroom in a whole new way. But it was not immediately clear what could be made of this new medium, what would prove to be its educational advantages in addressing, for example, the objects of our critique. Were the machines to be a transformative force in education, as many had claimed and few had delivered to date (Cuban, 2001)? Or were they simply another cause for critique, as the "digital divide" quickly became apparent within our communities and on a global scale (Norris, 2001)?

What I was struck by amid the hype and the hope was how the means of production, when it came to publishing, were going retail. Everyone their own blogger, photographer, musician, marketer, and file-sharer. More than that, everyone their own teacher and student, in ways that raised do-it-yourself and other hobbies to whole new levels.[6] At the same time, it was by no means clear where things were headed for educators, journalists, musicians, retailers, and many other forms of work. But rather than wait and see—until what point?—the critical transformative leader needs to risk a remaking of the world by trial and error, replete with false starts and blind alleys. Just so, I went after the educational promise I saw in this brave new world by working with others to build what turned out over a period of years to be three educational online platforms during the 1990s. It began with EdEx, which was designed for teachers to gather and exchange their best learning resources and materials as part of a professional community; only this was well before teachers had sufficient access or trust to engage in sharing what have since become known as "open educational resources" (OER) and that are still limited in their

---

5   Isaiah Berlin: "There is a line among the fragments of the Greek poet Archilochus which says: 'The fox knows many things, but the hedgehog knows one big thing'" (1953, p. 1).

6   My fumbling guitar work, for example, was entirely recast in the 1990s by the online sharing of amateurs' invented keyboard tablature that set out every known song by fret and string; in 1998 I formed a band with Joe Kincheloe, Ed O'Sullivan, and David Jardine, which Shirley Steinberg named "Tony and the Hegemones" (after Antonio Gramsci), that then rocked American Educational Research Association Conferences until Joe's tragically premature death in 2008.

educational impact. This was followed by a second platform known as Studio A. It was designed to help put students in a position to provide the technical support desperately needed by their high schools, with the platform enabling the students to manage their support projects and share what they learned; here it turned out that the schools while initially keen were leery of giving students such responsibility and of covering the platform development costs (Willinsky and Forssman, 2000). Then, in a third venture, this one deemed the Public Knowledge Project ("the right to know"), we sought to work with the local newspaper by finding and presenting relevant research to accompany journalists' coverage of educational issues, such as technology in the schools; this quickly led me to discover that, in light of publisher contracts with the library, such research could not be shared with the public.

It was this third blind alley of forbidden research access that stopped me cold. My first two efforts, with EdEx and Studio A, had faltered on the unrealistic expectations that I had of teachers, schools, and online systems. My third attempt stumbled over something else, namely, the structure of my own scholarly trade. I had to ask about what was wrong with this picture. How is it that research funded by the public and conducted to benefit the public, could not be shared with the public? How could we as education researchers have so little concern over who has access to what we hold to be such an important source of knowledge and learning? But then it also hit me that these restrictions, too, bore traces of the center–periphery binary in the distribution of knowledge, given that what could not be shared with the public was as likely to be unavailable in the global South. I decided to adjust the course of the newly formed Public Knowledge Project. As the century was about to turn, we dedicated our efforts, naively enough, to seeing how we could help move research and scholarship online with the goal of making it freely available to readers everywhere.

In setting my sights on altering the course of scholarly publishing, I was directing my work away from the study of schools and education.[7] Now note that this was not because I had discovered an issue of greater or more pressing urgency with scholarly publishing than what was going on in with the lives of children in classrooms. Rather, I took this new course because I thought I could see a clear and present path by which we might correct a disorder in the education system for which we researchers in the universities were directly responsible. I had been learning about how online systems work, after all, and thought that I might be able to offer journals and learned societies a platform through which they would enable them to provide greater openness in their inevitable move online. I soon realized, as well, that the alternative was a commercial

---

7   It was about this time that, as I recall it, Avner Segall stopped me on my bicycle, as he was waiting for a bus at the University of British Columbia, to ask me why I wasn't continuing the postcolonial work, even as he was exploring a "critical history" of his own at the time, in which he put "many of history's taken-for-granted procedures into question and challeng[ed] the classical notions of truth, reality, and objectivity" (1999, p. 358). I tried to explain how I was hesitant to go on pulling back one majestic tapestry after another, exposing the underlying mechanism behind what Segall characterizes as "a picture-perfect presentation of an unmediated, authorless past" (ibid.).

publishing industry, given to the corporate concentration of mergers and acquisitions that led to increasing prices, which were contributing to reduced access. Here was a political economy that I imagined being able to speak to in some small way, and then, after my colleagues everywhere had seen the light, I would get back to the schools and the children.

In looking back, I'd characterize it as a move from the study of education to that of learning. Now, learning today may seem to be all about measuring learning gains through high-stakes testing that provide results of statistical significance, if not student joyfulness. But the learning that I became involved in with this move to publishing draws on an older, much broader sense of the term. Let me offer an example. In a highly relevant passage for my shift in direction, Henry Oldenburg uses the term (following Francis Bacon's *The Advancement of Learning*) in his introduction and rationale for the first issue of the *Philosophical Transactions*, which appeared in London on March 6, 1665. Historically, it was only the second scholarly periodical to appear and proved the prototype for the many scientific journals that followed. Oldenburg explained on the front page: "It is therefore thought fit to employ the *Press*, as the most proper way to gratifie those, whose engagement in such Studies, and delight in the advancement of Learning and profitable Discoveries doth entitle them to the knowledge of what this Kingdom, or other parts of the World, do, from time to time, afford" (1665, 1).

I was much inspired by Oldenburg's belief that the printing press (issuing a periodical pamphlet) was the best means at hand for satisfying those who, by their interests in learning, had a natural right to such knowledge. This sense of technological fitness serving intellectual entitlement became my guiding star. For, in a sense, I dared to think it fit to employ the internet to this same end. This was not so much transformative leadership as getting behind what others, many others, had been making of the internet for some time. People were transforming, through email, file transfer protocols (FTP), and later the web, what had originally been a 1970s' pilot venture of the Defense Advanced Research Projects Agency (DARPA) intended to subvert the nuclear annihilation of American military communication channels by creating multichannel packet-switching webs across the nation.

In 1993, for example, Gene Glass, grasped email's potential for increasing the reach of research (much as he had in developing methods to harness the results of multiple studies; 1976) by using it to circulate what became one of the field's first open access or free-to-read journals *Educational Policy Analysis Archives*.[8] In 1999, Shawn Fanning released the file-sharing system Napster, which enabled people to share their music online, thoroughly altering people's perceptions of what to expect from the music industry (Ku, 2002). In 2001, Jimmy Wales and Larry Sanger started using a wiki to crowdsource what became Wikipedia, thereby demonstrating just how eager people were to collaborate in the sharing of what

---

8   In another turning point arising out of later-to-be-mentors, Gene Glass responded in 1999 to a survey that Larry Wolfson and I were conducting with journal editors on the cost of moving journals online with "nada, rien, nothing." He published the journal on a spare server that he'd slid under his desk and connected to the Internet.

they knew and could learn (Sanger, 2005). That same year, Lawrence Lessig, Hal Abelson, and Eric Eldred formed a set of Creative Commons licenses by which copyright holders—which is to say everyone who posted a blog or a picture—were able to clearly designate that, yes, others can use their work, while only asking in return a right of attribution (Lessig, 2003). And in 2001, the Public Library of Science, led by a distinguished team that included Nobel laureate Harold Varmus, began work on a an open access biomedical journal, for which authors paid an article processing charge (APC) if their articles are published, and which would, a few years later, become the highest ranking in its field (Brown, Eisen, and Varmus, 2003). There was room within the expansiveness of the internet, it seemed pretty clear, to provide a whole new level of access to knowledge, much as the nineteenth-century public library movement had sought to create the "arsenals of a democratic culture," as Sidney Ditzion put in some time ago (1947).

The lesson here proved to be all about bringing together the relevant bits one has learned about and what one hopes to wrest from the perceived possibilities. That is, I applied what I knew about journal publishing to what I had recently acquired about online workflow platforms and set out to design an online journal management and publishing system. It included support for each of the steps that journal editors undertook on a day-to-day basis, amid file folders, rolodex, spreadsheets, and printouts. All that it altered for the editor was moving the process online. Kevin Jamieson, an undergraduate student who worked with me over the course of his degree, released the platform as *open-source software*. The term emerged in the late 1990s and meant, as he taught me, that we applied a license to the system that protected its open status and that we designed it to be readily downloaded and easily installed on local servers, with instructions at every step for those new to online systems and even journal editing. We called the resulting software Open Journal Systems (OJS), which was released in 2002.[9]

Our initial focus was on helping print journals move their publishing process and content online, which we regarded as a first step in providing readers with open access, given the reduction in costs and the promise of increased readership that it offered. In the early days of the twenty-first century, even the move online proved a hard sell for journal editors. They politely sat enough through my demos and pitches; they often agreed with me in principle; then they went on with their work as they had before.[10] I came to see that it was not part of our work to call on each other to act on our convictions. It was a sobering experience, and I began to long for the days of postcolonial critiques.

Time, however, was on my side. With each passing year, it became clear to a few more editors that it was easier to work with reviewers and authors by email rather than mail, a few more authors saw that it was easier to send an electronic file rather than prepare four

9	It was preceded by Open Conference Systems in 2001 and followed by Open Monograph Press (OMP), released in 2014.

10	For example, in 2003–04, with support from a MacArthur Foundation Global Security and Sustainable Grant, I had the chance to demonstrate the OJS to journal editors and publishers, faculty and students in Argentina, Brazil, Hong Kong, Kenya, India, Philippines, and South Africa (without the imperial parallels lost on me), with the take-up coming many years after my visit was a distant memory.

copies along with the "original" to submission to the journal, and almost all production people found it easier to work from electronic files rather than key in a typescript paper. And as for readers, it took more time, but even they eventually realized that finding exactly what they were looking for the moment it was needed was a whole lot easier than locating the print journal, even if is was on their own bookshelves.

At the same time that journals began to move online, whether through commercial publishers or with such systems as the OJS, a very small, if growing, proportion of journals chose to set aside the subscription model and make the leap to open access. Over the course of the century's opening decade, open access took on the aspects of a movement, with the voices of advocacy coming from research libraries through SPARC (Scholarly Publishing and Academic Resources and Coalition) and dedicated open-access organizations, such as the PLOS (Public Library of Science). As a result of these efforts, I can, finally, invoke the critical transformative arena of policy studies. Research-funding agencies began to see the value and of having the research they sponsor circulate on an open-access basis. A big move came, after much lobbying by research libraries and activists, with the National Institutes of Health's Public Access Policy. What had begun as a largely ignored voluntary policy, became in 2008 a mandate that required funded researchers to make available an open access copy of their work, if only in its final draft form and after an up-to-twelve-month embargo, which was intended to protect the publisher's investment publishing the work. The Obama administration ordered the spread of this open-access mandate to all federal agencies involved in sponsoring research. Such policies have been adopted by the major research foundations and government funding agencies in other countries (Lange, 2016). In addition to government and foundation policies in favor of open access, it is fair to say that every major scholarly publisher also has seen the light and is looking for ways to capitalize on open access, largely through levying article processing charges for its set of open access titles. So while the majority of the literature remains in subscription journals, this critical transformation of scholarly publishing is now underway.[11]

To return, then, to the center–periphery binary of the postcolonial critique, it needs to be said that the Public Knowledge Project is part of the center, with its principal location at Simon Fraser University Library atop Burnaby Mountain on the unceded, traditional territories of the Coast Salish peoples. Its publishing tools follow the conventions of scholarly publishing that are descended from Henry Oldenburg's first venture with *Philosophical Transactions*, which in its earliest issues published scientific observations from the outer reaches of the empire.

---

11   The proportion of published articles that are freely available to online readers is only now approaching the halfway point, while this degree of open access is achieved through a variety of means, with a good share of it from authors posting rogue copies of their articles, which is forbidden by their publishers (Archambault et al., 2014). As for the final fifty percent, a number are working on how to bring about that final flip by which the roughly ten billion dollars' worth of subscription journals will offer universal open access to the whole of this body of knowledge. We at the Public Knowledge Project are working with journals and libraries to develop economic models for a subscription form of open access, going back to the historical origins of the subscription as form of sponsorship (see Willinsky, 2017).

Yet the asymmetry may be said to be loosely countered by, in this case, the taking up of the publishing tools in question to both provide local opportunities to further foster a research culture and to participate in the global knowledge exchange.[12] These tools are, by way of example, being used (a) by the Aboriginal Health Research Networks Secretariat to publish its *The International Journal of Indigenous Health* at the University of Victoria; (b) by the Vietnamese Ministry of Science and Technology to bring in 2007 virtually all of the country's journals online using a Vietnamese translation of the software (with currently 67 titles online); (c) by African Journals Online and Asia Journals Online to provide continent-wide platforms for local journals; (d) by Ranjini Mendis to launch *Postcolonial Text* in 2004 at Kwantlen Polytechnic University, one of the first journals to use the software, and later by Anne Hickling Hudson and Peter Mayo to start *Postcolonial Directions in Education* at the University of Malta in 2012; and (e) by some sixty percent of the more than 10,000 journals currently using OJS that are located in the global South, led by users in Brazil, with journals found on every continent. The openness of the software has enabled users to translate the system into twenty-five languages, and the journals are indexed, with their citations counted, in Google Scholar thanks to Anurag Acharya. Still, I have also discovered, to my dismay, that OJS has been used on more than one occasion to start so-called predatory journals, which, with questionable review or editorial services, charge authors APCs for "publishing" their work (Shen and Björk, 2015). This comes of lowering the entry bar while serving as a humbling reminder that every effort to tidy up some aspect of this messy world has its unintended consequences.

Over the course of these moves, from the postcolonial critique of the school curriculum to the online development of a publishing platform, the critical point may be that one needs to be more often transformed than transformative, more often chasing after elusive goals than exercising leadership in going after policies and political economies that continue to constrain educational opportunities. The trick of seeming to change only one thing is to focus on the one thing that you have reason to believe can change everything. It also helps to be both hedgehog and fox, which is to say, both ready to stay with a big idea and ready to be drawn to what seems a more promising path.[13] In my case, I've shifted over the years from the grand (if critical) theory of postcolonialism to matters of daily (editorial) practices and software licenses. And then back again, as it turns out, to big history. Over the last too many years, I have found myself chasing down questions of how and where this right to know and obligation to

---

12   Edward Shils on center and periphery: "Within any given society, the first inequality in the intellectual community is between those who create and those who consume" (1973, p. 360). It will be only when these [obstacles to the awakening of creativity in science, letters, scholarship] have been overcome that the present division of the world into intellectual metropolis and intellectual province will be superseded by an extension, on a universal scale, of the network of creative centers which is now a feature of Western intellectual life" (p. 371).

13   Berlin, further on the hedgehog and fox: "Of course, like all over-simple classifications of this type, the dichotomy becomes, if pressed, artificial, scholastics, and ultimately absurd.... It offers a point of view from which to look and compare, a starting point for genuine investigation" (1953, p. 2).

share among the learned has arisen. My efforts at answering these questions have led me to trace the course of what I term "the intellectual properties of learning" across the history of the Christian West, from Saint Jerome's fourth-century monastic publishing house to John Locke's seventeenth-century theory of property, as well as his active lobbying for learned books (Willinsky, in press). To set out one's course like this, from project to project in search of its arc presumes a certain lack of humility. This lack can only be justified by the hope that others find some finer, more focused point of their own critical transformative leadership in the way that João Paraskev has assembled this collection under this title.

References

Archambault, Eric, Didier Amyot, Philippe Deschamps, Aurore Nicol, Françoise Provencher, Lise Rebout, Guillaume Roberge. *Proportion of open access papers published in peer-reviewed journals at the European and world levels—1996-2013*. Montreal: Science-Metrix, 2014.

Arnold, Matthew. *Culture and anarchy: An essay in political and social criticism*. London: Smith, Elder, 1869.

Battiste, Marie, Lynne Bell, and L. M. Findlay. "Decolonizing education in Canadian universities: An interdisciplinary, international, indigenous research project." *Canadian Journal of Native Education* 26.2 (2002): 82–95.

Berlin, Isaiah. *The hedgehog and the fox: An essay on Tolstoy's view of history*. London: Weidenfeld and Nicolson, 1953.

Bhabha, Homi K. "'The beginning of their real enunciation': Stuart Hall and the work of culture." *Critical Inquiry* 42.1 (2015): 1–30.

Brown, Patrick O., Michael B. Eisen, and Harold E. Varmus. "Why PLoS became a publisher." *PLOS Biology* 1.1 (2003): e36.

Coombes, Annie E. *Rethinking settler colonialism: history and memory in Australia, Canada, New Zealand and South Africa*. Manchester: Manchester University Press, 2006.

Cuban, Larry. *Oversold and underused: Computers in the classroom*. Cambridge, Harvard University Press, 2001.

Ditzion, Sidney Herbert. *Arsenals of a democratic culture: A social history of the American public library movement in New England and the middle states from 1850 to 1900*. Chicago: American Library Association, 1947.

Glass, Gene V. "Primary, Secondary, and Meta-Analysis of Research 1." *Educational researcher* 5.10 (1976): 3-8.

Hegel, Georg Wilhelm Friedrich. *The Philosophy of history*. Trans. J. Sibree. New York: Dover, 1956.

Hickling-Hudson, Anne. "Striving for a better world: Lessons from Freire in Grenada, Jamaica and Australia." *International Review of Education* 60.4 (2014): 523–543.

Kincheloe, J. (2008). *Critical Pedagogy Reader*. New York: Peter Lang.

Ku, Raymond Shih Ray. "The creative destruction of copyright: Napster and the new economics of digital technology." *University of Chicago Law Review* (2002): 263–324.

Lange, Jessica. "Scholarly management publication and open access funding mandates: A review of publisher policies." *Ticker: The Academic Business Librarianship Review* 1.3 (2016): 15–27.

Lessig, Lawrence. "The creative commons." *Florida Law Review* 55 (2003): 763–793.

Loomba, Ania. "The everyday violence of caste." *College Literature* 43.1 (2016): 220–225.

McClintock, Anne. "The angel of progress: Pitfalls of the term 'post-colonialism'." *Social Text* 31/32 (1992): 84–98.

Mayo, Peter. "In defense of a liberal education." *International Review of Education* 62.2 (2016): 243–245.

Norris, Pippa. *Digital divide: Civic engagement, information poverty, and the Internet worldwide.* Cambridge: Cambridge University Press, 2001.

Paraskeva, João Menelau. "Michael W. Apple and the [curricular] critical studies." Trans. Google & J. Willinsky. *Curriculum without Borders* 2.1 (2002): 106–120.

Oldenburg, Henry. "The introduction." *Philosophical Transactions* 1, no. 1 (1665): 1–2.

Rizvi, Fazal. "Old elite schools, history and the construction of a new imaginary." *Globalisation, Societies and Education* 12.2 (2014): 290–308.

Said, Edward. *Orientalism.* New York: Pantheon, 1978.

Sanger, Larry. "The early history of Nupedia and Wikipedia: A memoir." *Open sources* 2 (2005): 307-38.

Schott, Thomas. "Tics between center and periphery in the Scientific world-system: Accumulation of rewards, dominance and self-reliance in the center." *Journal of World-Systems Research* 4 (1998): 112–144.

Shils, Edward. "Metropolis and center in intellectual life (1961)." In *The Intellectuals and the Powers and other Essays.* Chicago: University of Chicago Press, 1973, pp. 355–371.

Segall, Avner. "Critical history: Implications for history/social studies education." *Theory & Research in Social Education* 27.3 (1999): 358–374.

Shen, Cenyu, and Bo-Christer Björk. "'Predatory' open access: a longitudinal study of article volumes and market characteristics." *BMC Medicine* 13.1 (2015): 230.

Simon, Roger I. "Forms of insurgency in the production of popular memories: Columbus quincentenary and pedagogy of countercommemoration." In *Between Borders: Pedagogy and the Politics of Cultural Studies.* London: Routledge, 1994, pp. 127–144.

Snelgrove, Corey, Rita Dhamoon, and Jeff Corntassel. "Unsettling settler colonialism: The discourse and politics of settlers, and solidarity with Indigenous nations." *Decolonization: Indigeneity, Education & Society* 3.2, pp. 1–32 (2014).

Spivak, Gayatri Chakravorty. "Cultural pluralism?" *Philosophy & Social Criticism* 42.4–5 (2016): 448–455.

Willinsky, John. *The intellectual properties of learning: A prehistory from Saint Jerome to John Locke.* Chicago: University of Chicago Press, in press.

Willinsky, John. "Subscribing to open access for research and scholarship." (blogpost). *Slaw.ca*, January 13, 2017.

Willinsky, John. "High school postcolonial, and the students ran ahead." In Y. Kanu (Ed.) *Curriculum as Cultural Practice: Postcolonial Imaginations.* Toronto: University of Toronto Press, 2006, pp. 95–115.

Willinsky, John. *Learning to divide the world: Education at empire's end.* Minneapolis: Minnesota University Press, 1998.

Willinsky, John and Vivian Forssman. "A tale of two cultures and a technology: A/musical politics of curriculum in four acts." In C. Cornbleth (Ed.), *Curriculum, Politics, Policy: Cases in Context.* Albany, NY: State University of New York Press 2000, pp. 21-48.

CHAPTER NINETEEN

Can Post-Structuralist and Neo-Marxist Approaches Be Joined? Building Composite Approaches in Critical Educational Theory and Research

Thomas Pedroni[1]

Introduction and purpose

IN THE PAST two decades there has been considerable debate within and around education among post-structuralists and other critical theorists regarding issues such as agency, identity, the nature of power and the state, and the meaning and possibility of liberatory politics. My purpose in this essay is to assess the terms of this debate, demonstrating that the conversation among nonetheless been a productive one. Composite methods of analysis have emerged which further our ability to construct more nuanced understandings of our empirical subjects, and our capacity to form a more transformative educational vision that addresses structural issues of distribution as well as their intersection with exclusionary discursive practices.

My first task then will be to reconstruct the general terms of this conversation. In so doing, my primary objective will not be the production of a historical narrative of the evolution of these debates, yet I want to assert that my approach is not ahistorical either. It recognizes that these arguments have emerged over time and in response to local conditions and dynamics that are historically rooted. Having said this, my emphasis will be on broadly representing various positions that have issued from multiple contexts, sometimes intentionally in conversation with one another and sometimes clearly not. This strategy makes it possible for us to bring heterogeneous critical traditions to bear upon one other in a manner that a strict commitment to cotemporality or common geopolitical and cultural circumstances would not; it recognizes that it is precisely this type of juxtaposition that enables the productive misappropriation and creative misreading that frequently ushers in considerable breakthrough in critical

---

1   Keynote address, Department of Educational Leadership, University of Massachusetts Dartmouth, March 29, 2015.

research. While this argument seeks to validate imaginative critical and theoretical exploration, it is not an endorsement of historically irresponsible and epistemologically reckless scholarship. Some theoretical constructions cannot be expropriated from their cultural, geopolitical, and temporal contexts without considerable damage to both their utility and validity.

With this in mind, I want to foreground a set of broad themes that I explore as I move toward a conceptualization of how we might bring together post-structural and other critical analytical tools in ways that ultimately serve radically democratic educational and social purposes (while remembering Judith Butler's injunction that we deconstruct the very propositions which enable our action; so at the same time that I refuse to minimize my political objectives by wrapping "radically democratic" in scare quotes, I do acknowledge the provisional and potentially exclusionary nature of such a construction; Butler & Scott, 1992). One of these transitory themes will be an interrogation of precisely which contributive strategies within post-structuralism actually constitute innovation. Are there precursors to these approaches already within the very object of much of post-structuralism's critique—neo-Marxism?

A related wayside in this discussion will be an exposition of some of the misrepresentations of post-structuralist and neo-Marxist critical traditions in the respective polemics mounted against them. Too often such polemics have relied on anemic, reductive, and/or hyperbolic reconstructions of the object of their critique, thus offering little or no substantial contribution to the larger debate. In a similar vein, I draw attention to examples within critical educational scholarship of some of the debilitating consequences of partisanship for a singular conceptual strand, be it of a poststructural or a neo-Marxist inflection. Such works do less than they could to illuminate our empirical contexts or further our theoretical and political agendas.

Finally, I highlight some of the theoretical and empirical educational research that has been most successful in drawing together critical and post-structural analytical traditions in ways that are conceptually rigorous and fair at the same time that they further our understanding of their particular empirical context.

But first I provide an overview of some of the difficulties in critical (largely neo-Marxist) theoretical approaches in education that have served as a catalyst for many critical, poststructuralist, and postmodernist interventions.

Has neo-Marxism needed a post-structuralist reworking?

The raison d'être for many post-structuralist interventions in critical theoretical work in education derives from a set of inadequacies and dead-ends in neo-Marxism of which many neo-Marxist scholars were themselves quite cognizant. For example, much post-structuralist dissension is rooted in the classic problem in Marxism of adequately theorizing the relationship between the economic structure of a capitalist social formation and its ideological and cultural 'superstructure'. In Marx, as many neo-Marxist theorists have noted, this relationship is undertheorized and/or contradictory (Althusser, 1971, pp. 127 186; Avincri, 1968; Gramsci, 1971; Hall, 1996, pp. 25–46). Although Marx's intention was to 'turn Hegel on his head' by bestowing primacy to material relations of power as the driving force of history, rather than an idealized and non-material 'consciousness', Marx's incomplete formulations could not sufficiently explain to Marxists of the early and middle-20th century why the revolution against capital, which had been postulated as historically inevitable, had not yet transpired.

Culturally oriented Marxists of various traditions and geopolitical and cultural contexts of the early and middle-20th century grappled not only with the question of why the revolution that was to have come from a teleological playing out of contradictions inherent in material relations of power hadn't arrived but also with the rather ugly reality that in many ways capitalist relations of power and production had actually become more embedded in European social formations through developments in both material and institutional technologies and cultural political forms (Althusser, 1971). A common current in each of these strands was their interrogation and elaboration of the connection between a social formation's economic base and its superstructure. Each of these formulations was productive but in turn generated further conceptual problems. Many of these shortcomings have subsequently been addressed (both productively and partially) by post-structuralists.

For example, Louis Althusser had responded by attempting to theorize the importance of what he termed 'Ideological State Apparatuses' in the production and reproduction of unequal and capitalist relations of power (Althusser, 1971, pp. 127–186). What prevented revolution for Althusser was the overdetermined power of capitalist ideology to create (or interpellate) subjects who were amenable to established relations of power (Althusser, 1971, p. 174). Althusser found this power cycling through and 'realized' within various public and private institutions in civil society, including the schools, the media, trade unions, political parties, the family, and religion (Althusser, 1971, p. 143). For Althusser, Marx's teleological vision had not played out because the power of the capitalist state was vested in not just the material forces of production and the political branches of the state (the repressive state apparatuses) but also in the overdetermined ideology that formed compliant subjects through their relationships with institutions.

While Althusser contributed to Marxist theorizations by emphasizing the importance of the superstructure in maintaining and reproducing capitalist relations of production and power, his vision in the end replicated a notion of history without human agency and subsequently without the potential for social transformation. For Althusser, despite an occasional footnoted caveat, this process of ideological reproduction is smooth, efficient, and basically uncontested. Any resistance is either misguided or meaningless. The character of the overdetermined ideology is seamless and bereft of contradictions. Inadvertently, Althusser had constructed a Marxism of despair.

Earlier, and in another temporal, geopolitical, and cultural context, Antonio Gramsci had struggled with this same dilemma in Marxism (the relationship between the base and the superstructure), although perhaps more productively. In a formulation somewhat analogous to Althusser's notion of a bifurcated state consisting of both ideological and repressive state apparatuses, Gramsci posited 'two great floors' to the capitalist superstructure, that of 'political society' (e.g. the parliament, the police, the military) and that of 'civil society.' Within his theorization of civil society, Gramsci discovered and explicated a process of 'spontaneous' consent given by the great masses of the population to the direction imprinted on social life by the fundamental ruling class, a consent which Gramsci believed came into existence 'historically' from the prestige (and hence from the trust) accruing to the ruling class from its position and its function in the world of production (Gramsci, 1971). While this conceptualization enabled Gramsci to account for the continued success of the capitalist ruling classes, by depicting 'hegemony' as a historical process necessitating the continued 'winning' of the population's consent, Gramsci left the door open for subaltern agency and the possibility of social transformation. Through the fracturing of hegemonic alliances which instantiated this consent, and the formation of counter-hegemonic alliances, material relations of power within a social formation could be fundamentally altered (Gramsci, 1971).

While Gramsci's theorization was and continues to be quite productive in helping us to understand both the maintenance of current relations of class and gender, racial, and sexual power and their possible and actual contestation, it nonetheless contained problems and inadequacies to which post-structuralism has effectively responded.

But before I turn to these post-structural interventions, I want to speak to the ways in which the formulations of figures like Althusser and Gramsci have been productively subsumed into critical educational research.

Some of the earliest neo-Marxist research in education emerged in the work of scholars such as Paul Willis, Michael Apple, Samuel Bowles, and Herbert Gintis, who each sought to explain the vital role that educational institutions played in the reproduction of capitalist relations of power. For Bowles and Gintis, schools aided in the reproduction of capital in a rather functionalist way; they produced and reproduced 'human capital' by training and sorting workers into their designated place within the capitalist economic formation. Thus, schools 'corresponded' closely with the capitalist project (Bowles & Gintis, 1976; Cole, 1988). Similarly, in an empirical study of boys in a working-class school in the United Kingdom, Paul Willis described the ways in which students resisted the overt and hidden curriculum of the schools but in ways that were ultimately reproductive; for Willis, their resistance only further secured their matriculation into the dead-end economic slots which capital 'intended' for them (Willis, 1977). In *Ideology and Curriculum*, Michael Apple correspondingly emphasized the vital cultural role that schools played in the reproduction of capital in the United States (Apple, 1990).

While the neo-Marxist tradition in education has grown considerably in sophistication since these first early, limited, yet quite productive incursions—in part due to its increasing emphasis on contributions from Gramsci, various feminisms, critical race theory, queer theory, linguistics, and cultural studies—it is precisely the economic reductionism of this early period that has served as the object of critique for many post-structuralist theorists in education ever since. This neglect of both the productive importance of these earliest interventions, and the conceptual growth that has occurred in neo-Marxist critical education studies since this time, is evident in volumes such as Ian Hunter's *Rethinking the School*. Hunter asserts that Marxian theory in education conceptualizes the emergence of the modern school as "a means of serving the social requirements and economic interests of capitalist societies" (Hunter, 1994, p. 34). While neo-Marxist educational scholars do (correctly) underscore the role that schools have historically played in maintaining economic relations of power, Hunter's reductionism ignores the careful and nuanced portrait that neo-Marxists and neo-Gramscians of the past two decades have constructed of schools as sites of resistance, contestation, and identity production, in which complex struggles by an amalgamation of social movements concerning such fundamental questions as "what schools are for" and "what and whose knowledge should be taught" are embodied (Apple, 1993).

Notwithstanding such examples, there has been much in the post-structural literature that has been quite useful for critical educational work, and many neo-Marxist researchers have readily incorporated such concepts into their analyses. (As we shall discuss later, the question will still remain as to what degree these interventions, contrary to the assertions of some post-structuralists, are actually new to neo-Marxism and critical educational research.)

For example, much has been contributed to critical education studies by post-structuralism's emphasis on the process of identity formation, on the foregrounding of the ways in which relations of power are inscribed in and through discourse, and on its vigilant suspicion of reified notions of agency, the subject, and the meaning and possibility of 'liberatory' projects (Luke & Gore, 1992). Furthermore, poststructuralism has encouraged critical theorists to rework historical conceptions of the development of educational institutions that were embedded in linear narratives that underemphasized the complex aggregation of forces, dynamics, and interests that structured educational discursive practices (Wagner & Wittrock, 1989).

In many of these aspects, critical education studies was indeed in need of a fundamental reworking of some of its most basic concepts. For example, feminist educational theorists such as Elizabeth Ellsworth, Jennifer Gore, and Carmen Luke, utilizing insights garnered from poststructuralism's critique of the unitary Enlightenment (and masculinist) subject, powerfully challenged the figure of the sovereign critical and liberatory agent at the heart of the critical pedagogical project (Luke & Gore, 1992). Key critical pedagogical texts had problematically finessed the complex dynamics of power inherent in the relationship between the liberatory teacher and his or her students (Freire, 1970; Giroux, 1988; McLaren, 1989; Shor & Freire, 1987). Rather than recognizing a critical teacher who possessed power, and sought therewith to 'empower' his or her students, feminist post-structuralist educators demonstrated the multiaxiality of relations of power discursively constructing everyday classroom life. Following Michel Foucault and others, they asserted that the teacher did not possess power but rather was located and formed within complex webs of gender, class, race, sexual and institutional power (Butler, 1993; Foucault, 1979a; 1980). Similarly, the teacher's students, rather than being monolithically oppressed, were intersected by axes of power in complex ways that sometimes even privileged the discursive and material power of the students over the teacher and each other (Ellsworth, 1988; Luke & Gore, 1992). Finally, the 'redemptive' project of critical pedagogy and of the liberatory teacher was itself interrogated and shown to be riddled with problematic reinscriptions of exclusionary discourses.

Much work has also been done among post-structural educational theorists to highlight the discursive production of the 'individual' student on whose behalf critical educational as well as other 'progressive' and liberal projects are intended to intervene. The theoretical interventions of John Meyer, Ian Hacking, and David Armstrong, for example, have helped to draw attention to the ways in which schools can be identified as primary sites in which individuals and the very notion of individuality are 'fabricated' (Armstrong, 1994, pp. 222–236; Meyer, 1986, pp. 208–221). Among post-structuralists, Valerie Walkerdine has perhaps been among the most successful in demonstrating how discourses involving the school, the family, and the community have produced reified notions of childhood (or, in much of her work, girlhood) which put children in terrible quandaries as they try to negotiate among the multiple contradictory discourses simultaneously 'framing' them (Walkerdine, 2001, pp. 15–34). In fact, much productive research has been undertaken by the 'governmentality' school within critical and post-structural educational theory which has highlighted the relationship between the state and the social formation's need to produce 'governable' subjects and the construction of social scientific and educational discourses around the 'meaning' of childhood (Hultqvist & Dahlberg, 2001; Popkewitz & Bloch, 2001, pp. 85–118; Rose, 1999).

Another strand of useful post-structural or postmodern intervention has emerged around the analysis of changing modes of production, distribution, and consumption within new 'fast capitalist' and post-Fordist economies. Theorists such as David Harvey, John Clarke, Janet Newman, and Immanuel Wallerstein have used insights from both post-structural and more traditionally neo-Marxist conceptualizations of the cultural, economic, and political spheres to argue that the increasing globalization of capital, as well as the influence of new production and communication technologies and new managerialist discourses, have reshaped not only the functioning of global economic systems but also relationships of power within the workplace, the family, and schools, as well as between nation-states and capital (Clarke & Newman, 1997; Harvey, 1989; Wallerstein, 1974). As a result of these shifts, the coherence of the very meanings of terms like citizenship, the public sphere, and the sovereignty of the nation-state has been eroded and contested.

Many of these theorizations, situated simultaneously in both post-structuralism and other critical theories, including, perhaps most importantly, neo-Marxism, have most productively been brought into education by critical educational theorists such as Stephen Ball (1994), James Paul Gee (1999; Gee, Hull, & Lankshear, 1996), and Michael Apple (1996, 2001). Interestingly, none of these critical educational theorists would consider themselves a partisan of post-structuralism or postmodernism, and each would undoubtedly consider themselves to have benefited quite richly from various trajectories of thought within the neo-Marxist tradition. Which begs the next question that I would like to pose: How much of the post-structuralist claim to theoretical innovation in education and other fields is actually legitimate? Notwithstanding the assertions of many educational post-structuralists, how much of the agenda of post-structuralism (if there can be said to be such a thing) is actually a significant departure from neo-Marxist theoretical production?

The premature post-structuralism of neo-Marxism

For example, the claim is often made that neo-Marxist discourses necessarily but problematically reinscribe a notion of the sovereign Enlightenment subject (Hunter, 1994; Popkewitz & Brennan, 1998). Given this, it is ironic to find that it is precisely one of the most disparaged of the neo-Marxists (and rightly so to some extent), Louis Althusser, who introduced into French theorizations of Marxism the notion of a subject interpellated by and through ideology (Althusser, 1971, p. 174). In fact, the notion of identity as constituted within discourse—identity as the assumption of 'subject positions' produced within discourse—perhaps the centerpiece of much post-structuralist critique, is deeply rooted in Althusser's constructions.

Related to this, post-structuralist claims to innovation in our understanding of the instability of linguistic and discursive signifiers is similarly questionable. Working in the field of Marxist linguistics in the early 20th century, Mikhail Bakhtin and V. N. Volosinov (quite possibly the same individual) posited notions of the multiaccentual and heteroglossic character of language and discursive practice that continue to inform some of the most promising educational research today (Bakhtin, 1981, 1986; Gee, 1999; Gutierrez, 1997; Volosinov, 1973).

Furthermore, the notion of multiaxiality in relations of power within school settings, the centerpiece of Ellsworth's later successful criticism of critical pedagogy (Ellsworth, 1988), also predates post-structuralism. Michael Apple and Lois Weis, theorists within in fact predates most of the 'corpus' of the post-structural project. Michael Apple and Lois Weis, two of the most outspoken theorists within the neo-Marxist educational tradition, posited 'the parallelist position' as early as 1982 as a way of understanding the simultaneous workings of class, race, and gender within intersecting cultural, political, and economic spheres (Apple & Weis, 1983). This transcendence of some of the most problematic aspects of base/superstructure models in neo-Marxism *by neo-Marxists* is frequently under-acknowledged by partisans of post-structuralism in education.

Neo-Marxism has not been a static presence in the educational field; rather, its fluid development is further demonstrated by the subsequent revision of the parallelist position by Apple and Cameron McCarthy, as they postulated a non-synchronous parallelist position which allowed that raced, classed, and gendered identities, intersecting in a single individual, were not necessarily mutually reinforcing of one another; furthermore, in differing sociocultural contexts, one of the dynamics of identity (e.g., race) might take temporary precedence over the others.

Finally, while the call among post-structuralists for a non-linear reconceptualization of educational history is in itself quite understandable, its implicit claim that previous interpretations of educational history have been monolithically linear is not justifiable. For example, Herbert Kliebard's acclaimed history of the struggle over the American curriculum is exemplary of the power of non-linear history to come to terms with the sometimes strange aggregations of social movements and other historical forces behind the creation of a complex and contradictory American curriculum.

Has post-structuralism needed a neo-Marxist reworking?

While the degree to which post-structuralism represents a significant departure from neo-Marxism is in question, there is much in post-structural educational research that itself might benefit from a neo-Marxist reworking. For example, in the work of some post-structuralist researchers, 'discourse' is attributed with a monolithic and totalizing character that eerily parallels the vaunted position given to material relations of power and their expression in ideology in the most economistic readings of Marx.

Even in the work of one of the most brilliant post-structuralist theorists in education, Thomas Popkewitz, we find an elegant depiction of multiple and intersecting 'scaffolded' discourses within educational settings, which despite its complexity still does not allow for the possibility of tensions among multiple scaffolded discourses as they interpellate the teaching (or learning) subject (Popkewitz, 1998; Lindblad, Pettersson, and Popkewitz, 1999). That is, for Popkewitz these scaffolded discourses don't ever seem to rub up against each other, against the pre-assumed discourses of teachers-in-training, or even against the contexts into which they are localized. Although a recognition of scaffolded discourses might have been a starting point for reconstructing a post-structural sense of agency among subaltern individuals and groups, instead these only seem to cooperate in a singular and totalizing social architecture.

A similar assertion among some post-structuralist theorists in education—that all subject positions, and all educational interventions, produce ethically similar exclusions—presents further problems. While it is arguably correct and insightful that each discursive step toward inclusiveness produces new and often unanticipated exclusions, a relativist enunciation of such a position leaves educators and educational researchers in a zero-sum game in which there is no ethical way to be an educator or a researcher.

Even though, inevitably, the interventions we might produce to counteract exclusion will contain elements that produce new and unintended exclusions, here Judith Butler and Gayatri Spivak offer a contingent sense of possibility that moves us beyond a zero-sum game (Butler & Scott, 1992; Spivak, 1998, pp. 197–221).

Whereas a zero-sum game in relation to inclusion/exclusion leaves teachers and other educational practitioners stalemated, Butler and Spivak speak to the need for ethically committed people to contingently and strategically assume subject positions from which they might act, speak, and be heard (Butler, 1992, pp. 3–21; Spivak, 1998, pp. 197–221). While these subject positions are necessarily constructed and assumed, Spivak and Butler caution those so enabled to simultaneously deconstruct the very identities they take on, in order to bring attention to (and hopefully mitigate) the exclusions that are produced. Although their agent is not the universal and masculinist agent of the European Enlightenment—rather, it is contingent, fluid, and historically constructed— they do nevertheless preserve a manner in which we might envision a viable political project in which it is worth engaging.

Toward a composite approach in educational theory and research

Michel Foucault, one of the most referenced theorists of power among both post-structuralists and neo-Marxists, cautions us not to see discursive power as replacing more traditional, structural, and material concepts of power. He writes, "[I]n reality one has a triangle, sovereignty–discipline–government, which has as its primary target the population and as its essential mechanism the apparatus of security" (Foucault, 1979b, pp. 5–22). Thus, for Foucault, sovereign notions of power (and agency) still operate within a social formation in which the deployment of the normative gaze is nevertheless central (Rabinow, 1984). Foucault's almost exclusive emphasis on discursive technologies of power in his writings needs to be read, therefore, as a polemic against the French Marxist tradition from which he emerged and not as a reduction of all power to nonstructural forms.

While it may not be possible or even desirable to arrive at a clean "synthesis" of neo-Marxist and post-structural conceptions of power, it is clear that both structural and non-structural forms of power operate simultaneously within the social formation, producing patterns of inclusion and exclusion, and maldistribution of resources, sometimes in mutually reinforcing and sometimes in "non-synchronous" ways (McCarthy, 1998). Therefore, as Nancy Fraser and others have demonstrated, we can also envision that juxtaposing post-structural and other critical approaches in our analyses of our respective empirical contexts will prove much more useful than partisan efforts within a singular theoretical strand strand (Fraser, 1997, pp. 11–39). The injunction we should follow, then, may not be 'to Gramscianize Foucault while Foucauldianizing Gramsci' but rather to simultaneously Gramscianize and Foucauldianize our own analyses. Theorists and scholars as varied as Michael Apple, Stephen Ball, Jim Gee, Stuart Hall, Kris Gutierrez, and many others, both within and outside education, have made significant attempts, with varying degrees of success, to practice what we might call a 'neo-materialist post-structuralism' in their work.

For example, in their essay "Structuring the Postmodern in Education Policy", Michael Apple and Geoff Whitty call for critical educational researchers to embrace a series of insights and themes from postmodernism and post-structuralism, including the rejection of grand narratives predicated around singular causality, special attention to the 'pragmatic' and the 'local' as political sites, acknowledgment of the complexity of the power/knowledge nexus, and an extension of political concerns beyond what they call the 'holy trinity' of class, race, and gender. Furthermore, they argue for the post-structural emphasis on multiplicity and heterogeneity in our analyses, as well as its foregrounding of the decentered subject as a site of struggle (Apple & Whitty,1999).

Simultaneously, Apple and Whitty insist that we take seriously the economy as a massive structuring force; critical educational theorists must, for example, speak clearly about the structuration of class without reducing everything to a strict structural determinism. While post-structural theories are helpful in overcoming the tendency of overly structural theories to ignore the role of the local, the contingent, and individual propensities in accounting for what education does, nevertheless "there is a world of difference between emphasizing the local, the contingent and the non-correspondent and ignoring any determinacy or any structural relationship among practices" (Apple & Whitty, 1999, p. 29).

In the same way, Dennis Carlson and Michael Apple urge a composite neo-Gramscian and post-structural approach in their introduction to *Power/Knowledge/Pedagogy*:

> Gramscian discourse has highlighted the roles economic and technological forces and ideological struggles are playing in reshaping the "post-Fordist" cultural and political landscape; and Foucault's work focuses our attention on the role of the state and "expert" knowledge in constructing "normalized" citizens and subjectivity. (1998, p. 6)

The general theoretical and analytical aim of such researchers is to allow questions of identity formation to permeate their analysis without letting go of a realistic appraisal of economic constraints (Apple, 1996, pp. 42–67).

Equally productive instantiations of successful juxtapositions of critical and post-structural analytical approaches are to be found in the works and/or edited collections of other critical researchers within education, including Jim Gee, Chris Gutierrez, Joe Kincheloe, Shirley Steinberg, Nelson Rodriguez, Ronald Chennault, Geoff Whitty, Sally Power, David Halpin, and Stephen Ball.

Both Jim Gee and Kris Gutierrez have effectively incorporated analytical tools from Mikhail Bakhtin, Pierre Bourdieu, and Michel Foucault in their investigations of the way that both discursive and structural processes in the social formation infuse everyday classroom life, especially in regard to the reproduction, contestation, and exchange of cultural capital (Bakhtin, 1981, 1986; Bourdieu, 1984, 1991; Gee, 1999; Gutierrez, 1997). A number of contributors to a volume by Joe Kincheloe, Shirley Steinberg, and Nelson Rodriquez, on the other hand, have used post structural and neo-Gramscian analytics to examine the formation of hegemonic and counter-hegemonic racial and sexual identities in and around educational settings. Geoff Whitty, Sally Power, and David Halpin, as well as Stephen Ball, describe the ways in which privatizing discourses and the construction of quasi-markets in education have eroded not only public education but also the meaning of citizenship and the public sphere within the larger social formation (Ball, 1994; Whitty, Power, & Halpin, 1998).

Future directions: where do we go from here?

Although significant headway has been made within and around education in successfully bringing critical and post-structural approaches together in ways that help critical educational researchers illuminate their empirical contexts and identify possible spaces for radical social and educational transformation, there are moments in this composite project which still rest together uneasily, and are in need of further reworking.

While the conversation between Nancy Fraser, Judith Butler, and Seyla Benhabib regarding the possibility of a tenable reconceptualization of critical agency in light of post-structuralist interventions has been as fascinating as it has been productive, their project is as of yet incomplete (Butler, 1993, pp. 27–56; Fraser, 1997, pp. 207–224). A successful construction of a theory of subjectivity that is simultaneously nonessentializing yet politically possibilitarian has remained elusive. Stuart Hall has assisted in pointing to the continued inadequacies of post-structural theories of identity. Current attempts at this project, he argues, "offer us a formal account of the construction of subject positions within discourse while revealing little about why it is that certain individuals occupy some subject positions rather than others . . . Discursive subject positions become a priori categories which individuals seem to occupy in an unproblematic fashion" (Hall & Du Gay, 1996, p. 10). He continues (and I quote him at length because I believe he eloquently nails the tensions surrounding a theorization of the subject on the head):

> What I think we can see [in Discipline and Punish] is Foucault being pushed, by the scrupulous rigour of his own thinking, through a series of conceptual shifts at different stages in his work, towards a recognition that, since the decentring of the subject is not the destruction of the subject, and since the 'centring' of discursive practice cannot work without the constitution of subjects, the theoretical work cannot be fully accomplished without complementing the account of discursive and disciplinary regulation with an account of the practices of subjective self-constitution. It has never been enough—in Marx, in Althusser, in Foucault—to elaborate a theory of how

individuals are summoned into place in the discursive structures. It has always, also, required an account of how subjects are constituted; and in this
work, Foucault has gone a considerable way in showing this, in reference
to historically specific discursive practices, normative self-regulation, and
technologies of the self. The question which remains is whether we also
require to, as it were, close the gap between the two: that is to say, a theory
of what the mechanisms are by which individuals as subjects identify (or do
not identify) with the 'positions' to which they are summoned; as well as
how they fashion, stylize, produce and 'perform' these positions, and why
they never do so completely, for once and all time, and some never do, or are
in a constant, agonistic process of struggling with, resisting, negotiating and
accommodating the normative or regulative rules with which they confront
and regulate themselves. (Hall & Du Gay, 1996, pp. 13–14)

In some ways, then, post-structuralist theories of the subject have only deferred
the question of how the subject is constituted; the subject is 'hailed' and interpellated
through discourse, through the limited number of subject positions that are on offer,
and by the constraints embedded in each. But what is it in the subject that allows it to
be 'hailed' in the first place? Hall points to the realm of feminist work in psychoanalysis
(which Foucault had explicitly rejected) as a possible avenue for approaching this as of
yet unconcluded argument. For Hall, this question is only likely to be advanced "when
both the necessity and the 'impossibility' of identities, and the suturing of the psychic
and the discursive in their constitution, are fully and unambiguously acknowledged"
(Hall & Du Gay, 1996, p. 16).

Within education, we need a more complete and satisfactory theorization of the
constitution of the subject if we are to more fully comprehend, for example, the articulation of low-income parents with neo-liberal educational forms (the subject of my own
recent research; Pedroni, 2003).

Another area requiring fuller development within composite approaches is suggested by Ernesto Laclau and Chantal Mouffe, who emphasize the necessity of reworking
Gramscian and other neo-Marxist conceptualizations of the social, so as to remove what
they call the 'epistemological obstacles' to the full realization of neo-Marxism's radical
political and theoretical potential. They write,

It is only when the open, unsutured character of the social is fully accepted,
when the essentialism of the totality and of the elements is rejected, that this
potential becomes clearly visible and "hegemony" can come to constitute
a fundamental tool for political analysis on the left. These conditions arise
originally in the field of what we have termed the 'democratic revolution',
but they are only maximized in all their deconstructive effects in the project for a radical democracy, or, in other words, in a form of politics which is

founded not upon dogmatic postulation of any 'essence of the social', but, on the contrary, on affirmation of the contingency and ambiguity of every 'essence', and on the constitutive character of social division and antagonism. (Laclau & Mouffe, 1985, pp. 192–193)

Interestingly, although aspects of his work are highly problematic, Michele de Certeau seems to offer us a few conceptual tools with which to approach some of the remaining difficulties regarding subjectivity and the social. Although de Certeau's theory of power has the problem of positing strict binaries between essential categories such as "weak" and "strong" and "tactics" and "strategy", and although his theory of power is uniaxial, ahistorical, and essentially immune to transformative collective counter-hegemonic struggle, nevertheless he offers a notion of subaltern agency that has the advantages of being discursively produced, nonessential in regard to "the social", yet cast within relations of power (de Certeau, 1984). De Certeau is quite intriguing in his exploration of the manner in which fluid and ephemeral identities are tactically asserted and performed. Not surprisingly, though, he is still unable to account for how the 'hailed' subject is itself constituted as a desiring yet nonessential agent. Thus, a reworking of de Certeau may be helpful, but not sufficient, in addressing some of these concerns.

A final area which needs further attention in post-structural and critical juxtapositions concerns the question of how we, as critical educational researchers, epistemologically ground both our empirical research claims and our political projects. The radical constructivist position, argued for by French historian of science Bruno Latour and supported by educational post-structuralists such as Thomas Popkewitz, maintains that science claims succeed or fail in their quest to "gain reality" depending on the capacity of the involved scientists to "hold together as many elements as they can", by which Latour means things like institutional and agribusiness support support (Latour, 1999, p. 164; Popkewitz & Brennan, 1998). While there is much to be said for an analytics that draws our attention to the role that institutional forces play in determining what research questions are funded and asked, and therefore what knowledge is produced, Latour's position seems to vacate the possibility that scientists (or social scientific researchers, for that matter) can legitimately make claims on empirical grounds.

The opposite position from Latour's idealism would be a naive positivist position, with which Marx's materialism has sometimes quite wrongly been associated (Avineri, 1968, pp. 65–77). Here, there is essentially no intermediary space between human consciousness and external reality. Through the use of proper methods, researchers can gain access to raw 'factness' in a permanent and enduring way. Post-structuralists and other non-positivists (including Marx himself) have rightly criticized this position for its naiveté regarding the complex ways in which financial and social capital influence what knowledge is ultimately constructed. Furthermore, these critics have contended, positivism disregards the always mediated relationship between linguistically and discursively constituted human consciousness and 'external reality.' Finally, post-structuralists and other non-positivists have convincingly argued that facts are always 'materialized' (at least in part) as an effect of the discourses we construct about them (Butler, 1993; Harding, 1991).

As a general rule, post-structuralists such as Butler seem to concur with Latour's radical constructivist approach, although Butler and Spivak have argued for "contingent" and "strategic" truth claims based around ethical and political imperatives (Butler, 1993; Spivak, 1988). Therefore, according to Butler and Spivak, although we cannot ground our empirical and juridico-political claims epistemologically in "science", we can provisionally support them through their relationship to other ethical claims.

However, I would argue that none of these avenues—the radical constructivist, the positivist, or the 'contingent'—are entirely adequate for critical educational projects situated in post-structural and critical theoretical approaches. Is there nothing other than ethics and the weight of institutional power that would allow us to argue that some claims are better than others? If not, why do we involve ourselves in empirical research? As with Hall's concerns about agency and subjectivity, we are left here with a dilemma. While we want to (and do) recognize the validity of many of the constructivist arguments concerning the 'materialization' through discourse of exclusionary and oppressive 'facts', nevertheless, as critical educational researchers, we need an epistemological foundation other than mere contingency from which to make our empirical and political claims.

I concur with Jim Gee's (1999) argument that "humans construct their realities, though what is 'out there' beyond human control places serious constraints on this construction (so 'reality' is not 'only' constructed)" (p. 94). However, Gee does not intend this to apply to social research contexts. Instead, he outlines four elements which, taken together, constitute validity for social research involving discourse analysis: convergence, which is reminiscent of the concept of 'triangulation,' agreement, among 'native speakers' and discourse analysts, coverage, or the reading's applicability to other contexts, and linguistic details, or connection to known linguistic structures. For Gee, validity in discourse analysis is a social, not individual, process (Gee, 1999, p. 95).

While there is much in this account that is compelling, Gee runs into problems that are homologous to those Hall raised concerning the "hailed subject". Deferring the moment of validation of empirical claims to 'the social' only begs the question: How, then, is the disposition of the community of 'validators' regarding empirical claims itself constituted? And so we are right back again in the moment of needing to ground claims in some sort of empirical relationship with 'reality'. Entire social scientific communities in agreement about an empirical claim can be and have been 'wrong'. In such a scenario, what is it that enables us to assert that a claim is faulty, other than either an even larger community of dissenting experts, institutional muscle, or ethically based and contingent assertions? It seems that 'external reality', even one involving human construction, does exert a disciplining force, even if quite muted, on the truth claims that can be made about it. Clearly, if this is so, there is a need for a neo-materialist reworking of the epistemology of research claims that reasserts a kind of ephemeral and highly conditional critically realist epistemology.

In closing, our critical educational projects will continue to benefit from the debate among post-structuralists and neo-Marxists to the degree that we incorporate elements from both poststructural and critical neo-Marxist traditions in creative yet theoretically rigorous ways. Additionally, we should more fully theorize the agency of the subaltern subject and the nonessential character of the social through a critical reappropriation and reworking of ideas from sources such as de Certeau and psychoanalysis. Finally, we need to construct a critically realist epistemology which brings us beyond relativism and moral provisionalism at the same time that it recognizes key constructivist insights.

Without denying the existence of real tensions within, between, and among various critical theoretical traditions in and around education, this essay acknowledges that there have been serious and successful attempts at disciplined drawings from each of these traditions in ways that allow their analyses to complement each other. In the coming years, such composite approaches will become increasingly important in furthering our ability to construct more nuanced understandings of our empirical subjects, as well as our capacity to form a more transformative educational vision that addresses structural issues of distribution and their intersection with exclusionary discursive practices.

References

Althusser, L. (1971). *Lenin and philosophy and other essays.* New York: Monthly Review Press.

Apple, M. W. (1990). *Ideology and curriculum, second edition.* New York: Routledge.

Apple, M. W. (1993). *Official knowledge: Democratic education in a conservative age.* New York: Routledge.

Apple, M. W. (1996). *Cultural politics and education.* New York, NY: Teachers College Press.

Apple, M. W. (2001). *Educating the "right" way: Markets, standards, God, and inequality.* New York: RoutledgeFalmer.

Apple, M. W., & Weis, L. (1983). *Ideology and practice in schooling.* Philadelphia: Temple University Press.

Apple, M. W. & Whitty, G. (1999). Structuring the postmodern in education policy. In D. Hill, P. McLaren, M. Cole, & G. Rikowski (Eds.), *Postmodernism in educational theory: Education and the politics of human resistance.* London: Tufnell Press.

Armstrong, D. (1994). Bodies of knowledge/knowledge of bodies. In C. Jones & R. Porter (Eds.), *Reassessing Foucault: Power, medicine, and the body.* London: Routledge.

Avineri, S. (1968). *The social and political thought of Karl Marx.* Cambridge, UK: Cambridge University Press.

Bakhtin, M. (1981). *The dialogic imagination.* Ed. M. Holquist; trans. M. Holquist and C. Emerson. Austin: University of Texas Press.

Bakhtin, M. (1986). *Speech genres and other late essays.* Ed. C. Emerson and M. Holquist; trans. V. W. McGee. Austin: University of Texas Press.

Ball, S. (1994). *Education reform: A critical and post-structural approach.* Buckingham, England: Open University Press.

Bourdieu, P. (1984). *Distinction: A social critique of the judgement of taste.* Cambridge, MA: Harvard University Press.

Bourdieu, P. (1991). *Language and symbolic power.* Cambridge, MA: Harvard University Press.

Bowles, S., & Gintis, H. (1976). *Schooling in capitalist America.* New York: Basic Books.

Butler, J. (1992). Contingent foundations: Feminism and the question of postmodernism. In J. Butler & J. W. Scott (Eds.), *Feminists theorize the political* (pp. 3–21). New York: Routledge.

Butler, J. (1993). *Bodies that matter: On the discursive limits of "sex".* New York: Routledge.

Butler, J., & Scott, J. W. (Eds.). (1992). *Feminists theorize the political.* New York: Routledge.

Carlson, D., & Apple, M. W. (Eds.). (1998): *Power/knowledge/pedagogy: The meaning of democratic education in unsettling times.* Boulder, CO: Westview Press.

Clarke, J., & Newman, J. (1997). *The managerial state: Power, politics and ideology in the remaking of social welfare.* London: Sage Publications.

Cole, M. (Ed.). (1988). *Bowles and Gintis revisited.* New York: Falmer Press.

de Certeau, M. (1984). *The practice of everyday life.* Berkeley: University of California Press.

Ellsworth, E. (1988). *Why doesn't this feel empowering? Working through the repressive myths of critical pedagogy.* Paper presented at the Tenth Conference on Curriculum Theory and Curriculum Practice, Dayton, Ohio, October 26–9.

Foucault, M. (1979a). *Discipline and punish: The birth of the prison.* New York:Vintage Books.

Foucault, M. (1979b). Governmentality. *Ideology and Consciousness, 6,* 5–22.

Foucault, M. (1980). *The history of sexuality: Volume one: An introduction.* New York: Vintage Books.

Fraser, N. (1997). *Justice interruptus: Critical reflections on the "postsocialist" condition.* New York: Routledge.

Freire, P. (1970). *Pedagogy of the oppressed.* New York: Continuum.

Gee, J. P. (1999). *An introduction to discourse analysis: Theory and method.* London: Routledge.

Gee, J. P., Hull, G., & Lankshear, C. (1996). *The new work order.* Sydney: Allen and Unwin.

Giroux, H. (1988). *Schooling and the struggle for public life: Critical pedagogy in the modern age.* Minneapolis: University of Minnesota Press.

Gramsci, A. (1971). *Selections from the prison notebooks of Antonio Gramsci.* Trans. Q. & G. Smith. New York: International Publishers.

Gutierrez, K. (1997). Global politics and local antagonisms: Research and practice as dissent and possibility. In P. McLaren, *Revolutionary multiculturalism: Pedagogies of dissent for the new millennium.* Boulder, CO: Westview Press.

Hall, S. (1996). The problem of ideology: Marxism without guarantees. In D. Morley & K.-H. Chen (Eds.), *Stuart Hall: Critical dialogues in cultural studies.* New York: Routledge.

Hall, S., & Du Gay, P. (Eds.). (1996). *Questions of cultural identity.* Thousand Oaks, CA: Sage Publications.

Harding, S. (1991). *Whose science? Whose knowledge? Thinking from women's lives.* Ithaca, NY: Cornell University Press.

Harvey, D. (1989). *The condition of postmodernity.* Cambridge, MA: Blackwell.

Hultqvist, K., & Dahlberg, G. (Eds.). (2001). *Governing the child in the new millennium.* New York: Routledge Falmer.

Hunter, I. (1994). *Rethinking the school: Subjectivity, bureaucracy, criticism.* New York: St. Martin's Press.

Laclau, E., & Mouffe, C. (1985). *Hegemony and socialist strategy.* London: Verso.

Latour, B. (1999). *Pandora's hope: Essays on the reality of science studies.* Cambridge, MA: Harvard University Press.

Lindblad, S, Pettersson, D. &. Popkewitz, Th. (1999). *Numbers, education, and making society: International assessments and its expertise.* New York: Routledge.

Luke, C., & Gore, J. (Eds.). (1992). *Feminisms and critical pedagogy.* New York: Routledge.

McCarthy, C. (1998). *The uses of culture.* New York: Routledge.

McCarthy, C. & Apple, M. W. (1988) Race, class and gender in American educational research: Toward a nonsynchronous parallelist position. *Perspectives in Education* 4, no. 2: 67–69.

McLaren, P. (1989). *Life in schools: An introduction to critical pedagogy in the foundations of education.* New York: Longman.

Meyer, J. W. (1986). Myths of socialization and of personality. In T. C. Heller, M. Sosna, & D. E. Wellbery (with A. I. Davidson, A. Swidler, & I. Watt) (Eds.), *Reconstructing individualism: Autonomy, individuality, and the self in Western thought* (pp. 208–21). Stanford: Stanford University Press.

Popkewitz, T. S. (1998). *Struggling for the soul: The politics of schooling and the construction of the teacher.* New York: Teacher's College Press.

Popkewitz, T. S., & Bloch, M. (2001). Administering freedom: A history of the present: Rescuing the parent to rescue the child for society. In K. Hultqvist & G. Dahlberg (Eds.), *Governing the child in the new millennium* (pp. 85–118). New York: RoutledgeFalmer.

Popkewitz, T. S. & Brennan, M. (Eds.). (1998). *Foucault's challenge: Discourse, knowledge, and power in education.* New York: Teachers College Press.

Rabinow, P. (Ed.). (1984). *The Foucault reader.* New York, NY: Pantheon Books

Rose, N. (1999). *Powers of freedom: Reframing political thought.* Cambridge: Cambridge University Press.

Shor, I., & Freire, P. (1987). *A pedagogy for liberation: Dialogues on transforming education.* Granby, MA: Bergin and Garvey Publishers.

Spivak, G. C. (1988). Subaltern studies: Deconstructing historiography. In G. C. Spivak, *In other worlds: Essays in cultural politics* (pp. 197–221): New York: Routledge.

Volosinov, V. N. (1973). *Marxism and the philosophy of language.* Cambridge, MA: Harvard University Press.

Wallerstein, I. (1974). *The modern world-system.* New York: Academic Press.

Whitty, G., Power, S., & Halpin, D. (1998). *Devolution and choice in education: The school, the state, and the market.* Buckingham: Open University Press.

Willis, P. (1977). *Learning to labor: How working class kids get working class jobs.* New York: Columbia University Press.

CHAPTER TWENTY

Education and Equality: Learning to Create a Community[1]

Ana Sanches Bello

SOMETIMES, EVEN IDEAS designed to make our lives better can get worn out from overuse. They become so hackneyed, distorted, misrepresented and misinterpreted that we cease to see ourselves reflected in them, while the absence of a shared definition hinders debate and understanding between groups and individuals. One such idea is the long sought-after concept of equality, the eternal desideratum of social change for the people deprived of it.

In order to explain a concept accurately, it is important to understand its origin. Ideas do not come out of nowhere nor are they the fruit of a single mind; ideas are based on a specific interpretation of the social and historical context. Although the concept of equality has been around since classical times, consensus regarding its meaning had still not been established by the eighteenth century. Rousseau defended the idea of a social contract among all members of society as an antidote to the medieval crisis of political legitimacy. He maintained that human beings are born free and equal but did not acknowledge women as possessors of the human faculty of reason. Condorcet, by contrast, championed the concept of universal reason and used it to reject all forms of discrimination against women. In the nineteenth century, the concept of equality continued to be contested by both the suffragette movement and Marxist economic analyses of social inequality.

The idea of equality emerged as an attempt to restore the principles of dignity and justice in radically broken societies. Since the earliest formulations of the concept, there has always been a tendency to see the victims of inequality as at least partly responsible for their own disadvantage. As arguments against social inequality have evolved, so too have discourses of victim-blaming. In order to correct the disparity of privilege between certain social groups, the principle of equality must take into account both the equal value of individuals and the range of differences between them. As Celia Amorós observes, 'the right to difference clearly presupposes the principle of equality; otherwise,

---

1   Revised keynote address at 1st TRED—Transformative Researchers and Educators for Democracy—Annual Pre-conference. Department of Edcuational Leadership, University of Massachusetts Dartmouth, November 15, 2012, Woodland Commons.

my difference would not be recognised and valued by others as worthy of the same respect as what I perceive as *his or her difference* from me' (1997, 430). This moral presupposition forms the basis of the idea that all individuals *have the right to have rights*, for it is only by recognising that *other people* do not have to be like *me* that the principle of egalitarian reciprocity is assured (Benhabib, 2004). Equality is not merely a question of morality, however, but entails practices conducive to the preservation of difference, as in the unequal redistribution of basic goods in order to guarantee the equality of all citizens (Fraser and Honneth, 2006; Rawls, 1999).

Equal treatment does not mean identical treatment, therefore. Treating a group of people as identical denies them the possibility of individual development. No group can ever be identical; however small the differences between us, it is our individuality that makes us great and allows us to use our reason to construct a fairer, more dignified existence. Regardless of this obvious distinction, however, equality and sameness are frequently represented as synonyms of each other in discourses from across the academic (and not so academic) spectrum. Language reveals that this is not the case: comments such as 'gypsies don't like working', 'immigrants come to steal our jobs' or 'women are very sensitive' represent all members of the group as identical, but not as equals, either among themselves or in relation to other social groups. What they do share is a position of inequality in society. While equality is frequently thought of as a political idea, possibly for historical reasons, it is in fact a moral belief in the human ability to be fair, free, good and kind to others. It is the idea that we must seek to treat others according to the same moral principles we apply to ourselves (Valcárcel, 1994).

The idea of equality invokes in us the equally complex concept of *citizenship* and the consensus view of citizenship as a collective public good. The concept of citizenship has evolved from the ancient Greek democratic model of participation in the public sphere, to a modern citizenship of rights that delegitimises subjection and protects citizens' civil, political and social right to participation (Camps, 2007). According to Marshall's (1965) famous classification, there are three types of citizenship: civil, political and social. Civil citizenship refers to the specifically legislated rights of citizens. Political citizenship concerns the right to participate in the exercise of political power, both indirectly, as by voting, and directly, by running for or holding political office. Social citizenship, a construct of the twentieth century, refers to the right to different social services, such as education, health, employment and social insurance, with the implication that failure by a society to guarantee any of these conditions is to deny its members their full rights as citizens.

Implicit in a citizenship conceived of as a type of globalised localism or subaltern cosmopolitanism is the possibility of reconstructing human rights in terms of diversity (Santos, 2010). This leads us to two questions, however: First, is universalism possible in complex, culturally diverse societies? And, even if it is, is it possible to establish a list of human rights? John Rawls's (1999) famous list of basic human rights contains: the right to life (including means of subsistence and security), the right to freedom (freedom from slavery, serfdom, forced occupation, and sufficient liberty to ensure freedom of conscience and thought), the right to personal property, and the right to formal equality (that is, that similar cases be treated similarly). Martha Nussbaum (2012) proposes a context-responsive universalist framework that may be applied in any culture but takes into account contextual preferences and beliefs. Her framework is intended as a way to measure quality of life and formulate a theory of social justice. This so-called capabilities approach should be flexible enough to allow people of all cultures and particularities to live with dignity and justice.[2]

The capability approach was first articulated by Amartya Sen (1980), though from a more economic perspective than Nussbaum's, and has been used extensively as a measurement tool in UN Human Development reporting.[3] As well as the contrasting scope of their work, Sen and Nussbaum also differed in relation to the possibility of compiling a list of core capabilities, which Sen considered too normative to apply across a range of

---

2   Nussbaum's list of the core capabilities for human functioning is as follows: *Life.* Being able to live to the end of a human life of normal length; not dying prematurely, or before one's life is so reduced as to be not worth living. *Bodily health.* Being able to have good health, including reproductive health; to be adequately nourished; to have adequate shelter. *Bodily integrity.* Being able to move freely from place to place; to be secure against violent assault, including sexual assault and domestic violence; having opportunities for sexual satisfaction and for choice in matters of reproduction. *Senses, Imagination, and Thought.* Being able to use the senses, to imagine, think, and reason – and to do these things in a 'truly human' way, a way informed and cultivated by an adequate education, including, but by no means limited to, literacy and basic mathematical and scientific training. Being able to use imagination and thought in connection with experiencing and producing works and events of one's own choice, religious, literary, musical, and so forth. Being able to use one's mind in ways protected by guarantees of freedom of expression with respect to both political and artistic speech, and freedom of religious exercise. Being able to have pleasurable experiences and to avoid non-beneficial pain. *Emotions.* Being able to have attachments to things and people outside ourselves; to love those who love and care for us, to grieve at their absence; in general, to love, to grieve, to experience longing, gratitude, and justified anger. Not having one's emotional development blighted by fear and anxiety. (Supporting this capability means supporting forms of human association that can be shown to be crucial in their development.) *Practical reason.* Being able to form a conception of the good and to engage in critical reflection about the planning of one's life. (This entails protection for the liberty of conscience and religious observance.) *Affiliation. a).* Being able to live with and toward others, to recognize and show concern for other human beings, to engage in various forms of social interaction; to be able to imagine the situation of another. (Protecting this capability means protecting institutions that constitute and nourish such forms of affiliation, and also protecting the freedom of assembly and political speech.) b) Having the social bases of self-respect and nonhumiliation; being able to be treated as a dignified being whose worth is equal to that of others. This entails provisions of nondiscrimination on the basis of race, sex, sexual orientation, ethnicity, caste, religion, national origin. **Other species.** Being able to live with concern for and in relation to animals, plants, and the world of nature. *Play.* Being able to laugh, to play, to enjoy recreational activities. *Control over one's environment.* a) Political. Being able to participate effectively in political choices that govern one's life; having the right of political participation, protections of free speech and association. b) Material. Being able to hold property (both land and movable goods), and having property rights on an equal basis with others; having the right to seek employment on an equal basis with others; having the freedom from unwarranted search and seizure. In work, being able to work as a human being, exercising practical reason, and entering into meaningful relationships of mutual recognition with other workers. (2011, 33–34).

3   Sen's list of capabilities, defined as substantive freedoms, comprises the ability to live to old age, the ability to engage in economic transactions and the ability to participate in political activities. Development is thus understood in terms of capability to function, while the absence or deprivation of capabilities is seen as an indicator of poverty.

contexts. For Seyla Benhabib (2008), the difficulty lies in how to specify the legal rights and protections of each individual in a world of contrasting systems of law and unequal observance of human rights.

Legal universalism might therefore be defined as a non-essentialist justificatory universalism that includes the right to life, freedom and physical safety and integrity, as well as the right to some form of personal property and possession, freedom of expression and association, freedom of religion and conscience, and the right to employment, health, education, and cultural and political self-determination (Benhabib, 2008). As Benhabib also notes, resistance to a universal definition of human rights derives from the postmodern belief in the impossibility of universalism and rejection by contextual minorities of what they perceive as an attempt to impose cultural norms from elsewhere. As a way of overcoming cultural prejudices and stereotypes, she speaks of the need to protect communicative freedom and promote open debate (2008, 187). The role of the education system in this process is vital, as we shall see.

Communicative freedom is guaranteed by human rights protections against cruelty, oppression and degradation, which are in turn made possible by the right to subsistence and political freedom (Gutman, 2003). As Victoria Camps explains, human rights are about guaranteeing a minimum standard of *good living* for all humanity. Human rights are for everybody, but they have a special meaning for those who are unable to assert them (1994, 23).

Universalism is thus an aspiration to find a shared description of the world for an array of different experiences. The Enlightenment image of shared humanity is no longer adequate, however, but must be reformed to take into account the demands of groups and individuals who do not see themselves reflected in it. Postmodernism has made an important contribution to the remapping of concepts of universality, citizenship and human rights which were not originally designed with such a multiplicity of human contexts and experiences in mind. Benhabib (1992) talks about weak and strong postmodernism: while weak postmodernism is compatible with social movements working for greater dignity, justice and solidarity, with strong postmodernism, no alliance is possible, since its 'death of metaphysics' thesis precludes all criticism of any institution, practice or tradition other than through appeals to the self-legitimation of the group being analysed. Strong postmodernism eliminates the possibility of cultural questioning: certain cultures are constructed as ideal, idyllic or exemplary, and all external criticism is construed as a personal attack on one's culture and all who identify with it. However, cultural questioning exposes the contradictions inherent in every culture and is a vital way of expanding our understanding to see how our own and any culture can improve its members' lives. Weak postmodernism acknowledges the validity of all cultures without exception and places explicit value on their different ways of thinking. Though it is often easier to judge others than to think critically about our own habits, customs and traditions, these alternative perspectives help us to question, rethink and refocus the way we live our lives. Cultural questioning is thus one of the strengths of living together as a society, allowing us to see past what Paulo Freire (1973) calls the 'alienation of ignorance' (the idea that ignorance is always present in others, not me) to realise that the other is just as capable as I of thinking, questioning and judging.

Jean Baudrillard (1997) and others argue that most universal values have been lost as a result of globalisation, and that the very idea of universalism is all but dead. However, even the most convinced champions of diversity must be aware of our common cause as citizens of a world that requires bonds between people in order to exist, and a culture of dialogue to survive.

Public policy and the promotion of shared spaces

Truly public policy should be aimed at ensuring access to real citizenship for all members of society. Guided and governed by the moral principle of equality, egalitarian public policy can never be decontextualised from the lives of the citizens for whom it is created: their sex, financial status, religious beliefs, values, and so on. It must take into account the obstacles faced by certain groups to establishing patterns of behaviour that would allow them to live in equality, and seek ways to ensure the equality and well being of all citizens collectively, while recognising and respecting their individual differences.

Egalitarian social and economic policy is strongly criticised by neoconservative sectors of society, who believe that state intervention limits individual freedom and the possibility of economic progress and see the state itself as a communist social-ist-inspired system of oppression. The widespread currency of this idea obscures the alternative analysis of public life proposed by Jürgen Habermas in his *History and Critique of Public Opinion* (1994). Though slightly dated in some of its evidence and conclusions, the central thesis of the work contains two main principles: that political participation is based on the idea of the state as a place for the production and circu-lation of ideas, including those opposed to the prevailing state model itself, and that political participation can never be based on market principles, since the public sphere is a space for reflection and debate, not buying and selling (Fraser 2011).

Certain social groups (such as women, cultural minorities, non-heterosexual groups, etc.) continue to be denied access to and/or obstructed from participating in the public sphere. Equality of opportunity to participate in public life can only be achieved through the kind of egalitarian social policies continuously demanded by disempowered groups.[4] This demand is based on a belief in the state as the only institution capable of

---

4   Feminism, for example, stresses the importance of public services as one of the mainstays of real equality. Helga Maria Hernes (1990) explains the need for a strong public sphere for women in relation to three different female subject positions: as clients, because the welfare state improves quality of life and reduces unpaid work; as employees, because the state offers a more protective employment model than the private sector; and as citizens, because it gives them a voice of their own, allowing them to formulate and express their priorities based on their needs as women.

protecting workers' rights, ensuring equal treatment in the public and private spheres, and promoting public practices that improve the lives of all citizens.

One of the most aggressive social discourses against egalitarian policies is the argument that they simply do not work. In *Responsibility for Justice* (2011), Iris Marion Young examines the increasingly common view of poverty as a personal problem, rather than a social one. Young traces this shift in focus to the rise of conservative ideology in the 1980s that placed the burden of responsibility for poverty on the poor themselves.

The process of globalisation promoted by neoliberal ideology helps ideas such as these spread far, wide and faster than ever. In addition to the discourse of individual responsibility and its disregard for the structural causes of social injustice, globalisation itself is increasingly presented as a *sine qua non* of individual freedom (Maquieira 2002). More and more, personal freedom is identified with the omnipresent sense of unrestricted communication, the elimination of oppressive boundaries and interconnections between individuals without state interference or regulation. What this generic ideal ignores, however, is the huge number of people left out by globalisation, the cracks in a neoliberal model that provokes forced migrations in search of a better life, the accumulation of wealth in the hands of a few, the impoverishment of millions and the depletion of quality universal healthcare. The globalisation paradox signals the breakdown of the social contract and the emergence of a huge breach between those who view globalisation in terms of economic success, social recognition and unlimited travel options and those who find themselves sinking deeper and deeper into social inequality. The World Social Forum (WSF) offers an alternative to the dominant neoliberal model of globalisation in the form of counter-hegemonic globalisation (Santos 2008). WSF is a global network of civil society organisations in search of a common set of principles; a movement of movements working together to influence public policymaking. This counter-hegemonic alternative rejects the 'top-down' leadership of finance capitalism and the neoliberal state, and advocates instead a 'bottom-up' approach led by social movements of resistance against cultural and economic capitalist globalisation, and support for democracy and social justice (Kellner 2005).

The relativist tenets of globalisation also lead to the fragmentation of identities, and the search for communities of refuge (Bauman 2001) constructed in opposition to other identities. Identity is equated with cultural membership and the identification with or rejection of certain cultural characteristics based on their perceived value. The neoliberal agenda is thus fuelled by a discourse of clash and confrontation that scapegoats cultural difference and displaces the need for dialogue (Naïr 2006). However, the same discourse turns a blind eye to society's social, economic, political, educational and employment problems and the new forms of slavery emerging in the most economically developed countries (Sassen 2003).

The process of globalisation has intensified the focus on identity as an ontological category. Rather than highlighting the mixed, hybrid, heterogeneous nature of our culturally interconnected world, the discourse of identity is increasingly framed in terms of cultural purity and homogeneity. This discourse is shared by neoliberal globalisers and anti-globalisers (those who deny that globalisation has any positive influence) alike (Bilbeny 2002), with the result that legitimating identities and resistance identities produce the same result: the concretisation of pre-established identities.[5] Ensuing from this closed conception of identity is the perception of cultures as closed, solipsistic, unmoving and immovable entities, which in turn gives rise to misunderstandings and rivalries between groups.

Public policy has a vital role to play in safeguarding against conflicts and violence within society, by ensuring respect for cultural pluralism and tolerance among group members. It should neither promote nor discourage the identities associated with a particular culture, but seek to provide citizens with context-appropriate opportunities for communication and interaction between them. In order for these proposals to have a real effect, they should be many and varied and subject to public debate. They should ensure respect and protection for all cultures and for the way we live together as a society: promoting understanding between cultures, working to eliminate prejudices and stereotypes and trying to make life better for all members of the community.

There is no shortage of discourses that attempt to portray cultures as diametrically opposed, communicationally incompatible and even incapable of coexisting with one another, on the grounds of *the other*'s purported lack of reason, understanding and compassion. As Norbert Bilbeny (2002) points out, however, most civic values are common across all cultures.[6] What can give rise to confrontation are certain moral discrepancies between cultures, as in questions of women's rights, freedom of expression and the death penalty. Of these, the issue of the role of women in society is without doubt the most heavily represented in the media and consequently most prominent in the social consciousness. Sirin Adlbi Sibai (2016)[7] refers to these as 'technologies of power': covert ways of controlling subjectivities and inter-subjectivities worldwide using binary discourses that divide more than they unite. The tensions surrounding the issue of women's rights across the world's media are largely due to the emblematisation of women as carriers of the

---

5   Manuel Castells (2001) highlights three categories of identity: legitimating identity, resistance identity, and project identity. Legitimating identity interiorises the cultural norms of the dominant institutions of society and reproduces them at a social level. Resistance identity emerges when a group sees itself as oppressed and devalued, and reacts by constructing counter-discourses of resistance against the dominant group and/or institutions. Project identity is formed when social actors construct a new identity based on their own and whatever other cultural materials they have available to them. It is concerned with transforming individuals and constructing a new social model.

6   Bilbeny (2002) proposes the following list of civic values which he considers common to most cultures: rejection of lies and betrayal; respect for the elderly and the integrity of childhood; condemnation of drug trafficking and political corruption; prohibition of incest and rape; condemnation of slavery and torture; punishment of theft and fraud; condemnation of murder and massacre; rejection of evil witchcraft and ritual human sacrifice; rejection of vampirism and cannibalism; rejection of pederasty and human trafficking; discredit of tyranny and colonialism; opposition to threats and extortion; belief in justice and the sovereignty of public power; care for the sick and respect for the dead; condemnation of defamation and duelling; disapproval of the breaking of pacts and promises; rejection of the revelation of secrets.

7   The concept of "Technologies of power" is founded by Michael Foucault in 1979.

cultural essence and symbols of identitarian purity. In all cultures, explicitly or otherwise, the social norms for men and women are different. The rules for women are always associated with notions of care, decency and self-sacrifice (Valcárcel 2008), and represent the moral values that give a culture its identity. These culturally assigned norms are the focus for most of the social debate around the uniform, culturally invariant role envisioned for women of all backgrounds and beliefs. The rejection by women from all around the world of their culturally determined role in society has given rise to ideological confrontations of many kinds, which vary from situation to situation according to the different contexts and conceptions of oppression and differing priorities for improvement. In Nigeria, for example, women are used as a barometer of religious orthodoxy (Anwar 2008). In Sudan, as the director of the Institute of Women, Gender and Development Studies at the Ahfad University for Women, Balghis Badri (2008), explains, the question of women's rights has become a battleground for two opposing world views: on one side, belief in freedom of thought, judgement and action; and on the other, belief in the ability of one social group to control the lives of others. In Tunisia, Iran and Morocco, views about women are a reflection of a particular ideological stance and a source of internal conflict among reactionary and reformist-revolutionary groups alike. These conflicts highlight the unwillingness of hegemonic groups to accept their progressive loss of power as a result of globalisation and the new challenges and projects being assumed by women from around the world, both individually and collectively.

Globalisation can also help to create alliances between groups from different contexts by visibilising situations of oppression that are not bound by geopolitical borders. To offer just one example, the view of women as objects of sexual exploitation and oppression sees the female body as something to be controlled and subject to rape if the moral norms of part of the community are not observed. This reality is not unique to any one culture: judges who acquit a rapist on the grounds that the victim was not dressed 'appropriately' (that is, showing leg above the knee) are applying the same principle of 'modesty' that requires a Muslim woman to wear a hijab in order to avoid being harassed by men who claim to be standard-bearers for their culture.

In her compelling *Breaking the Silence* (2006; originally published in French as *Ni Putes Ni Soumises*, 2004), Fadela Amara tells of the French Arab women in the Parisian banlieues who tore back the veil of silence around these forms of oppression and whose courage cost some of them their lives. Their struggle contrasts with other Muslim women's defence of the hijab as a symbol of liberation that allows women to be judged on their intellect, not their physical appearance (Adlbi Sibai 2016). This repoliticisation of the hijab as a symbol of liberation can make it difficult to form alliances between women from the same culture or between cultures, since the problematisation of patriarchal privilege is seen as secondary to cultural allegiance. But can the hijab really be seen as a symbol of liberation when it entails submission to the objectifying gaze and will of patriarchal power? I believe that, instead of submitting to masculine definitions of morality, we should attempt to transform them and force our male interlocutors to look at women in a different way. What is clear is that the repercussions of showing or hiding one's body are much greater for women than men (of any culture) when it comes to maintaining the respect of their community.

The example of women's activism highlights the need for public policymaking that guarantees that proposals on behalf of groups excluded from full equality will be debated honestly, advisedly, and without reference to hegemonic stereotypes. Public policy must seek to reconcile individual freedoms with the common good.

Equality in schools: learning about the common good

Over two hundred years after Kant's contention that education should be moral as well as instrumental, designed to help children to develop into critically thinking adults, education policy continues to be more concerned with solving technical and bureaucratic issues than engaging with questions of ideology (Rizvi and Lingard 2013). As a result of this, far more media coverage of public policy is devoted to discussing administrative questions than the model of education needed to create a more just and equitable society. While analyses of the causes of inequality in education from feminist, anti-racist and other critical perspectives have made an important contribution to the debate, the fact remains that these discussions rarely reach beyond the bounds of academia and fail to address the practical, technobureaucratic pressures facing most educators on the ground.

Focusing public debate on technical and bureaucratic issues is a way of obviating discussion of the need for education policies that encourage teachers to think of education, not merely as the transmission of supposedly neutral, objective or impartial knowledge, but as the formation of young people with the attitudes and aptitudes necessary to make decisions about life according to their own criteria (albeit within parameters predefined by the curriculum). Official education policy seems to suggest that the sole purpose of schools is to teach the subjects that the capitalist system has deemed necessary for the education of society's children, irrespective of their social value or relevance. What is forgotten along the way is the indispensable duty of ethical education to prepare society's members to live in accordance with the principles of democratically constructed citizenship.

Meanwhile, education policy is increasingly promoting the idea of a 'need' to move schools out of the public sphere and into the private sphere. The case for separation is founded on two premises: market demand and cultural conflict. The discourse of market demand is clear from the reconceptualisation of education as a service, not a right, and the styling of the debate as a choice between state and public, not public and private. The idea of non-state public education redefines public education as a service that meets citizens' need for education, regardless of who regardless of who runs or finances it (Díez 2007; Rizvi and Lingard 2013; Torres 2001). The motivation behind this redefinition is financial profit on the part of multinational companies who have already gained a foothold in the education sector and now hope to manipulate public opinion by referring to their activities as a 'public service'.

Cultural conflict is put forward as another reason to segregate children according to ethnicity, religion, socio-economic group, and so on. As a result, pupils are denied the chance to live together, to learn about the reality of social diversity, or to learn how to deal with cultural differences through dialogue. Prior to the twenty-first century, educational discourse was based on the construction of pupils as actors with a fixed identity within a national framework of citizenship (Popkewitz 2005). This was the foundation of the public's trust in education and of the three pillars of public education: 1. Replacement of myths with accurate information; 2. The Kantian precept that every human being is an end in him or herself, never to be used as a means by others; and 3. Education is an instrument with which to remind free, equal individuals of their moral duties as autonomous, responsible, responsive beings (Valcárcel 1997).

Today, the duty of education to form citizens has been replaced by the production of technically trained workers and consumers, as evinced by the elimination of philosophy and the humanities from the school curriculum (Torres 2017). While schools cannot be expected to teach children everything about the world in all of its complexity, it should provide pupils with the basic cultural knowledge and principles needed to offer precise, critical interpretations of the diverse social reality around them, and to ensure their development into free-acting citizens. It is to these objectives that instrumental learning should be geared, not economic interests.

Creating community with a heterogeneous curriculum

Minority ethnic groups, human rights movements, radically new conceptions of equality, and new mass media are challenging and changing our traditional idea of citizenship. The struggle between hegemonic and counter-hegemonic models is being fought out in the arena of identity, yet global citizenship implies the tacit acceptance of the diverse world in which we live. Just societies build a meaningful sense of shared citizenship among their members and put in place the instruments of inclusion necessary to achieve it. Schools have an undeniable role in this process of creating and learning to live together as a society and promoting diversity as a positive, gratifying experience. As one of the main socialising institutions in society, the education system is also the most effective means of promoting mutual understanding and positive interaction. Becoming aware of the existence of different cultures and different ways of approaching public and private issues is the first step towards respecting *the other*'s right to express his or her own opinion, which is the basis of any productive dialogue. According to Nussbaum (2001), the single most important lesson of multicultural education is to make children realise how much important knowledge they are unaware of and to remind them that their traditions are only a small part of the much broader world in which they live. School must lead this change and help to overcome the stereotypes, prejudices, taboos and clichés that have made diversity a source of division. A good starting point is to educate children to be free, independent and self-confident. The development of debate skills among pupils is also key: presenting arguments and counter-arguments, hearing other people out and not dismissing their ideas out of hand no matter how unreasonable they may sound at first, looking for information from reliable sources and using that information to deepen our understanding of the reality around us, never merely to fill pages.

Diversity in schools is not merely an ethical or civic question but also leads to improved student performance, as attested by numerous studies on the positive effects (in terms of educational outcomes) of heterogeneous learning environments (OECD-UNESCO 2003, 2007, 2010; Dupriez 2010; Duru-Bellat 2002; Oberti 2012; Taut and Escobar 2012). Diversity in the classroom teaches children about the world in which they live. In the business world, large companies and multinationals have realised the growing importance of sourcing management teams from across a range of social and cultural backgrounds. Their newfound interest in multiculturalism is purely economic, of course, a business strategy aimed at expanding their customer and user base and growing their profits.

This complex interconnected world has brought with it new questions and uncertainties that only a new kind of knowledge can answer. We need to harness our diversity of experience and understanding to find solutions to the myriad challenges facing society today, including climate change, religious intolerance, endangered species, agricultural development and food shortages, women's rights, deforestation and world hunger. Failure to understand or take into account different cultural or religious perspectives may limit our ability to participate effectively in international business and political debates (Nussbaum 2001).

Diverse learning environments are one of the building blocks of a more integrated society, while at the same time offering pupils the chance to broaden their minds, compare ideas, consider the world from a more cosmopolitan perspective, think about issues in a more complex way and question their own opinions. The experience of diversity in the classroom helps pupils to realise that they are not the centre of the world, that their cultural traditions and practices are the result of a long process of change and (not always peaceful) integration between cultures. They learn that their culture is only one small part of a much vaster world.

In contrast to the purported role of schools as purveyors of objective, unalterable truths, experts point to a hidden curriculum of norms, values and beliefs that the teachers themselves are not always consciously aware of (Torres 1991). According to this hidden curriculum, schools are perceived as places devoid of difference, in which all pupils are judged according to the same standards, regardless of culture, ethnicity, religion, gender, economic situation, and so forth. The education system is held up as a bastion of equality of opportunity and has as one of its basic tenets the equal status of all its members. What this precept overlooks, however are the impact social inequality can have on pupils' lives and expectations and the affront, in some cases, to their identity.

In the compulsory education system, academic success is predicated on children's assimilation of the norms and standards of the dominant culture. In a democratic system of education, schools should study the situation of each new pupil in order to identify and address inequalities from the outset. An education system based on truly democratic values is one in which schools become institutions of change, not sites for the reproduction of cultural stereotypes.

Judgements about cultural, ethnic, religious and sexual diversity are implicit in all aspects of the learning and teaching process, from curricular content to relations and relationships within the classroom. Looks, gestures, jokes, pranks, comments (consciously made or otherwise), graffiti and flyers tell us a lot about normative attitudes to difference. The implicit hierarchy of values in every culture manifests itself in the denigration and *othering* of attitudes and behaviours that do not conform to the hegemonic norm. One of teachers' most important functions is the development of positive relationships among pupils as part of their education as self-sufficient, responsible citizens and human beings.

Shared learning encourages pupils to take each other seriously, to treat each other's ideas and opinions with respect, and never to look down on, humiliate or ignore a classmate because of his or her different culture. In order to achieve this, teachers need to think critically (and consensually) about the values they wish to foment in their pupils: rejection of violence, equal opportunities for girls and boys to express their thoughts and worries, empathy and respect for others and cooperation, not competition. Too often, sadly, the dream of democratic education founders on the reality of educational practices and relations within the school community.

Conclusion

Shared citizenship can only be achieved when society's children are provided with a truly shared curriculum. Far from seeking to orient student learning according to a single, homogenising perspective, shared curriculum recognises diversity and attempts to redress the exclusion of non-hegemonic cultural knowledge. Pupils taught according to a shared curriculum should feel safe and encouraged, not hurt or affronted by the learning they receive.

Shared curriculum should be founded on the principle of what Benhabib (2008) terms communicative freedom, which can only exist when people learn to listen to each other in conditions of openness, trust and mutual respect. Communicative freedom means learning to maintain communicative relations with other people, finding the best and most complete information available to support our opinions and realising that those opinions may change in the light of new arguments. Effective communication always entails acknowledging the equal validity of the *other*'s point of view, listening without prejudice and remaining open to altering one's own position. For Adela Cortina (2009), truth and justice should be used as adjectives, not nouns: rather than simply value truth and justice, we should think about what is just and true. Communicative freedom must be made part of the learning experience for schoolchildren in order to bring us closer as a society to the ideals of truth and justice.

The hegemonic cultural patterns ingrained by socialisation can make it difficult for members of a culture to perceive some of its failings and contradictions. For this very reason, we need to allow other cultures to look at our way of life and listen to, analyse and reflect on their opinions and suggestions. In *Scheherazade Goes West*, Fatema Mernissi recalls her grandmother's advice as one of the most important lessons of her life: that meeting a stranger is a chance to understand both others and oneself better and that '[t]he more you understand a stranger and the greater is your knowledge of yourself, the more power you will have' (2001, 1). The encouragement of open-minded thinking and the avoidance of stereotyped assumptions about other cultures should be one of the primary core goals of our education system. As Alain Touraine warns, '[a] modern society drastically reduces much of its creativity, but also its realism, if it does not combine a rational spirit with knowledge of the personal, psychological and social history of each individual' (2005, 164). Integrating the rational and the personal in this way should be one of the guiding principles of education, in order to enable children to behave and see themselves as active citizens.

As educators, we must help children to deconstruct, re-examine and seek alternatives to dominant cultural identities. In today's individualistic society, schools are the institution with the greatest capacity to nurture and facilitate communication and interaction between people with different identities, providing pupils with a safe, open space in which to engage in constructive dialogue based on mutual knowledge of each other. At a policy level, the focus of education needs to shift away from identity creation towards helping pupils to challenge pre-existing identities and supporting them in their own process of self-building.

Reflective learning and practice of responsible, participatory, democratic citizenship, equality, peaceful coexistence, non-violent resolution of conflict, emotional intelligence, development of basic skills and attitudes and preparation for adult life are not only essential for pupils' personal and interpersonal development but are the bedrock of a truly public education system.

Schools today have a dual responsibility: to act as a counterweight to social inequalities of origin; and to help pupils to question and reconstruct the knowledge, attitudes and behaviours they assimilate through their social interactions outside of school.

References

Adlbi Sibai, Sirin (2016). *La cárcel del feminismo. Hacia un pensamiento islámico decolonial*. Madrid: Akal.

Amara, Fadela (2004). *Ni Putes Ni Soumises*. Paris: La Découverte.

Amorós, Celia (1997). *Tiempo de feminismo. Sobre feminismo, proyecto ilustrado y postmodernidad*. Madrid: Cátedra.

Anwar, Zainah (2008). 'La organización Sisters in Islam y los derechos de la mujer en Malasia'. In *La emergencia del feminismo islámico* (pp. 211–228). Barcelona: Oozebap.

Badri, Balghis (2008). 'Feminismo musulmán en Sudán: un repaso'. In *La emergencia del feminismo islámico* (pp. 189–210). Barcelona: Oozebap.

Baudrillard, Jean (1997). *Le Paroxyste Indifférent*. Paris: Grasset et Fasquelle.

Bauman, Zygmunt (2001). *Community: Seeking Safety in an Insecure World*. Cambridge: Polity.

Benhabib, Seyla (2008). 'Otro universalismo: sobre la unidad y diversidad de los derechos humanos'. *Isegoría. Revista de Filosofía Moral y Política*, 39, pp. 175–203.

Benhabib, Seyla (2004). *The Rights of Others: Aliens, Residents and Citizens*. Cambridge: Cambridge University Press.

Benhabib, Seyla (1992). *Situating the Self: Gender, Community, and Postmodernism in Contemporary Ethics*. New York: Routledge.

Bilbeny, Norbert (2002). *Por una causa común. Ética para la diversidad*. Barcelona: Gedisa.

Blackmore, Jill (2005). 'Globalización. ¿Un concepto útil para la teoría del replanteamiento feminista y las estrategias en la educación?' In Burbules, N and Torres, C.A. *Globalización y Educación. Manual Crítico* (pp. 101–122). Madrid: Editorial Popular.

Camps, Victoria (1994). 'La igualdad y la libertad'. In Valcárcel, Amelia (comp.), *El concepto de igualdad* (pp. 17–28). Madrid: Pablo Iglesias.

Camps, Victoria (2003). 'La ciudadanía como libertad'. *El Valor de la Palabra. Revista anual de pensamiento*, 3, pp. 19–23.

Camps, Victoria (2007). *Educar para la ciudadanía*. Sevilla: Fundación Ecoem

Castells, Manuel (2001). *La era de la información*. Madrid: Alianza.

Cortina, Adela (2009). *Ética de la razón cordial. Educar en la ciudadanía en el siglo XXI*. Oviedo: Nobel.

Díez, Enrique (2007). *La globalización neoliberal y sus repercusiones en la educación*. Barcelona: El Roure.

Dupriez, Vincent (2010). *Methods of Grouping Learners at School*. Paris: UNESCO.

Durkheim, Emile (2002). *La educación moral*. Madrid: Morata.

Duru-Bellat, Marie (2002). *Les Inégalités Sociales à l'École*. Paris: Éducation et Formation.

Fraser, Nancy (2011). *Dilemas de la justicia en el siglo XXI: Género y globalización*. Illes Balears: Tecsed.

Fraser, Nancy and Honneth, Axel (2006). *¿Reconocimiento o redistribución?* Madrid: Morata.

Freire, Paulo (1973). *Education for Critical Consciousness*

Freire, Paulo (1992). *Pedagogía del oprimido*. Madrid: Siglo XXI.

Gutman, Amy (2003). 'Introducción'. In Ignatieff, M. *Los derechos humanos como política e idolatría* (pp. 9–28). Barcelona: Paidós.

Habermas, Jürgen (1994). *Historia y crítica de la opinión pública. La transformación estructural de la vida pública*. Barcelona: Gustavo Gili.

Hernes, Helga Mª (1990). *El poder de las mujeres y el estado de bienestar*. Madrid: Editorial Vindicación Feminista.

Kant, Immanuel (1991). *Pedagogía*. Madrid: Akal.

Kellner, Douglas (2005). 'Globalización y nuevos movimientos sociales: lecciones para una teoría y pedagogías críticas'. In Burbules, N and Torres, C.A. *Globalización y Educación: Manual Crítico* (pp. 211–230). Madrid: Editorial Popular.

Lledó, Emilio (2009). *Ser quien eres. Ensayos para una educación democrática*. Zaragoza: Prensas Universitarias.

Maquieira, Virginia (2002). *Mujeres, globalización y derechos humanos*. Madrid: Cátedra.

Marshall, T.H. (1965). *Class, Citizenship and Social Development.* New York: Anchor.

Mernissi, Fatema (2001). *Scheherazade Goes West.* Washington: Washington Square Press

Naïr, Samir (2006). *Diálogo de culturas e identidades.* Madrid: Universidad Complutense.

Nussbaum, Martha (2012). *Crear capacidades. Propuesta para el desarrollo humano.* Barcelona: Paidós. (English versión: 2011. Creating capabilities, The Belknap Press of Harvard University Press)

Nussbaum, Martha (2001). *El cultivo de la humanidad. Una defensa clásica de la reforma en la educación liberal.* Barcelona: Paidós.

Nussbaum, Martha (2000). *Las mujeres y el desarrollo humano.* Madrid: Herder.

Oberti, Marco. (2012). *L'École dans la Ville. Ségrégation, Mixité, Carte Scolaire.* Paris: Sciences Po.

OECD-UNESCO (2010). *PISA 2009 Results: Overcoming Social Background – Equity in Learning Opportunities and Outcomes (Volume II).* Paris: Organisation for Economic Cooperation and Development.

OECD-UNESCO (2007). *Science Competencies for Tomorrow's World. Pisa 2006.* Paris: Organisation for Economic Cooperation and Development.

OECD-UNESCO (2003). *Literacy Skills for the World of Tomorrow. Further Results from PISA 2000.* Paris: Organisation for Economic Cooperation and Development.

Popkewitz, Thomas (2005). 'La reforma como administración social del niño'. In Burbules, N and Torres, C.A. *Globalización y Educación: Manual Crítico* (pp. 123–150). Madrid: Editorial Popular.

Rawls, John (1999). *The Law of Peoples.* Cambridge: Harvard University Press.

Rawls, John (1995). *Teoría de la justicia.* Mexico: FCE (Fondo de Cultura Económica).

Rizvi, Fazal and Lingard, Bob (2013). *Políticas educativas en un mundo globalizado.* Madrid: Morata.

Santos, Boaventura de Sousa (2010). *Descolonizar el saber, reinventar el poder.* Montevideo: Trilce.

Santos, Boaventura de Sousa (2008). 'El foro Social Mundial y la izquierda global'. *El Viejo Topo,* 240, pp. 39–62.

Sassen, Saskia (2003). *Contrageografías de la globalización. Género y ciudadanía en los circuitos transfronterizos.* Barcelona: Traficantes de Sueños.

Sen, Amartya. (1980). Èquality of What?. In *The Tanner Lecture on Human Values,* I, 197–220. Cambridge: Cambridge University Press.

Taut, Sandy and Escobar, Jorge (2012). *El efecto de las características de los pares en el aprendizaje de estudiantes chilenos de enseñanza media.* Chile: Centro MIDE UC.

Torres, Jurjo (1991). *El curriculum oculto.* Madrid: Morata

Torres, Jurjo (2001). *Educación en tiempos de neoliberalismo.* Madrid: Morata.

Torres, Jurjo (2017). *Políticas educativas y construcción de personalidades neoliberales y neocolonialistas.* Madrid: Morata.

Touraine, Alain (2005). *Un nuevo paradigma para comprender el mundo de hoy.* Paidós: Barcelona.

Valcárcel, Amelia (1994). 'Igualdad, idea regulativa'. In Valcárcel, A. (Comp.) *El concepto de igualdad* (pp. 1–16). Madrid: Editorial Pablo Iglesias.

Valcárcel, Amelia (1997). *La política de las mujeres.* Madrid: Cátedra.

Valcárcel, Amelia (2008). Feminismo en el mundo global. Madrid: Cátedra.

Young, Iris Marion (2011). *Responsabilidad por la justicia.* Madrid: Morata.

PART V
THE STRUGGLE TO
DEMOCRATIZE EDUCATION

CHAPTER TWENTY-ONE

The Freirean Factor[1]

Gustavo E. Fischman and Sandra R. Sales

ALMOST SINCE ITS publication in English, *Pedagogy of the Oppressed* has generated quite visceral debates not only about the content and orientation of Freire's work but also about how to understand his ideas and particularly about the role of the translations in promoting understanding or generating more controversies. Undoubtedly we are discussing a unique intellectual and a singular case. How many authors can generate this type of debate and questions: Was he a Marxist? Christian? Sexist? What is the main contribution of Freire: a literacy technique, an educational philosophy or a theory of education? Is there a pedagogical program, or a system for teaching and learning? When asked which of those denominations he felt most comfortable with, *"None of them"*, he answered. "I didn't invent a method, or a theory, or a program, or a system, or a pedagogy, or a philosophy. It is people who put names to things" (Torres, 1997, p. 2).

Perhaps the first questions to consider are: Why bother thinking about Freire today? Who cares about the accuracy or lack of it in the translation of his books? In 2018 after 50 years of the original publication of *Pedagogy of the Oppressed*, there is a large industry of people profiting from translating and repeating Freire's ideas—we are well aware that this text is another small contribution to such industry—but we firmly believe that contemporary social scientists could greatly benefit from reflecting about Freire's long term powerful conceptual, pedagogical, and political impact and in particular about the role of translations in the social sciences.

Before getting directly in commenting about Freire's work it is important to situate our perspective. Today it is rare to find a college that is not asking faculty to provide annual reports of their scholarly output, measured by such yardsticks as the number of articles

---

1   In his two-day successful seminar "How to Get Published", Gustavo Fischman worked closely with students, mentoring them through the several complex problems such as how to structure a paper, an article, a chapter, a book, a book review, the reviewing process, the appropriate journal or academic publishing house. As a result, UMD graduate students voice work, most of them minorities,—and the intricate educational issues related with South Coast Massachusetts—have been able to be present at major annual academic meetings and publishing houses. Needless to say, that, due to the explicit critical orientation of the program, during the seminar the work and though of Paulo Freire was examined. "The Freirean Factor" is thus a tribute in gratitude for the commitment and constant support provided to our students. A word of gratitude to the authors as well as to Taylor and Francis and Annabel Flude and Hannah McCluskey for granting permission free of charge to reprint Fischman, G. & Sales, S. (2018) The Freirean Factor. *International Studies in Sociology of Education, 27* (4), pp., 438–444.

published in high impact factor journals, provide their H factors, citations obtained, money obtained through grants, and recognition of awards. For the social sciences and humanities, and particularly for large numbers of scholars working in and researching using languages other than English, this convergence between demands for increased productivity, oriented to obtain higher rankings and accountability appear as almost utopian, generating what appears to be increasingly unsolvable challenges (Collini, 2012; Fischman & Ott, 2016). We call this phenomenon the *simplimetrification* of social sciences research because it confuses continuous increases of countable items (more articles, more citations in harder-to-publish journals) with scholarly impact and scientific relevance,[2] but there are no clear and compelling indicators that the quality, access, relevance, and usability of social sciences scholarship have significantly improved. Paulo Freire's long-lasting influence and especially the use, of his ideas through translations are perhaps the best example of the limits and the risks of the simplimetrification of contemporary academic life.

The first ironic twist is that we strongly believe that Paulo Freire, as a scholar, activist, and intellectual committed to the ideas and ideals of freedom, democracy, and equality, would not really care much about how his ideas are cited or not cited. We suspect that Paulo Freire would be laughing at the fact that *Pedagogy of the Oppressed* has gained a truly iconic scientific status. Using data from Google Scholar, Elliot Green's (2016) study shows that Freire are currently the third-most cited author in the social sciences category, ahead of authors such as Anthony Giddens, Pierre Bourdieu, Michel Foucault, or Noam Chomsky. It is also interesting to observe that the English and Spanish versions of this iconic book have a substantially higher number of citations than the original Portuguese version. In terms of translations, it is also quite curious how the Wikipedia pages about *Pedagogy of the Oppressed* in Spanish, Portuguese, and English highlight distinctive aspects of Freire's work. In English Freire appears described an *"educator"* and the book as "containing a detailed Marxist analysis." On the page in Spanish Freire is introduced as *"educador, pedagogo y filósofo"* (educator, pedagogue and philosopher) and the book has a "Marxist orientation," whereas on the Portuguese page Freire is presented as *educador and filosofo* (educator and philosopher) and there is no mention to Marxism in the introductory paragraphs. Another quite poignant example of the importance of the translations in terms of dissemination of the work and of serious engagement with Freire's ideas happened in 2018 during the celebration of the 50 years of the publication of *Pedagogy of the Oppressed*. In March 2018 there was a campaign launched by a coalition of conservative educators against Freire's ideas and to eliminate the honorific title given by the Brazilian Federal Senate to Freire as "protector of Brazilian education" (Federal Law n.º 12.612/2012). At the same time at the annual convention of American Educational Research Association, the largest gathering of educational

2   It is important to acknowledge that there are many scholars and organizations who recognize the limitations of the simplistic models and seek to broaden definitions of scholarly impact like the signatories of San Francisco Declaration on Research Assessment (DORA, http://www.ascb.org/dora/) and the Leiden Manifesto for Research Metrics (http://www.leidenmanifesto.org/). See also O'Neill (2016), Simons (2008), and Vanclay (2012).

researchers in the world, 65 academic sessions were devoted to discuss the ideas of this Brazilian educator, and the Paulo Freire Special Interest Group has over 1000 members and is one of the biggest in this scholarly organization.

It makes us very happy to know that a book written in Portuguese by a Brazilian educator, who was harshly criticized for his hybridity,[3] not being "rigorous" enough, and for using convoluted language, which has proved to be very difficult to translate, is still among the most discussed books in social sciences, transcending language and geographies. Granted, why a book is among the most read and cited needs to be considered cautiously and with a critical perspective, considering that it is well established that *Pedagogy of the Oppressed* has been, according to some Freirean scholars, very often mis-cited and poorly translated (Bartlett, 2005; Glass, 2001; McCowan, 2006).

We are also convinced that Paulo Freire, instead of lamenting the multiple and even contradictory interpretations that his work provoked, welcomed multiplicity, hybrid understandings, and readers' carnivalesque intercultural translations and appropriations of his ideas and ideals. We thoroughly agree with Freire's thinking: "Deep down, this must be every author's true dream—to be read, discussed, critiqued, improved, and reinvented by his/her readers" (1998, p. 31). Freire's desire to be reinvented can also be seen through Boaventura de Sousa Santos's description of the processes of intercultural translation of certain authors: "Because it is a work of mediation and negotiation, the world of translation requires that the participants in the translation process defamiliarize themselves to a certain extent vis-à-vis their respective cultural backgrounds. In the case of North/South translations, which tend to be also Western/non-Western translation, the task of defamiliarization is particularly difficult because the imperial North has no memory of itself as other than imperial and, therefore, as unique and as universal" (223).

The second ironic twist is that using the simplistic models of research accountability, Freire may not qualify as a "highly productive" scholar in the Brazilian context because he committed four "research sins": (a) published books, which today in Brazil and many other countries are essentially considered inferior to journal articles and in many cases "don't count"; (b) wrote many pieces with the deliberate attempt to communicate his ideas outside academic contexts, a practice that is mostly ignored in the current system of academic accountability; (c) his works were translated multiple times which in many cases will be ignored as "double-dipping"; and (d) his work was never shy to engage in the politics of education, a point that generated and still generates constant criticisms to his ideas.

---

3   The hybrid character of Freire's writing was also a source of a frequent criticism. As Daniel Schugurensky has noted in a review of Freire's contributions: "In the writings of Freire we find, for instance, elements of Socratic maieutics, philosophical existentialism, phenomenology, Hegelianism, Marxism, progressive education and liberation theology. Together with Marx and the Bible are Sartre and Husserl, Mounier and Buber, Fanon and Memmi, Mao and Guevara, Althusser and Fromm, Hegel and Unamuno, Kosik and Furter, Chardin and Maritain, Marcuse and Cabral. Even though Freire was influenced by these and other authors, his merit was to combine their ideas into an original formulation" (1998, p. 23).

If people continue buying, copying, translating, and quoting—both properly or improperly—the key ideas of this seminal 50-year-old book, it is because it retains a sense of freshness and pedagogical allure that makes us think that somewhere at this very moment, a teacher, a professor, a popular educator, or an activist will declare that he or she is implementing a Freirean program inspired by *Pedagogy of the Oppressed*. We think this seemingly constant processes of translations/reinventions would have made Freire smile, but nonetheless it is important to inquire into the translation processes. How much do you lose or win with translation? Nita Freire's answer to Carmel Borg and Peter Mayo's questions about translation is worth quoting extensively:

> He used words of such beauty and plasticity, organized in phrases and these in turn in the context of the totality of the text, with such aesthetic and political force that, I repeat, they cannot be transposed so easily into other languages because a language cannot be translated literally. And it is important to emphasize that his language is extraordinarily beautiful, rich and full of his particular way of being. . . . Another problem for translators who did not know Paulo well is the fact that his language is loaded with his feelings, since he never provided a dichotomy between reason and emotion. Paulo was a radically coherent man: what he said contained what he felt and thought and this is not always easy to translate. There are emotions whose meaning can only be well perceived, understood and felt inside a certain culture. And we Brazilians are unique in this way. I think this is so, isn't it? Without any prejudice, I think it is difficult for translators who have only studied the Portuguese language, albeit accurately, to express Paulo in all his aesthetic and even cultural-ideological richness. (Nita Freire in Borg & Mayo, 2000, pp. 110–111)

Nita Freire points to potential and real problems with the translations, but we want to note the enormous advantages of translating Freire's works. In spite of the often-mentioned problems with Freire's translations (Darder, 2002; Mayo, 1999; Schugurensky, 1998, 2015), it is hard to deny that several generations of literacy workers, classroom teachers, popular educators, and university professors have found inspiration in the notion of not just applying but also reinventing a Freirean approach to education.

If *Pedagogy of the Oppressed* and other writings by Paulo Freire are still inspiring teachers, educators, and administrators, it is in large measure because the shortcomings of the "banking model" (Freire, 1998) remain the norm, not the exception, and because even today, teachers are willing to commit and affirm that another school experience—one that is more democratic, open, tolerant, and creative (as well as effective!)—is not only achievable but also necessary. Freire's political-pedagogical discourse, with all its shortcomings and blind spots, still provides both ideal and achievable goals. Freirean language helps popular educators, teachers and students, schools and communities to reflect about oppressive regimes, words, feelings, and institutions and to participate in the conscious development of just and creative educational opportunities as part of a new perspective of a participatory democratic life and a sustainable planet (Fischman & Sales, 2010). A renewed commitment to justice and fairness in society and schooling is a welcome movement for socially relevant knowledge, for respecting different perspectives on the sciences and the arts, for encouraging educational spaces where disagreement is not punished, where love and a desire to know thrive, and where a passion for radicalizing democracy and creating more just alternatives is welcomed.

To be clear, Freire's ideas and continuous intellectual relevance do not need to be demonstrated exclusively with the number of citations and translations, but not considering that the interest to translate and high volume of citations are also indicators of relevance is a mistake. The biggest challenge to developing more usable social science research is not to produce more or better data. The field is already doing that. Rather, we need to keep working on multiple translations that reinvent Freire's path of asking big questions rooted in ethical and political commitments while maintaining analytical rigor and attention to multiple forms of evidence. As social scientists we also need to confront the sense of comfort that the current system of simplistic incentives provides, where the rewards are the same for publishing scholarship that concludes with the statement "more research is needed" as they are for producing knowledge that may eventually bring value to a scientific field, help practitioners and professionals to improve practices or provide rigorous evidence to families, communities, and policymakers. We could move in this direction by expanding our debates beyond the important, yet insufficient, question, "How we are going to assess this research?" and carefully consider the questions we ask about research responsibility, relevance and impact. Social sciences programs need to avoid simplistic solutions that end up producing more and mattering less and engage in reflecting about the Freirean Factor by asking the significant questions about research and about translation: For whom, and to what end?

References

Bartlett, L. (2005). Dialogue, knowledge, and teacher-student relations: Freirean pedagogy in theory and practice. *Comparative Education Review, 49*(3), 344–364.

Borg, C., & Mayo, P. (2000). Reflections from a" third age" marriage: Paulo Freire's pedagogy of reason, hope and passion an interview with Ana Maria (Nita) Freire. *McGill Journal of Education/Revue des sciences de l'éducation de McGill, 35*(02), pp.?

Collini, S. (2012). *What are universities for?* ??: Penguin UK.

Crow, M. M., & Dabars, W. B. (2015). *Designing the new American university*. Baltimore, MD: JHU Press.

Darder, A. (2002). *Reinventing Paulo Freire: A pedagogy of love*. Cambridge, MA: Westview Press.

DORA (2012). San Francisco Declaration on Research Assessment. http://www.ascb.org/dora/

Fischman, G. E., & Ott, M. (2017) Access, equity and quality trends in Latin America's Public universities. *International Journal of Educational Development, 58*, 86–94. https://doi.org/10.1016/j.ijedudev.2016.11.002

Fischman, G. E., & Sales, S. R. (2010). Formação de professores e pedagogias críticas. É possível ir além das narrativas redentoras. *Revista Brasileira de Educação, 15*(43), 7–20.

Freire, P. (1993). *Pedagogy of the Oppressed* (New rev. 20th-anniversary ed.). New York: Continuum.

Freire, P. (1998). *Pedagogy of hope: Reliving the* Pedagogy of the Oppressed. New York: Continuum.

Glass, R. D. (2001). On Paulo Freire's philosophy of praxis and the foundation of liberation education. *Educational Researcher, 30*(2), 15–25.

Green, E. (2016). What are the most-cited publications in the social sciences (according to Google Scholar)? http://blogs.lse.ac.uk/impactofsocialsciences/2016/05/12/what-are-the-most-cited-publications-in-the-social-sciences-according-to-google-scholar/ Accessed May 22, 2016.

McCowan, Tristan (2006). Approaching the political in citizenship education: The perspectives of Paulo Freire and Bernard Crick. *Educate, 6*(1), 57–70.

Mayo, P. (1999). *Gramsci, Freire, and adult education: Possibilities for transformative action.* London & New York: Zed Books.

O'Neill, J. (2016). NISO recommended practice: Outputs of the alternative assessment metrics project. *Collaborative Librarianship, 8*(3), 4.

Schugurensky, D. (2015). *Paulo Freire.* NY: Continuum.

Schugurensky, Daniel (1998). The legacy of Paulo Freire: A critical review of his contributions. *Convergence 31* (1 & 2): 26.

Simons, K. (2008). The misused impact factor. *Science, 322* (5899), 165. doi:10.1126/science.1165316.

Torres, R. M. (1997). The million Paulo Freires. *Convergence,* "A Tribute to Paulo Freire", 31(1–2).

Vanclay, J. K. (2012). Impact factor: Outdated artifact or stepping-stone to journal certification. *Scientometric, 32*(2), 211–238.

CHAPTER TWENTY-TWO

Teacher Education as an
Inclusive Political Project[1]

Jurjo Torres Santome

ANY DISCUSSION OF teacher training and development in Spain must take into account the educational principles espoused by the Ministry of Education, and how these policies are enacted in the education system. The time has come to talk about how teacher training and development policies are affected by parallel policy decisions in relation to compulsory curriculum content and performance standards, indicators and measurement formulae across all subjects and educational levels.

Standardisation, assessment and measurement systems encourage teachers to conceptualise their work, needs and development in very similar terms to the performance and assessment criteria applied to their pupils. Teachers nowadays are subject to veiled and explicit rankings based on completed six-year terms, government funding for innovation projects, school and student results, and so on. These metrics of performance and productivity have a decisive influence on the construction and orientation of teachers' training needs and choices based on the selection of courses and seminars offered by the education authorities and certain authorised entities. The choice of development course, seminar, workshop or conference is made according to a particular model of professionalism in which teachers have no say. Their professional activities, strategies and improvement needs are determined by agencies and individuals from outside the profession. What little decision-making power they have is reduced to a list of 'official' options in which they have no real input or influence.

The monitoring and assessment methods used by the government and Ministry of Education inspection services have a pivotal effect on the direction of the education system. At present, school and teacher 'productivity' is defined, classified and measured by instruments designed to promote a specific model of 'educated citizenry' and the professional performance required to achieve it. Compounding this is the lack of clarity and transparency in relation to the criteria used by key decision-making bodies, such as the National Institute of Educational Assessment (INEE),[2] the National

---

1   Revised keynote address at 1st TRED—Transformative Researchers and Educators for Democracy—Annual Pre-conference. Department of Edcuational Leadership, University of Massachusetts Dartmouth, November 15, 2012, Woodland Commons.
2   http://www.mecd.gob.es/inee/

Agency for Quality Assessment and Accreditation (ANECA)[3] and other regional assessment agencies. The opacity of these bodies precludes any chance of democratic debate in relation to the selection criteria and internal mechanisms used for internal committee appointments or the rationale behind the indicators and instruments created to measure and analyse data (a situation widely denounced by teachers).

The techniques, instruments and technologies used by these agencies are designed to shape our common sense view of education and the professional ideals that determine the meaning and direction of the teaching profession. It is these agencies that decide what teachers quantify and assess, how they do it and to what end. Assessment instruments and indicators thus play a major role in the construction of subjectivities and conceptions about education.

Assessment bodies such as those referred to earlier monitor performance through testing technologies such as questionnaires and objective tests. Without even the veneer of democratic debate, positivism is held up as an incontestable reality in which numbers are the sole dogma. Anything that cannot be measured or valued quantitatively is minimised or ignored. Everything becomes subject to quantitative monitoring and checks: professional performance, organisation performance and productivity, the physical health and performance of the human body and social relations (rankings, number of articles published in specialist journals and ranking of same, number of followers and interactions on Facebook, Twitter, Instagram, etc.).

Positivist models and technologies for creating numerical comparisons and hierarchies give governments a huge say in how education is shaped and practised. Published test results in relation to specific concerns and interests force educators to focus on and give priority to teaching how and what the government wants them to.

Too often, the true meaning and purpose of education get forgotten along the way. For the most part, the only time they are talked about at all is when the ministry produces a new draft bill or decree, and even then their presence is reduced to the typically rhetorical statement of intent in the preamble or introduction. Beyond that, however, the ideals of the education process become blurred and diluted amid the specific conditions of implementation, their teleological nature untranslatable into numerical standards. Discussion and proposal of alternatives to the prevailing model are usually limited by quantifiable interests, particularly when those interests bear the mark of organisations such as the Organisation for Economic Co-operation and Development (OECD); World Bank; International Monetary Fund (IMF); World Trade Organization (WTO); World Economic Forum (Davos); International Association for the Evaluation of Educational Achievement (IEA)[4]; Organisation of Ibero-American States for Education, Science and Culture (OIE); Spanish Confederation of Business Organisations (CEOE); National Institute for Educational Assessment (INEE); and others.

---

3   http://www.aneca.es/
4   La IEA is the organisation responsible for overseeing TIMSS (Trends in International Mathematics and Science Study) and PIRLS (Progress in International Reading Literacy Study), among other study cycles.

The authority attributed to reports by the OECD and others, propagated, in turn, by a wide network of compliant mainstream media, is crucial to the construction of common sense among citizens. The conception of value in terms of measurability overlooks and invisibilises unquantifiable dimensions of life such as morality, ethics and values. Effectively obviated from the discussion, they are either dispensed with or reduced to well-sounding yet ultimately meaningless catchwords, empty vessels ready to be filled at will.

The current *culture of inspection* and its systems of assessment are impoverishing education by imposing intellectual and ideological self-censorship on its subjects, thus smoothing the path to greater commercialisation and mental recolonisation.

There is nothing innocent about comparative assessment. The information and interpretations obtained from these tests is used by governments to justify their particular definitions of good and bad education, performance outcomes and student and teacher failure. The same culture of continuous assessment and inspection also extends to the different institutions of professional training and development for educators. The fundamental aim is to construct a narrative of failure in relation to the public education and teacher training model, in order to leave the way open for the kind of economistic salvationist formulae promoted by national government agencies and supranational organisations, including greater opportunities for private business and the privatisation of the teacher training sector as a whole (Peters, Paraskeva & Besley, 2015; Reese, 2013).

Positivist assessment instruments play a vital role in changing people's expectations and turn their attitudes, options and preferences away from public institutions and professionals in favour of all things private. With the manipulated backing of popular opinion, public education institutions, together with the training and development of those who teach in them, are taken over by a private sector with very different ideas about the knowledge and resources teachers need and what they should pass on to their pupils.

In order for their positivist vision of education to prevail, the education authorities and their national and international economic mentors must first convince families and teachers that the education system is not working. They must be made to believe that the system is unfit for purpose and that substandard public preschool, primary, secondary, vocational and university education in Spain is ultimately to blame for the country's economic and unemployment problems.

The true purpose of education, however, is to create critical, thoughtful, creative human beings, not mechanical followers of certain 'authorised truths'. Real education equips people against indoctrination and dogmatic thinking. Critical, thoughtful living involves questioning and reflecting on received information, theories, models, opinions, truths, traditions, and so on; debating democratically; and seeking moral and ethical consistency in one's arguments. Informed, creative, competent citizens should understand that the problems, dilemmas, doubts and situations of life can be solved in different ways. They must be conscious that creativity requires divergent, critical thought, imagination and enaction of alternatives to the ideas and routines of everyday life.

A philosophy that prizes critical thought and reflection must consider the extent to which certain cultures and realities have been silenced and/or deformed by hegemonic conceptions of education. To combat and ensure against these exclusions, the education authorities and teacher training and development institutions must start placing much more emphasis on fair, inclusive education policies and treating education as an *inclusive political project* designed to identify and overcome impediments to educational access, democratic participation and success. It is no secret that admission practices in many schools are shamefully selective and undeniably racist. The marginalisation and ghettoisation of Roma (gypsy) culture is just one example of the failure by schools to acknowledge the cultural reality of a part of their community, a reality that has been present in Spanish life for centuries.

The discriminatory policies and practices suffered by the Roma community in Spain have been the subject of strong criticism by the Council of Europe 'Commission against Racism and Intolerance' (ECRI).[5] As yet, however, no satisfactory measures have been taken to rectify the situation identified by the Commission. In February 2011, ECRI issued the following findings and 'strong recommendations':

> Problems in education include the uneven distribution of immigrant and Roma pupils and continued existence of 'ghetto' schools. (p. 7)

> ECRI has received consistent reports of 'ghetto' schools of immigrant or Roma children in certain parts of the country, and discriminatory practices in the admissions procedures, enabling publicly funded private schools to pick and choose pupils. (p. 18)

> ECRI strongly recommends that the Spanish authorities review the way in which pupils are admitted to public and publicly funded private schools and take other necessary measures to ensure an even distribution of Spanish, immigrant and Roma pupils in the various schools. (p. 18)

> ECRI strongly recommends that the positive contribution of the Roma people to Spanish history and culture should be a compulsory part of the curriculum for all pupils in Spain. The teacher training syllabus should also include this component. (p. 19)

Despite the publication of the report in 2011 and the repetition of its findings and recommendations in 2014,[6] to date, both papers have been largely ignored in Spain, most notably among teachers and the gypsy community itself. More unsettlingly, however, is the apparent obliviousness of state and regional governments alike to the report's

---

5   ECRI – Report on Spain, 8 February 2011 (4th monitoring cycle) www.coe.int/ecri http://www.coe.int/t/dghl/monitoring/ecri/country-by-country/spain/ESP-CBC-IV-2011-004-ESP.pdf
http://www.coe.int/t/dghl/monitoring/ecri/country-by-country/spain/esp-cbc-iv-2011-004-eng.pdf
6   ECRI (2014). ECRI Conclusions on the Implementation of the Recommendations in Respect of Spain Subject to Interim Follow-Up (adopted on 5 December 2013) http://www.coe.int/t/dghl/monitoring/ecri/library/publications.asp

existence, given the absence of any move to action its 'strenuous recommendations'. The government's treatment of such issues as questions of minor importance illustrates the institutional racism at work within the Spanish state, born out of an inherently racist culture and a hypocritical political system that touts equality of opportunity as its watchword.

The question of gypsy children's welfare in Spain first came to the fore in the second half of the 1970s, when small groups of politically minded and thus more socioculturally aware teachers began to draw attention to the serious shortcomings in official education policy in respect of marginalised communities such as the Roma. This was the decade in which Roma children started to become a regular presence in ordinary schools (having previously attended the famous 'bridge schools' for gypsies or received no formal schooling of any kind), but the teachers they encountered knew nothing about Roma culture, except for their own deeply engrained prejudices against the community. They had no training in multiculturalism or information or teaching resources to draw on, no understanding of the Roma people's contribution to Spanish history and culture and no contact with anybody from among the gypsy community or cultural mediators to turn to for guidance. On the whole, Roma pupils were greeted by an atmosphere of hostility or, at best, one of charity, tolerance and do-goodery; neither was the appropriate, professional response to meet the challenge. The Association for Teaching with Gypsies was set up at the end of the 1970s as a way for teachers of gypsies from different regions of Spain to pool their experiences, share problems and develop their teaching skills collectively, in order to improve dropout rates and offer pupils a better, more relevant education. Despite these good intentions, however, most of the teachers in the association were non-gypsies, which made it hard for them to engage with and motivate Roma parents to join and participate in the school community.

As a result of pressure from progressive teachers' groups, the education authorities in Spain slowly began to incorporate elements of the association's ideas into their official programmes. Nevertheless, this was usually confined to psycho-pedagogical supports aimed at improving gypsy integration in ordinary schools, or training and development courses for teachers in the newly created Teacher Training Centres. It never translated into social, educational or cultural policies or measures designed to stimulate and facilitate access to teacher training colleges and faculties of education for Roma men and women. Developments in this direction would help gypsy children to feel a sense of belonging in their schools, and non-gypsy children to get to know, interact with and work side by side with professionals and people in general from the Roma community.

For all their talk of teacher training and integration, the authorities have never attempted to tackle one of the key obstacles to inclusive education in Spanish schools: the representation of Roma history, achievements and realities in the cultural content of the school curriculum. Instead, a methodology of textbook analysis (similar to that applied in the case of sexist curriculum content) was used to establish the presence or absence of people of gypsy ethnicity, what subjects they appeared in and how they were referred to (on the rare occasions they were even mentioned).

In the face of this climate of marginalisation, certain members of the teaching profession and the gypsy community remained committed to eradicating the institutionalised racism within the education system. As part of their efforts, they created the first curricular materials to include the history and culture of the Roma people. For the most part, however, the new teaching units were rarely used except as supplements to the compulsory content set by the ministry and regional departments of education or by the most politically and socially aware teachers in their classes with gypsy pupils.

Experts have criticised on numerous occasions the culturally (and otherwise) skewed nature of the official curriculum which pupils are required to follow and the colonialist, classist, racist, sexist, militarist and developmentalist bias found in textbooks and other teaching materials.

Truly inclusive education, aimed at the personal development, socialisation and civic insertion of pupils, depends to a large extent on the selection of cultural content for the curriculum they will be required to follow. It is important to remember that the curriculum is necessarily selective in this regard, which is why critical analysis processes and techniques in relation to culture and curriculum content should be compulsory parts of teacher training and development syllabuses. Up to now, this has not been the case. As highlighted by Ladson-Billings (1994: 52), the basis of a successful education is for teachers to look on cultural identity, not as an obstacle to be overcome or shaken off but as an asset to learning and a foundation on which to build and shape new knowledge.

In attempting to promote a model of inclusive education, teachers frequently find themselves faced with what seems like an impossible dilemma: Should they focus on teaching the skills and cultural content prescribed by the official curriculum, despite the feeling that they are pushing out the pupils' culture and replacing it with another, or should they encourage and nurture the pupils' natural culture by listening to them and promoting intercultural dialogue in the classroom? The following situation described by Delpit (1995: 18) illustrates the conflicting priorities faced by many educators: 'Progressive white teachers seem to say to their black students, "Let me help you find your voice. I promise not to criticise one note as you search for your own song". But the black teachers say, "I've heard your song loud and clear. Now, I want you to harmonise with the rest of the world." Their insistence on skills is not a negation of their students' intellect, as is often suggested by progressive forces, but an acknowledgement of it: "You know a lot; you can learn more. Do It Now!"'

The difficult choice facing teachers stems from the completely decontextualized nature of the official curriculum (and the textbooks that entrench that irrelevance even further), with compulsory cultural content that bears virtually no relation to the cultural experience of most pupils and, as such, holds little interest or attraction for them. To bridge this gulf, it is essential for teachers to develop certain aspects of their personalities, such as discretion, moderation, honesty, impartiality, courage, patience, generosity and good judgement, in order to allow them to establish a positive interpersonal relationship with each and every pupil.

Despite recent improvements, serious deficiencies remain in relation to teacher training for inclusive education. While significant advances were made with the extension of the qualification period from three to four years, good intentions aside, an opportunity to introduce more specifically inclusive measures was lost, with no firm attempt made to put in place programmatic reforms against the prevailing culture of racism, sexism, classicism and colonialism.

Teacher training should take place in full and explicit consciousness and acknowledgement of the political nature of all social professions. First and foremost, teachers are citizens, and it is the interplay between the civic and professional aspects of their personality that determines their performance and motivation. Teacher training must kindle new life in both, since all educational projects are ultimately concerned with instilling a particular model of citizenship. When we talk about education, curriculum and the work of teachers in schools, what we are really talking about is the kind of society we want to create: the kind of people who live in it and how they interact with each other and the kind of skills, knowledge and abilities that make up citizenship. Recent decades have seen the relentless advance of neoliberalism, conservativism and neocolonialism, and with it, the edging out and eclipsing of *homo politicus* by *homo economicus, consumens, debitor* and *numericus.* All that defines us as humans and makes us equal – public, democratic debate, concern for others, the search for consensus – has been diminished and curtailed by the advance of technologies designed to compare and pit people against each other, champion self-starters, privatise and commercialise human life, reduce people to customers with wealth-indexed access to opportunity and turn us all into robots.

Being a teacher-citizen involves demanding truly democratic education policies for the training and development of skilled, informed, fair, inclusive, caring, critical, public, democratic and eternally optimistic teachers who believe that all children, teenagers and people in general have the right and the ability to succeed.

Psycho-pedagogical reductionism in teacher training

The importance placed on external student assessment, the exclusion of explanatory variables, and the direct link drawn between test results and quality of teaching, have made test skills, content and performance standards the focus of schoolwork for pupils and teachers alike. The same obsession with quantitative comparisons that characterises these assessments has also taken hold of the teaching methods and criteria used in relation to content designed to meet the demands of the labour market and the economic and financial sectors.

The decisions teachers take, the work they do and the knowledge they consider important for their pupils' education are depoliticised. The real needs of the community are ignored and no thought is given to what knowledge might help us to understand better how society works or how social dysfunction and injustice might be tackled. People stop questioning how priorities are established or who decides what issues to address first or at all. Eventually, society is taken over by a culture of utilitarian pragmatism at the service of big corporations and international economic organisations. In education, the vocabulary and learning activities used by teachers exhibit the same instrumentalist philosophy in the form of capitalist, neoliberal values such as competition, rivalry and individualism. In its obsession with student scores and school rankings, the education system has forgotten the need for collaborative professionalism in teaching and the transformative power of *professional capital*. Professional capital is the product of *human capital* (capital built out of the talents of individuals), *social capital* (capital created as a result of cooperation and team work) and *decisional capital* (the accumulated wisdom and experience of many years of professional decisions taken in a range of complex, practical and shared situations) (Hargreaves and Fullan, 2014). The catchcry of 'scientific evidence' proclaimed with positivist zeal by neoliberal organisations intent upon discrediting and privatising public teacher training colleges and faculties, obviates the idea of professional capital and reduces education to the mere production and training of workers, rather than the creation of skilled, informed, critical, thoughtful, optimistic, democratic citizens.

Notwithstanding their purported efficiency, positivist pedagogies actually increase the paperwork load of teachers and school administrations. Teaching staff and principals assume that academic success can be achieved by implementing standardised, universal protocols, created with no input from the individual schools themselves. Copied from those used in companies and factories, these protocols fail to take into account the additional social dimensions at play in contexts of human and educational interaction (intellectual, ethical, moral and political). Yet these dimensions must be highlighted and discussed, and opinions and legitimate sociopolitical differences teased out, in order to arrive at a deliberative, democratic consensus for the benefit of the whole community. Though rarely stated explicitly, decisions about the purpose of the project, the priorities to be addressed and its adaptation to the specific reality of the community, city, neighbourhood, student personality, and so on. are an inherent part of all educational protocols.

The ultimate aim of standardisation policies and performance indicators is to redirect the teaching profession. This new conception of the role and function of educators undermines or dispenses with the philosophical, sociological, political, ethical and aesthetic aspects of teacher training and development and replaces them with the precept of immediate practicality. The discourse of efficiency, objectivity, neutrality and apolitical education used to justify the quantitative measurement of learning is merely a smokescreen to disguise the democratic blackout underway since the 1980s. School communities (teachers, pupils and families) have been disempowered and educators have been deprofessionalised under the management and collusion of number-crunching principals and the argument that no reasonable alternatives are possible.

The growing use of critically, practically and theoretically unsubstantiated expressions such as 'good practice', 'enterprise', 'educational innovation', 'proved evidence', and so on. is indicative of a dangerous reductionism that replaces educators with 'coaches' whose only function is to apply standardised formulae, protocols and measurement tests, incentivise competition through comparison, and encourage activity for activity's sake, with no serious, verifiable arguments or methodology to support them.

Even with the best information available, professional activity in social sectors such as education are always subject to *uncertainty* and *unpredictability*. The only thing certain in these situations is that prejudice, false expectations, semi-unconscious personal desires, bias, ignorance, and so on will always have a role to play. For this very reason, it is essential that the teacher training received by future professionals bring them into contact with more information, theories and experiences from a wide range of fields, sources and realities; encourage teamwork with other teachers and specialists; and form part of a continuous process of learning and development. Knowledge changes and advances all the time, which is why teachers should be curious and eager to discover the full possibilities of whatever research, development or work they encounter in relation to educational experience.

Up until the 1980s, assessment and analysis of teacher training and development in colleges and faculties received little or no attention. The lack of any serious, theoretical examination of the question on the part of education authorities meant that biases, omissions and other problems within the system remained undetected. The legacy of those deficiencies in the analysis and development of teacher training policy is still felt to this day.

Researchers have warned for years of serious deficiencies in the cultural education received by teachers, especially those working at preschool and primary level. University syllabuses place a very significant emphasis on the pedagogical and psychological aspects of teacher training. While their place and role in the syllabus are essential, there is an urgent need for these programmes to be expanded to include more sociological, cultural and scientific content, as recommended by the vast majority of experts in this area.

If teachers are expected to stir in their pupils a passion for culture in its myriad forms and contexts, it is only logical that they, too, should receive meaningful training and education in these areas. However, this very idea has been dislodged by the reductionist emphasis on the psychological, pedagogical and didactic aspects of teacher training and practice across all subjects and educational levels. Teachers in charge of their pupils' humanistic and scientific education are being trained according to a minimalistic, filtered concept of curriculum and learning. The traditional goals of education have been replaced by a new set of priorities.

Traditionally, the person with the most knowledge about a subject was considered to be the best qualified to introduce, explain and encourage interest in it among his or her pupils. That changed when teacher training authorities decided that after secondary education, teachers were sufficiently expert in arts, humanities, experimental science and mathematics and that what they needed was training in areas they knew nothing about: child and youth development psychology, psychology of learning, theory and history of education, sociology of education, general and specific didactics and educational technology.

For decades, experts have argued that teaching requires more than just knowledge of the subject being taught. In a bid to overcome traditional models of education focused on memorising information, formulae, theories and other knowledge and offer pupils a more relevant, rounded and meaningful educational experience, it was assumed that what teachers needed was more training in the areas they apparently knew least about. This new approach placed greater emphasis on equipping teachers with the knowledge necessary to help children learn more effectively, including questions such as the construction of knowledge in pupils' minds, influence of pupils' cognitive structures and types of intelligence on methodologies and resources, strategies for motivating pupils and maintaining their interest, tasks to promote learning, ethical education, and so on. Yet however important these pedagogical, psychological, didactic, philosophical and sociological aspects of teacher training may be, they are not sufficient by themselves: teachers must also be educated in the cultural aspects of their subjects and disciplines.

Psychologistic policies and reforms in education began in earnest with the LOGSE (General Governance of the Education System Act) in 1990. The new law introduced a number of positive changes, such as the extension of compulsory education from the age of 6 to 16, a commitment to make education more comprehensive, the inclusion of preschool from the ages of 0 to 6 as an official stage of education, and support for the inclusion of pupils with disability in ordinary classrooms. At the same time, however, it brought with it an ideology of constructivist learning as a panacea for all the ailments of the system, from dropout and failure rates to obstacles to learning in general. Despite the miracles promised by the law, day-to-day life in schools remained virtually unchanged, and there was no discussion of the cultural grounding received by pupils as part of their civic education or how to inspire in them a passion and curiosity for cultural content in all areas of the curriculum. The newest members of the teaching profession have been trained according to an official policy of constructivist learning, translated years later into the skills model introduced by the LOE (Education Act) of 2006 and continued by the LOMCE (Improvement of the Quality of Education Act) seven years later. The technocratic and psychologistic ideas encapsulated by these laws have given rise to a new vocabulary of terms whose actual significance is unclear but which serve to distract attention away from more fundamental questions, such as the selection of cultural content. With the progressive implantation of psychologistic approaches, more critical, emancipatory theories and pedagogies have been steadily sidelined or reduced to empty slogans and catchphrases (Apple, 2001; Darder, Mayo & Paraskeva, 2016; Gimeno Sacristán, 2010; Saltman, 2014; Torres Santomé, 1991).

Although teachers were slow to question the policies of a government known for its progressivism, the education reforms introduced by the Spanish Socialist Party (PSOE) opened the door for the conservative, neoliberal and neocolonialist direction of political decision-making by the Popular Party government that succeeded it, as well as the deprofessionalisation of teachers by subjecting their work to regular auditing-style inspection and measurement (Au, 2011).

Policies of this kind pave the way for an acritical education system and the disappearance of fair, ethical curriculum planning. What is even worse is that a large number of less politically aware teachers do not even realise that this is happening. The principle of fairness disappears from education when teaching staff are no longer able to discuss and analyse democratically the reasons for their selection of cultural content, methodologies and activities, classroom interactions, expectations with regard to student ability and performance or ways to engage families, pupils and other social groups in the school community.

The reductionist technocratism of current reforms focuses exclusively on psycho-pedagogical content, ignoring the need for a thorough analysis of all that is said, omitted, distorted, exaggerated and assumed about history, culture and reality. Not alone that, but the blame for these omissions, distortions and lies is laid with the pupils. The only purpose served by this kind of education is cultural assimilation: forcing people to renounce their cultural identity, persuading them of its inferiority and convincing them to doubt its very authenticity.

Teacher training and development programmes also fail to address the reality and importance of cultural fusion in today's society. The gap in cultural understanding remains enormous, with activities organised in the name of multiculturalism, interculturality, inclusivity, and others amounting to little more than cultural fairs or markets, when they should be part of more far-reaching political, cultural, economic, professional or educational projects aimed at subverting the roots and causes of segregation, colonialism and marginalisation.

Similarly absent from the education system are languages that form part of the culture and day-to-day reality of many pupils, such as Caló, Arabic and other non-official languages of the state. In acknowledging the long-standing injustice of this situation, we must also be aware of associated problems, such as the scarcity of qualified teachers and teaching materials. Policies aimed at promoting educational fairness must include forceful measures against this type of injustice. Another area in which the educational authorities have been dragging their feet is in the incentivisation of people from minority cultures to study a teaching degree or people from the cultures' countries of origin to come to Spain to work within the education system. Increasing the presence of teachers from minority ethnicities in ordinary schools is a powerful way of providing role models for minority pupils, visibilising silenced, marginal realities and demonstrating to pupils that all human beings are equal.

In order to offer children a solid cultural grounding and shape them into critical future citizens, teachers themselves must receive a critical education with a solid base in theory, practice and experience. In recent decades, however, 'practice, practice, practice' has been the mantra of teacher training (regardless of how repetitive that practice might be), to the point that many teachers view theory as a pointless abstraction. Yet there is an important difference between valid, well constructed theory and the kind of religious, metaphysical discourses used to indoctrinate teachers ill equipped to defend themselves. For a person without theoretical markers or critical faculties, it is much harder to arrive at a sound, reasonable judgement about the representations, perceptions, prejudices, intuitions, assessments and proofs that constitute our reality. Our human capacity to question, analyse, distinguish and judge is diminished when we forget about or lose our commonsense view of the world.

Teachers in training require a solid theoretical grounding in philosophy, sociology, ethics, educational theory, didactics, and others that will allow them to devote their time at university to deconstructing and reassessing the scientific, cultural, social and popular knowledge they receive as part of their education; to becoming more aware of the ethical and political aspects of knowledge; and to attuning their senses to detect the presence of privileged national and group interests in the selection of cultural content, procedures and values, to the detriment of the common interests that make us a society. Teacher training should equip and enable teachers to detect epistemicide, bias and hierarchies of knowledge; to construct public, common knowledge using dialogic educational philosophies (Habermas, 1999, 2013); and to assess how well qualified their training has made them to empower pupils from the most deprived and marginalised sectors of society. With greater knowledge comes greater critical awareness of the need for constant vigilance against the kind of unwitting biases that often affect our decision-making. In this sense, Wallenstein (2013: 18) warns of 'the Heisenberg principle writ large: the process of investigation, the procedure through which the observations are made, transforms the object of investigation. Under certain circumstances, it transforms it so much that the data obtained are quite unreliable'. Neoliberal, conservative and neocolonialist groups and organisations invest much time and effort in promoting this very dynamic: in designing tactics and campaigns aimed at hollowing out and depoliticising the language of motivation and mobilisation. Thus, for example, the concept and philosophy of 'empowerment' may have radically different meanings, depending on the ideological context in which it is used: for the left, empowerment refers to equipping citizens to work together to combat and reverse situations of oppression and injustice; for the right, it means producing rational economic and business actors (Cruikshank, 1999: 68).

The quest for critical pedagogy and curricular optimism

In these times of depoliticisation and technocratism, critical pedagogy has become an *ethical, political practice* involving the presentation and promotion of ideals and aspirations for a better world. To nurture this conception of the world as shared experience and horizons, schools must offer relevant, meaningful and motivating cultural content about the society we want to live in. Informative didactic resources and strategies should be properly conceived and suited to each level of learning, and aimed at encouraging pupils to imagine and design better futures. A solid curricular project must aim to make pupils aware of how we, our community, other people and the environment are portrayed and judged.

When we talk about politics, we have to accept the need for free, open-minded collective debate and that the 'other' also has something interesting to say which may force us to reassess and even change our opinions, actions, decisions and feelings. When an issue is political or politicised, it means that there are competing discourses, understandings and judgements at play: social groups who are silenced because they think differently; groups that are subordinated yet continue to struggle to make their voice heard and take their place in the conversation. Open political debate forestalls fundamentalisms and dictatorial solutions by ensuring a voice for the vulnerable: supposed enemies and criminals, 'disposable' citizens and victims of fatwas. In its absence, when people are silenced and their will suppressed, alternative, often 'illegal' forms of resistance emerge, which in turn lead to an escalation of repressive police measures designed to keep the powerful safe.

When something is 'public', it means that it is shared by all members of the community and should therefore be open to free debate and criticism. Public debate serves to highlight one of the basic actions of democracy and the commitment to equal rights and opportunities for all: the fight against oppression, injustice and inequality.

In recent decades, education reforms have been attacked as 'politicised' by the most conservative, neoliberal and religiously fundamentalist sectors of society, in an attempt to confuse citizens and discredit political thought and practice. Their efforts have not been without reward, as witnessed in the significant depoliticisation of education (in the most negative sense). Their strategy consists of convincing families, teachers and pupils to look upon politics as something negative, ignoring the fact that the purveyors of the message are themselves salaried politicians and members of the different parliaments and ministries. When politics is degraded in this way, it is as a result of fear of people practising their citizenship and participating in the organisation and management of society. The action of 'depoliticising' the education system distracts attention away from its most essential and defining aspects so that neither teachers nor families nor pupils consider how they can help to create a more just, egalitarian, participatory, caring, inclusive and democratic society through education.

The source of the feelings of helplessness and anxiety experienced by many young people nowadays may be traced, at least in part, to the cultural manipulations presented to pupils through the official curriculum. The ease with which neoliberal governments and large corporations have managed to expropriate, privatise or destroy public services and resources (including education, health, social services, retirement pensions and public buildings and spaces) is indicative of a widespread sense of defeatism within society. This is what happens when education becomes disempowering, incapacitating and domesticating, denying pupils access to truly relevant learning or the procedures needed to investigate how to transform reality, overcome difficulties and find reasons for optimism about the future.

Teaching means creating conditions for pupils to make knowledge their own: to construct its meaning for themselves, transform their initial knowledge, develop new concepts, understand theories, acquire and develop new procedures, and so on. In recent years, numerous psychological theories have argued for pupils to be placed at the centre of the education system, reasoning that each pupil has his or her own learning speed, prior knowledge, interests, intelligences, desires, ways of feeling, capacities and expectations. However, this total focus on the child and his or her needs leads us into the territory of the individualistic, selfish and even innatist philosophies so favoured by conservatives and neoliberals nowadays. An individualistic approach to learning (focusing on individual learning speed, knowledge, interests, expectations, etc.) isolates education from the social realities and influences of the pupil's situation and bases its methods (albeit implicitly) on an ideology of giftedness and natural talent. The giftedness perspective assumes that each person is the exclusive product of the aptitudes with which they are born; the social possibilities of their personality come encoded in their genetics. In a classist, racist, neocolonialist, sexist, individualistic society, explanatory models of this kind are a perfect justification for segregation and social exclusion.

In most cases, differences between pupils are based on factors of class, nationality, ethnicity, gender and sexuality rather than genetics. The ideology of giftedness naturalises differences between individuals while disregarding the political, social and familial factors responsible. It ignores the unique circumstances of each family, how they occupy their free time, their financial, social, cultural, symbolic and informational capital, and so on. Economic disadvantage affects children's physical and emotion growth and socialisation processes, while cognitive development is further impacted by the poverty of cultural stimuli to which they are exposed. The discourse of giftedness has proved a particularly effective strategy for depoliticising education and reducing it to just another consumer service for a critically unimaginative clientele.

Teachers and cultural workers have a vital role to play in helping to expose the hidden agenda of neoliberal, conservative, neocolonialist policies; promote debate and alternative hypotheses; and stand up to injustice in all its forms. It is their job to stimulate the collective imagination to seek out fairer, more inclusive and more sustainable alternatives and possibilities.

As public intellectuals, critical educators have a responsibility to try to change their world: to realise that what happens in the classroom has repercussions for the rest of society, and remain alert to the non-democratic, authoritarian structures, forces and dynamics attempting to redirect society and the education system.

Emancipatory education requires integrated curricular projects and an optimistic attitude to pupil abilities. Children should be treated and accepted as intelligent, curious, interested and passionate about everything worth knowing. Curricular projects should be based on the principle of interdisciplinarity, with the aim and ability to make children dream. Education means helping pupils to know about the world they live in, to understand what makes it the way it is and to imagine a better future. All educational practice should inspire children with a sense of possibility, based on active learning methodologies.

A pedagogy of optimism and empowerment looks at the past and present together to show that innovation and the struggle for a fairer, better society have always been necessary for success: 'Exemplary use of memory involves using the past with a view to the present, learning from injustices suffered in the past in order to struggle against those committed in the present, and separating oneself from the "I" in order to move towards the other' (Todorov, 2008: 31). Calling up memories makes sense when we have a reason to do so, when there is a need to know exactly what happened and why in order to understand and find a solution to problems in the present that affect our rights, recognition or participation: 'Everyone has the right to recover the past, but there is no reason to create a cult of memory for memory's sake; sacralising memory is another way to render it sterile. Once the past is recovered, we must ask questions such as: how will we use it, and to what end?' (Todorov, 2008: 33). One of the injustices of the world in which we live is that only those in power have the ability to decide what gets preserved and what gets left out, thereby ensuring 'certain privileges for themselves within society' (Todorov, 2008: 53).

Critical, empowering pedagogy requires methodologies that stimulate a critical, optimistic attitude and encourage pupils and teachers to think about how to build towards a better future: to ask what they can do, where to help, with what resources and how. Limiting education to questions of who did what, when and where leads to passivity, a sense of marginalisation from history and society and disempowerment. Integrated, interdisciplinary curriculum planning is, therefore, essential in order to connect as many levels of learning as possible. Emancipatory education is always both critical and optimistic, giving pupils the confidence to continue learning and improving.

The education system must move away from models and discourses of failure. There will always be pupils whom schools find it difficult to understand, motivate or provide with a learning curriculum to suit their skills, interests and knowledge, but there is no barrier to learning that cannot be overcome. In this case, the solution is for teachers and specialists to work together to identify the strengths and weaknesses of each pupil and find alternative strategies that adapt more effectively to their particular needs and circumstances.

Pupils' chances of success cannot be modelled in negative terms. Negative expectations go against the inherently optimistic march of science, which is based on the belief that every problem has a solution; you just have to figure it out. Discourses of negativity represent people's chances of success in life, individually or as a group, as in some way predestined or even genetically encoded. The exaggerated individualism of this perspective reinforces the unfair and immoral logic of 'every person for him or herself', and leads to a paradigm of blame according to which members of the most deprived groups are viewed as responsible for their own circumstances of disadvantage and the deficiencies of their education.

A large proportion of pupils considered problematic and even anti-social come from families in situations of social and economic disadvantage or are experiencing some complex interpersonal, social, medical or labour-related difficulty. Children living on the front line of tension and inequality frequently feel unwanted at school and rejected or unappreciated within their local and home environments. The accumulation of negative experiences throughout their lifetime quickly leads to a self-concept of failure and the search for alternatives, including violence and/or other disruptive or hostile behaviours.

The omissions of the curriculum and many of the materials used to teach it make schools a site of inequality for many children from Roma, immigrant (documented or otherwise), refugee, ethnically distinct and economically disadvantaged backgrounds, leaving them isolated, invisible and disengaged. Immediate action is needed to address the lack of serious, respectful information and educational resources about the history and cultures of these silenced communities. Pupils from low cultural and economic backgrounds are often disadvantaged further by their own manners and appearance, which cause fellow pupils and even teachers to withhold love, care, support and solidarity (Lynch, Baker and Lyons, 2014), and they are rarely made the centre of the teacher's time or attentions, except to watch for misbehaviour. Teachers must become aware of what is happening and take steps to forestall the perversely classist, racist, colonialist, sexist and homophobic forms of common sense to which we have been a party since our days as students.

The commitment by schools to just curriculum planning requires that teachers be consciously and actively guided in their professional practice by ethical principles such as intellectual integrity and impartiality, moral courage, respect, humility, tolerance, trust, responsibility, justice, honesty and solidarity (Torres Santomé, 2009: 74–75).

Educational optimism requires good professionals capable of identifying and understanding the social, cultural, political, employment and health circumstances that make everyday life more challenging for children from disadvantaged backgrounds. Teachers should not ignore the problems facing their pupils but help them to formulate a response and make them more aware of the political nature of their situation and what they can do about it. It is also important for pupils in situations of poverty to understand, first, that they must be prepared to work hard in order to solve their problems (Wrigley, 2007: 157), but equally that there are a host of institutions, organisations and individuals (teachers included) working side by side with them, their families and their communities to overcome the injustices they face.

We live in a world in which people need to be active, critical and responsible and equipped with all the information, knowledge and procedures necessary to act at a local, national and global level in accordance with their rights and obligations as citizens. Education is and must be the key to achieving that objective.

By showing pupils how social groups in other countries have succeeded in overcoming forms of discrimination similar to those witnessed and experienced in Spanish society, optimistic pedagogies teach pupils to hope and how to formulate solutions to the problems in their own lives. Those objectives can only be realised, however, when the system itself becomes fully democratic. As Rudduck and Flutter (2007: 116) have pointed out, '[p]erhaps the most challenging dimension is the need for pupils to learn about citizenship in a structure that offers them experience of the principles of citizenship'.

Securing and perfecting democratic gains is a continuous process that requires informed, educated, critical, alert, ethically committed, idealistic citizens, with faith in a future that we can make possible together.

Public, political, social and educational activism is needed now more than ever to stand up against the new neoliberal, conservative and neocolonialist common sense and the radical education reforms introduced by the People's Party government with the backing of business and finance organisations, the Roman Catholic church, and supranational neoliberal organisations such as the OECD, the World Bank, the IMF and others. In an effort to produce new generations of *homo numericus*—competitive, enterprising individuals, obsessed with numerically measurable standards of quality and excellence, and shaped to meet the labour needs of financial and economic corporations—increased emphasis is being placed within the curriculum on content and subjects that feed the globalised capitalist market and the processes of colonisation. The OECD and its triennial PISA (Programme for International Student Assessment) surveys play a crucial role in this redirection of the education system (Torres, 2011: 186–200). PISA drops an 'information bomb' (Virilio, 2016) of test findings on all participating states on the same day, which are sold to the public as a true and objective statement of the quality of the education system in each country. Astutely, the programme highlights the weak points of each in order to force people to accept the reforms recommended by the OECD and uses league tables of overall performance to portray certain countries ranking very poorly in relation to others.

What I have attempted to highlight in this analysis are the intimidation measures used to frighten citizens into accepting whatever policies and solutions the government proposes. The fear constructed during the earliest years of education becomes ingrained in the individual, leading to a demobilised citizenry and the abdication of civic rights and responsibilities. The engine of history has passed from the mass social organisation of previous centuries to the capacity for intimidation possessed by those in power and the capacity for resignation of ordinary citizens. With the encroachment of neoliberalism and neocolonialism, hope and resistance have lost ground and been replaced by despair, passivity, conformism and resignation. Democracy and the institutions on which it is founded have become a mutated sham of what they once were.

The course of history never did run straight, however, and official policies and intentions can never fully prevent people from thinking, imagining and creating ways to put aside passivity and act to change the world.

More and more citizens are refusing to accept the status quo and are willing to fight for a different kind of society, a different kind of world. They realise that, in order to exercise our rights and obligations as citizens, people in today's world must be equipped with all the information, knowledge and procedures necessary to act at a local, national and global level. We must know and understand our responsibilities as citizens. Society needs an insurgent citizenship to denounce and reject the empty democracy demanded by authoritarian neoliberal, conservative, neocolonialist models and take up the fight for shared, public values and real democracy based on justice, participation, inclusivity and solidarity. The role of education in this exciting endeavour is to create and encourage mentalities and imaginations more attuned to the aspirations, needs, interests and desires of an able, autonomous, critical, democratic, sympathetic and caring, anti-sexist, anti-classist, anti-racist, inclusive, optimistic, sensitive citizenry, dedicated to the pursuit of greater social justice and democracy. Education systems, teachers, families, pupils and society in general must be persuaded that a different world is possible. That yes, we can.

References

Apple, Michael W. (2001). *Política cultural y educación*. Madrid: Morata.

Au, Wayne (2011). Teaching under the New Taylorism: High-Stakes Testing and the Standardization of the 21st Century Curriculum. *Journal of Curriculum Studies*, Vol. 43 (N° 1), pp. 25-45.

Cruikshank, Barbara (1999). *The Will to Empower. Democratic Citizens and Other Subjects*. Ithaca, New York: Cornell University Press.

Darder, Antonia, Mayo, Peter & Paraskeva, João (Comps) (2016). *International Critical Pedagogy Reader*. New York: Routledge.

Delpit, Lisa (1995). *Other People's Children. Cultural Conflict in the Classroom*. New York: The New Press.

Gimeno Sacristán, José (Comp.) (2010). *Saberes e incertidumbres sobre el currículum*. Madrid: Morata.

Habermas, Jürgen (1999). *La inclusión del otro. Estudios de teoría política*. Barcelona: Paidós.

Habermas, Jürgen (2013). *Teoría de la acción comunicativa. Tomo I. Racionalidad de la acción y racionalidad social. Tomo II. Crítica de la razón funcionalista*. Madrid: Trotta.

Hargreaves, Andy & Fullan, Michael (2014). *Capital profesional. Transformar la enseñanza en cada escuela*. Madrid: Morata.

Ladson-Billings, Gloria (1994). *The Dreamkeepers. Successful Teachers of African American Children*. San Francisco: Jossey-Bass.

Lynch, Kathleen, Baker, John & Lyons, Maureen (2014). *Igualdad afectiva: amor, cuidado y justicia*. Madrid: Morata.

Peters, Michael A., Paraskeva, João M. & Besley, Tina (2015). *The Global Financial Crisis and Educational Restructuring*. New York: Peter Lang.

Reese, William J. (2013). *Testing Wars in the Public Schools. A Forgotten History*. Cambridge. Harvard University Press.

Rudduck, Jean & Flutter, Julia (2007). *Cómo mejorar tu centro escolar dando la voz al alumnado*. Madrid: Morata.

Saltman, Kenneth J. (2014). *The Politics of Education. A Critical Introduction*. New York: Routledge.

Todorov, Tzvetan (2008). *Los abusos de la memoria*. Barcelona: Paidós.

Torres Santomé, Jurjo (1991). La Reforma educativa y la psicologización de los problemas sociales. In Isidoro Alonso Hinojal et al. (Eds). *Sociedad, Cultura y Educación. Homenaje a la memoria de Carlos Lerena Alesón*. Madrid. Centro de Investigación y Documentación Educativa (CIDE – Ministerio de Educación y Ciencia) and Universidad Complutense de Madrid, pp. 481-503.

Torres Santomé, Jurjo (2005). *El currículum oculto* (8th ed.) Madrid: Morata.

Torres Santomé, Jurjo (2009). *La desmotivación del profesorado* (2nd ed.) Madrid: Morata.

Torres Santomé, Jurjo (2011). *La justicia curricular* (2nd ed.) Madrid: Ediciones Morata.

Virilio, Paul (2012). *La administración del miedo*. Madrid: Pasos Perdidos.

Wallerstein, Immanuel (2013). *Capitalismo histórico y movimientos antisistémicos. Un análisis de sistemas-mundo* (1st reprint). Madrid: Akal.

Wrigley, Terry (2007). *Escuelas para la esperanza. Una nueva agenda hacia la renovación*. Madrid: Morata.

CHAPTER TWENTY-THREE

Walkouts Teach U.S. Labor a New Grammar for Struggle[1]

Lois Weiner

LIKE THE ARAB Spring, the U.S. "education Spring," was an explosive wave of protests. Statewide teacher walkouts seemed to arise out of nowhere, organized in Facebook groups, with demands for increased school funding and political voice for teachers. Though the walkouts confounded national media outlets, which had little idea how to explain or report on the movements, for parent and teacher activists who have been organizing against reforms in public education in the past four decades, the protests were both unexpected and understandable. What was surprising was their breadth of support (statewide), their organizing strategy (Facebook), and their breathtakingly rapid spread.

For most of the far-Right, the West Virginia, Oklahoma, Kentucky, Arizona, and North Carolina walkouts showed greedy public employees exploiting their job security to get pay and benefits better than hardworking taxpayers have. However, teachers won wide popular support, even from Republicans, forcing the media-savvier elements of the Right to alter their tone. The American Enterprise Institute (AEI) posted a blog with a sympathetic tone pushing the same stance: "While teachers are justly frustrated by take-home pay, their total compensation is typically a lot higher than many teachers realize. That's because teacher retirement and health-care systems are much more expensive than those of the taxpayers who pay for them—whether those taxpayers work in the private or public sector." Shedding crocodile teachers for teachers who are underpaid and retirees without adequate pensions, AEI rejects the idea more school funding would help. What's needed is tweaking neoliberalism's (failed) policy of "merit" pay. As I explain later, policies that link teacher pay to their "performance," judged by students' scores on standardized tests, underlies much teacher anger. The AEI authors, who write for people in education, adopt the bouncy, cheerleader-like prose to argue the real challenge is "how to pay terrific and invaluable teachers more appropriately." Teachers now understand these policies force them to compete against one another for elusive bonuses which replace funding pay schedules for everyone that are based on years of experience and education.[i]

---

1   Keynote address, Department of Educational Leadership, University of Massachusetts Dartmouth, October, 18, 2013, Woodland Commons.

From the start in West Virginia, local coverage of the state walkouts was impressively accurate. Reporters interviewed teachers, school workers, and parents, hearing from them how and why their movement had gained momentum, noting they were not only protesting salaries, health care, and pensions but also the need for increased school funding for school supplies and improvements to dilapidated facilities. In contrast, national media were clueless about how the walkouts had been organized, relying on interviews and press releases from union officers and politicians. Few reports explained that in these "right to work states" both the American Federation of Teachers (AFT) and the National Education Association (NEA), the two national teachers unions, had state affiliates with a tiny number of dues-paying members and state union officials did not speak for the protestors. Though the AFT president showed up for a few publicity opportunities, in all of these states the AFT affiliate is far smaller than the NEA and is essentially irrelevant politically in teacher union politics. One singular aspect of the walkouts is that they were organized from below, outside of (and despite) attempted control by state union officials. Though teachers and other school workers who were local union activists were often leaders, they were part of the movement, not its masters. The many activists with whom I communicated in the course of the "education Spring" all concurred that if the unions had been doing what they should have, the Facebook-based movements wouldn't have been needed. Though participants were understandably uncomfortable expressing their dissatisfaction with the unions in public during the walkouts, in private conversations teachers were quite explicit that their unions were "irrelevant," "out of touch," and "useless." Teachers in Oklahoma and Kentucky told me they had never been approached to join a union until the Professional Organization of Educators signed them up. They learned once the agitation for the walkouts began and this "union" responded to the calls for action with the same arguments as the far-right teacher-bashers that this was a front group for the billionaires who controlled the state legislature.

Coverage in liberal media and some Left publications tried to make these walkouts fit the mold of "bread and butter" labor struggles. While accounts were accurate in noting that reduced state funding was the immediate root of low teacher pay, a unifying demand in the walkouts, the stories ignored other, equally important sources of teachers' frustration and anger, profound changes in schools and teaching because of bipartisan reforms in the past ten years and the unions' acquiescence to them. The walkouts have brought to the surface widespread frustration and anger about policies that teachers see making their jobs and fulfillment of the reasons they chose to teach almost impossible.

Despite the flood of stories in popular and Left publications, most analysis has missed key lessons of these walkouts, including how gender and race influenced the movement, why these walkouts exemplified workers' self-organization, and how collective bargaining both restrains and protects class struggle, issues I discuss in more detail elsewhere.[ii] When these elements are included, the walkouts suggest a new grammar for labor struggle that can challenge the Right's legal and political attacks on unions everywhere, the South included.

Teacher Self-Organization Replaces Unions Missing in Action

West Virginia began the wave of statewide walkouts, inspiring similar campaigns in Oklahoma, Kentucky, and Arizona. Teachers in Denver closed schools in Jefferson County for a day to mass in their state capital, and North Carolina teachers held a one-day protest in which 25,000 people participated. While there were major similarities, the movements also differed in significant ways because of geography, history, demographics, and the state's balance of political forces.

My knowledge of the walkouts is drawn from published reports as well as my ongoing involvement with activists as an adviser and supporter on the Facebook pages, in phone calls with organizers, and videoconferences with protestors. The movements followed the same pattern: A handful of teachers and other school employees, including some union activists, frustrated about their unions (in)action, created a Facebook group limited to people who were teachers and school employees in the state. Often an auxiliary group or page was established to provide information and support, but decisions about strategy in votes conducted in surveys were restricted to the closed Facebook pages, to those risking their jobs in taking action. Participants shared information, strategy, and voted. No distinction was made on the Facebook page between those who were or were not union members, although many joined the unions in the course of the walkouts. Discussions became more political by the hour; remorseful, angry posts by people who had voted for the governors who subsequently ridiculed and insulted them were common. A post questioning where the money would come from to fund salary increases might be answered with a suggestion to use the lottery, followed shortly by an activist knowledgeable about the Right's control of tax policy with more information about a progressive alternative, generally in the form of a link to a website. Many participants self-identified as Republicans and as conservatives. Many identified religious faith, assumed to be Christianity, as a powerful support, and in West Virginia thousands joined in prayer each day at a designated time, asking for guidance and strength.

The reason I refer to these actions as "walkouts" is that the organizers adopted a strategy that avoided the language of striking although the protests took a form that relied on unity and solidarity no less than in a strike. Teachers phoned in to their schools saying they would not be present, using personal days or sick days *en masse* to force schools and districts to close until all or much of the state's school districts announced they would be closed. Superintendents, who are almost always former teachers, were often sympathetic to the walkouts. In West Virginia, school workers other than teachers were included in the movement from the start, using what one activist called "wall to wall" organizing. Detroit teachers closed their schools in May 2016, a school system under state control, using the "sick out," which, like using personal days to close schools, avoids, at least temporarily, some of the legal problems of a walkout in a state that outlaws teachers' strikes.

National media, including a labor reporter who represents himself as a savvy insider, consistently assumed that state union officials spoke for the movements, missing a dynamic that made the "education Spring" so special in U.S. labor: those whom union officials say they represent were actually in control much of the time, reversing the typical hierarchy of union officials telling members/workers what to do. In West Virginia union officials tried—and failed—to broker a deal with the government without checking in with the Facebook organization. The movement was sufficiently well organized and unified that it held strong in rejecting the settlement, forcing union officials to back down after they announced—and the *New York Times* reported—the walkout had been ended. In Oklahoma and Kentucky the movements were more fragmented, less well organized, and the teachers and school workers leading the Facebook groups less politically experienced. Officers of the Oklahoma and Kentucky NEA affiliates made backroom deals to end the walkouts, claiming to have polled members. But as the postings on the Facebook pages showed, the vast majority of walkout participants had no opportunity to weigh in on the settlement, either on the Facebook page or in the union poll. The reaction to the substance of the settlements was, at best, very mixed. However, the anger at union officials' usurpation of what was almost unanimously agreed was protestors' right to decide how and when to return to work was expressed quite strongly. Those who were the most active felt the most blindsided and betrayed by the unions' actions. Though deeply disappointed with the settlements, which relied on regressive taxes and provided relatively little new money, Oklahoma and Kentucky teachers lacked sufficient organization, even in the cities where they were strongest, to continue the walkouts without union help. "How could we have missed that the union would do this?" one anguished Oklahoma activist asked me.

In Arizona activists developed a collaborative relationship with the NEA affiliate, which "played nice," as one leader told me. A small AFT local, on the other hand, played a "rogue" role, calling for walkouts separate from the unified "Red for Ed" movement so as to claim leadership of the movement. Activists in all the states mentored one another, and in Arizona leaders referred to what had occurred in the Chicago Teachers Union (CTU) 2012 strike. They developed a consensus that the walkout was the first round in building a movement that had initiated what would be an ongoing struggle that involved political education, electoral action, and building a stronger, responsive union by recruiting and engaging teachers who had lost their fear of standing up and being heard. Unlike in the other states, in North Carolina the May 16 statewide protest in the capitol planned well beforehand in a process initiated by Organize 2020, a statewide reform caucus in the NEA affiliate.

One tension in all the states was balancing direct action with the hope that electoral activity would bring solutions. As teachers massed in the state capital in the tens of thousands, their protests suggested a possibility of a reenactment of what had occurred in Madison, Wisconsin. In Madison teachers and other public employees occupied the state legislature in response to the legislation that revoked the right of public employees to bargain collectively. Their occupation ended when union officials persuaded them to leave the building, to adopt what proved to be an unsuccessful electoral strategy, recall of the governor, Scott Walker. In Kentucky one contingent of teachers and education activists were alert to the possibility of an occupation and packed bags with clean underwear. This possibility of a "Madison—with a different ending," the shorthand I used in my discussions with walkout leaders, explains why national media clung to the myth that union officials spoke for teachers and the corollary, that workers can't achieve their goals through direct action but must instead rely on the ballot box. In her press conference announcing that the Oklahoma Education Association (OEA) had agreed to support legislation (which the movement had previously rejected), the OEA president said the union "had achieved all it could with a walkout" and would "shift their efforts to supporting candidates in the fall elections who favor increased education spending." Yet the biggest pieces of legislation passed before the walkout, not during it, so the movement's strength had not yet been tested. No press questioned how or why the electoral strategy would succeed in Oklahoma or Kentucky when the traditionally liberal and labor-friendly state of Wisconsin had failed to recall Walker, allowing the GOP to destroy collective bargaining for public employees.[iii]

The walkouts enjoyed huge popular support, from conservative Republicans to socialists. A new generation radicalized by the Sanders campaign, especially members of Democratic Socialists of America (DSA), made their presence felt by organizing support. Progressive watchdog groups were also important allies in identifying legislation that needed to be stopped—or should be passed—in each state. Save Our Schools Kentucky, an education advocacy group that has strong connections with progressive and "good-government" organizations in the state, did much of the planning that the NEA affiliate did not, serving as an auxiliary to the Facebook group of teachers and other school employees, led by a charismatic school worker.

Liberalism's Rip Van Winkle Slumber and Partial Awakening

Liberals have (mostly) been awakened from their neoliberal somnolence, discovering that reforms supported enthusiastically by both parties, masked in the rhetoric of creating educational opportunity, were aimed at destroying public education. Still, an exchange in *Dissent* about what was progressive in neoliberalism reveals that even socialists are not yet clear about the real aims and meaning of the neoliberal project.[iv] Their confusion seems to me related to a fearfulness about confronting head-on the role of the Democratic Party and therefore aligning with popular movements, often people fighting on issues of social oppression, that are pushing for a fundamental political break from both parties and the political status quo.

There should be no doubt on the Left about the need to reject all of the bipartisan reforms that have been imposed on U.S. schools. As I explain elsewhere, the project's key elements include privatizing the education sector, eliminating democratic oversight of schools, and making teaching a revolving door of low-paid, minimally educated teachers who will teach to tests over which students, parents, and teachers have no voice. In all of the states having walkouts, teachers were aghast that state legislators moved to allow anyone with a B.A. to teach, removing requirements for teaching credentials, because of a "teacher shortage" artificially induced by low pay and poor working conditions in schools. In fact, U.S. state legislatures have been carrying out policies the World Bank has demanded from the global South for decades, destroying teaching as a career.[v] Though teachers understood that the "shortage" could be solved by funding schools and increasing salaries, even they missed how elimination of certification requirements connects to testing and privatization, pillars of the neoliberal project.

In a lavishly funded global propaganda campaign orchestrated by powerful elites, teachers have been attacked for a huge range of social and educational problems over which they have no control. As many comments on the Facebook pages showed, frustration and anger that fueled the explosiveness of the walkouts was due in good part to policies and rhetoric that assume "teacher quality" is all that matters in student learning and can be measured accurately by students' scores on standardized tests. Oklahoma's "teacher of the year," one of the fifty teachers given this award and invited to meet privately with Education Secretary Betsy DeVos, told DeVos her "choice policies," meaning charter schools and private schools receiving vouchers, were draining traditional public schools of resources in his state. When DeVos suggested students were fleeing low-performing schools, the Oklahoma music teacher, who had voted for Trump, responded that government policies "taking all the kids that can afford to get out and leaving the kids who can't behind" is what "created the bad schools." The Montana and California teachers of the year expressed dismay after the meeting at DeVos's comments opposing teacher strikes. "She basically said that teachers should be teaching and we should be able to solve our problems not at the expense of children. . . . For her to say at the 'expense of children' was a very profound moment and one I'll remember forever because that is so far from what is happening."[vi]

Teacher anger at being held responsible for student learning while facing policies that undercut their ability to do their jobs is clearly not limited to the "red states." An array of conditions, not just reduced funding, created the perfect storm for direct action that spread so quickly. Some teachers were inspired by student protests over gun violence, but for many years courageous teachers and parents have been allies in the "opt out" of testing movement to stop standardized testing. The Bad Ass Teachers (BATS), organized on social media, banded together in "red states" and "blue" to fight the attacks on teachers' dignity as workers because teachers unions have not adequately defended the profession. Nationally, funding of teachers' salaries mostly comes from local districts, supplemented by state revenues, but much of teachers' work is directly controlled by state law. Although federal mandates have squeezed the states—with little resistance from Democrats—states still have leeway in deciding who can teach, what is taught and how. States generally fund teachers' pensions and health benefits, either entirely or to a considerable extent. Therefore, *every* state is susceptible to statewide mobilizations by teachers, though the presence or absence of collective bargaining rights is certainly a factor in explaining the walkouts.

Collective bargaining legislation that was passed in the 1960s and 1970s is a mixed bag. It gave teachers unions stability and the strength to negotiate improved wages and benefits for members, but the legal framework also created a highly circumscribed scope of bargaining, ceding to school boards and administrations the right to decide most issues that affect teachers' work and students' learning. Even under the best of circumstances, when they have public support for increased school funding, with the best unions, teachers have a very difficult time using collective bargaining to make significant changes in their work. Improving schools is complex, as even elements of the far Right that want a fully privatized public school system now acknowledge, because privatization has failed to boost students' test scores. Teacher unions generally focus on what officials see as most winnable "bread and butter" for reasons both political and practical. In places the unions have collective bargaining, the narrowed scope of bargaining has been worsened by the business union model, which has encouraged member indifference and inactivity when not deepening frustration. Thus business unionism has simultaneously weakened the unions' capacity to protect teachers' interests and intensified the constraint of struggle.

The Walkouts and Teacher Unionism's Transformation

The assumption that the state teachers unions in the "red states" spoke for the movement obscured an extremely important political aspect of the walkouts: They were round two in the struggle to transform teacher unionism. Whether knowingly or not, these grassroots movements challenged the premises on which teachers unions have operated for four decades, a fact missing in most reportage and analysis. Even stories correctly noting links between the walkouts' and the CTU's path-breaking 2012 strike omitted reference to how the Caucus of Rank and File Educators (CORE) won CTU leadership by mobilizing union members to fight for a different kind of union, altering the CTU's priorities, narrative, and operation and in so doing presenting a challenge to the business unionism of both AFT and NEA. [vii]

CORE's successful struggle launched a wave of reform caucuses, which is challenging leadership in urban locals and statewide, supported by a network associated with Labor Notes. In Los Angeles and Boston (AFT locals), as well as the state of Massachusetts (the NEA affiliate), union activists who identify with CORE's "social justice" orientation and organizing model have been elected union presidents. In other cities, reform caucuses sometimes share leadership with the older guard. Key "red state" activists have now joined this reform network. They are a new, vibrant ally for the CTU and like-minded reformers, in a group that is supported by Labor Notes. [viii]

Gender wasn't discussed much but it should be because the walkouts showed its powerful potential to reinvigorate and democratize teachers unions. While CORE was able to win the votes of teachers in elementary schools, has organized in their schools, and has had a remarkable program of political education, as is true in most teachers unions, its leadership and base were mostly white and male high school teachers, with some crucial exceptions, the most powerful being Karen Lewis, CTU's beloved African American president. What has been game-changing in the "red state" walkouts is the participation and politicization of women, especially female elementary school teachers. The movement's power was "women power." Though female teachers didn't discuss gender on the Facebook pages, with the exception of a few postings about paternalistic (my word, not theirs) male principals, and most answered gender wasn't a factor in their participation when the question was first posed, after some reflection they identified a range of gender-related issues, from who did housework and shopping for the family while they were protesting in the state capital, to the ways their work and intelligence were devalued in the society. They were ferociously protective of "their kids" (the term elementary school teachers especially use for their students), making sure they had meals when schools were closed. This speaks to their view of teaching as nurturing, traditionally the mother's role. Their participation is #MeToo brought to teacher unionism, a response to the deterioration and devaluation of teachers' work. One of the best analyses of any of the walkouts, which captured the union's attempt to "domesticate" the struggle, explained how gender configured the West Virginia protest. "If the vast majority of women strikers did not regard themselves to be feminists, feminism, to paraphrase a revolutionary, certainly was not disregarding the strike. The strike, the conditions that led to the strike, the way the strike unfolded were all deeply gendered." [ix]

Perhaps the most dangerous omission in the walkout narrative and subsequent analyses is the salience of race and racism and teacher unionism's historic failure to engage with systemic racism in education and the society. Pyrrhic strikes in 1960s and 1970s that pitted teachers against civil rights activists, perhaps most violently in Newark, New Jersey, and New York City, accelerated the unions' demise as democratic, militant organizations capable of winning substantial victories for members. [x] That pattern was interrupted when CORE, which had organized against school closings in the Black community, foregrounded the gross inequities the city perpetuated against students of color in its 2012 strike, with its program for the schools "Chicago children deserve."

The strategic and moral importance of teacher unions fusing a commitment to antiracism work with their narratives about what's wrong with public education can't be overstated. Tulsa and Oklahoma City were strongholds of the walkouts in Oklahoma, yet in both places the local union was unwilling or unable to articulate demands that would speak directly to the aspirations and apprehensions of Black residents, parents, and students, who are educated in intensely segregated neighborhoods and schools. In Kentucky, the deal the state union brokered allowed the governor to move to take over the Louisville schools. In being "race blind" the movements failed to connect with one of their most powerful potential allies. As a co-thinker involved in supporting the Kentucky teachers astutely observed in our conversation about racism's invisibility even among socialists, we have a chance "to get race right this time, and if we don't, it's over."

The movements created in the "education Spring" face the challenge of how to discuss and act on systemic racism, reflected in every aspect of school life I can think of, while maintaining unity among teachers. Almost one-quarter of AFT members nationally voted for Trump; one-third did so in the NEA. The national statistics about teacher union members voting for Trump don't even reflect how teachers in the South, not members of unions, voted. A color-blindness that obscures racism is not only a problem for teachers and teachers unions but also for the Left, including socialists, as shown by omission of analysis of race in reports about the walkouts and an article about the "progressive potential" of the Scholastic Aptitude Tests (SATs) that ignored the origins of standardized testing in Eugenics. [xi]

Stating the need for "quality education for all" as do the unions—at their best— avoids confronting the legacy of labor's and the education establishment's complicity in accepting government policies that have created and sustained racial segregation in housing, schools, and the labor market.[xii] Expecting support in economic struggles without giving it to communities of color and immigrants on social battles is a dangerous illusion for teachers unions. When workers mobilize and see the need to have allies, they become open to topics that are otherwise not welcomed. In conversations with teachers in Oklahoma and Kentucky, I asked if they had support among parents. The White teachers all thought their locals (in large cities) had done a solid job in getting support, but when I asked the African American teachers to comment, they dissented, saying they had heard community and other teachers express ambivalence about supporting the walkout because the local hadn't been there for the community. For teachers' organizations with collective bargaining or without it, winning the trust of parents who feel estranged from schools and often teachers personally, especially White teachers of students of color, requires being physically present in community struggles against racist policies, fighting school closures but also police brutality and deportations.

Organize 2020 is an important model in this and other regards. This statewide caucus used social media and the excitement of the previous walkouts to build a one-day protest in the state capital and in so doing greatly expand its on-the-ground presence statewide. Its leadership understands the caucus's purpose as long term, building a democratic union based on socially progressive ideals, including an explicit rejection of racism. It has developed alliances with community groups, and when the North Carolina Association of Educators, the lethargic, passive state union, refuses to take action members need, the caucus steps in as best it can given its scarce resources and carries out the plan. Though the North Carolina walkout was just one day, Organize 2020 mobilized teachers on the basis of demands that were race-conscious and that addressed tax breaks for the corporations and wealthy. [xiii] The caucus sees a role for the state's teachers in rebuilding labor in the state. It brings CORE's ideas to its work but looks for strategies that fit its situation.

Teacher Unionism in a Trump Administration

Since the "excellence reforms" in education in the 1990s, when the neoliberal project in the country was begun with the warning the U.S. was a "nation at risk" of falling behind in a global economy, liberals have joined conservatives in embracing strategies to use education as "the one true path out of poverty," as Arne Duncan, Obama's secretary of education phrased the ideological assumption driving educational policy. Despite overwhelming evidence that poverty and unemployment are endemic to a global economy in which workers globally are forced to compete for low-wage jobs requiring relatively little education, liberals and the labor establishment have embraced an exclusively economic rationale for public education that has subverted its other social purposes. While the Left has rightly emphasized education's limited potential to ameliorate poverty and its inability to create jobs, socialists have been less willing to grapple with the complicating reality that schooling can make a difference in terms of individuals' life prospects. So while "teacher quality" is one of the many factors that affect what students learn and we should be concerned about having well-prepared teachers in our schools, good teaching cannot be accurately measured by students' standardized test scores or created or sustained in environments that undercut teachers' exercise of their judgment, the hallmarks of the last decade's reforms.[xiv] We need only look at how wealthy elites educate their children—in schools with small classes, with teachers who are paid well and given considerable autonomy working in properly maintained buildings and schools offering courses of study that include the arts—to see that education counts. The policies that have created "choice," that is, privatized schooling, have resonated with low-income parents and communities of color because they want their children to have the same opportunity affluent parents demand for their kids, to attend college so as to compete for the diminishing number of good jobs.

However, during the 2016 primaries and election, bipartisan consensus about education being the best way to end poverty and improve the nation's economy was shattered. Both Donald Trump and Bernie Sanders, campaigning on diametrically opposed premises about capitalism, argued for economic policies to alleviate inequality. In so doing they implicitly rejected education as the "one true path out of poverty." Education reform as a jobs policy was jettisoned. Moreover, Trump's and the GOP's embrace of policies supporting White supremacy, misogyny, anti-immigrant sentiment, and pseudo-Darwinian ideas about "natural ability" have completely undercut the currency of the Democratic Party's claims that education reforms it has supported are a viable way to make U.S. society more equal. The rhetoric masking privatization and "choice" as a method of increasing opportunity for racial minorities has been ditched by the GOP, stripping the Democrats of their cover for supporting privatization.

Trump and the GOP have been met with outrage and opposition in the streets, and though the "resistance" has not been able to turn protest into political victories, these movements present an opportunity for teachers unions and a dilemma for existing national leadership. Teachers unions feel pressures from social justice movements to confront the Trump administration, not "sit at the table" as they have in collaborating with previous administrations. The political tightrope the NEA and the AFT walk was illustrated by an episode shortly after DeVos was approved as secretary of education. The AFT and NEA mobilized with petitions and phone calls to Congress to block her appointment, raising expectations that the unions would use their power to wage an all-out fight against the GOP and Trump. But when parent and community activists blocked DeVos from entering a Washington, D.C. school, AFT President Weingarten tweeted a reprimand to the protestors for blocking the school, and she invited DeVos to visit schools with her to engage in dialogue. Weingarten also met with Steve Bannon before he was ousted, an encounter reported (uncritically) in *The Intercept* with Weingarten's stance that it was an opportunity to understand Bannon's entreaties to support Trump.[xv] So while the AFT and the NEA endorse the ideas of "social justice" unionism and provide financial support for Journey for Justice, an alliance that includes well-respected community activists, Weingarten's meeting with Bannon suggest the AFT leadership's willingness to desert allies in communities of color should union officials find that expedient.[xvi] And where the AFT goes, the NEA follows shortly, regardless of policies its convention endorses.

Though most activists in the "red states" don't see this—yet—these movements are laying the groundwork for a new labor movement in the South. What they need to do now is develop a truly progressive program for tax reform and provision of public services and figure out an electoral strategy that uses mobilizations and controls the politicians it elects. In West Virginia and in Jersey City, where teachers union conducted a one-day strike, health care was a key issue. To undercut the argument that unions, especially those representing public employees, are no different from other special interest groups, out for their own good, teachers have to use their political muscle to win "single payer" health care. Fighting for economic demands without embedding them in a social vision for improving working people's lives is a losing strategy that may win an occasional strike but depletes the reservoir of support that is needed to win the big battles.

One of the greatest contributions of this movement has been to redefine what it means to be a worker. Even the Left has had trouble understanding that teachers' work, though it is "women's work," is real work—that teachers are real workers. In the "turn to the working class" in the 1970s, socialists abandoned their activity in public employee unions with robust reform caucuses in order to influence industrial workers, in steel, auto, communications, transportation. In doing so, they decimated the radical presence in the AFT and the NEA. The walkouts have shown the Left its mistake in a turn to the working class that defined work, workers, and class in ways that ignored a huge swath, even then, of the workforce.

Teachers are fighting for the dignity of their work and the right to voice about their working conditions. They are defending education as a public good and their students' rights to have what the wealthy take for granted. This strike wave has demonstrated an intensity and scale of self-activity and organization of workers we have not seen in the US in decades. This movement of people who do "women's work," most of who are women, has confirmed—once again—Marx's dictum "the emancipation of the working class must be the act of the working class itself."

Notes

[i]   Frederick M. Hess and Amy Cummings (April 18, 2018). What's behind the teacher strikes? https://www.aei.org/publication/whats-behind-the-teacher-strikes/

[ii]   **How business unionism got us to Janus (November 9, 2017). In These Times.** http://inthesetimes.com/working/entry/20677/janus-right-to-work-union-labor; **West Virginia's school employees teach US labor a huge lesson (February 24, 2018). New Politics (online).** http://newpol.org/content/west-virginias-school-employees-teach-us-labor--huge-lesson. West Virginia Teachers Are Showing How Unions Can Win Power Even If They Lose Janus (February 24, 2018). In These Times (online). http://inthesetimes.com/working/entry/20940/west_virginia_teachers_show_how_to_win_power_after_janus. **West Virginia's strike is no 'wildcat.' Getting the language right (March 4, 2018). New Politics (online).** http://newpol.org/content/west-virginia-strike-no-wildcat. Why support the strike of Jersey City teachers? (March 16, 2018). New Politics (online). http://newpol.org/content/why-support-strike-jersey-city-teachers. Labor renaissance in the heartland (April 6, 2018). The Jacobin (online) https://jacobinmag.com/2018/04/red--state-teachers-strikes-walkouts-unions. **The Red State Walkouts. An analysis - and homage - to the work of teachers** (April 6, 2018). New Politics (online). http://newpol.org/content/red-state-walkouts. Inside the closed Facbook pages where the teacher strikes began (May 18, 2018). In These Times (online). https://jacobinmag.com/2018/04/red-state-teachers-strikes-walkouts-unions

[iii] Dana Goldstein and Elizabeth Dias (April 12, 2018). Oklahoma Teachers End Walkout After Winning Raises and Additional Funding. *The New York Times.* https://www.nytimes.com/2018/04/12/us/oklahoma-teachers-strike.html

[iv]   Fraser, N. (2017, 2 January). The end of progressive neoliberalism. *Dissent.* https://www.dissentmagazine.org/online_articles/progressive-neoliberalism-reactionary-populism-nancy-fraser. Brenner, J. (2017, 14 January). There was no such thing as "progressive neolberalism." *Dissent.* https://www.dissentmagazine.org/online_articles/nancy-fraser-progressive-neoliberalism-social-movements-response.

[v]   Susan Robertson (2000). *A class act. Changing teachers' work, globalisation and the state.* New York: Falmer Press.

[vi]   Rebecca Klein (May 1, 2018). Nation's Top Teachers Confront Betsy DeVos In Private Meeting. HuffPost. https://www.yahoo.com/lifestyle/nation-top-teachers-verbally-s-par-134944008.html?.tsrc=fauxdal

[vii] Maurice BP-Weeks, Stephen Lerner, Joseph A. McCartin, & Marilyn Sneiderman (April 24, 2018). Before the Chalk Dust Settles: Building on the 2018 Teachers' Mobilization. American Prospect. http://prospect.org/article/chalk-dust-settles-building-on-2018-teachers%E2%80%99-mobilization

[viii] Ellen David Friedman (May 27, 2018). What's behind the teacher walkouts? The Jacobin. https://www.jacobinmag.com/2018/05/teacher-strikes-labor-movement-education

[ix]　Tithi Bhattacharya (March 6, 2018). Bread and roses in West Virginia. https://www.versobooks.com/blogs/3669-bread-and-roses-in-west-virginia

[x]　Marjorie Murphy (May 11, 2018). Militancy in many forms: Teachers strikes and urban insurrection, 1967-74. https://www.versobooks.com/blogs/3798-militancy-in-many-forms-teachers-strikes-and-urban-insurrection-1967-74

[xi]　Wayne Au (April 14, 2018), The socialist case against the SAT. The Jacobin. https://www.jacobinmag.com/2018/04/against-the-sat-testing-meritocracy-race-class

[xii]　Richard Rothstein (March 25, 2014), Segregated housing, segregated schools. Education Week. https://www.edweek.org/ew/articles/2014/03/26/26rothstein_ep.h33.html

[xiii] Michelle Gunderson (May 25, 2018). North Carolina Teachers Shut Schools and Flood the Capital for a Day. Labor Notes http://www.labornotes.org/2018/05/north-carolina-teachers-shut-schools-and-flood-capital-day

[xiv] Marilyn Cochran-Smith, Elizabeth Stringer Keefe, Wen-Chia Chang, and Molly Cummings Carney (May 24, 2018). NEPC Review: 2018 State Teacher Policy Best Practices Guide (National Council on Teacher Quality, March 2018) http://nepc.colorado.edu/thinktank/review-teacher-quality

[xv]　Rachel Cohen and Ryan Grim (November 1, 2017). Steve Bannon tried to recruit teachers union to Trump's agenda while in the White House. *The Intercept.* https://theintercept.com/2017/11/01/steve-bannon-aft-teachers-union-randi-weingarten/

[xvi] *Journey for Justice Alliance.* https://www.j4jalliance.com/memb

Culturally Responsive Teaching: Learning to Teach Within the Context of Culture[1]

Fernando Naiditch

The New Face of the American Classroom

A *WASHINGTON POST* headline in August 2014 stated that the academic year that was about to start was the first in history when the so-called minorities were going to be the majority in the American public-school classrooms: For the first time, minority students expected to be majority in U.S. public schools this fall *(Washington Post*, August 21, 2014).

This headline should have come as no surprise. Schools in the United States have changed dramatically over the past few decades. Student and teacher demographics point to a large sociocultural distance between teachers and the students that they teach. While approximately 80% of the nearly 4 million American public-school teachers are still primarily white, over 50% of the nation's approximately 51 million public-school students are children of diverse racial and ethnic background (National Center for Education Statistics [NCES], 2016). This vast contrast between the racial and ethnic makeup of the student population and their teachers is evidence of an even larger gap in the languages, cultures, and socioeconomic statuses represented in the American classrooms today.

According to the NCES's report *The Condition of Education*, not only are over 50% of school-age children in the United States today ethnic minorities, many of them also struggle with poverty, health, living, and social issues, and come from homes where English is not the language spoken by their parents. In the academic year 2011–2012, approximately 23.2% of elementary and 9.7% of secondary school children attended high poverty public schools. In 2016, 19.1% of public-school children under age 18 were living in poverty. The effect of poverty becomes even more meaningful when we consider that, in 2016, almost 25% of public-school students were eligible for free or reduced-price lunch. These numbers only confirm what many researchers have already shown over the years: family income is the number one predictor of academic achievement and fighting poverty should be at the center

---

1   Keynote address, Department of Educational Leadership, University of Massachusetts Dartmouth, November 29, 2016, UMass Law School.

of every discussion on ways of improving education and closing the achievement gap (e.g. Davis-Kean, 2005; Rothstein, 2008; Reardon, 2011).

The number of children who come from linguistically diverse homes has also increased over the years. According to the Census Bureau/2013 American Community Survey, 1 in 5 students speaks a language other than English at home. With at least 20% of families speaking another language at home and in their communities, we can also see great variation in cultural practices and in the different ways of acting in society and interpreting the world that will be reflected in schools.

The demographics that reflect the face of the American classroom today reaffirm the urgent need to prepare educators who can incorporate multiple viewpoints in their teaching, who can bring diverse voices into the educational conversation, and who can use family knowledge and community as a resource.

In order to create schools that promote and value diversity and prepare teachers who can effectively address the needs of a changing society, we need to shift our priority towards educational equity. A society needs to guarantee equal opportunity as well as the means for all children to succeed if it aims to educate its youth to excel and to become active citizens of a democracy. Above all, there needs to be a serious effort to address and eliminate racial and socioeconomic disparities in society.

We may still be far from achieving equity in our educational system, but we need to remind ourselves that when schools fail their students, our nation fails its citizens. The high percentage of children who are failing in school, the growing dropout rate, and the low scores on standardized testing point to the immediate need to address a chronic illness that the educational system seems to be perpetuating. Moreover, socioeconomic and demographic variables should be considered when developing and implementing educational programs.

Given the context of diversity that characterizes schools across the country, a culturally and linguistically relevant approach to education appears as a sound response and as a philosophical orientation that addresses this change in school culture and that offers some directions on how to go about promoting equity and creating a culture of educational excellence.

In this essay, I discuss basic principles of culturally and linguistically responsive pedagogy and how they can contribute to more equitable educational opportunities for all of America's public-school students. As a teacher educator, my concern is with preparing teachers to deal with the reality of the American classroom effectively and purposefully. Educational change implies examining and addressing the complex relationships among cultural, political, social and economic variables that affect the teaching and learning that occur in schools. In order to do so, culturally responsive teaching is more than a pedagogical approach—it is a vision of what schools can become and how they can and should be for *all* students.

Understanding Culture and Diversity

Culture is one of those terms that serve as a large category, a concept that encompasses so many interpretations, definitions, and understandings that one may need to qualify it before being able to define it. People usually point to elements that make up a culture. They identify specific food, music, clothing, and dance, and they also point to linguistic, cultural, social, and even religious practices.

When asked what culture means to them, my students tend to qualify it both in terms of personal and collective meanings based on their life experiences and knowledge of the world. Therefore, terms such as *subculture, counterculture,* and *micro* and *macro cultures* are useful, as they help us identify more precisely the cultural elements that we relate to and that define us as members of the different groups we associate ourselves with: from being humans to being citizens of different nations, members of various communities, social groups, professional associations, clubs and sports organizations, organized religions, political parties, artistic and self-expression circles, and so on. The meaning of culture develops from our ability to make an otherwise abstract concept more tangible and transform it into something we can relate to and identify in concrete personal and collective practices.

What definitions of culture have in common is that they all focus on identifying characteristics, knowledge, patterns, behaviors, and interactional patterns of a group of people that have developed historically and that are learned through a process of socialization. Social scientists argue that culture is a much more complex concept that encompasses a people's whole way of life—from the objects that characterize their customs and inventions to the ideas that describe them as a civilization. This is why it is common to find a description that involves layers of meanings: cultures and subcultures.

One of the most frequently cited definitions of culture comes from the British anthropologist Sir Edward Burnett Tylor, who defined culture as "that complex whole which includes knowledge, belief, art, morals, law, custom, and any other capabilities and habits acquired by man as a member of society" (Tylor, 1924). His definition includes three important elements on describing and understanding culture: culture is acquired, an individual acquires culture as a member of a particular society, and culture is a complex interplay of elements (concrete and abstract).

Banks and Banks (2015) adds that "most social scientists today view culture as consisting primarily of the symbolic, ideational, and intangible aspects of human societies. The essence of a culture is not its artifacts, tools, or other tangible cultural elements but how the members of the group interpret, use, and perceive them. It is the values, symbols, interpretations, and perspectives that distinguish one people from another in modernized societies; it is not material objects and other tangible aspects of human societies. People within a culture usually interpret the meaning of symbols, artifacts, and behaviors in the same or in similar ways" (p. 5–6).

In sum, culture is the shared knowledge of a society, common beliefs and values, a set of accepted behaviors as well as the products and artifacts that they create and reproduce systematically. Understanding culture as a set of learned patterns is essential for any teacher in a multicultural setting where many different traits will be displayed and acted upon and need to be interpreted as a learning opportunity rather than a hindrance.

The understanding of culture inevitably leads us to that of diversity. Because we all have different cultures, belong to different groups, carry out different practices, display different behaviors and represent different ideals and values, we are all diverse. Like culture, diversity is personal and collective. We are all individuals and we all display group differences. When talking about diversity, people can be talking about categories such as age, gender, sexual orientation, race, and ethnicity, as well as our opinions, abilities, experience, values, and beliefs.

Gardenswartz and Rowe (2003), who have written extensively about diversity, especially in the workplace and in business settings, have developed a model of the dimensions of diversity that is widely used in diversity trainings. Their model helps us visualize the different aspects and layers of diversity and how they relate to internal or external factors. They start the model from an inner circle and identify internal, external, and organizational dimensions that characterize diversity, as can be seen in Figure 24.1 below:

FIGURE 24.1.: FOUR LAYERS OF DIVERSITY
MAJ (2015), ADAPTED FROM GARDENSWARTZ AND ROWE (2003)

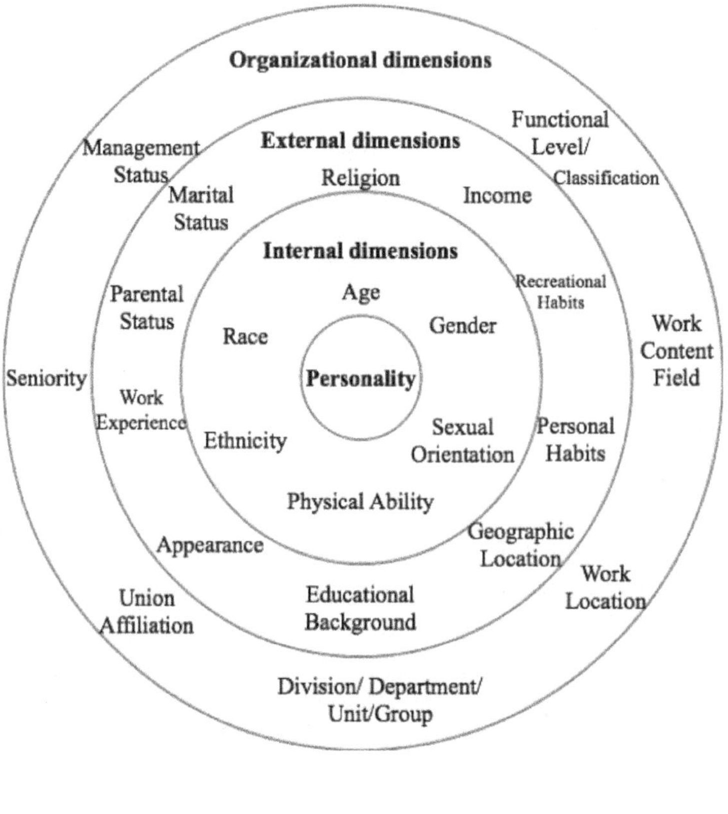

In the model, diversity starts with individuality. We are all different individuals with different personalities that affect the way we go about the world and relate to people on personal and professional levels. The internal dimension of diversity describes features that we are born with. People may choose to change their gender, but most of these features accompany us through life.

The external dimension refers to factors that have more to do with personal choice and aspects of our lives we are not born with but develop as we live. Factors such as education, work experience, marital status, habits, residence, income, leisure activities, religion, or belief describe who we are and how we live our lives. The organizational dimension refers to features that relates us to our professional activities and describe our line of work as well as employment history, which is how the world sees the way we express our craft. Gardenswartz and Rowe (2003) have created a way to systematize the different aspects of diversity. These categories only define us at a specific moment in time, which means that other features may be added as we grow and evolve, experience new things, or change the course of our lives.

Taken together, all these dimensions describe the way we present ourselves to the world and the way the world sees us. Whether we are born with certain features, develop them as we grow, and change some of them throughout our lives, they are sill part of who we are and the way we are seen and judged by others. Because we are all judged based on our appearance, choices, and behavior, we need to be aware of all these features and make sure they are included in an education program. Given the diversity in American classrooms today, teachers need to develop not only an awareness but also different instructional strategies and educational approaches to make sure they their pedagogy is respectful and inclusive of every student in the classroom and that every student is given an equal opportunity to succeed independently of how they express any of the categories of diversity.

In the classroom, both teachers and students present themselves as whole individuals, which means we are our race, ethnicity, socioeconomic class, language or linguistic variety, sex, gender identity and expression, and sexual orientation, as well as our cultural, political, religious, and social affiliations. This presents a challenge for many teachers who need to commit to recognizing and valuing diversity in the classroom, but it is also an opportunity to act and demonstrate that the value of a multicultural society lies in the fact that we all contribute with different perspectives, backgrounds, and history. Diversity is what makes a society stronger and more capable to address and deal with the problems it is presented in novel, creative, and diverse ways.

Multicultural Education: Dimensions and Approaches

In the United States, multicultural education is seen as a result of the civil rights movement of the 1960s (Banks, 2004) and the focus is on reforming the nation's schools. Because of the *Brown vs. Board of Education of Topeka* decision of 1954, the idea that schools could be separate but equal no longer prevailed. The decision itself did not necessarily guarantee equal opportunity and social justice (Ladson-Billings, 2006). Instead, the racial, ethnic, and socioeconomic gap became even wider (Bell, 2004).

Gay (2004) recognizes that in trying to describe multicultural education, one comes across a variety of definitions which can vary in terms of content, focus, and orientation. Based on Banks's (2004) tripartite definition of multicultural education, she identifies the following categories:

- Multicultural education as a philosophy, concept or idea: a set of beliefs and values that represent ethnic and cultural influences on lifestyles, experiences, and identities of a group. As a philosophy, multicultural education encompasses cultural pluralism and educational equality and excellence.

- Multicultural education as a process: an approach to education that places multiculturalism as a continuous and systematic element within a more comprehensive understanding of education. As a process, multicultural education should not be developed as a program or method but as a progressive course of ideas and actions.

- Multicultural education as a reform movement: a structural and procedural change in education that reflects the larger change in society—social cultural, ethnic, racial, and linguistic diversity. As a movement, multicultural education focuses on empowering individuals towards social action and transformation.

Historically, the concept of multicultural education and the ways we understand it have evolved and developed to consider societal changes and evolution. Grant and Sleeter (2008) identify five major approaches to the development of multicultural education:

1. **Teaching the Exceptional and Culturally Different:** developed in the 1960s, this approach focuses on the academic achievement of ethnic minorities and students from lower socioeconomic status as well as students with limited English proficiency and those with special needs.

2. **Human Relations:** this approach was developed as a result of desegregation and focuses on improving race relations and promoting tolerance by fostering positive intergroup relationships and interaction.

3. **Single-Group Studies:** also developed in the 1960s, this approach focuses on developing in-depth studies of specific groups, such as ethnic or women's studies, aiming at raising social consciousness of and about those groups.

4. **Multicultural Education:** the actual term was coined in the 1970s, and the focus is on the relationships among culture, ethnicity, language, gender,

handicap, and social class in developing educational programs. Cultural diversity and equal opportunity are at the core of multicultural education.

5. **Education that is Multicultural and Social Reconstructionist:** this is a more recent approach that is in fact an extension of multicultural education and embraces social action. The curriculum should focus on active student participation in addressing social issues (such as racism, sexism, classism) and in developing problem-solving skills.

As a movement, multicultural education represented a contrast to the prevalence of Anglo-European views around which school curricula were centered and a shift to including the perspectives of culturally disadvantaged populations. According to Bennett (2011) four broad principles guided the movement:

1. The theory of cultural pluralism

2. The ideals of social justice (which would end different forms of oppression)

3. Affirmation of all cultures in the process of teaching and learning

4. Visions of educational equity and excellence (which would lead to the academic achievement of all children)

Of all these principles, cultural pluralism seemed to carry the heaviest weight in the development of multicultural education, particularly in view of America being a country of immigrants. Cultural pluralism embraces the democratic principles that guided the foundation of the United States by giving all groups of immigrants the right to maintain their heritage—culture, language, and religion. Although national identity was an important aspect in the assimilation of immigrant groups, it was also seen as a compromise as immigrants integrated into the American society. Ethnic minorities were expected to participate in the life of the society by exercising some level of acculturation, but they were also allowed to maintain and affirm their home culture.

Also at the heart of the multicultural education movement is the struggle to end racism and any other form of oppression (which includes issues of class, gender, disabilities, sexual preference) and to eliminate any structural element in society that creates or reinforces socioeconomic inequalities. In America, there is a need to redress issues of racial inequities in a society that has been guided by white privilege. Proponents of multicultural education argue that white privilege is so deeply rooted in American society that it goes beyond issues of racial oppression to also include the experience of whites, which is seen as "normal" rather than "advantaged." They believe that only by providing these experiences for people of color will we bring them up to white ("normal") standards and address racial discrimination.

As an approach to teaching and learning, multicultural education envisions equity in the school system, proposes reform in the curriculum, and calls for a commitment to social justice. In a diverse society centered on principles of cultural pluralism, there is a need to respect students as individuals as well as members of a subgroup or an ethnic minority. This translates into embracing differences in the classroom and developing pedagogical practices that reflect acceptance to differences in the way students communicate, learn and relate to the materials at hand and to each other. Moreover, it also implies the need for equity and academic excellence and achievement of all students who should be given equal opportunities to reach their fullest potential and succeed.

In "Genres of Research in Multicultural Education," Bennett (2001) describes four interactive dimensions of multicultural teaching and designs a framework for the multicultural classroom, as depicted in Figure 24.2 below:

FIGURE 24.2.: A CONCEPTUAL FRAMEWORK OF MULTICULTURAL TEACHING

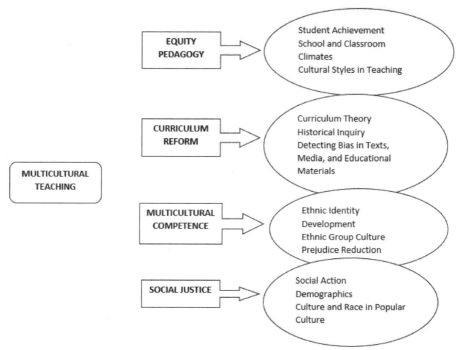

The first dimension, Equity Pedagogy, refers to the one of the tenets of multicultural education which is the development of classroom practices and climate that will foster student achievement by creating equal learning opportunities for all children. Ethnic minorities and low-income students are particularly relevant in creating equity pedagogy, as they have been the student population that has been historically neglected or segregated. In setting high standards and expectations for all students, schools need to ensure that all children are continually progressing. In order to do so, they need to attend to individual as well as group differences and promote a variety of teaching and learning strategies to include diverse learning styles and ways of knowing.

The second dimension, Curriculum Reform, requires teachers to rethink the content and scope of their lessons by questioning the curriculum. Many schools adopt ethnocentric views in the way they select and deliver content, and students may end up learning one single perspective instead of being exposed to multiple possible ways of analyzing an issue. This prevents students from understanding different sides of an issue and from developing critical thinking skills. An example of that comes from history classes where students learn about historical events from the perspective of the "winner" or the white Anglo-European man. In order to understand global interdependence, multiple worldviews are necessary and even contradictory views should be presented to students. The classroom should be a space of inquiry and the development of new and comprehensive knowledge.

The third dimension, Multicultural Competence, requires teachers to develop both an awareness and a sensitivity to cultural differences and multiple ways of relating to the world, interpreting phenomena, organizing knowledge, developing literacy (oral and written), and communicating and interpreting meanings. Given that American classrooms are filled with students from the most varied cultural, linguistic, ethnic, and racial background, teachers who truly want to reach those students need to learn about who they are, their families and communities, their *ways with words* (Heath, 2006). Moreover, many teachers do not share the same background as their students and the only way to understand and implement pedagogical practices that incorporate their ways of learning may be to immerse themselves in the life of the community they teach. Students may also be going through the process of becoming interculturally competent, as they try to make sense of the new culture they are being exposed to, and their attitudes, behavior, and ways of thinking may be characteristic of an interculture (Naiditch, 2006a; Kramsch, 2000).

The fourth dimension, Social Justice, reflects the movement towards a socially just world, that is, the struggle for a society based on human rights and equality. In order to achieve a more socially just society, we need to work towards eliminating economic and social differences and promote practices that advocate for equal opportunity and outcomes. Social justice also assumes the inclusion and acceptance of groups whose voices have been historically silenced. Teaching for social justice requires confronting our social views on issues of gender, class, race, ethnicity, age, sexual orientation, and any other form of oppression and discrimination.

Clearly, the multicultural education movement and the dimensions developed by Bennett (2001) for Multicultural Teaching are embedded in ideological and political views. These reflect larger democratic principles of equality, equity, social justice, and respect for human dignity, which provide the basis for life in an organized society. Life in a democratic society also implies that all citizens, regardless of race, ethnicity, age, gender, sexual orientation, religion, or lifestyle, are entitled to their basic civil liberties and to equal educational opportunities. Pluralism of ideas and opinions is encouraged, and the classroom should be the place where all these values are passed on from generation to generation. In this context, teachers need to reconsider their roles, especially because teaching within these four dimensions requires an understanding of their responsibility as guardians of these values and principles who need to make sure students get the education they are entitled to.

The Multicultural Classroom:
Funds of Knowledge and Culturally Responsive Teaching

Teaching students from diverse backgrounds requires more than applying several learning strategies or teaching techniques that will address different learning styles and ways of knowing. Not that these are not important. On the contrary, a successful teacher needs to be able to identify diversity in the classroom and devise pedagogical procedures to address diverse learners and their learning styles.

Apart from teaching methods, though, teachers in multicultural classrooms need to develop a deep understanding of how students' home language, culture, values, and system of beliefs influence and, in many cases, determine, the teaching and learning that takes place in the classroom. Culturally responsive teaching is a philosophical orientation to teaching and learning that takes into account the interconnection of different aspects and dimensions of diversity and empowers students on intellectual, social, and emotional levels by making use of cultural references to convey and develop knowledge, skills, and dispositions.

Ladson-Billings (1994) first introduced the term as culturally relevant teaching as a result of her study on pedagogical practices and instruction in elementary classrooms where students not only maintained their cultural identity but also used it as a reference to relate to the material. The teachers in her study displayed a number of characteristics that reflected not only their experience, but mainly their ability to transform curriculum into classroom pedagogy that "spoke" to the students, that highlighted their backgrounds and that made use of their history as central to their learning. The students' academic success was closely related to their being able to respond to the classroom activities and content by making use of their ways of learning and knowing.

These ways of learning and knowing have been systematized through the notion of funds of knowledge. Moll and his colleagues define funds of knowledge as "historically accumulated and culturally developed bodies of knowledge and skills essential for household or individual functioning and well-being" (Moll et al., 1992, p. 133).

Funds of knowledge reflect the ways of knowing of a particular society or community and represent how knowledge is understood, what knowledge is valued, and what knowledge is passed on through the generations. Culturally responsive teachers learn about the funds of knowledge of their students by engaging in the communities where they teach, by getting to know the families, their histories, and their ways of leaning, knowing, communicating, and interacting. This knowledge gained from crossing the street and getting to know the community and its families is used as the basis for the work developed in the classroom (Naiditch, 2013). Teachers use students' and families' funds of knowledge as an asset, as a resource for classroom teaching and learning.

In order to fully understand the concept, let us look at an example from a literacy lesson developed at an elementary school in New Mexico, as described by Johnson (2004). The community that the school served included many minority students from low socioeconomic background. Through a quick-write, the teacher was able to find out what students knew about medicinal folk remedies. The theme of the unit and lesson was decided based on information gathered in the community. While learning about the families, the teacher interacted with many students and parents who shared information about remedies they used at home to cure certain ailments. This is a topic that resonates with many people who come from cultures where it is more common to cure certain illnesses with home remedies, plants, and herbs and where medication is only used as a last resource.

Having learned about this fund of knowledge, the teacher decided to transform it into classroom practice by doing research on the topic and learning more about it, by selecting texts and materials that reflected that knowledge, but, most important, by developing her lessons using her students as the experts in the room. Because no one knew more about it than the families themselves, they became a rich resource for the classroom, and they shared their knowldge, expertise, and experience with it. A unit or a lesson that is developed from students' funds of knowledge also keeps students interested and motivated. As a result, they engage realistically with the content, and learning becomes more authentic and meaningful.

Students expanded the topic by reading about it, discussing, doing additional research, interviewing family members, and even bringing them to the classroom as guest speakers. At the end of the unit, the students even published a book (Book of Medicinal Folk Remedies). The topic of medicinal folk medicine also brings about more questions to be investigated. Teachers can develop it even further by comparing medicinal practices (herbal, holistic, traditional) and types of medical practices (homeopathy, allopathy, and Ayurveda), and this can create interdisciplinary lessons and bring together teachers of several content areas to broaden the theme and develop different skills.

The aim of the teacher in New Mexico was to develop her students' literacy, but she was free to decide on how to achieve this aim by choosing themes that reflected the funds of knowledge of the community. Her choice empowered her students and their families by creating strong links between the knowledge of the school and the home and by relating the everyday life of the community to the work that is done in the school. This created an authentic learning context and valued the knowledge that many times is underestimated or ignored by the school.

Funds of knowledge are the basis of a culturally responsive curriculum. A culturally responsive teacher is a researcher who comes to know students and their families in new and distinct ways.

They need to understand that the households of their students is filled with rich cultural and cognitive resources and that these resources can and should be used in their classroom to provide culturally responsive and meaningful lessons that tap into students' prior knowledge. More important, culturally responsive teachers have high expectations and look at the families that they serve with positive lenses—as opposed to a deficit model that associates minority and marginalized students with perceived weaknesses and an inability to succeed.

Gay (2000) describes culturally responsive teaching as being validating, comprehensive, multidimensional, empowering, transformative, and emancipatory. Culturally responsive teaching is validating primarily because teachers use students' background knowledge, prior experiences, and cultural capital to adapt their pedagogy and make it appropriate and accessible for students. The premise is that one should teach to students' strengths in order to be effective and help learners achieve academically. Gay identifies the following characteristics in culturally responsive teaching:

- It acknowledges the legitimacy of the cultural heritages of different ethnic groups, both as legacies that affect students' dispositions, attitudes, and approaches to learning and as worthy content to be taught in the formal curriculum

- It builds bridges of meaningfulness between home and school experiences as well as between academic abstractions and lived sociocultural realities

- It uses a wide variety of instructional strategies that are connected to different learning styles

- It teaches students to know and praise their own and each others' cultural heritages

- It incorporates multicultural information, resources, and materials in all the subjects and skills routinely taught in schools (Gay, 2000, p. 29)

As can be seen in Gay's description, culturally responsive teaching brings students' lives, homes and communities into the classroom and uses them as resources to develop activities that reflect a variety of meanings and a variety of sensory opportunities (visual, auditory, tactile) for learners to relate to the material. The multidimensional aspect of culturally responsive teaching refers to the fact that teachers need to attend to multiple dimensions of teaching and learning, such as the curriculum, the content, the context, classroom atmosphere, relationships between teacher and students and among students themselves, instructional techniques, and assessment. Moreover, culturally responsive teaching needs to integrate content across disciplines. Collaboration between teachers should be encouraged and units of study should be integrated so that students study a certain topic from multiple perspectives, from the language arts to the social studies class. Teaching across content areas also makes content more meaningful and relatable from the learner's point of view.

Banks (1994) has claimed that in order for education to empower students, particularly marginalized groups, it must be transformative. This statement resonates with Freire's (1970) views of empowerment and teaching for social action. Freire argued for multiple voices to coexist in the classroom. These voices represent not only pluralism or diversity but also the actual existence and acknowledgment of multiple identities in the classroom that need to be affirmed, recognized, valued, and respected.

Freire's critical approach to education looks at learners as *subjects* who need to be empowered to elaborate on and express their views. This view takes their reality into account and encompasses each individual student and the personal and collective histories in a classroom. The Freirean praxis presupposes a shared dialogue of experiences among educators and students in order to understand social, political, and economic context and create new knowledge and possible solutions for the challenges one faces. Culturally responsive teaching echoes Freire's praxis by exercising dialogue as a way of potentially transforming social condition. Teaching students to think critically requires strengthening the dyad "comprehension-action" (Freire, 1992) and assessing its effectiveness in transforming social and power relationships.

Within the framework of culturally responsive teaching, empowerment also encompasses academic achievement as measured by students' ability to take initiative, persevere, self-motivate, and more importantly, to believe that they can succeed. This is why this approach is also emancipatory. It shows students that there is no single truth and inspires learners to search for their truth and consider, compare, and contrast possible interpretations on the way.

Villegas and Lucas (2002) have identified six salient qualities for the culturally responsive teacher that serve as a framework for schools and teachers who wish to find an effective response to address the needs of an increasingly diverse student population. Their framework includes the following guidelines:

1. Understanding how learners construct knowledge: teachers need to help students build bridges between their prior knowledge and experiences as they work on making sense of new ideas and experiences at school.

2. Learning about students' lives: to engage students meaningfully, teachers need to learn about their students' experiences outside of school, their family life, activities, concerns, the value they place on schooling, and so on.

3. Being socioculturally conscious: teachers need to be aware that students' worldview is not universal and is shaped by their experiences and universe, which may differ drastically from that of the teacher. Being socioculturally conscious may help prevent miscommunication.

4. Holding affirmative views about diversity: teachers who do not believe in students' ability to achieve or who have low expectations regarding their students' accomplishments will end up preventing these students from succeeding.

5. Using appropriate instructional strategies: teachers need to try out and experiment with a variety of strategies in order to reach their students and motivate them to learn.

6. Advocating for all students: teachers are ethically committed to advancing their students' lives by helping them learn and by speaking on their behalf when necessary.

These guidelines reflect the qualities that culturally responsive teachers should cultivate and apply in their teaching. These are important guidelines because they recognize students as capable learners and capitalize on their previous experiences and background knowledge—on what students bring with them to the classroom. Being able to build from students' real-life experiences and relate new knowledge to the outside world, students' families and communities makes learning a relevant and more meaningful enterprise. It also engages students in the process of learning and motivates them to extend their learning experiences and opportunities beyond the walls of the classroom.

Putting it All Together: Developing Culturally Responsive Lessons

Growing up in a dictatorship, the history lessons I had in school reflected what we knew as the official history of the country, an edited version of history, that is, the history approved and sanctioned by the government. In a democratic society like the United States, however, it is our job to ensure that history becomes histories and that the classroom reflects the many viewpoints, historical perspectives, and the voices of the people from all walks of life who have contributed to building and enriching this nation.

The social studies classroom is a good starting point to understand what a culturally responsive lesson can look like in practice. Marginalized populations do not get a voice in textbooks, and the curriculum focuses on history as told from the perspective of the "winner." My generation grew up in an era of knowledge transmission where history was only about events, personalities, and dates. Knowing history meant knowing to identify who, what, when, where, and sometimes how. The emphasis was on the chronological review of the national history, which always started with the arrival of the white European colonizers (who were referred to as "discoverers" then). The national history was the history of the largest national group with its dominant linguistic and cultural hegemony.

In a culturally responsive classroom, this traditional and ethnocentric approach to the study of history is replaced by critical thinking and analysis and deep inquiry-based learning. Students are encouraged to question and to understand historical events from multiple viewpoints considering all the characters and all the possible interpretations of facts. The teachers also need to question: Whose "history" is privileged in the curriculum and in textbooks? Why?

A culturally responsive social studies classroom uses multiple sources of information to develop understanding and to interpret history—taking into account, of course, the role and reliability of primary and secondary sources in documenting history. A classroom like this can be truly multicultural and inclusive, which means replacing an ethnocentric view of history that privileges what is considered "mainstream" to incorporate a pluralistic view of a nation and its people, its multiple languages, and its distinctive cultures.

This example of the social studies classroom illustrates the role schools should take to ensure inclusive and multicultural education, to promote diversity, to encourage the practice of using multiple sources of information, and to consider different perspectives. Schools need to do more to prepare students for life in a world characterized by ethnic, cultural, linguistic, religious, and socioeconomic diversity. Students need to see themselves represented in the curriculum and in all aspects of their education.

Therefore, culturally responsive teaching should be implemented across content areas. Whether it is by reading multicultural literature and questioning the literary canon, or by developing a unit that focuses on social justice mathematics by studying the relationship between SNAP (Supplemental Nutrition Assistance Program) and labor force participation among low-income households, teachers need to learn to find opportunities in diversity in order to include everyone in the curriculum; to make content accessible and critical, meaningful, and relevant; and to ensure a high quality education.

Moreover, when diversity is seen as an asset, it increases the number of solutions that a collection of people can find by creating different connections among groups. Our students are growing up in a more diverse world and need to learn to navigate it appropriately. They can only do so by exploring sources, factors, facts, reasons, causes, and consequences as well as their identities and histories.

Above all, culturally responsive teaching is a major disposition and a responsibility that teachers need to embrace in order to develop teaching and learning goals to promote respect and understanding, to improve race relations, and to protect civil liberties.

References

Banks, J. A. & Banks, C. A.M. (2015). *Multicultural education: Issues and perspectives.* Hoboken, NJ: Wiley. (9th Edition).

Banks, J. (2004). Multicultural Education: Historical Development, Dimensions and Practice. In: Banks, J. & C.M. Banks. (Eds.). *Handbook of Research on Multicultural Education.* San Francisco, CA: Jossey-Bass. pp. 3–29.

Banks, J. (1994). The Canon Debate, Knowledge Construction and Multicultural Education. In: Banks, J. (Ed.). *Multicultural Education, Transformative Knowledge, and Action: Historical and Contemporary Perspectives.* New York, NY: Teachers College Press. pp. 3–29.

Bell, D. (2004). *Silent Covenants:* Brown v. Board of Education *and the Unfulfilled Hopes for Racial Reform.* Oxford: Oxford University Press.

Bennett, C. I. (2011). *Comprehensive Multicultural Education: Theory and Practice.* Boston, MA: Pearson Education, Inc.

Bennett, C. I. (2001). Genres of Research in Multicultural Education. *Review of Education Research,* 72(2), pp. 171–217.

Davis-Kean, P. E. (2005). The influence of parent education and family income on child achievement: The indirect role of parental expectations and the home environment. *Journal of Family Psychology,* 29(2), pp. 294–304.

Freire, P. (1992). *Pedagogia da esperança: Um reencontro com a pedagogia do oprimido.* São Paulo, SP: Editora Paz e Terra S/A.

Freire, P. (1970). *Pedagogy of the Oppressed.* New York, NY: Continuum International Publishing Group.

Gardenswartz, L., & Rowe, A. (2003). *Diverse Teams at Work: Capitalizing on the Power of Diversity.* Alexandria, VA: Society of Human Resource Management.

Gay, G. (2004). Curriculum Theory and Multicultural Education. In: J. A. Banks & C.A. McGee Banks (Eds.). *Handbook of Research on Multicultural Education.* New York, NY: Macmillan. pp. 25–43.

Gay, G. (2000). *Culturally Responsive Teaching: Theory, Research & Practice.* New York, NY: Teachers College Press.

Grant, C., & Sleeter, C. (2008). *Turning on Learning: Five Approaches for Multicultural Teaching Plans for Race, Class, Gender and Disability.* Somerset, NJ: Wiley.

Heath, S. B. (2006). *Ways with Words: Language, Life and Work in Communities and Classrooms.* Cambridge: Cambridge University Press.

Johnson, S. I. (2004). Using Funds of Knowledge to Create Literacy Lessons. *Making Connections: Language, Literacy, Learning.* Department of Language and Cultural Equity, Albuquerque Public Schools. pp. 1–2.

Kramsch, Claire. 2000. *Context and Culture in Language Teaching.* Oxford: Oxford University Press.

Ladson-Billings, G. (2006). The Meaning of *Brown* . . . for now. In: Ball, A. (Ed.). *With More Deliberate Speed: Achieving Equity and Excellence in Education – Realizing the Full Potential of* Brown v. Board of Education *Part II.* Somerset, NJ: Wiley-Blackwell. pp. 298–313.

Ladson-Billings, G. (1994). *The Dreamkeepers: Successful Teachers of African American Children.* San Francisco, CA: Jossey-Bass.

Maj, Jolanta. (2015). Diversity Management's Stakeholders and Stakeholders' Management. *Proceedings of the 9th International Management Conference, 9,* pp. 780–793.

Moll, L. C., Amanti, C., Neff, D., & González, N. (1992). Funds of Knowledge for Teaching: A Qualitative Approach to Connect Households and Classrooms. *Theory into Practice, 31*(2), pp. 132–141.

Naiditch, F. (2013). Cross the Street to a New World. *Phi Delta Kappan, 94*(6), pp. 26–29.

Naiditch, F. (2006). *The Pragmatics of Permission: A Study of Brazilian ESL Learners.* Dissertation Abstracts International 67-05A.

Rothstein, R. (2008). Whose Problem is Poverty? *Educational Leadership, 65*(7), pp. 8–13.

Tylor, E. B. (1924) [orig. 1871]. *Primitive Culture.* New York, NY: Brentano's.

Villegas, A. M. & Lucas, T. (2002). *Educating Culturally Responsive Teachers: A Coherent Approach.* Albany, NY: SUNY Press.

Websites Cited:

National Center for Education Statistics: https://nces.ed.gov/

National Center for Education Statistics–The Condition of Education Report: https://nces.ed.gov/programs/coe/

United States Census Bureau–American Community Survey (ACS): https://www.census.gov/programs-surveys/acs/

CHAPTER TWENTY-FIVE

National Learning Standards, Global Agenda, and Teacher Education

Álvaro Moreira Hypolito[1]

THE *NATIONAL LEARNING Standards*[2] is the result of long-standing conflicts around the definition of a National Curriculum for Brazilian education. Since the 1990s, after the approval of the 1988 Constitution and the beginning of the discussion of a new LDB,[3] the debate has intensified over what the curriculum for basic education should be—a debate which at times is direct, other times less so. Soon after the approval of the new LDB in 1996, this debate grew stronger with the discussion of the National Curriculum Parameters (Silva and Gentili, 1996; Brasil, 1997). Since then, there has been a series of debates, actions, movements, criticisms, and defenses (not always explicit) regarding the necessity of a national curriculum.

In this sense, we first had the creation of definitions of the *National Curriculum Parameters, Parameters in Action*, and the *National Curriculum Guidelines*. However, given its low acceptance at schools and among researchers in the field, other concepts such as "learning expectations" and "learning rights" were introduced during the debate of the last *National Education Plan* (PNE)—either to confuse or to reintroduce the theme of the national curriculum. In any case, there has always been, even if surreptitiously, a move towards the definition of national standards until a proposal for a BNCC was reached (Hypolito, 2014, 2015). Owing to the fact that the *National Association of Graduate Studies and Research in Education* (ANPEd) and its *Curriculum Division* (GT-Currículo) have always opposed defining a national curriculum, it was defended by the Ministry of Education and Culture, and by more and more influential "think tanks"—whether via non-governmental entities, foundations or private consultancies—and by many academics, generally foreign to the field of the curriculum.

The movement *Todos pela Educação* (All for Education) has played a decisive role in the educational agenda in recent years, especially for Brazilian education to become compatible with the global agenda (Martins, 2016). That movement and the entities that revolve under its influence, as well as various government bodies and associations

---

1   Keynote address, Department of Educational Leadership, University of Massachusetts Dartmouth, Spring, 2012.
2   Hereinafter referred to as BNCC due to its spelling in Portuguese (Base Nacional Curricular Comum).
3   The Law on Brazilian Education.

of educational leaders, have come to play a decisive role in the approval of the National Learning Standards (Avelar and Ball, 2019). The Mobilization for the BNCC is an example of this type of articulation.

In order to contribute to the discussion on the BNCC related to a global agenda and to teacher education, this text is organized into three sections: (i) the first aims to present some relationships between global policies and national curriculum policies, (ii) the second aims to relate the National Learning Standards to broader national policies and (iii) and the final section discusses these policies and teacher education.

A global agenda to be accomplished locally

Through documentary analyses carried out by researchers, well-defined contributions are presented, expressed by multilateral agencies, with the intention of defining an education project that is articulated with a global education project.

Since at least 2001, the Global Education Reform Movement (hereinafter GERM) has been organized to strengthen educational reforms through what is called the effectiveness of educational systems. It is structured around three principles of educational policy: standards, accountability, and decentralization. These GERM principles are briefly presented in Table 25.1, according to Verger et al. (2018).

In the three highlighted axes, the guidelines for the policies to be pursued are defined. In terms of standardization, a national curriculum that sets quality standards is prescribed based on national assessments with achievable goals and learning standards. In terms of decentralization, the transfer of competences and responsibilities to local levels of the school system administration is advocated so that national assessments then serve to hold authorities accountable and to control them at their different levels of competence. This decentralization aims to make management teams and schools answerable to performance assessments, thereby permitting remote government assessment systems to be used through results management. In terms of accountability, both in the sense of responsibilization and rendering of accounts, educational actors are made accountable for their performance through evaluations with consequences. Such is intended to be achieved by both administrative accountability, in which the results of the exams are linked to awards or sanctions in the form of salary incentives or financial/material resources for schools, and market accountability, in which the results are used for both school-choice policies and for the encouragement of competition between schools.

TABLE 25.1.: THE ROLE OF NATIONAL ASSESSMENTS WITHIN THE GERM

GERM principle	Definition and main policies	Role of national assessments	
Standards	Prescription of a national curriculum and establishment of quality standards	National assessments used to make sure schools meet and adhere to evaluable learning standards	
Decentralisation	Transfer of competences and authority from the central government to lower administrative levels	National assessments used to control state, regional, provincial and local authorities	
	Devolution of managerial and/or pedagogical responsibilities to principals and schools	National assessments used to govern at a distance a range of autonomous providers through the principles of outcomes-based management	
Accountability	Educational actors made responsible for their actions/results through some form of evaluation linked to consequences.	*Administrative accountability*	Test results attached to incentives or sanctions for schools, principals and teachers
		Market accountability	Test results used to inform school choice and promote school competition

As can be seen, the theme of the national curriculum is associated with standardized assessments and testing processes, and is directly linked to these policies based on a program of global reform.

In order to highlight other aspects of this project and to relate it to a broader agenda, two World Bank documents are discussed. Weiner and Compton (2016) analyze the World Bank document "Great teachers: How to raise student learning in Latin America and the Caribbean", authored by Bruns and Luque (2015), and underline some five premises that they consider to be the common ground of this document. According to the authors, the premises are

- Premise 1: Poverty in Latin America and the Caribbean can be most effectively reduced through educational reform.

This shows that although investments in education are low and insufficient in the region, the myth that education is the redemption of all types of evil still persists. The solution of social inequality is shifted from economics and politics to educational reform. The problem of poverty is now supposedly solved by an educational reform solution: improve the quality of the school. The quality of the school is obviously conceived as quality dependent on tests, assessments, and the market.

- Premise 2: Latin America and the Caribbean constitute a single political, economic, social and educational context in which the same educational policy can be applied with equal, positive effect.

This second premise reaffirms global reform. Given that a wide region such as Latin America and the Caribbean constitute a unique context, the same educational policy could be applied without prejudice and with only minor adjustments. Therefore, it would suffice to transfer policies considered globally to local contexts. Ball (2010, 2013), considering the different actors and contexts, as well as the dynamics specific to each context, prefers to call such processes "policy mobility" and "non-transference", in the sense that such policies are displaced and adapted according to global interests and locations. Furthermore, global policies only shift, move and are accepted because they coincide with the interests of local elites and because some of them have more power than others in global relations. It is therefore important to know who globalizes whom (Santos, 1995, 2002). Clearly, this is always an imposing process, structurally scheduled based on socioeconomic interests in the development of global capitalism, and that the premise posed as a clear and perfect possibility is a lure to justify the reform itself, as if different contexts did not require different educational alternatives.

- Premise 3: Improving teacher quality, as captured by students' scores on standardized tests and value-added measures (vam), is the most effective lever to improve educational outcomes in Latin America and Caribe.

Reducing the evaluation of the quality of teaching to standardized test results and even measures of added value is to reduce the quality of teaching to multiple choice tests. In a previous study, Ivo and Hypolito (2017) demonstrate that a same early education teacher used to teach in two public schools—one with the best and the other with the worst according to the Basic Education Development Index (hereinafter, IDEB[4]) in the municipality. That imposes the unavoidable fact that the performance in the exams is related to many factors and that the quality of the teaching cannot be assessed by simplistic metrics. The working and salary conditions that the teaching profession is subjected to are very uncertain. Brazilian public schools in general feature very precarious conditions, the financing of public education is very poor and insufficient, and teacher training is subject to rules and conditions far from what is considered adequate. In fact, this premise is absolutely inadequate to assess teaching quality.

- Premise 4: Poor teacher quality, as measured by teachers' use of instructional time, demonstrates that the composition of the teaching force should be changed.

The measure used to indicate low teaching quality according to teaching time is highly criticized by authors like Weiner and Compton (2016). In addition to the imprecision of the instruments used and their inadequacy for being applied out of context (instrument created and tested in the USA, applied to classes of children from developing countries), the authors further show on pages 8 and 9 of the referred article that both the instrument and the research that initiated the World Bank report are criticized in this particular aspect by another document of the Bank itself and is not mentioned in the report expressing premise 4. Furthermore, the study does not take into account

---

4   The Basic Education Development Index.

other studies that have demonstrated that children and teachers in the same cultural context can increase proficiency with the development of a culturally relevant pedagogy, in which teaching times do not coincide with the metrics of studies with out of context quantitative biases.

- Premise 5: The primary obstacle in improving education by raising teacher quality is the political power of teacher's unions, which therefore must be greatly weakened.

This last premise expresses the political view long emphasized by neoliberalism: the teaching unions are corporate, they do not understand the need for reform, they hinder and boycott any initiative to improve the quality of education and so on. Such arguments are well known.

In fact, teachers unions have been an important basis for resistance to reforms and the only way to improve teachers' working conditions in Brazil. Trade unions have been crucial in demanding more funding for public education, improving working conditions and educational provision both in terms of physical-material conditions at schools and of guaranteeing autonomy of work and freedom of expression in education. In periods like the one we are experiencing, much of the criticism addressing teachers has been redirected to neoconservative content, and groups such as Free Brazil Movement and Non-Partisan School (School without Party) have been taking the lead in the attacks on teaching. (see Lima and Hypolito, 2019)

This may be another demonstration of the neoliberal, neoconservative alliance with populist-authoritarian groups and sectors of the middle class, an alliance that Apple (1996; 2000; 2006) has been warning us of since the last decade of the previous century. It concerns the growth of what he calls Conservative Modernization, and many of us are surprised that it is hegemonic among us. For this alliance, teaching unions are a threat to traditional, conservative and religious society.

Following this same line, or at least connected to it, we have the report published by the World Bank *A fair adjustment: efficiency and equity of public spending in Brazil* (2017). After a decade of economic growth, Brazil began to go into a crisis that remains until today with an economy run by economists from financial groups. With this report, the World Bank indicates a series of measures for a "fair" adjustment. Among them, there are some for the educational field, which are worth transcribing to illustrate the scope of these policies.

Suggestions for the educational field include reforms to increase, according to the well-known vision of the bank, efficiency and equity in order to reduce tax cost. As stated in the report, regarding elementary and secondary education it is possible to save around 1% of the gross domestic product by improving efficiency at these levels of education, without compromising the services provided.

448 CRITICAL TRANSFORMATIVE EDUCATIONAL LEADERSHIP AND POLICY STUDIES

Some options of reform to increase efficiency at these levels of education are summarized below:

(i) Allow student-teacher ratios in the more inefficient schools to gradually rise to efficient levels through teacher attrition. On average, frontier levels of efficiency would be reached by 2027 for primary and lower secondary education if retiring teachers are not replaced and by 2026 in upper secondary. This step alone could save up to 0.33 percent of GDP. A further recommendation for those municipalities who need to replace retiring teachers, is to limit the hiring of new "professores concursados", whose dismissal is extremely difficult (and who create significant costs as they can retire early with a full pension).

(ii) Scale-up and share positive experiences in school management that have already demonstrated strong results across various states and municipalities. Some interventions as the appointment of school directors by performance and experience (not political indications), bonus-pay to teachers and school staff based on school performance, tailoring policies at the state level to specific local needs, sharing experiences and best practices to highlight high performing schools are some of the good examples that could be emulated. Contracting the provision of education services to private providers might also enhance performance and efficiency in public education spending. Charter schools are likely to have more flexibility in human resource management. Because they can be penalized for bad performance, they will make hiring, firing and teachers 'promotion and salary decisions based on performance and not tenure or seniority. However, new federal, state and municipality legislation may be needed to allow for PPPs in primary education. (World Bank, 2017, pp., 132–3)

The recommendations in this report are known to many managers and certain suggestions have been applied or have already been attempted to apply in some of the municipal or state education systems. It is certainly hard to believe that such recommendations were made by education specialists—made with the approval/endorsement of some. The proposal of increasing the number of students per class to "balance" the number of teachers is something completely unrealistic in the educational context of the country, where large groups are a current fact and problem. Nonetheless, here class size wouldn't be the greatest issue, as class management is usually pedagogically difficult even with smaller groups given the unfavorable social conditions, economic and cultural differences found in many communities. The failure to replace teachers who are retiring will cause chaos in many systems.

In addition to being a legal guarantee, democratic management was an achievement of many social movements and teachers. For this reason, the election of school principals and councils is considered to be a very successful experience in many public schools and is often associated with improving school and student performance (Leite *et al.*, 2012). This achieved in a more positive way for communities than by the political-administrative behaviorist models of compensation, prizes and punishments—differing from the suggestions of the Bank document, such as school performance bonuses in the form of payments. Democratic management practices and successful collective pedagogical projects are not disseminated—only good managerial pragmatic practices are widely recommended.

The privatization of services and schools, either by increasing public–private partnerships or by encouraging charter schools, are experiences that have already been very thoroughly analyzed and have shown poor results as demonstrated, for example, by Ravitch (2011) when examining education in the USA and by Freitas (2018) when discussing Brazilian national policies such as *Education Business Reform*. In both the USA and Brazil, the positioning in the performance classification in the Programme for International Student Assessment (PISA) exam (OECD's international assessment system) has shown little change for several years. In the Brazilian case, it has been so for decades. After a few decades of managerialism in education, the advances in improving the quality of education in Brazil are meager—not to say shameful—in the face of the investment of millions of *reais* (R$) in federal, state, and municipal assessment systems.

BNCC as a global/local policy

It is in this local and global context that the BNCC curricular reform was created, with the support of groups and institutions linked to the movement All for Education and by lobbies of profit and non-profit foundations, institutes and entities, with well-defined interests around a billion-dollar educational market involving the sale of teaching materials, private consultancies and the provision of services so as to replace what is currently accomplished by schools and the public education system.[5]

The model is the managerialism intended by GERM and neoliberal policies. This model involves public–private partnerships, with the outsourcing of the production of teaching materials and sale of *sistemas apostilados*[6], with the inclusion of educational management systems in the form of applications or digital platforms, monitoring all administrative and educational systems, removing the control over what should be taught and how it should be taught from the schools and from the teachers. Following this line of work, the promise is that the quality of teaching will reach the best IDEB rates. In order to better ascertain the progress of this improvement, it is necessary to trigger actions of accountability and responsibilization so that the "society" can verify, as close as possible to real time, the performance of its children's education. For this dynamic to be true, it is essential and crucial that a broad evaluation system coexist with such actions, which can be referred to as a large-scale evaluation system. Currently models of

---

5 See the article by Avelar and Ball (2019), which presents the mapping of theses active groups in educational policies of Brazil.
6 A kind of booklet system produced by private groups adopted by several education public systems.

tests and evaluations of this type have become almost a rule for states and municipalities, although there is already a very complex system organized at the federal level.

It is in this environment that policies of control over textbooks and the use of various types of teaching materials are now required on a scale basis, in order to make all materials the object of the market, including those distributed through public networks. As mentioned earlier, such policies include management systems that are very much in use and are very profitable, as many charge for the number of passwords used to access the system (Silva, 2018).[7]

These dynamics proposed for public education are successful only if they are accompanied by standardized tests and exams recommended by the current evaluation systems. It is with this logic that a national curriculum base becomes essential.

Many of the arguments in defense of a base are attractive because they present a seducing discourse: How can the children of the working class, the poor, those with little cultural capital, be left without the right to learn? How can they gain valuable knowledge if a common curriculum is not guaranteed? Many respectable academics, in my view, went down this road to nowhere and worked hard to obtain the best possible product in terms of curriculum quality. Many were part of both the first and second versions of the BNCC. As to the third version, it was very conservative and did not absorb many of the liberal precepts for public education.

Apple (2000) warned that the definition of official knowledge means the exclusion of subaltern voices and cultures. The confluence of interests around the definition of a national curriculum or official knowledge can be very contradictory. Many aspects are negotiable. Others are nonnegotiable. While neoliberal groups may not be prejudiced against LGBT minorities, neoconservative and religious groups can be very homophobic and racist. It is because of these contradictions that control over textbook content is no small feat, as it involves publishing views on gender, family, evolutionism and creationism, among many controversial themes around the curriculum (Apple, 2006).

As a general rule, the definition of a national curriculum presupposes a cultural homogenization, as some voices will be silent and others may be deafening. One can move towards curricular impoverishment. For the curricular justice to be fair and with a better distribution of knowledge, it often needs to be uneven. You cannot accept a poorer standard of school for the poor.

The third version of the BNCC has more influence and control by neoconservative and populist-authoritarian groups. Virtually the entire group that was linked to the academy had either withdrawn or been excluded. The resulting version, in addition to the problems arising from any nationally based idea, also contains very backward and conservative content. This due to the fact that even if groups that aligned with neoliberal policy occupied positions in the Department of Education, they were unable to stop the influence of more

---

7   I recommend this dissertation for presenting data which is very compelling in regards to privatization processes, private consultancies and the use of platforms in public education systems in Brazil (Silva, 2018).

conservative groups, such as the movement Non-Partisan School. The theme around gender has been dropped entirely, for instance.

That being said, neoliberal groups supported the election of the current president, driven by the illusion that they would keep control over more neoliberal policies such as the BNCC, evaluation systems, national tests and teacher training and even negotiate the appointment of the future minister. However, religious and conservative groups acted decisively to block more liberal appointments and imposed a more ideologically conservative agenda, which aligned more with the principles of the Non-Partisan School, of creationism and of a conservative gender vision, attacking what they call gender ideology. We are currently experiencing a time when certain interests are at stake at the Department of Education and Culture (hereinafter, MEC).

Currently, the MEC still experiences internal problems arising from these disputes, but it already expresses ultra-liberal and neoconservative policies on basic and secondary education, withdrawing resources from both and promising privatist policies for universities.

In this environment that is still uncertain in many ways, the very implementation policy of the BNCC is confusing on the part of the MEC and many states and municipalities are awaiting initiatives. Currently, the strategy for actions related to the BNCC remains unknown, and the partnership with foundations and entities that would have a role in this implementation process (such as advising the states) has still not been defined.

BNCC and teacher education

At moment, schools are riddled with policies that increasingly intend to subject it to the market and to neoconservatism. Notwithstanding, control over daily school life largely involves controlling teacher education.

Thus, the effects of managerialism and conservatism on the curriculum, management and teaching are profound and affect the school routine. The evaluation policies reinforce this conservative appeal over the school, but resistance is present in the teaching actions and the reinterpretation and translation of policies as analyzed by Ball, Maguire, and Braun (2012). One of these actions involves teacher education.

The new guidelines for undergraduate teaching programs approved by the National Education Council (hereinafter CNE) that should be implemented in all universities have been postponed and suspended, suggesting that new guidelines are being considered but not discussed. The guidelines approved by the CNE went through a very comprehensive discussion process. It is a proposal that tries to solve an old impasse in teacher education programs: make the increase in the general course load compatible with the increase in theoretical hours of foundational learning and increase the hours of practice, without any dichotomy in training.

What has been observed as a training trend in the context of reforms is the lightening of teacher education programs, either as shortened or condensed and simplified degrees taught by universities of doubtful quality or as distance education and cheap programs aimed at a market-focused training.

From the point of view of the method, the national policy of teacher education had been converging towards a logic very close to that of the BNCC. The dynamics would be something as described in Figure 25.2.:

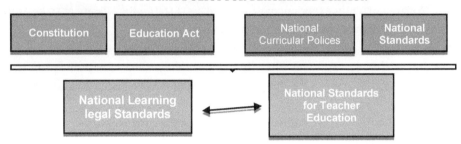

FIGURE 25.2.: LEGAL ARTICULATION FOR BNCC
AND NATIONAL POLICY FOR TEACHER EDUCATION

One of the arguments that attempts to support the legal imposition of the BNCC is the determination by law of the need for a *National Curriculum Policy.* In response, we have already had a national curriculum policy with the Parameters and the National Guidelines, which was enough for schools to develop their work and was already criticized by many as a type of national curriculum. The literature on this issue is vast. However, it has always been insufficient for those who advocate that a managerial education geared towards the interests of the billion-dollar market is necessary in order to improve the quality of public schools. We do not yet have a BNCC for teacher education programs, but this may be the next step for some, because for other groups that advocate for the need to deregulate teacher training—in the sense that any person with a degree in any area with rapid training can be a teacher—we already have programs like Teach for All, Teach for America, Teach First and Teach Brazil.

The teaching education models adopted by the program Teach For All are strategies strongly sponsored and supported by corporations and the new private philanthropies. Teach for All is a global plan, a more articulated version of Teach For America (USA) and Teach First (England and countries under its influence). The Brazilian version is Ensina! Brazil. Teach for All describes itself as "a global network of social entrepreneurs working to expand educational opportunities in their countries [. . .] its mission is to expand educational opportunities internationally by increasing and accelerating the impact of these social ventures"(Ball *et al.,* 2013, p. 17, note 1).

The program Ensina Brasil is part of the Teach for All network and presents the following proposal: recruit graduates from good universities, carry out a basic training of 250 hours with a continuing training portion consisting of 1830 hours and teach in vulnerable schools with remuneration as shown on the program homepage.[8]

8   Ensina Brazil webpage, https://www.ensinabrasil.org/, accessed on 06/08/2019, available at: https://docs.wixstatic.com/ugd/033518_2ce100c1f5954515975bf10f9a192b37.pdf.

This type of program is not incompatible with the BNCC curriculum policy. Ensina Brasil is in line with supporters of neoliberal managerialist policies. The program is supported or has partners such as Itaú Social, Insper, Lemann Foundation, Elos Educacional, Kroton, among others.[9]

The purpose is to remove teacher education from universities and show that it is possible for newly trained young graduates to become teachers for a short period of two or three years. There is no contradiction with the BNCC, as it is enough to apply materials and packages previously oriented to achieve the curriculum provided in the BNCC. Currently, given the legal possibility of outsourcing core activities and voluntary work, it has become more flexible and possible for these young recruits to be paid by city halls as developers of temporary work and with grants provided by partner entities. The goal for this type of program is not longevity but to make teaching and training more flexible. In this sense, teacher training in university programs based on teaching and research is threatened and could be replaced by programs that are cheaper and "lighter." As the improvement of working conditions and wages that could attract talented young people to the profession is not envisaged in the midterm, there is a real possibility that programs of this type and mediocre courses will gain space in teacher training. The irresponsibility of these policies is huge, because, unlike what the reformists may claim, such policies are not based on evidence.

What this text attempts to show is that there is a global agenda that is being structured locally, based on hegemonic groups, which are not always cohesive, and are at sometimes more liberal, now more ultraliberal, now neoconservative and authoritarian, but which have been successful in imposing their agenda that assumes multiple ways of meeting the dictates of the market and conservative interests. BNCC is at the center of these interests and, from my viewpoint, has served both to deepen market interests and interests around the control over knowledge, with conservative ideological advances.

Resistance has been strong and may be long, but one cannot give up the search for a social, collective, culturally relevant education that seeks curricular and social justice.

References

Apple, M. W. (1996). *Cultural politics and education*. Bukingham: Open University Press.

Apple, M. W.(2000). *Official knowledge*. New York: Routledge

Apple, M. W. (2006). *Educating the right way: Markets, standards, God, and inequality* (2nd ed.). New York: Routledge.

Avelar, M., & Ball, S. J. (2019). Mapping new philanthropy and the heterarchical state: The Mobilization for the National Learning Standards in Brazil. *International Journal of Educational Development*, n. 64, p. 65–73.

Ball, S. J. (2010). New states, new governance and new education policy. In: Apple, M. W., Ball, S. J., & Gandin, L. A. (2010). *The Routledge international handbook of the sociology of education*.

Ball, S. J. (2013). *Global Education Inc: New policy networks and the neoliberal imaginary*. New York: Routledge

---

9   Strong foundations and/or institutes funded by big corporations, such as banks, financial institutions, educational private sector, and so on.

Ball, S. J., Bailey, P., Mena, P., Del Monte, P., Santori, D., Tseng, C-Y., Young, H., & Olmedo, A. (2013). A constituição da subjetividade docente no Brasil: um contexto global. *Revista Educação em Questão*, Natal, v. 46 n. 32, p. 9–36, maio/ago.

Ball, S. J., Maguire, M., & Braun A. (2012). *How schools do policy – policy enactments in Secondary Schools*. London: Routledge, 2012.

Brasil. (1997). Secretaria de Educação Fundamental. *Parâmetros curriculares nacionais: introdução aos parâmetros curriculares nacionais*. Brasília: MEC/SEF.

Bruns, B.; Luque, J. (2015). *Great teachers: How to raise student learning in Latin America and the Caribbean*. Washington, DC: World Bank. Access in 06/01/2019, available in: https://openknowledge.worldbank.org/handle/10986/20488

Freitas, L. C. (2018). *A Reforma Empresarial da educação: nova direita, velhas ideias*. São Paulo: Expressão Popular.

Hypolito, A. M. (2014). Currículo e projeto político-pedagógico: implicações na gestão e no trabalho docente. *Cadernos de Educação*, Brasília, n. 26, p. 11-26, jan./jun. Disponível em: http://cnte.org.br/images/stories/cadernos_educacao/cadernos_educacao_26.pdf

Hypolito, A. M. (2015). Trabalho docente e o novo Plano Nacional de Educação: valorização, formação e condições de trabalho. *Cadernos CEDES*, v. 35, p. 517–534.

Ivo, A. e Hypolito, A. M. (2017). Sistemas de avaliação em larga escala e repercussões em diferentes contextos escolares: limites da padronização Gerencialista. *RBPAE*, v. 33, n. 3, p. 791–809, set./dez.

Lima, I. G. e Hypolito, A. M. (2019). The expansion of neoconservatism in Brazilian education. *Educação e Pesquisa*. São Paulo, v. 45, e190901.http://www.scielo.br/pdf/ep/v45/en_1517-9702-ep-45-e190901.pdf. DOI: http://dx.doi.org/10.1590/S1678-463420194519091

Leite, M. C. L., Hypolito, A. M., Dall'igna, M., Cossio, M. F., & Marcolla, V. (2012). Gestión escolar democrática: una construcción contextualizada en escuelas municipales de la ciudad de Pelotas, RS, Brasil. *Revista Mexicana de Investigación Educativa*, v. 17, p. 89–113.

Martins, E. M. (2016). *Todos pela Educação? Como os empresários estão determinando a política educacional brasileira*. Rio de Janeiro: Editora Lamparina.

Ravitch, D. (2011). *The death and life of the great American school system: How testing and choice are undermining education*. Boulder: Basic Books.

Santos, B. S. (1995). *Toward a new common sense: Law, science, and politics in the paradigmatic transition*. New York: Routledge.

Santos, B. S. (2002). *A Globalização e as Ciências Sociais*. São Paulo: Cortez Editora.

Silva, M. E. (2018). *Redes de influência em Mato Grosso – O Estado e as Parcerias Público-Privadas e a reconfiguração da política educacional da Rede Estadual de Ensino*. Pelotas: UFPel, Tese de Doutorado.

Silva, T. T., & Gentili, P. A. A. (Org.) (1996). *Escola S. A.: quem ganha e quem perda no mercado educacional do neoliberalismo*. Brasília, DF: CNTE (Confederação Nacional dos Trabalhadores em Educação).

Verger, A., Parcerisa, L., & Fontdevila, C. (2018) The growth and spread of large-scale assessments and test-based accountabilities: A political sociology of global education reforms. *Educational Review*, v. 71, no. 1, pp. 1–26. doi:10.1080/00131911.2019.1522045

Weiner, L., & Compton, M. (2016). Understanding the aims and assumptions of the World Bank's report "Great Teachers" for Latin America and the Caribbean. *Critical Education*, v. 7, no. 11. Accessed 01/06/2019, from https://ices.library.ubc.ca/index.php/criticaled/article/view/186145/185383

World Bank. (2017). *A fair adjustment: Efficiency and equity of public spending in Brazil. Vol.1 - Overview*. Access in 06/01/2019, available in http://documents.worldbank.org/curated/en/643471520429223428/pdf/Volume-1-Overview.pdf

About the Author

João M. Paraskeva is a Professor and founding Chair of the Department of Educational Leadership and of the Doctoral Program in Educational Leadership and Policy Studies at the University of Massachusetts, Dartmouth. A former middle school and high school teacher in the southern Africa region, he was also a Professor at the University of Minho, Portugal; Honorary Fellow of the University of Wisconsin—Madison; Visiting Professor at the University of La Coruna, Spain; Visiting Professor at Federal University of Pelotas, Brazil; Visiting Professor at the University of Florence, Italy; and visiting Professor at Miami University, Oxford, Ohio. Founder of the journal *Curriculum Sem Fronteiras*, his latest books are *Conflicts in Curriculum Theories: Challenging Hegemonic Epistemologies* (New York: Palgrave; 2011/2014); *Curriculum: Whose Internationalization?* (New York: Peter Lang; 2015); *Curriculum: Decanonizing the Field* (New York: Peter Lang; 2015); *Curriculum Epistimicides* (New York: Routledge; 2016, which won an AERA Critic's Choice Book Award); *Towards a Just Curriculum Theory: The Epistemicide* (New York: Routledge; 2018); and *The Generation of the Utopia. Decolonizing Critical Curriculum Theory* (New York: Routledge; 2020). His work has been translated in Greece, Portugal, Korea, China, Spain, Finland, and Brazil.